Lecture Notes in Computer Science 14022

Founding Editors

Gerhard Goos
Juris Hartmanis

Editorial Board Members

Elisa Bertino, *Purdue University, West Lafayette, IN, USA*
Wen Gao, *Peking University, Beijing, China*
Bernhard Steffen ⓘ, *TU Dortmund University, Dortmund, Germany*
Moti Yung ⓘ, *Columbia University, New York, NY, USA*

The series Lecture Notes in Computer Science (LNCS), including its subseries Lecture Notes in Artificial Intelligence (LNAI) and Lecture Notes in Bioinformatics (LNBI), has established itself as a medium for the publication of new developments in computer science and information technology research, teaching, and education.

LNCS enjoys close cooperation with the computer science R & D community, the series counts many renowned academics among its volume editors and paper authors, and collaborates with prestigious societies. Its mission is to serve this international community by providing an invaluable service, mainly focused on the publication of conference and workshop proceedings and postproceedings. LNCS commenced publication in 1973.

Pei-Luen Patrick Rau
Editor

Cross-Cultural Design

15th International Conference, CCD 2023
Held as Part of the 25th International Conference, HCII 2023
Copenhagen, Denmark, July 23–28, 2023
Proceedings, Part I

Springer

Editor
Pei-Luen Patrick Rau
Department of Industrial Engineering
Tsinghua University
Beijing, China

ISSN 0302-9743   ISSN 1611-3349 (electronic)
Lecture Notes in Computer Science
ISBN 978-3-031-35935-4   ISBN 978-3-031-35936-1 (eBook)
https://doi.org/10.1007/978-3-031-35936-1

This Springer imprint is published by the registered company Springer Nature Switzerland AG
The registered company address is: Gewerbestrasse 11, 6330 Cham, Switzerland

Foreword

Human-computer interaction (HCI) is acquiring an ever-increasing scientific and industrial importance, as well as having more impact on people's everyday lives, as an ever-growing number of human activities are progressively moving from the physical to the digital world. This process, which has been ongoing for some time now, was further accelerated during the acute period of the COVID-19 pandemic. The HCI International (HCII) conference series, held annually, aims to respond to the compelling need to advance the exchange of knowledge and research and development efforts on the human aspects of design and use of computing systems.

The 25th International Conference on Human-Computer Interaction, HCI International 2023 (HCII 2023), was held in the emerging post-pandemic era as a 'hybrid' event at the AC Bella Sky Hotel and Bella Center, Copenhagen, Denmark, during July 23–28, 2023. It incorporated the 21 thematic areas and affiliated conferences listed below.

A total of 7472 individuals from academia, research institutes, industry, and government agencies from 85 countries submitted contributions, and 1578 papers and 396 posters were included in the volumes of the proceedings that were published just before the start of the conference, these are listed below. The contributions thoroughly cover the entire field of human-computer interaction, addressing major advances in knowledge and effective use of computers in a variety of application areas. These papers provide academics, researchers, engineers, scientists, practitioners and students with state-of-the-art information on the most recent advances in HCI.

The HCI International (HCII) conference also offers the option of presenting 'Late Breaking Work', and this applies both for papers and posters, with corresponding volumes of proceedings that will be published after the conference. Full papers will be included in the 'HCII 2023 - Late Breaking Work - Papers' volumes of the proceedings to be published in the Springer LNCS series, while 'Poster Extended Abstracts' will be included as short research papers in the 'HCII 2023 - Late Breaking Work - Posters' volumes to be published in the Springer CCIS series.

I would like to thank the Program Board Chairs and the members of the Program Boards of all thematic areas and affiliated conferences for their contribution towards the high scientific quality and overall success of the HCI International 2023 conference. Their manifold support in terms of paper reviewing (single-blind review process, with a minimum of two reviews per submission), session organization and their willingness to act as goodwill ambassadors for the conference is most highly appreciated.

This conference would not have been possible without the continuous and unwavering support and advice of Gavriel Salvendy, founder, General Chair Emeritus, and Scientific Advisor. For his outstanding efforts, I would like to express my sincere appreciation to Abbas Moallem, Communications Chair and Editor of HCI International News.

July 2023   Constantine Stephanidis

HCI International 2023 Thematic Areas and Affiliated Conferences

Thematic Areas

- HCI: Human-Computer Interaction
- HIMI: Human Interface and the Management of Information

Affiliated Conferences

- EPCE: 20th International Conference on Engineering Psychology and Cognitive Ergonomics
- AC: 17th International Conference on Augmented Cognition
- UAHCI: 17th International Conference on Universal Access in Human-Computer Interaction
- CCD: 15th International Conference on Cross-Cultural Design
- SCSM: 15th International Conference on Social Computing and Social Media
- VAMR: 15th International Conference on Virtual, Augmented and Mixed Reality
- DHM: 14th International Conference on Digital Human Modeling and Applications in Health, Safety, Ergonomics and Risk Management
- DUXU: 12th International Conference on Design, User Experience and Usability
- C&C: 11th International Conference on Culture and Computing
- DAPI: 11th International Conference on Distributed, Ambient and Pervasive Interactions
- HCIBGO: 10th International Conference on HCI in Business, Government and Organizations
- LCT: 10th International Conference on Learning and Collaboration Technologies
- ITAP: 9th International Conference on Human Aspects of IT for the Aged Population
- AIS: 5th International Conference on Adaptive Instructional Systems
- HCI-CPT: 5th International Conference on HCI for Cybersecurity, Privacy and Trust
- HCI-Games: 5th International Conference on HCI in Games
- MobiTAS: 5th International Conference on HCI in Mobility, Transport and Automotive Systems
- AI-HCI: 4th International Conference on Artificial Intelligence in HCI
- MOBILE: 4th International Conference on Design, Operation and Evaluation of Mobile Communications

List of Conference Proceedings Volumes Appearing Before the Conference

1. LNCS 14011, Human-Computer Interaction: Part I, edited by Masaaki Kurosu and Ayako Hashizume
2. LNCS 14012, Human-Computer Interaction: Part II, edited by Masaaki Kurosu and Ayako Hashizume
3. LNCS 14013, Human-Computer Interaction: Part III, edited by Masaaki Kurosu and Ayako Hashizume
4. LNCS 14014, Human-Computer Interaction: Part IV, edited by Masaaki Kurosu and Ayako Hashizume
5. LNCS 14015, Human Interface and the Management of Information: Part I, edited by Hirohiko Mori and Yumi Asahi
6. LNCS 14016, Human Interface and the Management of Information: Part II, edited by Hirohiko Mori and Yumi Asahi
7. LNAI 14017, Engineering Psychology and Cognitive Ergonomics: Part I, edited by Don Harris and Wen-Chin Li
8. LNAI 14018, Engineering Psychology and Cognitive Ergonomics: Part II, edited by Don Harris and Wen-Chin Li
9. LNAI 14019, Augmented Cognition, edited by Dylan D. Schmorrow and Cali M. Fidopiastis
10. LNCS 14020, Universal Access in Human-Computer Interaction: Part I, edited by Margherita Antona and Constantine Stephanidis
11. LNCS 14021, Universal Access in Human-Computer Interaction: Part II, edited by Margherita Antona and Constantine Stephanidis
12. LNCS 14022, Cross-Cultural Design: Part I, edited by Pei-Luen Patrick Rau
13. LNCS 14023, Cross-Cultural Design: Part II, edited by Pei-Luen Patrick Rau
14. LNCS 14024, Cross-Cultural Design: Part III, edited by Pei-Luen Patrick Rau
15. LNCS 14025, Social Computing and Social Media: Part I, edited by Adela Coman and Simona Vasilache
16. LNCS 14026, Social Computing and Social Media: Part II, edited by Adela Coman and Simona Vasilache
17. LNCS 14027, Virtual, Augmented and Mixed Reality, edited by Jessie Y. C. Chen and Gino Fragomeni
18. LNCS 14028, Digital Human Modeling and Applications in Health, Safety, Ergonomics and Risk Management: Part I, edited by Vincent G. Duffy
19. LNCS 14029, Digital Human Modeling and Applications in Health, Safety, Ergonomics and Risk Management: Part II, edited by Vincent G. Duffy
20. LNCS 14030, Design, User Experience, and Usability: Part I, edited by Aaron Marcus, Elizabeth Rosenzweig and Marcelo Soares
21. LNCS 14031, Design, User Experience, and Usability: Part II, edited by Aaron Marcus, Elizabeth Rosenzweig and Marcelo Soares

47. CCIS 1836, HCI International 2023 Posters - Part V, edited by Constantine Stephanidis, Margherita Antona, Stavroula Ntoa and Gavriel Salvendy

https://2023.hci.international/proceedings

Preface

The increasing internationalization and globalization of communication, business and industry is leading to a wide cultural diversification of individuals and groups of users who access information, services and products. If interactive systems are to be usable, useful and appealing to such a wide range of users, culture becomes an important HCI issue. Therefore, HCI practitioners and designers face the challenges of designing across different cultures, and need to elaborate and adopt design approaches which take into account cultural models, factors, expectations and preferences, and allow development of cross-cultural user experiences that accommodate global users.

The 15th Cross-Cultural Design (CCD) Conference, an affiliated conference of the HCI International Conference, encouraged the submission of papers from academics, researchers, industry and professionals, on a broad range of theoretical and applied issues related to Cross-Cultural Design and its applications.

A considerable number of papers were accepted to this year's CCD Conference addressing diverse topics, which spanned a wide variety of domains. A notable theme addressed by several contributions was that of service and product design for the promotion of cultural heritage and local culture. Furthermore, a considerable number of papers explore the differences in cultural perceptions of technology across various contexts. Design for social change and development constitutes one of the topics that emerged this year, examining the impact of technology on society, for vulnerable groups, for shaping values, and in promoting social movements and folk beliefs. Another growing topic is that of sustainable design, which delves into methodologies, cultural branding, and design for sustainability in various areas such as travel, transportation and mobility, climate change and urban public spaces. Emerging technologies, future-focused design and design of automated and intelligent systems are also prominent themes, exploring culturally informed innovative design methodologies, User Experience aspects and user acceptance angles, as well as evaluation studies and their findings. Furthermore, papers emphasized the design of technological innovations in domains of social impact such as arts and creative industries, cultural heritage, immersive and inclusive learning environments, and health and wellness.

Three volumes of the HCII 2023 proceedings are dedicated to this year's edition of the CCD Conference:

- Part I addresses topics related to service and product design for cultural innovation, design for social change and development, sustainable design methods and practices, and cross-cultural perspectives on design and consumer behavior.
- Part II addresses topics related to User Experience design in emerging technologies, future-focused design, and culturally informed design of automated and intelligent systems.
- Part III addresses topics related to cross-cultural design in arts and creative industries, in cultural heritage, and in immersive and inclusive learning environments, as well as cross-cultural health and wellness design.

Papers in these volumes were included for publication after a minimum of two single-blind reviews from the members of the CCD Program Board or, in some cases, from members of the Program Boards of other affiliated conferences. I would like to thank all of them for their invaluable contribution, support and efforts.

July 2023   Pei-Luen Patrick Rau

15th International Conference on Cross-Cultural Design (CCD 2023)

Program Board Chair: **Pei-Luen Patrick Rau,** *Tsinghua University, P.R. China*

Program Board:

- Na Chen, *Beijing University of Chemical Technology, P.R. China*
- Zhe Chen, *Beihang University, P.R. China*
- Kuohsiang Chen, *Fuzhou University of International Studies and Trade, P.R. China*
- Wen-Ko Chiou, *Chang Gung University, Taiwan*
- Paul L. Fu, *Wish Inc., USA*
- Zhiyong Fu, *Tsinghua University, P.R. China*
- Hanjing Huang, *Fuzhou University, P.R. China*
- Yu-Chi Lee, *Ming Chi University of Technology, Taiwan*
- Xin Lei, *Zhejiang University of Technology, P.R. China*
- Sheau-Farn Max Liang, *National Taipei University of Technology, Taiwan*
- Pin-Chao Liao, *Tsinghua University, P.R. China*
- Rungtai Lin, *National Taiwan University of Arts, Taiwan*
- Po-Hsien Lin, *National Taiwan University of Arts, Taiwan*
- Na Liu, *Beijing University of Posts and Telecommunications, P.R. China*
- Ta-Ping (Robert) Lu, *Sichuan University – Pittsburgh Institute, P.R. China*
- Liang Ma, *Tsinghua University, P.R. China*
- Xingda Qu, *Shenzhen University, P.R. China*
- Huatong Sun, *University of Washington Tacoma, USA*
- Hao Tan, *Hunan University, P.R. China*
- Pei-Lee Teh, *Monash University Malaysia, Malaysia*
- Lin Wang, *Incheon National University, South Korea*
- Hsiu-Ping Yueh, *National Taiwan University, Taiwan*
- Runting Zhong, *Jiangnan University, P.R. China*
- Xingchen Zhou, *Beijing Normal University, P.R. China*

The full list with the Program Board Chairs and the members of the Program Boards of all thematic areas and affiliated conferences of HCII2023 is available online at:

http://www.hci.international/board-members-2023.php

HCI International 2024 Conference

The 26th International Conference on Human-Computer Interaction, HCI International 2024, will be held jointly with the affiliated conferences at the Washington Hilton Hotel, Washington, DC, USA, June 29 – July 4, 2024. It will cover a broad spectrum of themes related to Human-Computer Interaction, including theoretical issues, methods, tools, processes, and case studies in HCI design, as well as novel interaction techniques, interfaces, and applications. The proceedings will be published by Springer. More information will be made available on the conference website: http://2024.hci.international/.

General Chair
Prof. Constantine Stephanidis
University of Crete and ICS-FORTH
Heraklion, Crete, Greece
Email: general_chair@hcii2024.org

https://2024.hci.international/

Contents – Part I

Design for Social Change and Development

Sustainable Design Methods and Practices

Cross-Cultural Perspectives on Consumer Behavior

Contents – Part II

Culturally-Informed Design of Automated and Intelligent Systems

Contents – Part III

Cross-Cultural Design in Arts and Creative Industries

Cross-Cultural Design in Cultural Heritage

Cross-Cultural Design in Immersive and Inclusive Learning Environments

Cross-Cultural Health and Wellness Design

Service and Product Design for Cultural Innovation

A Study on the Innovative Design of Fuzhou "FU" Cultural Tourism Products Based on Design Heuristics

Xin Cao[1,2](✉) ⓘ, Yen Hsu[2] ⓘ, and Weilong Wu[2] ⓘ

[1] Fujian Province, Fuzhou University of International Studies and Trade, 28, Yuhuan Road, Shouzhan New .0 District, Changle District, Fuzhou 350202, China
caoxindesign@163.com

[2] The Graduate Institute of Design Science, Tatung University, No.40, Sec. 3, Zhongshan N. Road, Taipei City 104,10461, Taiwan

Abstract. Innovative design methods for cultural products have gradually become a research hotspot in the international design community. At present, most of the products in the market are designed to reflect cultural connotations through the simple use of traditional patterns, or even the direct application of traditional product styles to modern product design, without fully considering the characteristics of human aesthetic needs. In this study, we propose card-based design heuristics for Fuzhou's "Fu" cultural tourism products by searching keywords and database to integrate past excellent Fuzhou "Fu" cultural tourism products and similar cases, using KJ method and cluster analysis method to classify and filter these cases, extract and summarize their design heuristics. The design heuristic of Fuzhou "Fu" cultural tourism products is proposed. The aim is to provide a theoretical basis and design reference for the design of Fuzhou " Fu" cultural tourism products.

Keywords: Innovative Design · Design Heuristic · Cultural Product

1 Introduction

Innovative design for cultural products is gradually becoming a research hotspot in the international design community. In Japan, culturally oriented products are considered as a strategic approach for the domestic market. Emphasizing cultural significance and demonstrating the aesthetic value of traditional culture in products can enhance people's interest in conservation. For example, Indonesia's cultural heritage angklung, a musical instrument made of bamboo, has been successfully conserved through cultural products that promote cultural values and awareness. Some companies and design studios use symbolic meanings in their product designs to differentiate their products from others in order to gain a competitive position. Thus, culture can be a resource for generating and symbolic meaning.

P.-L. P. Rau (Ed.): HCII 2023, LNCS 14022, pp. 3–16, 2023.
https://doi.org/10.1007/978-3-031-35936-1_1

With the continuous reform and opening up of China and the cultural exchanges at home and abroad and across regions, and the continuous collision and exchange of various cultural trends of thought, culture gradually presents diversified characteristics, and because of this the embodiment of cultural connotations in product design is also necessary to enhance product quality and promote consumption. Yang et al. take Tunxi Old Street in Anhui Province as an example and propose three conditions that must be present in the development of tourism products in the historical district: traditional commercial street, shopping behavior, and popularity, and discuss the tourism development of this historical district. Taking Kaifeng City as an example, Xiaobai Li proposed a tourism product development strategy for the historic district of Kaifeng from the perspective of the functional division of the historic district.

The city of Fuzhou, the site of this study, is rich in humanistic and natural culture, and has the double advantage of resources, which can be found in the items on the national non-heritage list, and is widely distributed in five districts and eight counties, such as the shipbuilding culture in Mawei District, the historical and cultural street of Sanfang Qi Xiang in Gulou District, and so on. The tourism products with the background of culture in this area are called "Fu" cultural tourism products, and there are few studies on the design of "Fu" cultural tourism products.

The scope of this study is related to the field of product innovation design, where most of the research has been conducted by scholars proposing design methods that focus on improving existing products or developing new products, such as the methods of participatory design [1], ethnography [2], and empathic design [3]. These methods emphasize the incorporation of the human perspective into the design process and aim to design useful products by focusing on the needs of the user and by applying ergonomics.

Despite improvements in various design methods, design teams developing tourism products today still face many problems, one of which is the lack of design heuristics needed to generate concepts for problem solving solutions.

The ideal team for the design of a " Fu" cultural tourism product should include product designers and users [1, 4]. In most cases, product designers lack expertise in the type of sustainable product under consideration and experience with the target users. The use of a user-participatory human-centered design approach can effectively bridge this gap and can help designers understand and properly define design problems [2, 3, 5]. However, once the design problem is defined and moves to the problem-solving solution concept generation phase, the design team is likely to encounter a lack of design knowledge [6].

Currently, design teams rely heavily on the knowledge of team members to generate and explore solution concepts, and brainstorming methods seem to be the most commonly used design approach [7–9]. The problem is that the design knowledge within the design team may not be sufficient to explore the design domain effectively. Despite their design expertise, designers often do not have much practical experience in solving specific sustainable product design problems. With the wide variety of materials and processes used in " Fu" cultural tourism products, it is often difficult for designers with extensive design experience to solve specific product design problems in real life. In the absence of experienced professional designers involved in the design of projects with insufficient budgets, some production workers and users have designed the products themselves [10, 11]. However, they usually do not have the knowledge to generate solution concepts. Even though they understand the problem context and user needs, they are not design experts who specialize in creating problem-solution concepts. The lack of knowledge required by the design team to generate problem-solution concepts hinders the product development to some extent.

In order to solve the above problem of insufficient design knowledge within the design team, this study integrates past excellent tourism product cases by searching keywords and databases, extracts and summarizes their design methods, and proposes a design heuristic for "Fu" cultural tourism products. Previously, several scholars have proposed related design heuristics [6, 12–18].

The design heuristics were developed through research with experts, senior engineers and product designers, and analysis of award-winning products. Daly, Seifert [19] identified 77 design heuristics and provided illustrations and written descriptions on each design heuristic card, and several studies have demonstrated the effectiveness of this tool. However, the target group of this tool is broad, and Fuzhou "Fu" cultural tourism products have regional cultural characteristics, so this generic design heuristic is not applicable to Fuzhou "Fu" cultural tourism products. This generic design heuristic is not applicable to Fuzhou "Fu" cultural tourism products. It is significant to promote "Fu" cultural tourism product development through design heuristics.

In this study, we propose card-based design heuristics for Fuzhou's "Fu" cultural tourism products by searching keywords and database to integrate past excellent Fuzhou "Fu" cultural tourism products and similar cases, using KJ method and cluster analysis method to classify and filter these cases, extract and summarize their design heuristics. The design heuristic of Fuzhou "Fu" cultural tourism products is proposed. The content of this study is a design heuristic that brings together design knowledge and may inspire designers and help them conceptualize solutions for Fuzhou "Fu" cultural tourism products.

2 Literature Review

2.1 Cultural and Creative Products

In today's diverse society, products developed based on traditional design thinking are increasingly unable to meet the diverse needs of consumers, and cross-disciplinary collaboration and integration between industries and the shaping of consumer services and experiences have become breakthroughs in modern innovative design. 2018 World Design Organization (WDO) President Luisa Bochendo talks about how past concepts were more focused on production, and now in the midst of an electronic era and amidst electronic changes, products are becoming more and more intangible [2]. Industrial design has also evolved into a creative activity that cares about human needs, focuses on humanistic concerns, and integrates technology, business, innovation, research, and consumers across resources. All these reveal that human-centeredness and cross-border integration have become the inevitable trend of design development.

Among the wide range of industrial design, the design of cultural and creative products is an important part of it, which is a carrier of cultural heritage and a product of the integration of culture and technology. The development of cultural and creative products should consider not only the shape, material, technology and structure, but also visual design, experience design, brand planning, marketing and management, etc. A good cultural and creative product can not only realize the creative expression of cultural connotation, but also map the essence of human life and values under the contemporary cultural system. The pursuit of human-oriented concept and cross-border integration are the charm of industrial design.

Cultural and creative products are products with physical forms based on culture and derived from cultural symbols, and are an important part of cultural consumption. It can be divided into several categories according to themes, such as tourism cultural and creative products, animation and game derivatives, and theme-specific souvenir products, etc. It can also be distinguished by attributes for different purposes such as selling or giving away. Its soul lies in the clever combination of culture and innovation.

With the strong advocacy of China's national policy, there has been a boom in the public's attention to traditional culture, and a large number of trendy cultural and creative products have emerged that combine tradition with modernity and are well-made and in line with the current trend. For example, the MOLLY palace beast series, the Chinese Taipei Imperial Palace Jade Cabbage umbrella, and the "I know" paper tape, etc. They present the traditional dull style in a relaxed and entertaining manner, and closely combine with the trendy culture, making the presentation of traditional culture more innovative and creative, and creating explosive products that integrate tradition and modernity.

In some countries where cultural and creative industries are developed earlier, the market is relatively mature and there are many excellent cases worthy of reference. For example, Bearbrick, the most famous block bear of Japanese toy company MEDICOM, takes bear as the prototype, carefully designed in many aspects such as color, pattern and style, and integrated with trendy elements, street culture and movies across the border, and cooperated with famous artists, designers and popular brands to form a distinctive hip play image, which is very popular in the market. Then there are the Mona Lisa series of art derivatives from the Louvre in France, the Little Yellow Duck from the British Museum, the Titanic Cultural and Creative Experience, etc. Most of them start from current market trends and design cultural and creative products with unique cultural connotations and in line with contemporary needs.

Faced with the opportunity of the explosion of cultural and creative industries at home and abroad, China's cultural and creative industries are facing the problems of insufficient creativity and one-sided pursuit of economic benefits. For example, USB flash drives with blue and white porcelain elements, mugs with landscape paintings, and so on, are hardly meeting the actual needs of the market due to the homogenization of traditional patterns. In the design process, we should try to get rid of the status quo of single design method, old-fashioned form, narrow carrier limitation, and lack of practical functions, and explore the traditional Chinese culture in depth, actively explore the innovative design methods of cultural and creative products in the new era, integrate culture into public life, and enhance national self-confidence and cultural identity.

2.2 "Fu" Culture

The culture of "Fu" is a folk culture system formed by the changes and development of China's civilization over thousands of years of history. The auspicious concept of "Fu" is the ideal pursuit of survival and life for Chinese people. This pursuit runs through people's lives and influences their attitudes towards life and their understanding of nature, thus becoming the goal that most Chinese people aspire to and pursue throughout their lives. Here, through the interpretation of the relationship between the "Fu" culture and tourism product design, we try to explore the design principles and methods of combining cultural connotation and tourism products, integrate the "Fu" culture into the information and concept of the products, and give them a unique traditional Chinese cultural concept and connotation. The design principles and methods of combining cultural connotations with tourism products are explored.

Fuzhou city has a profound human and natural cultural heritage and has the advantage of double resources, which can be found in the items on the national non-patrimonial heritage list, which are widely distributed in the five districts and eight counties, such as the Shipbuilding Culture in Mawei District, the Three Square Seven Lane Historical and Cultural Street in Gulou District, and so on. The governments of the districts and counties have seized the opportunity to apply for the creation of many cultural industry parks, historical and cultural streets, industrial parks such as: One Paeonia Garden in Gulou District, Strait Industrial Design Creative Park in Jin'an District, Lacquer Space, Youth Club, etc.; cultural streets such as: Three Square Seven Lanes, Shang Shang Shang Hang, Zhu Zi Fang, etc. The cultural and creative industries have leapt to become an emerging economic force to meet the people's growing pursuit of spiritual culture. However, most of the product designs in the current market reflect the cultural connotation through the simple use of traditional patterns, or even the direct application of traditional product styles in modern product design, without fully taking into account the aesthetic needs of people, and the connotation of the traditional "Fu" culture and the thematic ideas to be reflected in the product design are not The overall operation level is superficial and ignores the essence of design, resulting in a general lack of cultural connotation in modern design.

The culture of "Fu" is a combination of people's concept and behavior of praying for good fortune and the visual symbols, which is a symbol of people's aspiration for a happy life. The application of "Fu" culture in modern tourism product design is not only reflected in the individual graphic symbols, but also in the package as a whole. It can form an overall conventional symbol system, thus satisfying the common wishes reflected by the "Fu" culture, i.e., seeking, receiving, cherishing and blessing, as the principle of integrating modern tourism product design with the "Fu" culture, which can highlight the cultural connotation of tourism products. The cultural connotation of tourism products can be highlighted.

2.3 Design Heuristics

Fu et al. [20] defined design heuristics as "context-dependent instructions based on intuition, tacit knowledge, or empirical understanding that provide direction to the design process to increase the chances of reaching a satisfactory, but not necessarily optimal, solution. "Design heuristics also have other terms, such as design principles and rules of thumb [21], common sense [22], strategies [23], and short cuts [24].

Several different design heuristics have been proposed in this field, such as SCAMPER [14], TRIZ 40 inventive principles [12] and 77 Design Heuristics [13, 18, 24].

77 Design Heuristics was developed by analyzing award-winning innovative products and identifying recurring solution principles [13]. Similar to the TRIZ40 invention principle, it provides 77 design inspirations that can be used to solve a variety of design problems. 77 Design Heuristics is designed to help designers better explore solution areas and develop generic solutions. Research has confirmed that 77 Design Heuristics can effectively generate innovative and unique design solutions [13, 18].

The design heuristics described above are all generalized problem solving strategies and are not specific to a particular product category. As a result, designers have to experimentally test each design heuristic without knowing the success rate of each design heuristic in solving a specific design problem. The contradiction matrix of TRIZ defines a set of contradictions between engineering parameters and formulates each of its principles to target a different class of contradictions. However, many designers use TIRZ only as a general-purpose problem-solving strategy and do not use its contradiction matrix.

A large number of previous design heuristics studies can greatly help designers to generate novel and useful ideas [13, 18, 25]. However, little research has been conducted on design heuristics for the design of "Fu" cultural tourism products. In this study, we analyze existing cultural creative products and patents to inspire designers' creativity and help them conceptualize solutions for "Fu" cultural tourism products in the concept generation stage.

3 Development of "FU" Cultural Tourism Product Design Heuristics

In order to solve the above-mentioned problem of insufficient design knowledge of product designers, this study uses the KJ method to extract and summarize design heuristics from past excellent product cases by searching keywords and databases, and proposes a design heuristic for the cultural tourism product "Fu". It is a design heuristic that brings together design knowledge that may inspire product designers and help them conceptualize ideas. The heuristic is derived from the experience of analyzing examples of products that have met the requirements in the past [15–17]. This study builds on Hwang and Park (2018), who proposed a design heuristic to assist in product concept generation for target X [6], to propose a design heuristic for constructing a "Fu" The step-by-step process of constructing a design heuristic for "Fu" cultural tourism products is divided into the following three steps.

3.1 Search of Keywords

This study entered the keyword search phase to find products and patents that meet the needs and functions. The choice of keywords determines the search results and the quality of the extracted design heuristics.

This study conducted a case search using two categories of keywords. The first category includes adjectives describing product characteristics such as "cultural," "creative," and "tourist," while the second category includes nouns such as "product," "souvenir," and "commodity" and their synonymous singular and plural forms. The lexicon used in this study includes Roget's thesaurus [26], which can be used to identify synonyms and singular-plural forms.

The search formula combines the keywords of each category with the Boolean operator OR, and then further connects each combined keyword with the operator AND.

In addition to searching for keywords, it is also necessary to have the appropriate database or computer aids available. Also using Google search engine helps to search for relevant and specific product examples, as well as prestigious competitions such as International Design Excellence Awards (IDEA), Red-Dot Product Design Awards and iF Product Design Awards. Award-winning entries.

3.2 Pre-processing Data

After selecting keywords and databases, relevant product cases and patents are searched. Then, the selection is performed using predefined criteria. The criteria include: 1. Relevant products or patents that meet the design requirements; 2. Three criteria of economic, environmental and social that meet the design requirements. After screening, duplicate or very similar cases are merged.

The format used to describe products and patents varies. Therefore, it is important to standardize their formats: 1. The problem that the product or patent addresses. 2. How the product or patent solves that problem. The process of format standardization can help designers understand the product or patent of an invention [27] and help in the subsequent processing of data integration and discovery of design heuristics.

3.3 Discovering Design Heuristics Using the Kawakita Jiro (KJ) Method

After the design heuristics are summarized from the products and patents collected in the previous phase, the designers or a team of experts in the related fields work together to integrate and analyze them using the Kawakita Jiro (KJ) method, which helps designers organize large amounts of unordered data and find hidden meanings in them by summarizing the data. The analysis process is as follows.

1) Prepare a small card for each product or patent that describes how it solves the targeted design problem using the standard format identified in the previous phase, and require each card to have a simple and easy-to-understand description. The cards are then placed on a large work surface so that all participating members can see them all.
2) The participating members worked individually and in silence. They look for cards that are similar to each other according to a specific design problem and place the cards close to each other on the table. This was repeated until there was no possibility of regrouping. Each participant can adjust the cards of the others after grouping until there is no disagreement. If a card can belong to more than one group, it can be copied in different groups.

3) Participants discuss the card grouping pattern on the work surface. If necessary, smaller changes can be made to the grouping results. Participants examine the similarities between each card based on their design features. Participants then describe the commonalities expressed in each group's card design in design heuristics format. Figure 3 provides a set of case studies illustrating how design heuristics information can be extracted from a group of products or patents.

4) Participants combined the design heuristics summarized by each group into large groups. Participants examined the similarity of design heuristics in each large group and generalized their commonalities with higher-level design heuristics. Then, large groups that were similar to each other were brought closer together to form super-groups until no further grouping was possible. This grouping operation forms a tree hierarchy diagram of design heuristics in which the lowest to the highest level of design heuristics is shown. The highest level of design heuristics is Level 1 design heuristics, followed by Level 2 design heuristics at the next lower level, and so on down the hierarchy. The development process is shown in Figure 1, which provides the different levels of design heuristic knowledge.

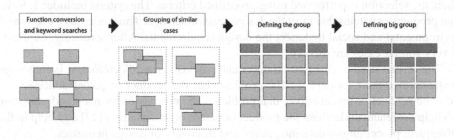

Fig. 1. Development process of "Fu" cultural tourism products.

A total of 276 examples were searched from the keywords in this study. Subsequently, among the 276 examples, 169 examples that met the above criteria were selected and retained, and each example was converted to a standard format. Finally, the KJ method as shown in Fig. 1 was used for group analysis.

As shown in Table 1, a total of 12 design heuristics and their detailed descriptions were identified as a result of this study. The number of examples for these 12 design heuristics ranged from 6 to 25 examples, with significant differences between the number of examples. The design heuristics were used to help designers or design teams generate conceptual solutions for the "Fu" cultural tourism product, and this study created a manual as a design aid, which contains examples of each design heuristic and its textual descriptions.

Figure 2 provides an example of how design heuristics can be extracted from a set of similar cases. The example shows four cases in the same group using the KJ method, all of which fall under the category of "educational sensitization" design heuristics, calling for a greater awareness of sustainability through product design, which is educational in some way.

Table 1. Twelve design heuristics for "Fu" cultural tourism products.

No	Design heuristics	Description	No. of examples
1	Function integration	By effectively integrating mature folk art with modern products and bringing their respective strengths into play, to find a new product carrier for traditional art to thrive	16
2	Process combination	Combine two different folk arts or traditional crafts to design new cultural products	18
3	Material substitution	While retaining the essential characteristics of the original products, we give full play to the superiority of new materials and technologies	24
4	Technology integration	A design method in which new technology is directly implanted into the original product. Through the implantation of technology, the original product is improved in terms of appearance and function	12
5	Change of shape	Design by changing the form, color, structure, material, sound and smell of the original product, or changing the way it is used	8
6	Image reinvention	The existing traditional culture that does not have material entities or craft techniques, such as legends, tales, myths, folk tales, etc., is reshaped with visual images or product appearance that meet the aesthetic needs of modern society	15
7	Simulated situation	With the support of design and technology, the products are used as props to simulate the reproduction of artistic situations or traditional tropes	8

(continued)

Table 1. (*continued*)

No	Design heuristics	Description	No. of examples
8	Simulated original	By creating conditions through imitation, tourism products are preserved so that people can gain experience of local traditional culture and lifestyle while using the products and feel the culture in the process of participation	16
9	Fusion of ancient and modern	Creating quality cultural and creative products that combine tradition and modernity to meet the lifestyle and aesthetic needs of people today has become a hot topic	14
10	Fun experience	The traditional and heavy cultural connotation is transformed into an open and relaxed emotional factor in a narrative way to create a pleasant psychological experience for consumers	7
11	Educational probation	We spread traditional culture through our products to achieve the purpose of science popularization and education	6
12	Branding	High-quality products as the carrier, user-centered, make every effort to build a deeply customized platform, and present a three-dimensional and full brand image clearly in front of users	25

In this study, the final design heuristics are presented to designers in the form of a small card that describes each design heuristic in the form of an illustration with text. It can be used to assist in the conceptual design of the cultural tourism product "Fu", and can also be used in conjunction with other general principles to promote creativity in the product [28–31]. During conceptual design time, designers can quickly generate design ideas and generate more ideas from that design idea [32–34]. The standard brainstorming approach usually does not require the use of any design aids, but relies on the designer's own design knowledge, and design heuristics can be used at this stage to facilitate the generation of design ideas.

This study validated the design heuristic for the "Fu" cultural tourism product using three assessment criteria (novelty, quality, and quantity) that have been widely used to assess design ideas in previous studies [6, 35–40]. Novelty refers to the fact that an idea is more unusual than other ideas. Quality refers to the feasibility of an idea and how close

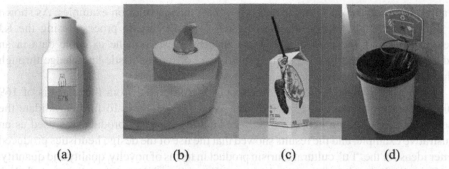

| (a) | (b) | (c) | (d) |

Fig. 2. An example illustrating the extraction of a design heuristic from a group of similar examples.

it is to the intended design goals. The novelty and quality of each idea are quantified through subjective ratings by experts. For novelty assessment, this experiment used the rarity metric proposed by Viswanathan and Linsey (2011), as shown in Eq. 1, in addition to the subjective scoring by experts. For the quantitative assessment, the total number of different ideas generated by subjects in each group was counted separately. Among them, the novelty and quality assessment metrics were only for individual ideas.

$$\text{Novelty} = 1 - \text{frequency} = 1 - \frac{\text{number of ideas in a bin}}{\text{total number of ideas}} \tag{1}$$

The evaluation metrics used in this study used a 7-point equal measure scale (1 = extremely low, 7 = extremely high) to subjectively determine the novelty and quality score of each idea, where score 1 indicates the lowest score and score 7 indicates the highest score, as shown in Fig. 3.

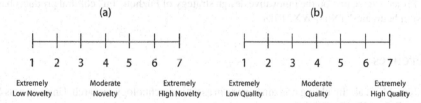

Fig. 3. Subjective rating scales for idea novelty and quality evaluations: (a) novelty scale, (b) quality scale.

The experimental results of this study show that the use of the design heuristic generates better ideas for the "Fu" cultural tourism products in terms of novelty, quality and quantity.

4   Conclusion

This study proposes a design heuristic for "Fu" cultural tourism products, which can assist in generating ideas. It is a collection of design inspirations that can provide useful help and guidance for solving the design problems of "Fu" cultural tourism products. It is an experience derived from the analysis of past design solution examples. As shown in Fig. 1, this study proposes a step-by-step design heuristic process, using the KJ method to extract the corresponding design heuristics from the example data in an inductive manner, and then presenting multi-level design heuristic knowledge through a hierarchical organization.

As shown in Table 1, 12 design heuristics were derived from the analysis of 169 cultural creative product cases found from keyword searches. To further validate the usefulness of the design heuristics, the "Fu" cultural tourism product was used as an illustrative example, and the results showed that the use of the design heuristics produced better ideas for the "Fu" cultural tourism product in terms of novelty, quality and quantity.

Overall, design heuristics can be a positive aid to the conceptualization of "Fu" cultural tourism product design. Design heuristics can be used as a solution to the current lack of professional conceptualization tools and low R&D investment in cultural and creative product development, and can play an important role in supporting sustainable product design activities. In order for the design heuristics proposed in this study to have a real impact, design heuristics need to be developed that cover a wide range of cultural creative product types, which may require the concerted efforts of a large number of people. Currently, this research project is developing several design heuristics for use in other cultural and creative product designs.

This study presents the final set of design heuristics in the form of a small card for designers, teachers and students in colleges and universities to use as a reference, with each design heuristic described in the form of an illustration with text. The cards describe each design heuristic in the form of illustrations and text. The aim is to provide a theoretical basis and design reference for the design of Fuzhou "Fu" cultural tourism products.

Funding. This research was supported by the Fuzhou University of International Studies and Trade Project "Research on the innovative design strategy of Fuzhou "Fu" cultural products based on design heuristics" (No. FWX21018).

References

1. Allen, M., et al.: Involving domain experts in assistive technology research. Univ. Access Inf. Soc. **7**(3), 145–154 (2008)
2. Carmien, S.P., Fischer, G.: Design, adoption, and assessment of a socio-technical environment supporting independence for persons with cognitive disabilities. In: Proceedings of the SIGCHI Conference on Human Factors in Computing Systems (2008)
3. Chen, C.-B.: An empathic approach in assistive technology to provide job accommodations for disabilities. In: Stephanidis, C. (ed.) HCI 2011. CCIS, vol. 173, pp. 363–367. Springer, Heidelberg (2011). https://doi.org/10.1007/978-3-642-22098-2_73
4. Allsop, M.J., et al.: The engagement of children with disabilities in health-related technology design processes: identifying methodology. Disabil. Rehabil. Assist. Technol. **5**(1), 1–13 (2010)
5. Meiland, F., et al.: Participation of end users in the design of assistive technology for people with mild to severe cognitive problems; the European Rosetta project. Int. Psychogeriatr. **26**(5), 769–779 (2014)

6. Hwang, D., Park, W.: Design heuristics set for X: a design aid for assistive product concept generation. Des. Stud. **58**, 89–126 (2018)
7. Gulliksen, J., Lantz, A.: Design versus design-from the shaping of products to the creation of user experiences. Int. J. Hum.-Comput. Interact. **15**(1), 5–20 (2003)
8. Sharples, S., et al.: Medical device design in context: a model of user–device interaction and consequences. Displays **33**(4–5), 221–232 (2012)
9. Steen, M., Kuijt-Evers, L., Klok, J.: Early user involvement in research and design projects–A review of methods and practices. In: 23rd EGOS colloquium (2007)
10. Hersh, M.A.: The design and evaluation of assistive technology products and devices part 1: Design (2010)
11. Lhotska, L., et al.: Student projects in assistive technologies. In: 2014 Information Technology Based Higher Education and Training (ITHET). IEEE (2014)
12. Altshuller, G., Altov, H.: And suddenly the inventor appeared: TRIZ, the theory of inventive problem solving. Technical Innovation Center, Inc. (1996)
13. Daly, S.R., et al.: Assessing design heuristics for idea generation in an introductory engineering course. Int. J. Eng. Educ. **28**(2), 463 (2012)
14. Eberle, B.: Scamper on: Games for Imagination Development. Prufrock Press Inc. (1996)
15. Hwang, D., Park, W.: Development of portability design heuristics. In: DS 80-4 Proceedings of the 20th International Conference on Engineering Design (ICED 15), vol. 4: Design for X, Design to X, Milan, Italy, 27–30.07.15 (2015)
16. Singh, V., et al.: Design for transformation: Theory, method and application. In: International Design Engineering Technical Conferences and Computers and Information in Engineering Conference (2007)
17. Weaver, J., et al.: Transformation design theory: a meta-analogical framework. J. Comput. Inform. Sci. Eng. **10**(3), 031012 (2010)
18. Yilmaz, S., et al.: How do design heuristics affects outcomes? In: DS 70: Proceedings of DESIGN 2012, the 12th International Design Conference, Dubrovnik, Croatia (2012)
19. Daly, S.R., et al.: Comparing ideation techniques for beginning designers. J. Mech. Des. **138**(10), 101108 (2016)
20. Fu, K.K., Yang, M.C., Wood, K.L.: Design principles: literature review, analysis, and future directions. J. Mech. Des. **138**(10), 101103 (2016)
21. Li, C., Tan, S., Chan, K.: A qualitative and heuristic approach to the conceptual design of mechanisms. Eng. Appl. Artif. Intell. **9**(1), 17–32 (1996)
22. Rechtin, E., Maier, M.W.: The art of Systems Architecting. CRC Press (2010). https://doi.org/10.1201/9781420058529
23. Pearl, J., Intelligent search strategies for computer problem solving. Addision Wesley, 1984
24. Yilmaz, S., et al.: Cognitive heuristic use in engineering design ideation. Age, vol. 15, p. 1 (2010)
25. Chulvi, V., et al.: Influence of the type of idea-generation method on the creativity of solutions. Res. Eng. Design **24**(1), 33–41 (2013)
26. Jarmasz, M., Szpakowicz, S.: Roget's thesaurus and semantic similarity. Recent Advances in Natural Language Processing III: Selected Papers from RANLP, 2004, p. 111. (2003)
27. Ross, V.E.: A model of inventive ideation. Thinking Skills Creativity **1**(2), 120–129 (2006)
28. Ahmad, S., et al.: Sustainable product design and development: a review of tools, applications and research prospects. Resour. Conserv. Recycl. **132**, 49–61 (2018)
29. Chiu, M.-C., Chu, C.-H.: Review of sustainable product design from life cycle perspectives. Int. J. Precis. Eng. Manuf. **13**(7), 1259–1272 (2012)
30. Go, T., Wahab, D., Hishamuddin, H.: Multiple generation life-cycles for product sustainability: the way forward. J. Clean. Prod. **95**, 16–29 (2015)
31. Ramani, K., et al.: Integrated sustainable life cycle design: a review. J. Mech. Des. **132**(9), 091004 (2010)

32. Baruah, J., Paulus, P.B.: Effects of training on idea generation in groups. Small Group Res. **39**(5), 523–541 (2008)
33. Glier, M.W., et al.: Distributed ideation: idea generation in distributed capstone engineering design teams. Int. J. Eng. Educ. **27**(6), 1281 (2011)
34. Kohn, N.W., Smith, S.M.: Collaborative fixation: effects of others' ideas on brainstorming. Appl. Cogn. Psychol. **25**(3), 359–371 (2011)
35. Nelson, B.A., et al.: Refined metrics for measuring ideation effectiveness. Des. Stud. **30**(6), 737–743 (2009)
36. Oman, S.K., et al.: A comparison of creativity and innovation metrics and sample validation through in-class design projects. Res. Eng. Design **24**(1), 65–92 (2013)
37. Shah, J.J., Kulkarni, S.V., Vargas-Hernandez, N.: Evaluation of idea generation methods for conceptual design: effectiveness metrics and design of experiments. J. Mech. Des. **122**(4), 377–384 (2000)
38. Shah, J.J., Smith, S.M., Vargas-Hernandez, N.: Metrics for measuring ideation effectiveness. Des. Stud. **24**(2), 111–134 (2003)
39. Smith, S.M., et al.: Empirical studies of creative cognition in idea generation. Creativity and innovation in organizational teams, pp. 3–20 (2006)
40. Wodehouse, A., Ion, W.: Augmenting the 6-3-5 method with design information. Res. Eng. Design **23**(1), 5–15 (2012)

From Pattern to Imagery Correlation: An Evaluation Method for the Redesign of Liangzhu Patterns Based on GRA-TOPSIS

Yuxin Ding, Yun Wang[✉], Longfei Zhou, Lingyan Zhang, and Yunjia Chen

Design Innovation Center, China Academy of Art, Hangzhou 310013, China
20202602@caa.edu.cn

Abstract. With the development of the progress of science and technology and the frequent cultural exchanges, the "image" has gradually converged. Traditional patterns with regional and national characteristics are receiving more and more attention in international cultural exchanges. Liangzhu culture, a world heritage site, is not only tangible evidence of the origin of Chinese civilization but also a valuable resource for design research. In order to solve the problem of inheriting the cultural connotation of the original cultural relics through pattern innovation, this research takes the semi-deity and animal pattern of Liangzhu jade cong as the research object from the perspective of the relevance of the cultural relic connotation and the design object. The visual cognition of Liangzhu pattern was obtained by the aesthetic preference rating scale and eye movement experiment, while the cultural imagery correlation was determined using the Analytic Hierarchy Process (AHP). Then, the above three factors were integrated by the GRA-TOPSIS evaluation method to construct an evaluation model of the correlation between the innovative patterns and the cultural connotation of the original cultural relics. As a result, the optimal solution with both modern aesthetics and cultural imagery was obtained to provide objective data support for the selection decision of the traditional pattern design based on cultural relics.

Keywords: Liangzhu pattern · Imagery correlation · GRA-TOPSIS

1 Introduction

1.1 Background

Modernization is now sweeping the world. In addition to increasing productivity and efficiency, external forms such as products and internal habits are rapidly becoming homogenized. Moreover, 'a thousand cities', one way has become a common case. Clearly communicating who I am in this highly internationalized world has become a challenge. Traditional patterns as a symbolic presence allow the viewer to recognize the past and present as distinct from other nationalities. According to relevant literature, traditional patterns, as specific cultural attributes, can awaken the viewer's awareness and shared memory. It also reflects traditional cultural aesthetic perception, symbolizes cultural connotations and conveys visual emotional semantics, bringing invaluable value to cultural creative product design [6].

At present, the traditional pattern is an important link to establish modern aesthetic and cultural imagery and has become an important source of creative design. However, there are still some deficiencies in the process, such as directly using the original pattern without redesigning, resulting in no distinctive visual characteristics and modern aesthetics, and lack of correlation between pattern innovation and the cultural connotation of the original cultural relics. In recent years, many experts and scholars have done related research on the traditional pattern, part of which is to deconstruct and reorganize the units of the original pattern and extract personal images for redesign. Liu extracted the core texture of Qiang embroidery patterns, using shape Grammar to evolve the basic graphic elements and designs a new texture scheme [10]. Li et al. taking Fengyang Phoenix painting as an example sorted out the relevant theories of geometric abstraction of cultural symbols, and redesigned the Phoenix painting, applying the theory of abstraction to the practice of product design, obtaining a practical operation method model [7]. Liu et al. [11] took traditional Chinese textile patterns as the research object, used conditional generative confrontation network model and computer-aided technology, and introduced deep learning conditional generative confrontation network model to classify and generate Chinese traditional textile patterns.

In addition to the redesign of the pattern itself, evaluation is an indispensable part of the pattern design process. An effective evaluation of the redesigned pattern is conducive to innovative design without changing its connotation so that the pattern can not only attract users, but also It is better to enter the mass market without losing the original cultural color. There are two basic approaches currently being adopted in research into design evaluation. One is formula evaluation method, and another is experimental evaluation method. The formula evaluation method uses mathematical formulas to calculate the index and obtain objective and quantitative judgments, such as principal component analysis [15], fuzzy evaluation method and analytic hierarchy process [3], extension semantics [5], GRA-TOPSIS evaluation method [12,18], Li et al. [8] studied the comprehensive evaluation and ranking of industrial design schemes through gray relational analysis and entropy weight method; however, the aesthetic feeling of products in the actual process, comfort and other factors are difficult to accurately quantify and express. Hsiao et al. (hsiao2012online) proposed an online evaluation model to replace the actual operation survey of product availability, using Multidimensional Scaling (MDS) to identify affordance attributes and their associated weights, K-means clustering, and analytic hierarchy process (AHP) method analyzes the product and evaluates the availability; constructs an online product availability evaluation model that can specifically quantify the availability level.

1.2 Overview of Liangzhu Culture

On July 6, 2019, Liangzhu was inscribed as a UNESCO World Heritage Site [13]. It is characterized by highly sophisticated jade artifacts, elaborate pottery, and well-planned cities and canals. The iconic jade artifacts of the Liangzhu Culture, including bi discs, cong tubes, and huang discs, demonstrate a high level of technical skill and aesthetic sensibility, and have come to symbolize the cultural achievements of the period [17,19]. The jade cong (Fig. 1), which seamlessly blends form and function, beauty and material, is the most exemplary and impactful of them all [9].

Fig. 1. The most representative Liangzhu jade cong-Fanshan M12:98

At the same time, the finely crafted decorations on Liangzhu jade cong add a touch of mystery to the piece, while the abstract and stylized lines bring the image to life and make the vessel truly come alive. These four corner prisms are typically filled with a standardized imagery of two types that may be repeated in similar size, in rows up and down the implement. The two types of imagery represent what are simplified versions of semi-deity and animal pattern (Fig. 2).

Fig. 2. Msemi-deity and animal pattern

The semi-deity symbol is identified by circular eyes, often with side slits, abended mouth, and a headdress formed by three lateral bands. The animal is defined by large eye sockets and circular pupils, a raised nasal ridge and a banded mouth, sometimes varied with an additional upward and downward set of fangs [4], the side padding is some spiral patterns. As time went on, the patterns became more simplified, and the image of the deity was often represented by its eyes. Today, the Liangzhu Culture remains an important cultural legacy of ancient China, and its artifacts are highly valued. This research focuses on Liangzhu Jade Cong as the subject of study to address the low correlation between cultural creative design and traditional cultural artifacts, leading to a reduced public recognition of design objects and subjective decision-making by designers. The visual recognition of the pattern is assessed through an aesthetic experience rating scale and eye movement experiment, while the cultural image correlation is evaluated through the Analytical Hierarchy Process. The GRA-TOPSIS evaluation method is employed to integrate these three factors to establish a comprehensive ranking system. This model aims to objectively evaluate the correlation between innovative design and the cultural significance of traditional cultural artifacts, providing a basis for informed decision-making in traditional pattern design solutions based on cultural relics.

2   Research Process

2.1   Research Process

The research process is divided into three stages, and the research process is shown in Fig. 3. First, after determining the target cultural relics, collect image samples of cultural relics in detail through literature, bibliography, web pages, historical materials. Then, the visual cognition of the cultural relics are deeply analyzed from the perspectives of shape, pattern, color, material, and craftsmanship, and the image model of the cultural relics is constructed through research. The patterns on the original cultural relics are extracted and designed to evolve. Then, the heat map of the pattern and the gaze time was obtained through the eye movement experiment, and the degree of preference was obtained through the questionnaire survey to obtain the aesthetic preference evaluation; the correlation between the pattern and the style intention of the original cultural relic was obtained through the analytic hierarchy process. Finally, combined with the evaluation of the above three aspects, a comprehensive evaluation of the redesigned pattern is obtained according to GRA-TOPSIS, and a pattern that not only conforms to modern aesthetics but also inherits the characteristics of traditional cultural relics is obtained.

2.2   Selection of Experimental Samples

In order to achieve the correlation analysis and aesthetic preference between patterns and original cultural relics, it is necessary to analyze the cultural imagery of traditional cultural relics. In this study, 12 valid samples of Liangzhu jade cong were collected through the "Liangzhu Digital Cultural Relics Database",

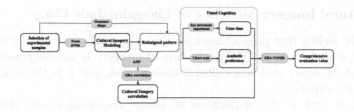

Fig. 3. Research process

Fig. 4. Cultural Imagery Modeling Sample

historical materials, web pages, and field photography. They were classified from the shape dimension, and the legend of Liangzhu jade cong was obtained (Fig. 4).

At the same time, the shape grammar was used to redesign the animal face pattern on the Liangzhu jade cong, and 12 patterns were obtained. And the patterns were divided into three groups according to the figure-ground relation set $M = \{M_1 - M_4\}$, $N = \{N_1 - N_4\}$, $O = \{O_1 - O_4\}$, as shown in (Fig. 5)

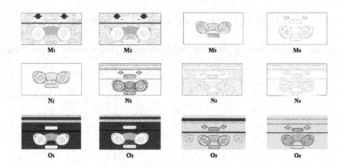

Fig. 5. Redesigned patterns sample set

2.3 Cultural Imagery Modeling of Liangzhu Jade Cong

Image is the feeling that people have about a certain thing, and it is a projection of emotion and thought [2]. The generation of imagery is usually closely related to personal life experience and cultural background, and it is the reproduction of perceptual experience.

The first part is the acquisition of image cognition about the original Liangzhu jade cong. Invite 30 people to conduct user research, including 5 archeology professionals, 20 designers, and 5 art researchers. This part of the subjects is recorded as user group A. Subjects can use adjectives to describe and evaluate Liangzhu jade cong according to its shape, characteristics, implication, and feelings. Adjectives can be single or multiple, and the formed image adjective set $U \in \{U_1, U_2, U_3, \cdots, U_n\}$ Due to individual differences, many adjectives may be generated. A total of 52 perceptual samples were collected this time. Repeated words in U_1-U_{52} were removed and similar words were clustered. The remaining There are 18 imagery adjectives in total, and the initial set of imagery adjectives $U\prime \in \{U_1, U_2, U_3 \cdots U_{18}\}$ is obtained.

In the second part, for the sake of style consistency, 5 subjects were selected from user group A, including 2 design professionals, 2 archaeologists, and 1 art researcher. as user group B. The imagery value of 18 words was evaluated using the Likert Scale method. The evaluation score adopts a 5-point system, and the results are summarized. Through comprehensive data analysis, it is found that the average value of the four words: mysterious, stately, sophisticated, and religiousis relatively high, so these four imagery adjectives are used as the final Imagery, Liangzhu culture jade cong imagery adjective evaluation see (Table 1).

Table 1. Likert scale score sheet(partial)

subjects	Mysterious	Quaint	Stately	Orderly	Sophisticated	Heavyweight	Quiet	Sharp	Religious
M1	4.8	4.5	4.5	4.2	4	3.9	3.8	3	3.5
M2	5	4	2.5	2.7	3	3.3	2.3	2.45	4.2
M3	5	4	2.5	2.7	3	3.3	2.3	2.45	4.2
M4	4	1	4.8	3	4.6	5	1	1	4
N1	4.3	2.1	4.6	3.2	3.1	3.8	1.2	2.1	4.8
N2	4	5	4.3	4	3	2	2	2	3
N3	4.5	4.5	5	4.2	4	4.3	4	4.8	4.3
Average	4.43	3.52	4.28	3.55	3.86	3.72	2.38	2.57	4.03

3   Visual Cognition of Patterns

Pattern, as a symbolic existence, has a strong image correlation, which can touch people's heartstrings in a moment. Whether it is the bison in the murals of the Altamira Cave or the patterns of the Liangzhu culture, it expresses the artistic language of the ancient ancestors. In this regard, through the study of visual cognition, we can examine the aesthetic preference and image cognition behind the decoration of cultural relics.

3.1 Visual Cognition

At present, visual cognition research is mainly carried out through subjective evaluation and objective measurement. Subjective evaluation includes in-depth interviews, questionnaires [20], and focus groups [1] semantic differential scale [16]. Subjective evaluation presents low technical barriers, allowing for the identification of problems and the capture of participants' subjective cognitive information. However, its limitation lies in the dependence of the evaluation results on the knowledge and experience of the test subjects and their familiarity with the relevant field.

Physiological measurement involves the combination of EEG technology and eye tracking experiment, infrared imaging, and other methods to detect changes in participants' physiological indicators. Among the above methods that can obtain the physiological indicators of the subjects, the eye-tracking experiment is the most effective way to analyze and obtain the attention information of the subjects [14]. It can objectively analyze consumers' aesthetic preferences for products through factors such as gaze time, gaze point, and pupil diameter. In this part, eye-tracking experiment and questionnaire methods will be combined to explore people's aesthetic preferences and the distribution of attention points for different target patterns

3.2 Eye Movement Experiment Evaluation and Preference Measures Model

Evaluation Model of Eye Movement Test. The eye tracker was used to evaluate and measure the subjects' feedback on different experimental samples, so as to identify their potential, intuitive physiological feedback. The eye movement indicators obtained from it were:

$$Y(b_i, c_i, E) = \begin{bmatrix} y(b_1, c_1, E) & y(b_1, c_2, E) & \cdots & y(b_1, c_m, E) \\ y(b_2, c_1, E) & y(b_2, c_2, E) & \cdots & y(b_2, c_m, E) \\ \vdots & \vdots & \ddots & \vdots \\ y(b_n, c_1, E) & y(b_n, c_2, E) & \cdots & y(b_n, c_m, E) \end{bmatrix}$$

Preference Value Evaluation Model. Set Subject as evaluation of scheme M_1 is $P_a M_1$, then the set of subjects $(a_1, a_2, \cdots, a_n)$respectively evaluating schemes$(M_1, M_2, \cdots, M_n)$ in turn is :

$$P = \begin{bmatrix} p_{1,1} & p_{1,2} & \cdots & p_{1,m} \\ p_{2,2} & p_{2,2} & \cdots & p_{2,m} \\ \vdots & \vdots & \ddots & \vdots \\ p_{n,1} & p_{n,2} & \cdots & p_{n,m} \end{bmatrix}$$

The comprehensive score of subject i is

$$P = \frac{p_{1,i} + p_{2,i} + \cdots + p_{n,i}}{n}$$

3.3 Eye Movement Experiment

1. Participants
   The subjects were 18–40 years old, 6 of them were male and 6 were female. All participants were in good health, and no color blindness (both partial and total), abnormal trichromatism, or night blindness was found. Visual acuity or corrected visual acuity of at least 1.0.
2. Apparatus
   The experiment was conducted in a quiet, comfortable, well-lit, and temperature-appropriate space; the subjects sat in a comfortable posture and avoided moving various parts of the body to reduce disturbance. The experimental apparatus is SteelSeries Sentry, The data sampling frequency 30 Hz, and using infrared compensation lighting technology, experiments can be carried out under any lighting conditions to ensure the accuracy and stability of the test. Experiments are carried out by Pro Display XDR.
3. Stimuli
   As shown in Fig. 5. The base color of each image is white and the pixel size is the same (600 × 900). Grayscale images were processed with Adobe Photoshop CC to eliminate the influence of color on cognitive judgments.
4. Experiment process
   The study was comprised of two parts: an eye-tracking experiment and a preference questionnaire. The eye-tracking experiment involved the use of an eye-tracking instrument to capture binocular data, with five points on the display screen being calibrated. The experiment began after the subjects were provided with accurate information and understood the instructions. The pictures were presented in a random order, each viewed for 10 s, with an average of 2 min per experiment. After the eye movement experiment, the participants rated the 12 patterns in the test materials on aesthetic preference through a five-point Likert scale questionnaire. The 12 subjects participated in the experiment in sequence until completion
5. Data processing of experimental results
   Eye movement data were statistically analyzed by Analysisone software. According to the purpose of the experiment, excluding unreasonable experimental data, the statistical data include the gazes points, the gaze time, etc. Aesthetic preference is the statistical mean of the subjective scale. Use Excel to organize data and use spss26 to analyze relevant mathematical statistics knowledge. The Heat map of gaze time are below (Fig. 6).

4 Analysis of Cultural Imagery Based on Grey Correlation Analysis

4.1 Method

Construction of Comparison and Reference Sequences. The first step is to determine the reference sequence (parent sequence) and the comparison

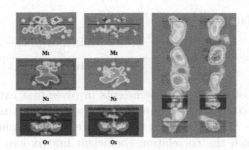

Fig. 6. Heat map of gaze time(partial)

sequence (subsequences). The reference sequence Y serves as the benchmark for subsequent correlation ranking and is typically generated from the best value in the comparison sequence when addressing comprehensive evaluativity issues. In the pattern design factor selection, it is assumed that the designer needs to choose the most representative design factors among the m factors to be evaluated, with the preferential ranking of these design factors being linked to the n evaluation indexes.

Comparison sequence of each design factor: $X_i = X_i(k)\ k = 1, 2, \cdots, n\ i = 1, 2, \cdots, m$

Reference sequence set according to the cultural image of Liangzhu jade cong: $Y = Y(k)\ k = 1, 2, \cdots, n$

Data Normalization. The original data is normalized to reduce the difference in the absolute values of the data and to unify it to a similar range. There are various evaluation indices for evaluating the design factors of the pattern of the evaluator. The data of different factors also have different magnitudes, so they cannot be directly compared. Normalization methods such as initial value method and mean value method are commonly used to process the data. In order to facilitate the solution, the mean value method is adopted to normalize the data of each evaluation index, and the values of each sequence are compared with the average value of the entire sequence.

$$X_i k = \frac{x_i(k)}{\overline{x_i}} \tag{1}$$

Calculating Correlation Coefficient. The correlation coefficient measures the degree of association between two system elements and the degree of association between the reference sequence and the comparison sequence at each point in the sequence curve. If the correlation coefficient is large, the degree of association between the comparison sequence and the reference sequence is large, indicating a closer connection between the design factor and the cultural relic. After processing the original data, the correlation coefficient is calculated according to formula(2).

$$\xi_i(k) = \frac{\min\limits_{i} \min\limits_{k} |y(k) - x_i k| + \rho \min\limits_{i} \min\limits_{k} |y(k) - x_i k|}{|y(k) - x_i k| + \rho \min\limits_{i} \min\limits_{k} |y(k) - x_i k|} \tag{2}$$

The calculation of correlation coefficients involves first extracting the reference sequence and comparison sequence and then subtracting them to obtain the difference value. This allows us to calculate the maximum and minimum difference, from which the correlation coefficient matrix can be obtained. The correlation coefficient, ρ, is in the range $(0, \infty)$, with smaller values indicating higher resolution. The range of ρ is usually $(0, 1)$ and its specific value can be determined based on the situation. It is commonly set to $\rho = 0.5$.

Calculation and Sorting of Correlation Degree. When calculating the correlation degree, since the correlation coefficient is the value of the correlation between the comparison sequence and the reference sequence at each moment (i.e., the points in the curve), its numbers are not just one. However, too much dispersed information will not be convenient for overall comparison, so it is necessary to centralize the correlation coefficients at each moment into one value, i.e., take its average value, as the quantitative representation of the correlation between the comparison sequence and the reference sequence, and the average value i is referred to as the correlation degree of $Y(k)$ and $X_i(k)$:

$$\gamma_i = \frac{1}{n} \sum_{k=1}^{n} \xi_i(k) 1, 2, \cdots, n \tag{3}$$

In the formula, n is the dimension of each vector, that is, the number of features of each element. The results are obtained by sorting the correlation and analyzing the relationship between the sub-sequence and the mother sequence. Therefore, the importance of each design factor can be sorted by correlation degree, reflecting the mapping degree between the design factor and the culture.

4.2 Specific Process

Construction of Comparison Sequences and Reference Sequences. Construction of comparison sequences. Thirty people were invited for user research, including 5 archaeology professionals, 20 designers, and 5 fine arts researchers, and this part of subjects was recorded as user group A. Subjects evaluated the three M, N, O groups using $U\prime$. The evaluation scores were evaluated using a 5-point scale, and the results were summarized and the mean values were taken as a comparison sequence. Construction of the reference sequence. Five experts were invited, two of whom were design professionals, two were archaeologists, and one was a fine arts researcher, and this part of the subjects was recorded as user group B. The subjects evaluated the three M, N, O groups using $U\prime$. The evaluation scores were evaluated using a 5-point scale, and the results were summarized and the mean values were taken as a reference sequence.

The results are shown in 2.

Table 2. Construction of comparison sequences and reference sequences

Scheme	Mysterious	Stately	Sophisticated	Religious
$M1$	3.30	3.53	3.52	4.45
$M2$	3.45	3.55	3.53	4.48
$M3$	2.30	1.73	2.12	2.27
$M4$	3.25	3.10	3.17	2.98
$N1$	3.97	3.88	4.17	3.70
$N2$	4.27	4.08	3.93	4.32
$N3$	3.32	3.10	3.12	3.23
$N4$	3.70	2.87	3.18	3.42
$O1$	3.83	3.37	3.12	3.58
$O2$	3.02	3.25	2.55	3.65
$O3$	2.82	2.67	2.50	3.12
$O4$	3.52	3.12	3.27	3.17
reference	3.39	3.19	3.18	3.53

Data Normalization. According to formula (1), the data in Table 2 is normalized to obtain matrix I_i'

$$I_i' = \begin{bmatrix} 0.97 & 1.11 & 1.11 & 1.26 \\ 1.02 & 1.11 & 1.11 & 1.27 \\ 0.68 & 0.54 & 0.67 & 0.64 \\ 0.96 & 0.97 & 1.00 & 0.85 \\ 1.17 & 1.22 & 1.31 & 1.05 \\ 1.26 & 1.28 & 1.24 & 1.22 \\ 0.98 & 0.97 & 0.98 & 0.92 \\ 1.09 & 0.90 & 1.00 & 0.97 \\ 1.13 & 1.06 & 0.98 & 1.01 \\ 0.89 & 1.02 & 0.80 & 1.03 \\ 0.83 & 0.84 & 0.79 & 0.88 \\ 1.04 & 0.98 & 1.03 & 0.90 \\ 1.26 & 1.28 & 1.31 & 1.27 \end{bmatrix}$$

Calculation of Correlation Coefficients. Based on formula (2), calculate the correlation coefficients between the comparison sequence and the reference sequence on each indicator, obtaining the matrix $\xi_i\prime$:

$$\xi_i\prime = \begin{bmatrix} 0.58\ 0.67\ 0.83\ 0.81 \\ 0.61\ 0.67\ 0.84\ 0.80 \\ 0.41\ 0.35\ 0.45\ 0.47 \\ 0.57\ 0.55\ 0.68\ 0.61 \\ 0.79\ 0.81\ 0.85\ 0.86 \\ 0.94\ 0.92\ 1.00\ 0.88 \\ 0.58\ 0.55\ 0.67\ 0.68 \\ 0.69\ 0.50\ 0.69\ 0.74 \\ 0.73\ 0.62\ 0.67\ 0.80 \\ 0.52\ 0.58\ 0.52\ 0.83 \\ 0.48\ 0.47\ 0.51\ 0.64 \\ 0.63\ 0.55\ 0.72\ 0.66 \end{bmatrix}$$

Correlation Calculation and Ranking. Finally, the correlation of each design factor with the original artifact is obtained according to formula (3).

Table 3. Cultural relevance of each scheme

	M_1	M_2	M_3	M_4	N_1	N_2	N_3	N_4	O_1	O_2	O_3	O_4
value	0.12	0.12	0.07	0.10	0.14	0.16	0.10	0.11	0.12	0.10	0.09	0.11

5   GRA-TOPSIS Comprehensive Evaluation

5.1   AHP Method

The Analytic Hierarchy Process (AHP), introduced by American operations researcher Thomas Saaty in the 1970s is a systematic and hierarchical analysis method that combines both qualitative and quantitative methods. The AHP method was utilized by Linqi Zhao et al. [18] to establish a judgment matrix and determine the relative weights of each cultural image and objective evaluation index. The steps involved in the AHP process include:

1. Development of a hierarchical analysis model
2. Establishment of a judgment matrix
3. Hierarchical ranking and assessment of consistency

5.2   GRA-TOPSIS Evaluation Method

Define the Decision Matrix. The evaluation indexes are established, and the m pattern options are ranked and optimized one by one. The evaluation values of the m alternatives form a decision set, denoted as $A = \{A_1, A_2, \ldots, A_m\}$. The k_{th} The evaluation value A_i of the i_{th} pattern alternative corresponding to the value of the evaluation index under the kth index is defined as $\omega_i(k), (i = 1, 2, \ldots, m; k = 1, 2, \ldots, n)$, the decision matrix is defined as $\omega = [\omega_i(k)]_{n \times m}$.

Standardize the Decision Matrix. In the evaluation of Liangzhu patterns, the nature of each evaluation index is different, and there are mainly two types of evaluation indexes, benefit-type and cost-type. The larger the value of benefit type, the better; the smaller the value of cost type evaluation index, the better. In order to eliminate the influence of different dimensions of indicators, firstly, the cost-type indicators are processed positively, i.e., the largest evaluation indicator value under the kth indicator is selected, and the alternative evaluation indicators of each pattern under this indicator are subtracted. The maximum value of the evaluation indicator under the kth indicator is selected, and the alternative evaluation indicators under the indicator are subtracted:

$$x_i(k) = \max_{1 \le j \le m} \{\omega_j(k)\} - \omega_i(k) \tag{4}$$

Subsequently, the processed decision matrix $\omega = [\omega_i(k)]_{n \times m}$ is transformed into a normalized decision matrix $X = [x_i(k)]_{n \times m}$ through normalization procedures:

$$Z_{ij} = \frac{x_{ij}}{\sqrt{\sum_{i=1}^{n} x_{ij}^2}} \tag{5}$$

Determine the Positive Ideal and Negative Ideal Solution. The determination of positive and negative ideal solutions involves evaluating a total of n Liangzhu pattern evaluation indicators. The maximum evaluation values of m solutions constitute a positive ideal solution, designated as A^+. Conversely, the minimum evaluation values of m solutions, when evaluating the n Liangzhu pattern evaluation indicators, form the negative ideal solution, designated as A^-. Upon normalization of the decision matrix, the positive and negative ideal solutions are represented as $Z^+ = \{z^+(1), z^+(2), \cdots, z^+(n)\}$ and $Z^- = \{z^-(1), z^-(2), \cdots, z^-(n)\}$, respectively, which:

$$z^+(k) = \max_{1 \le i \le m} \{z_i(k)\} \tag{6}$$

$$z^-(k) = \min_{1 \le i \le m} \{z_i(k)\} \tag{7}$$

Calculating Gray Correlation Desgree. In the k_{th} indicator, the correlation coefficient of the positive ideal solution of the i_{th} Liangzhu pattern design solution A is:

$$\gamma(z^+(k), z_i(k)) = \frac{\min_i \min_k |z^+(k) - z_i(k)| + \rho \max_i \max_k |z^+(k) - z_i(k)|}{|z^+(k) - z_i(k)| + \rho \max_i \max_k |z^+(k) - z_i(k)|} \tag{8}$$

where ρ is the discriminant coefficient, generally $\rho = 5$. In the k_{th} indicator, the correlation coefficient of the negative ideal solution of the i_{th} Liangzhu pattern design scheme A is:

$$\gamma\left(z^-(k), z_i(k)\right) = \frac{\min\limits_{i}\min\limits_{k}|z^-(k) - z_i(k)| + \rho\max\limits_{i}\max\limits_{k}|z^-(k) - z_i(k)|}{|z^-(k) - z_i(k)| + \rho\max\limits_{i}\max\limits_{k}|z^-(k) - z_i(k)|} \tag{9}$$

Let the vector of index weights to be evaluated $\omega = (\omega_1, \omega_2, \ldots, \omega_n)$, and the gray correlation between the i_{th} solution A and the positive ideal The gray correlation of the solution is :

$$\gamma\left(Z^+, Z_i\right) = \sum_{k=1}^{n} \omega_k \cdot \gamma\left(z^+(k), z_i(k)\right) \tag{10}$$

The gray correlation of the i_{th} solution Ai with the negative ideal solution is:

$$\gamma\left(Z^-, Z_i\right) = \sum_{k=1}^{n} \omega_k \cdot \gamma\left(z^-(k), z_i(k)\right) \tag{11}$$

Calculating Euclidean Distance. The Euclidean distance between the i_{th} element A and the positive ideal solution is:

$$d\left(Z^+, Z_i\right) = \sqrt{\sum_{k=1}^{n} \omega_k \cdot \left(z^+(k) - z_i(k)\right)^2} \tag{12}$$

$$d\left(Z^-, Z_i\right) = \sqrt{\sum_{k=1}^{n} \omega_k \cdot \left(z^-(k) - z_i(k)\right)^2} \tag{13}$$

Integration of Gray Correlation Degree and Euclidean Distance Normalization Normalize $\gamma(Z^+, Z^i)\gamma(Z^-, Z^i), d(Z^+, Z^i), d(Z^-, Z^i)$.

$$R\left(Z^+, Z_i\right) = \frac{\gamma\left(Z^+, Z_i\right)}{\sqrt{\sum_{k=1}^{n} \gamma\left(Z^+, Z_i\right)^2}} \tag{14}$$

$$R\left(Z^-, Z_i\right) = \frac{\gamma\left(Z^-, Z_i\right)}{\sqrt{\sum_{k=1}^{n} \gamma\left(Z^-, Z_i\right)^2}} \tag{15}$$

$$D\left(Z^+, Z_i\right) = \frac{d\left(Z^+, Z_i\right)}{\sqrt{\sum_{k=1}^{n} d\left(Z^+, Z_i\right)^2}} \tag{16}$$

$$D\left(Z^-, Z_i\right) = \frac{d\left(Z^-, Z_i\right)}{\sqrt{\sum_{k=1}^{n} d\left(Z^-, Z_i\right)^2}} \tag{17}$$

When the values of $D(Z^-, Z_i)$ and $R(Z^+, Z_i)$ are larger, the evaluation plan tends to the positive ideal solution. On the other hand, when the values of $D(Z^+, Z_i)$ and $R(Z^-, Z_i)$ are larger, the evaluation plan tends to approach the negative ideal solution. By combining the grey correlation and Euclidean distance, we get:

$$E\left(Z^+, Z_i\right) = \alpha D\left(Z^-, Z_i\right) + \beta R\left(Z^+, Z_i\right) \tag{18}$$

$$E\left(Z^-, Z_i\right) = \alpha D\left(Z^+, Z_i\right) + \beta R\left(Z^-, Z_i\right) \tag{19}$$

where α and β reflect the decision-maker's preferences for location and shape, $\alpha + \beta = 1$, $\alpha, \beta \in [0.1]$.

Calculating Similarity. The relative similarity of the $i_t h$ member A_i is:

$$S_i = \frac{E\left(Z^+, Z_i\right)}{E\left(Z^+, Z_i\right) + E\left(Z^-, Z_i\right)} \tag{20}$$

In this formula, the larger the value of S_i the better the solution.

5.3   Evaluation Process

Table 4. The comparison matrix

	Cultural imagery relevance	Gazing Point	Aesthetic Preference
Cultural imagery relevance	1	2	2
Gazing Point	$\frac{1}{2}$	1	1
Aesthetic Preference	$\frac{1}{2}$	1	1

Indicator Weights. The matrix can be obtained from Table 4.

$$A = \begin{bmatrix} 1 & 2 & 2 \\ \frac{1}{2} & 1 & 1 \\ \frac{1}{2} & 1 & 1 \end{bmatrix}$$

According to the method adopted by Zuo et al. [?], A is normalized twice to obtain the eigenvectors of A eigenvector W

$$W = (0.5, 0.25, 0.25)^T$$

It has been verified that:

$$\lambda_{\max} W = 3$$

$$CI = 0$$

$$CR = 0$$

Decision Matrix. Thirty subjects were selected to evaluate 12 different patterns of Liangzhu cultures. The gender distribution of these subjects was 13 males (43%) and 17 females (57%). Among them, 18 had Master'sDoctorate degrees (60%) (Tables 5 and 6).

Table 5. The scores of each scheme under three indicators.

scheme	culture imagery correlation	gaze time	aesthetic preference
O_4	0.58	0.67	0.83
O_3	0.61	0.67	0.84
O_2	0.41	0.35	0.45
O_1	0.57	0.55	0.68
N_4	0.79	0.81	0.85
N_3	0.11	2.00	3.03
N_2	0.09	2.00	3.13
N_1	0.10	2.17	3.20
M_1	0.12	0.83	3.60
M_2	0.11	2.33	3.88
M_3	0.10	3.17	4.17
M_4	0.16	2.67	3.18

Due to the difference in dimensions between distance metrics and simplicity and richness of cultural heritage metrics, the decision matrix was standardized according to Eq. (5), as shown in the table.

Table 6. Standardized score of each scheme under the 3 indexes.

scheme	culture imagery correlation	gaze time	aesthetic preference
O_4	0.27	0.28	0.26
O_3	0.22	0.28	0.27
O_2	0.26	0.31	0.28
O_1	0.30	0.12	0.31
N_4	0.28	0.33	0.34
N_3	0.26	0.45	0.36
N_2	0.40	0.38	0.28
N_1	0.35	0.24	0.33
M_1	0.26	0.35	0.22
M_2	0.18	0.21	0.23
M_3	0.31	0.17	0.24
M_4	0.31	0.17	0.31

Determining the Ideal Positive and Negative Solutions. Selecting the ideal positive and negative solutions from all the evaluation data sets, resulting in the ideal positive and negative solutions.

$$z^+(k) = \{0.40, 0.45, 0.36\}, z^-(k) = \{0.18, 0.12, 0.22\}$$

Calculating Grey Correlation Degree. Based on formula (14), (15), (16) and (17), calculate the grey correlation of each Lianzhou pattern scheme with the positive ideal solution and the negative ideal solution. The calculation results are shown in Table 7.

Table 7. Grey correlation degree between Liangzhu pattern scheme and ideal scheme.

Schemes	Gray Correlation Degree	
	Positive Ideal Solution	Negative Ideal Solution
O_4	0.56	0.64
O_3	0.56	0.66
O_2	0.59	0.61
O_1	0.57	0.77
N_4	0.70	0.53
N_3	0.91	0.48
N_2	0.74	0.53
N_1	0.67	0.57
M_4	0.57	0.70
M_3	0.47	0.82
M_2	0.51	0.76
M_1	0.58	0.68

Calculating the Euclidean Distance. According to Formulas (6), (7), (12), and (13), calculate the Euclidean distance between each design solution of the Lianzhou weave pattern and the positive and negative ideal solutions. The calculation results are shown in Table 8.

Integration of Gray Correlation Degree and Euclidean Distance. Due to the different dimensions of the grey correlation degree and Euclidean distance, the grey correlation degree and Euclidean distance between each Liangzhu pattern design scheme and the positive and negative ideal solutions are normalized according to formulas (14), (15), (16) and (17), as shown in Table 9.

Define $\alpha = \beta = 0.5$ according to formulas (18) and (19). Then, the grey correlation degree and Euclidean distance are combined. The results are shown in Table 10. Finally, the relative similarity of the integrated grey correlation degree and Euclidean distance is derived according to formula (20), as shown in Table 3.

Table 8. Euclidean distance between Liangzhu pattern design scheme and ideal solution.

Schemes	Euclidean Distance	
	Positive Ideal Solution	Negative Ideal Solution
O_4	0.13	0.11
O_3	0.15	0.09
O_2	0.13	0.12
O_1	0.18	0.10
N_4	0.10	0.14
N_3	0.10	0.19
N_2	0.06	0.20
N_1	0.11	0.15
M_4	0.13	0.13
M_3	0.21	0.05
M_2	0.17	0.10
M_1	0.16	0.10

Table 9. Normalized grey correlation degree and Euclidean distance between Liangzhu pattern scheme and ideal solution.

Schemes	Gray Correlation Degree		Euclidean Distance	
	Positive Ideal Solution	Negative Ideal Solution	Positive Ideal Solution	Negative Ideal Solution
O_4	0.12	0.13	0.55	0.54
O_3	0.11	0.14	0.65	0.46
O_2	0.12	0.12	0.53	0.57
O_1	0.12	0.14	0.76	0.49
N_4	0.14	0.11	0.44	0.70
N_3	0.16	0.11	0.40	0.94
N_2	0.18	0.10	0.23	1.01
N_1	0.15	0.11	0.47	0.73
M_4	0.12	0.14	0.56	0.64
M_3	0.10	0.17	0.87	0.24
M_2	0.12	0.13	0.70	0.48
M_1	0.13	0.13	0.66	0.52

Calculating Similarity. As shown in Table 11, based on the GRA-TOPSIS method, the overall ranking results of the various design scenarios are $N_2 > N_3 > N_4 > N_1 > M_4 > O_2 > O_4 > M_1 > M_2 > O_3 > O_1 > M_3$. The results show that N2 retains the pattern's main outline andcenter fill pattern, which best conveys the design image; N4, composed of the mainoutline and simplified patterns, is most in line with modern aesthetic preferences. Themost visually exciting design is the N3, which comes with a graphic background, and the N2, which has a good balance of the three dimensions. It is also interesting tonote

Table 10. Integrated GRA-TOPSIS evaluation score compared with ideal solutions.

Schemes	Integrated GRA-TOPSIS	
	Positive Ideal Solution	Negative Ideal Solution
O_4	0.33	0.33
O_3	0.39	0.29
O_2	0.33	0.34
O_1	0.44	0.32
N_4	0.29	0.40
N_3	0.30	0.52
N_2	0.19	0.56
N_1	0.31	0.42
M_4	0.34	0.39
M_3	0.48	0.20
M_2	0.40	0.32
M_1	0.39	0.32

that the results for the simpler M3 and M4 do not seem satisfactory, so it may be assumed that pure simplification is not exceptionally applicable.

Table 11. Liangzhu pattern scheme similarity Degree

Schemes	O_4	O_3	O_2	O_1	N_4	N_3	N_2	N_1	M_4	M_3	M_2	M_1
Similarity Degree	0.50	0.43	0.51	0.42	0.58	0.64	0.74	0.58	0.53	0.29	0.44	0.45

6   Dissusion

The cultural and traditional patterns of utensils serve as a nation's defining characteristic and source of cultural richness. This study investigates the correlation between traditional heritage and cultural and creative design products by utilizing subjective and objective evaluations. The results aim to improve the cultural image characteristics of these products, provide a theoretical reference, and meet modern aesthetic needs while preserving traditional culture. To a certain extent, it gets rid of the shortcomings of the artificial extraction method relying on subjective experience, helping to enhance the cultural image characteristics of products. In the new era, traditional patterns should satisfy the dynamic relationship of the big situation so that the excellent traditional culture can be carried forward and inherited. The limitations of the study include the lack of cross-cultural evaluation and the omission of gender and population factors in the eye movement experiment. Further research is needed to design and apply the evaluated patterns and conduct additional evaluations for verification.

References

1. Alahmadi, T., Drew, S.: Subjective evaluation of website accessibility and usability: a survey for people with sensory disabilities. In: Proceedings of the 14th International Web for All Conference, pp. 1–4 (2017)
2. Bryson, N., Holly, M.A., Moxey, K.: Visual Culture: Images and Interpretations. Wesleyan University Press, Middletown (1994)
3. Chen, Y., Liu, Y., Liu, T., Wen, B.: Comprehensive evaluation for product quality generalized based on fuzzy analytic hierarchy process. In: 2009 Second International Conference on Intelligent Computation Technology and Automation, vol. 2, pp. 672–675. IEEE (2009)
4. Childs-Johnson, E.: Speculations on the religious use and significance of jade cong and bi of the liangzhu culture. Liangzhu: Late Neolithic Jades, pp. 2–16 (2012)
5. Hu, S., Jia, Q., Wang, Y., Dong, L., Lao, Y.: Redesign research of traditional cultural symbols based on eye-movement experiments and extensible semantics. Art Design (8), 4 (2021)
6. Lee, Y.J.: Exploration of local culture elements and design of cultural creativity products. J. Stat. Manag. Syst. **13**(4), 823–834 (2010)
7. Li, H.: The application of geometric abstraction of Chinese traditional cultural symbols in the design of daily utensils-taking fengyang phoenix painting as an example. In: Cross-Cultural Design. Applications in Learning, Arts, Cultural Heritage, Creative Industries, and Virtual Reality: 14th International Conference, CCD 2022, Held as Part of the 24th HCI International Conference, HCII 2022, Virtual Event, June 26-July 1, 2022, Proceedings, Part II. pp. 387–399. Springer (2022). https://doi.org/10.1007/978-3-031-06047-2_28
8. Li, X., et al.: decision making model of industrial design scheme optimization based on multi-level grey comprehensive evaluation method and its application. J. Graph. **42**(4), 10 (2021)
9. Liu, B.: Power and beliefs. In: Liangzhu Jade Artifacts: Legal Instrument and Royalty, pp. 99–150. Springer, Singapore (2022). https://doi.org/10.1007/978-981-19-0292-5_3
10. Liu, L.: Application of qiang embroidery's innovation pattern design based on shape grammar. Packag. Eng. **41**(24), 7 (2020)
11. Liu, M., Zhou, B.: Innovative design of Chinese traditional textile patterns based on conditional generative adversarial network. In: Culture and Computing: 10th International Conference, C&C 2022, Held as Part of the 24th HCI International Conference, HCII 2022, Virtual Event, June 26-July 1, 2022, Proceedings. pp. 234–245. Springer, Cham (2022). https://doi.org/10.1007/978-3-031-05434-1_15
12. Quan, H., Li, S., Wei, H., Hu, J.: Personalized product evaluation based on gratopsis and kansei engineering. Symmetry **11**(7), 867 (2019)
13. wikipedia: liangzhu culture – wikipedia the free encyclopedia (2022). https://zh.wikipedia.org/w/index.php?title=online. Accessed 20 Dec 2022
14. Wu, C., Song, S., Min, Y., Fei, B.: A study on the aesthetic preference of bamboo weaving patterns based on eye movement experiments. Available at SSRN 4108604
15. Yang, C., Sun, S., Liu, Z., Chai, C.: Decision-making model of product design based on principal component analysis. China Mech. Eng. **22**(18), 6 (2011)
16. Yang, W., Su, J., Qiu, K., Zhang, X., Zhang, S.: Research on evaluation of product image design elements based on eye movement signal. In: Harris, D. (ed.) HCII 2019. LNCS (LNAI), vol. 11571, pp. 214–226. Springer, Cham (2019). https://doi.org/10.1007/978-3-030-22507-0_17

17. Ying, Z.: The dawn of the oriental civilization: Liangzhu site and liangzhu culture (2007)
18. Zhao, L., Wang, Z., Zuo, Y., Hu, D.: Comprehensive evaluation method of ethnic costume color based on k-means clustering method. Symmetry **13**(10), 1822 (2021)
19. Zhixin, S.: The liangzhu culture: its discovery and its jades. Early China **18**, 1–40 (1993)
20. Zhu, L., Li, C., Zhu, Z.: Research on design style of cartoon medical science interface based on kansei engineering. In: Marcus, A., Wang, W. (eds.) HCII 2019. LNCS, vol. 11583, pp. 597–606. Springer, Cham (2019). https://doi.org/10.1007/978-3-030-23570-3_44

Construction and Design Application of Taohuawu New Year Woodblock Prints Color Database

Yiao Fang[1], Zhengqing Jiang[1(✉)], Ruihan Zhang[1], and Liangyu Gu[2]

[1] East China University of Science and Technology,
Shanghai 200030, People's Republic of China
jiangzhengqing@ecust.edu.cn
[2] Nanjing Audit University, Nanjing 211815, People's Republic of China

Abstract. It is proposed in this study that an approach of color application strategy based on the user kansei images can help convey the cultural connotation of cultural products. A Continuous Fuzzy Kano Model is used to study which factor is more important among the main factors affecting user evaluation. The study shows that the color factor has a more significant impact, and the color of cultural products is determined as the primary research object. The K-means clustering algorithm extracts the representative colors of Taohuawu New Year Woodblock Prints. Then, we studied consumers' kansei evaluation of different colors by semantic differential method, and the experimental results were used for design. The user-centered color design strategy of cultural products is expanded and applied to the design of cultural products. Through the analysis of user satisfaction and perception, it is proved that a color application scheme has high user satisfaction, which can meet the needs of user visual satisfaction and cultural connotation transmission.

Keywords: Taohuawu New Year Woodblock Prints · Continuous Fuzzy Kano Model · Cultural Design · Customer Satisfaction · Kansei Image

1 Introduction

Currently, consumers' consumption motivation is not limited to function and appearance. They hope that the products can reflect certain cultures and tastes. Therefore, increasing the cultural value of products can effectively enhance consumers' willingness to consume. At the same time, it can also better spread and protect the excellent traditional culture.

Most scholars' research is directed at how to extract the cultural factors in traditional culture more accurately. These cultural factors mainly include form, color, pattern, allegory, line, pattern, etc., among which the research on pattern design is relatively affluent. The current research on cultural product design is mainly based on the theory of "three levels of culture" [1], which consists of three levels of culture: inner, middle, and outer [2]. Su et al. [3] applied the tortoise snake pattern of longevity to the teapot product

P.-L. P. Rau (Ed.): HCII 2023, LNCS 14022, pp. 38–51, 2023.
https://doi.org/10.1007/978-3-031-35936-1_3

design through the study of user preference evaluation. Chen Xiang et al. [4] also studied from the user's point of view, extracting the characteristics of the skin shadow pattern through eye-movement experiments and applying them to the design. Chen Manru et al. [5] collected data on the color of familiar Qin cadence faces and studied user kansei evaluation of different red color values to provide some color-matching suggestions. Yang Mei et al. [6] constructed a Dunhuang mural color network model and applied it to product design.

Homogeneous studies mainly extract relevant colors directly through clustering algorithms. However, there will still be many similar colors after extraction, and the final color selection relies on expert experience, which will be more subjective and ambiguous and may indirectly affect the design results. Therefore, optimizing the objectivity of color used in the design process is necessary to prevent designers' subjective preferences from influencing the semantic communication of cultural products. In this paper, we study color use strategies in cultural products through user kansei images to improve cultural image communication's rationality and accuracy.

2   Study on the Importance of Cultural Elements of Cultural Products

2.1   Taohuawu New Year Woodblock Prints Culture

Taohuayu New Year Woodblock Print is one of the most widely circulated types of Woodblock Prints in southern China, and its influence is quite profound [7]. Originating in the Jiajing period of the Ming Dynasty, the early Taohuayu New Year Woodblock Prints inherited the engraving and printing techniques of the Song Dynasty and were fresh and elegant in style. During the Qianlong period of the Qing Dynasty, with economic development, the quality of Taohuawu New Year Woodblock Prints reached a peak in sales. Taohuawu New Year Woodblock Prints generally embody the local people's spiritual beliefs and cultural psychology, reflecting their aspirations and pursuit of a better life [9].

In general, the development of this art through the vicissitudes can be roughly divided into two stages. The first period, from the late Ming and early Qing dynasties to the Taiping Heavenly Kingdom period, is known as the Changmen Kusu Prints, and the works were elegant in style, with delicate and elegant pictures, focusing on perspective and light and shadow. The works after the Taiping Heavenly Kingdom were mainly aimed at the urban underclass and peasants. The pictures were relatively rough. A detailed comparison of the two periods is shown in Table 1.

Through the preliminary user preference experiment, it is found that users prefer Changmen Kusu Prints [14] to the works after the Taiping Heavenly Kingdom, so the research in this paper is mainly based on Changmen Kusu Prints.

Table 1. Comparison of two major periods of Taohuawu New Year Woodblock Prints

	Changmen Kusu Prints	Taohuawu New Year Woodblock Prints
Period	Early Qing Dynasty ~ Taiping Heavenly Kingdom	Taiping Heavenly Kingdom ~ Now
Time background	Social stability, Economic development, Cultural prosperity	Social unrest, The economic downturn
Artistic features	The work is magnificent, pays attention to perspective, light and shadow are finely portrayed, and has an elegant style	The style is festive and warm, bright and simple, with strong contrast
Consumers	Upper-class citizens, Foreigners	Underclass urban citizens, farmers

2.2 Continuous Fuzzy Kano Model

The Kano model is a method for studying user needs proposed by Professor Noriaki Kan [10]. It is a qualitative study of user needs through a two-way questionnaire in which users answer their feelings about a feature from both positive and negative perspectives so that user needs can be categorized into five types: must-be, attractive, one-dimensional, indifferent, and reverse. In this way, it is possible to understand the user's needs for a specific product and guide the design. The Kano model is one of the most widely used models and methods in the design field [11].

Many scholars have proposed optimization strategies for the Kano model, among which the fuzzy Kano model has many applications. Fuzzy Kano uses the principle of fuzzy mathematical affiliation to replace the original "whether" with a fuzzy interval [0,1], in which the user can fill in the approval degree of the option. In this way, the users' evaluation preferences can be more precisely understood. However, in general, fuzzy Kano is still a qualitative study, which only makes the process of user judgment precise by fuzzy mathematics, and the final result is only a qualitative conclusion. Considering the shortcomings of existing methods, Liya Wang [12] proposed a continuous fuzzy Kano method, which allows users to choose more values between "like" and "deserve," which considers the complexity of the original user's judgment. It also means that they established a quantitative algorithm to calculate specific user satisfaction values (see Fig. 1).

Based on the questionnaire outcome, the subordination matrix U_n of the user's preference for different satisfaction levels can be constructed (see Eq. 1). Its calculation is mainly based on fuzzy set theory: the closer the user chooses the point to the standard answer, then the higher his affiliation to this standard answer. F_n represents the matrix of positive questions, Dn represents the matrix of negative questions, i denotes the i-th standard answer under positive questions, and j denotes the j-th standard answer under negative questions.

$$U_n = F_n \times D_n = \left(u_{nij}\right)_{5\times5} \tag{1}$$

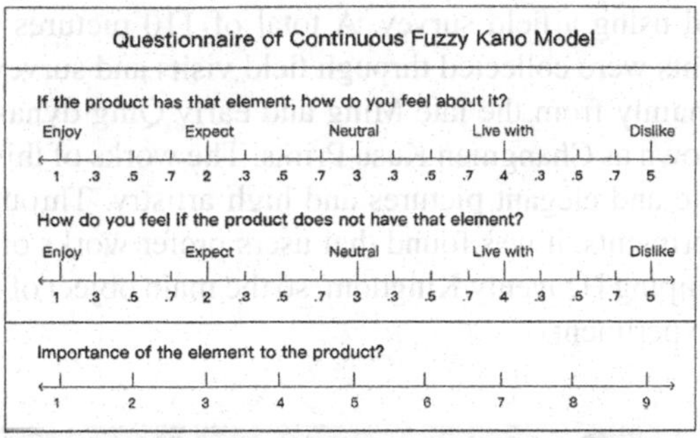

Fig. 1. Questionnaire of Continuous Fuzzy Kano model

After that, we can calculate individual satisfaction (S_n). According to the evaluation table of the Kano model, we can express the contribution of each combination to user satisfaction by assigning different "impact values" to the 25 combinations [11]. This influence value can be adjusted to the actual situation, and WU [11]created a standard matrix of influence values.

$$NIV = (v_{ij})_{5 \times 5} = \begin{bmatrix} 0 & 0.200 & 0.250 & 0.300 & 0.500 \\ -0.100 & 0 & 0.050 & 0.075 & 0.900 \\ -0.125 & -0.025 & 0 & 0.1 & 1.000 \\ -0.150 & -0.038 & -0.050 & 0 & 0.800 \\ -0.250 & -0.450 & -0.500 & -0.400 & 0 \end{bmatrix} \tag{2}$$

Using the impact value weighting gives the individual satisfaction formula:

$$S_n = \sum_{i=1}^{5} \sum_{j=1}^{5} v_{ij} \times u_{nij} \tag{3}$$

Finally, the user satisfaction index (EI) can be calculated, which is the average of all participants' satisfaction with an element, and ω_n represents the weight value given by the n-th user, and the data range is [0,1].

$$EI = \frac{\sum_{n=1}^{N} \omega_n \times S_n}{N} \tag{4}$$

When EI > 0.1, the element is judged to be a charm type and above demand, which is of research value and significance. When it is less than 0.1, it is considered to be a non-differentiated demand, which has a relatively small effect on improving user satisfaction.

2.3 Experiment on User Satisfaction of Taohuawu New Year Woodblock Prints Elements

According to the theory of cultural hierarchy [1], the artistic characteristics of Taohuawu New Year Woodblock Prints were combined to determine the "color," "gesture," and "pattern" of the external level and the "symbolic meaning" of the internal level. "The study was conducted using a field survey. A total of 110 pictures of Taohuawu New Year Woodblock Prints were collected through field visits and surveys (see Fig. 2). The selected styles are mainly from the late Ming and early Qing dynasties to the Taiping period, which are known as Changmen Kusu Prints. The works of this period are elegant in style, with delicate and elegant pictures and high artistry. Through the preliminary user preference experiments, it was found that users prefer works of this period [14] to woodcuts after the Taiping Heavenly Kingdom, so the main object of study is Changmen Kusu Prints in this experiment.

Fig. 2. Pictures of Taohuawu New Year Woodblock Prints

In the color extraction experiment, we chose to extract the colors from the picture of *Maguxianshou*, which is a representative work of the mid-Qing period, showing a high artistic standard, with a detailed portrayal of the characters and elegant colors. After extracting the colors through the K-means algorithm, the primary colors, black and light brown, were excluded. The matching colors blue-violet and orange-red were selected as the experimental colors. After sorting statistics of the collected samples for the patterns, we found that various traditional patterns were widely used, among which the *Wan Zi* and the *Flower and Grass* pattern were used with great frequency especially, so we extracted these two pattern elements. For the gesture, we mainly extracted the facial gesture. We selected the facial images of two representative works, *Maguxianshou* and *Yituanheqi*, as the experimental objects, and the extracted elements are shown in Fig. 3.

The experiment was conducted mainly using the continuous fuzzy Kano method described previously, and 42 questionnaires were finally obtained. The Cronbach's α coefficient of the questionnaire was 0.835. Its value is above 0.8, indicating that the scale's reliability was excellent.

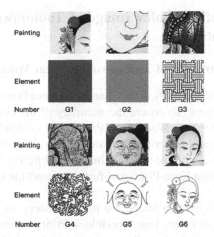

Fig. 3. Extracting of Traditional Elements

2.4 Analysis of Experimental Results

The experimental results were processed using a script coded in Python to process the experimental data. The user satisfaction index (EI) was obtained after processing, and the value represents the average user satisfaction with a particular element. The experimental results are shown in Table 2.

Table 2. Evaluation index data

	Number	Description	Satisfaction index (EI)
Color	G1	#5D619F	0.0738
	G2	#EF8457	0.1100
Patterns	G3	*Wan Zi*	0.0198
	G4	*Flower and Grass*	0.0256
Gesture	G5	*Yituanheqi*	0.0139
	G6	*Maguxianshou*	0.0556

In the experiment, the user satisfaction of the two patterns is low, and they are both " indifferent qualities," which is less effective in improving user satisfaction. User satisfaction with the two postures is average and belongs to the " indifferent qualities." However, the difference between them is large, which shows that the specific form has a relatively significant impact on user satisfaction. User satisfaction with both colors is higher among the experimental elements, and one of the colors is "attractive qualities," which means that consumers are more satisfied with the color element in cultural product design today. This result also prompts us to study users' preference for the color element in cultural products more carefully.

3   Determination of the Color Image of Taohuawu New Year Woodblock Prints

3.1   Color Element Extraction of Taohuawu New Year Woodblock Prints

The object of the experimental study is the Changmen Kusu Prints, a genre of Taohuawu New Year Woodblock Prints. To ensure the accuracy of the color image, we use 110 images of Taohuawu New Year Woodblock Prints shot at standard color temperature and brightness as the original material. First, we use the clustering algorithm to extract a single picture. Then we can divide the color hues into different categories to obtain the color database of Changmen Kusu Prints and further extract the representative colors of Changmen Kusu Prints.

Since the colors used in each image are not consistent, to be able to convey the whole style of the Taohuawu New Year Woodblock Prints, we used the color extraction results of a single image as a basis to further integrate the whole representative colors for the user image research experiments. The experiments are mainly conducted by the k-means image clustering algorithm, which can extract specific colors. Then, randomly select specific numbers(k) of pixel points from the picture as clustering centers, thus calculating the gap between each pixel point and each preset clustering center so that similar colors can be clustered into a set [15]. We implemented the experiment with a python program coded by us. After comparing the experiments, we found that when k is 12, we can extract most of the main colors, so we extract all 12 theme colors in the first step of extraction. Figure 4 shows the case of extracting one image. By extracting the color of one image by one, we obtain the color database of Changmen Kusu Prints.

Fig. 4. Single picture color extraction

Through statistical analysis and a literature survey of the picture elements of Taohuawu New Year Woodblock Prints [8], we found that the color used in most paintings showed a certain regularity. The first is the background color. Most of the background color is the original beige color of the paper. Secondly, the lines often use pure black fine lines. The subject of the painting is usually filled with only two to three colors. And the colors in the painting can be divided into blue, green, yellow, red, and black, according to the hue and lightness (see Table 3).

Based on the color database taken out before, the optimized color feature database of Changmen Kusu Prints is obtained by classifying the color values according to the

Table 3. Color system of Taohuawu New Year Woodblock Prints

Color	Description
Beige	Background color
Blue	Clothing accessories, etc.
Green	Plants or clothing, etc.
Yellow	Flowers and clothing decoration, etc.
Red	Wood products and clothing
Black	Main color of the picture

hue. Each series's representative color can be extracted using the K-means clustering algorithm. When the k value is set at 5, we can extract most of the commonly used colors effectively. In this way, we obtain Changmen Kusu Prints' color feature database, as shown in Fig. 5.

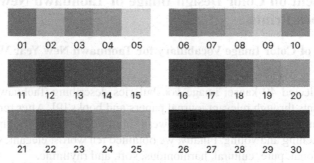

Fig. 5. Color feature database of Changmen Kusu Prints

3.2 Coding of Experimental Color Objects for Taohuawu New Year Woodblock Prints

According to different needs, colors can be represented using different color quantization systems [16]. The RGB color system was used in previous experiments to facilitate digital processing, but the mode could not reflect the color features visually. Therefore, we used the HSB mode to quantify the extracted color feature database of Changmen Kusu Prints, which uses H for hue (0°–360°), S for saturation (0%–100%), and B for brightness (0%–100%). This conforms to the pattern of color perception by the human eye and facilitates generalization, which can improve the scientific nature of the data (see Table 4).

Table 4. Color element coding

Code	H°	S%	B%	Code	H°	S%	B%	Code	H°	S%	B%
A1	35	35	67	C11	235	41	67	E21	68	35	61
A2	37	28	83	C12	216	41	44	E22	120	8	43
A3	35	20	69	C13	217	30	55	E23	128	10	58
ßßßA4	39	23	76	C14	224	17	52	E24	155	14	67
A5	39	18	92	C15	200	10	80	E25	100	12	75
B6	32	58	75	D16	359	40	56	F26	288	50	4
B7	32	60	89	D17	1	63	61	F27	212	59	11
B8	32	41	91	D18	8	49	75	F28	260	12	20
B9	48	36	90	D19	1	32	89	F29	240	10	26
B10	49	41	73	D20	21	37	88	F30	320	4	29

4 Experiment on Color Design Image of Taohuawu New Year Woodblock Prints

4.1 Selection of Color Image Vocabulary for Taohuawu New Year Woodblock Prints

Firstly, we collected 40 kansei image vocabularies describing Taohuawu New Year Woodblock Prints through relevant journal papers and books [9]. After removing some semantic repetitions, the remaining words were submitted to seven designers and three experts for screening and voting. Finally, we obtained ten words: elegant, simple, calm, delicate, traditional, pure, cultural, harmonious, soft, and rhythmic.

Then we reduced the dimensionality of these image vocabularies, and the experimental process mainly used factor analysis, using SPSS software to quantify the data of kansei image [17]. From the 120 data samples, 12 pictures of Changmen Kusu Prints were randomly displayed in the questionnaire. After inviting users to view these pictures, they rated the degree of conformity to the ten image vocabularies. The questionnaire is a 7-point Likert scale. Finally, this experiment collected 45 questionnaires. First, the KMO value and Bartlett's spherical test were used to identify whether the data were suitable for factor analysis.

The results show that the KMO value was 0.820, which is larger than 0.5, indicating that the data are suitable for factor analysis. Bartlett's spherical test approximate chi-square value is 283.109, with a degree of freedom of 45. The probability of significance is 0.000, which is less than 0.01, indicating a correlation between the factors. The correlation between the factors is suitable for factor analysis.

By rotating the component matrix of the image vocabularies, we find that there are two factors with eigenvalues greater than one, so the ten image words can be categorized into two types of images. In the first category of images, those with more substantial influence are calm, delicate, and pure, which mainly describe the texture and expressiveness of the image and can be classified as "elegant" image. In the second category of images, the more influential ones are antique and traditional, which mainly describe a sense of culture and age of the picture and can be classified as "classical" image. Therefore, the "elegant" and "classical" factors represent people's primary impression of Changmen Kusu Prints (Table 5).

Table 5. Rotating elements of image vocabulary

Image vocabulary	Elements	
	1	2
Elegant		.835
Simple		.933
Calm	.776	
Delicate	.836	
Traditional		.510
Pure	.772	
Cultural		.504
Harmonious	.658	
Soft	.708	
Rhythmic		.519

4.2 Quantitative Analysis of Color Elements and Users Kansei Image in Taohuawu New Year Woodblock Prints

To study the quantitative relationship between each color in the experimentally derived color database and user image [18], we drew 30 illustrations with the same image but different color schemes based on the experimentally derived six groups of 30 colors. We invited users to evaluate the conformity between these experimental samples and the two images. The questionnaire is a 5-point Likert scale, and 54 questionnaires were collected, including 20 users with design backgrounds and 34 general users. Then we analyzed the experimental data by Spearman correlation analysis in SPSS 26.0 tool. The Spearman correlation analysis was conducted using the dummy variable assignment method with two images as the dependent variables and 30 color factors as the independent variables, which resulted in the correlation between the elements of each group and the two kansei images.

In the Spearman correlation analysis, the normal range is -1 to 1. If the correlation coefficient is positive, it indicates a positive correlation of the color factor with kansei image, and the larger the value, the higher the correlation. If the correlation coefficient is negative, it indicates a negative correlation of the color factor with kansei image, and the smaller the value, the smaller the correlation. The specific data are shown in Table 6.

Table 6. Correlation between color series and images

Color	Relevance of image	
	Elegant	Classical
Beige(A)	0.010	0.134
Yellow(B)	0.030	−0.082
Blue(C)	0.154	0.130
Red(D)	0.014	−0.079
Green(E)	0.135	0.005
Black(F)	0.121	0.019

According to the average values of each element, we found that blue, green, and black can enhance the sense of elegance in terms of "elegant" image, and individual colors such as C05, E05, and D04 have a stronger sense of elegance. Combined with the quantitative value analysis, this paper discovers that the current consumers more often think that the color's high brightness and low saturation have more elegant senses. In terms of "classical" image, the application of beige and blue can enhance the classical sense of design in consumers' subjective feelings. E03, F01, and other low saturation, low brightness, and low color are more likely to give users a sense of classical and scored higher.

5   Design Practice and Verification

5.1   Design Positioning and Solution Display

To verify the above experimental results, we selected the "elegant" imagery as the experimental object and designed the related cultural and creative products based on it. First, we decided to use *ZhixiangYituanheqi* as the design theme [8], a recurring theme in Taohuawu New Year Woodblock Prints. Its origin is *Yituanheqi*, created by Mianshen Zhu, Emperor Xianzong of the Ming Dynasty. He expresses the desire for political stability in this picture. Later on, the symbolic meaning was more inclined to the meaning of "harmony," expressing the people's desire for a better life. We hope to design a cultural and creative product that meets the "elegant" image and satisfies users' preferences based on *Yituanheqi*.

Chunlei Chai [13] suggested that consumers may prefer cultural products with modern design elements rather than traditional cultural elements. Therefore, we integrated modern elements in the allegory and image to make it more relevant to contemporary life and aesthetics. We designed a modern character dressed entirely in modern clothes, with only the posture referencing traditional *Yituanheqi*. As for the symbolic meaning, we added design modern decorative elements and text to fit the current mainstream work topic to resonate with users.

The main goal of the color application is to design a product in line with modern aesthetics and reflect the characteristics of Taohuawu New Year Woodblock Prints. In applying color, we mainly use the blue and red series with higher scores of elegant images. The specific color selection is based primarily on the average score of users in the research on the conformity of color and image. We selected some colors with high Elegance scores, C15, D19, and E25, and brought a sense of elegance through the comprehensive application of these colors. According to previous research, we designed a pillow that matches the relevant user kansei image (see Fig. 6).

Fig. 6. Design solutions in line with "elegant" image

5.2   Design Evaluation

To verify whether the effect of color used in the product design and the end of the experiment are consistent, we invited users to evaluate the conformity of the design and the two imageries. We experimented with questionnaires and collected 126 questionnaires in total. Among them, 82% thought that the "elegance" scheme was in line with elegance, and 70% were in line with the Classical, as shown in Table 7.

The experiments' results validate the design's actual effect and the experimental process's consistency.

Table 7. Evaluation results of two schemes

Category	Particularly consistent	Fairly consistent	Consistent	Not consistent	Exclusive
Elegant	15.7%	42.1%	23.9%	12.7%	4.8%
Classical	12.7%	24.0%	31.0%	22.2%	7.1%

6 Conclusion

This paper determines the importance of color image in cultural product design by the Continuous Fuzzy Kano Model. We extracted and summarized the color application system of Taohuawu New Year Woodblock Prints by a clustering algorithm. The color application scheme for different images was derived based on this color database and the user's Kansei image study. Finally, the color scheme is applied in the pillow design to verify the validity of the extracted color factors and prove the reliability of the color database construction method based on color classification and clustering algorithm.

Based on traditional Taohuawu New Year Woodblock Prints, the article hopes to help designers better introduce traditional elements into modern life and consumer markets to meet consumers' growing cultural and aesthetic needs by constructing a digital design element database. Since the culture of Taohuawu New Year Woodblock Prints itself has a long history with many styles and factions, this paper is hard to study Taohuawu New Year Woodblock Prints comprehensively. In addition, different people have various color preferences, which may affect the experimental results. To enhance the study's scientific, subsequent research may need to study more user preferences from different cultural backgrounds and regions.

References

1. Leong, B.D., Clark, H.: Culture-based knowledge towards new design thinking and practice: a dialogue. Des. Issues **19**(3), 48–58 (2003). https://doi.org/10.1162/074793603768290838
2. Hui, C., Xiao, Q., Bingjian, L., Xu, S., Yang, L.: Literature review on cultural and creative product design method research in China: An Analysis of Themed Papers Published by the J. Packag. Eng. **43**(12), 339–347 (2022). https://doi.org/10.19554/j.cnki.1001-3563.2022.12.042
3. Jianning, S., Fangran, R., Rong, S., Wenjin, Y., Xiaowu, L.: Turtle-shaped and serpentine long-lived cultural product design based on user preference evaluation. Packag. Eng. **40**(24), 33–38 (2019). https://doi.org/10.19554/j.cnki.1001-3563.2019.24.005
4. Xiang, C., Yue, L.: Culture factor extraction and design application of shadow play based on satisfaction analysis. J. Graph. **40**(5), 953–960 (2019). https://doi.org/10.11996/JG.j.2095-302X.2019050953
5. Manru, C., Fengjuan, W.: Analysis of the color image of Qinqiang facial makeups. Packag. Eng. **38**(14), 69–75 (2017). https://doi.org/10.19554/j.cnki.1001-3563.2017.14.017
6. Mei, Y., Jinsong, L., Yiyan, W.: Construction and application of color network model of Dunhuang traditional fresco. Packag. Eng. **41**(18), 222–228 (2020). https://doi.org/10.19554/j.cnki.1001-3563.2020.18.028
7. Jie, T.: Multi-sensory perspective of traditional arts and crafts creative product design and development. Master, East China University of Science and Technology (2016)
8. Ning, Z.: Modern Design Performance of Taohuawu New Year Paintings. Master, Shanghai University (2016)
9. Ming, L.: Taohuawu new year woodblock prints and Wu folk culture. J. Soochow Univ. Philos. Soc. Sci. Edn. **2**, 86–90 (1993). https://doi.org/10.19563/j.cnki.sdzs.1993.02.020
10. Kano, N., Seraku, N., Takahashi, F.: Attractive quality and must-be quality. J. Jpn. Soc. Qual. Control. **14**(2), 39–48 (1984)

11. Senlin, Y., Xiyue, C.: Innovative design of outdoor speaker based on Fuzzy-Kano model. Packag. Eng. **41**(24), 202–208 (2020). https://doi.org/10.19554/j.cnki.1001-3563.2020.24.029

12. Ming, W., Liya, W.: A continuous fuzzy Kano's model for customer requirements analysis in product development. J. Eng. Manuf. **226**(3), 535–546 (2012). https://doi.org/10.1177/0954405411414998

13. Chunlei, C., Defu, B., Lingyun, S., Yu, C.: The relative effects of different dimensions of traditional cultural elements on customer product satisfaction. Int. J. Ind. Ergon. **48**(10), 77–88 (2015). https://doi.org/10.1016/j.ergon.2015.04.001

14. Dai, F., Jiang, Z., Fang, Y., Guan, X.: Research on user's subjective preference of Taohuawu New Year painting based on CycleGAN. In: Long, S., Dhillon, B.S. (eds.) Man-Machine-Environment System Engineering: Proceedings of the 22nd International Conference on MMESE, pp. 44–53. Springer Nature Singapore, Singapore (2023). https://doi.org/10.1007/978-981-19-4786-5_7

15. Yujing, C.: The Study of Chinese Traditional Color Characteristics Based On Big Data Technology. Master, Zhejiang University of Technology (2015)

16. Minghui, L.: Product Color Design Based on Generative Adversarial Network Systematic Approach.Master, Hebei University of Technology (2019)

17. Nianwen, W., Ruidan, Q.: Research on shape design method of ceramic tea set based on user intention. J. Graph. **39**(6), 1175–1182 (2018). https://doi.org/10.11996/JG.j.2095-302X.2018061175

18. Yixiang, W.: Research on Product Form Design Process Based on Construction and Evaluation of Miryoku Factors. Doctor, East China University of Science and Technology (2016)

Gaze Interaction Design for Displaying Characters of Taiwanese Glove Puppetry

Tsuen-Ju Hsieh[1]([✉]), Yun-Ju Chen[2], Chun-Cheng Hsu[3], and Hsiao-Yu Lo[3]

[1] National Tsing Hua University, 101, Section 2, Kuangfu Road, Hsinchu 300, Taiwan
tracy.tjhsieh@gmail.com
[2] National Taipei University of Business, 321, Sec. 1, Jinan Road, Taipei 100, Taiwan
[3] National Yang Ming Chiao Tung University, 1001, University Road, Hsinchu 300, Taiwan

Abstract. Taiwanese Glove Puppetry is a traditional performance art form deeply rooted in Taiwanese culture. Glove puppetry has cultural and historical significance, and its visual design and craftsmanship of puppet design make it a promising area of focus for engagement. This study demonstrates the potential of gaze interaction to enhance the audience's understanding and appreciation of traditional puppetry characters. The interaction was implemented with eye-tracker Tobii Nano and Unity SDK. The puppet costume design's intricate details, and the symbolic patterns are displayed and emphasized through the gaze-based user interface. By merging traditional art forms with eye-tracking technology, this study presents the potential for a more meaningful and engaging experience that deepens one's appreciation of Taiwanese Glove Puppetry.

Keywords: Taiwanese Glove Puppetry · gaze interaction · puppet · eye tracking

1 Introduction

Puppetry, a traditional performing art form, has been popular in various cultures and histories worldwide and typically encompasses different types such as marionettes, glove puppetry, shadow puppetry, and pod-head puppetry [1]. Taiwanese glove puppetry theatre, which originated from the Fujian region of China and was later developed with its unique character design and script, is an exemplar of this ancient art form [2, 3]. Contemporary Taiwanese puppetry has incorporated modern technologies, such as 3D animation, while renouncing traditional on-site performances of glove puppetry to appeal to a broader audience. For example, Pili International Multimedia has produced a popular modern puppetry drama series, Thunderbolt Fantasy, and has broadcasted it through mass media channels like television and movies [4, 5].

Nevertheless, the art of traditional glove puppetry, characterized by live performances and handcrafted puppets and stage props, faces a significant risk of extinction. The decrease in the audience of traditional Taiwanese glove puppetry can be attributed to several interplay factors, including the competition from modern entertainment and the widening talent gap among live performers and artisans for creating puppets and stage props [2]. Like many ancient performance arts, the scripts of Taiwanese puppetry

P.-L. P. Rau (Ed.): HCII 2023, LNCS 14022, pp. 52–61, 2023.
https://doi.org/10.1007/978-3-031-35936-1_4

commonly feature historical figures and folk legends, while the performance primarily takes place in religious settings such as temples. The theme and venue are usually not favored by young audiences exposed to global culture and the internet.

The National Center for Traditional Arts of Taiwan conducted a survey that revealed that over 60% of the traditional performing arts audience have either studied or are learning traditional arts [6]. This report indicates that audience familiarity with the art form is a significant factor driving attendance. However, for potential audiences with limited knowledge of glove puppetry's religious and historical contexts, it may be helpful to showcase specific elements of the art form instead of staging full puppet performances. Glove puppetry's visual design and craftsmanship appreciation value make it a promising area of focus to engage those without relevant backgrounds. In addition to its cultural and historical significance, puppet theatre offers an added layer of artistic value in the exquisite craftsmanship involved in creating the puppets, stages, and props. The handcrafted wooden stage and intricate puppet head carving and costume making are exemplified in Figs. 1 and 2, respectively.

Fig. 1. A handcrafted wooden glove puppetry stage, also known as "彩樓" in Chinese, preserved in the National Taiwan Museum

Taiwanese glove puppetry features five basic types of characters: Sheng, Dan, Jing, Mo, and Chou, as well as a supporting character type called "Za." Costume design defines each character's role, with unique facial expressions, colors, and patterns distinguishing them and conveying their personalities. The patterns on the costumes draw on traditional symbols and motifs to reflect each character's attributes [2, 3]. These costume patterns hold symbolic meaning and enhance the performance's cultural significance and aesthetic appeal.

Traditional glove puppetry requires intricate craftsmanship, but the art is often underappreciated due to the distance between the stage and viewers and the limited interaction with the audience. Viewers typically have little opportunity to observe the puppets up

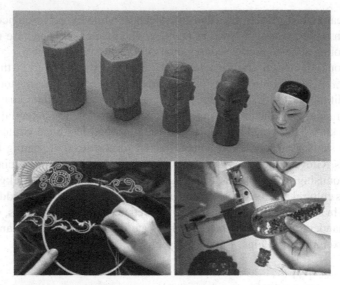

Fig. 2. The example process of making a puppet for traditional Taiwanese glove puppetry

close and appreciate the details of their design. Several previous studies have explored ways of increasing the interactivity of puppetry by incorporating technology into glove puppetry, including using IoT talk [7], virtual reality systems [8], and leap motion to manipulate virtual puppets [9, 10].

In response to this trend, our study aims to present the design elements of glove puppetry characters to the audience through gaze interaction. Compared with the previous methods, our approach is unique in integrating eye-tracking technology into an interactive exhibit [11], enabling viewers to engage actively with the puppets by tracking their gaze. The present gaze-based user interface highlights the intricate details of the puppets' costumes, patterns, and embroidery, providing a deeper understanding of these elements' cultural significance and symbolism.

2   Method

2.1   Element Design of Puppet Character

In our eye-tracking interactive exhibit of glove puppetry characters, we use traditional Taiwanese glove puppetry design elements as the visual content in our interactive script. We obtain glove puppetry design elements in two ways. The first way is by scanning high-quality 2D images of physical glove puppets, followed by 2D graphic and animation techniques. For example, as shown in Fig. 3, we present the elements of a puppet costume collected and preserved by the Seidan Sha Glove Puppetry Foundation(西田社布袋戲基金會). This puppet typically plays the role of a young maid in a wealthy household, dressed in green clothing adorned with exquisite floral and phoenix embroidery fitting her social status and age. These patterns can be further digitized and transformed into animations responding to the viewer's gaze. By utilizing eye-tracking interactive technology, viewers can enlarge to observe the details of the puppetry costumes through their visual attention, thereby increasing their attention to the value of the craftsmanship of the glove puppetry art.

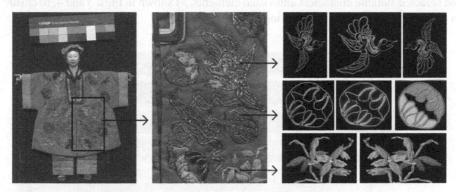

Fig. 3. The embroidery patterns on the puppet's clothing were obtained through high-resolution digital imaging using digital archiving technology and then transformed using digital drawing and animation techniques.

The second way is by designing characters using 3D computer graphics. Figure 4 illustrates two virtual puppet characters representing Princess Iron Fan and Sun Wukong in the traditional Chinese myth "Journey to the West." The character's appearance and accessories were designed using 3D modeling and animation, referencing the character's joint appearances and characteristics in Taiwanese glove puppetry scripts [10]. We then created animation materials to showcase the puppet's movements and make them responsive to the viewers' gaze, enhancing their understanding and impression of the characters.

Fig. 4. The 3D puppet character design of Princess Iron Fan and Sun Wukong in "Journey to the West."

2.2 Development of Gaze-Based Puppet Display Interface

The development process of the proposed gazed-based puppet display interface is given in Fig. 5. To create an engaging interactive showcasing puppet design, we first produced and selected suitable characters and visual elements, as shown in Figs. 3 and 4, to ensure an enjoyable and educational viewing experience.

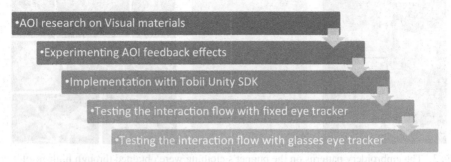

Fig. 5. Process of developing the gaze-based puppet display interface

Next, we researched those visual materials to estimate the viewers' Areas of Interest (AOI). Specifically, in our research on image AOI, we used eye-tracking data to analyze users' visual focus and attention as they interacted with the displayed puppet. In Fig. 6 are two puppet costumes. For example, the left is a young female character's costume, and the right is a costume for the Thunder God character with a bird-head. The heatmap analysis of the eye-tracking data revealed that most viewers' gazes were concentrated on specific symbols and ornaments, which can serve as natural interaction points. Using this information, we created gaze interaction areas allowing users to view the displayed puppet seamlessly and effectively and avoid the Midas touch problem [12].

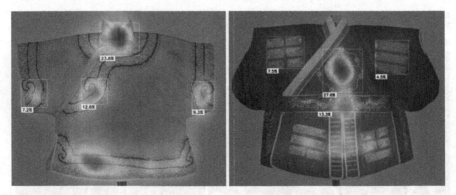

Fig. 6. The puppets' costumes were analyzed using eye-tracking measurements to identify Areas of Interest (AOI).

In Fig. 7, we demonstrate an example of using the black collar button on the costume on the left side of Fig. 6 (attracting approximately 24% of attention) as an interaction starting point. To evaluate the effectiveness of this interaction point, we conducted tests with 14 participants, and 12 of them could smoothly activate the costume display within 5 s without any prompting or instruction.

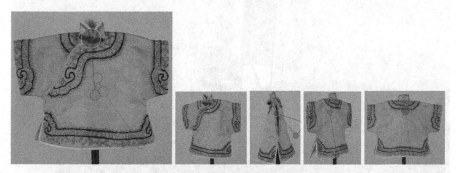

Fig. 7. An example of testing the measured AOI as an interactive point

After determining the exhibit materials and appropriate interactive design, we utilized Tobii Unity SDK to implement the gaze-based interaction. Incorporating the eye tracker with Unity allowed us to create a seamless and responsive interface for users to engage with the exhibit puppet character. To evaluate the exhibit's effectiveness, we conducted interactive experience tests with two types of eye trackers, the fixed eye trackers Tobii Nano, as shown in Fig. 8, and the glasses eye tracker Tobii G3, as shown in Fig. 9. Tobii Nano is a small and portable eye tracker that has a sampling rate of 60 Hz with an optimized spatial resolution of 0.4° and wrapped in a track box of 20 × 15 × 20 cm, while Tobii G3 is a wearable eye tracker that has a higher sampling rate and spatial resolution packaged in a black framed glass. These two commercialized eye-tracking devices enable developers to capture the users' eye movements [13].

Considering the "non-contact" aspect and the maintenance and equipment costs when exhibiting this artwork in museums or galleries, we decided to use a fixed eye tracker. After testing the interactive experience of both wearable (glasses-style) and fixed eye trackers, we conducted interviews. We found that participants generally preferred the fixed eye tracker because it only required them to sit down to begin the experience without needing to wear it. We further improved the gaze-control accuracy based on the previous relative study [14, 15].

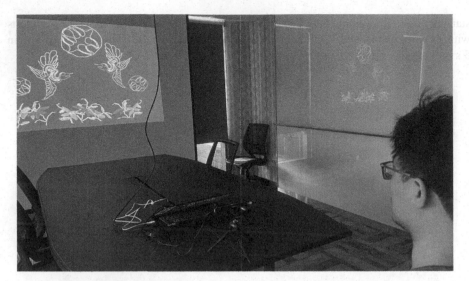

Fig. 8. Testing the interaction flow with the fixed eye tracker Tobii Nano

Fig. 9. Testing the interaction flow with glasses eye tracker Tobii G3

3   Results

Figure 10 shows the spatial layout of the interactive exhibit, which utilizes a wooden board projection, a fixed Tobii Nano infrared eye tracker, and a directional speaker. This setting is for single-user interaction. The viewer sits in front of the display table containing the eye tracker and computer host. The 3D puppets and the zoomed-in details are projected onto a wooden board cut in the shape of a puppet theater, shown in Fig. 1. Although other viewers can observe from the surrounding area, the eye tracker can capture only one person at a time to interact with the projection through the gaze.

The gaze-based puppet character display's interaction flow is depicted in Fig. 11. The process starts with the infrared camera detecting a viewer approaching and activating the projection display screen. Eye-tracking calibration is conducted briefly before the 3D puppets are projected onto the stage board. The audience gazes at one of the characters,

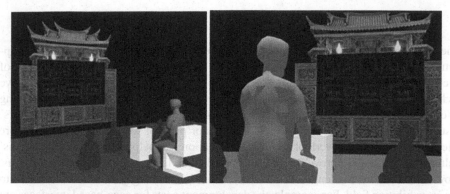

Fig. 10. Spatial layout of the interactive exhibit

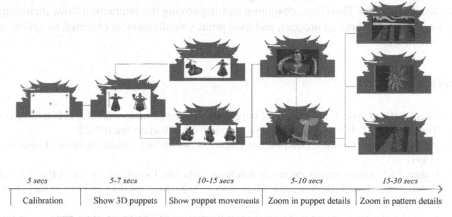

5 secs	5-7 secs	10-15 secs	5-10 secs	15-30 secs
Calibration	Show 3D puppets	Show puppet movements	Zoom in puppet details	Zoom in pattern details

Fig. 11. Interaction flow of the gaze-based puppet character display

then begins to perform movement routines while the other character shrinks and moves out of the stage. If the audience continues to focus on the character's movements, the details of the puppet are zoomed to enlarge.

Additionally, if the audience focuses on the character's costume details, the details are further expanded into a 2D image mode, revealing intricate embroidery patterns. The audience can then gaze at specific embroidery symbols, which trigger the symbol to transform through 2D animation. If the audience loses interest or their visual attention is no longer focused on specific characters or costume details, the interaction ends, and the audience exits the interactive viewing experience.

This interactive artwork will be exhibited in two joint exhibitions in 2023 and 2024, with the curated theme of technology-based contemporary puppetry. One exhibition will occur at the Kaohsiung Museum of Fine Arts, an important cultural and artistic venue in Taiwan. It is expected to attract hundreds to thousands of art enthusiasts who have never experienced gaze-based interaction exhibitions. During the exhibition, the researchers of this study will collect visitors' experience data as a reference for research to optimize the gaze-based interactive exhibition design.

4 Discussion

The study presents a novel application of eye-tracking technology in performance puppetry art, enhancing audience engagement and appreciation. Apart from the utility of eye-tracking technology in creating interactive artwork, it is also a suitable assistive technology for application in the exhibition design of inclusive museums. By collecting interactive data, curators and relevant researchers can gain in-depth insights into visitors' visual behavior and understand which artworks or parts of works have received more attention or have been overlooked. This information can help evaluate art exhibitions' cultural benefits and improve future exhibition design, layout, and explanation systems. However, there are challenges to overcome when introducing gaze-based interfaces to the art exhibition field. For example, the development costs for gaze-based interfaces are still relatively high, and the current eye-tracking interaction process may be unfamiliar to viewers. This calibration process may affect the viewer's experience and acceptance of gaze interaction. Therefore, designing and improving the interaction flow, including the user guide, calibration process, and gaze point visualization, is essential to optimize its smoothness.

References

1. Chen, F.P.L., Clark, B.: A survey of puppetry in China (summers 2008 and 2009). Asian Theatre J. **27**(2), 333–365 (2010). https://doi.org/10.1353/atj.2010.a413122
2. Hsieh, C.P.: The Taiwanese Hand-Puppet Theatre: A Search for its Meaning. Brown University (1991)
3. Cohen, M.I.: Glove puppet theatre in Southeast Asia and Taiwan ed. by Kaori Fushiki and Robin Ruizendaal. Asian Theatre J. **35**(2), 500–502 (2018). https://doi.org/10.1353/atj.2018.0046
4. Chen, J.Y.H.: Transmuting tradition: the transformation of Taiwanese glove puppetry in Pili productions. J. Oriental Soc. Australia **51**, 26–46 (2019)
5. Silvio, T.: The aesthetics of Pili puppetry fan fiction. Popular Culture in Taiwan: Charismatic Modernity **3**, 149 (2010)
6. National Center for Traditional Arts: Survey Report on the Participation and Consumption of Traditional Performing Arts in 2017. Taiwan Institute of Economic Research (2018)
7. Lin, Y.B., Luo, H., Liao, C.C., Huang, Y.F.: PuppetTalk: conversation between glove puppetry and internet of things. IEEE Access **9**, 6786–6797 (2021)
8. Chou, W.H., Li, Y.C., Chen, Y.F., Ohsuga, M., Inoue, T.: Empirical study of virtual reality to promote intergenerational communication: Taiwan traditional glove puppetry as example. Sustainability **14**(6), 3213 (2022)
9. Lin, C.Y., Yang, Z.H., Zhou, H.W., Yang, T.N., Chen, H.N., Shih, T.K.: Combining leap motion with Unity for virtual glove puppets. In: 2018 IEEE International Conference on Artificial Intelligence and Virtual Reality (AIVR), pp. 251–255. IEEE (2018)
10. Luo, H.Y., Liu, L., Hsu, C.C.: A study of virtual puppet design in virtual reality and augmented reality. In: 2022 CID International Design Conference, Yunlin, Taiwan (2022)
11. Ramirez Gomez, A., Lankes, M.: Eyesthetics: making sense of the aesthetics of playing with gaze. In: Proceedings of the ACM on Human-Computer Interaction, 5(CHI PLAY), pp. 1–24 (2021)

12. Velichkovsky, B., Sprenger, A., Unema, P.: Towards gaze-mediated interaction: collecting solutions of the "Midas touch problem." In: Howard, S., Hammond, J., Lindgaard, G. (eds.) Human-Computer Interaction INTERACT '97. ITIFIP, pp. 509–516. Springer, Boston, MA (1997). https://doi.org/10.1007/978-0-387-35175-9_77

13. Stein, N., Niehorster, D.C., Watson, T., Steinicke, F., Rifai, K., Wahl, S., Lappe, M.: A comparison of eye tracking latencies among several commercial head-mounted displays. i-Perception **12**(1), 2041669520983338 (2021)

14. Niu, Y.F., et al.: Improving accuracy of gaze-control tools: design recommendations for optimum position, sizes, and spacing of interactive objects. Hum. Factors Ergon. Manuf. Serv. Ind. **31**(3), 249–269 (2021)

15. Niu, Y., et al.: Enhancing user experience of eye-controlled systems: design recommendations on the optimal size, distance and shape of interactive components from the perspective of peripheral vision. Int. J. Environ. Res. Public Health **19**(17), 10737 (2022)

Study on the Application of "White and Black" Concept to Ceramic Luminaire Design

Yi-Fu Hsu(✉)

Graduate School of Creative Industry Design, National Taiwan University of Arts, New Taipei City 22058, Taiwan

Abstract. The concept of "White And Black" in Laozi's thought has had a great influence on Chinese culture and has formed a unique aesthetic form in the field of calligraphy and painting. This study uses the aesthetic form of "White And Black" to convey this concept through ceramic works. The research review explored the connotation and art form of "White And Black", and formed the theoretical framework of this study based on "communication theory" and "cultural and creative design process", and used the aforementioned theory as the evaluation criteria and selected works that fit the concept of "White And Black" as stimuli for the questionnaire survey. The research found that using potter's works as stimuli can convey the connotation of "White and Black" better than general merchandise. Moreover, the performance of the stimuli in "Technical Level" and "Semantic Level" will greatly affect the "Effect Level". Therefore, this study suggests that the key to convey the concept of "White And Black" through pottery works is to master the expression of "Technical Level" and "Semantic Level", especially the "Semantic Level" has a greater influence on the "Effect Level" and is an important key to the viewer's perception of the connotation of the work.

Keywords: Lao Tzu Thought · White And Black · Ceramic Craft · Cognitive Evaluation

1 Introduction

Laozi's thoughts have had a profound impact on Chinese culture, covering a wide range of fields, and even have an impact on other countries. For example, in the Japanese tea ceremony culture, Okakura Tenshin [1] believes that the greatest contribution of Taoism to Asian life culture is in the field of aesthetics.

The concept of "White And Black" is derived from "Knowing the white and keeping the black is the way of the world." in Chapter 28 of "Tao Te Ching." [2] Black and white are very representative colors, with black representing "yin" and white representing "yang", and forming a set of "yin and yang" theory [3]. Taoist thought had a great influence on the development of art in later times, and in the field of painting and calligraphy it formed a unique aesthetic form and aesthetic value, which also extended to the expression of ceramic painting [4].

© The Author(s), under exclusive license to Springer Nature Switzerland AG 2023
P.-L. P. Rau (Ed.): HCII 2023, LNCS 14022, pp. 62–71, 2023.
https://doi.org/10.1007/978-3-031-35936-1_5

The art of painting and calligraphy has long been closely associated with ceramics [5]. However, how to make the public perceive such connotations through the works is undoubtedly a major challenge. This study will help to solve this problem by discussing the mechanism of coding and decoding. In this study, we will evaluate the public's perceptions of ceramic luminaries that use the concept of "White And Black". In this study, the public will conduct two cognitive experiments, one on ceramic luminaires created by potters who understand the concept of "White And Black" and the other on mass-produced luminaires on the market that fit this concept. We will assess people's cognition at the Technical Level, Semantic Level, and Effect Level to identify the elements that affect people's cognition, and use the results to draw conclusions and recommendations that will help bring the work or product closer to the people, and help with other related designs or research in the future.

2 Literature Review

2.1 "White and Black" in the Art of Calligraphy and Painting

Since ancient times in China, the concept of "White And Black" has formed a form of expression and aesthetic connotation in the art of painting and calligraphy [3]. In calligraphy and painting, the elements of a picture are not only black, but also "white" is equally important, because the black in a picture needs white to set it off, forming an interdependent relationship, just like the concept of "the creation of emptiness and reality" as Lao Tzu said [6]. Therefore, in addition to thinking about the colors, lines, shapes and compositions, the creator also needs to consider the gaps that he wants to leave on the surface of the painting. This artistic expression allows the work to be full of imagination. As Da Zhongguang said, "White and black complement each other, and where there is no painting on the surface, it becomes a beautiful realm [6–8]. This study is mainly based on the art form of ink painting as a reference, and therefore will be directed toward this area of literature.

"White And Black" is a unique aesthetic form in Chinese ink painting, which often uses the expression of "leaving white space" to deal with the situation you want to create in the picture, and uses the relationship between real and virtual scenery to convey the state of mind, especially in landscape painting, which implies the connotation of nature and is closely related to the thought of Laozi [9, 10]. Therefore, Chinese landscape painting is not only a copy of the external environment, but also a manifestation of philosophical thought.

The Song Dynasty was a period of great artistic and cultural development, and the expression of white space was flourishing in the Song Dynasty [11]. Unlike the "panoramic form of landscape painting", the white space was more emphasized and used in the Southern Song Dynasty. White space has become an expressive technique to show the mood of the painting. The white space not only complements the shapes drawn with ink and brush, but also gives the viewer more room for imagination. This expression of "nothing is better than something here" also presents the spirit of Taoist thought of "The Great Way is invisible.

Ma Yuan was a famous artist of the Southern Song Dynasty and one of the most important artists in the history of Chinese ink and wash art. He excelled in using the art form of leaving white space to create the mood of his works, and has a very important position in Chinese landscape painting. Ma Yuan's landscape paintings prefer to place visual emphasis in the corners of the composition, with large areas of white space, forming a unique aesthetic style [12]. Ma Yuan's blank space is not blank, but the state of mind and emotion in the creator's mind. Ma Yuan's artistic creation presents an artistic conception of "less is more". The so-called "simplification" does not mean simplification, but the artist uses appropriate white space to set off the most refined brush and ink in the picture, so as to present the focus of the picture and convey the creator's emotions and ideas. Therefore, Ma Yuan's works often use refined shapes and symbols to set off the full emotion of the whole work, bringing the audience a concise and concise feeling [13]. This form of silent expression often gives the viewer a meaningful feeling and leaves more room for the viewer's imagination.

2.2 Ceramic Art Creation and Cognition

When people view a work, they are in fact in dialogue with the creator. The creator uses the work's viewable external form to convey its meaning, and the two are complementary to each other. The public experiences the "content" through the "form"; the "content" enriches the "form" and is more touching to the heart [14]. From another perspective, the work can be seen as the result of "coding" by the creator. Through the external form of the work, the public understands the meaning that the creator wants to express, which in turn leads to the public's emotional resonance with the work. This process can be seen as the process of "decoding" by the public. A channel of communication is formed between creators, the public and works [15].

The three mental models proposed by Norman [16] can be extended into three models: the creator's model, the users' model, and the ceramic artwork [17]. The creator's model is the transformation of abstract concepts into concrete forms to form works, while the users' model is the process of decoding the meaning of the work through the aesthetics of its external form. The creators use symbols or forms familiar to the public, taking into account their cultural backgrounds, to help them understand the message of the work [18, 19]. By perceiving the external form (Technical Level) of the work to understand its semantic meaning (Semantic Level), the public will finally be able to connect and resonate with the internal feeling (Effect Level) [15, 20]. The above principles and models can also be applied to the analysis and evaluation of ceramic artworks.

3   Materials and Methods

3.1   Stimuli

The main purpose of this study is to investigate the public's perception of the "White And Black" concept when applied to ceramics, and the result of the public's perception of the appearance of the work. Therefore, this paper is not concerned with the assessment of public preferences for the works. The focus of this paper is on the translation of abstract thought into the cognitive study of ceramic artworks, and therefore, we have made the concept of knowing white and keeping black the central theme of this study. We will also follow this principle when selecting the objects for this study.

Figure 1 shows the original works selected for this study and the two sets of works generated or selected based on the form and connotation of the original works.

- The author invited experts in the field of craftsmanship and aesthetics to select three landscape paintings from the Song Dynasty (Row 1 in Fig. 1) under the theme of "White And Black".
- The three pieces of ceramic lamps made by the craftsman according to the stylistic forms and connotations of the reference works are shown in the second row in Fig. 1.
- In this study, three pieces of mass-produced luminaires were selected from the market according to the style and connotation of the original product, which fit the theme and are of the same type, as shown in the third row in Fig. 1.

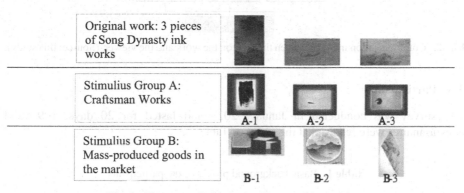

Fig. 1. Two sets of stimulants. (Source: this study).

3.2 Research Design and the Content of the Questionnaire

The general public may not have a deep understanding of Laozi's philosophy, but they are no strangers to the art of calligraphy and painting. Therefore, when people look at any work of art, they will first understand it by its appearance, then think about its meaning, and finally reach the emotional connection. Therefore, in line with the communication model (see Fig. 2) constructed by the related discussion mentioned in this paper, the three levels of the concept of "White And Black" presented in the middle of the model are the evaluation criteria of this study, which also assesses the perceptions and feelings of the test subjects towards the different works.

The author drafted the questionnaire for this study, and after repeated discussions and corrections by experts in the fields of art, craft, and design, the survey was formally conducted. In order to avoid unnecessary interference with the survey, the works in the questionnaire were named with letters of the alphabet, and detailed descriptions of the contents of the works were avoided, so that the participants could only respond to each work with their most direct perceptions and feelings.

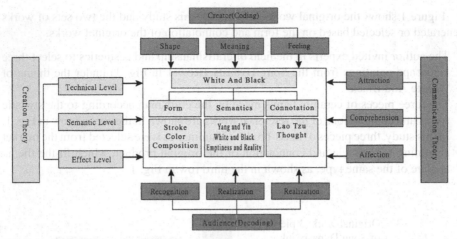

Fig. 2. Communication matrix between the creator, the work and the viewer. (Source: this study).

3.3 Participants

The survey was conducted in January 2023 and lasted for 20 days. 109 valid questionnaires were received at the end (see Table 1).

Table 1. Basic background profile of the participants.

Category		n (%)
1. Gender	Male	26(23%)
	Female	83(76.1%)
2. Age	Under 29	82(75.2%)
	30–39	4(3.7%)
	Over 40	23(21.1%)
3. Educational Attainment	Below high school	3(2.8%)
	Specialties and Universities	92(84.4%)
	Master or above	14(12.8%)
4. Background	Artistic Design Background	95(87.2%)
	Non-Artistic Design Background	14(12.8%)

N = 109

The main focus of this study is to assess the cognitive outcomes of the public through viewing the external form of the work. However, the possible cognitive differences between participants from different backgrounds will be further investigated in future studies and will therefore not be addressed in this paper.

3.4   Research Procedures

This study is divided into several stages. First, we explore and sort out the relevant literature to understand the connotation of the concept of "White And Black" and analyze and summarize the forms of its expression in the field of painting and calligraphy. Secondly, a model of communication between the creator, the viewer and the work was constructed based on the relevant literature. Based on this model, a questionnaire was developed and then a survey was conducted. Finally, the participants' responses were analyzed and discussed, and the conclusions and recommendations for follow-up research were summarized (see Fig. 3).

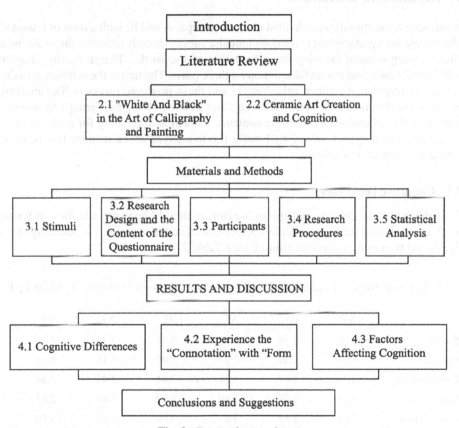

Fig. 3. Research procedures.

Participants in the survey were asked to read the instructions carefully before responding to the questions. People were asked to rate six works in relation to the brush strokes, color expression, white space effect, and the content of the work. The study used Likert's 5-point scale, which assigns a score from a minimum of 1 to a maximum of 5 based on the individual's perception of the work.

3.5 Statistical Analysis

The questionnaires in this study were initially examined and met the requirements for a valid questionnaire, and were used to conduct relevant statistics and analyses. First, we used descriptive analysis to statistically analyze the background information of the participants, second, we used independent sample t-testing to analyze the cognitive differences between group A and group B, and finally, we used regression analysis to analyze whether the Form and Meaning of all stimuli had a significant effect on Feelings and which attribute had the most significant effect on Feeling.

4 Results and Discussion

In this study, the stimuli were divided into two groups, A and B, with a total of 6 works. The people who participated in the questionnaire survey directly reflected the evaluation after viewing without knowing the connotation of the works. Therefore, this chapter will conduct data analysis and discussion on three parts. The first is the difference in the public's perception of ceramic artists' works and mass-produced products. The analysis includes the differences in Form, Meaning, and Feeling of the two groups of stimuli. The second is to analyze whether the audience's Form and Meaning for each stimulus have a significant impact on Feeling. Finally, it is to analyze which attribute has the most significant impact on Feeling.

4.1 Cognitive Differences

From the data of the three control groups, we can see that although the data show different levels of significant reflection, people's perception of stimulus group A is generally more significant than that of stimulus group B (see Table 2).

Table 2. Comparison of the cognitive differences between the works of Group A and Group B.

	A1	B1	A2	B2	A3	B3
Stroke	2.90	2.56	3.05	2.62	3.43	3.32
Color	3.21	2.49	3.43	3.02	3.18	2.98
Composition	3.34	2.67	3.26	3.41	3.42	3.34
Semantics	2.71	2.97	3.86	3.09	3.66	2.65
Connotation	2.81	2.86	3.9	3.09	3.23	3.16

4.2 Experience the "Connotation" with "Form

Analyzing the data obtained after the participants viewed Group A and Group B, the F value of each stimulus showed a high value, while the value obtained for significance was below 0.05. This shows that form and semantics have a significant effect on feeling (see Table 3).

Table 3. The influence of form and semantics on feelings.

	F	Significance
A1	42.447	0.000[b]
A2	21.117	0.000[b]
A3	31.911	0.000[b]
B1	36.071	0.000[b]
B2	102.855	0.000[b]
B3	29.746	0.000[b]

4.3 Factors Affecting Cognition

We can find from the data that although other attributes also have different degrees of influence, the attribute of Semantics has a significant impact on the comparison of Connotation. From the Significance data of each stimulus in Table 4, only the data of Semantics, in each stimulus the response of the object is presented below the value of 0.05. This consistency shows that this attribute has a certain influence on the Connotation of the work.

Table 4. Factors affecting the communication of the content of the work.

	Stroke	Color	Composition	Semantics
A1	0.114	0.159	0.167	0.518
Significance	0.192	0.034	0.027	0.000
A2	0.080	0.087	−0.007	0.550
Significance	0.247	0.180	0.920	0.000
A3	0.150	0.086	0.089	0.533
Significance	0.079	0.374	0.312	0.000
B1	−0.053	−0.086	0.421	0.538
Significance	0.536	0.384	0.000	0.000
B2	0.038	0.072	0.139	0.761
Significance	0.587	0.276	0.690	0.000
B3	0.164	0.067	0.189	0.516
Significance	0.143	0.507	0.081	0.000

5 Conclusions and Suggestions

5.1 Conclusion

Most human beings rely on their senses to understand the world, and most of the external information is obtained through the eyes. No matter it is a scenery of nature, an art work, a commodity, etc., as long as there is a viewable appearance, through the color, line, texture, structure and other attributes of the appearance, it may be transformed into a meaningful message to the viewer. Therefore, the meaning and connotation of a work needs to be conveyed by the form. The creator's understanding of the subject matter and its transformation into a formal symbol that expresses the relevant message is the most basic condition for conveying the message of the work, and it is also the code formed by the author through his personal experience and emotion. Through the clues provided by the form, the public is able to deduce the meaning of the work in their minds and understand the connotation and idea of the work.

This study found that the work presents its semantic meaning and connotation through its external form. However, once all the external formal attributes of the work are discussed independently, although the effect of the attributes can still be obtained, the meaning of the work cannot be fully conveyed, just as in a painting, you are asked to understand the meaning of the painting only by the feeling of lines or colors. This is an imposition. In addition, from the results of the study, we can find that although the single external form attribute will affect the conveyance of the semantic meaning and connotation, but usually not too strong, and the public through the viewing of the overall effect of the work, generally can understand the work to express the semantic meaning, and then trigger the feeling of the connotation of the work. Therefore, whether you are engaged in graphic design, three-dimensional creation or product design, as long as you can master the external form, it will enhance the audience's understanding of the semantic meaning of the work and strengthen the public's feeling of experiencing the connotation of the work.

5.2 Suggestions

After the preliminary drafting of the questionnaire for this study was completed, it was found that many participants could not understand the vocabulary of Lao Tzu's philosophy in the questionnaire questions, and this problem was especially obvious among the young people. Such a situation will cause the participants to not be able to truly understand the meaning of the questionnaire, and of course it will not be able to reflect the participants' real thoughts and feelings after viewing the stimuli. After discussing and suggesting with experts in related fields, I amended the sentence of the topic to a more understandable word, but the author believes that there is still a gap between the true feeling and understanding of the spirit and connotation of Laozi's philosophy, so I will continue to carry out relevant research in the future, better fixes for such problems will be proposed.

References

1. Okacho, T.: The Way of Tea. Walkers Cultural Enterprise, Ltd., New Taipei City (2018)

2. Chen, G.Y.: Laozi's Present-day Commentary and Commentary. The Commercial Press Ltd., New Taipei City (1986)

3. Chen, J.F.: An Analysis of the Concept of "Black and White" in Traditional Chinese Painting. Visual Forum **5**, 86–103 (2010)

4. Xu, X.D.: A brief analysis of the role of white shoublack in ceramic painting. Ceram. Stud. **137**(35), 109–111 (2020)

5. Wang, P., Locke, J.: The transmission and development of Song Dynasty landscape painting in modern ceramic landscape painting. Tiangong **24**, 88–90 (2022)

6. Wang, M.G.: The beauty of knowing white and keeping black. J. Zhejiang Univ. **4**(5), 97–101 (1991)

7. Zhang, S.H.: An Exploration of Deng Shi Ru's Aesthetic Practice of "White as Black", pp.9–10. MingDao University Department of Chinese Culture and Communication, Changhua County (2017)

8. Da, Z.G.: Painting Chyuan. People's Art Publishing House, Beijing (2018)

9. Chen, C. X.: A Study of Six Dynasties Painting Theory, Taipei (1991)

10. Zong, B.: Preface to the Painting of Landscapes, in the first volume of the Chinese Painting Series, Taipei (1984)

11. Yang, L.: An analysis of the beauty of blankness in black and white art of Qing Hua. Jingdezhen Ceram. **4**, 15–16 (2016)

12. Liu, Y.Y.: Exploring the aesthetic interest of "knowing white and keeping black" in landscape painting. Art Appreciation **36**, 13–14 (2018)

13. Gao, J.H.: History of Chinese Painting. Hsiung Shih Art Books Co., Ltd, Taipei (1987)

14. Lin, R., Lee, S.: Turning "Poetry" into "Painting": The Sharing of Creative Experience. Taiwan University of Arts, Taipei, Taiwan (2015)

15. Lin, R., Qian, F., Wu, J., Fang, W.-T., Jin, Y.: A pilot study of communication matrix for evaluating artworks. In: Rau, P.-L. (ed.) CCD 2017. LNCS, vol. 10281, pp. 356–368. Springer, Cham (2017). https://doi.org/10.1007/978-3-319-57931-3_29

16. Norman, D.A.: The Design of Everyday Things. Basic Books, New York, NY, USA (2002)

17. Sun, Y.K., Lin, H.Y., Lin, R.: A pilot study on reproduction and sustainable development under the promotion of crafts: taking weaving in Taiwan as an Example. Sustainability **14**, 13116 (2022)

18. Jakobson, R.: Language in Literature. Harvard University Press, Cambridge, MA, USA (1987)

19. Fiske, J.: Introduction to Communication Studies. Routledge, London, UK (2010)

20. Lin, C.-L., Chen, J.L., Chen, S.J., Lin, R.: The cognition of turning poetry into painting. US China Educ. Rev. B **5**, 471–487 (2015)

A Study on the Application of Urban Imagery Posters – A Case Study of Shanghai City Posters

Yi-Hang Lin[(✉)]

Graduate School of Creative Industry Design, National Taiwan University of Arts,
New Taipei City 220307, Taiwan
yh1206203323@163.com

Abstract. The study or creation of "urban imagery" benefits from a city's long and deep cultural roots in the promotion and construction of the city, which can sustain and promote specific development and consolidate the achievements made. This study uses documentary analysis and questionnaire survey as the research method, In the process of cultural emotional cognition, various factors and cultural aspects of different respondents can intuitively feel the expression of the city impression and the sense of identification with the city, and these six evaluation attributes have their own attraction to the respondents. This is directly related to each person's cultural cognition, and factors such as respondents' cultural background, personal experience and impression of the city will influence the choice of city posters, Shanghai designers create a variety of styles of city posters because of local cultural identity and deep thinking about the city's history and humanity. Overall, the cognitive process of the respondents will be reflected in the posters with clear urban imagery, mainly in the specific visual symbols, clear urban imagery and clear urban landmarks presentation.

Keywords: Poster Research · Cognitive Patterns · Urban Imagery · Shanghai Culture

1 Introduction

1.1 Research Background

"A city is an object perceived (and appreciated) by millions of people of all walks of life and personalities, and a product of the hands of all people." Kevin Lynch suggests that cities create their own urban culture and symbolic imagery in the process of development. In recent years, Shanghai, where the researcher has conducted case studies, has also developed a rich urban imagery through its history and culture, characteristic exhibitions, and stages of urban development, which are presented by many designers.

Among them, in order to promote Shanghai to the world, the Shanghai Municipal Government invited 23 local designers to design city imagery posters in 2017, with a design focus on showcasing internationally renowned Shanghai characteristics or local culture. Shanghai has enough well-known local characteristics and urban landmarks to

P.-L. P. Rau (Ed.): HCII 2023, LNCS 14022, pp. 72–82, 2023.
https://doi.org/10.1007/978-3-031-35936-1_6

be understood in the analysis process, and has a unique local "Shanghai" culture in terms of urban culture. Through data collection and appreciation, it is found that there are few relevant cognitive studies on urban poster factors, which can also bring deeper design inspiration and creative ideas to the poster series cognitive studies.

1.2 Motivation and Purpose of the Study

This study is to collect and summarize 26 cases of urban imagery posters designed by Shanghai designers, and to study their posters by six attributes: Image, Color, Copy Content, Layout, Creativity, and Urban Culture, to understand how to express urban imagery through poster visualization and design. It is hoped that this study will give more people a clearer understanding of the imagery of posters and a deeper understanding of urban style design, and that the results of this study will provide a reference for subsequent urban imagery researchers in their research and creation.

2 Literature Review

2.1 Theoretical Analysis of Urban Imagery

2.1.1 Urban Imagery Concept and Elements

Kevin Lynch [1] in "Imagery of the City" argues that the visual qualities of the city focus on the clarity of the landscape, or "Recognizability", mainly the extent to which the various parts of the city are readily identifiable and can be organized into a coherent context. Therefore, in the process of creation, the relevant symbols are recognizable and can be better recognized by the viewers. Through interviews, sketches and drawings, Lynch further summarized the five major elements that make up urban imagery: Path, Edge, District, Node and Landmark. For cities, the greater the clarity of these five elements, the more distinctive and memorable they are [1].

In addition to the construction of hardware facilities, local characteristics such as celebrations, folk culture, and art activities are also factors in creating urban imagery and style, and natural scenery plays a significant role in shaping urban imagery [2].

2.2 Five Elements of Urban Imagery and Localization Relevance

The clear tone of urban imagery is an important trend in the development and external promotion of a city. The creation of "urban imagery" requires a clear positioning of urban development and an understanding of the characteristics of the city, as well as a connection to the five constituent elements.

The key points of "localization" in creative works are "content", "form" and "material". Each creator has a different idea of "content", which is related to the creator's "creative idea" and "expressive content". Among them, there is a deeper connection with "urban landmarks" and "districts" among the five elements of urban imagery, which are better presented in the process of localized expression [3].

2.3 Poster Design Related Theory and Creation

2.3.1 Poster Design Components

The components of poster design are divided into three parts, which are graphics, text, and color [4]. As the city poster design message is presented in a concise flat form, creating a visual symbol to strengthen the distinctive urban imagery, which is conducive to the audience to understand the characteristics of the city, the use of images, colors, text, composition and other forms of expression, the arrangement to achieve the desired visual effect. Therefore, the images used in the creation of the poster include specific symbolic signs, text is matched with images, and color is an important prerequisite for the visual impact and artistic impact of the design, all three are indispensable.

During the analysis of the urban imagery posters, it was found that "urban land-marks", "urban local culture", and "natural landscape" were mostly used as symbolic components in the images, text, colors, and arrangement. The name of the city can be displayed in both English and Chinese, and the title can be creative to make it more promotional. The colors are displayed according to the city's own positioning and urban characteristics. The most important thing is to master the characteristics of the theme and express the creativity with the most appropriate technique [5].

2.3.2 Related Shanghai Urban Imagery Poster Creation

This study is based on six posters with the most prominent attributes and four posters selected by the researcher to analyze how the posters express their city impressions by six attributes and preferences: image, color, Copy Content, layout, creativity, and city impression (cultural connotation). The purpose of looking at different urban imagery and dotted line poster design is to understand the connotation and meaning in poster design. In this way, the scientific basis for "coding" and "decoding" will be obtained by comparison in the subsequent study [6] (Table 1).

2.3.3 Emotional Reflections on Urban Imagery Poster Design

The city is created by human beings, and human activities and history have influenced all aspects of the city. The different streets and landscapes are the most direct way to distinguish and understand different cultures. Therefore, in the creation of the poster design skills to convey more than "skills" level, because the "design" and the times, the surrounding environment, the combination of human thought to truly express its value and design style. Designers must address different themes, solve difficulties and design eye-catching, innovative, and engaging works. At the same time, the designer must have an in-depth understanding of social trends, and may even try to lead the trend and drive the style of design [4, 5]. In the process of designing imagery into visual symbols through flat forms, we found it more difficult to simplify urban imagery than complex designs, and the process of recognizing it through case studies became the main axis of creation. Norman proposed the concept of Emotional Design in three psychological processes: instinctive level, behavioral level and reflective level. Instincts and behavioral levels are subconscious and are the basis of basic emotions. Conscious thinking, decision making. And higher order emotions occur at the reflective level.

Table 1. Sample of Shanghai Urban Poster Study

Poster&Properties				
Image	Color	Copy Content	Layout	Creativity
Poster&Properties				
City Culture	Creativity2	Image2	Layout2	Creativity3

(Source: https://www.sohu.com/a/197374945_768832. Collated from this study)

Therefore, the design must consider these three levels, which can determine a person's cognitive and emotional state. In this study, the cognitive theory was integrated with the three levels of the psychological history model into a communication matrix framework for poster creation (Fig. 1), so that it could be easily evaluated and analyzed with the three different levels in the subsequent research phase [7].

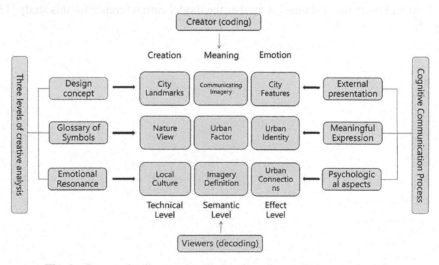

Fig. 1. Communication matrix of urban imagery applied to poster study.

2.4 Outline of Communication Theory and Cognitive Model

2.4.1 Roland Barth Barth's Theory of Symbolism

Roland Barthes Barth's symbology elevates Sothir's theory to the first level and proposes a second level: implicit meaning, myth, and symbol [8]. Symbols may also be connotive. The connotive signs carry a deeper set of meanings. In the process of methodological interpretation emphasized by Barthes (1977), the stuium and punctum are reflected differently, depending on the level of understanding of each individual. In the case of photographs, for example, the stuium is a culturally influenced interpretation method, so as to interpret the symbols in the photographs; while the punctum is a kind of sensual point in the images, which will make the viewer break away from the habitual viewing habits. When creating a poster by coding (coded), and punctuation will give the viewer a different visual and psychological experience. Therefore, a broad understanding of cultural dynamics is required in the process of interpretation [9].

2.4.2 Cognitive Model and Analysis of Works

In Roland Barthes' linguistic analysis of symbols, the importance of visual communication in which pictorial symbols are more deeply rooted than textual symbols comes from their naturalization. In the process of creating posters, designers use many city landmarks or natural landscapes as graphic symbols, which is part of the coding process. How to integrate the urban imagery with the designer's personal experience to achieve the creative goal needs to be conveyed through coding [10]. Among the studies by related researchers [11, 12], three cognitive levels were proposed: 1. Form perception, whether the respondents see; 2. Meaning perception, whether the respondents see and understand; 3. Inner feeling, whether the respondents identify with the message. The focus is on whether the third level can accurately convey the message. The cognitive model of readership was explored in depth by Lin, R. T. in 2015. The cognitive model of "Turning Poetry into Painting" is used as the model case reference for this study [13] (Fig. 2).

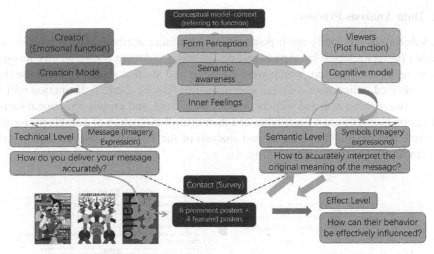

Fig. 2. Cognitive model of emotional research on urban imagery posters

3 Research Methods and Procedures

3.1 Research Methodology and Framework

This study uses documentary analysis and questionnaire survey as the research method to compile research literature on the composition and layout principles of poster design, urban imagery, communication theories and cognitive patterns, and to design a questionnaire based on the cognitive patterns of the research sample. In the quantitative research process, we conducted a questionnaire survey with the people we know around us, and conducted a multi-dimensional questionnaire survey on the Image, Color, Copy Content, Layout, Degree of Creativity, and Urban Culture awareness process of the city imagery posters, and analyzed the relevant results to draw conclusions and recommendations (Fig. 3).

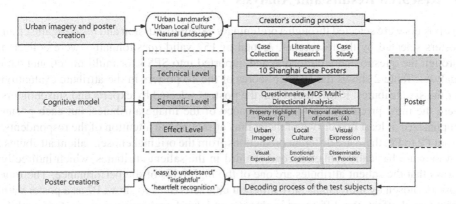

Fig. 3. Research Framework

3.2 Data Analysis Process

The subjects of this study are 6 posters with prominent attributes and 4 individually selected posters selected by experts and design stakeholders in Shanghai city imagery posters as a control group, which were analyzed and studied separately, and the data were collected online with a design questionnaire. Among them, a distinction will be made between those with and without design background, and a multi-directional survey will be conducted through 6 attributes and their overall evaluation of a single poster will be asked, and the final comparison and analysis of the 10 posters will be made on the differences between the attributes (Fig. 4).

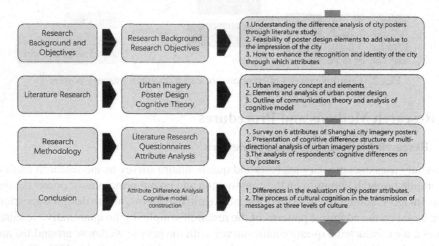

Fig. 4. Data analysis process of urban imagery poster sentiment study

4   Research Results and Analysis

Six posters were selected through a preliminary expert discussion and tested against four posters selected by the researcher. A total of 152 valid questionnaires were collected through the questionnaire collection and imported into SPSS for multi-directional data analysis. Table 2 shows the average scores of the 10 posters in the attribute evaluation for the six attributes. It was found that the posters selected by experts and stakeholders were the most prominent in the performance of the image attributes, but each poster emphasized at least one or two of them, thus attracting the attention of the respondents. From P2 to P6, there are different predictions from the original chosen salient attributes, but they are basically ranked second or third in the salient attributes, which indirectly shows that the salient attributes are one of the highlights of the performance. The four posters chosen by individuals have different characteristics to show, P7 as a poster with great visual effect, the difference is obvious and good performance in creativity, while P8, P9 and P10 are the highest values chosen by the test subjects in the attributes of layout, image and copy. Therefore, the image of Shanghai city poster is the best attribute to interpret the city imagery, while the average score of creativity is above 3, which is enough to show that the attention to creativity is the focus of city poster design.

Table 2. Average score of attribute evaluation of 10 posters

	p1	p2	p3	p4	p5	p6	p7	p8	p9	p10
f1 (圖像)	3.93	4.00	3.47	4.05	3.88	4.32	2.52	3.83	3.93	3.57
f2 (色彩)	3.52	3.57	3.34	3.89	3.64	4.07	2.39	3.77	3.72	3.57
f3 (文案)	3.64	3.66	3.37	3.84	3.55	3.82	2.81	3.71	3.78	3.79
f4 (編排)	3.41	3.75	3.26	3.88	3.82	3.88	2.62	4.01	3.86	3.64
f5 (創意)	3.58	3.83	3.32	3.81	3.82	3.59	3.05	3.80	3.88	3.76
f6 (文化)	3.43	3.59	3.42	3.96	3.65	3.85	2.49	3.69	3.78	3.43

After inputting the data in Table 2 into the MDS multivariate analysis, the multivariate structure of cognitive differences was presented, as shown in the figure above, Figure P1–P10 are 10 research posters, F1–F6 are 6 attributes, and 10 posters are divided into four vectors. P1, P3 group (first quadrant) and P4, P6 group (second quadrant), where most of the posters P2, P5, P8, P9 together represents the poster in different attributes have similarities in copy, layout, creativity is quite close; and P10 is close to the creative attributes, P7 due to various factors, the difference is significant (Fig. 5).

Throughout the 10 study samples, P6 became the most prominent poster in the image, and also had the highest rating, in that it specifically showed the factors of Shanghai city landmarks and regions, and also showed the respondents' personal preference for the image in poster recognition. P1 is in second place in terms of image performance, which is basically in line with the previous prediction; when the angle between image and layout is close to 90°, it means that the correlation between the two is almost non-existent, and it also shows that the layout and creativity factors are missing in the specific design of the image presentation; In the color attribute and cultural attribute P4 is outstanding, because there is a contrast between the old and new houses outside the sea shows the continuous heritage and development of sea culture; in the third quadrant is a collection of four posters P2, P5, P8, P9, which shows that these four posters in the attributes of copy, layout and creativity are not very different, and the respondents' awareness and preference for these three attributes is more intuitive; P3 and P10 posters in the overall attributes will be relatively weak but still be able to show the focus of some attributes, while P7 in the visual expression and other attributes above and other posters performance is very different. It shows that too simple or avant-garde design is

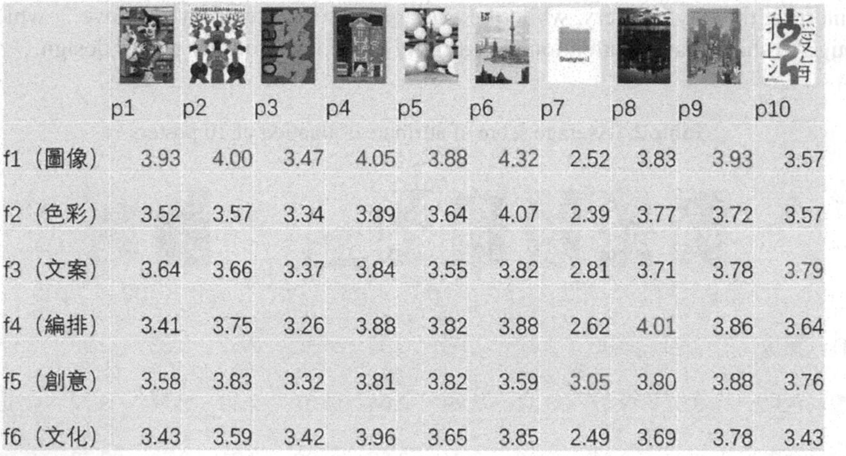

	p1	p2	p3	p4	p5	p6	p7	p8	p9	p10
f1 （圖像）	3.93	4.00	3.47	4.05	3.88	4.32	2.52	3.83	3.93	3.57
f2 （色彩）	3.52	3.57	3.34	3.89	3.64	4.07	2.39	3.77	3.72	3.57
f3 （文案）	3.64	3.66	3.37	3.84	3.55	3.82	2.81	3.71	3.78	3.79
f4 （編排）	3.41	3.75	3.26	3.88	3.82	3.88	2.62	4.01	3.86	3.64
f5 （創意）	3.58	3.83	3.32	3.81	3.82	3.59	3.05	3.80	3.88	3.76
f6 （文化）	3.43	3.59	3.42	3.96	3.65	3.85	2.49	3.69	3.78	3.43

Fig. 5. MDS Analysis of Spatial Structure

not enough to attract the attention of the respondents in the process of expressing urban imagery.

Finally, in the questionnaire survey, "What is the overall rating of this poster? (One Sample T Test in Table 3), we can see the intuitive feelings of the respondents towards the city poster. Among them, P4, P6, P8, P9 as the average of the top three city posters in the "Technical Level" of the expression of the direct observation of the appearance of perception, and in the second level of meaning recognition can understand that it is describing the characteristics of the city of Shanghai, the city culture and then conveyed to the inner feelings, the test subjects understand the city in the heart to achieve a sense of identity. In the process of cultural awareness, the expression of city impressions and the sense of identification with the city can be intuitively felt in the face of various factors and cultural aspects of different test subjects, making the six assessment attributes particularly important.

Table 3. 10 posters for the overall evaluation of the One Sample T Test

Variable	M	SD	t
a7	3.59	1.064	41.553
b7	3.62	0.962	46.352
c7	3.34	1.256	32.806
d7	3.92	0.903	53.551
e7	3.75	1.044	44.295
f7	3.90	1.015	47.395
g7	2.70	1.423	23.430
h7	3.82	0.991	47.568
i7	3.82	1.011	46.633
j7	3.64	1.153	23.430

$^{*}p < .05.$ $^{**}p < .01.$ $^{***}p < .001.$

5 Results and Discussion

This study is a cognitive study of poster attributes for urban posters based on a cognitive model. The first case study of design differences in urban posters was conducted through literature exploration and cognitive theory. Six attribute rating models were constructed to analyze the variability of respondents' ratings after viewing these posters and the visual deficiencies of the posters. Finally, through a questionnaire survey, which of the individual attributes of these posters can enhance the recognition and identity of the city in which they are located, the following are the results of the study.

5.1 Research Conclusion

In the analysis of the case study, the importance of the six attributes (Image, Color, Copy Content, Layout, Creativity, and Urban Culture) that were constructed through the study of literature can be realized, and the difference in design is the weight of the different attributes. These attributes are common to poster design elements, except for urban cultural expression which is a specific attribute. The analysis allows the researcher to confirm the importance of the design elements in the poster design, and the process of cognitive attention to the visual expression should be clear, preferably figurative expression.

From the responses of the questionnaire survey, it can be seen that the posters selected by experts in advance have outstanding performance in the selection of "images", because the performance of images is the most intuitive to observe the shape perception, which is also related to the public's understanding of the city and cultural awareness, which also reflects the connotation of the posters to the "city landmarks", "city architecture", "sea culture" to the intuitive awareness of the respondents. However, the average score of "creativity" remained above average in the overall rating of the attributes, indicating that the "creativity" performance of Shanghai city posters was recognized by the respondents in order to attract their attention.

A structure chart of cognition was constructed by statistical methods and multidimensional scale analysis, and the results of the analysis can interpret the respondents' preference for city poster cognition, with the attributes concentrated in the second and third quadrants. This means that there is a certain relevance in "color", "culture", and "text" for the attribute of "image", but there is a lack of relevance in "layout" and "creativity". Because the emphasis on the degree of creativity and arrangement may lack the figurative visuals, therefore, in order to enhance the recognition and identity of the city, the emphasis on one or two of the six attributes can have a significant effect on the recognition of the poster.

Cultural cognition process through the local designers in Shanghai to the importance of home culture, the creative expression of urban culture and the respondents face Shanghai impression posters received by the city cultural expressions, posters visual elements and other factors to achieve the cognitive process of urban imagery poster emotional research. By accurately conveying information at three levels: form perception, semantic awareness, and inner feelings, the city's impressions and sense of identification with the city can be intuitively felt by the various factors and cultural aspects of the test subjects from different backgrounds.

References

1. Lynch, K.: The Image of the City. MIT press (1987)
2. Chiang, H.M.: A Study on the Urban Image — Tainan City as an Example. D. thesis, Department of Architecture, National Cheng Kung University (2001)
3. Liao, C.C., Lin, R.T., Lin, C.Y.: Explore the localized poster design from the cultural awareness point of view. In: The 10th National Conference on Technical and Vocational Education, Business Category, pp.37–46 (1995). [in Chinese, semantic translation]
4. Lin, P.-C.: Poster Design Techniques. Introduction to Poster Design. Published by Taipei Fine Arts Museum, Taipei, Taiwan (1993)
5. Yuan, M.-L.: Introduction to Poster Design. Introduction to poster design. Published by Taipei Fine Arts Museum, Taipei, Taiwan (1993)
6. Shanghai is a place of fascination and individuality. 23 masters have created 26 posters for Shanghai. https://www.sohu.com/a/197374945_768832 (1 Dec 2022)
7. Norman, D.A.: Emotional Design. Basic Books, New York (2005)
8. Barthes, R.: Elements of Semiology (A. Lavers & C. Smith, trans.). Jonathan Cape, London, UK (1967)
9. Rose, G.: Visual Methodologies: An Introduction to Researching with Visual Materials. British Library Cataloguing in Publication data, London, UK (2006)
10. Fiske, J.: Introduction to Communication Studies. Routledge, London, UK (1990)
11. Chen, S.J., Yen, H.Y., Lee, S.M., Lin, C.L.: Applying design thinking in curating model a case study of the exhibition of turning poetry into painting. J. Des. 21(4), 1–24 (2016). [in Chinese, semantic translation]
12. Lin, C., Chen, S., Lin, R.: Efficacy of virtual reality in painting art exhibitions appreciation. Appl. Sci. 10(9), 3012 (2020). https://doi.org/10.3390/app10093012
13. Lin, R.T., Lee, S.M.: Poetic and Pictorial Splendor. National Taiwan University of Arts, New Taipei City (2015). [in Chinese, semantic translation]

From Eating to Cooking: A Case Study of the Development of the TiMAMA Deli & Café and the Creative Reproduction of Taste Based on the Mother's Menu

Yikang Sun[1]([envelope]) [iD], Huiting Lin[2], and Rungtai Lin[3] [iD]

[1] College of Art and Design, Nanjing Forestry University, Nanjing City 210037, China
sunyikang120110@hotmail.com
[2] TiMAMA Deli and Cafe, Taipei City 114, Taiwan
[3] Graduate School of Creative Industry Design, National Taiwan University of Arts, New Taipei City 22058, Taiwan
rtlin@mail.ntua.edu.tw

Abstract. Due to the fast pace of work, people are often unable to eat at home. While eating out is convenient, it does entail some health hazards, and it is easy to make eating a formality, simply a means of filling the stomach. It is advisable to turn eating a good meal into a ritual, or to lend it a sense of ceremony. More importantly, good food can inspire people's love for their parents and homes. A restaurant named the TiMAMA Deli and Café in Taipei is used as an example in this study. By communicating with the restaurant's founders, we were able to obtain first-hand information, and then use concepts such as design psychology and communication theory to develop a theoretical framework. Employing a qualitative research method, this study addresses two issues: i) the creation of a feasible model for design thinking in order to intervene in cuisine regarding the relation between form and ritual; ii) overcoming consumers' inherent prejudice against frozen food in order to adapt to the new restaurant business model that emerged during the pandemic period. The results show that the operating model of this restaurant will spread to its peers. Moreover, we wish to draw increased attention to the connotations surrounding eating, which can be summarized as feelings of warmth towards, and love of, home.

Keywords: Eating and Cooking · Home and Family · Transforming Creative · Cognitive Ergonomics · Commercial Operations · Form and Ritual

1 Introduction

People who work fast-paced jobs are often forced to simplify the important process of eating, such as by consuming fast food. Furthermore, many people relocate away from their hometowns for work. For these people, the privilege of eating at the same table as their families becomes a luxury. It is for this reason that many people return home during the holiday season, to eat meals prepared by their parents.

P.-L. P. Rau (Ed.): HCII 2023, LNCS 14022, pp. 83–95, 2023.
https://doi.org/10.1007/978-3-031-35936-1_7

Despite the convenience of eating outside the home, it is important to consider whether these foods are healthy. Although most restaurants are paying increased attention to food safety and are reducing the amount of oil and seasoning used in the cooking process, eating out often can incur some health risks. In addition, such a way of eating, especially when eating alone, can lead people to ignore the meanings associated with eating. In other words, one no longer experiences the pleasure of tasting food. This is one reason why families reunite on specific holidays and gather to enjoy food, which is always an evocative experience. Therefore, the question arises as to whether restaurant cuisine can allow guests to feel the warmth of home, or the taste of a mother's cooking [1, 2].

COVID-19 began to spread around the world in late 2019, and, during the worst phase of the pandemic, many countries required restaurants to reduce their opening hours or even banned people from dining in restaurants. As a result, many restaurants have had to develop take-home meal boxes or frozen foods such as those considered in this study, which can be eaten after a simple and convenient reheating process. What is more, the quality of these frozen foods is not compromised, which allows guests to enjoy a variety of cuisines at home. As the pandemic eases, many stores continue to sell their own frozen food to expand sales channels to those who may not be able to dine in restaurants [3].

Restaurants have offered frozen packaged food for some time. Initially, consumers were skeptical, worrying about the quality of the food and its poor taste after freezing. Because of the pandemic, the sales of frozen food have increased significantly. The pandemic may end in the future, but the way people eat has changed. The question of whether restaurants will take this opportunity to highlight the value of frozen food merits closer attention. For consumers, the ability to enjoy delicious food at home without having to go to a restaurant is undeniably appealing. In addition, it is necessary to distinguish between frozen food and food delivery. Delivery refers to the process whereby a restaurant prepares the food and a courier delivers it to the customer's home (e.g., Uber EATS and Foodpanda). During this process, the food may become cold, which greatly affects the taste. Frozen food, on the other hand, is often packaged using new technologies such as rapid freezing, and customers need to heat it up before eating. It is advisable to turn eating a good meal into a ritual, or lend it a sense of ceremony. More importantly, good food has the ability to inspire people's love for their parents and homes.

In short: eating is the form, and cooking is the ritual. Life without rituals is just living.

The following two issues are discussed in this study:

(1) The creation of a feasible model for design thinking that is capable of intervening in cuisine in terms of the relation between form and ritual.
(2) Overcoming consumers' inherent prejudices against frozen food in order to adapt to the new restaurant business model that emerged during the pandemic.

2 Theoretical Framework

Customers are increasingly concerned with the shopping or spending experience [4–7]. Due to the large number of similar services in the market, it has become extremely important for stores to increase customer loyalty (see Fig. 1). Stores must address customers' needs, as well as the evolving trends in these needs [8–10]. In short, in addition to constantly improving the items they provide, stores also need to keep track of how customers feel. Good communication is essential.

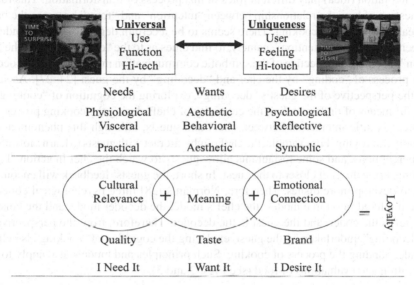

Fig. 1. From "Time to Surprise" to "Time to Desire". (Source: Reprinted with permission from [11]. Copyright 2013 Lin)

In addition to preparing delicious dishes, chefs must consider many other details. Such questions include how to style both dishes and the decoration and furnishings of the restaurant, how to develop new dishes on a regular basis, and how to design menus that are easy for guests to use. Most important is the question of whether chefs can treat guests like family. Therefore, a good chef may need to possess many qualities. This study argues that these people should combine the characteristics of artists, designers, and psychologists. The core element here is creativity [12–18], this encourages customers to spend money, and allows restaurants to engage in continuous innovation.

Encoding and decoding are widely used in various fields of study [19, 20], and their mechanisms can also be applied to the interpretation of cooking. During the tasting process, guests are in fact participating in a conversation with the chef. Communication theory can further explain this phenomenon. This study believes that guests' ability to successfully 'decode' is an important aspect of communication. Good communication is essential in helping the guest to better understand the chef's ideas and the connotation of delicious foods. Cooking is an expression of the chef's creative intentions. Through this process, their imagination, thoughts, and feelings are reproduced. The purpose of these delicacies is to express ideas and communicate them to the guest in order to ensure that there is an understanding between the chef and the guest [21].

The process whereby a chef prepares high-quality food is akin to that whereby a painter creates a painting, or a designer imagines a product. Therefore, cooking food is an expression of the chef's pursuit of beauty. It has the following two mutually influencing characteristics: i) the "connotation" is experienced through "form"; ii) the "form" is enriched by "connotation". Thus, as with painting [22, 23], cooking has a "form" context that transforms an abstract "connotation" into a concrete "form". Form (style) and connotation (idea) play different roles in this process of transformation. This raises the question of how the relationship between "intention" and "form" becomes the basis for creative thinking in cooking. There seems to be a certain degree of correspondence between "form" and "intention", namely, to find clues as to the "connotation" in the "intention". From the perspective of the symbolic communication model, "cooking" occurs in the process of "coding" by the chef and "decoding" by the guest [24–27]. As such, from the perspective of the guest's "decoding", exploring the cognition of "cooking" is a helpful means of understanding the creativity of chefs during the cooking process.

There is little interaction between chefs and guests, although this phenomenon is gradually improving. For example, the chef might interact with guests to learn more about their perceptions, and some restaurants allow guests to watch the chef in action. These measures bring the chef closer to the guest. In short, the guests' feedback will encourage chefs to develop more dishes. Therefore, Norman's [28] three psychological concepts can be modified into three modes: the chef's mode, the decoder mode, and the cuisine. The chef is the coder, and the guest is the decoder. Therefore, from the perspective of the "decoding" undertaken by the guest, exploring the cognition of "cooking" is helpful for understanding the process of cooking. Such principles and models also apply to our observation and evaluations of food (see Figs. 2 and 3).

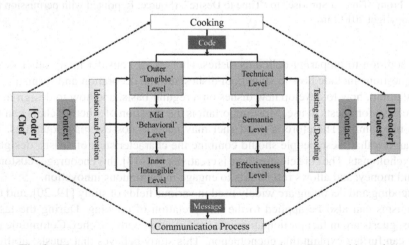

Fig. 2. The communication matrix for evaluating cuisines (Source: this study)

Integrating the above concepts and theories, this study proposes the theoretical framework shown in Fig. 4.

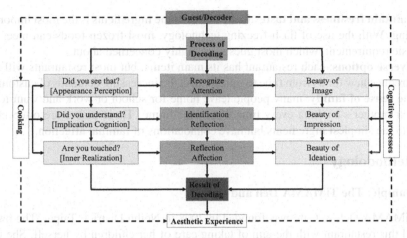

Fig. 3. The cognitive model of the decoder's perception of cuisines. (Source: this study)

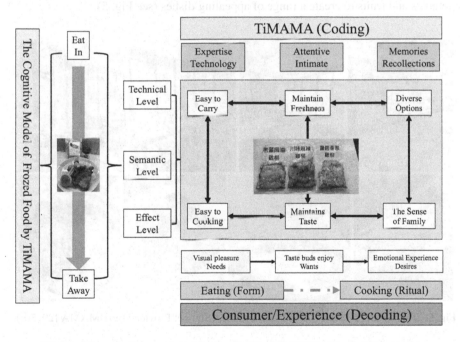

Fig. 4. The cognitive model of frozen food by TiMAMA. (Source: this study)

The components of this structure are further developed into the questions in the questionnaire. The properties outlined in Fig. 4 are explained below:

(1) **Easy to carry and cook**: occasionally, guests pick up their food from restaurants, and people bring simple utensils to cook with when they go camping. In these cases, the frozen food will be popular if the packaging is lightweight and easy for people to carry.

(2) **Maintain freshness and taste**: the freshness of the ingredients is the most important thing. With the use of flash-freezing technology, most frozen foods can meet this basic requirement, which most guests are highly concerned about.

(3) **Diverse options**: each restaurant has its main items, but most restaurants will also introduce new foods from time to time to meet the increasing demands of customers.

(4) **The sense of family**: many people leave home for school or work and want to eat their mother's cooking every time they come home. These dishes are often made with the simplest ingredients but have connotations of familial affection.

3 Methodology

3.1 Sample: The TiMAMA Deli and Café

The TiMAMA Deli & Café was founded in 2008 in Neihu District, Taipei. The owner opened this restaurant with the aim of taking care of her children by herself. She uses local ingredients and a variety of home-made sauces, and combines a variety of fresh vegetables and fruits to create a range of appealing dishes (see Fig. 5).

Fig. 5. The layout of TiMAMA and their cuisine. (Source: Provided by TiMAMA [29, 30])

In recent years, she grew concerned with the stressful and hard work undertaken by parents who prepare food for the household, leading to the launch of a frozen food series (see Fig. 6). These foods allow parents to create a variety of delicious dishes in a relaxed and simple way, so that the family can spend time together while enjoying their food.

The strengths, features, and creative ingenuity of TiMAMA mainly concern the following two aspects:

(1) Sourcing and making food to the strictest standards, and approaching customers with the attitude of cooking for one's own family.

Fig. 6. Some frozen food series. (Source: Provided by TiMAMA [29, 30])

(2) Various types of frozen food are provided, and consistent quality is maintained, as the restaurant seeks to break down customer bias against frozen food.

3.2 Questionnaire Design

The questionnaire consists of three parts (see Table 1). The first part addresses respondents' basic data, including their gender, age, eating style, and whether they have ever purchased frozen food. The second part consists of nine questions, and asks respondents to make judgments based on their subjective feelings; a seven-point Likert scale was used, with scores ranging from 1 ("very low") to 7 ("very high"). In the third part, respondents are invited to add new opinions and suggestions.

3.3 Participants

A total of 71 customers who had dined at TiMAMA participated in this survey (64 women and 7 men). Since only one of the respondents was aged between 18 and 30, this person was combined with the 31–50 age group. There were 21 respondents over the age of 51. Most of the participants were regular customers of the restaurant and found out about the survey from the owner. A total of 48 respondents (67.61%) left additional comments. Moreover, 85.8% of participants had purchased frozen food sold by TiMAMA. Therefore, although the number of participants was fairly small, their feedback had good reference value.

3.4 Data Analysis

Respondents' habits related to cooking, eating out, and buying frozen food were recorded. Then, the results of the respondents' subjective assessments of frozen food were obtained and their mean and SD were calculated. The Statistical Package for Social Science (SPSS) was used to conduct analyses of variance.

Table 1. The content of the questionnaire.

Part I	
Gender	☐Female ☐Male
Age	☐18-30 ☐31-50 ☐up 51
I-1. Do you often cook?	☐Yes ☐No ☐Occasionally (1-2 times a week)
I-2. Do you often eat out?	☐Yes ☐No ☐Occasionally (1-2 times a week)
I-3. Have you ever bought frozen food?	☐Yes ☐No ☐Occasionally (1-2 times a week)
I-4. Have you ever bought frozen food from TiMAMA?	☐Yes ☐No ☐Occasionally (1-2 times a week)
Part II	
II-1. Do you think there are many frozen foods to choose from on the market?	Very Low ☐1 ☐2 ☐3 ☐4 ☐5 ☐6 ☐7 Very High
II-2. What do you think of the taste of frozen foods?	Very Low ☐1 ☐2 ☐3 ☐4 ☐5 ☐6 ☐7 Very High
II-3. What do you think of the quality of the frozen foods on the market?	Very Low ☐1 ☐2 ☐3 ☐4 ☐5 ☐6 ☐7 Very High
II-4. Does TiMAMA offer a wide range of frozen foods?	Very Low ☐1 ☐2 ☐3 ☐4 ☐5 ☐6 ☐7 Very High
II-5. Is there a big gap between the frozen food sold by TiMAMA and the food it makes in-store?	Very Low ☐1 ☐2 ☐3 ☐4 ☐5 ☐6 ☐7 Very High
II-6. Is the quality of frozen food sold by TiMAMA guaranteed?	Very Low ☐1 ☐2 ☐3 ☐4 ☐5 ☐6 ☐7 Very High
II-7. Are the frozen foods sold by TiMAMA easy to cook?	Very Low ☐1 ☐2 ☐3 ☐4 ☐5 ☐6 ☐7 Very High
II-8. Can you feel the shopkeeper's intention in the frozen food sold by TiMAMA? (e.g., Feel the warmth of home or feel the smell of dishes made by your mother)	Very Low ☐1 ☐2 ☐3 ☐4 ☐5 ☐6 ☐7 Very High
II-9. Is TiMAMA's intention and the frozen food it sells worth recommending?	Very Low ☐1 ☐2 ☐3 ☐4 ☐5 ☐6 ☐7 Very High
Part III	
If you have other opinions or suggestions, please let us know. If not, please fill in "None".	

4 Results

4.1 Respondents' Cooking Habits and How Often They Eat Out and Buy Frozen Food

Table 2 shows the cooking habits of the respondents and data relating to how often they eat out and buy frozen food:

(1) In most families, the mother is responsible for preparing three meals a day. There is a high proportion of women among the respondents, so the number of people who cook regularly is higher (61.97%); about 28.17% of respondents cook 1–2 times a week

(2) The number of people who eat out often is close to 50%, and 42.25% of the respondents eat out 1–2 times a week. Only 8.45% of respondents do not eat out.

(3) The proportion of respondents who have purchased frozen food is high (92.96%); additionally, 85.92% of the respondents had purchased frozen food sold by TiMAMA.

Table 2. Respondents' cooking habits and how often they eat out and buy frozen food (n = 71).

Question		n/%
I-1. Do you often cook?	Yes	44/61.97%
	No	7/9.86%
	Occasionally (1-2 times a week)	20/28.17%
I-2. Do you often eat out?	Yes	35/49.30%
	No	6/8.45%
	Occasionally (1-2 times a week)	30/42.25%
I-3. Have you ever bought frozen food?	Yes	66/92.96%
	No	2/2.82%
	Occasionally (1-2 times a week)	3/4.23%
I-4. Have you ever bought frozen food from TiMAMA?	Yes	61/85.92%
	No	8/11.27%
	Occasionally (1-2 times a week)	2/2.82%

4.2 Respondent's Subjective Assessment of Frozen Food

The mean and SD of respondents' subjective evaluations of frozen foods is shown in Table 3. It is clear that responses were positive for the TiMAMA-related questions. Since most of the respondents regularly visit this store, it is reasonable that they would give it a high rating.

Table 3. The mean and SD of respondents' subjective evaluations of frozen foods (n = 71).

Questions	Mean (SD)
II-1. Do you think there are many frozen foods to choose from on the market?	5.70 (1.38)
II-2. What do you think of the taste of frozen foods?	4.03 (1.08)
II-3. What do you think of the quality of the frozen foods on the market?	4.11 (1.08)
II-4. Does TiMAMA offer a wide range of frozen foods?	5.15 (1.32)
II-5. Is there a big gap between the frozen food sold by TiMAMA and the food it makes in-store?	3.63 (1.61)
II-6. Is the quality of frozen food sold by TiMAMA guaranteed?	6.32 (0.84)
II-7. Are the frozen foods sold by TiMAMA easy to cook?	6.49 (0.67)
II-8. Can you feel the shopkeeper's intention in the frozen food sold by TiMAMA? (e.g., Feel the warmth of home or feel the smell of dishes made by your mother)	6.56 (0.60)
II-9. Is TiMAMA's intention and the frozen food it sells worth recommending?	6.68 (0.55)

4.3 Differences in Views Between Different Respondents

Since there was only one respondent aged between 18 and 30, this respondent was combined in a group with respondents aged 31–50 for ease of analysis. The t-test found that there were no differences in views between respondents of different genders and ages. ANOVA is a means of revealing differences in views between respondents.

The results showed that there was no difference in perceptions among respondents who regularly cooked or ate out. However, respondents gave different assessments of some of the issues related to whether they had purchased frozen food and whether they had purchased frozen food sold by TiMAMA (see Tables 4 and 5).

Table 4. The differences in perceptions between respondents at different frequencies of buying frozen food (n = 71).

		SS	df	MS	F	Multiple Comparisons
II-1. Do you think there are many frozen foods to choose from on the market?	BG	13.804	2	6.902 1.750	3.944*	1>2
	WG	118.985	68			
	Total	132.789	70			
II-2. What do you think of the taste of frozen foods?	BG	11.080	2	5.540 1.042	5.316**	1>2; 3>2
	WG	70.864	68			
	Total	81.944	70			

Table 5. The differences in perceptions between respondents who have purchased TiMAMA and sold frozen food at different frequencies (n = 71).

		SS	df	MS	F	Multiple Comparisons
II-2. What do you think of the taste of frozen foods on the market?	BG	9.583	2	4.792 1.064	4.503*	1>2
	WG	72.361	68			
	Total	81.944	70			
II-7. Are the frozen foods sold by TiMAMA were easy to cook?	BG	3.822	2	1.911 .411	4.654*	1>2; 3>2
	WG	27.924	68			
	Total	31.746	70			

5 Discussion

Although the number of people who cook their own meals is not small, a significant proportion of respondents still eat out regularly. In addition, most people have bought frozen food at one time. This shows that the market prospects for frozen food are still broad. It is not difficult for restaurants to invest in this field, but how to differentiate themselves requires careful analysis. Otherwise, they can easily be overtaken by other competitors. TiMAMA's cooking philosophy may seem complicated, but the key is perseverance and adherence to the business's original principles.

Respondents did not rate commercially available frozen foods highly. This indicates that there is still potential for the improvement or enhancement of these products. Respondents were satisfied with the frozen food sold by TiMAMA, which once again proved that TiMAMA's culinary philosophy is successful. However, since the respondents are all TiMAMA customers, further investigation is needed to determine whether other consumers have the same views. In addition, many people may be biased against frozen foods, believing that these foods are not fresh enough, or are of poor quality.

Therefore, the feedback of respondents who have purchased frozen foods is more valuable than the feedback of those who have not. It is necessary for vendors to gather the opinions of these people through a return visit or other means.

The 48 respondents made a number of new proposals, which focused on 2 main areas: 1) respondents hoped that TiMAMA would increase the variety of food products; 2) these people want the cooking instructions provided on the packaging of the product to be further simplified, or for the font size of the text to be increased to make it easier to read.

Of course, there are also minor problems, such as not particularly liking the taste of a certain food. This shows that, at least among the respondents who participated in this study, the acceptance of frozen food is at a relatively high and stable level. These people hope that TiMAMA will develop more products, a reasonable and natural demand from the consumer's perspective. However, for merchants, while developing new products can enhance their competitiveness, there may also be associated risks. In addition, as mentioned above, this type of frozen food can be eaten after a simple preparation process, but respondents may not be sufficiently familiar with how to handle it. At a suitable time in the future, the store could invite these people to the restaurant to demonstrate how to prepare the food in a practical setting. This intervention would also bring the restaurant closer to its guests. All of the comments made by respondents were fed back to TiMAMA.

6 Conclusions

COVID-19 has had an impact on many industries, with the restaurant industry being the hardest hit. The frozen food ordering services launched by restaurants, and represented by TiMAMA, generated a new business model, which not only increases revenue, but also allows consumers to taste a variety of delicious foods at home. More importantly, TiMAMA takes eating, which is a mundane activity, to the extreme, giving foods a personal touch such that they have a positive impact on the emotions of consumers. In other words, when food is regarded simply as a necessity, eating is simply a question of going to a convenience store and buying a loaf of bread. The findings of the present study suggest that the ritual of eating, as well as the meaning and warmth behind these foods, can be enjoyable aspects of people's daily lives.

Acknowledgement. The author would like to thank TiMAMA for its support, especially for providing all kinds of figures free of charge. In addition, we would like to thank the 71 respondents for their enthusiastic participation.

References

1. Perez, M.H.: Reflections on family traditions. Smith Coll. Stud. Soc. Work **71**(2), 323–328 (2001). https://doi.org/10.1080/00377310109517632
2. Schneiderman, G., Barrera, M.: Family traditions and generations. Fam. Commun. Health **32**(4), 354–357 (2009). https://doi.org/10.1097/fch.0b013e3181b91fe3
3. Pine, B.J., Pine, J., Gilmore, J.H.: The Experience Economy: Work is Theatre & Every Business a Stage. Harvard Business School Press, Boston, MA, USA (1999)

4. Keiningham, T., et al.: Customer experience driven business model innovation. J. Bus. Res. **116**, 431–440 (2020). https://doi.org/10.1016/j.jbusres.2019.08.003
5. Pennington, A.: The Customer Experience Book: How to Design. Measure and Improve Customer Experience in Your Business. Pearson, London, UK (2016)
6. Shaw, C., Ivens, J.: Building Great Customer Experiences. Palgrave Macmillan, London, UK (2004)
7. Zaki, M., Neely, A.: Customer experience analytics: dynamic customer-centric model. In: Maglio, P.P., Kieliszewski, C.A., Spohrer, J.C., Lyons, K., Patrício, L., Sawatani, Y. (eds.) Handbook of Service Science, Volume II. SSRISE, pp. 207–233. Springer, Cham (2019). https://doi.org/10.1007/978-3-319-98512-1_10
8. Maslow, A.H.: A theory of human motivation. Psychol. Rev. **50**(4), 370–396 (1943). https://doi.org/10.1037/h0054346
9. Maslow, A.H.: The farther reaches of human nature. J. Transpers. Psychol. **1**(1), 1–9 (1969)
10. Maslow, A.H.: Motivation and Personality. Harper, New York, NY, USA (1954)
11. Lin, R.: Prologue- From curatorial design to creative brokerage. J. Des. **18**(4), i–ix (2013). [in Chinese, semantic translation]
12. Hsu, C., Lin, R.: A study on cultural product design process. J. Des. **16**(4), 1–18 (2011). [in Chinese, semantic translation]
13. Hsu, C., Chang, S., Lin, R.: A design strategy for turning local culture into global market products. Int. J. Affect. Eng. **12**(2), 275–283 (2012). https://doi.org/10.5057/ijae.12.275
14. Hsu, C., Fan, C., Lin, J., Lin, R.: An investigation on consumer cognition of cultural design products. Bull. Japan. Soc. Sci. Des. **60**, 39–48 (2014)
15. Leong, B.D., Clark, H.: Culture-based knowledge towards new design thinking and practice—A dialogue. Des. Issues **19**(3), 48–58 (2003). https://doi.org/10.1162/074793603768290838
16. Lin, R.: Transforming Taiwan aboriginal cultural features into modern product design: a case study of a cross-cultural product design model. Int. J. Des. **1**(2), 45–53 (2007)
17. Lin, C., Chen, S., Hsiao, W., Lin, R.: Cultural ergonomics in interactional and experiential design: conceptual framework and case study of the Taiwanese twin cup. Appl. Ergon. **52**, 242–252 (2016). https://doi.org/10.1016/j.apergo.2015.07.024
18. Norman, D.A.: Emotional Design: Why We Love (or Hate) Everyday Things. Basic Books, New York, NY, USA (2005)
19. Hall, S.: Encoding and decoding in the television discourse. In: Gray, A., Campbell, J., Erickson, M., Hanson, S., Wood, H. (eds.) CCCS Selected Working Papers, pp. 386–398. Routledge, Abingdon, UK (2007)
20. Lloyd, R.: Cognitive maps: encoding and decoding information. Ann. Assoc. Am. Geogr. **79**(1), 101–124 (1989). https://doi.org/10.1111/j.1467-8306.1989.tb00253.x
21. Lin, R., Qian, F., Wu, J., Fang, W.-T., Jin, Y.: A pilot study of communication matrix for evaluating artworks. In: Rau, P.-L. (ed.) CCD 2017. LNCS, vol. 10281, pp. 356–368. Springer, Cham (2017). https://doi.org/10.1007/978-3-319-57931-3_29
22. Lin, C., Chen, J., Chen, S., Lin, R.: The cognition of turning poetry into painting. US-China Educ. Rev. B **5**(8), 471–487 (2015). https://doi.org/10.17265/2161-6248/2015.08b.001
23. Lin, R., Lee, S.: Turning "Poetry" into "Painting": The Sharing of Creative Experience. National Taiwan University of Arts, New Taipei (2015). [in Chinese, semantic translation]
24. Barthes, R.: Elements of Semiology. Jonathan Cape, London, UK (1967)
25. Craig, R.T.: Communication theory as a field. Commun. Theory **9**(2), 119–161 (1999). https://doi.org/10.1111/j.1468-2885.1999.tb00355.x
26. Fiske, J.: Introduction to Communication Studies, 3rd edn. Routledge, London, UK (2010)
27. Jakobson, R.: Language in Literature. Harvard University Press, Cambridge, MA, USA (1987)
28. Norman, D.A.: The Design of Everyday Things. Basic Books, New York, NY, USA (2002)

29. TiMAMA Deli & Café: https://www.facebook.com/timama2008/. Last accessed 19 Jan 2023. [in Chinese, semantic translation]
30. TiMAMA Deli & Café: https://www.timama.com.tw/. Last accessed 19 Jan 2023. [in Chinese, semantic translation]

Research on the Characteristic of Speculative Design in Contemporary Jewelry

I. Ting Wang(✉)

School of Department of Crafts and Design, National Taiwan University of Arts, Taipei, Taiwan
etinw@ntua.edu.tw

Abstract. Speculative design, with the evolution of the times, encourages critical and independent thinking abilities. It is a debate on various possibilities with assumptions and questions, instigating contemplation and discussion. With the background coming from Critical design, Speculative design advocates a more open approach, inviting people to think and discuss actively. Meanwhile, Contemporary jewelry is a highly experimental and artistic form of creation emerging from the Western countries, combining unique craft techniques with experimentation of materials and criticism of values to become an expression of thought. This study takes the theories of Speculative design such as design fiction, critical design, and thought experiments to explore how a framework of methodology or tools is created to support the ideas at the conscious level, First, based on the literature study of Speculative design theories responding to the homogeneity with contemporary jewelry, the theoretical structure, questionnaire survey, and in-depth interview are carried out. Secondly, through in-depth interviews with 16 experts, we explore their perspectives on contemporary jewelry, the relationships between contemporary jewelry and the body, and the importance of craft value in contemporary jewelry, summarize the experts' perspectives and exploration of jewellery characteristics, and further revise the questionnaire model. The research results show that speculative design, as a jewelry design method, has nine characteristic attributes engages more dialogues and reflections using implications, debate, ask, thus providing a framework for inference in the context of inferential reasoning.

Keywords: Speculative design · Contemporary jewelry · Design thinking

1 Introduction

1.1 Research Background and Motives

Speculative design, which is distinct from the field of interactive design, has been expanding in the design field in recent years and was first introduced in 2013 by British designers Anthony Dunne and Fiona Raby in Speculative Everything: Design, Fiction, and Social Dreaming. The term speculative design encapsulates this overlapping discipline between art and design. The book explores non-realist aesthetics, non-realist maps, thought experiments, design fiction, functional fiction, critical theory, and future speculation in the field of design.

© The Author(s), under exclusive license to Springer Nature Switzerland AG 2023
P.-L. P. Rau (Ed.): HCII 2023, LNCS 14022, pp. 96–110, 2023.
https://doi.org/10.1007/978-3-031-35936-1_8

The term "speculative design" also has different definitions in design field. It is usually referred to as speculative design which frames reality in a way that predicts the future. However, contemporary jewelry as a branch of applied art was first seen in Europe in the 1950s to 1970s. Contemporary jewelry creators define new styles of art and philosophy with boldness and independence, using anti-traditional and non-stereotypical pure art forms for self-awareness, philosophical reflections, and new material experiments. It is not a skill but a reflection. Therefore, it is appropriate to use the term "speculative design" as a keyword to explore the field of contemporary jewelry design, which discusses various possibilities in a hypothetical and questioning way, which is the essence of contemporary jewelry conceptual thinking. In turn, we explore whether contemporary jewelry can meet the categorical attributes of speculative design, and summarize the characteristics of contemporary jewelry to provide a reference practice model for goldsmith creators to expand jewelry design in their creative development.

1.2 Research Purpose

As a new form of artistic expression, contemporary jewelry exists at the intersection between design, art, and craft. By applying the theory of speculative design, this study investigated the model of practice that can be referred to as the development of jewelry creation. The purpose of this study is described as follows:

a) To assess the applicability of speculative design theory to the future development of contemporary jewelry design.
b) To construct a speculative design model that can be used as a reference in contemporary jewelry creation.

2 Literature Review

Contemporary jewelry attempts to cross the boundaries of design mediums and processes, often challenging the viewer's perception not only in the selection of topics, but even jumping out of the shackles of social ethics, cultural stereotypes, and present-day philosophies, as opposed to traditional design based on existing scenarios to solve existing problems. Unlike the human-centered, problem-solving methodology of design, Speculative design reflects on the future to give shape to the present and is not driven by market demand. In the 20th century, the entire history of Western thought was also influenced by technological progress, whether in the fields of art, design, or craft, immersed in the realm of scientific progress. The period used design as a medium of study, with an emphasis on the interaction of multiple cross-domains, such as the new media, science, art, design, literature, and biology field. This study responded to possibilities by asking questions, which in turn manipulates the design output of thought experiments, prompting a clearer view. Or, it attempted to intersect across domains and summarized three orientations of design fiction, critical design and thought experiments as the medium of this study. In addition, through the theoretical foundation of speculative design, this study also explored a referenceable model of thought experiments applicable to contemporary jewelry creation, triggering people to pay attention to contemporary jewelry designs and opening up a dialogue of more possibilities.

Exploring the Value of Design Fiction. Design fiction is used in the field of human computer interaction research with HCI, combining technology with an interactive design that allows the viewer to imagine and learn between fiction and science fiction. Julian Bleecker sees Science Fiction as a methodology for designing genres that involve imagining the future in terms of the issues of concern, how the objects created are to be used, or speculating on the development of events. At the same time, he emphasizes that Fiction is based on facts. It can be traced back to the influence of narratology, from science fiction, film scripts, storylines, and textual narratives, observing that the text (e.g., inspired by science fiction and film narratives) drives thoughts, raises questions, and opens discussions, a discursive future that is needed for design today [1]. Dourish Paul and Genevieve Bell [4], in the practice of Science Fiction, provided fictional prototypes of things that bring technology and design fiction into the plot through scenes and situations to highlight more of the importance of reasoning about future technologies or future worlds. Dunne and Raby [2] proposed that props in speculative design have the pattern of synecdoches. It was established by William J.J. Gordon, an American psychologist, and its core concept is to make familiar things new by combining them and; to make novel things familiar by combining them. This concept helps the viewer to think and generate different views.

In summary, design fiction talks more about the importance of technology for conceptual thinking, while providing more inferences for future imagination based on real-world technological developments, and suggesting other possibilities of time, space, and value with design fiction.

Using Critical Design as a Reflection. In the past 20 years, critical design has been widely promoted in the field of design. Throughout its development and lineage, art, design thinking, and philosophical thought have been a reactionary force in this evolution, countering each other against the dominant ideas and values of its society. Jakobsone mentioned that critical design initially originated from academic studies and can be part of design studies as well as pedagogy. It focuses on cognition and empirics and reveals its purpose through the design of works and deliberately provokes controversial design practices [8]. Malpass [9] talked about critical design with a particular focus on the object of design and the social, cultural, and moral aspects of the present, with an aim of stimulating the imagination of the viewer and conveying messages within it.

In their book, *Speculative Everything,* Dunne & Raby [2] referred to critical design as a position, an attitude, rather than a methodology. And the term critique, not in a negative sense, is a guide to how things might look, offering an alternative to things. Malpass [9], on the other hand, argues that critical design is a design practice that attempts to challenge user perceptions in order to trigger transformation. It challenges traditional design with new assumptions in an attempt to change the image in the user's mind. Dunne & Raby [2] emphasized the need for critical design to be relevant to life because of its ability to disrupt the mind. If critical design is too bizarre in its conception, it can easily be considered as art. If it is to be based on the attributes of design, critical design has to emphasize the suggestive nature of the product so that things can change and be different.

Critical design lies in the exploration of two value levels, as several scholars have talked about. Critical design, on the other hand, looks at the development of trends in the field today and challenges the openness of the designer's mind. It mostly uses subversion, challenge, and questioning as verbs to expand its design thinking toward the contemporary.

Methodology of the Thought Experiment. Thought experiments are closer to conceptual design than to traditional design. In *Heterocosmica: Fiction and Possible Worlds,* Lubomir Dolzel writes: "Our real world is surrounded by an infinite number of other possible worlds" [5]. Dunne & Raby suggested that Fiction enters the realm of possible worlds as soon as it departs from the way things are now. In this regard, the literary theory focuses on the semantics of reality and unreality. Art, on the other hand, is fascinating in its ability to push fiction to its limits in terms of conception and idea building. Thought experiments explore the importance of designing prototypes, experimenting with transformations to facilitate thinking through the dimensions of social needs and perceptions, political economy, moral and ethical judgments, and social values, thinking about alternatives, ironies, critiques, questioning, reflecting, and even provoking the possibility of an alternative design [3]. In their book of *Speculative Everything,* Dunne and Raby [2] talked about possible methodologies for thought experiments, which can be explored in three ways: (1) reductio ad absurdum-assuming an argument, extrapolating it to the extreme, and thus producing absurd results. (2) counterfactual set a story, or change the historical events, like "what if...... Could have happened". (3) ask questions- from a concept of exploration to "what if...... Would have been" the idea, the operation is mostly seen in the film, to an excuse to detach from reality, embracing a way of thinking that defies common sense.

Thought experiments as a methodology explore the nature of things through imagination, emphasize the importance of process exploration, and try to reach the purpose of research with different paths. For design, thought experiments provide an alternative for design thinking, or even the integration and role exchange between different fields, which is more forward-looking than the setting through scenes and events as design interventions.

2.1 Contemporary Jewelry as an Expression of Design

Jewelry, with definition usually associated with preciousness and personal adornment. From historically, jewelry has the value preservation of gemstones and precious materials, and is generally to be a symbol of wealth [6]. Including the body decoration and beauty, from the scars produced by tribal peoples on the body through rituals, they will become jewelry in the cultural meanings.

The history of contemporary jewelry dates back more than 60 years to 1960. It began in the second half of the 20th century, and its beginnings are seen as a progressive art movement. In the early 19th century, jewelry design was more formalized, maintaining the craftsmanship and technicality. In the mid and late period focused on new concepts and media experimentation of jewelry, more boundaries of the body discussed extend emphasizing social value and ecological reflection. in mid-20th century, contemporary jewelry really began to take shape as an established field.

Artists in various fields rebelled the traditional art expressions, resulting in new position and creative perspectives and also began to free jewelry from the shackles of traditional values, thus making jewelry a new form of artistic expression. Unger & Smeets [10] discuss Jewellery are wearable objects and as such pre-eminently suitable as signs of position within a society. Dormer & Turne [6] mentioned that jewelry not only reflects the popularity of consumption and fashion, but also reflects political, social and cultural changes. design.

Scholar pointed out that jewelry becomes an object that translates the artist's intentions and conveys them to the wearer, and then the wearer conveys the artist's words to the world [7]. From then on, jewelry artists no longer consider traditional precious jewelry expression forms and material value, but also reflect on the value of jewelry, explore body wearing, and participate in interventions with viewers.

3   Research Method

Throughout the development of contemporary jewelry education and creation in Taiwan, in the face of globalization and the border lessness of art information, it is difficult to establish one's own pulse. While searching for the contemporary jewelry context, the researcher attempted to sort out the classification of its creative forms to provide a way to establish a context and think about the creation and implementation of metalsmithing in Taiwan.

3.1   Research Structure

This study aims to clarify the characteristics of contemporary jewelry by selecting design fiction, critical value, and thought experiments in speculative design. These characteristics parallelly correspond to contemporary jewelry homogeneity correspondence and participate in the exploration through the narrative nature of conceptual texts, the reflective nature of value criticism, and the participatory nature of synesthetic cognition. Through textual analysis, expert interviews, and questionnaires, the works of jewelry creators from European countries and recent jewelry creators were compiled to fill in the nine components of the three theoretical perspectives of speculative design in this study. Furthermore, the presentation of the concepts, techniques, and contexts of contemporary jewelry was cross-referenced at the level of thinking to construct characteristic indicators of contemporary jewelry. In this study, textual analysis, case studies, and expert interviews were conducted, in which two expert cases were selected, and the cases were selected in accordance with the components of speculative design. After the pre-testing and revision of the questionnaire, expert interviews, and focus interviews, a qualitative-quantitative mixed method were used to organize and cross-analyze the findings of this study. The flow chart of this study is shown in Fig. 1.

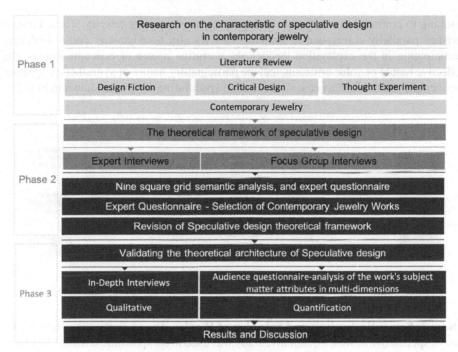

Fig. 1. Flow chart of the study structure

3.2 Research Process

The research steps will be divided into three stages. In the first stage, text analysis will be conducted for Speculative design, and the theoretical structure of Speculative design will be constructed. In the second stage, for the questionnaire design of the expert interviews, the group focus interviews, and the selection criteria of the samples, their key features are defined using books and journal literature relevant to contemporary jewelry. After sorting the group focus interview data, the semantic deficiencies of the nine square grids will be modified. Through the expert questionnaire, nine works were selected by comparing the nine semantic attributes of Speculative design from the 18 works. In the third stage, the audience questionnaire was widely distributed and the sample size of expert interviews was increased simultaneously. Continuing with the cross-analysis in a qualitative way, we further understand the differential views between experts and audiences and clarify the characteristics of contemporary jewelry, expecting to help stimulate thinking in the field of jewelry creation.

Phase 1: Literature Analysis. Using the theories related to Speculative design as the material for textual analysis, this study extracted the important attributes mentioned by experts and scholars, such as design fiction, value criticism, and thought experimentation, to form the nine elements of the grid. The case study was selected by compiling the works of pioneering jewelry creators in European countries and recent jewelry creators to correspond to the constituent elements of this study. The presentation of the concepts, techniques, and contexts of contemporary jewelry were cross-referenced at the level of thinking to construct characteristic indicators of contemporary jewelry. These characteristics parallelly correspond to contemporary jewelry homogeneity correspondence. Participation in the exploration through the narrative nature of conceptual texts, the reflective nature of value criticism, and the participatory nature of synesthetic cognition were employed for the theoretical structure of speculative design, as shown in Fig. 2.

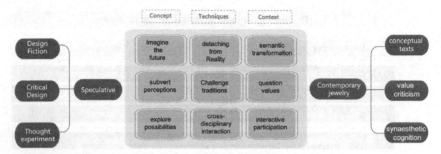

Fig. 2. The theoretical architecture of Speculative design

Phase 2: Semantic Analysis and Selection of Works. Based on the theoretical structure of speculative design, a qualitative study was used to compile nine semantic headings and word definitions through literature exploration (as shown in Table 1). The sample was selected from 18 pieces of jewelry works, each subdivision corresponding to 1–2 pieces of works, corresponding to the nine semantic features. Meanwhile, five contemporary jewelry designers, artists, curators, and scholars with more than 12 years of experience were invited to conduct expert interviews and expert questionnaire design. A total of nine samples were selected through interviews with experts and scholars in various fields for subsequent audience questionnaire design.

Case Selection. Based on the theoretical architecture of speculative design, the nine semantic features presented in the vertical axis design fiction, critical value, thought experiment, and the horizontal columns of Concepts, Techniques, and Context, were selected by experts and the samples are as follows:

a.) Design fiction: Electronic tattoos created by Taiwanese creator Hsian-Liu Kao of MIT Media Lab, the work "Energy Addicts" created by Israeli architect Naomi Kizhner, and the work "Ciao" created by German artist Bischoff Manfred.

b.) Critical design: The work "Ring#488" by German artist Karl Fritsch, the work. "Jewellery under the Skin" by Australian artist Peter Skubic, the work "Gold Makes Blind" of German conceptual artist Otto Kunzli

c.) Thought experiment: The work "Brooch" by Italian artist Francesco Pavan, the work "Large Propeller" by Sweden artist Pierre Degen, and the work "Chew your Own Brooch" by Dutch artist Ted Noten.

The works were selected by experts, and their concepts, techniques, and contexts were addressed, followed by quantitative research questionnaires to understand the differences between the viewers' thinking and the researchers' own inductive predictions,

Table 1. Characteristic semantics and word definitions

Semantic Title	Word Definition
f1. imagine the future	The design incorporates technology in an interactive way, or asks hypothetical questions, speculates on the possibility of the development of events, and creates works with future concepts.
f2. detaching from Reality	By challenging the human perceptions and stereotypes of the established world, and detaching from the concept of common sense and facts, we reconstruct a world view to extend the archetype of design.
f3. semantic transformation	Focusing on the correlation between the object and the narrative, the concept of transformative design through itself, the grammatical meaning, symbolic forms, and material vocabulary are embedded in the work.
f4. subvert perceptions	Overturning and changing existing formal facts and aesthetic perceptions, making conscious changes, and proposing practices and ideas that are different from the norm.
f5. challenge traditions	The traditionally established value determinations arising from the evolution of society and culture are questioned by the creators with their personal views in relation to the mainstream value perceptions.
f6. question values	In response to several different opinions, we clarify the contradictions between the perceptions of facts through rational and logical responses, and make self-identified statements of conclusions.
f7. explore possibilities	By subverting traditional techniques or experimenting with the mediums used to support the ideas, the possibilities and new values between the theory and the mediums vibrate.
f8. cross-disciplinary interaction	The systematic integration of two or more dissimilar fields, through the intersection of conceptual knowledge and technical experience between the different fields, and the stimulation and impact of knowledge, leads to new thinking and new results.
f9. interactive participation	Through the design of the process of inviting the viewer to interact, the power is given back to the viewer for them to take ownership of the work. Through the presentation, experience, and interaction of the work, the viewer is triggered to think about the connection between their inner emotions and cognition.

and the differences between the experts' questionnaires and the public's interviews. The model construction was then examined through MDS multi-directional analysis.

4 Model Evaluation and Analysis

4.1 Introduction of Contemporary Jewelry Works

After micro-adjustment by expert focus interviews, questionnaire pre-testing, and semantics of discursive attributes, the works were selected in the category of European regions, including Germany, Switzerland, Taiwan, Israel, Austria, Netherlands, and Italy. The works of jewelry dating from 1975–2016 nearly 40 years, corresponding to the attributes of a total of 9 jewelry works, as shown in Table 2.

Table 2. Description of Contemporary jewelry Works

No.	Work	Description
P0 1	Electronic Tattoo	MIT Media Lab host Hsin-Liu Kao, the design concept originated from the popular tattoo culture in Taiwan, imitating popular culture such as metal jewelry tattoos, made using conductive metal materials, and designed using the same principles as circuit boards, allowing users to turn their skin into a touchpad that can remotely control devices such as smartphones, or transfer data through near field communication (NFC), making The human body as a personalized technology interface becomes possible.
P0 2	Energy Addicts	Israeli designer Naomi Kizhner hypothesized a scenario of energy scarcity through her work in 2013. She designed a series of curious devices that use the flow of human life-sustaining blood to generate energy. Considered as a pioneering piece of Anthropocene design, these installations use a mix of gold, biopolymers, and electrical conductors embedded in the skin to provoke thoughts about the future possibilities of contemporary design.
P0 3	Ciao	Manfred Bischoff's brooch *Ciao* is a masterpiece that marries goldwork with modern graffiti art, infusing contemporary goldwork with a vocabulary of swiftness and improvisation. As a whole, Manfred Bischoff's goldwork is narrative, philosophical, and poetic.
P0 4	Ring#488	As a skilled goldsmith, Karl Fritsch's mastery of all traditional techniques allows him to create seemingly crude, even unfinished goldsmithing pieces, for example, by gluing ore into clumps or leaving the surface of a mold grayish-brown to reveal its special flavor, playing with the diverse styles of goldsmithing with wit and humor.
P0 5	Jewellery under the Skin	Peter Skubic has implanted a small stainless-steel piece in his own lower arm. In this work, Peter Skubic talks about the relationship between jewelry and the body field, using the implanted steel piece to raise the idea of the visibility and invisibility of jewelry, and to convey the concept of invisible jewelry, which also refers to the existence of the decorative function of jewelry, and the intimate relationship between jewelry and the body field, while questioning the decorative and wearing style. The viewpoint. This jewelry presents the ultimate materialization as invisible, existing only in our imagination.
P0 6	Gold Makes Blind	The famous Gold Makes Blind from 1980 attempts to make the viewer think about the definition of value by encasing a precious material, gold, in a cheap rubber.

(continued)

Table 2. (*continued*)

P0 7	Brooch	Pavan combines different metals to create a woven effect. His jewelry is characterized by repetitive geometric structures, created using materials such as gold and silver. Wearable Object Square Frame
P0 8	Square Frame	In the early 1980s, Degen explored the relationship between the object and the wearer through the scale of the work. By exploring the symbiotic and expressive relationship between materials, techniques, symbolic power, the object, and the wearer, the design expresses an intimate relationship between the jewelry and the creator or wearer.
P0 9	Chew Your Own Brooch	Ten Noten's work "To Chew Your Own Brooch", published in 1998, transforms an everyday, worthless material into something precious. Thus, value is placed on the process of making and the sensory experience of chewing gum, in which the creator gives sovereignty back to the viewer, while reverting to a secondary passive role. This work allows the viewer to build a viewing experience that turns from participatory to dominant.

4.2 Characteristics of Contemporary Jewelry Recommended by Experts

Through the questionnaire design of qualitative interview, 18 attributes of contemporary jewelry were selected, and the interviewed experts were invited to select the corresponding characteristics for the introduction of the works (with the possibility of double selection), and the statistics were counted to select the corresponding nine semantic characteristics of contemporary jewelry characteristics which are futurity, topicality, emblematic, subversive, experimental, critical, craftsmanship, artistry, and participatory. In addition, the most contemporary characteristics were selected through expert interviews in response to the diverse development of contemporary jewelry, and the results show that the most contemporary characteristics are, in descending order of importance, materiality > topicality > artistry > experimentation > technicality.

4.3 Analysis of Cognitive Assessment Matrix

The audience's perception of contemporary jewelry design needs to be studied based on the assessment matrix, corresponding to the nine attributes in the assessment matrix, nine questions were proposed to assess the rationality of Speculative design theory, and the nine questions were corrected by the expert pre-test questionnaire to present the negative question f2 [detaching from reality] as the positive question f2 [based on reality], where questions 1–3 were based on the design fiction (imagine the future, based on reality, and semantic transformation), 4–6 questions were based on critical values (subvert perceptions, challenge traditions, question values), and 7–9 questions were based on thought experiments (explore possibilities, cross-domain integration, and interactive participation). A total of 216 valid questionnaires were collected for this study. Based on the cognitive assessment matrix of speculative design applied to contemporary jewelry, the overall reliability of the questionnaire was first analyzed and observed. For the overall questionnaire, Cronbach's alpha value for the overall reliability performance was 0.739 on a five-point Likert scale, indicating that this questionnaire has analyzable reliability.

To test the reliability and validity of speculative design applied to the cognitive assessment matrix of contemporary jewelry, its validity construction was tested by factor analysis, and its correlation analysis is shown in Table 3. For design fiction, there were three attributes of f1, f2, f3. Among them, one factor was extracted after factor analysis, totaling three questions, with an eigenvalue of 1.355, explained variance of 45.2%, and factor loadings of .606 to .763. For critical design, there were three attributes of f4, f5, f6. Among them, one factor was extracted after factor analysis, totaling three questions, with an eigenvalue of 1.719, and an explained variance of .606 to .763. For the thought experiment, there were three attributes of f7, f8, f9. Among them, one factor was taken after factor analysis, and the total of three questions had an eigenvalue of 1.516, with an explained variance of 50.5% and the factor loadings of .611 to .763. The eigenvalues of all three attributes were the overall factor loadings ranged from .606 to .821, and the overall was greater than .5, which passed the validity test.

Table 3. Validity analysis of the questionnaire

Dimensions	Properties	Factor loadings	Commonality	Eigenvalue	Explain the amount of variation
Design fiction	f1	.763	.582	1.355	45.2%
	f2	.637	.406		
	f3	.606	.367		
Critical design	f4	.716	.513	1.719	57.3%
	f5	.821	.674		
	f6	.730	.533		
Thought experiment	f7	.611	.373	1.516	50.5%
	f8	.763	.583		
	f9	.748	.560		

4.4 Spatial Analysis of Characteristic Attributes of Contemporary Jewelry Works

As shown in Table 4, the mean of nine attributes with contemporary jewelry pieces is presented to explore the rationality of generalizing the nine characteristic attributes with jewelry pieces. This study will explore the analysis through the viewpoint of Speculative design, and the chart shows that the highest mean score of jewelry pieces corresponds to their attributes, which can infer the difference between the perceptions preferred by the audience and the researcher's expectations.

According to the chart, p2 shows the lowest score in the f2 (based on reality) dimensional attribute. f2 was defined as a design that conforms to reality; its work was based on the premise of hypothetical and fictional design; its concept was based on the flow of life-sustaining blood to generate energy to form a device. The concept of the device was based on the flow of life-sustaining blood to generate energy. It shows the audience's preference for realistic imagination in the reverse sense of the word, scoring.

high reasonableness. On the other hand, p8 had the highest score on f5 (Challenging Tradition) with a mean of 4.59 and the predicted mean of 4.31 for f8 (Cross-Domain Integration), so it can be assumed that there is a difference between the characteristics and attributes on the research surface, and the work shows that it is more critical in the form of challenging tradition than different artistic views. Combination. This study shows that the semantic analysis predicted by the researcher is similar to the numerical view shown in the audience questionnaire, which is relevant to the application of contemporary jewelry views.

Table 4. Mean Scores of the characteristics in each of 9 works

	P 01	PO 2	PO 3	PO 4	PO 5	PO 6	PO 7	PO 8	PO 9
f1 Imagine the future	4.38	3.82	1.87	1.72	2.99	2.12	2.38	2.14	2.26
f2 Stand in reality	3.50	2.85	3.62	3.27	2.35	3.37	3.93	2.35	3.39
f3 Semantic transformation	3.75	3.90	4.02	3.76	3.79	4.20	3.72	4.11	4.11
f4 Subvert perceptions	3.25	3.61	3.20	3.96	4.44	4.14	2.85	4.36	4.23
f5 Challenge traditions	3.81	4.31	2.69	3.63	4.68	2.58	2.66	4.59	3.05
f6 Question values	4.01	3.91	3.07	3.73	3.64	4.46	3.69	3.58	3.80
f7 Explore possibilities	3.26	3.85	3.31	3.60	2.58	3.16	4.62	2.46	2.92
f8 Cross-domain convergence	3.70	3.96	3.66	3.79	4.23	3.98	3.40	4.31	4.04
f9 Interactive participation	3.71	3.54	2.71	2.81	3.59	3.00	2.62	4.07	4.29

The matrix was statistically calculated with SPSS software, and the MDS was calculated to form a two-dimensional spatial diagram to show the relationship between each piece and attribute, which provides the values of nine jewelry pieces in the first and second dimensional coordinates. Its nine pieces express the relationship between stimuli and attributes in a pattern of point coordinates with vectors, as shown in Fig. 3. This study is to explore the audience's views on jewelry pieces and to structure the analysis of their classification clusters as a basis and reference for jewelry design.

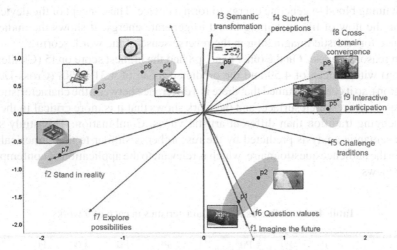

Fig. 3. Cognitive space distribution of the 9 works and 9 characteristics

The cognitive space diagram shows that there are works distributed in all four quadrants, which are divided into five classification clusters. The nine works can be further explored in terms of their attributes, and correspond to the characteristics of jewelry works suggested by experts, in order to explore the cognitive analysis of works in the order of audience characteristics. The work in the cluster, p9 (*Chew your own brooch*), talks about the relationship between body and space in a new form, so the gray block is named the "Body Interaction" cluster. p5 (*Jewelry under the skin*) and p8 (*Wearable Object Square Frame*) consider the relationship between jewelry and the body as an artistic conceptual manipulation, constantly changing the way the body corresponds to the body, critiquing the traditional meaning of jewelry in terms of wearing, as well as the relationship of mutual subjectivity in art forms. Therefore, the green block is named the "Art Field" cluster. The works of p1 (*Electronic Tattoo*) and p2 (*Energy Addicts*) talk about science and technology, they focus on the presentation of the scenario, usage context, and social environment of the product, and emphasize on the two qualities of criticality and experimentation in terms of overlapping properties for future design. In terms of overlapping attributes, the two qualities of criticality and experimentation are emphasized to facilitate future design thinking, hence the name of the pink block as the "Future Speculation" cluster. Work p7 (*Brooch indicates*) that the technicality of contemporary jewelry is in a two-way flow, one is the spiritual continuation of the maker's own traditional craftsmanship, and the other is the spiritual unity of the imagination of the flow of consciousness that remains in the state of physical labor and creation, so the purple block is named "Craft Technology". The works p 4 (*Ring #488*), p 6 (*Gold*

Makes Blind), and p3 (*Ciao*), all of which are clearly functional, are in the form of pins, rings, and bracelets, respectively, emphasizing critical, symbolic, and subversive correspondence to the use of material speculation in thought experiments. The blue block is therefore named the "design concept" cluster.

The research shows that contemporary jewelry is at the intersection of design, art, and craft, constructed in a relationship of correspondence between wearability, the relevance of size, and strategic thinking involving the body as consciousness. Its future speculation, as a talk about the uniqueness of Speculative design, lies in the design that explores the issues and implications that arise in scientific research, ultimately inviting the viewer to unfold the possibilities of imagining the future in a contextual level.

5 Conclusions

As an independent artistic expression in the field of design, contemporary jewelry is located at the intersection of the three fields of design, art, and craft. It expands and integrates with each other in the multidisciplinary fields of formal aesthetics, conceptual perception, science, and technology.

Contemporary jewelry originates from the traditional jewelry's intention to promote contemporary thinking. Speculative design and contemporary jewelry have a commonality and similar characteristics and attributes, clarifying the theory and methodology of Speculative design will help the creator's preliminary thinking and deduction in the dimensions of design fiction, critical design, and thought experiment, this study crossed related theories to come up with nine discursive trait attributes, namely, imagining the future, detaching from reality, semantic transformation, subverting perception, challenging tradition, questioning value, exploring possibilities, cross-disciplinary interaction, and interactive participation, which have been selected by experts to correspond to nine characteristics of contemporary jewelry, namely, futurity, topicality, emblematic, subversive, experimental, critical, craftsmanship, artistry, and participatory. The experts concluded that the top five characteristics of contemporary jewelry are materiality > topicality > artistry > experimentality > technicality, the selection of the highest votes by the experts in this study for materiality also indicates the importance of the material vocabulary of contemporary jewelry in the field of craftsmanship to be explored in depth. With regard to the qualitative and quantitative mixed methods of research and cross-analysis of the characteristic indexes of contemporary jewelry, the conclusion from the result of the research:

a) The three major configurations of speculative design theory correspond to the characteristics of contemporary jewelry.
b) The nine attributes of speculative design could be used as reference for the future of contemporary jewelry practice, with emphasis on the uniqueness of the body as conveyance of art, the craftsmanship of material experimentation, and the symbolism of functional semantics in jewelry.

The importance of contemporary jewelry in this era is to revitalize the solidified traditional craftsmanship employing speculative design as a methodology, starting from the connection between technology and the concept of body-spirituality. As for the relationship and creation of materials and forms, they are the transmission of the creator's ideas which exist in a fluid and interactive way. Art and experimentation, as characteristics of this era, are about uniqueness and change of times, and cannot just stay in the shackles of traditional craftsmanship. In contemporary jewelry, the body is not only the main character but also the subject of thoughts and actions, while the level of thought touches on the relevance of culture and art.

References

1. Bleecker, J.: Design fiction: A short essay on design, science, fact, and fiction. In: Machine Learning and the City: Applications in Architecture and Urban Design (2022)
2. Dunne, A., Raby, F.: Speculative Everything: Design, Fiction, and Social Dreaming. MIT press (2013)
3. Dunne, A., Raby, F.: Speculative Everything: Design, Fiction, and Social Dreaming. Sm, H. Ciao Wei Ho Studio LTD., Taipei (2019). (Translation Chinese)
4. Dourish, P., Bell, G.: "Resistance is futile": reading science fiction alongside ubiquitous computing. Pers. Ubiquit. Comput. 18(4), 769–778 (2013). https://doi.org/10.1007/s00779-013-0678-7
5. Doležel, L.: Heterocosmica: Fiction and Possible Worlds. Johns Hopkins University Press (1998)
6. Dormer, P., Turner, R.: The New Jewelry: Trends+ Traditions. Thames and Hudson (1994)
7. Hushka, R.: Subjective Objects Psychoanalyzing Jewelry (2010)
8. Johannessen, L.K.: The young Designer's Guide to Speculative and Critical Design. Norwegian University of Science and Technology (2017)
9. Malpass, M.: Contextualising critical design: towards a taxonomy of critical practice in product design. Nottingham Trent University, United Kingdom (2012)
10. Unger, M., Smeets, T.: Jewellery in Context. A Multidisciplinary Framework for the Study of Jewellery. Arnoldsche Verlagsanstalt GmbH (2019)

Study on the Effect of the New Media Marketing Methods of the Palace Museum's Cultural and Creative Products—Take "Gugong Taobao" as an Example

Ruxin Wang[1] and Fang Liu[2(✉)]

[1] The University of Edinburgh, Edinburgh EH8 9YL, UK
[2] Xi'an Jiaotong Liverpool University, No. 111, Renai Road, Suzhou, Jiangsu, China
Andyberry@163.com

Abstract. The development of new media technology provides new methods for the marketing and promotion of cultural and creative industry. The Palace Museum has seized the opportunity to use new media platforms to extensively promote its cultural and creative products. A series of innovative marketing methods have not only successfully promoted the products, but also propagandized the history and culture of the Palace Museum itself. However, the cultural and creative development of the Palace Museum is still in its development stage, and there probably exist some deficient points in its marketing and promotion on new media platforms. In order to provide valuable suggestions for the new media marketing and promotion of the Palace Museum's cultural and creative products, and also to provide reference for the innovation of publicity methods of the cultural and creative industry in the future, this research takes "Gugong Taobao" as an example to investigate and study the actual effectiveness of the marketing methods which have been used by the Palace Museum's cultural and creative products in the new media era. The research found that the marketing of "Gugong Taobao" lacks effective interaction with consumers, and many consumers are generally not motivated to participate in the interactive activities and are not willing to further share and spread cultural and creative products information of "Gugong Taobao". The research indicates that effective interactive activities can greatly improve the marketing influence of creative products.

Keywords: Cultural and Creative Industry · "Gugong Taobao" · New Media Marketing Strategy · The cultural and creative products of the Palace Museum

1 Introduction

1.1 New Media Technology and Museums' Cultural and Creative Industry

The development of new media technology has modified the way information is transferred, which has also influenced the traditional cultural industry. The utilization of new media such as WeChat, Microblog and App, which are generated based on the Internet, have increased people's enthusiasm for cultural products and online consumption,

P.-L. P. Rau (Ed.): HCII 2023, LNCS 14022, pp. 111–127, 2023.
https://doi.org/10.1007/978-3-031-35936-1_9

which have also promoted the marketing methods of cultural industry to become varied, innovative and personalized [1]. The development of cultural and creative industries is a manifestation of the innovation and inheritance of a country's history and culture. According to Chen's report [2], we can identify cultural and creative products as products that originated from the core of traditional culture, become products with both cultural significance and market value through creative adaptation and transformation. As public institutions that record the culture and history of a country or a region, museums play an important role in the development of cultural and creative industries. Relying on their rich collection of historical resources, the museums create a series of cultural and creative products through creative design. The dissemination of these cultural and creative products enables the public to understand the spiritual connotation of the museum, to continue the vitality of the cultural relics, and to create economic, cultural and social values [3].

The combination of new media technology and marketing strategy has brought new vitality to the cultural and creative industry of museums. As one of the most important heritage conservation units in China, the Palace Museum's cultural and creative development started in 2008 and has successfully promoted its products by implementing a series of marketing strategies combined with new media technologies. Its cultural and creative products have generated over $1 billion in economic revenue annually since 2018. The successful cultural and creative product development and marketing strategies of the Palace Museum make it a representative of the development of China's cultural and creative industry, and has led lots of museums to learn from it.

1.2 The New Media Marketing Strategy of the Palace Museum

In order to disseminate culture and attract the attention of young people, the Palace Museum has innovated the content and form of its cultural and creative products and carried out a series of online marketing activities. "Gugong Taobao" is the official brand established by the Palace Museum for cultural and creative industry development. It mainly sells and publicizes the cultural and creative products of the Palace Museum by using new media marketing strategy, and spreads the history and culture of the Palace Museum in the form of e-commerce. The marketing strategy of "Gugong Taobao" in the early days of its establishment did not significantly improve the popularity and sales of its cultural and creative products. This situation has changed since 2015, when "Gugong Taobao" changed its marketing mode and applied the concept of integrated marketing communication to the new media platform. It began to utilize popular topics and the network structure of the community to connect consumers and rapidly spread the information of its cultural and creative products [17]. The articles published by "Gugong Taobao" on Microblog began to introduce cultural and creative products in a humorous and humorous style, of which the content usually connects with diverse topics of popular interest and current events. The official account leaves messages to interact with readers in a cordial tone, and gains consumer demand from the comments to improve the products development. These innovative marketing methods have effectively raised the popularity of cultural and creative products of the Palace Museum, and successfully attracted a large number of fans on Microblog and Taobao platforms.

   This research takes the new media marketing strategy of "Gugong Taobao" as the main research object. It was found that the amount of repost, likes and comments of "Gugong Taobao" on Microblog platform has shown an obvious decline since 2019. As of December 2018, the average number of likes of "Gugong Taobao" on Microblog platform is between 2,000 and 4,000 per month, and many posts which introduce new products received an average of 5000 to 10000 likes. The maximum amount of reposts of a single message posted by "Gugong Taobao" on Microblog received up to 26000. However, the number of reposts, likes and comments of "Gugong Taobao" on Microblog has dropped to between 100 to 300 per month as of February 2022. Meanwhile, the number of topics and discussions related to the Palace Museum's cultural and creative products are also decreasing on social platforms. This condition probably reveals that there exist some problems with the new media marketing strategy of the cultural and creative products of the Palace Museum.

   This research aims to investigate the actual effect of the new media marketing strategy currently implemented by "Gugong Taobao" from the perspective of consumers. In order to improve the new media marketing methods of cultural and creative industry of the Place Museum, the research also attempts to provide logical suggestions based on research findings and related theories.

2   Literature Review

2.1   Related Theories About New Media Marketing

The emergence of new media technology has innovated the traditional marketing theory. The marketing of 4Ps, which was proposed by Jerry McCarthy in the 1960s, summarizes the marketing elements as four parts including Product, Price, Place and Promotion [7]. With the development of new media technology, the deficiency of 4P theory, which is only focusing on the elements of the enterprise itself and ignoring the psychological factors of consumers, has been improved by new media marketing. Influenced by new media technology, Robert Lauterborn proposed The Marketing Theory of 4Cs in 1990. The 4C theory is guided by consumer demand and summarized the elements of marketing as Consumer, Cost, Convenience and Communication [5]. This theory advocates that marketing strategy needs to be guided by market requirements and try to satisfy consumers' needs. It also reveals that the core of marketing has changed from enterprises to consumers gradually [10].

   Integrated Marketing Communication (IMC), which originated from the 1980s, has a core idea that marketing strategy should give priority to consumers and integrate all useful information of enterprises to promote products with various communication methods[11]. During the 1980s and 1990s, numerous authors attempted to describe the concept of IMC, among which Don E Schultz's [6] definition was most widely accepted. Schultz claimed that IMC can be used to determine the behaviors of consumers and maintain their trust in products. With the development of new media, IMC theory has been innovated and extended the concept of Internet Integrated Marketing Communication and the theory of 4I [1]. Don E Schultz [6] proposed the four principles of Internet marketing strategy, which are Interesting, Interests, Interaction, Individuality. It emphasizes the role of new media in marketing strategy and optimizes the original marketing concept [13].

Following these principles in the practice of marketing strategy can achieve the marketing targets effectively.

2.2 Literature Related to "Gugong Taobao"

Most of the literature recognized the success of the Palace Museum's new media marketing strategy and summarized the main marketing channels and methods of it. Song [1] mentioned that the Palace Museum has innovated the content of its products, the technology used, and the way of publicity based on the theory of new media marketing. The Palace Museum has applied the theory of Integrated Marketing Communication, making full use of its website, WeChat, Weblog, Taobao, live broadcast and other resources to create an interesting and creative temperament of its products, while also promoting cultural knowledge [1]. Shi and Sun [28] proposed that the online marketing strategy of "Gugong Taobao" is carried out by using the mode of "Weblog + Taobao", which combines social media platform and e-commerce platform. Liang [16] explained that "Gugong Taobao" posts product introductions in the form of "text + product pictures" on Weblog platform to attract users' attention, and using Taobao platform to sell products conveniently and receive consumers' comments and feedback directly. Compared with traditional marketing strategy, the idea of integrating social platform and e-commerce platform can continuously transmit the culture and brand image of the Palace Museum to consumers, which enhances consumers' sense of identity with the cultural and creative products of the Palace Museum [15].

The marketing content of the Palace Museum's cultural and creative products on the new media platform is also the focus of many papers. Shi and Sun [28] summarized the new media marketing strategy of "Gugong Taobao" into four parts, which are combining products' information with popular social topics, cooperating with other platforms, interacting with consumers and readers, and utilizing the Palace Museums' cultural elements and collections to marketing. It can be explained as follows.

The main content of articles that have been published on Weblog by "Gugong Taobao" combines products' information with popular online topics. These articles aim to attract young readers who are the target consumers of "Gugong Taobao", and successfully raise consumers' interest in the Palace Museum's culture and creative products [28]. Sun and Wang [15] claimed that compared with traditional marketing methods in which consumers unilaterally accept information, interaction that is supported by new media technology is more efficient in communication, which can successfully win readers' recognition. They mentioned that the way of communicating with consumers by using the tone of famous historical figures on social media can better raise consumers' interest, because the anthropomorphic way of communication can enhance consumers' trust in the brand [15]. Shi's [14] research mentioned that the marketing of museums should always pay attention to the needs and attitudes of consumers. The museum needs to interact and communicate with consumers through new media platforms to continuously attract audiences, and also utilize the function of repost to widely spread products and stabilize fans [14]. Huang and Wang [17] mentioned that "Gugong Taobao" can widely publicize its unique brand image by cooperating and customizing cultural and creative products with popular IP or other fields. Cooperation with popular IP probably helps "Gugong Taobao" to find potential consumers and enhance brand popularity [17].

Utilizing the cultural elements of the Palace Museum to design creative products that have the practicability not only meet the material needs of consumers, but also generate emotional empathy of ideology and culture with consumers [17].

2.3 Untried Things in Existing Research

From the perspective of the research method, most of the previous literature are qualitative research. The research results often come from authors' own theoretical analysis and subjective thinking, which lacks the support of realistic data. In addition, many previous literatures focus on the perspective of enterprises and cultural and creative developers. There exists little research focus on the actual effect of platform marketing from the perspective of consumers and audiences. Although there are many authors summed up the main reasons for the success of "Gugong Taobao", most studies did not systematically summarize the shortcomings of the Palace Museum's new media marketing strategy, and only put forward some general and vague suggestions for its future development. What's more, some studies of the new media marketing methods of the Palace Museum's cultural and creative products are still confined to analyze the marketing strategies of the Palace Museum in 2016 and 2017. There are few studies which analyze the current situation of the marketing strategy of the Palace Museum. According to these studies, this research utilized a quantitative method to collect data and aims to evaluate the effect of marketing strategy of "Gugong Taobao" from the perspective of consumers.

3 Methods

3.1 Aims and Objectives

As an official representative of the Palace Museum's CCI, "Gugong Taobao" is the main research object of this study. The research has investigated the data and information of "Gugong Taobao" on both Weblog and Taobao platforms. It has been found that the numbers of repost, likes and comments of "Gugong Taobao" on Weblog has decreased extremely from 2019 to 2022, which shows an opposite trend with the data between 2015 and 2018. After browsing and analyzing articles that have been published by "Gugong Taobao", the research found that the main content and published form of articles did not change much compared with previous information. The study aims to figure out possible reasons for this phenomenon, and it might indicate that there are some problems or things that need to be improved in the new media marketing method of "Gugong Taobao" in recent years.

One of the objectives of this research is finding out whether there exist points that need to be improved in the marketing methods of the Palace Museum's CCI on new media platforms. The research investigated the actual effect of new media marketing strategy that has been implemented by the Palace Museum on the Microblog and Taobao platforms from the perspectives of consumers and audiences, and provided valuable suggestions for the future development of the new media marketing strategy of the Palace Museum. On the basis of the research on the CCI of the Palace Museum, this study also summarized valuable new media marketing methods that can be used as references for the publicity of cultural and creative products in other fields.

3.2 Research Design and Reliability

This research studied the question in an explanatory sequence. It first used the methods of quantitative to collect data, and then used a qualitative approach to analyze results and data. In this research method, an online questionnaire was designed based on academic theories, and published to collect data. In the phase of analyzing data, investigation of contents published by "Gugong Taobao" on new media platforms were carried out to provide a better understanding of the collected data.

The research utilized the WenJuanXing online platform to design and publish the questionnaire. Many researchers have proposed various research frameworks to evaluate the effectiveness of social media marketing and the behavior of consumers, including the AESAR mode, the theory of the formation process of media influence. This study referred to these theories and mathematical models to design the questionnaire. And the research framework, theoretical modes and content that were utilized in the method of this study are reliable, which have been tested for reliability.

The AESAR mode divided the influence of Weblog marketing to users into five main stages, which are Awareness-Engagement-Sentiment-Action-Retention [20]. It evaluates the new media marketing effect of enterprises from five aspects: attracting users' attention, encouraging users' participation, improving users' attitude, driving users' behavior and realizing user retention [20]. According to this mode, the questionnaire of this study evaluated the new media marketing effect of "Gugong Taobao" by investigating the attitudes and behaviors of interviewees in these five stages.

In addition, by analyzing domestic and international relevant theories, domestic scholars have summarized the formation process of media influence into four stages, which are Contact-Cognize-Convince-Secondary Transmission [21]. The theory of the formation process of media influence has been tested for its reliability by using SPSS software with 1824 samples, the investigation of correlation coefficient and significance parameter shows that this theory has good validity [21]. This theory provides measuring standards for the realization of the influence of media marketing at each stage, which could also be used to measure the effect of new media marketing methods of "Gugong Taobao" in this questionnaire.

The design of this questionnaire also took the research of Qi [22] as a reference, which investigated the communication effect of the Palace Museum's brand image by utilizing a series of evaluation models and Likert Scale in a quantitative method. Therefore, this study utilized the Likert scale to investigate the respondents' assessment of each statement, which provides five critical answers (including strongly disagree, disagree, not sure, agree, strongly agree) to indicate the degree of positivity[18]. The content of the questionnaire can be summarized as follows.

Degree of awareness of the products of the Palace Museum
Degree of awareness of the new media marketing strategy of "Gugong Taobao"
Attitude towards the new media marketing methods of "Gugong Taobao"
The possibility of participating in the marketing campaign of "Gugong Taobao"
The enthusiasm for spreading the corresponding content of "Gugong Taobao"

The investigation of the blogs and content published by "Gugong Taobao" was carried out based on the result from the questionnaire. Its main purpose is to understand the specific reasons for respondents to make corresponding choices, and provide more reasonable explanations and basis for data analysis.

In order to ensure the reliability of the data obtained in this study, this study utilized the SPSS platform to evaluate the credibility of the data. The reliability analysis of SPSS software is mainly used for the reliability analysis of quantitative research. It utilized various kinds of analysis coefficients to study the intrinsic and extrinsic reliability of scales [23]. This study utilized Cronbach coefficient to evaluate the reliability of the questionnaire. If the calculated Cronbach is bigger than 0.9, it indicates that the questionnaire is highly reliable. There might exist problems with the design of the questionnaire if the Cronbach is between 0.7 and 0.8, and the questionnaire needs to be redesigned if the Cronbach is lower than 0.7 [23]. The questionnaire of this study received a coefficient of 0.942, which indicates that the questionnaire has good reliability.

3.3 Participants

The number of participants in this study was 182, among which 16.48% were males and 83.52% were females. The research population primarily included young people aged 18–25. The viewpoint of this group might be more valuable for this study, because the main target consumers of the cultural and creative products of the Palace Museum are young women [19]. This research selected the most representative blogs published by "Gugong Taobao" to conduct analysis and investigation of their content, form and the condition of consumer interaction, which aims to provide a better understanding of the collected data.

3.4 Procedure

This study discusses the new media marketing strategy of "Gugong Taobao" according to the following procedures. Firstly, this study defined the concepts and definitions related to new media marketing and CCI of the Palace Museum by collecting and analyzing literature, and investigated the specific contents of the new media marketing carried out by "Gugong Taobao" through practical investigation.

For the next step, the research utilized a questionnaire to investigate consumers' perception, understanding and attitudes to the new media marketing strategy of "Gugong Taobao", which aimed to investigate the effectiveness of its communication. The marketing of museums' cultural products should realize the expression and exports of cultural value while obtaining economic income [8], which indicates that the investigation of the new media marketing of "Gugong Taobao" needs to integrate both economy and culture perspectives. Therefore, the questionnaire not only investigated consumers' purchase of the products, but also contained the investigation of consumers' understanding of the cultural elements of the Palace Museum that the products contained.

Then the research collected questionnaire data and analyzed the data combined with the content published by "Gugong Taobao" on new media platforms. The investigation of the published content probably helped to provide a better description of the data collected from the questionnaire and support the statement of the research. This research analyzed the results in combination with relevant literature and academic theories, in order to evaluate the actual effectiveness of the new media marketing methods implemented by

"Gugong Taobao" and find out the reasons why consumers show such attitude towards the new media marketing strategy of "Gugong Taobao".

For the last step, the study provided appropriate suggestions for the future improvement of the new media marketing strategy of "Gugong Taobao" depending on the results of the study. Meanwhile, the discussion of this study probably provided some valuable ideas for the development of new media marketing of other social fields.

3.5 Feasibility Analysis

The method of the research still needs to be improved. The research mainly investigated the actual effectiveness of new media marketing applied by "Gugong Taobao", and the possible problems of it. The research pays more attention to the marketing strategy that has been utilized on the Microblog platform, and focuses on the attitude of consumers towards these marketing methods. This research is probably not able to provide a particularly scientific and systematic analysis and summary for the reasons and solutions of the problems that exist in the new media marketing of "Gugong Taobao", and this requires further research to investigate. The participants of this research are mainly the young women who are the target consumers of the Palace Museum CCI. It needs to conduct broader surveys with more participants, if future research wants to comprehensively investigate the attitudes of all kinds of consumers towards the new media marketing strategy of the Palace Museum. In addition, the research didn't find a scientific method to investigate the cultural communication effect of the new media marketing methods of "Gugong Taobao", and it only roughly investigated consumers' satisfaction with the cultural introduction of "Gugong Taobao" by using the questionnaire survey. What's more, the number of participants might influence the final result of the research. Although the questionnaire of the research gains an appropriate Cronbach coefficient, increasing the number of participants is more helpful for the authenticity and accuracy of the final result.

4   Results

4.1   Cognition of the Palace Museum CCI

The questionnaire investigated respondents' basic understanding of CCI of the Palace Museum. 34.07% of the respondents consider that they have a certain understanding of the Cultural and Creation products of the Palace Museum. There are 56 respondents who know little about the CCI of the Palace Museum, and there are about 63 respondents who know nothing about it, which takes an account of 34.62%. The data probably indicates that the popularity of cultural and creative products of the Palace Museum still needs to be improved.

The study also investigated from which new media platforms consumers are more likely to access information about the Palace Museum's cultural and creative products. 71.43% of the respondents prefer Taobao as the primary way for them to get in touch with and learn about the CCI of the Palace Museum. Taobao ranks first among all the selected media channels, and the number of respondents who choose Microblog ranks second, accounting for 67.03%. This may indicate that most people get to know the information about the cultural and creative products of the Palace Museum through Microblog or Taobao platforms. It might reveal that the marketing has a greater influence on Taobao and Microblog platforms than other channels and are more widely accepted by consumers.

4.2 Attention and Interest Generation

In order to investigate consumers' attention to "Gugong Taobao", the study recorded the number of followers of "Gugong Taobao" on both Microblog and Taobao platforms. It has 98.9 thousand followers on the Microblog platform, and has 8.33 million followers on Taobao as of May, 2022. The questionnaire also investigated respondents' attention to its official account on the two platforms, which shows that there are only 13.19% of the respondents following the Microblog account of "Gugong Taobao" and 36.26% following the Taobao account. The questionnaire also investigated the popularity of the Palace Museum's cultural and creative products on the Microblog platform, and wanted to find out whether it could continually attract target consumers' attention. Only 26.92% of the respondents show that they usually witness people talking about the Palace Museum's cultural and creative products online, while 34.07% of the respondents keep the opposite view. In addition, it was found that 30.22% of the respondents are willing to search "Gugong Taobao" on their own initiative, and the percentage of people who hold different views on this issue reaches 44.5%. The collected data indicates that the attention "Gugong Taobao" received from the two media platforms is not high enough. The online account and marketing content of "Gugong Taobao" on Microblog are less attractive to consumers than its account on the Taobao platform.

The research found that the marketing content released by "Gugong Taobao" on the two online platforms can be summarized as pictures of products, photos of the Palace Museum's cultural relics collection, popularization of knowledge related to culture and history, product promotion articles combined with social hot spots and lottery activities. The questionnaire surveyed respondents' attitudes towards these marketing contents. 79.17% of the respondents are interested in the pictures of products, which is the most popular choice. An equal percentage of respondents choose photos of the Palace Museum's cultural relics collection and popularization of knowledge related to culture and history are similar, which are about 62.5%. In addition, 83.33% of the respondents think that pictures of cultural and creative products published by "Gugong Taobao" can motivate them to buy the products. These results might indicate that the form of publishing pictures is useful for products promotion of "Gugong Taobao".

4.3 Impact on Behaviors

The interaction between consumers and enterprises is a factor in evaluating the effectiveness of media marketing. This study surveyed the interaction situation between consumers and "Gugong Taobao" on new media platforms, and also investigated their attitudes towards the secondary transmission of the marketing content of "Gugong Taobao".

The investigation found that the number of comments and reports in the comment section of "Gugong Taobao" on Microblog has gradually decreased since 2019. The average number of comments and repost on the Microblog platform was respectively 88.5 and 109.5 in 2021. On the Taobao platform, the average number of comments for products that sell more than 1,000 units a month is approximately twenty thousand, and the products that sell less than 1000 a month received around 5000 comments.

The collected data shows that 37.5% of the respondents are willing to leave comments in the comments section of "Gugong Taobao" on Microblog, and there are only 28.57% of the respondents who want to share their feedback and experience after buying cultural products from Taobao platform. Meanwhile, 41.67% of the participants show that they like to share the information that was released by "Gugong Taobao" on Microblog with others online, and there are 42.86% of the participants are willing to share the online links of the products that they like to their friends.

In addition, the online activities of lottery, discount and live broadcast are the main interactive activities launched by "Gugong Taobao" on Microblog and Taobao platform to encourage users to participate. The questionnaire investigated the respondents' enthusiasm for participating in these three kinds of interactive activities. The result shows that 66.67% of the respondents who follow the account of "Gugong Taobao" on Microblog are willing to participate in the lottery on Microblog. There are 36.26% of the respondents who think the discount offered by "Gugong Taobao" is a good deal and worth attending. While there exist 43.96% of the respondents have a neutral attitude to these promotions and do not particularly want to participate, and 19.78% of people indicate that they are not willing to participate in these activities. Only 6.6% of the respondents show that they usually buy products of "Gugong Taobao" through online live, while 74.73% of the respondents show an opposite attitude to the live events of "Gugong Taobao".

Because the Microblog platform has realized a direct link with the e-commerce platform, "Gugong Taobao" can directly provide the purchase link of the cultural and creative products on the Microblog, which aims to create a convenient way for consumers who browse the marketing content to purchase directly. The questionnaire investigated the actual situation of consumers purchasing cultural and creative products in this way. The result shows that 58.33% of the respondents will purchase the cultural and creative products directly through the link provided by "Gugong Taobao" on Microblog platform. 20.83% of the respondents are not sure about it, and 20.83% of the respondents show the attitude that they won't buy the products in this way.

4.4 Perception of Cultural Communication

The evaluation of marketing effect of cultural and creative industry needs to integrate economic sales and cultural communication comprehensively. The questionnaire respectively investigated consumers' perception of cultural knowledge dissemination when browsing the contents of "Gugong Taobao" through Microblog and Taobao platform. The result shows that 64.84% of the respondents who have ever purchased cultural and creative products from "Gugong Taobao" consider that they could learn about the cultural background and history of the Palace Museum from the products introduction interface. There are 29.67% of the respondents who demonstrate a neutral attitude, and only 5.5% of the respondents are opposed to this statement.

4.5 Unexpected Result

Some of the data collected by the questionnaire differed from the assumptions originally made in the study. Because the frequency of publishing articles also influences the marketing effect of enterprise, the study investigated consumers' satisfaction with the frequency of updating articles of "Gugong Taobao". It was found that the frequency of updating information on Microblog of "Gugong Taobao" is erratic. The investigation shows that 34 original articles were published by "Gugong Taobao" on Microblog in 2018. A total of 60 original information was released by "Gugong Taobao" in 2021, while it only posted two tweets in 2022 as of June 2022. The frequency of publishing new content on Microblog of "Gugong Taobao" is unstable, and the total number of articles might not be enough. According to this situation, the study provided a hypothesis that consumers might be unsatisfied with the update frequency of "Gugong Taobao" on Microblog platform, while the collected data of the questionnaire shows that only 8.34% of the respondents are not satisfied with it and 41.67% of them show a neutral attitude. Half of the participants show that they are satisfied with the update frequency of "Gugong Taobao" on Microblog platform.

5 Discussion

The present quantitative research was conducted aiming to find out the actual effectiveness of the new media marketing of "Gugong Taobao". "Gugong Taobao" utilizes the new media marketing mode of "Microblog + Taobao" to advertise and promote its cultural and creative products.

A series of pictures and articles published by "Gugong Taobao" can effectively attract consumers' attention and raise their interests in cultural and creative products. However, consumers are generally not motivated to participate in the interactive activities and further share and spread cultural and creative information of "Gugong Taobao". There is a huge difference in the number of followers of "Gugong Taobao" between on Microblog and Taobao, which may indicate that it lacks loyal fans on microblog platforms, and it is difficult to attract and stabilize consumer groups continuously. Meanwhile, the content released by "Gugong Taobao" probably enables some consumers to learn about certain cultural knowledge of the products, but they may not have a clear and complete understanding of these cultural knowledge. In general, the observation might indicate that the new media marketing effect of "Gugong Taobao" still needs to be improved. Based on the findings obtained from the questionnaire and the content published by "Gugong Taobao", this study combined literature and theory to analyze the new media marketing effect of "Gugong Taobao" in more depth, and attempted to discuss the reasons for these situations.

5.1 Main Findings

The lack of effective interaction with consumers in the new media marketing strategy of "Gugong Taobao" is the first and most important finding of this study. Interaction is one of the four principles of mainstream marketing theory in the Internet era, which have been concluded as Interesting, Interests, Interaction, Individuality by Don E Schultz [6]. The status of marketing subjects and users has changed with the development of new media technology, and users' right to speak has been constantly improved. This indicates that how to communicate and interact with users well has become the key point of implementing new media marketing [24]. According to the research of Zhao and Zhu [20], interaction runs through the stages of Engagement and Sentiment in the formation of enterprises' marketing influence on Microblog platform. In these phases, the enterprises need to regularly launch discussion topics about related products and carry out online activities such as lottery or voting to attract consumers to leave comments, repost and participate. Meanwhile, it is necessary to receive the feedback of consumers from their comments which reflect their attitudes to the products, interactive activities and brand image. The enterprises need to improve the marketing content based on the requirements of consumers [20].

Based on these theories, the number of comments, repost and participation in the activities are significant factors to evaluate the interactive effect of the new media marketing of "Gugong Taobao". The declining trend in the number of comments and repost indicates that the interactivity of the contents released by "Gugong Taobao" on Microblog is weakening. The questionnaire data also showed that consumers generally lack interest and enthusiasm in engaging in interactive activities of "Gugong Taobao", which include leaving comments and sharing information. The purpose of carrying out interactive activities is to stabilize customers' attention to the brand, improve the public's sense of participation and experience, and increase the number of loyal customers for the brand [13]. As the collected data reveal that many consumers lack the motivation to continually follow and search related content about "Gugong Taobao" on their own initiative, it indicates that the purpose of implementing interaction has not been fully realized.

In addition, effective interactive activities can help enterprises improve the content and quality of services according to consumers' feedback. It was recorded that "Gugong Taobao" has changed the names of some cultural and creative products according to users' comments and suggestions [17]. For instance, "Gugong Taobao" has changed the name of a fridge magnet to "LengGong" in 2016 according to the comments of consumers, which successfully attracted consumers and met their expectations of the brand. The current decline in the number of comments and reposts of "Gugong Taobao" might negatively affect its acceptance of consumers' feedback and influence its ability to improve the services. This reveals that the new media marketing methods of promoting consumers' participation and interaction of "Gugong Taobao" are not very effective and need to be improved.

The research also found that some new media marketing methods carried out by "Gugong Taobao" did not motivate consumers to buy products. "Gugong Taobao" fully uses a variety of new media to promote cultural and creative products in multiple channels based on Integrated Marketing Communication, and livestreaming is one of the methods it has been utilized [1]. "Gugong Taobao" regularly introduces its cultural and creative products by utilizing live broadcast on the Taobao platform, which takes the advantage of directly displaying the products and timely interaction with consumers. However, the research found that the activity of live broadcast of "Gugong Taobao" on

Taobao platform was not attractive to users and had no great effect on promoting customers to buy cultural and creative products. The collected data shows that only 6.6% of respondents buy products from the live broadcast of "Gugong Taobao", and 25.28% of the respondents think the live broadcast is useful for them to buy products. It indicates that the live broadcast strategy implemented by "Gugong Taobao" has little effect on product promotion, and further investigation is needed to analyze the reasons.

The ability of "Gugong Taobao" to attract consumers' attention and promote consumers to spread and promote the information of products to others probably needs to be improved, which is another finding of this research. According to the theory of the formation of media influence, the phase of secondary communication is the final result of media influence, and also the beginning of the next stage when new users are exposed to the content of communication [27]. In this process, consumers recognize the marketing content of the enterprises and are willing to spread and promote information of its products on their own initiative [21]. In the context of new media marketing, users play a dominant role in the dissemination of marketing content. Consumers' sharing and dissemination of product information is feasible to help enterprises gain potential target users, but also potentially affect the brand image of the enterprises [8]. Accordingly, the ability to guide consumers to spread and share information is a factor in evaluating the effect of new media marketing. In this research, approximately 42% of the respondents said that they would like to share the blogs of "Gugong Taobao" on Microblog and usually share links of products to their friends. The result shows that consumers are comparatively acceptable to the marketing content of "Gugong Taobao", and the possibility for consumers to further spread and promote cultural and creative information about the Palace Museum is moderate. It presumably requires "Gugong Taobao" to come up with creative marketing methods to better attract consumers' attention and encourage them to participate in the dissemination of marketing information.

5.2 Possible Reasons Analysis

According to previous literature and the data collected by the study, this research summarized several possible reasons for the decline of the interactivity of "Gugong Taobao". Firstly, the contents published by "Gugong Taobao" have become less interesting, and the content may not be understandable to consumers, which fail to attract consumers' attention. Previous research mentioned that the innovative products, humorous words and illustrations have attracted a lot of attention and greatly increased the popularity of "Gugong Taobao" since 2015 [1]. The content of most articles published by "Gugong Taobao" combined with popular online hot topics to introduce products in a lively tone, and it aims to create an atmosphere of entertainment and create a youthful brand image [25]. This innovation of marketing content successfully promoted many users to leave comments and repost articles of "Gugong Taobao", and has deepened consumers' identification with the Palace Museum brand [26].

However, the data of this questionnaire shows that more respondents now think they cannot empathize with the articles and words released by "Gugong Taobao" and aren't motivated to interact with it. The research investigated the blogs and found that "Gugong Taobao" truly uses a lively and humorous tone in its blog posts, but most of the contents are in the form of multiple pictures with only a few words for introduction and explanation. In addition, the research found that although the copywriting of most blogs of "Gugong Taobao" utilized a humorous tone, the content of the words lacked the combination with popular social events. This might confuse consumers to understand the message that the blog wants to express, and it might be difficult for readers to notice the interesting point. Despite the fact that the pictures posted by "Gugong Taobao" contain textual explanations of the products or cultural relic, and the text in the pictures sometimes combine with popular online phrases to add interest, the lack of explanation might distract consumers and make consumers miss the information in the pictures. Although the official account of "Gugong Taobao" later published an introduction to the names of the characters in the murals in the comments section, this form of blog probably confused readers who haven't read it carefully. And the incomplete explanation failed to achieve the purpose of attracting consumers and spreading cultural knowledge. This condition is different from the description of previous literature, which probably indicates that the interactive marketing strategy of "Gugong Taobao" has not been improved and updated with the times.

Irregular update frequency of contents might influence the new media marketing effect of "Gugong Taobao". The Palace Museum CCI needs to continuously generate content with high quality and carry out long-term interaction with consumers, so that consumers can deepen their understanding of the culture of the Palace Museum and buy the cultural and creative products finally [15]. In order to maintain users' attention to products, enterprises need to publish new topics on Microblog to generate discussion with consumers regularly [20]. After browsing the content published by "Gugong Taobao" on Microblog, this study found that "Gugong Taobao" sometimes publishes only one article or blog a month, and sometimes publishes five to ten blogs a month. The number of blogs published by "Gugong Taobao" is not stable each month. The investigation also found that some consumers expressed their confusion and dissatisfaction with the frequency of articles being published in the comments section of some blogs of "Gugong Taobao". For example, some users leave comments about the update frequency in the comment section of the blog published on April 5, 2021. @做尼啦left the comment that, "You haven't updated information for a long time". And several users left comments to express their confusion about the update frequency in the comment section of blog published on February 10th, 2022. However, the questionnaire data shows that almost a half of the respondents are satisfied with the update frequency of "Gugong Taobao". It can be speculated that the reason for this condition may be that the respondents did not pay enough attention to the contents published by "Gugong Taobao", which leads to certain problems in the questionnaire data. The discrepancy between the questionnaire data and investigation might reveal that further research is needed to investigate this condition.

Based on the analysis results, the research can provide some possible suggestions for the improvement of new media marketing of "Gugong Taobao". Firstly, the new media marketing of "Gugong Taobao" needs to find useful ways to improve the effectiveness of interaction with consumers. The articles and blogs published by "Gugong Taobao" can add more explanatory words to introduce and explain the content in detail, which aims to make the readers understand and probably learn cultural knowledge from the blogs. In addition, the update frequency of "Gugong Taobao" needs to be regular. It needs to interact with consumers continually to make them fully understand the cultural value of this brand and become willing to share and spread the products information. Furthermore, the marketing content of "Gugong Taobao" needs to grasp the opportunity to find popular events and design the content that can effectively attract consumers. More studies need to be carried out to find useful ways to improve the effect of the Palace Museum's new media marketing strategy.

6 Conclusion

The main purpose of this research is to investigate the effectiveness of marketing methods implemented by "Gugong Taobao" on new media platforms, which is a representative brand of the Palace Museum's cultural and creative industry, from the perspectives of consumers. The research was conducted with a quantitative method to collect data, and utilized a qualitative approach to analyze the result. An online questionnaire has been designed and published based on academic theories and literature about new media marketing and museums' cultural and creative industry to investigate the attitudes, understanding and participation of consumers to the new media marketing of "Gugong Taobao" on the Microblog and Taobao platforms. Then the research collected all the data and analyzed the result with the support of related literature. After summarizing the actual effect of the new media marketing implemented by "Gugong Taobao" and the problems reflected in the questionnaire, the study also attempted to analyze possible reasons for the condition and provide several suggestions for the improvement of new media marketing strategy of "Gugong Taobao".

The most important finding of this research is that the marketing of "Gugong Taobao" lacks effective interaction with consumers, which probably influences its marketing effect. It was found that although the pictures and content published by "Gugong Taobao" can attract consumers' attention and raise their interests, many consumers are generally not motivated to participate in the interactive activities and are not willing to further share and spread cultural and creative products information of "Gugong Taobao". The research also found some possible reasons, which related to the content posted by "Gugong Taobao" on the Microblog and the update frequency of the blogs.

With the development of new media technology, new media marketing strategy is widely used in various industries and fields of society. Although the main object of this study is the cultural and creative products of the Palace Museum, the analysis and investigation of the effect of new media marketing can also be applied to other fields. Some findings of this study indicate that enterprises should pay attention to the interaction with consumers when promoting products by utilizing new media marketing. Effective interactive activities can greatly improve the marketing influence of products, and it probably promotes the wider dissemination of the products information.

In conclusion, this research investigated the effect of new media marketing methods of "Gugong Taobao", and it was found that there exist things that need to be improved in the interaction of marketing strategy. Further studies of the Palace Museum's cultural and creative industry need to be conducted.

References

1. Song, Q.: Research on new media marketing strategy of Forbidden City series cultural product 故宫系列文化产品的新媒体营销策略研究, 山东大学 (2018)
2. Chen, Z.: "Take-away culture" – Definition and classification of cultural and creative products and "3C resonance principle" "带得走的文化"——文创产品的定义分类与"3C共鸣原理". Modern Commun. 现代交际 (02), 103–105 (2017)
3. Zhang, Y.: The study of cultural and creative product development and design based on museum resources 基于博物馆资源的文化创意产品开发设计研究. Suzhou (2015)
4. Wu, L.: Research on the application of cartoon image in the cultural and creative industry of the Palace Museum 卡通形象在故宫文创产业中的运用研究. JiangXi (2018)
5. Man, Y.: Marketing strategy analysis of museum cultural and creative products based on 4C marketing theory 基于4C营销理论下博物馆文创产品营销策略分析. Identif. Apprec. Cultu. Relics 文物鉴定与鉴赏 22, 130–132 (2021)
6. Don, E.S., Philip, J.K.: Communicating Globally: An Integrated Marketing Approach. China Machine Press (2012)
7. Wang, R.: Analysis of new media marketing strategy based on 4I theory—take SY food company as an example 基于4I理论的新媒体营销策略分析 (2020)
8. Tang, Y., Li, L.: Research on marketing Strategy of museum cultural creation in the perspective of new media 新媒体视野下的博物馆文创营销策略研究. DongNan Cultu. 东南文化 (05), 104–109 (2019)
9. China Internet Network Information Center: The 49th Statistical report on Internet Development in China. http://www.cnnic.net.cn/hlwfzyj/hlwxzbg/hlwtjbg/202202/t20220225_71727.htm. Last accessed 21 Mar 2022
10. Yu, X., Feng, S.: Comparative analysis of 4P, 4C and 4R marketing theories 4P, 4C, 4R营销理论比较分析.Productivity Res.生产力研究 (3), 248–249 (2002). https://doi.org/10.19374/j.cnki.14-1145/f.2002.03.099
11. Yang, L.: Integrated marketing strategy of traditional media and new media based on media convergence background 基于媒介融合背景的传统媒体与新媒体的整合营销策略. Cult. Ind. 文化产业 (09), 7–9 (2022)
12. Zhao, Y.: A review of integrated marketing theory 整合营销理论研究综述. News World新闻世界 (05), 198–199 (2012)
13. Hu, J., Dai, Y.: Public digital cultural service marketing based on 4I principle of Network integrated marketing 基于网络整合营销4I原则的公共数字文化服务营销. Libr. Forum 图书馆论坛 (06), 25–33 (2021)
14. Shi, J.: An analysis of the Network marketing strategy of museum cultural creative products – taking the Palace Museum cultural creative products as an example 博物馆文化创意产品网络营销策略的分析——以故宫文创产品为例. Mod. Market. 现代营销 (06), 86–87 (2019). https://doi.org/10.19921/j.cnki.1009-2994.2019.06.061
15. Sun, Y., Wang, F.: Research on the design and promotion of museum cultural creative products from the perspective of marketing communication – A case study of the Palace Museum 营销沟通视角下博物馆文化创意产品设计及推广研究——以故宫博物院为例. Cult. Artistic Res. 文化艺术研究 11(02), 1–7 (2018)
16. Liang, Y.: Study on network communication of cultural and creative products in China's museums 我国博物馆文化创意产品网络传播研究. XiangTan (2017)
17. Huang, Y., Wang, Y.: The Magnificent change of "Gugong Taobao" – a case study of integrated marketing of cultural and creative brands under the background of new media 故宫淘宝的华丽转身——新媒体背景下的文创品牌整合营销案例分析. Reform Opening up 改革与开放 (04), 13–14 (2018). https://doi.org/10.16653/j.cnki.32-1034/f.2018.04.007

18. Qi, L.: Statistical analysis and comprehensive evaluation of Likert scale 李克特量表的统计学分析与模糊综合评判. Shandong Sci. 山东科学 **19**(02), 18–28 (2006)
19. Huang, S., Cao, X., DuanMu, Q.: Marketing planning analysis of cultural and creative products of the palace museum 故宫文创产品的营销策划分析. Operat. Manag. 经营与管理 (12), 54–57 (2020). https://doi.org/10.16517/j.cnki.cn12-1034/f.2020.12.008
20. Zhao, A., Zhu, J.: Research on evaluation of enterprise micro-blog marketing effect] 企业微博营销效果评估研究,JiangSu Bus. Discuss. 江苏商论 (01), 89–92 (2012). https://doi.org/10.13395/j.cnki.issn.1009-0061.2012.01.012
21. Zheng, L.: Analysis on media influence multiplicative index and its validity 媒介影响力乘法指数及其效度分析. Journalism Commun. 当代传播 (06), 20–23 (2010)
22. Qi, J.: Research on the effect of cultural and creative brand communication of the palace museum in the new media era 新媒体时代故宫文创品牌传播效果研究. Guide Journalism Stud. 新闻研究导刊 (24), 222–223 (2020)
23. Zhang, M., Tian, M.: The application of reliability analysis in questionnaire design 信度分析在调查问卷设计中的应用. Stat. Dec. 统计与决策 (21), 25–27 (2007)
24. Liu, J.: Strategies for live steaming marketing of popular science journals based on 4I theory 基于4I理论的科普期刊网络直播营销策略探究. China Acad. J. Electron. Publishing House 中国科技期刊研究 (03), 320-327 (2022)
25. Hao, S.: "New" Marketing in the Era of New Media – A case study of "Gugong Taobao" 新媒体时代下的"新"营销——以"故宫淘宝"为例. Media Market. 新媒体研究 (21), 51–52. (2016). https://doi.org/10.16604/j.cnki.issn2096-0360.2016.21.026
26. Zhang, Q.: A brief analysis of the new media marketing model of cultural and creative products – taking "Gugong Taobao" as an example 浅析文创产品的新媒体营销模式——以故宫淘宝为例. Guide to Journalism Stud. 新闻研究导刊 (21), 66–67 (2016)
27. Chen, M., Qiu, T., Xie, Y.: Scientific construction of microblog influence evaluation index system 微博主影响力评价指标体系的科学构建. J. Zhejiang Univ. 浙江大学学报 (02), 53–63 (2014)
28. Shi, L.G., Sun, Z.H.: Network marketing analysis of cultural and creative products in the Palace Museum in the age of social media社交媒体时代故宫文创产品的网络营销分析. J. Mudanjiang Normal Univ. (Philos. Soc. Sci. Edn.)牡丹江师范学院学报(哲学社会科学版) (06), 18–25 (2018). https://doi.org/10.13815/j.cnki.jmtc(pss).2018.06.003

Research on the Influence of Traditional Mythological Animation on the Spread of Festival Culture – A Case Study of Nian Beast

Junying Wang🆔 and Jun Wu(✉)🆔

School of Art and Design, Division of Arts, Shenzhen University, Guangdong Shenzhen 518061, People's Republic of China
2210506023@email.szu.edu.cn, junwu2006@hotmail.com

Abstract. The atmosphere and influence of traditional Chinese festivals have been weakening in recent years, especially the Spring Festival, the largest traditional festival in China, which is getting colder and colder. Traditional festivals as an important carrier of the heritage of Chinese national culture, it is necessary to promote and develop. As a popular form of artistic expression for young people, animated films are mostly based on rich Chinese myths, legends, and allusions, which can better spread the spiritual connotation of traditional Chinese festival culture. *Mr.Nian* is the only Chinese Spring Festival themed animated film in recent years, so this research takes *Mr.Nian* animated film as an example to explore the cognitive differences between different audiences, and the impact on the spread of festival culture. The research results are as follows: 1. Women rated the elements of the film significantly higher than men; 2. Audiences majoring in liberal arts rated the film significantly higher than those majoring in art and science; 3. Young people identified more with the traditional cultural features of the film than middle-aged people; 4. Freelancer and student had a better experience of the film and rated it higher; 5. Traditional mythology-themed animation have an effective impact on the spread of festival culture.

Keywords: Traditional Myth · Festival Spread · Nian Beast · Animated Film · Cognitive Differences

1 Introduction

Chinese traditional festivals have ancient origins, which not only clearly record the colorful social production life of Chinese nation, but also accumulate the profound historical and cultural connotations. Although young people have a wide awareness of traditional festivals, the depth of cognition is not optimistic. Most youth do not understand the cultural connotation of traditional festivals, but only stay on the surface, lacking the accuracy of cognition. 31% of youth are blind follower and follow the public's preferences, 32% of youth like traditional festivals because of holidays, 54% of youth think that the content of festival forms is simple, stuck to tradition, no novelty, and nothing special [1, 2]. The survey shows that 67.65% of college students think that Chinese animation is

© The Author(s), under exclusive license to Springer Nature Switzerland AG 2023
P.-L. P. Rau (Ed.): HCII 2023, LNCS 14022, pp. 128–139, 2023.
https://doi.org/10.1007/978-3-031-35936-1_10

more attractive to young people, and that animation is interesting, attractive, diverse and expressive, making it easier for audience to understand and accept. 33.38% of students think that watching an excellent Chinese animation is very helpful to enhance their cultural self-confidence, and 97.11% of college students think that Chinese animation can effectively spread and promote excellent traditional culture. Chinese animation builds a bridge between youth and excellent Chinese traditional culture, allowing them to get in touch with the values contained in excellent traditional culture, creating favorable conditions for young people to develop cultural confidence [3].

The legend of the Nian beast is widely spread in Chinese folk tales and is inextricably linked to the traditional Chinese New Year [4]. The elements of the Nian beast legend: fierce beasts, gods, couplets, red light, firecrackers, and window flowers, etc., all contain people's good wishes for exorcising demons and warding off evil spirits and praying for good fortune and peace. And then in the process of people's oral transmission, influenced by the cultural customs of different regions, with many versions of different Nian beast story, including the begging old man with candle flame, red clothes, firecrackers to scare away the version of the Nian beast more widely spread [5], and in Guangdong, Nian was scared off by people beating drums and gongs on New Year's Eve using bamboo and paper Nian beast heads, the Southern lion culture of Guangdong is also related to the Nian Beast legend [6]. These Nian beast stories present the human characteristics of different regions and contain rich ethnic cultures. This research attempts to take *Mr.Nian* animated film as an example to analyze the influence of ordinary audience's attention and preference to different factors on the correct perception and dissemination of animation content through quantitative research and questionnaire interviews. This research aims to explore:

1. To explore the audience's cognition of the Nian beast story and Nian culture.
2. Differences in audience's cognition of various elements of the *Mr.Nian* animated film.
3. Differences in audience's cognition of the overall rating of the *Mr.Nian* animated film.

2 Literature Discussion

2.1 The Spread of Festival Culture

Traditional festivals are gradually formed in the process of long-term national historical development, and they are an important part of national cultural heritage, an important carrier of national cultural traditions inheritance, and an important force to unite social groups [7]. However, the development of new media has changed the spatial sense of people's lives, and the rituals and celebrations of traditional festivals have shifted from offline to online, lacking the interactivity of real scenes, while the proliferation of entertaining and vulgar contents in the Internet has diluted the mainstream traditional culture, and people's customs and concepts of festivals have gradually faded away [8]. Many of the traditional festivals hosted by the government have made the festival traditions with rich and varied customs more similar [9]. The change of festival forms, the extreme scarcity of people's attention, and the solidification and serious loss of festival content have all become dilemmas in the spread of traditional festival culture. Festivals and myths are twin sisters originating from primitive worship, and in their development, they have influenced each other with an intimate relationship. Myths add romance to festival culture, and festival culture in turn provides a medium for spreading myths [10]. Rituals are usually staged at the festival site because of the strong connection between rituals and myths [11]. Traditional Chinese festivals have been developed in the following ways: the proliferation of primitive beliefs, the attachment of myths, legends and characters, the borrowing of existing folk rituals, and the incorporation of dietary customs. Myths and legends explain the origin and meaning of festivals and add vivid characters and deep emotions to the transmission of festive customs, such as the burning of firecrackers at Chinese New Year, which originated to ward off evil spirits and later developed into the legend of driving away the Nian beast. Without these perceptible stories and emotions, the festival heritage may be boring, or even impossible to pass down. In the development of festival culture, people consciously perform roughly the same activities at the same time in the form of conventions and experience festivals cultural in similar rituals. This cyclical festival behavior regularly enhances the people's awareness and recognition of the cultural connotations, values, and behavioral norms embedded in traditional festivals, and even sometimes people do not know the origin of the festivals but still repeat the same festive activities [12]. "Chinese traditional culture is the 'root' and 'soul' of our nation....... To inherit and promote traditional culture well, it is necessary to speak clearly about the excellent Chinese traditional culture's historical origin, development vein, and basic direction" [13]. To explore the spread of traditional festival culture, it is not only necessary to understand the historical origin of traditional festivals, but also to pay attention to the profound cultural connotation and national spirit of traditional festivals, so as to better spread Chinese traditional festival culture and establish cultural confidence and national self-confidence.

2.2 The Significance of Traditional Mythological Theme Animation

China has a long history and many ethnic groups, and the myths passed down in China are not only abundant in number, but also rich in variety and themes. These myths have been handed down for thousands of years and contain the philosophy, art, beliefs, customs and value system of the Chinese people, which have a profound influence on Chinese society and culture and people's daily life [14]. Myths and folk tales are records of human commonalities, the embodiment of ethnicity, and the interweaving of real life and fantasy of working people [15]. In the primitive society period when productivity was not developed, people were often unable to explain the fickle phenomena in nature, so they had mythological stories and corresponding ritual practices in order to appease their minds and fight against nature, trying to explain and fight against the treacherous natural phenomena with the mysterious power of myths and legends [12]. Traditional myth is the legend that people deify and personify the natural objects, containing a large amount of human reverence and fantasy for nature, while animation film is a kind of plastic art, the objects shot in animation film are designed and processed by artists, which are virtual and non-real, and can express the beautiful fantasy and distinctive moral meaning of mythology through the virtual design of animation film to the fullest extent [16]. It is necessary for Chinese animated films to draw materials from the rich myths, legends and tales, to incorporate the valuable essence of culture and content into the creation of animated films, and to subconsciously penetrate the essence of traditional

Chinese culture into the consciousness of youth [17]. Mythology itself not only has a permanent artistic charm and a profound influence on the development of various ethnic arts, but also has profound emotional connotations and educational significance. Many stories can reflect great emotional power, and animation with the spirit of mythology can show various states of nature, society and life, so that the audience can have an initial understanding of those good qualities in mythological stories such as loyalty, bravery, wisdom and perseverance, and play a good guiding role [18]. Therefore, in addition to its unique artistic expression, the traditional mythology-themed animated film also contains rich cultural connotation and humanistic emotion, which has certain cultural value and educational value, while myths and legends and festivals are mutually influencing and developing together, so it is very necessary to study the influence of traditional mythology-themed animated film on the spread of festival culture.

2.3 Differences in Audiences' Cognition of Festival Culture

Culture is inherently intercultural, influencing, learning from, adapting and dialoguing with each other; it is rooted in every aspect of economic, political, social and environmental activities, and valuing the functioning of culture makes an important contribution to sustainable development and the achievement of national development goals [19]. Chinese animation should be rooted in traditional Chinese culture and spread Chinese values and spirit. However, in the era of rapid development and progress of digital technology, how to integrate traditional Chinese cultural themes with contemporary technological means and common concerns of people to create national style animation with cultural identity and enhance cultural exchange is the purpose of cultural communication in film [20]. New media is the main way for young people to obtain information [21]. The modularity that comes with the development of new media has changed the preferences of young people, who see a work as a combination of multiple modules, free to combine or cut in any way they want, and youth enjoy this cultural sharing and interaction [22]. Movies allow people to break the time limit and get in touch with the real context constructed by the film and have an impact on behavior [23]. Cognitive differences exist across individuals, and the specific role of traditional culture in cultural transmission and the specific impact on youth thinking is not yet known; it is important to fully recognize cognitive differences in order to facilitate the transmission of traditional culture [24]. Audiences have different physiological reactions and aesthetic standards, which should be scientifically configured in combination with multiple factors of the film, trying to attract the audience's attention at the first time and stimulate their desire and curiosity to watch [25].It is of great significance to follow the trend of The Times, explore quality traditional culture, analyze audience preferences, and interpret and innovate them in a contemporary way to spread Chinese national style animation [4]. Therefore, due to the difference of audience's aesthetic preference favorite, it is an important research topic to explore the audience's preference pattern for different traditional mythological theme animations and enhance the effect of animation on the spread of festival culture.

3 Research Methods

3.1 Questionnaire Design

Mr.Nian is an animated film about Chinese Spring Festival released in 2016, which tells the story of a traditional Chinese mythological character, the Nian Beast, who originally wanted to destroy the Spring Festival, but after an adventure and getting along with a little girl, Shaggy, who was looking forward to her father's return home for the Spring Festival, he realized his responsibility and self-worth, triggered his inner goodness, and saved the Spring Festival together with the gods, and the film conveyed the meaning of the Spring Festival to the audience. This research adopts self-made questionnaires to analyze the differences in audience's cognition of the Nian beast animated film according to the relevant theories of communication and art. The questionnaire design was based on the previous research and was self-designed [26, 27]. The questionnaire has five independent variables, including gender, age, education, professional background, and occupation; eight dependent variables, including the film element evaluation, the film shows the characteristics of traditional culture, the recognition of the film's mythological adaptation, the preference for the film, the willingness to recommend the film to others, the film helps you to recognize traditional Chinese New Year culture and customs, to further understand the intention of Chinese traditional festival culture and the expectation of this kind of animation film in the future. A five-point scale is adopted for ratings (1 = strongly disagree, 5 = strongly agree).

This research adopts online questionnaire, and the link is: https://www.wjx.cn/vm/tOHrhy5.aspx# The respondents are all viewers of the film *Mr.Nian*. Before answering the questionnaire, the purpose of this research and the specific rules for filling in the questions have been informed, and voluntarily filled in the questions after obtaining consent.

3.2 Situation of the Questionnaire Samples

A total of 211 questionnaires were collected in this research, and 134 valid questionnaires were obtained after removing invalid ones. As for gender: 52 (38.81%) were male and 82 (61.19%) were female. In terms of age: 18 (13.43%) were 17 years old or younger, 75 (55, 97%) were 18–28 years old, 27 (20.15%) were 29–39 years old, 9 (6.72%) were 40–50 years old, and 5 (3.73%) were 51 years old or older. Education: 34 have high school/junior high school education or below, 57 have college/undergraduate education, and 43 have master's degree or above. Professional background: 37 are related to arts, 31 to science, 22 to engineering, 30 to art, and 14 to other industries. Occupation: 85 students, 8 related to state agencies and institutions, 14 general business units, 11 commercial and service industry personnel, 5 related to agriculture, forestry, fishery and water conservancy, 6 freelancers, and 5 others.

4 Research Results

4.1 Differences in Audience Gender in the Trait Measurement of the Animated Film *Mr.Nian*

The audience's gender was used as the self-variable term, and 7 overall assessments and 25 film elements of film animation were used as the dependent term, and independent sample t-tests were used to test the results, The results are shown in Table 1. No significant differences were found between genders in the evaluation of the qualities of the animated film *Mr.Nian* in the seven overall assessment questions; significant differences were found in the evaluation of the film elements of visual effects, stimulating imagination, situational atmosphere, and story core, and the ratings of women were significantly higher than those of men. One of the climaxes of the film is that in order to help the little girl Shago perform on the stage for her father, the Nian beast unites with many gods to create a tropical rainforest stage with magic power, and the scene is very fantastic. Women are sensitive, they are more interested in romance, ambience and emotional expression, so they will have a better experience of the visual effects, imaginative space, plot atmosphere and story.

Table 1. T-test analysis of gender and characteristic evaluation differences

Questions	Gender	N	M	SD	T	Scheffe comparison
Visual effects	Man	52	3.29	1.177	-2.354^*	Man < Women
	Women	82	3.74	.940		
Stimulate imagination	Man	52	3.15	1.211	-2.432^*	Man < Women
	Women	82	3.63	1.048		
Plot atmosphere	Man	52	3.31	1.164	-2.296^*	Man < Women
	Women	82	3.76	1.061		
Story kernel	Man	52	3.15	1.258	-2.386^*	Man < Women
	Women	82	3.65	.998		

* $p < 0.05$.

4.2 Analysis of Audience's Different Education on Each Variable Measure

The analysis of the audiences' education with the total rating of the film and the evaluation of each element shows that the audiences with different education do not show significant differences in their cognition of animated films. It can be seen that the scores of audiences with different educational backgrounds are relatively close and do not show significant differences, which means there is a relatively consistent opinion. The film tells the story of the heroine Shago's father who cannot go home to visit because he works outside, and the Nian beast saves the Spring Festival together with the gods to help Shago see her father in the New Year. The surface of the film is that the Nian beast saves the Spring Festival, but in fact it conveys Shago's desire for family love and strong expectation for family reunion, which is the meaning of the New Year. The theme of the film is clear, and people with different educational backgrounds can directly receive the core content conveyed by the film, achieving a good communication effect.

4.3 Analysis of Audience's Different Age on Each Variable Measure

The analysis of the audiences' age on the evaluation of each variable are shown in Table 2. There were significant differences in the evaluation of the elements of expression of thematic cognition and in the overall evaluation of traditional cultural characteristics (F = 3.639, p < .01). The comparison shows that people in the age group 17 and below and those in the age group 18–28 have a higher degree of agreement with the traditional cultural features presented in the animated film than those in the age group 40–50, who are in the stage of having old and young children, under economic pressure, and are more interested in material satisfaction, and most of them are not well educated and have a low level of understanding of traditional culture. Unlike middle-aged people aged 40–50 who need to solve the problem of food and clothing when they were young, young people under 17 and 18–28 have no worries about food and clothing, and focus on spiritual pursuits, and they know more about traditional culture than middle-aged people.

Table 2. Analysis table of significant difference variance for age and characteristic tests

Questions	Source of variation	SS	Df	MS	F	Scheffe comparison
Thematic cognition	Between Groups	14.208	4	3.552	2.560*	
	Within Groups	179.016	129	1.388		
	Total	193.224	133			
Traditional cultural characteristics	Between Groups	16.053	4	4.013	3.639**	1 > 4
	Within Groups	142.276	129	1.103		2 > 4
	Total	158.328	133			

* p < 0.05. ** p < 0.01.

4.4 Analysis of Audience's Different Majors on Each Variable Measure

The results are shown in Table 3. It can be seen that audiences with different majors showed significant differences in the evaluation of the film's communication elements of character personality vividness, intensity of emotional infection, and state of mind transformation, and there were no significant differences in the seven total rating questions. The comparison of the means shows that audiences of liberal arts-related majors have the highest ratings in the evaluation of the above three film elements, and audiences of engineering majors have the lowest ratings in the film's character's distinctive personality and intensity of emotional infection. The audiences of arts-related majors are emotional, and their emotions are more likely to be caused to fluctuate and infected by the film's emotions. The audiences of engineering-related majors are rational and pay more attention to the logical thinking of the film. Audiences of art-related majors rated the lowest on the communication of the film's state of mind transition. The audiences of art-related majors have undergone rigorous professional training in art, they have professional and rational consideration of various elements, and are more demanding of the film elements, so their ratings are lower.

Table 3. Analysis table of significant difference variance of major and characteristic tests

Questions	Source of variation	SS	Df	MS	F	Scheffe comparison
Distinct character	Between Groups	9.675	4	2.419	2.572*	
	Within Groups	121.340	129	.941		
	Total	131.015	133			
Intensity of emotional infection	Between Groups	11.330	4	2.833	2.491*	
	Within Groups	146.707	129	1.137		
	Total	158.037	133			
The transfer of mood	Between Groups	11.927	4	2.982	2.441*	
	Within Groups	157.543	129	1.221		
	Total	169.470	133			

* $p < 0.05$. (1 = related to liberal arts, 2 = related to science; 3 = Engineering related, 4 = art related, 5 = other)
Character personality distinct average comparison:
1(4.22) ≻ 5(4.07) ≻ 4(3.73) > 2(3.41) > 3(3.00)
Intensity of emotional infection average comparison:
1(3.97) > 5(3.93) > 2(3.48) ≻ 4(3.40) > 3(3.32)
Values of mood transitions average comparison:
1(3.92) > 5(3.64) ≻ 2(3.52) > 3(3.27) ≻ 4(3.13)

4.5 Analysis of Audience's Different Occupations on Each Variable Measure

The results are shown in Table 4. Audiences with different occupational backgrounds showed significant differences in the evaluation of four elements of the film: character design, scene combination, action performance, and spatial environment. And there were no significant differences in the seven total rating questions. The comparison of the means shows that the freelance groups all have higher ratings than other groups with different occupational backgrounds. Freelancers have a high degree of time freedom, and they are more knowledgeable and have a more unique experience of the elements in the film. Students rated the film's character design, scene combinations, and action performances higher, and the general corporate group rated it lowest. Students' world is simple and pure, while ordinary enterprise groups have rich social experience, so they will consider various elements of the film from more diversified aspects and have higher requirements. In terms of character design, those engaged in agriculture, forestry, fishery and water conservancy have significantly higher ratings than those in state institutions, general enterprises and service industries. Workers and farmers are simple and honest, but due to the limitations of their living environment and the narrowness of social interaction, most of them have limited knowledge. And just because workers and farmers don't watch many films, they tend to have a higher evaluation of the film design. In terms of the film's spatial environment, those engaged in the service industry scored significantly higher than those engaged in national institutions, agriculture, forestry and animal husbandry.

Table 4. Analysis table of significant difference variance of occupation and characteristic tests

Questions	Source of variation	SS	Df	MS	F	Scheffe comparison
Role design	Between Groups Within Groups Total	12.823 116.013 128.836	6 127 133	2.137 .913	2.340*	
Scene combination	Between Groups Within Groups Total	12.250 110.265 122.515	6 127 133	2.042 .868	2.351*	
Action performance	Between Groups Within Groups Total	15.609 150.846 166.455	6 127 133	2.60211.188	2.190*	
Space environment	Between Groups Within Groups Total	17.117 117.096 134.209	6 127 133	2.852 .988	3.093**	

* $p < 0.05$. ** $p < 0.01$. (1 = students, 2 = government organs and public institutions related, 3 = general enterprises, 4 = business and service personnel, 5 = agriculture, forestry, husbandry, fishing and water resources related, 6 = freelancers, 7 = others)
Character design average comparison:
6(4.50) > 7(4.20) > 1(3.78) > 5(3.60) > 4(3.36) > 2(3.25) > 3(3.14)
Scene combination average comparison:
6(4.50) > 7(4.20) > 1(3.72) > 4(3.55) > 2(3.25) > 5(3.20) > 3(3.14)
Action performance average comparison:
6(4.17) > 7(4.00) > 1(3.87) > 2(3.50) > 5(3.20) > 4(3.18) > 3(3.00)
Space environment average comparison
7(4.20) > 6(4.17) > 4(4.00) > 1(3.74) > 3(3.29) > 5(2.80) > 2(2.75)

5 Conclusions

Based on the above research, it can be seen that viewers from different backgrounds have similar and different cognitive experiences of the animated film *Mr.Nian*. The conclusions of this research are as follows:

1. Audience's different genders have significant differences in the evaluation of visual effects, stimulating imagination, scene atmosphere and film elements at the core of the story; And women scored significantly higher than men. Compared with men, women have more delicate emotional perception ability and pay more attention to the visual effects, atmosphere and emotional expression in the film.
2. There is no significant difference in the cognition of audiences with different educational backgrounds to animated films. Audiences of different ages have significant differences in the traditional cultural characteristics shown in the film. Young people rated the traditional cultural features shown in the film higher and middle-aged people rated it lower. The youth group lives in a different era and has different interests than the middle-aged and older groups. As a form of artistic expression favored by young people, animated films are more attractive to young people, and young people receive the cultural features conveyed by animation to a higher degree. Young people are the new force for national construction, and the animation film builds a bridge for the youth to understand and absorb the excellent traditional Chinese festival culture, enhances the cultural confidence of the youth, and can effectively spread and promote the excellent traditional Chinese festival culture.
3. Audiences with different majors show significant differences in the evaluation of the film's distinctive character personality, intensity of emotional infection, and the conveying elements of mind transformation. Audiences of liberal arts majors have the highest ratings, and those of engineering majors have the lowest ratings. Audiences with liberal arts-related majors are emotional and tend to focus more on the emotional expression of the film's story, while audiences with engineering-related majors are rational and focus more on the logic of the characters' story behind the film.
4. Audiences with different occupations show significant differences in the evaluation of the elements of character design, scene combination, action performance, and spatial environment of the film; in general, freelancers have the highest ratings, because freelancers have a freer life, they are more knowledgeable and have rich experiences, and they have deeper experience in the elements of character design, scene, action performance, and spatial environment of the film. Secondly, students rated each of these elements higher than those engaged in state institutions, general enterprises, agriculture, forestry and animal husbandry. Students' feelings and expressions about the elements of the film are more simple and direct, while those who have been working for a long time have rich social experiences, and their feelings about the elements of the film will be more diversified and delicate, and more demanding.
5. In terms of willingness to learn more about traditional festival culture after watching the film, factors from different backgrounds did not show significant differences, It shows that the theme of the film to promote the traditional festival Spring Festival is distinct, which can arouse the festival culture perception of audiences with different

backgrounds, and they are willing to further understand the traditional Chinese festival culture, so as to achieve good festival culture communication effect.

Research suggestion: The purpose of this research is to explore and discuss the cognitive differences of audience groups with different backgrounds on the *Mr.Nian*. Because only one film is selected as the study case, it is an important research topic to improve the audience's cognition and communication of traditional festival culture through animated films, which can be further discussed by more cases in the future.

Funding. The authors gratefully acknowledge the support for this research provided by the General Projects of Guangdong Provincial Social Science Planning under Grants, No. GD22CYS12.

References

1. Chang, X., Zhou, Y.: Investigation report on the status quo of traditional festivals and suggestions on inheritance. J. Commun. Univ. China (Nat. Sci. Ed.) (05), 26-32 (2019)
2. Du, J.: The status quo, problems and countermeasures of college students' cognition of traditional festivals. Indus. Sci. Forum (06), 97–98 (2015)
3. Zhu, R.: Chinese animation: an effective vehicle for enhancing cultural confidence of university students. In: 2022 8th International Conference on Humanities and Social Science Research (ICHSSR 2022), pp. 377–383. Atlantis Press (2022)
4. Ge, S.: Analysis on traditional cultural communication strategies of domestic animated films – A case study of domestic animated films after 2015. China Press (04), 68–69 (2022)
5. Wu, D.: Happy Reading of Chinese Folk Tales, vol. 212. Democracy and Construction Press, Beijing (2020)
6. Zeng, Y., Liu, X., Deng, L.: The Legend of Lingnan, vol. 146. Guangdong Education Press, Guangzhou (2012)
7. Xiao, F.: Traditional festivals: an important national cultural heritage. J. Beijing Normal Univ. (Soc. Sci. Ed.) (05), 50–56 (2005)
8. Xu, W., Zheng, J.: Traditional festival culture communication in the new media era from the perspective of communication ceremony. New Media Res. (19), 81–82+96 (2019)
9. Ao, H.: Predicament and countermeasures of modern inheritance of the Torch Festival of Yi Nationality in Yunnan. J. South-Central Univ. Nationalities (Humanit. Soc. Sci. Ed.) (03), 34–38 (2019)
10. Han, Y., Guo, X.: Chinese Historical Stories · Social Customs Series: Festival and Custom Historical Stories, vol. 16. Social Sciences Academic Press, Beijing (2011)
11. Falassi, A.: Festival: definition and morphology. Time out of Time: Essays on the Festival vol. 1 (1987)
12. Zeng, Y.: Analysis on the generation and development mode of Chinese Traditional festivals. J. Honghe Univ. (06), 62–66 (2021)
13. Micro platform of Party construction network. http://politics.people.com.cn/n1/2022/0603/c1001-32437873.html. Last accessed 3 Feb 2023
14. Yang, L., An, D., Turner, J.A.: Handbook of Chinese mythology. Abc-clio 48–52 (2005)
15. Shao, Y.: Cultural Tradition Reconstruction of Domestic Animation, pp. 60–61. Ph.D. Dissertation, Zhejiang University (2012)
16. Xiao, L.: The Traditional Aesthetic style of Chinese animated films and its Cultural Origin, p. 5. Ph. D. Dissertation, East China Normal University (2006)

17. Wang, H., Fu, L.: The influence of chinese animated films on the moral education of Chinese teenagers. In: Chistyakova, O., Roumbal, I. (eds.) Proceedings of The 7th International Conference on Contemporary Education, Social Sciences and Humanities (Philosophy of Being Human as the Core of Interdisciplinary Research) (ICCESSH 2022), pp. 188–195. Atlantis Press SARL, Paris (2023). https://doi.org/10.2991/978-2-494069-43-5_23

18. Wang, Q.: The Influence and significance of Chinese fairy Tales on animation creation. Fine Arts Rev. (10), 191 (2010)

19. Albernaz, M.F.S., Bandarin, M.F., Hosagrahar, J.: Why development needs culture. J. Cultu. Heritage Manag. Sustain. Dev. 1(1), 2 (2011)

20. Whyke, T.W., Mugica, J.L., Brown, M.S.: Contemporizing the national style in Chinese animation: the case of nezha (2019). Animation **16**(3), 157–174 (2021)

21. Yang, T.: Application of digital animation technology in traditional cultural communication in the new media era. Cultu. Indus. **26**, 58–60 (2022)

22. Takumasa, S.: Where are we going now? Subculture in East Asian cities and the heart of youth. Cult. Stud. **34**(2), 208–234 (2020)

23. Achugar, M., Duffy, P.B.: The affective construction of others' experience: A cross-cultural comparison of youth's (2021)

24. Haselton, M.G., Nettle, D., Murray, D.R.: The evolution of cognitive bias. In: Buss, D.M. (ed.) The Handbook of Evolutionary Psychology, pp. 1–20. Wiley (2015). https://doi.org/10.1002/9781119125563.evpsych241

25. Yang, Y., Zheng, M.: The value and application of digital media art in Film and television Animation. Media Forum (16), 64–66 (2022)

26. Wu, J., Gao, Y., Tsai, S.B., Lin, R.: Empirical study of communication of audience cognition of environmental awareness. Sustainability **10**(6), 1803 (2018)

27. Lin, R., Qian, F., Wu, J., Fang, W.-T., Jin, Y.: A pilot study of communication matrix for evaluating artworks. In: Rau, P.-L. (ed.) CCD 2017. LNCS, vol. 10281, pp. 356–368. Springer, Cham (2017). https://doi.org/10.1007/978-3-319-57931-3_29

Virtual Display and Cross-Cultural Communication of Hejia Village Relics in Digital Media

Yanmin Xue, Ping Zhang(✉), and Mei Xue

School of Art and Design, Xi'an University of Technology, Xi'an, Shaanxi, China
915728096@qq.com

Abstract. In recent years, the development of cultural industries under digital media has been extremely rapid, making full use of modern information technology such as "Internet +" to promote the integration of heritage conservation with modern technology and innovation, which has consequently expanded cultural exports worldwide, and cross-cultural communication has received widespread attention. The Hejiacun Treasures excavated in Hejiacun, Xi'an, Shaanxi Province, is a precious physical evidence of the exchange and mutual appreciation between Chinese and Western civilizations through the Silk Road, which plays an important role in cross-cultural communication and carries the mission of national cultural dissemination. How the virtual display of Hejiacun Treasures in digital media can be known and accepted by more cross-cultural users, and how we can meet the needs of cross-cultural users in terms of digital experience, cultural communication, and interaction design, are the key points to achieving effective communication. In this paper, we propose a Unity3D engine-based heritage conservation and dissemination of the Hejia Village, with emphasis on its cultural dissemination methods, from the perspective of internal and external cultural dissemination, with "cultural relics guide", "education and fun", etc. "digital creativity" and other learning-use-innovation three levels to create a virtual display platform to achieve cultural dissemination, and build a diversified cultural exchange platform for Hejiacun Treasures. The study of the innovative application of the virtual display of the Hejiacun Treasures, provides a reference for the dissemination of cultural soft power and the construction of digital platforms.

Keywords: Hejiacun Treasures · Virtual Display · Digital Media · Unity3D · Cross-cultural Communication

1 Introduction

The Hejiacun Treasures were discovered in October 1970 in Hejiacun, a southern suburb of Xi'an, Shaanxi Province, and contains a total of more than one thousand artifacts, including gold and silver artifacts, gold and silver and copper coins, onyx ware, glazed ware, crystal ware, white jade cups, and gold jewelry [1]. The discovery of the relics fully demonstrated the prosperity of the Tang Dynasty and was called an epoch-making

P.-L. P. Rau (Ed.): HCII 2023, LNCS 14022, pp. 140–158, 2023.
https://doi.org/10.1007/978-3-031-35936-1_11

great archaeology. Since 1970, these precious excavated artifacts have been collected in the Shaanxi Provincial Museum. The museum attaches great importance to their display, setting up special exhibition halls, and since 2022 has been displaying them by theme, hoping to present them to the audience in multiple directions. With the development of digital technology, "through the virtual display of cultural relics in three dimensions, diversification, to maximize the information of traditional cultural relics, as an extension of the spatial and temporal dimensions of cultural relics" is a useful supplement and expansion of the exhibition of cultural relics, with the characteristics of virtual, open, universal and scalable [2]. Virtual display as a branch of virtual reality, widely used mainstream virtual display technology are VRML (Virtual Reality Modeling Language) technology, Cult3D technology, Quest3D technology, and Unity3D technology. Among them, the advantage of the Unity3D platform is that there is no need to download the client, and it can be directly released for web browsing for a direct experience [3].In October 2018, the General Office of the Central Committee of the Communist Party of China and the General Office of the State Council issued "Several Opinions on Strengthening the Reform of Cultural Relics Protection and Utilization", which stated that we should strengthen scientific and technological support, fully utilize information technologies such as the Internet, big data, cloud computing, and artificial intelligence, and promote the "Internet + Chinese civilization" action plan [4], i.e., we should apply Digital information technology should be applied to the protection, research, and display of cultural relics. Wang Ping [5] analyzed the user experience design elements of the excellent cultural heritage-themed APP and summarized the humanized design methods and strategies of the cultural heritage themed APP in terms of function settings and interface settings, and the design of the cultural heritage themed APP should adhere to the user-centered approach, fully consider the functional issues, information combination methods and interface visual effects of users in the process of use, and also meet the national emotional needs of users. Let users experience the beauty of Chinese design. Shenyang Imperial Palace Museum digital culture and creativity [6] based on digital media technology and experience design of digital culture and creativity product design and development of new ways, innovative construction of the Shenyang Imperial Palace image data network platform, the use of mobile positioning and big data targeted design development. Feng Tingting [7] and others used gesture recognition methods to complete the study of human-computer interaction systems to improve the effectiveness and accuracy of the virtual display of digital museums. These are the performance forms of the virtual display of cultural relics, while the virtual display of Hejiacun Treasures is still in the primary display stage, with a relatively single form, which is not attractive enough to the audience and difficult to meet the audience's sense of its experience.

This paper discusses the virtual display of Hejiacun Treasures culture, combines the advantages of the virtual display of domestic outstanding cultural relics, and builds a design study based on three levels of learning, use, and innovation from the perspective of inner and outer cultural communication [8] to expand the audience browsing experience, bring into play the social benefits of cultural heritage, and promote the integration of cultural industry and related industries.

2 Research on the Status of Virtual Display of Chinese Traditional Cultural Relics

2.1 Digital Media Research

Today's virtual display form of cultural relics is built based on the traditional display form of extension, with the help of a variety of digital media display means, such as PC network platforms, intelligent mobile terminal information technology, virtual reality, holographic projection, and other technical means to achieve the digital display and dissemination of cultural relics. In recent years, online exhibition has become a new trend, the virtual display of cultural relics is mainly based on the PC network platform and intelligent mobile terminals in two forms, the application of cultural relics to the Forbidden City Museum, Dunhuang Grottoes Digital Museum, Samsung Pile Museum, etc. as representatives.

Research Methods. Using the literature method and comparative study method, web research and comparative study were conducted on two forms of the PC web platform and smart mobile terminal respectively to study and analyze the characteristics of virtual display of cultural relics under different media.

PC Network Platform for Virtual Display of Cultural Relics. PC network platform of the virtual display is the most traditional form of the digital media display, but also the earliest form used, through the Internet information technology will be museum cultural relics related to text information, picture information, and other information materials on display, its interactivity lies in the click of the mouse for operation, according to the route planned by the designer for interactive viewing, the entire network platform to show the page layout, heritage information, the color balance, sound effects, so that the virtual environment effect is significantly enhanced, the display method can bring in and experience, focusing on humane design, emphasizing the audience's feelings experience, making the design of the subject from the object to people, is the traditional form of physical exhibitors in the past changed to human-computer interaction or several forms of communication information transfer.

In 2013, China's first 360° panoramic virtual museum opened with the opening of the Chinese Art Palace Art Digital Museum [9], laying a good foundation for digital archive management and network applications of precious collections. The Dunhuang Caves Digital Museum-"Digital Dunhuang"-is the most representative of the web platform display methods, which includes caves and murals (see Fig. 1). Users can choose different caves to browse according to the name of the site, cave form, era, each cave has a 720° panoramic roaming, displaying the picture fine reproduction are very high, the user immersive viewing, with a strong sense of three-dimensional, not only to expand Dunhuang publicity at the same time reduce the degree of damage to the frescoes and caves of tourists in the field, greatly protect the original historical appearance of Dunhuang. The virtual world of the Forbidden City in the National Palace Museum, "Forbidden City Beyond Time and Space", is the first 3D virtual restoration world in China to showcase cultural and ancient sites through the Internet, allowing visitors to browse the multidimensional Forbidden City architecture, ancient relics, and ancient figures through the Internet, and to access site details by clicking on the page. The "Virtual Exhibition of

Han Huo's Tomb Murals" in the digital exhibition hall of Shaanxi History Museum is amazing, with not only vividly animated explanations but also interactive games of "restoration of cultural relics", making the overall display experience very good (see Fig. 2).

Fig. 1. Digital Dunhuang

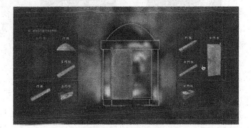

Fig. 2. Virtual Exhibition of Han Hugh's Tomb Murals

Virtual Display of Cultural Relics on Mobile Smart Terminals. The rapid development of mobile intelligent terminals, virtual display through app programs, and small programs, is an important way of digital media display and dissemination, this mode of dissemination and display is more convenient and extensive, and the audience is more comprehensive.

The Daily Palace app and the Digital Palace app, both launched by the Forbidden City Museum, are popular with audiences. The "Daily Palace" is a simple and concise daily push of cultural relics from the collection of the Forbidden City, penetrating traditional heritage information into people's lives, which is more inclined to the popularization of knowledge; the "Digital Palace" app contains not only a digital relics library, panoramic view of the Forbidden City, ceramics museum, etc., but also a derived game "Pocket Palace maker" (see Fig. 3), in the dissemination of culture at the same time also increases the fun, and no need to download the APP, the mobile smart web page can meet the online display. The Sanxingdui Pile Museum has launched a VR genie guide app (see Fig. 4), which selects 15 of the most important and interesting artifacts, each with a multimedia voice explanation and one or two questions using text and voice expressions, allowing the audience to gain a deeper understanding of the Sanxingdui artifacts, in addition to the accompanying quiz module, to achieve the interactive experience of knowledge consolidation.

Fig. 3. The "Digital Palace" app

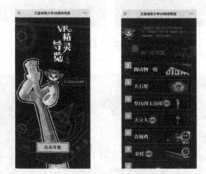

Fig. 4. "Sanxingdui Pile Museum" applet.

By comparing the two digital media, the PC terminal has a large screen, a wider field of view, and is more designable and easy to operate, so this paper adopts the PC terminal to realize the design of the virtual display platform of Hejiacun Treasures.

2.2 Hejiacun Treasures Research

Research Methods. Using the online research method and field research method, the online and offline research of Hejiacun Treasures is used to analyze the current situation of the virtual display of Hejiacun Treasures and sort out its shortcomings.

Research Results. Research shows that since 2022, the overall content of the Shaanxi History Museum's Hejiacun Treasures exhibition hall is divided into six sections, namely, "the use of the chapter, food and beauty, jade and neon clothing, pleasure and interest, the silk road story, the great artisan". Each section has a novel intention and clear classification. Very few precious artifacts are equipped with intelligent screens to give visitors an interactive Experience (see Fig. 5), and some of the artifacts are displayed in three dimensions by rotating in all directions so that each part of the artifact can be clearly viewed, and the modeling structure is displayed by using animation to achieve intuitive and simple interaction, showing the communication and interactivity of the virtual display, which plays a reference value in the design of the virtual display Platform of Hejiacun Treasures. In the virtual panoramic roaming of Hejiacun Treasures (see Fig. 6), the overall browsing route is carried out in accordance with the six sections of the physical exhibition hall classification, and the exhibition environment is also designed with reference to the physical exhibition hall.

But the overall view, the display of heritage is mainly physical, the display of information is not comprehensive; virtual display involves very few exhibits, has not formed a system, the form is also relatively single, and the depth is not enough, for the dissemination of culture focused on the external dissemination of culture, that is, cultural relics pattern, modeling characteristics, the meaning behind the cultural relics conveyed by the internal cultural communication to be explored and displayed. The panoramic view of the exhibition environment is not novel enough, and can not facilitate the content they want to watch, the form of cultural relics display only stuck in the flat picture, can not make the audience better view the three-dimensional state of cultural relics, the interaction between the audience and cultural relics is not strong, effective communication is not strong.

Fig. 5. Virtual interactive interface of the Hejiacun Treasures collection pavilion

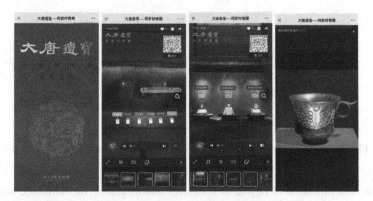

Fig. 6. Panoramic tour of the Hejiacun Treasures collection

2.3 User Requirement Research

Research Methods. The questionnaire method was used to design a web-based questionnaire to understand the audience's perceived expectations and desired ideas for the virtual display of Hejiacun treasures.

Research Results. A total of 200 questionnaires were distributed, with 124 valid questionnaires, and the results of the study were as follows.

When it comes to the audience's level of knowledge about the heritage culture of Hejiacun Treasures, nearly 42% are unaware of it, as shown in the pie chart (see Fig. 7).

From the ring diagram, it can be seen that among the people who know about the relics of Hejiacun Treasures, they acquire knowledge through visiting museums, online channels, news, and introduction by friends, and the fewest people learn about them through the virtual display technology (see Fig. 8).

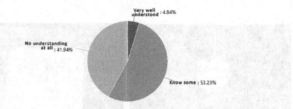

Fig. 7. The level of public awareness of the heritage culture of Hejiacun Treasures

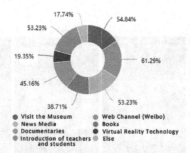

Fig. 8. Through what channel did you know about the Hejiacun Treasures

For the dissemination of Hejiacun Treasures and treasures, the audience would like to see continuous innovation in the form and content of the display, knowledge gained from the exhibition, enhanced promotion of Hejiacun Treasures, and learning of the cultural spirit (see Fig. 9).

For the virtual display of Hejiacun Treasures in the way of experiential interaction, the viewers' demand points include virtual model interactive display, video animation, derivative games, digital collections, etc. (see Fig. 10).

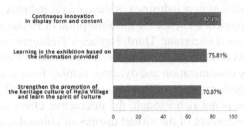

Fig. 9. For the dissemination of cultural heritage with Hejiacun Treasures more hope

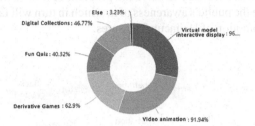

Fig. 10. Hope virtual display experience interactive way

Interviews were conducted with some of the respondents who completed the questionnaire, and the main questions were grouped into two areas.

No Access to Valid Information. Restricted by time, it is impossible to visit the library and view the artifacts at any time, while having access to little effective information to go deeper.

The Content Lacks Interest Heritage display content single, the lack of interactivity between the cultural relics and the audience, and therefore can not deepen the impression of the audience.

3 Design of Virtual Display Platform for Hejiacun Treasures

3.1 The Raise of the Question

Facing the double logic of social change and media change in the new era, people's values, moral standards, and behaviors have changed accordingly, and effect-oriented cultural communication inevitably brings problems such as loss of cultural cultivation and dysfunctional cultural communication [10]. At present, there are three main aspects of the lack of cross-cultural communication during the virtual display of Hejiacun Treasures: First, the cross-cultural communication of Hejiacun Treasures is out of order, and the interpretation of Hejiacun Treasures culture by the masses of different regions is not enough, and the influence is not far-reaching enough, which has to a certain extent solidified the cultural communication path, and undoubtedly led to the reduction of Hejiacun Treasures cultural identity and cultural self-confidence; Second, the audience of Hejiacun Treasures cross communication is narrow in scope. Coupled with the current impact of the epidemic, the issue of new industries in the cultural industry is quite concerning, in this epidemic environment audience for the absorption of Hejiacun Treasures culture, the popularization effect is uncertain; Third, Hejiacun Treasures culture virtual display dissemination form has limitations, focusing on the external culture dissemination, the lack of internal culture dissemination and dynamic display form is not sufficient, resulting in tourists users whether visiting offline Museum or online exhibition, understanding the content of heritage is not rich enough, the interactive effect is not strong, lack of interest. Therefore, the content of the virtual display of cultural relics should be a perfect blend of external cultural communication and internal cultural communication (see Fig. 11). Therefore, it is necessary to solve the problem of how to display the Hejiacun Treasures to enhance the public's awareness of it, which in turn will facilitate the cultural preservation and promotion of Hejiacun Treasures.

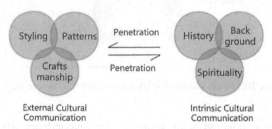

Fig. 11. External cultural communication and internal cultural communication

To address the above-mentioned shortcomings, and to achieve a more comprehensive and in-depth cultural dissemination effect of the Hejiacun Treasures, we propose to build a virtual display platform based on the Unity3D engine through the PC side to realize the platform design for the protection and dissemination of the Hejiacun Treasures, pay attention to its cultural dissemination methods, and build a diversified cultural exchange platform for the Hejiacun Treasures by creating a virtual display platform with three levels of learning-use-innovation such as "cultural relics guide", "fun and education", and "digital creation" from the perspective of internal and external cultural dissemination.

3.2 Design Framework

Chinese cultural history is profound and long-standing, and my historical relics heritage represents the cultural symbols of China, and the Silk Road of the Tang Dynasty tied the eastern and western countries and regions together. The Hejiacun Treasures are representative of the heyday of the Tang Dynasty, and the Tang Dynasty's gold and silver artifacts are the most famous. To meet the needs of the audience to understand the Hejiacun Treasures, this paper selects some representative Hejiacun Treasures, whose main types are footware, drinking ware, and daily necessities (See Fig. 12).

Fig. 12. Hejiacun Treasures Sample Selection

Through the network research to review relevant Hejiacun Treasures information, organize the Hejiacun Treasures related to modeling characteristics, patterns, historical and cultural, to make full preparation for the design of the virtual display platform. Using 3D modeling technology and combined with the Unity3D system, the virtual display platform was developed (see Fig. 13).

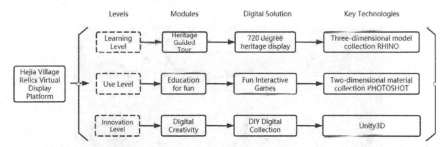

Fig. 13. Design framework for the virtual display platform of Hejiacun Treasures

The design of the whole virtual exhibition platform should meet the following three points.

From the Display Effect. The virtual display should give realistic restoration to the cultural relics as far as possible, to enhance the visual impact of users; set up diversified path selection, so users can choose the visit route according to their own needs when viewing the exhibits in the virtual environment, or selectively participate in the interaction of the virtual display according to their interests.

From the Interaction Aspect. Multiple mobilizations of the user's visual, auditory, and tactile sensory experience, so that the display of heritage information is more comprehensive, and three-dimensional, to strengthen the user's emotional experience, resulting in a strong sense of participation and identity.

In Terms of Virtual Display Content. Focus on the combination of cultural heritage intrinsic cultural communication and external cultural communication, to achieve "technology + culture" perfect integration. serious history and culture combined with interesting scenes should be kept rigorous, to better balance the relationship between the history of cultural relics and cultural communication.

3.3 Main Development Process and Content

Data Acquisition. Firstly, Hejiacun Treasures were transformed into digital models. The collection of artifact models was mainly modeled on a 1:1 scale using rhino software (see Fig. 14) to ensure the accuracy of the 3D virtual relic effect. The built 3D model was rendered for mapping.

Fig. 14. Three-dimensional model

Pattern Extraction. To facilitate the development of the later platform game, the sample model shown by the 2D software photoshop for pattern extraction is mainly divided into plant patterns, animal patterns, and people patterns, the following Table 1 is the sample artifacts extracted patterns.

Table 1. Sample artifact extraction pattern sheet.

Sample Artifact Patterns
Botanical pattern
Animal pattern
Character pattern

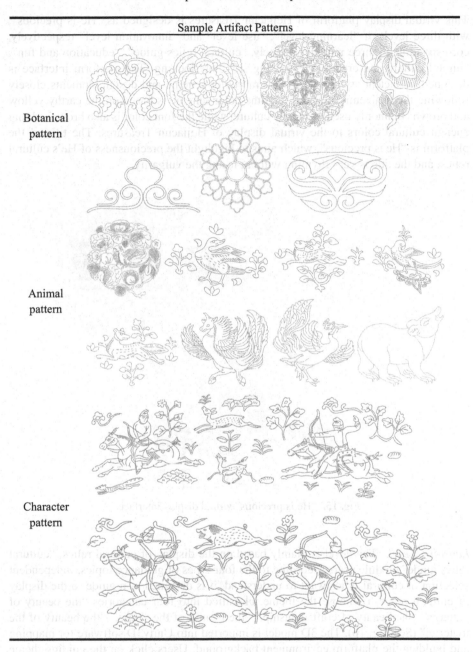

3.4 Platform Levels

This virtual display platform of Hejiacun Treasures is designed as "He is precious", with three levels of "learning level", "use level" and "innovation level" respectively, corresponding to three modules, namely, "cultural relics guide", "education and fun", "digital culture and creativity" (see Fig. 15), interlocking. The platform interface is designed in ancient style, with the overall color scheme and design elements closely following the Hejiacun Treasures, and the color scheme is based on the earthy yellow and brown commonly used in ancient culture, while the font color is also brown, adding ancient cultural colors to the virtual display of Hejiacun Treasures. The title of the platform is "He is precious", which aims to highlight the preciousness of He's cultural relics, and the title is very rhyming without losing the vulgarity.

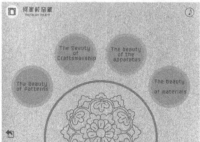

Fig. 15. "He **is precious**" virtual display interface

Learning Level. This level is mainly based on the display of cultural relics, "cultural relics guide" module users according to the four types of guidance topics, independent selection of cultural relics want to understand, it is designed as a guide to the display of cultural relics to choose the theme, classified into four categories "the beauty of patterns" "the beauty of craftsmanship," "the beauty of the shape," "the beauty of the material" (See Fig. 16). The 3D model is imported into Unity3D software for mapping and building the platform environment background. Users click on the guiding theme to enter the hyperspace environment of the heritage display (See Fig. 17), breaking the traditional digital museum exhibition environment, a novel form of display (see Fig. 18) will bring a different tour experience. Users will fully understand and appreciate the basic information of the relics such as name, age, color, classification, production process,

Pattern, etc. (see Fig. 19), accompanied by multimedia explanation, this module has an interactive experience, and users can zoom in and out, 720o all-round rotation of the relics. It also has a section to expand the history, background, and spirit of the relics, such as the hidden history and culture, allusions, and poems behind the Hejiacun Treasures (see Fig. 20), which can provide more professional information points for relics lovers or professionals. Since most of the visitors aim at sightseeing and learning, a large number of information displays are limited for such people, and the design also takes into account the simplification of exhibit information to achieve diversified information transmission.

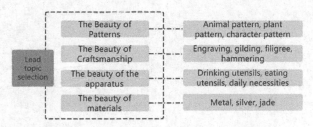

Fig. 16. Heritage display guide theme selection

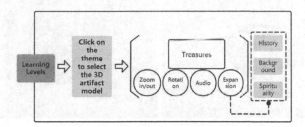

Fig. 17. Learning Level

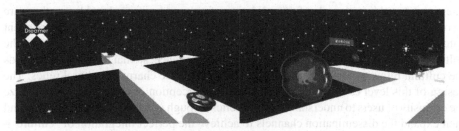

Fig. 18. Hyperspace scenes

Use Level. This level of user interaction experience as the center, "FUN" module focuses on the learning level of further understanding, mainly after the user understands the basic letter of heritage "people" and "things" "connection", the user clicked on the "education and fun" to expand the interaction of cultural heritage (see Fig. 21), that is, the user for the learning level of understanding of cultural heritage learning knowledge to answer

Fig. 19. Basic heritage information display

questions, to achieve the role of consolidation of cultural heritage. In addition, there are also designed relics patchwork games (see Fig. 22), the user through the independent patchwork of cultural relics, one can be more familiar with the structural part of the cultural relics, while having a sense of game fun experience, so that the user understands the cultural relics no longer walk around, but can feel the charm of cultural relics. The design of this level can deepen the user Group's perception of cultural relics, mobilize the curiosity of users to understand cultural relics through virtual display technology, and then expand the dissemination channels to achieve the perfect integration of "culture + technology". The use level emphasizes the interactive experience effect, leaving a deep impression on users through a simple interactive experience.

Innovation Level. The Learning and Use Level is a Process for the General Public to learn more about the cultural relics, while innovation is a redesign process based on the design elements of the cultural relics, focusing on patterns and motifs, and users build their digital products. After users click on "DIGital Creations" (see Fig. 23), they can DIY their digital collections based on the pattern library provided by the platform, attach their

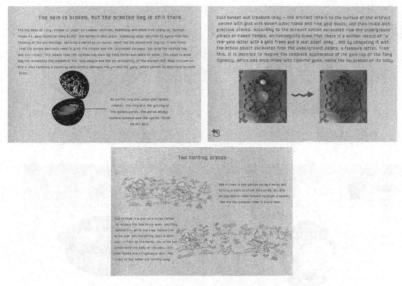

Fig. 20. Heritage Expansion

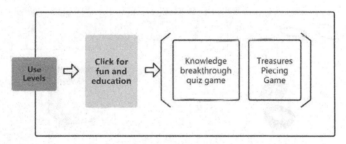

Fig. 21. Use level.

favorite patterns to postcards, commemorative stamps, and calendars (see Fig. 24), write down their messages to the cultural relics for the Hejiacun heritage showcase experience, and generate exclusive pictures with with the "he is precious" virtual display platform QR code, users can share the virtual display platform of Hejiacun Treasures to promote to anyone anywhere, to spread the Hejiacun Treasures cultural. The innovation level uses digital technology to break the traditional form, and the customized design process will give users an extremely strong sense of experience, both learning about cultural relics and feeling the infinite charm brought by Hejiacun Treasures, with immersive participation in the whole innovation process, and the generated exclusive digital cultural and creative products can play a role in sharing and promotion, expanding the user group of Hejiacun Treasures culture and promoting the development of the cultural industry.

The design process of this virtual display platform of Hejiacun Treasures realizes the inner and outer communication of culture, and promotes Hejiacun Treasures to

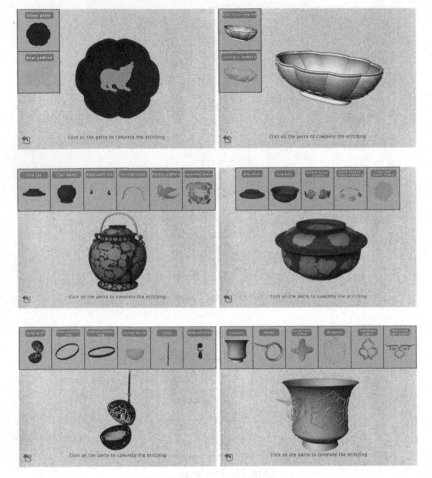

Fig. 22. Artifact Piecing Game

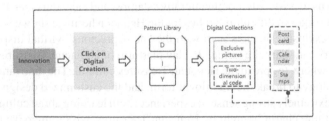

Fig. 23. Innovation level.

audiences all over the world, with three levels of "learning, using and innovation", forming a better system, achieving the gradual penetration of interest dimension, emotional dimension, and spiritual dimension, understanding Hejiacun Treasures from a diversified perspective, and giving users a rich experience.

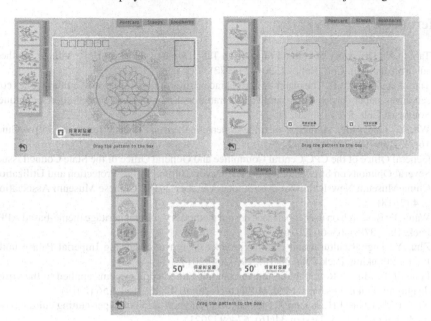

Fig. 24. Digital Collections

4 Conclusion

The virtual display platform of Hejiacun Treasures designed with the Unity3D engine proposed in this paper is different from the traditional display method, breaks the boundary between the traditional information disseminator and the audience, focuses on the combination of inner culture and outer culture dissemination, takes the three levels of learning, using and innovation as the design route, promotes the improvement of the cultural value of Hejiacun Treasures, and plays an important role in the protection and dissemination of Hejiacun Treasures. The integration of "culture + technology" in digital media provides a strong reference value for the study of the virtual display of Hejiacun Treasures, increases the Public's attention to Hejiacun Treasures from another perspective, and plays an important role in promoting the conservation and innovative work of cultural dissemination of Hejiacun Treasures. It can also promote the cross-cultural dissemination of Hejiacun Treasures in China, promote the exchange and mutual appreciation of Chinese and Western civilizations, and promote the integration of national cultural diversity.

References

1. Tan, Q.X.: Discovery of cultural relics from Tang Dynasty cellars in Hejia Village, southern suburbs of Xi'an. Cult. Relics **1**, 30–42 (1972)
2. Tian, J.H., Zhang, J.P.: The planning and characteristics of the exhibition of cultural relics conservation: paper carries a thousand years - traditional memory and conservation techniques. Southeast Cult. **5**, 13–18 (2021)
3. Wu, X., Gao, H.H.: A review of three-dimensional virtual display research. Softw. Guide **16**(2), 190–191 (2017)
4. General Office of the CPC Central Committee and General Office of the State Council issued Several Opinions on Strengthening the Reform of Cultural Relics Protection and Utilization. China Museum Newsletter (No. 374 in total, October 2018). Chinese Museum Association, p. 4 (2018)
5. Wang, P.: Research on user experience design methods of cultural heritage theme-based APPs. Pack. Eng. **37**(8), 63–66 (2016)
6. Zhu, Y.: Digital cultural and creative product design of Shenyang Imperial Palace under Internet thinking. Pack. Eng. **38**(18), 200–204 (2017)
7. Feng, T.T., Mu, J.: Research on human-computer interaction systems applied to the virtual display of digital museums. Modern Electr. Technol. **42**(15), 154–156 (2019)
8. Xue, Y.M., Chen, J.H., Huang, C.: Preservation and activation of paper-cutting culture based on digital technology. Design **34**(16), 67–69 (2021)
9. Lv, X.Y.: Research on digital restoration and virtual display of Hubei Provincial Museum. Technol. Innov. **2**, 51–52 (2018)
10. Zhou, K., Zhang, Y.: The function and path of cultural communication of non-traditional tourism under the threshold of ritual view. J. Shandong Univ. (Philos. Soc. Sci. Edn.) **4**, 40–46 (2022)

Design for Social Change and Development

As with Wine, Life Gets Better with Age. Redefining Mobile User Interface (UI) Components in the Age-Friendly Design Transformation

Qihe Chen[1], Mengyi Zhang[1], Mingyang Zhang[1], Ruonan Huang[1], Jingyu Pang[1], An Yang[1], Jing Yang[1], Hongyuan Yi[1], Weikun Yuan[1], Chengwen Zhang[1], Guohao Zhang[1], Yike Zhang[1], Zhejun Zhang[1], Juan Jimenez Garcia[2], Yuan Gao[3], Shifang Hou[3], Qi Liao[3], Senming Yang[3], and Di Zhu[1(✉)]

[1] Faculty of Psychology, Beijing Normal University, Beijing 100875, China
di.zhu@bnu.edu.cn

[2] School of Industrial Design, Carleton University, Ottawa K1S5B6, Canada

[3] Department of Design, Beijing Instant Design Technology Co., Ltd., Beijing 100102, China

Abstract. Due to the lack of experience in the age-friendly design transformation, small and medium-sized enterprises typically do not have relevant research capabilities for pursuing relevant data to meet the standards. Currently they rigidly apply the standard requirements in the process of this transformation, resulting in imbalance in design effect and experience. Reflecting on the literature and user studies, we describe project-based learning (PBL) practice and three sets of novel contexts, target user groups, and design solutions to support future age-friendly design. The overall evaluation was positive, with some valuable suggestions for the user interactions and features.

Keywords: Older Adults · User eXperience · Human-Centered Design · User Interface Design · Square Dance · Choral Singing · Intergenerational Dating

1 Introduction

Since the new century, the proportion of older adults has been expanding along with the dramatic increase in global per capita life expectancy [1–3]. Its global population is expected to more than double by 2050. At the same time, the Internet has gradually integrated into our lives, bringing pleasant experiences in many aspects, such as socialization, entertainment, and education. However, while most people enjoy the convenience of the Internet, older adults have difficulty quickly integrating into this Internet carnival. Many researchers have explored the reasons for this 'isolation' in the Internet age [4, 5]. First, at the user level, they have reduced cognitive ability and are less receptive to new things. Second, at the product level, many digital products lack consideration for this user group in terms of hardware and software, e.g., redundancy of features and difficulty in learning. The texts, graphics, and interactions do not meet their cognitive

P.-L. P. Rau (Ed.): HCII 2023, LNCS 14022, pp. 161–171, 2023.
https://doi.org/10.1007/978-3-031-35936-1_12

characteristics. Research shows that the use of the Internet can enhance the cognitive ability, self-perception of competence, and social support for older adults [6, 7]. This means that age-friendly design is necessary and beneficial. Although the degree and scope of digital applications for older adults are far less than that of young people, the growing size of the group dictate that we cannot ignore their needs.

Older adults need to fulfill their lives through sports and exercise, entertainment programs, and other activities [8, 9]. Caused by changes in family members and job situations (i.e., retirement), their social and emotional needs become difficult to be met [10, 11]. Driven by the above context, square dance, choral singing, and intergenerational dating have become three mainstream daily activities of Chinese older adults [12–14]. This study strives to improve the experience of social activities for older adults through digital applications.

Since the spring of 2022, a collaboration with JS.Design (js.design/home) took place to co-create age-friendly mobile applications, e.g., functionality definitions, visionary scenarios, and concept designs. The research team consisted of various stakeholders, including product managers, designers, teachers, and students. We adopted a human-centered design (HCD) process [15, 16] for designing and developing user experience (UX) applications [17–20]. This HCD process requires close and timely collaboration with experts in the fields of human-computer interaction (HCI), engineering psychology, industrial design, sociology, and cultural anthropology. The key aspects are expressiveness of products, usability, aesthetics, meanings of product forms, and design in a socio-cultural context [21]. According to the general effects of the aging process, designers have figured out several potential design solutions, includes improve illumination, keep it simple as possible, and inclusive [22, 23]. This study aims to understand the needs of older adults by investigating the current aging trend in China's society and redefining mobile application design based on cognitive psychology theories.

2 Methodology

In the fall semester of 2022, 15 graduate students of Master of Applied Psychology (MAP) worked in teams of five on a design brief. Regular workshops, review sessions, and company visits took place, ensuring that the results provide the research team with key design and growth opportunities. To achieve this overarching goal, we sought to answer the following research questions.

1. What are the trends and user interactions of future online collaboration?
2. What are the characteristics of the target user groups (i.e., older adults)?
3. What are the typical user scenarios and journeys?
4. What are the new design concepts to enable future online collaboration?

2.1 The Fourth Classroom

Intending to cultivate UX talents with applied and innovative abilities to meet the demands of the development of contemporary society, the essential mission of higher education teaching is to meet the urgent needs of talents in the community and to make the utmost of the advantages of scientific research in universities, to lead the development of a career in the future and provide the preliminary training of entering society for students. The concept of the Fourth Classroom [24] links universities and the society. It introduces the actual and complicated social professions in higher education teaching. In this way, students are deeply immersed in the role of pre-profession, and with the guidance from teachers, they can realize their role adaptation and shift from a college student to a professional. The Fourth Classroom has four characteristics: 1) the circulation mode of research-production-learning, 2) the interdisciplinary scientific research advantages, 3) the results-oriented mass innovation and entrepreneurship education, 4) the pluralistic and open fields and time. It is a beneficial attempt and exploration to deepen the reform of higher education and cultivate UX talents with applied abilities.

2.2 The Corporate Partner

JS.Design is a complete set of solutions to achieve efficient collaboration according to the actual needs of different roles of user interface (UI) design teams, providing the platform's service capabilities to more application scenarios (see Fig. 1 for an impression). The platform is a professional UI design tool that is used by opening a browser, providing native Chinese users with services closer to local needs and more user-friendly. This tool respects users' existing operating habits, with low learning costs and stress-free tool conversion. The platform brings together a variety of complementary design materials, which can inspire designers and improve the efficiency of their output. Currently, the product maintains a rapid iteration rhythm of more than a tiny up-date per day and one big update per week on average. The research and development team are now actively expanding to improve the current efficiency and environment and define a new standard for future design and collaboration between industry and research. They provided a great resource to the student teams, who can access a wealth of knowledge through their knowledge and social network. They often met with the student teams biweekly.

Fig. 1. The UI of JS.Design.

2.3 Transdisciplinary Student Teams

The participating students came from different backgrounds and disciplines. All students had core competencies in their respective fields, and some had prior project-based learning (PBL) [25] experience in academia or industry. Unlike many other academic psychology projects, students must design digital UI with usability, desirability, and learnability. The students gave full play to their strengths in their respective areas of expertise. For example, psychology students led team members to conduct user studies and design students led them to brainstorm UI design. This diversity allowed the students to think and make from multiple perspectives when solving problems. This way of thinking and doing provided new possibilities of innovating age-friendly UI. Through this transdisciplinary learning experience, the students learned from each other and gained new knowledge and skills.

2.4 The Design Brief Assignment

Aging is an inevitable trend, and age-friendly design cannot be ignored in social life. To promote PBL, one design brief was assigned by the corporate collaborator. It is expected that through this project collaboration, the UI components can be redesigned and modified for aging. Relevant theoretical guidance should be compiled to reduce the subsequent design modification cost and improve the design efficiency while guaranteeing UX. Practical product design pipeline should be considered, including user interviews, personas, design ideation, prototyping, and mockups.

3 Results

Table 1 lists the mapping of the personas (i.e., target user groups) [26], contexts of use [27–29], and the key jobs-to-be-done (JTBD) [30] applied. Because of the COVID-19, many social activities have been transferred into online formats, however, many activities cannot be held. Therefore, older adults want to dance with friends at home. Many applications support online singing, however, older adults report that sing along lose the connection with others. Therefore, creating immersive singing atmosphere is essential. Intergenerational dating is common in Beijing and Shanghai. However, they visit the dating corners to find appropriate dating resources. They complain about the resource's quality. Therefore, information resources and guarantee privacy should be ensured. Below, research scopes, personas, concept designs, and user testings are presented for all results.

Table 1. Mapping of the teams, personas, and JTBDs of the results.

Team	Persona	JTBD
1	Square dance lovers, 60–75	Dance with friends at home where there are limitations of COVID-19 and space
2	Choral singing lovers, 55–70	Immerse in emotion and experience of the choral singing atmosphere
3	Parents need intergenerational dating, 55–65	Access to rich dating resources and guarantee privacy and security

3.1 Team 1: Square Dance

Square dance is a popular leisure activity among older Chinese adults and plays a positive role in improving their health and achieving active aging. However, due to the impact of COVID-19 and the limitation of activity space, helping them perform online square dance activities has become an urgent problem to be solved.

Through preliminary research interviews, the target users are the retired group aged 60–75, who can use smartphones independently. They love to exercise, socialize with friends, enrich their lives, and enhance their dancing skills through square dancing. They need a more straightforward and convenient way to learn, mix, and record their dance online.

They currently try to do this using video conferencing software and instant messengers. However, current solutions must improve to avoid low age-appropriateness, low immersion, and low interactivity. To solve this problem, this team has designed a mobile application to dance together online and learn to dance quickly. This application helps them do square dance smoothly and efficiently and get an excellent online experience through multi-angle video teaching, practice assistance, and dancing together on the same screen. See Figs. 2 and 3 for an impression.

Fifteen target users underwent usability testing using a 26-question UEQ and low-fidelity UI [31, 32]. The results showed that all dimensions scored average and above. The efficiency, reliability, and novelty dimensions were all "excellent." Based on their subjective feedback, the final UI design was improved by adding a video recording view, changing gesture interaction to voice to prevent accidental touches, and simplifying buttons that consumed visual resources.

3.2 Team 2: Choral Singing

Affected by COVID-19, choral activities in parks could not carry out as usual. Although major music, live streaming, and Karaoke mobile applications have launched large-print and offered senior versions, the emotional support and singing experience of singing alone differs from that of choral singing.

The target users are music-loving older adults aged 55–70. They have plenty of time, feel lonely and bored, and want to continue to develop their interests. Due to COVID-19, they are members of several choirs but have not participated in face-to-face activities for a long time.

Fig. 2. The user scenario.

Fig. 3. The UI designs.

For this reason, this team designed a choral mobile application to help them achieve immersive choral singing. See Figs. 4 and 5 for an impression.

12 target users tested the primary features of low-fidelity UI. Judging from their subjective feedback, most of them accepted the new design. The results showed that the pragmatic dimension had a low score, and the hedonic dimension had a high score. An updated iteration of the UI design was conducted based on the feedback and scores.

3.3 Team 3: Intergenerational Dating

Older adults with intergenerational dating needs are limited by time and space due to COVID-19 when looking for a match for their children at dating corners. They have attempted to solve this problem, such as introducing blind dates to their children through friends and browsing dating websites. However, these solutions have issues such as a need for more resources, untrue information, and difficulty securing privacy and safety.

Based on research and user interviews, the target user group is older adults aged 55–65 who need to give their children a match. They live in first- and second-tier cities and have secondary school or above education level. Because their children are usually

Fig. 4. The user scenario.

Fig. 5. The UI designs.

busy at work, they volunteer to help them go on blind dates, hoping their children can find partners soon.

This team designed an online intergenerational dating mobile application to access rich dating resources, guarantee privacy and security, gain emotional respect, and enable efficiency and convenience. See Figs. 6 and 7 for an impression.

12 target users performed usability tests on low-fidelity UI and primary features. From the results, the pragmatic dimension had a low score, and the hedonic dimension had a high score. They generally found this new design unique and novel and enjoyed experiencing it. They found the settings feature complex and wanted to enhance its ease of use.

Fig. 6. The user scenario.

Fig. 7. The UI designs.

4 Discussion and Reflection

4.1 The Fourth Classroom

The students have adopted the innovative model of the Fourth Classroom and worked closely with the corporate partner to produce digital age-friendly projects. In the actual process, they identified real-world problems in field research and teamwork. The PBL approach enabled them to gain working skills in UX design, such as prototyping and interview research. At the same time, they gradually deepened their understanding of age-friendly UI design components, which reflected innovative learning outcomes of the Fourth Classroom.

4.2 Transdisciplinary Learning

As students from liberal arts, business, engineering, design, psychology, and other disciplines collaborated and completed the projects, perspectives from different disciplines collided, providing a wealth of inspiration and experience in integrating transdisciplinary perspectives in the HCD process. The students brought their respective strengths to bear, providing diverse perspectives and expanding each other's horizons, which led to a comprehensive understanding and appreciation of the complexity of the problems. Not only that, but the collision between different disciplinary perspectives also brought new inspiration and stimulated new and exciting ideas. In addition, these different perspectives brought about some differences in the collaboration process. For example, it was challenging for the students to balance the exciting ideas and the rigorous science. However, it also provided them with experience in collaboration. This helped them to deeply understand the epistemological and methodological differences between different disciplines so that they could better achieve their common goals.

4.3 Collaboration Between University and Corporate Partner

The university-corporate collaboration approach provided ample practical opportunities for students to align with the industry. However, simultaneously, there are certain limitations in the implementation. The university valued the development and progress of students in the project process, and everything served the goal of student growth. The corporate partner focused more on results and outputs, and the goal was to obtain viable solutions. Both sides needed to form a common landing point to achieve win-win development. This way of teaching inevitably brought time conflicts. Both sides must often communicate with students and provide guidance and assistance separately. In some cases, one party was significantly ahead of the other, leaving students with a distinct sense of fragmentation and affecting the progress and quality of teaching. This required both sides to keep communication channels open and to communicate in real-time about progress and problems encountered to avoid such issues.

4.4 What if We Start All Over

The students used proven research and analysis methods to implement the age-friendly UI design of three mobile applications for square dancing, choral singing, and intergenerational dating. Some less-than-satisfactory feedback also emerged from this study, and the students could certainly do better if they started over. Because older adults rarely engaged in choral, sports, and dating activities online, it was often difficult for the students to gain direct experience in context. In most cases, they had to observe and interview offline-related activities for their pain points and needs. This required the interviewers to conduct enough visits and surveys and have great insight to uncover the suitable needs from the original research materials. Therefore, the interview sample size and depth could be much larger. If starting over, the students should accumulate more on the preliminary research and interviews to sort out a better design logic and interaction workflow to provide sufficient guidance for subsequent work.

Acknowledgment. We would like to thank the students at UX Program of MAP at Faculty of Psychology at Beijing Normal University and the designers at Department of Design at Beijing Instant Design Technology Co., Ltd.

References

1. Chatterji, S., Byles, J., Cutler, D., Seeman, T., Verdes, E.: Health, functioning, and disability in older adults: present status and future implications. Lancet **385**(9967), 563–575 (2015)
2. Tang, M., Wang, D., Guerrien, A.: Effect of "freedom of choice" on task performance and well-being during leisure activity: an intercultural study among older adults in China and France. Int. J. Aging Hum. Develop. **95**(2), 187–204 (2022)
3. Wang, Q., Wang, D., Li, C., Miller, R.B.: Marital satisfaction and depressive symptoms among Chinese older couples. Aging Ment. Health **18**(1), 11–18 (2014)
4. Hunsaker, A., Hargittai, E.: A review of Internet use among older adults. New Media Soc. **20**(10), 3937–3954 (2018)
5. Chen, B., Huang, Y., Wang, D., Deng, W.: Comparison of performance-based observed assessment, self-report, and paper–pencil measures of everyday problem solving in Chinese older adults. J. Adult Dev. **26**(2), 129–138 (2019)
6. Huai, Q., Liu, X., Peng, H.: Processing mode and processing contents in older and younger adults' sunk cost decision-making. Curr. Psychol. 1–14 (2022)
7. McGinley, C., Myerson, J., Briscoe, G., Carroll, S.: Towards an age-friendly design lens. J. Popul. Ageing 1–16 (2022)
8. Manini, T.M., Pahor, M.: Physical activity and maintaining physical function in older adults. Br. J. Sports Med. **43**(1), 28–31 (2009)
9. Hu, T., et al.: The influence of "small private online course+ flipped classroom" teaching on physical education students' learning motivation from the perspective of self-determination theory. Front. Psychol. **13** (2022)
10. Green, L.R., Richardson, D.S., Lago, T., Schatten-Jones, E.C.: Network correlates of social and emotional loneliness in young and older adults. Pers. Soc. Psychol. Bull. **27**(3), 281–288 (2001)
11. Charles, S.T., Carstensen, L.L.: Social and emotional aging. Annu. Rev. Psychol. **61**, 383–409 (2010)
12. Seetoo, C., Zou, H.: China's guangchang wu: the emergence, choreography, and management of dancing in public squares. TDR/the Drama Rev. **60**(4), 22–49 (2016)
13. Beynon, C., Heydon, R., O'Neill, S., Zhang, Z., Crocker, W.: Straining to hear the singing: toward an understanding of successful intergenerational singing curriculum. J. Intergenerat. Relationships **11**(2), 176–189 (2013)
14. Chen, J., Jordan, L.P.: Intergenerational support and life satisfaction of young-, old-and oldest-old adults in China. Aging Ment. Health **22**(3), 412–420 (2018)
15. Liu, W., Lee, K.P., Gray, C.M., Toombs, A.L., Chen, K.H., Leifer, L.: Transdisciplinary teaching and learning in UX design: a program review and AR case studies. Appl. Sci. **11**(22), 10648 (2021)
16. Norman, D.: The design of everyday things: Revised and expanded edition. Basic books (2013)
17. Jimenez Garcia, J., Castilla, C., Aguirre, J., Martinez, J.P., Liu, W.: Experiences in the design of localized eHealth tools for users facing inequality of access to healthcare. In: International Conference on Human-Computer Interaction, pp. 130–148 (2022)
18. Zhu, Y., et al.: Wellbeing and healthcare: exploring ways of interactive prototyping with mental process. In: International Conference on Applied Human Factors and Ergonomics, pp. 123–127 (2021)
19. Zhu, D., et al.: Designing a mobile application for working memory training through understanding the psychological and physiological characteristics of older adults. Sustainability **14**(21), 14152 (2022)

20. Long, K.M., et al.: Understanding perspectives of older adults on the role of technology in the wider context of their social relationships. Ageing Soc. 1–24 (2022)
21. Zhu, D., Wang, D., Huang, R., Jing, Y., Qiao, L., Liu, W.: User interface (UI) design and user experience questionnaire (UEQ) evaluation of a to-do list mobile application to support day-to-day life of older adults. Healthcare **10**(10), 2068 (2022)
22. Zhu, D., et al.: Envisioning the future trends of smart assistive devices to support activities of daily living for older adults with disabilities. In: International Conference on Human-Computer Interaction, pp. 454–466 (2022)
23. Zhu, D., et al.: Social inclusion in an aging world: envisioning elderly-friendly digital interfaces. In: International Conference on Human Interaction and Emerging Technologies, 1082–1087 (2021)
24. Liu, C., et al.: From theory to practice: on the connotation and characteristics of 'the Fourth Classroom.' Res. Teach. **41**(6), 1–6 (2018)
25. Liu, W., Byler, E., Leifer, L.: Engineering design entrepreneurship and innovation: transdisciplinary teaching and learning in a global context. In: International Conference on Human-Computer Interaction, 451–460 (2020)
26. Ferreira, B., Silva, W., Oliveira, E., Conte, T.: Designing personas with empathy map. In: SEKE, vol. 152 (2015)
27. Visser, F.S., Stappers, P.J., Van der Lugt, R., Sanders, E.B.: Contextmapping: experiences from practice. CoDesign **1**(2), 119–149 (2005)
28. Gray, C.M., Hasib, A., Li, Z., Chivukula, S.S.: Using decisive constraints to create design methods that guide ethical impact. Des. Stud. **79**, 101097 (2022)
29. Ohashi, T., Auernhammer, J., Liu, W., Pan, W., Leifer, L.: NeuroDesignScience: systematic literature review of current research on design using neuroscience techniques. Design Comput. Cogn. 575–592 (2022)
30. Lucassen, G., Keuken, M.V.D., Dalpiaz, F., Brinkkemper, S., Sloof, G.W., Schlingmann, J.: Jobs-to-be-done oriented requirements engineering: a method for defining job stories. In: International Working Conference on Requirements Engineering: Foundation for Software Quality, pp. 227–243 (2018)
31. Schrepp, M., Hinderks, A., Thomaschewski, J.: Applying the user experience questionnaire (UEQ) in different evaluation scenarios. In: International Conference of Design, User Experience, and Usability, pp. 383–392 (2014)
32. Encinas, E., Durrant, A.C., Mitchell, R., Blythe, M.: Metaprobes, metaphysical workshops, and sketchy philosophy. In: CHI Conference on Human Factors in Computing Systems, pp. 1–13 (2020)

Building the Knowledge Base of Folk Beliefs Based on Semantic Web Technology

Yu-Liang Chi[1(✉)] and Han-Yu Sung[2]

[1] Department of Information Management, Chung Yuan Christian University, ChungLi, Taiwan
maxchi@cycu.edu.tw
[2] Department of Allied Health Education and Digital Learning, National Taipei University of Nursing and Health Sciences, Taipei, Taiwan

Abstract. There are various folk beliefs (religions) in Chinese society. Due to the current limited system for querying beliefs and the lack of intelligent content editing, it is difficult for the public to retrieve in-depth information. The purpose of this research is to develop a knowledge-based system, using semantic web technologies to develop a knowledge base, and then using chatbots as the front end to provide user-friendly knowledge queries. The three designs include: (1) Upgrade existing open data to linked Data in the form of RDF resources; (2) Build a knowledge model to describe the knowledge composition and relationship of folk beliefs. This knowledge model is established by OWL to support logical reasoning. Linked data and knowledge model are finally combined into a knowledge base; (3) Develop a chatbot system to utilize the power of knowledge bases. In conclusion, this study verifies the utility of knowledge base in knowledge composition, relationship description and reasoning by establishing the application of folk beliefs.

Keywords: Semantic web · Knowledge base · Linked data · Folk religions

1 Introduction

This study focuses on folk beliefs in Taiwanese society, which are largely inherited from the Chinese. In addition to traditional Buddhism, Confucianism, and Taoism, other beliefs are mostly derived from ancient animistic beliefs, legends, ancestor worship, etc. In addition, factors such as social groups, natural environment, and changes in ruling power will also affect beliefs. Unlike organized religions such as Christianity, Islam, and Judaism, folk beliefs usually do not have specific leaders or strict organizations. Altars and ancestral halls are centered to seek specific benefits and harmony in life. The diversity of folk beliefs in Taiwan can be seen from the monasteries, temples, churches, and ancestral halls that can be seen everywhere. However, due to the wide variety of deities, most people only have a rough or piecemeal understanding. For example, what religion or deity is worshiped in this temple, what are the customs, celebrations, and history. Taken together, the content of these beliefs is made up of intertwined knowledge. Therefore, the topic of this research is how to develop the intelligent application of folk beliefs in the form of knowledge base.

P.-L. P. Rau (Ed.): HCII 2023, LNCS 14022, pp. 172–182, 2023.
https://doi.org/10.1007/978-3-031-35936-1_13

In order to establish a knowledge application system for Taiwanese folk beliefs, this study utilizes Semantic Web technology for development. Three main tasks include: (1) Upgrade existing open data to linked Data. Government open data and other open resources such as DBpedia, Wikidata, etc. will be collected. The data will be represented by the Resource Description Framework (RDF); (2) Build a knowledge model. Knowledge extraction and modeling are performed on the collected facts, including the formation of classes, attributes and logical relationships between classes. The knowledge model uses Web Ontology Language (OWL); (3) Develop chatbot applications as a means of interacting with users. This system includes natural language processing tools to analyze user intentions and retrieve knowledge bases. In short, the chatbot provides a friendly environment for interaction, and the knowledge base acts as a smarter brain, providing queries and supporting reasoning.

2 Literature Review

The goal of the Semantic Web is to transform the traditional web page content into a link network with data as the unit, which is called the "Web of data" [1, 5]. Under this framework, the data is transformed into a resource type, which can be recognized by the computer system and contains other links that can be connected to the outside world. The resources can be continuously extended to another resource, providing computer systems a wider operating space [12, 15]. In order to ensure smooth operation, all participants must follow a unified agreement or specification. The World Wide Web Consortium (W3C) is the authoritative organization for formulating specifications; therefore, the so-called Semantic Web "technology" can also be understood as the relevant protocol specifications formulated by W3C [4, 8]. The following is a brief description of several specifications used in this program:

- Resource Description Framework (RDF). This framework actually defines a standard data model, which provides a unified description of resources on the Internet. The data model is composed of subject, predicate, and object. In principle, these three items must be expressed by URI. The portal site where RDF data set is placed is called endpoint, which It can handle SPARQL query requests sent by the outside world [10].
- SPARQL, which is a language specification specially formulated for querying RDF data sets. Its syntax and functions are similar to the SQL language used by relational databases. In application, users must write query commands in SPARQL syntax, and send queries to RDF data endpoints through any platform that supports the HTTP protocol [3, 13].
- Web Ontology Language (OWL). Information science often applies ontology to the event composition of real world, such as file management, taxonomy, etc. [14]. OWL is a language specification that uses the ontology method to provide the vocabulary needed to describe semantics. Finally, OWL is often used to define upper-level concepts or models, and RDF is used to edit lower-level data instances. Because both OWL and RDF are XML-based markup languages, they can compatible in syntax.

• Linked data is the specific practice of Semantic Web technology in the data layer. Traditional data formats such as csv, excel, or associated databases can first obtain RDF-based data through conversion tools, and then improve the quality of the data to become linked data [11]. Several methods to improve data quality are: (i) the subject of an RDF triple must be expressed using a URI; (ii) the predicate of an RDF triple should use a common and referable vocabulary to facilitate machine interpretation; (iii) the object of an RDF triple should possibly be resources of type URI rather than universal literals. Linked Open Data (LOD) is to publish linked data as open data, which is the most ideal form of data for Semantic Web technology [6, 7], Linked Open Data Cloud (LOD Cloud) has collected thousands of data endpoints, spanning government, geography, media publishing, life sciences, social networks, etc. Among them, DBpedia, the most commonly used, transposes Wikipedia content into linked data providing users with SPARQL queries and using the necessary resources for free [2].

3 Research Design

The core topic of this study is to organize and deal with the intertwined relationship of "folk beliefs", that is, to support logical operations and even reasoning. Therefore, we have introduced a number of technologies from the Semantic Web series. We initially used Taiwan's Taoism and its related deities as the experimental scope to test the effectiveness of the research design. The design structure of this study is shown in Fig. 1. It is mainly divided into three blocks, including: (1) making linked data, (2) building knowledge models, and (3) developing chatbots. The first two blocks will eventually be combined into a knowledge base to provide external system links (refer to the middle part of Fig. 1). The third block is the development of chatbots, which provide users with more intelligent queries by linking to the knowledge base (refer to the arrow line in the lower half of Fig. 1). The detailed design is described in the following sections.

3.1 Making Linked Data

Traditional machine-readable data is mainly used for limited or closed data processing. W3C recommends upgrading existing data as a resource to meet the data quality requirements of the new generation. Because many datasets have existed for a long time, they are usually obtained through data transformation. This research is divided into the following three processes:

• Collect and analyze data. Folk beliefs often contain some partial, circulated or fragmented information. Due to limited research time and expertise, we do not conduct factual research on the content of the materials. Therefore, we only collect government open data and other open resources. Table 1 is part of the data set obtained from the official data open platform. We have counted the number of records, screened important fields, and noted the download location of the data set. The original data format is xml and csv. After analyzing the content of the data, many important information and knowledge associations are found, such as temples and gods, sects, and related notes on celebrations. These interrelationships can provide materials for building models.

In the following sections, we select "Temple" and "Festival" and other data sets for experimental description.

Table 1. Open data sets related to folk beliefs

Data set name	Main items and download locations
Temple list	Temple name, main deity, administrative area, address, sect, organizational type, coordinates… (available at https://data.gov.tw/dataset/8203)
Church list	Church name, administrative area, address, organizational type, (available at https://data.gov.tw/dataset/8204)
Temple festival	Festival title, religious group, sect, festival type,. (available at https://data.gov.tw/dataset/8209)
Church status	Registered foundation, registration status, quantity,. (available at https://data.gov.tw/dataset/13949)
Temple Organization	Organizational type, number of temples, foundation name,. (available at https://data.gov.tw/dataset/13954)

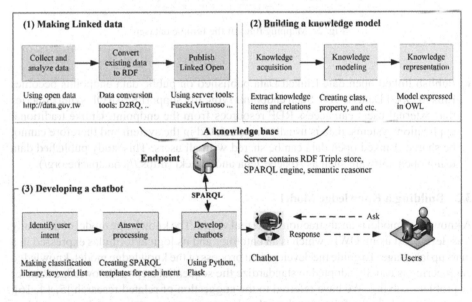

Fig. 1. The architecture of research design

Convert existing data to RDF resources. Data conversion usually changes the original data into the target format by defining mapping rules. RDF data conversion is how to express it as a "resource". Therefore, the focus is on converting the content into the data model of RDF. This research has used OpenRefine and D2RQ conversion tools respectively, and has experienced the advantages and disadvantages of different ways of making mapping rules. When the data source is stored in the associated database, it is more direct and convenient to use the revised D2RQ. Figure 2 is a mapping example of the temple data set, which has modified the initial mapping rules from D2RQ. The annotations in the figure include the establishment of identifiable subjects, revision of interpretable predicates, and changing link data to object.

Fig. 2. Mapping rules of the temple dataset

- Publish linked open data Linked Data published on public data endpoints becomes Linked Open Data (LOD). Such endpoints typically support SPARQL syntax queries that external users can access RDF resources from the endpoint. Unlike traditional application systems, data is usually encapsulated in the system and therefore cannot be shared. Linked open data can be shared with all users. This study published data using open software such as Apache Jena and Fuseki (https://jena.apache.org/).

3.2 Building a Knowledge Model

A knowledge model is an abstraction of the real world. The knowledge model of this study was developed using OWL, which is an ontology and its logical formulas expressed in a markup language. To guide the development process of the knowledge model, knowledge engineering is usually adopted to standardize the sequential steps of knowledge transfer or problem solving. We have referred to the suggestion of related research [5, 14, 16], which will include the following three development processes: knowledge acquisition, knowledge modeling and knowledge representation, as described below.

Knowledge Acquisition. According to a research survey, about 49.3% of the people in Taiwan believe in traditional folk religions, followed by 14% for Buddhism, 12.4% for Taoism, and only 13.2% for those who have no religious beliefs, leaving about 10% of the people Believe in Christianity, Islam, or other religions. On the other hand, there is a kind of worship of ancestors in Chinese society. In traditional Confucianism, the family is an important social system, so ancestor belief has special significance. Three major categories of folk beliefs including organized religion, folk religion, and ancestors or saints will be regarded as basic knowledge elements. These categories and members will be used as the content of ontology construction. Taoism is the native religion of Chinese culture. After a long period of evolution, Taoism and folk beliefs have gradually become connected and developed into polytheism. More than a thousand deities or saints have derived various temples. These deities or saints will be incorporated into the classes and hierarchies of the ontology.

Knowledge Modeling. In the preceding knowledge acquisition, knowledge elements are collected as sources for constructing ontology. This study uses Protégé for knowledge model development. The tool can edit ontology models and allows various types of plugins to extend functionality, such as visualization graphs and inference engines. Ontology uses terms such as concepts, attributes, and instances in theory, while it is called classes, attributes, and individuals in Protégé [17]. Figure 3 is a class structure diagram edited by Protégé, which contains three subviews: Class hierarchy on the left, Annotations on the upper right corner, and Description on the lower right corner. The ontology modeling process is as follows:

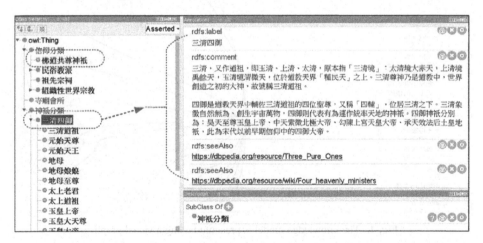

Fig. 3. Editing a knowledge model with Protégé

Class Hierarchy View. Create classes and hierarchies based on the previously obtained knowledge elements. The first layer includes belief classification, deity classification, temples, etc. The belief classification and deity classification expand down to a total of three layers. Temples are reserved to connect the facts. Classes are divided into two types: primitive class is represented by a solid circle same as most classes in the current figure. Defined class is represented by a solid circle with a congruent symbol (≡), which class is used for inferring implicit knowledge.

Annotations View. Add various descriptions to a class. For example, add three annotations to the dotted ellipse mark on the left side of Fig. 3, including: (1) use the predicate *rdfs:label* to annotate the common name; (2) use the predicate *rdfs:comment* to annotate the historical background of the deity;(3) use the predicate *rdfs:seeAlso* to annotate two linkable resources.

Description View. The formal definition of a class uses this view to edit logic axioms. According to the type of primitive class or defined class, use "necessary condition" or "necessary & sufficient condition" respectively.

3.3 Knowledge Representation

Knowledge models usually need to be tested and revised repeatedly. Using a visual knowledge map can simplify the verification of knowledge models [9]. Protégé can plug-in graph tools, such as OntoGraf, OWLViz, VOWL, etc. Figure 4 is a partial screenshot of using OntoGraf to present the category structure and containment relationship.

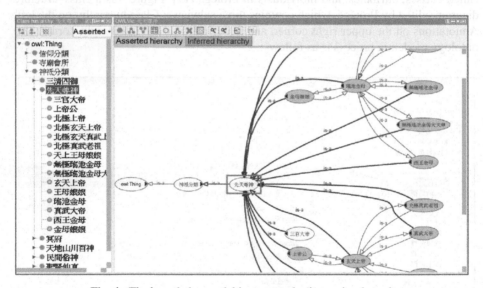

Fig. 4. The knowledge model is presented using a visual graph

The factual knowledge edited by RDF and the knowledge model edited by OWL are combined into a knowledge base. Since this knowledge base conforms to the Semantic Web architecture, it supports logical operations and reasoning. The completed knowledge base is configured on the Jena Fuseki server in Turtle format. Because the server is a web endpoint, everyone can retrieve the information. Figure 5 shows that the content of the knowledge base is presented in Turtle format but the syntax still follows the OWL specification.

```
696
697  ###  http://example.org/Religion#三清四御
698  ex:三清四御 rdf:type owl:Class ;
699        rdfs:subClassOf ex:ForkDeities .
700
701  ###  http://example.org/Religion#三清祖師
702  ex:三清祖師 rdf:type owl:Class ;
703        rdfs:subClassOf ex:道教 ;
704        rdfs:label "三清祖師" .
705
706  ###  http://example.org/Religion#三清道祖
707  ex:三清道祖 rdf:type owl:Class ;
708        owl:equivalentClass ex:元始天尊 ,
709                            ex:道德天尊 ;
710        rdfs:subClassOf ex:三清四御 ,
711                        ex:道教 ;
712        rdfs:comment "三清，又作道祖，即玉清、上清、太清，原本指「三清境」：太清境大赤
```

Fig. 5. The knowledge base is expressed in Turtle format based on OWL syntax

4 Develop Chatbot Applications

To response to users' questions about folk beliefs, this research develops a chatbot as a front-end application. By simulating human dialogue to judge intent and then activate the knowledge base to reply. The chatbot consists of two designs: (i) Identify user intent. By analyzing the question entered by the user, estimate the type of question and analyze the similar intent; (ii) Answer processing. According to the identified intent, design the corresponding SPARQL query template. This SPARQL will communicate with the knowledge base on the endpoint. Detailed design instructions are as follows:

4.1 Identify User Intent

In order to identify the intent of the input sentence, Fig. 6 is the design of the relevant process. First of all, "Chinese word segmentation" uses the Jieba package as a word segmenter. The input sentence is disassembled and segmented, and then the part of speech of the vocabulary is marked according to a pre-established keyword list; secondly, "similarity analysis" continues to represent words as vectors. Count the number of occurrences of each word and compare the similarity with the "problem classification model library of problems". Finally, this mechanism will determine the intent of the user's question.

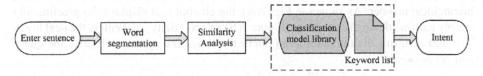

Fig. 6. Process design for identifying User's intent

4.2 Answer Processing

This mechanism will use SPARQL instructions to retrieve RDF endpoints according to the user's intentions. In order to increase flexibility and retrieval efficiency, 19 question intentions have been defined in the pre-work. According to the intentions, the corresponding SPARQL query templates are designed one by one and wrapped in In the program. Table 2 is two examples of SPARQL query templates, which correspond to different intents. The parameters in the examples have been underlined and bolded. For example, "{temple}" in the left column must be replaced with a temple name, and "{deity}" must be replaced with a deity name. Both names are obtained by disassembling the sentences entered by the user.

Table 2. Example of a SPARQL query template

Query the name of the deity of a temple?	Query which religious group a specific deity belongs to?

Prefix ex: <http://example.org/Religion#>
 Prefix dc: <http://purl.org/dc/elements/1.1/>
 Prefix rdfs: <http://www.w3.org/2000/01/rdf-schema#>
 Prefix vcard: <http://www.w3.org/2006/vcard/ns#>
   Select distinct ?ans
   WHERE {
    ?s vcard:organization-name ?name;
     dc:subject ?g.
    ?g rdfs:label ?ans.
    filter (contains(str(?name), '*{temple}*'))
 }
	Prefix ex: <http://example.org/Religion#>
	 Prefix org: <http://www.w3.org/ns/org#>
	 Prefix rdfs: <http://www.w3.org/2000/01/rdf-schema#>
	   Select distinct ?ans
	   Where {
	    ex:**{deity}** rdfs:subClassOf ?o.
	    ?o org:classification ?p;
	     rdfs:label ?ans.
	    filter (contains(str(?p), 'religious group'))
	 }

4.3 Question Answering Experiment of Chatbots

This study uses Python and Flask kits to develop a chatbot using a knowledge base. We design two types of operation interfaces, including hierarchical guidance and natural language questioning. The following shows how the chatbot operate:

Hierarchical Guidance Questioning. This design is to assist users who are inexperienced or do not know what to ask. The system guides and confirms questions in a hierarchical manner. As shown in Fig. 7(A), the chatbot first displays the greeting and simply narrows down the questions. Figure 7(B) selects "deity" and enters the next layer. The user confirms the intention in an interactive way. The system will drive the query and get answers.

Natural Language Questioning. This design allows users to input text questions, and the system judges the user's intention through disassembly, segmentation and analysis. The system will send the appropriate SPARQL query to the knowledge base, and the retrieval results will be sent back to the user. Figure 8(A) demonstrates a question of "What is another name for emperor Guan-Sheng-di?". The retrieval results are shown below the question. Figure 8(B) demonstrates another question of "Is Guan-Sheng-di the same as Guan-Sheng-di-Jun?". The retrieval results are shown below the question.

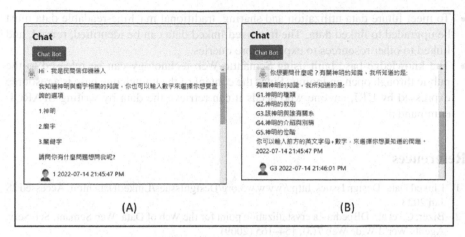

Fig. 7. Hierarchy-guidance questioning design

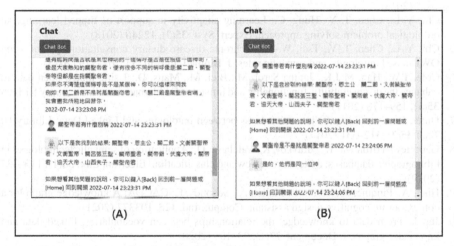

Fig. 8. Nature language questioning design

5 Conclusion

In this era of "Data is king", the open data of the public sector has its own value. Proper use of this data will demonstrate its benefits. This study introduces Semantic Web technology to construct the knowledge base application of "folk beliefs". We particularly emphasize the application in knowledge modeling and reasoning. Here are three ideas to share:

- The knowledge model edited by OWL provides logical operations. This model describes how knowledge is composed with an ontology-based hierarchical structure. The logical formula of the model is used to define the knowledge content and the relationship between elements. Therefore, the model can use the reasoning engine to perform knowledge inference.

- To meet future data utilization and sharing, traditional machine-readable data must be upgraded to linked data. The improved linked data can be identified, reused, and linked to other resources to expand more queries.
- The knowledge base built using Semantic Web technology can be released to the public through open endpoints. Since the content of the knowledge base is a resource expressed by URI, anyone who needs it can retrieve the data by writing SPARQL commands.

References

1. Linked Data- Design Issues. http://www.w3.org/DesignIssues/LinkedData.html. Accessed 28 Jan 2023
2. Bizer, C., et al.: DBpedia - a crystallization point for the Web of Data. Web Semant. Sci. Serv. Agents World Wide Web 7(3), 154–165 (2009)
3. Buil-Aranda, C., Arenas, M., Corcho, O., Polleres, A.: Federating queries in SPARQL 1.1: syntax, semantics and evaluation. Web Semant. Sci. Serv. Agents World Wide Web 18(1), 1–17 (2013)
4. Chi, Y.-L., Chen, T.-Y., Hung, C.: Learning adaptivity in support of flipped learning: an ontological problem-solving approach. Expert. Syst. 35(3), 12246 (2018)
5. Chi, Y.-L., Chen, T.-Y., Tsai, W.-T.: A chronic disease dietary consultation system using OWL-based ontologies and semantic rules. J. Biomed. Inform. 53, 208–219 (2015)
6. Cole, T.W., Han, M-J.K., Janina Sarol, M., Biel, M., Maus, D.: Using linked open data to enhance the discoverability, functionality and impact of Emblematica Online. Library Hi Tech 35(1), 159–178 (2017)
7. Dutta, B.: Examining the interrelatedness between ontologies and Linked Data. Library Hi Tech 35(2), 312–331 (2017)
8. Georgieva-Trifonova, T., Zdravkov, K., Valcheva, D.: Application of semantic technologies in bibliographic databases: a literature review and classification. Electron. Libr. 38(1), 113–137 (2019)
9. Huet, A., Pinquié, R., Véron, P., Mallet, A., Segonds, F.: CACDA: A knowledge graph for a context-aware cognitive design assistant. Comput. Ind. 125, 103377 (2021)
10. Jia, J.: From data to knowledge: the relationships between vocabularies, linked data and knowledge graphs. J. Document. 77(1), 93–105 (2020)
11. Karagiannis, D., Buchmann, R.A.: Linked Open Models: extending Linked Open Data with conceptual model information. Inf. Syst. 56, 174–197 (2016)
12. Khan, S.A., Bhatti, R.: Semantic Web and ontology-based applications for digital libraries: an investigation from LIS professionals in Pakistan. Electron. Libr. 36(5), 826–841 (2018)
13. Loizou, A., Angles, R., Groth, P.: On the formulation of performant SPARQL queries. Web Semant. Sci. Serv. Agents World Wide Web 31, 1–26 (2015)
14. Ontology Development 101: A Guide to Creating Your First Ontology. https://protege.stanford.edu/publications/ontology_development/ontology101.pdf. Accessed 28 Jan 2023
15. Sung, H.-Y., Chi, Y.-L.: A knowledge-based system to find over-the-counter medicines for self-medication. J. Biomed. Inform. 108, 103504 (2020)
16. Sung, H.-Y., Chi, Y.-L.: Applications of Semantic Web in integrating open data and bibliographic records: a development example of an infomediary of Taiwanese indigenous people. Electron. Libr. 39(2), 337–353 (2021)
17. A Practical Guide to Building OWL Ontologies Using Protégé 5.5 and Plug-ins. https://www.researchgate.net/publication/351037551_A_Practical_Guide_to_Building_OWL_Ontologies_Using_Protege_55_and_Plugins. Accessed 28 Jan 2023

Perceptions and Expectations of Women-In-Tech (WIT) Application: Insights from Older Women in Rural Areas

Chun Yong Chong[1]([✉]) [iD], Pei-Lee Teh[2] [iD], Shinyi Wu[3] [iD],
and Ewilly Jie Ying Liew[2] [iD]

[1] School of Information Technology, Monash University Malaysia, Bandar Sunway,
Selangor Darul Ehsan, Malaysia
chong.chunyong@monash.edu
[2] School of Business, Gerontechnology Laboratory, Monash University Malaysia, Bandar
Sunway, Selangor Darul Ehsan, Malaysia
{teh.pei.lee,ewilly.liew}@monash.edu
[3] Daniel J. Epstein Department of Industrial and Systems Engineering, Viterbi School of
Engineering, University of Southern California, Los Angeles, CA, USA
shinyiwu@usc.edu

Abstract. Digital learning platforms are notably an important tool for education and socialization. The ability to learn independently as one advances in age becomes critical for most rural communities. The Covid-19 Pandemic worsens the issues of economic inequality throughout the world, particularly for women. Options are few for older women who are eager to adapt and learn but are less technologically engaged. An iterative co-design approach was used to improve the design of the Women-in-tech (WIT) app embedded with Chatbot. The purpose of the WIT app is to help upskill older women through technology intervention, that is, capturing their upskilling need and providing relevant contents to them through the Internet. However, there are limited existing studies that provide relevant guidelines or good practices to aid in designing the Chatbot for technology upskilling among older women. Hence, a qualitative approach with in-depth interviews was undertaken with 15 rural women participants to help improve our learning platform of WIT in the area of design and functionality. WIT app could fill the gap in facilitating older women's transition planning and upskilling over time. The study can potentially be applied to future work that attempts to address similar problems in the same domain.

Keywords: Learning · Older adults · Rural areas · Women-in-tech

1 Introduction

The COVID-19 pandemic has caught the world by surprise and brought significant impacts to the labor market. A sharp rise in unemployment rate is one of the most prominent impacts when countries all around the world shut down their borders and

P.-L. P. Rau (Ed.): HCII 2023, LNCS 14022, pp. 183–200, 2023.
https://doi.org/10.1007/978-3-031-35936-1_14

impose movement restrictions [1]. In April 2020, the unemployment rate in the US is recorded at 14.9% and most importantly, the vulnerable groups (e.g., low/unskilled workers, elderly workers, etc.) are the most affected by the pandemic [2]. The same can be observed in Asia countries, which make up of mostly developing countries [3]. Existing studies [1, 4, 5] have found that the negative effects of COVID-19 differ due to different factors such as age groups, gender, employment type, education level, etc. The issues of inequalities in the global economy, especially on women, are further exacerbated by the pandemic [6, 7]. The work by Lokot and Bhatia [7] found that for women over the age of 55, there is very little job security during the pandemic because employers in most countries do not treat them as a viable option when it comes to employment opportunities.

Young people can delve into gig work but the same cannot be applied to older adults, particularly older women in rural areas. The wellbeing and employment of older women in developing countries are the key agenda of UN. As such, there is an urgent need to relook into strategies and effort which attempts to provide support to those who are negatively impacted by the COVID-19 pandemic and help them to realign their skillsets to join back the workforce. The issues of older women getting discriminated during the economic slowdown and pandemic is something well researched and documented in the past [8]. Especially in developing countries, women are often sidelined due to bias and perceived role in families and thus, limited support at the policy-level has captured their need in employability.

To help uplift their personal and technical skills, technology can play a very important role. Developing countries such as Malaysia and Thailand have witnessed rapid proliferation of affordable smartphones, social media usage, and rising user awareness to catch up with a fast-paced tech-savvy lifestyle [9]. For adults above 50 years old, technology advancement promotes their aging in place [10] to live independently within the community for as long as possible. The growing complexity confronting the ageing population, however, emerges from the tension between technology explosion, information overload, and socioeconomic restructuring towards a technology-centric society.

The World Economic Forum called for an urgent need to address this complex demographic shift particularly on older women's education and health as they tend to live longer, poorer, and alone in the society. In Malaysia, numerous older women are illiterate, financially insecure, and less digital savvy than average. The urgency is amplified by the COVID-19 pandemic, which has significantly affected older women given their fear and vulnerability to higher risk of infection, loss of employment, and loss of social support. With the lockdown conditions and closure of workplaces, alternatives should be provided for the less digitally connected older women who are willing to adapt and learn.

This study aims to use technology to establish new knowledge for creating user value, especially in the context of women-in-tech application for older women in the rural areas in the developing countries such as Malaysia. "Women-In-Tech" in our context is defined as using technology as an intervention to help uplift older women's skills. More concretely, using online resources such as e-book, video tutorials, and online reading materials to impart the relevant skills (such as cooking, presentation, marketing, etc.) to older women.

However, in order to provide targeted and focused contents to the audience, one of the most important steps is to understand their needs and requirements. One way to reach a huge number older women is through online Chatbot [11] that can capture their demographics and also their needs with minimal human intervention. Furthermore, due to the COVID19 pandemic, it becomes less likely to conduct face-to-face interview due to social distancing requirements and also to protect the wellbeing of these vulnerable groups. As such, with technology intervention such as Chatbot, it becomes possible to capture the requirements of older women remotely, without the need to conduct face-to-face meetings. However, we acknowledge that older adults who are not tech savvy might find it challenging to adopt to answering questions through Chatbots and other means of technologies. Hence, the design of Chatbot is one of the critical elements to ensure the success of the upskilling effort as older women are typically less tech-savvy and might find it challenging to maneuver the Chatbot application.

However, common best practices in developing Chatbot applications for older adults and women are still in their infancy, largely due to unclear users' requirements [12]. In this paper, we aim to explore the perceptions and expectations of older women in Malaysia regarding the use of Women-in-Tech app which embeds Chatbot to capture their upskilling needs through a qualitative study. Information and data gathered would then be used to propose a system design of Women-in-tech (WIT) solution that helps empower them to improve their employability through technology upskilling. The aims of this paper are two-fold. First, to design and develop a novel concept of a Women-in-Tech app for older women. Second, to investigate the perception and expectations of older women to understand the required customizations of Women-in-Tech app for user applications. Older women living in the urban areas are believed to respond and adopt new mobile applications differently from older women in rural areas. In this study, we frame our study to examine the perceptions and expectation of WIT application within the older women from the rural areas.

2   Background

2.1   Design Requirement for Women-In-Tech Chatbot

Maintaining a reasonable amount of activity rates and employment among older workers will not only help ensure a healthy lifestyle, but can also improve their position in the labor market [13]. With the COVID19 pandemic, older workers who are less competitive in the labor market tends to be at the receiving end which is a major concern among developing countries due to a looming pensions crisis involving an increasing proportion of the population who are pensioners needing the government's help to avoid poverty [14]. As such, the usage of technologies to provision the education and training needs among older adults becomes more and more popular among policy makers [15].

The women-in-tech (WIT) application is designed to provide an AI-powered learning and recommendation service that integrates three components namely, chatbot, recommender and forum. The first component, chatbot is an automated dialogue agent that helps in the information collection of older women's needs and practice toward technology. The second element is a recommender that is tasked to provide the selection of online learning options available for older women. Based on user's input, the recommender will propose related skill training module to the users. Finally, forums enable users to facilitate peer support in the online learning.

2.2 Chatbot Design

Target Users. In our context of Women-In-Tech, the target users are older women who are more than 50 years old intending to upskill themselves through the use of technologies. We assume that most of the users are less tech savvy due to their age profile, and also have very limited experience navigating for resources on the Web (i.e., Facebook, YouTube, etc.). Apart from that, we also assume that some of the users might have eyesight problems which motivate us to design the app with high contrast color with bigger font size to help with readability.

Purpose of the Chatbot. As mentioned in the earlier chapter, the goal of the Women-In-Tech project is to use smartphones as a medium to capture the upskilling requirements from older women. The usage of Chatbot is also meant to help minimize physical contact between the interviewer and interviewee during the COVID19 pandemic.

Through the Chatbot, we will capture demographic information about the participants, as well as their upskilling needs. This will allow us to provide follow-up materials and contents that are relevant to their needs (for example, providing tutorial videos related to cooking, baking, marketing skills, etc.).

2.3 Older Women's Technology Usage Constraints and Limitations

In order to come out with a Chatbot design that is generally accepted by older women, we first need to identify what are the challenges and pitfalls when it comes to technology usage among the target users. However, it is hard to generalize the usage constraints and limitations because the population in Malaysia is unique due to its diverse culture background [16]. The cultural experiences of Malaysian older women may shape their different expectations and challenges for using technology than older women in other countries. As such, we try to look for literature that pinpoint these kinds of constraints among the Malaysia older adults or women.

The work by Wong et al. [17] discussed the challenges of older adults in Malaysia when operating smartphones. The authors conducted a series of interview, observation, and questionnaire among 80 Malaysian older adults through a mixed-method approach. Some of the constraints and limitation faced by older adults as reported in the paper can be summarized as follow:

1. Non-intuitive icon design – visual cue is one of the most direct and dependent mode used by older adults when navigating smartphones. Hence, if the icon design is not intuitive and do not represent the purpose of the operation, older adults might find it challenging and difficult to navigate. For instance, in the work by Wong et al. [17] the authors found that 86% of the users find it hard to locate "missed call" because there are no visual cues that can help them locate the "missed call"

2. Complex operation – when being tasked to save a new contact to the smartphone, more than 30% of the participants find it hard because there are a lot of steps involved to save a new contact. As such, when designing apps for these group of users, developers are advised to ensure that users will need to perform the least number of steps to achieve the goal.
3. Usage of external app – when being tasked to install an app on Google Play store, more than 30% of the participants couldn't finish the task because it is hard for them to locate the target app, and the complicated process involved to install and use them. As such, this issue help motivate us to move away from standalone app when designing the Chatbot.
4. Reliant on family members – most of the older adults mentioned that they rely on their children when it comes to complicated tasks. As such, low learning curve and intuitive design becomes a crucial design element to encourage the usage among the older adults.

With all these constraints captured, we propose the design of our Chatbot in the next section.

3   Research Methodology

3.1   Initial Conceptualization

As discussed in Sect. 2.3, the usage of external app will further complicate the entire process. This is because if we were to launch a separate app on Google Play Store or Apple Store, the older adults will need to 1.) search for the apps on the relevant app marketplace, 2.) install the app and provide the credentials, 3.) register and use the app.

These extra steps will cause unnecessary issues and challenges for the older adults. As such, we have decided to develop a HTML-based website that works on both desktops and mobile phones, allowing the older women to access the Chatbot regardless of the platform that they choose to use. Figure 1 shows the front-page view of the Chatbot, where the left-hand side show the Desktop view while the right-hand side shows the view of the Chatbot when navigated on iPhone XR with 375 × 667 resolutions.

Understanding that visual impairment is also one of the main challenges faced by older women, we try to choose high contrast color (light blue and white background) to design the Chatbot. Apart from that, we have chosen font size 14–16px that are big enough when displayed on mobile view.

Figure 2 shows the landing page after the user login to the portal. They are greeted by three selection panels, namely the Chatbot, Recommender, and Forum. The Recommender page is meant to display videos and resources relevant to the users after they have completed the initial screening on Chatbot. The Forum page on the other hand, is meant for the older women to socialize and share ideas about the skills that they are planning to learn (or is learning at the moment) with other users. As the focus of this paper is on the design of the Chatbot, we will only focus on the first functionality.

Figure 3 shows an example of a screenshot to capture the participant's age, where the users can enter their age using on-screen keyboard. If the users fall outside the range of the target audience (less than 55 years old), they will be redirected to end the survey.

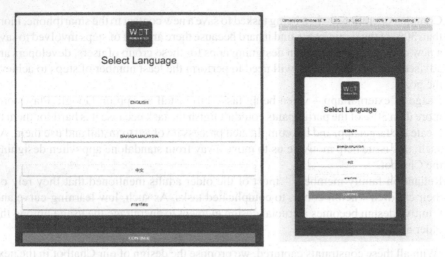

Fig. 1. Chatbot front page UI. Desktop view (left) and mobile view (right)

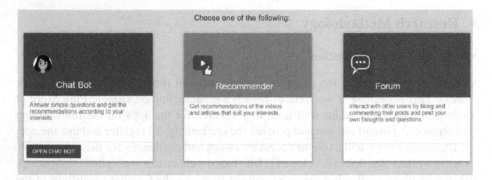

Fig. 2. Landing page of the Chatbot

In order to help improve the accessibility of the users when navigating the Chatbot, we also design to Chatbot to accept touch-based inputs, such as the ones shown in Fig. 4. The left-hand side of Fig. 4 shows selection based on two options, while the right-hand side shows selection based on 6 options. Users can touch the screen to choose their answers which helps minimize the complexity of the Chatbot.

3.2 Iterative Co-design Approach

Osborne et al. [18] proposed the co-design approach as "the voluntary or involuntary involvement of public service users in any of the design, management, delivery and/or evaluation of public services". Different from traditional software design, the idea of co-design is to engage the end users in the forming of ideas and solutions to solve a particular niche problem. Various work has shown success in the use of co-design in addressing technology challenges among the older population, due to its unique trait in

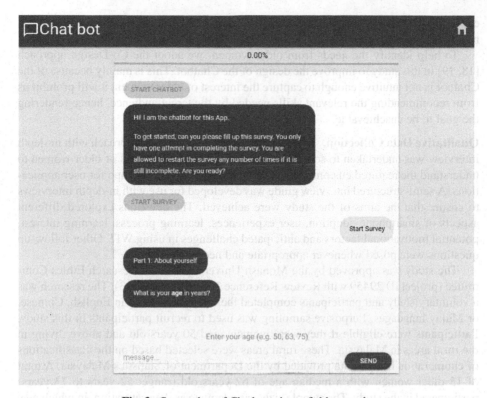

Fig. 3. Screenshot of Chatbot – input field example

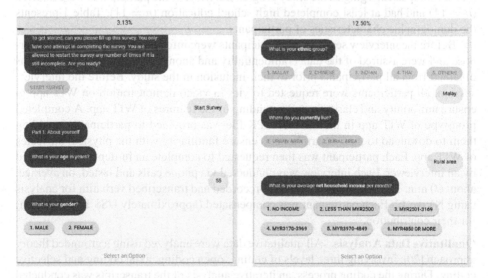

Fig. 4. Screenshot of Chatbot – touch-based selection to improve accessibility

capturing the essential needs of some targeted end users, ensuring all the functional and non-functional requirements can be fulfilled as much as possible [18].

To help identify the needs from older women, we adopt the Co-Design approach [18, 19] in this study to improve the design of the Chatbot. This is mainly because of the Chatbot is not intuitive enough to capture the interest of older women, it will prohibit us from recommending the relevant skills needed by the target audience, hence rendering the goal to be unachievable.

Qualitative Data Collection. In the current study, a qualitative approach with in-depth interview was undertaken to solicit the perception and expectations of older women to understand the required customizations of Women-in-Tech (WIT) app for user applications. A semi-structured interview guide was developed for use with in-depth interviews to ensure that the aims of the study were achieved. The questions explored different aspects of smartphone adoption, user experiences, learning process, learning interest, potential motivational factors and anticipated challenges in using WIT. Other follow-up questions were posed whenever appropriate and necessary.

The study was approved by the Monash University Human Research Ethics Committee (project ID 29459 with Review Reference 2021-29459-65513). The research was a voluntary study and participants completed the interviews either in English, Chinese, or Malay languages. Purposive sampling was used to recruit participants in this study. Participants were eligible if they were women aged 50 years old and above, living in the rural areas in Malaysia. These rural areas were selected based on the classifications of enumeration blocks data provided by the Department of Statistics Malaysia. A total of 15 older women with a median age of 62 years old (range: 52 years to 73 years) participated in the study. The sample size was adequate as data saturation, in which new themes stopped emerging as the study progressed. Most of the participants were married ($n = 14$) and had at least completed high school education ($n = 11$). Table 1 presents the demographic characteristics of participants.

Before the interview sessions, all participants were informed about the research purpose and were assured of the data confidentiality and anonymity. Informed consent was obtained from all participants prior to their inclusion in the study. Before the interview session, all participants were requested to view a video demonstration on WIT app to ensure uniformity and clarity in understanding of the features of WIT app. A completed prototype of WIT app in the form of APK file was provided to participants, enabling them to download to their smartphone to ensure familiarity with the physical attributes of WIT app. Each participant was then requested to complete an in-depth interview led by an interviewer. Each interview was conducted via phone calls and lasted, on average, about 60 min. The interviews were audio-recorded and transcribed verbatim for analysis using NVivo 12. Each participant was compensated (approximately US\$ 11 per person) for their contribution.

Qualitative Data Analysis. All qualitative data were analyzed using a grounded theory approach [20], involving three levels of coding: open coding, axial coding and selective coding. During the coding process, an iterative analysis of the transcripts was conducted and cross-checked by the research team until consensus on themes was achieved. In the following section, we discuss the aggregate results of the qualitative analysis for brevity. The codes are broadly summarized into four main categories: (1) Experience

Table 1. Participant demographic characteristics

Variables	Example	Frequency (n = 15)	Percentage (100%)
Median age, years	62 (range 52–73)		
Marital status	Married	14	93.3%
	Single	1	6.7%
Education	Primary School	4	26.6%
	Secondary/High School	9	60.0%
	Vocational/Technical Certification	1	6.7%
	University	1	6.7%
Ethnic Group	Malay	2	13.3%
	Chinese	9	60.0%
	Other Native (i.e., Bumiputera)	4	26.7%
Areas	Perak	2	13.3%
	Johor	8	53.3%
	Sarawak	5	33.3%
Living Status	Living with Someone at Home	14	93.3%
	Living Alone at Home	1	6.7%
Employment status	Working	5	33.3%
	Retired	5	33.3%
	Semi-retired	2	13.3%
	Not working	2	13.3%
	Not working but doing voluntary work	1	6.7%

and familiarity with smartphone and mobile app; (2) Purpose for learning and using mobile app; (3) Experience with the WIT user interface; and (4) Recommendations for improvement in WIT design.

1) Experience and familiarity with smartphone and mobile app

To explore older women's smartphone adoption and acceptance, participants were asked about their individual experiences in using smartphones and mobile applications. All participants owned a smartphone and had internet access, either home-based WIFI or mobile data plan. Although the participants were living in the rural areas, they used several applications related to online messenger (WhatsApp, Facetime), social networking services (Facebook), online game (Candy Crush), online video sharing services (Instagram), online banking (RHB online banking), online shopping (Lazada, Shopee), e-wallet app (Touch and Go, TnG), online meeting app (Zoom and Google Meet), contact tracing app (MySejahtera) and navigation map app (Google Maps). All the participants expressed that they know how to use the basic features of mobile applications. Notably, one participant who buys online spoke about how she overcomes the online payment issue with the use of cash on delivery payment method. These findings provide a good understanding of older women's smartphone usage and familiarity with specified mobile apps such as WhatsApp, YouTube and Zoom, thereby providing some key insights into the customization of WIT interface design. Sample quotes from participants on the mobile applications include:

> Sometimes we use video calls to chat on **WhatsApp**. Now, with video calls we can see the opposite party clearly. (T009, 52, Chinese)

> I only use facetime…When you shop for groceries, then something that the children wants to see, … you are not sure what is it, so I will use the **Facetime**. (T007, 66, Chinese)

> Oh, I occasionally look at their photos [on **Facebook**], sometimes if I am familiar with that person. There are some people who are very good at reporting the news and I would watch. (T010, 65, Chinese)

> I'm playing **Candy Crush**. (T007, 66, Chinese)

> I use **Instagram**, … to know some news because my interest are in politics and religion. (T005, 58, Chinese)

> For example, recently I felt that going to the bank to put cash is very troublesome, so I asked my children to teach me how to go **online to put cash** without going to the bank in person. I don't like going to the bank. (T005, 58, Chinese)

> I do shopping at **Lazada**, **Shopee** and **Shein**. (T012, 54, Bumiputra)

> I know how to **buy things online**, but I don't know how to pay for them…So when I go online, there is an option for payment to be made after they made the delivery and I can pay it myself (**cash on delivery**). (T011, 73, Chinese).

> When I go to 99 (Speed Mart) I use **TnG**. (T006, 73, Chinese)

> Especially haircut salons they usually have special promotions, and they **accept e-Wallet payments**. (T009, 52, Chinese)

> Many of my close friends around me are in their 60s. Actually, they can't, but because I attend a lot of online courses, so I use these two kinds, **Zoom** and **Google Meet**. I join groups of young people, so I have to learn how to use. (T005, 58, Chinese)

> I know how to use **MySejahtera**, I do every day whenever like I go to Tai Chi class every day and after that dance class. We need to use MySejahtera, we have to scan. (T011, 73, Chinese)

> Sometimes when I could not find the place, I will use the **Google Maps**. (T015, 54, Bumiputra)

Most of the participants are novice smartphone users who do not have the high procedural memory to navigate advanced features in their smartphone applications. Procedural memory is knowledge about how to perform activities such as following a recipe [21]. Majority of the participants expressed that they learn to use the features of the mobile applications with children's or friend's continual support.

My sons were the ones who taught. They would tell me where to press and all until it works. (T003, 65, Chinese)

When I'm not very sure then I will ask my children, my son, my friend. (T013, 57, Chinese)

(2) Purpose for learning and using mobile app

Analysis of the interview transcripts revealed that smartphones are an important tool for the participants to support their business operation. Some participants used WhatsApp to run their business, particularly when personal selling is not possible.

I used to sell at schools, but my husband has retired so most people don't know where we sell anymore. Then they would do posts, I would post [on Whatapps] my house location where I'd sell. (T014, 57, Bumiputra)

Some older people at normative post-retirement ages are often involved in various work and volunteer activities. The interview excerpts illustrate some older women have desire to relaunch their live with purpose, doing different activities such as volunteering in the church and starting new business that enable them to start a new part of their life. In doing so, they are motivated to learn how to use video call for meetings and how to start a food business after retirement. With this information, WIT could play an important role to facilitate older women's transition planning and upskilling over time.

In my church, I am responsible for teaching young people. So I have to use video call meetings. (T005, 58, Chinese)

Yes, all this while I'm working at the firm- this lawyer firm, so now I want to learn how to do my own business like this, cooking. (T013, 57, Chinese)

(3) Experience with the WIT user interface

Overall, the participants noted that the font size in WIT is readable except that an older woman with myopia visual impairment mentioned that she needed to enlarge the interface as the font size appeared to be small. The color contrast in WIT is acceptable. One participant proposed the use of icons to assist users who cannot read.

The wordings and all are very good, ... very clear. (T001, 70, Malay)

The font is quite small because I have glasses, my myopia is very serious, so sometimes I can't see so need to enlarge it so I can see. (T011, 73, Chinese)

The color is comfortable to the eyes. (T005, 58, Chinese).

Maybe like simple things that they can understand through the icons instead of reading. Because they cannot read. (T015, 54, Bumiputra)

The participants have divided opinions about the components of WIT. Some participants with higher levels of digital literacy felt that the content of WIT was rather basic. This feedback suggests that more advanced features should be made available for those who were interested in more learning contents. Other participants, however, felt that the level of information in WIT was suitable for them who live in the rural areas, and cautioned against information overload for those women aged above 60 years old.

*This app is suitable for those who are very new or they have no knowledge at all of using the apps. But for someone like me I feel like it is quite **basic**. (T017, 55, Bumiputra)*

*Maybe if it's in the city area, I would consider an expansion but this area is a little **rural**, so I think the current one (WIT) is **enough**. I am satisfied. (T014, 57, Bumiputra)*

*...that is good because that is the way how to communicate with let's say those people who are living in **rural areas**, to access those **resources**. (T012, 54, Bumiputra)*

*I think if it's those who are **older** than me, they **wouldn't be able to absorb** what you're talking about. There are so many things all at once, we wouldn't be able to absorb them. (T005, 58, Chinese)*

(4) Recommendations for improvement in WIT design

Additionally, participants were invited to provide recommendations on the user interface design of WIT. Some non-English speaking participants suggested WIT learning platform to include other languages such as Bahasa Malaysia to cater to users who did not have a good command of English. Some participants proposed it was important to create group- or partner learning features in WIT app to facilitate collaborative learning and discussion. Examples of group learning features include forum or breakout room. Some participants expressed the need to have onsite learning support and facilitator to provide guidance practice. The participants also emphasized the importance of allowing WIT users to learn for free. The participants acknowledged the presence of chatbot component in WIT app although some participants did not fully understand the role of chatbot. As such, it is important for the team to revisit the design of chatbot component in WIT for better clarity.

*When it comes to the English language, I do not really understand. But if it's in **Bahasa Malaysia**, I do understand a little bit. (T002, 70, Malay)*

*Like if it is a **group** of friends, it's nice to go together. Something we can **discuss together**. (T009, 52, Chinese)*

*If someone is teaching and they use their own phone and showing how to click, it wouldn't leave a deep impression. You **need to be there**, and assist them in pressing the buttons in their phone. (T005, 58, Chinese)*

If it's **free**, they will support it, and if it has a fee, maybe they'll consider it. (T005, 58, Chinese).

*Yeah, I saw that one. The **chatbot** survey. (T012, 54, Bumiputra)*

*You're going to introduce a new format, that is a **robot**. [referring to chatbot] (T009, 52, Chinese)*

*As you interact with the **robot**, it will provide a suitable **reaction**...(T010, 65, Chinese)*

4   Refined and Propose Design

The findings of qualitative research provide important insights into the continuous improvement in WIT design. The older women in rural areas made several suggestions for further development of the interface design and content of WIT app to better suit their needs.

Participants highlighted the importance for Women-In-Tech app to be made available in more languages, especially to cater for the major ethnicities in Malaysia. The need for support and help while using the app was essential, especially for those using the app without their children or family assistance. For ease of use and navigation, participants suggested meaningful icons to be used, as shown in Fig. 6.

Users tend to prefer more engaging ways of interacting with the app. As such, we implement two avatars – drawing avatar and human-like avatar, that can engage with the users verbally after each click on the chatbot, as shown in Figs. 9, 10 and 11. Participants suggested community-like engagement with their friends and family on the app to be updated on their learning progress and share helpful information, as shown in Fig. 7 and 8. The Women-In-Tech app will act as a main interface to facilitate digital socializing.

Below are the refined and proposed design:

1. Provision of multi-language options including English, Chinese, Malay and Thai (Fig. 5).
2. Build in magnifying glass feature, enabling users to enlarge words.
3. Use explicit and descriptive icons for links and buttons
4. Design interactive forum platform to enable instant messaging, audio and video calling and file sharing for collaborative learning.
5. Provision of both remote and onsite support for learning how to use WIT
6. Incorporate an expressive avatar with the chatbot feature to provide better clarification on the use of chatbot and generate interest to complete the chatbot survey.

Fig. 5. Screenshot of Chatbot – User multi-language selection

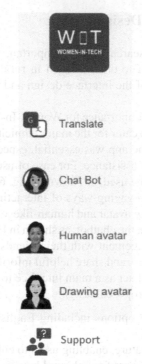

Translate

Chat Bot

Human avatar

Drawing avatar

Support

Fig. 6. Screenshot of Chatbot – onsite and remote support

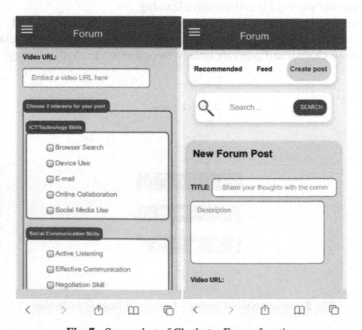

Fig. 7. Screenshot of Chatbot – Forum function

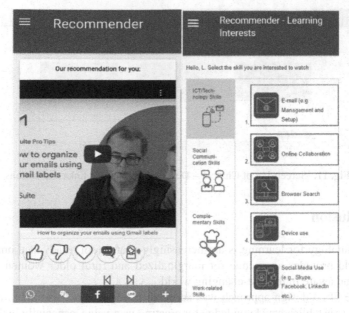

Fig. 8. Screenshot of Chatbot – Recommender Function

Fig. 9. Screenshot of Chatbot – Drawing Avatar

Fig. 10. Screenshot of Chatbot – Human Avatar

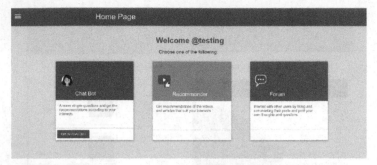

Fig. 11. Screenshot of Chatbot – Descriptive icons for links and buttons

5 Conclusion

Digital technology for learning is an increasingly useful tool to advance oneself. The digital world provides an avenue for marginalized and rural older women to remain informed and aware in the fast-changing world.

The use of co-design approach was adopted in this study. This study aims to use technology to establish new knowledge for creating user value, especially in the context of Women-In-Tech application for older women in the rural areas in the developing countries such as Malaysia.

In conclusion, this study identified the opportunities and expectations for older women adults in rural areas when engaging technology to establish new knowledge in Malaysia. Overall, participants were satisfied with their experience with the WIT app user interface as they had experience and were familiar using social media. Smartphones are generally used as a tool to run their business and be involved in various volunteering activities. WIT app could fill the gap in facilitating older women's transition planning and upskilling over time. Additional recommendation for improvement includes multi language options, advance learning contents feature, create group- or partner learning features in WIT app to facilitate collaborative learning and discussion and allow users to use it for free.

This study is not without limitations. First, the findings of this study were based on the gathered qualitative data. Due to the COVID19 pandemic, recruitment of participants was challenging especially when the older women are categorized as "vulnerable groups". Hence, the low number of participants can potentially affect the generalizability of our findings. Future research should explore the use of experimental design to run an intervention using WIT app, and survey questionnaire to assess the predictors of WIT adoption among the older women. Second, the present sample was collected with older women from rural areas in general. A promising future line of research would be to focus on the WIT adoption of older women who are working, volunteering or self-employed, as there are significant variations within the older women who engage in continuous learning and a range of purposeful activities through smartphone application.

Acknowledgment. This project is funded by the Monash University Malaysia-ASEAN Research Grant Scheme 2021 - 2023 (Grant Code: ASE000008). The authors express their gratitude to Ng

Li Shin, Elizabeth Lee Jia Huei, Eugene Yong You Jin, Joanna Renai Raja and Fionamae Raja for their assistance in data collection.

References

1. Kikuchi, S., Kitao, S., Mikoshiba, M.: Who suffers from the COVID-19 shocks? Labor market heterogeneity and welfare consequences in Japan. J. Japan. Int. Econ. **59**, 101117 (2021)
2. Kikuchi, S., Kitao, S., Mikoshiba, M.: Heterogeneous vulnerability to the covid-19 crisis and implications for inequality in Japan. Research Institute of Economy, Trade, and Industry (RIETI) (2020)
3. Yadav, A., Iqbal, B.A.: Socio-economic scenario of South Asia: an overview of impacts of COVID-19. South Asian Surv. **28**, 20–37 (2021)
4. Chaudhary, M., Sodani, P., Das, S.: Effect of COVID-19 on economy in India: Some reflections for policy and programme. J. Health Manag. **22**, 169–180 (2020)
5. Vegt, Ie., Kleinberg, B.: Women worry about family, men about the economy: gender differences in emotional responses to COVID-19. In: Aref, S., et al. (eds.) SocInfo 2020. LNCS, vol. 12467, pp. 397–409. Springer, Cham (2020). https://doi.org/10.1007/978-3-030-60975-7_29
6. Chatterjee, B., Caffarelli, L., Ranawana, A.: Grandmother, breadwinner, caregiver, widow, entrepreneur: COVID-19, older women, and challenges for the implementation of the women's economic empowerment agenda. Gend. Dev. **30**, 247–264 (2022)
7. Lokot, M., Bhatia, A.: Unequal and invisible: a feminist political economy approach to valuing women's care labor in the COVID-19 response. Front. Sociol. **5** (2020)
8. Ghosh, J.: Informalisation and women's workforce participation: A consideration of recent trends in Asia. Report on Gender Equality: Striving for Justice in an Unequal World, United Nations Research Institute for Social Development, Geneva (2004)
9. Poushter, J., Bishop, C., Chwe, H.: Social media use continues to rise in developing countries but plateaus across developed ones. Pew Res. Center **22**, 2–19 (2018)
10. Ball, M.M., et al.: Managing decline in assisted living: the key to aging in place. J. Gerontol. B Psychol. Sci. Soc. Sci. **59**, S202–S212 (2004)
11. Ryu, H., Kim, S., Kim, D., Han, S., Lee, K., Kang, Y.: Simple and steady interactions win the healthy mentality: designing a chatbot service for the elderly. Proc. ACM Hum. Comput. Interact. **4**, 1–25 (2020)
12. Fang, B., Chong, C.Y., Teh, P.-L., Lee, S.W.H.: Assessing the needs of mobility solution for older adults through living lab approach: an experience report. In: Rau, P.L.P. (eds.) Cross-Cultural Design. Applications in Business, Communication, Health, Well-being, and Inclusiveness. HCII 2022. LNCS, vol. 13313. Springer, Cham (2022). https://doi.org/10.1007/978-3-031-06050-2_24
13. Loretto, W.: Work and retirement in an ageing world: the case of older workers in the UK. Twenty-First Century Society **5**, 279–294 (2010)
14. Mayhew, K., Elliott, M., Rijkers, B.: Upskilling older workers. Ageing Horizons **8** (2008)
15. Findsen, B., Formosa, M. (eds.): Lifelong Learning in Later Life: A Handbook on Older Adult Learning. SensePublishers, Rotterdam (2011). https://doi.org/10.1007/978-94-6091-651-9
16. Poh, Z., et al.: What do users like about smart bottle? insights for designers. In: Rau, P.-L. (ed.) HCII 2019. LNCS, vol. 11577, pp. 325–336. Springer, Cham (2019). https://doi.org/10.1007/978-3-030-22580-3_24
17. Wong, C.Y., Ibrahim, R., Hamid, T.A., Mansor, E.I.: Usability and design issues of smartphone user interface and mobile apps for older adults. In: Abdullah, N., Wan Adnan, W.A., Foth, M. (eds.) i-USEr 2018. CCIS, vol. 886, pp. 93–104. Springer, Singapore (2018). https://doi.org/10.1007/978-981-13-1628-9_9

18. Osborne, S.P., Radnor, Z., Strokosch, K.: Co-production and the co-creation of value in public services: a suitable case for treatment? Public Manag. Rev. **18**, 639–653 (2016)
19. Sumner, J., Chong, L.S., Bundele, A., Wei Lim, Y.: Co-designing technology for aging in place: a systematic review. Gerontologist **61**, e395–e409 (2021)
20. Corbin, J.M., Strauss, A.: Grounded theory research: Procedures, canons, and evaluative criteria. Qual. Sociol. **13**, 3–21 (1990)
21. Fisk, D., Charness, N., Czaja, S.J., Rogers, W.A., Sharit, J.: Designing for Older Adults. CRC Press (2004)

"I Have Learned that Things are Different here": Understanding the Transitional Challenges with Technology Use After Relocating to the USA

Prakriti Dumaru[✉], Ankit Shrestha, Rizu Paudel, Arezou Behfar, Hanieh Atashpanjeh, and Mahdi Nasrullah Al-Ameen

Department of Computer Science, Utah State University, Logan, USA
{prakriti.dumaru,ankit.shrestha,rizu.paudel,abehfar,
hanieh.atashpanjeh,mahdi.al-ameen}@usu.edu

Abstract. In the age of globalization, international students from developing countries (for brevity, we term them as 'international students' in this paper, unless otherwise specified) have become an integral part of the U.S. education system. After relocation to the USA, first-generation international students undergo not only societal differences but also experience changes in the technology space - posing unique challenges for them. Our semi-structured interviews with 26 participants who were pursuing education at the time of our study, or had recently graduated informed us of their adaptation to the technology landscape in the USA; our analysis revealed the underlying challenges in light of the changes in policies, regulations, and social norms that our participants had experienced after geographic relocation. We identified the significance, and scopes of bridging the gap between the existing role of the U.S. institutions and the expectations of international students in helping them to navigate through the technology space in a foreign country. Overall, our findings provide valuable insights for the HCI community to understand the international students' challenges, needs, and expectations with technology use in the USA. We provide recommendations based on our findings and present guidelines for future research in these directions.

Keywords: International students · Technology use · Transitional challenges

1 Introduction

The use of digital technologies is an indispensable part of many government and private institutions in the USA, including the ones offering education, and health services for people. The international students in the USA–relocating from their native country to attain higher education–represent a large user base who need to avail services from these organizations [10,24]. While the technology space in their native country could be different from the USA, they experience the change

P.-L. P. Rau (Ed.): HCII 2023, LNCS 14022, pp. 201–220, 2023.
https://doi.org/10.1007/978-3-031-35936-1_15

in their interaction with technologies, as necessary to avail services from the U.S. organizations. In this context, the unfamiliarity, and lack of understandability could present unique challenges for them to cope with the technology used in a foreign country.

The differences in social norms and policy practices [4,48,53,56] that international students in the USA experience after geographic relocation aggravates the concerns about their transition to a new technology landscape. However, there is a dearth of existing literature to systematically investigate the needs, challenges, and expectations of international students as they navigate through the technology space in the USA. As we begin to address this gap, we focus on the international students from developing countries in this work, where recent studies [2,23,43,46,49] highlighted the situated technology use in developing countries resulting from the differences in societal background, cultural norms, technology infrastructure, and government policies. In particular, we investigated the following research question in our study: *What challenges do international students face, and what factors contribute to those challenges during their adaptation to the technology landscape in the USA?* While prior studies [26,38] focused on the navigation strategies of international students in an academic environment, we aimed to examine how they cope with unfamiliar technology not only in academic settings but also in personal computing environments during their transition to technology space in the USA.

We conducted semi-structured interviews with 26 participants in the USA who were pursuing education at the time of our study or had recently graduated. We found that their unfamiliarity with the new and advanced technologies in the USA, along with the prevalent conceptual models related to past technology use in their native country led them to experience a steep learning curve to blend in the technology ecosystem of the USA (see Sect. 4.1). Our findings point to the factors that increase the challenges of adaptation (see Sect. 4.1 and Sect. 4.1); for instance, the inadequate resources for the international pupil to get acquainted with online services, and lack of customized recommendations to avail services as per their preferences. Our study confirms the findings from prior work [31,55] on the difficulty in communicating with others due to the language barrier. We also found instances representing the challenges to assimilating to the formal setting in the U.S. academic culture, where a few participants were used to more informal communication with faculties and classmates before relocation, e.g., over online social media.

Our participants reported trust issues while navigating through the technology landscape in the USA, leading to the dilemma of obtaining a balance between availing services and disclosing personal information (see Sect. 4.2), which is impacted by various factors, including unfamiliarity, uncertainty, past experiences, and fear of scrutiny. Our study unpacks the inconveniences, cognitive burden, and fear of consequences of the participants fueled by the abundance, or dearth of choices with technology use in the USA as compared to their native country (see Sect. 4.3). For instance, the participants who could not access online social media in their native country, now having unrestricted access reported a cognitive burden to blend into the complex social media culture in the

USA. In several cases, our participants pointed to the complexity of the digital ecosystem in the USA, where they were habituated to a compact system in their country facilitated by a multi-purpose app. The participants, who were used to using pirated software and accessing movies, music, and games online without a subscription in their country, described their fear of consequences due to the strict copyright law in the USA.

Taken together, our findings advance the HCI community's understanding of the interplay between the challenges, needs, and expectations of international students. Based on our results, we provide recommendations to ease the transition of international students to a new technology landscape.

2   Related Work

The recent HCI research focused on understanding the interaction of students with technology [10,28,37,50,52] including the challenges of using remote technologies after the onset of COVID-19 [16,20]. Among these works, some have highlighted the difficulties of globalization for international students [10,14,41]. Additionally, other works have reported on challenges of collaboration with immigrants in general due to existing, socio-cultural, linguistic, and technological barriers [6,29,42,45]. Such challenges may be further exacerbated for students from developing countries due to a larger gap in the technology landscapes which motivates our study. Using our research question (see Sect. 1), we hope to address the existing gaps in the prior literature as discussed below.

In light of challenges originating from the changed technology landscape, we first focus on the prior works that reported the technology perceptions of the users in their home countries [2,47]. Fusilier et al. [21] reported the intentions of Indian students in using the Internet based on the technology acceptance model and the theory of planned behavior developed in the Western world. This implies that in order to encourage intentions of Internet usage, it appears worthwhile to create a sense that the technology is useful and easy to use among potential users. Chen et al. [15] reported that there is a lack of understanding of how Internet technologies operate among users in Ghana. Similarly, Al-Ameen et al. [1,2] unveiled the impact of local infrastructure, and social practices on HCI and privacy challenges in Bangladesh.

Second, we focus on the studies [1,3,5,27] that have explored the contrasting views of technology between the USA, Europe, and Asia. The study of Alsuhaibani et al. [3] reported on students' perceptions of significant identity change when coming to the UK from Saudi Arabia, and their choices about how to reconfigure their digital presence to represent and support this transition. Prior works [1,27] further highlighted the impact of the prevalent culture and infrastructure of the user on the technology usage behavior. While these studies provided the contrast between the perceptions based on region, they do not focus on the difficulties in transition for international students.

Several studies explored the changes in the technology landscape in academic settings and the challenges arising from it. In this context, Gunnarsson et al. [22] reported on the need for educating international students on how to cite and reference properly in order to help them avoid plagiarism. Jackson et al. [25] and Phillips et al. [40] have focused on the use of academic libraries by international students and their role in elevating their performance.

Another body of works [9,26,33,34,36] have focused on understanding the information and help-seeking behavior in international students to overcome their challenges. Several studies [51] reported the use of counseling services by international students to seek information and help for adjustment to the new environment. Similarly, the study of Oh et al. [36] examined the local information-seeking behavior of international students and the relationship between their behavior and their demographic and socio-national context. Additionally, Natalie et al. [34] revealed that international students seek information regarding local practices and internationally specific information for adaptation. In 2009, Ozturgut et al. [38] concluded from their review that the institutions of higher education in the USA were not meeting the needs of international students and were not using the research to drive practice in accommodating international students. There have been several works [13,22,54] that have focused on helping international students. Saw et al. [44] and Yuan et al. [54] have focused on the use of social media sites and the challenge of maintaining a presence and relationships between social network sites of their home country and the USA.

The prior work, as discussed above, highlighted the challenges of international students in dealing with the technology landscape in an academic environment and their efforts in coping with the challenges. Our study extends the exploration beyond the academic settings to uncover the unique challenges, needs, and expectations in the personal computing environment during the transition to the technology landscape in the USA.

Further, the differences in culture, values and ethics have a significant impact on the way academia, industry, and the general population use technology [48,56]. Several studies [31,33] reported that the adjustment challenges faced by international students are primarily attributed to English language proficiency and culture. Thompson et al. [48] revealed that emotional and cultural intelligence played an important role in enabling international students to integrate socially. Li et al. [31] reported that East Asian international students cope in a vastly different academic culture by forming their own peer academic subculture and limiting interactions with faculty members and domestic students. Such coping mechanisms can result in difficulties in communication and collaboration. The study of Khawaja et al. [26] reported adjustment, social isolation, English language skills, academic difficulties, unmet expectations, employment, culture shock and psychological distress to be the challenges faced by international students.

The challenges relating to technology usage are even more prominent in the context of international students from developing countries that have marked differences in infrastructure and culture compared to the USA. However, few studies have focused on understanding the different factors that impact international students from developing countries in their use of technology during their time of transition. Hence, through this research, we identified the unique

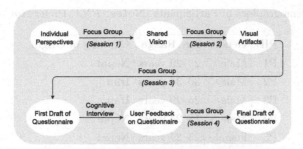

Fig. 1. Precursories to User Study

challenges faced by international students from developing countries, and the factors contributing to those challenges during their adaptation to the new technology landscape in the USA.

3   Methodology

3.1   Precursories to User Study

Probing and Scoping. We conducted two focus group sessions during probing and scoping (see Fig. 1). In the first session, we drew upon the preconceptions and knowledge of each author, with the acknowledgment of individual perspectives in a shared vision. The authors contributed their existing knowledge, brainstormed, and then reached a consensus as a group. In this way, we combined a speculative vision agreed upon by the team, as reflected in our research question (see Sect. 1). We then conducted a second focus group session, where based on the shared vision attained in the first session, we created visual artifacts, including the territory map and stakeholder map to establish our research focus.

Questionnaire Design. In our third focus group session, we prepared the initial draft of the questionnaire in light of our *probing and scoping* (see Sect. 3.1). During this focus group discussion, we brainstormed and identified the contexts leading to individual questions, followed by including sub-questions to attain in-depth responses from the participants.

In the next step, we aimed to gather feedback on the questionnaire that resulted from our focus group discussion, where we conducted cognitive interview [8,17] with two participants who are international students at our university. Here, we recruited participants from non-CS backgrounds so that we could understand the comprehensibility of technology-related terms used in our questionnaire, in addition to examining how the questions are perceived by participants in the context of our research goals. Then, we conducted the fourth focus group session, where we employed a set of changes (e.g., ensured consistency in the flow of questions, defined terms, opted for broader scope, induced articulation, etc.) to improve the structure and clarity of the questionnaire based on

Table 1. Demographics of Participants [**Notes:** *PNA*: Prefer Not to Answer]

PID	Gender	Age Range	Country of Origin
P1	Male	25–29 years	Nepal
P2	Male	30–34 years	Iran
P3	Male	25–29 years	Iran
P4	Male	18–24 years	Nepal
P5	Female	25–29 years	Nepal
P6	Female	18–24 years	India
P7	Male	35–39 years	Iran
P8	Male	25–29 years	Pakistan
P9	Female	25–29 years	Nepal
P10	Female	30–34 years	Morocco
P11	Male	25–29 years	Iran
P12	Male	25–29 years	Iran
P13	Male	25–29 years	Nepal
P14	Female	25–29 years	Nepal
P15	Male	25–29 years	Morocco
P16	Female	25–29 years	Bangladesh
P17	Female	25–29 years	India
P18	Female	25–29 years	Nigeria
P19	Male	30–34 years	Bangladesh
P20	PNA	25–29 years	Nepal
P21	Male	25–29 years	China
P22	Male	30–34 years	China
P23	Male	25–29 years	China
P24	Female	30–34 years	China
P25	Female	25–29 years	China
P26	Male	30–34 years	Iran

the participants' feedback in cognitive interviews. At the end of the fourth focus group session, we completed our final draft of the questionnaire, used during subsequent user study. The participants who took part in cognitive interviews did not participate in our main study (In this paper, the term 'study' refers to our main study with 26 participants, unless otherwise specified).

3.2 User Study

We conducted semi-structured interviews over Zoom (an online communication medium) with 26 participants in the USA between October 2021 and April 2022.

Participant Recruitment. In our study, we first recruited a few participants from the personal networks of authors, e.g., through social media posts, and email communication. We then used snowball sampling recruiting more participants from the recommendation of participants who had participated in this study. To take part in our study, a participant had to be at least 18 years old, whose primary reason for relocation to the USA was attaining higher education. While geographic relocation could occur for a wide range of reasons [30,32], we particularly focused on the first-generation international students in the USA, who were either pursuing their education at the time of our study, or had recently earned their academic degree in the USA. The study was approved by the Institutional Review Board (IRB) at our university.

Procedure. When a participant showed interest to take part in our study, we emailed them the Informed Consent Document (ICD). As they agreed to ICD, we scheduled a time for an online interview over Zoom. Interviews were audio recorded. Each interview was conducted by at least two authors in which the primary interviewer asked the questions whereas the secondary interviewer took notes and helped with devising the follow-up questions.

In our study, we asked participants about their experiences in technology use after their relocation to the USA, where they reported the challenges they had faced in their interaction with technology, and in protecting online security and privacy in the USA. We asked them about their perceptions of the policies and culture related to technology use in the USA, and differences with their native country in the context of technology landscape, social norms, and policy practices; the participants also shared their experiences and workarounds to deal with such changes after their relocation. In addition, participants reported their expectations from U.S. institutions in providing help for international students, especially at the early phase after their relocation. At the end, participants responded to demographic questionnaire. On average, each session took between 35 and 60 min. Each participant was compensated with a $15 Amazon.com gift card.

Analysis. We transcribed the audio recordings. We then performed thematic analysis [7,11,12] on our transcriptions, where we took an inductive approach. In this ground-up approach, codes are derived from the data without preconceived notions, which allows the narrative to emerge from the raw data itself without trying to fit into the preconceptions [7,11,12]. Each transcript was coded by two independent researchers, where they read through the transcripts of the first few interviews, developed codes, compared them, and then iterated again with more interviews until we had developed a consistent codebook. Once the codebook was finalized, two researchers independently coded the remaining interviews. After all interviews had been coded, both researchers spot-checked the other's coded transcripts and did not find any inconsistencies. Finally, we organized and taxonomized our codes into higher-level categories.

Demographics of Participants. We recruited 26 participants from 10 different universities located in the Northeastern, Central, Southwestern, Southern, and Northwestern region of the USA. Among them, 25 participants reported pursuing their education at the time of our study, when one participant had recently completed his education. Our participants are originally from Nepal, Iran, Bangladesh, India, Morocco, Nigeria, China, and Pakistan.

Table 1 presents the demographic information of our participants (men: 15, women: 10, did not report gender: 1). The age of our participants varied between 18 and 34. All participants except one (who preferred not to reveal current education level) had at least a four-year college degree; they are from diverse disciplines, including Biology, Chemical Engineering, Electrical Engineering, Chemistry, Education, Computer Science, Civil Engineering, and Architecture.

4   Findings

In this section, we present the findings from our user study. For consistency, we use these terms based on the frequency of comments in participants' responses: a few (0–10%), several (10–25%), some (25–40%), about half (40–60%), most (60–80%), and almost all (80–100%).

4.1   Technology Intervention

Many of the U.S. immigrants are foreign-born students who have relocated to the USA in pursuit of their higher studies on account of the scopes and opportunities in this country [10]. These students from different origins face radical changes in terms of their interaction with technology in different settings, leading to their perceptions and experiences around steep learning curve (Sect. 4.1), the pace of service (Sect. 4.1), and sense of seclusion (Sect. 4.1).

Steep Learning Curve. Digitization contributes to ease of navigation in academic settings with all the information available in an online platform. However, due to the unfamiliarity with new and advanced technologies, almost all of our participants found it difficult to assimilate into the technology-centered environment in U.S. universities. For instance, one of the participants (P10) referred to her initial experiences as an international student: *"It [student's digital ID] was something new for me, I was like how I can use this, I find it difficult to remember my ID number, I was like oh my god, I need to log in using this number, I have to use this number in the gym, with students, teachers...".*

Prevalent conceptual models of familiar technology present challenges while interacting with the new technology in an unfamiliar setting. Almost all of our participants compared the way they used to enroll in courses, take exams, and access documents; and stressed how these processes – digitized in the USA – are different from their native country. This leads them to experience a learning curve and allot substantial time to blend in and get used to the new technologies. One of our participants (P13) described his experience: *"...the university website and all those digitization...in our university [at participant's country of origin], we don't have those kinds of technology...So that's one of the areas I can say, we have to do everything manually in our universities...I cannot enroll through the online account from home, I need to go to university and I need to do all of those [access and enroll courses], you know, by going there. But in here [USA], I can do everything through the internet, from the computer."*

Our participants reported using several ways to figure out how to use the new tools and technologies. Some of them mentioned using hit-and-trial techniques and making notes of the mistakes for future reference. The participant, P10 said: *"...now I got used to it and learned to navigate in Canvas [online course management system]...and do whatever I need to do in Canvas by myself...".*

Most participants pointed to the availability of an IT center at their university, however, reported frustration with the delay in getting technical services and the lack of manpower in the IT center to provide assistance. Several participants also mentioned asking for help from their friends, classmates, and colleagues in the lab who were already familiar with the technology-centered environment at the university.

Pace of Service. Some participants expressed satisfaction with the pace of work in the USA resulting from digitization, in contrast to their country's over-reliance on paperwork leading to a long waiting time. One of them (P6) who recognized the significance of digitization in the governmental processes in the USA, said: *"In India, there is a long wait time definitely. I remember [for] getting my driver's license in India I went and waited for more than five to six hours, which was unpleasant. Here it [getting driver's license] was pretty quick because you can upload anything like I20, passport...very quickly...it was easy here [USA] compared to India."*

On the contrary, the participants from China pointed to the inconvenience in the USA resulting from having to make an appointment through a phone call instead of being able to do that online. They also reported annoyance with the need of sending documents through mail service in the USA, which varies from the experience in their native country where they could submit information directly through online applications or websites. One of our participants (P26) who completed his Master's study in Europe, pointed out that there are relatively more online applications to interact with the governmental services in Europe offering a faster service to the people compared to the USA.

Sense of Seclusion. The findings from our study present the challenges faced by international students to adapt to a new environment, which could relate to the lack of necessary resources for international pupils, the language barrier, and the shift from a semi-formal to a more formal academic setting. Most of our participants pointed to the lack of adequate resources for tax filing, especially the unavailability of usable and understandable tax filing software for international students. The participant, P22 reported: *"For some information, there are some tools out there but not enough resources for international students. For example, there is a lot of software for residents for tax filing but a limited resource for international students, so they get confused when they file it for the first time,* *and also finding someone outside to help them is costlier. So, if governmental institutions can provide more information about this, that will be very helpful."*

A few participants pointed to the lack of customized recommendations for the international population in the online crowd-sourced reviews when it comes to finding local restaurants and services that fit their preferences. The participant, P23 offered suggestions based on his experiences with Yelp: *"There's a difference with people's preferences...for example, in Yelp, we can set up a filter like, 'hey, what's an Asian people think of this restaurant?'...this can make me find one with more confidence...that United States people like that, but Asian people do not like that."*

Understanding and articulating were reported as challenges that emerged from the language barrier. About half of our participants mentioned their struggles with understanding others, as well as making their points and ending up in a completely different situation than intended. One of them (P12) referred to an incident: *"I wanted to transfer my new number to the old number, so I called the company [carrier provider]. I explained everything that I have joined a new plan, and I wanted to transfer my new phone number to the old number. They said, 'okay', and just five minutes later, I was removed from that family plan. So I don't know why but because of the language barrier, they got completely different compared to what I explained to them."*

One of the participants (P15) reflected on his experiences in Europe where he completed his Master's study. He was used to semi-formal academic settings in Europe that made him feel more connected, in contrast to more formal settings in the USA. He (P15) mentioned: *"When I went to Hungary, they were using Facebook, in classes. Like they had Facebook chats with the professor. In some classes, they would give them assignments in Facebook groups. Here, in the U.S., Discord is used, like, more often than not, but just between students..."*

4.2 Sphere of Trust

Our participants reported trust issues while interacting with day-to-day technologies after relocating to the USA, which can be attributed to several factors, including unfamiliarity (§4.2), uncertainty (§4.2), past experiences (§4.2), and fear of scrutiny (§4.2).

Unfamiliarity. Most participants referred to the changes in their day-to-day experiences after relocating to the USA, especially in the context of how they use online services. Due to unfamiliarity, the participants could not put trust in such services; one of them (P10) reflected on her online shopping experience: *"People are becoming like digital natives, if I can say this word, like people are here [USA], like, technology and the use of technology is a part of their life. Yeah, so it's there like they are sitting and they can order whatever they want this, but this, these processes [online shopping] are not something familiar back home, you need to go to the store, and you need to see things with your eyes. And that's something also that I felt when I first came here. I felt like how can I trust those* *people [online sellers]? How can I trust this store [online store]? I need to see a fabric if I want to buy a dress, I need to see the fabric. Is it true what I see in like on the website, so I didn't trust those websites [online shopping portal]..."*

Similarly, the participants expressed their frustration with the frequency of the spam calls, phishing emails, and online ads they get in the USA as compared to their native country.

Uncertainty. Availing services from an organization might demand the disclosure of personal information, where some of our participants reported a dilemma in obtaining a balance between the services to avail and personal information to be disclosed in the process. Here, our participants referred to the lack of trust in various organizations (e.g., hospitals, insurance, etc.) resulting in uncertainty about how their personal data would be handled by them. One of the participants (P6) mentioned an incident where she was trying to get car insurance and went through different websites to have an idea about the tentative cost, but those websites asked for sensitive information, including her Social Security Number (SSN) to give her the price quote which left her in bewilderment as she believes showing a price quote should not need her SSN. Another participant (P2) reported her surprise with the data collection practices while referring to an incident related to a healthcare center: *"Recently I wanted to make an appointment with the healthcare center, just for a regular physical checkup...they were basically asking a lot of information and I didn't understand what is the reason for having this much information like my salary just for a physical appointment with a physician."*

Past Experiences. Almost all of the participants exhibited confusion and frustration with the scam calls they received in the USA; one of them (P7) said: *"...there was one instance that was basically subject to identity theft...someone called me...pretended that they are calling from U.S. Department of State...then they started getting some information from me. In the middle of that phone call, I understood that there's something not right here...then I hung up the phone."*

Most of the participants who experienced scam calls or phishing emails were worried about their information being misused, including their SSN, and their credit scores being hampered. Further, the frequency of personalized ads has led our participants to believe that the data collection and sharing are more extensive in the USA as compared to their native country. One of our participants (P23) reported his concern about the data practices of a credit card company leading him to believe that his personal information was leaked: *"...my first credit card was a [anonymized; we would call it C-card]...[where] my name was [typed] wrong...I started to get some advertisements... in the mail...[with] exactly the [same] wrong name...I put on the C-card...So I'm pretty sure they like my information got sold or stolen from C-card...So that made me feel not happy."*

Another participant (P7) talked about his experiences of his stock account being hacked: *"The app I was using for investing in the stock market got hacked and someone got my login information and did transactions on my behalf and*

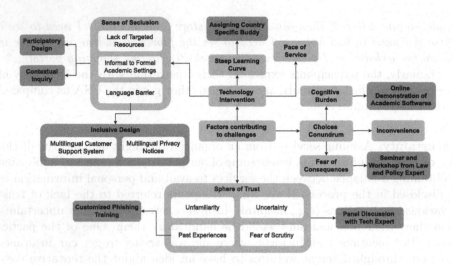

Fig. 2. Factors Contributing to Challenges of Adaptation and Implications. *Note:* The boxes in blue represent the findings from our study with international students, and the boxes in green represent the corresponding implications. (Color figure online)

stole my money...the admin noticed and contacted me, and blocked my account for a month, investigated and returned my money but my account was locked for a month, so I could not do any transactions."

Our participants reported expectations that the organizations would inform them whenever they provide information to third parties. While data collection practices are typically documented in the privacy policy, some participants pointed to the difficulty in understanding privacy policy due to lengthiness, and the use of technical and legal terms, which poses even greater challenges for them because of the language barrier.

Fear of Scrutiny. We found evidence where the participants reported a sense of estrangement after relocating to the USA, leading to the fear of scrutiny by others. For instance, P6 mentioned: *"I have a Facebook account but I don't use it often after moving to the U.S., I started using Facebook to search for rooms and roommates in college...I changed the privacy settings of Facebook so that people cannot send me a friend request or look at my profile for those who are not friends with me because sometimes people might look at your profile, and [landlords] might not give you the house [to rent], or don't want to be your roommate because you are from somewhere [outside of the USA]."*

4.3 Choices Conundrum

Our participants reported an abundance, or dearth of choices in the USA as compared to their native country in the context of technology use, which led them to experience inconveniences (§4.3), cognitive burden (§4.3), and fear of consequences (§4.3) during their initial phase of transition.

Inconveniences. Almost all participants from China referred to the multi-purpose application in their native country, which contributes to the ease of social communication, making payments, instant messaging, and online reservations. One of them (P22) mentioned: *"In China, we use WeChat a lot not only for messages but also for paying the ticket or other things. But in the U.S., we need to use different things to buy and pay for food and other things in the market, and also most people use a credit card here, even though there are some apps like Apple Pay but it is not very popular."*

They pointed to their inconvenience in the USA, like always carrying a credit card due to the unavailability of such multi-purpose applications, where they also referred to the confusion in making a choice arising from the availability of multiple applications for a single purpose (e.g., Facebook, Instagram, and Twitter for social communication).

Cognitive Burden. The need to learn, and interact with different applications for separate purposes added to the challenges of participants in coping with the technology landscape in the USA. For instance, one of our participants (P4) reflected on his experiences with the necessity of interacting with multiple tools in academic settings: *"Blackboard was pretty new to me when I started using it and I still can't get a hang of it sometimes. It's like messing up...there are multiple things that I have to keep track of. There's Blackboard, Piazza, June, Teams, Slack, Skype, and everything. And it's like all of it at once...and then I have to jumble between things, keep myself sane as well."*

A few participants mentioned that they had restricted access to social media applications in their native country due to the local policy related to censorship and content regulation. Upon relocating to the USA, they could exercise more freedom in accessing online social media, however, it also added cognitive burden to understand and blend into the complex social media culture, including how to present oneself in the virtual world, and initiate and maintain relationships in online platforms.

Fear of Consequences. Most of the participants mentioned limited access to free online content in the USA as compared to their native country, where they specifically referred to the websites and apps for downloading movies (e.g., Torrent), and live streaming of sports. Our participant, P4 shared his experiences with such restricted access: *"There are certain sites [for movie streaming and downloading] that are banned [in the USA]...I watched anime a lot growing up...but I never realized that these sites and Torrents were such a huge issue here [USA]. People distributed content like a game of thrones in pen drives and stuff back in my country but here if you want to access you have to get a subscription and anything else is illegal which can result in severe charges."*

Our participants talked about their realization that copyright is an important consideration in the USA in contrast to their native country, which instilled fear in them regarding financial penalties, legal issues, and possible immigration complications including deportation. In these contexts, a few participants talked about the importance of offering an organized learning opportunity to international students about copyright laws; P12 said: *"...the students from my country, when came here, may not just aware of those rights and the consequences of the copyright things...there should be something that makes the students aware of the copyright things and the consequences."*

5   Discussion

The United States has long been the top receiving country for international students, with a consistent growth in the number of students in the last decade [10]. In our study, we identified the challenges faced by international students and the factors contributing to those challenges during their initial phase of transition to the new technology landscape in the USA. In this section, we discuss the implications of our findings. (Figure 2 provides a highlight of the implications of our findings).

5.1   Enhancement and Increased Adoption of the Buddy System

The buddy system, commonly used in industry settings [19, 35, 39], is an onboarding and knowledge-sharing method used to orient new employees that involve assigning them to an existing employee who guides them during the first few weeks or months in their job [18]. It is intended to make them feel comfortable in their new roles by helping them to understand the workplace systems, processes, and culture.

While some universities have an existing support system for incoming students through peer mentorship and the involvement of volunteering organizations, we argue that these academic institutions could play a more active role to enhance the existing support system or introduce a new system if that is not in place. Based on our findings, we recommend the contextualization of the buddy system to the academic environment and go beyond the one-to-one mentoring that is more common in the industry setting [18]. We emphasize considering the unique challenges faced by international students with technology use in designing or enhancing a buddy system appropriate for a university; our study starts filling up this dearth in the existing literature to understand the struggles of international students to cope with the technology used upon relocating to the USA.

Our study points to the cognitive burden resulting from the necessity of interacting with multiple tools in academic settings (see §4.3), where the steep learning curve during the transition phase to a new technology space contributed to the challenges faced by our participants (see §4.1). Moreover, our findings on leveraging intermediate help with technology use indicate the need for an organized support system from the university, where prior study [1] presents the security risks emerging from scenarios around availing intermediate help. To address these challenges, the universities could pair an incoming student with a current student, where assigning a first-or second-year student could be helpful because of their more recent experiences with going through the transition period in the USA. To make the transition smooth while keeping the language barrier and cultural changes in consideration, we encourage future work to examine the benefits and challenges around assigning a buddy specific to the race, and native country of the new student. Further, the universities could initiate mentoring and supporting international students before they arrive in the USA through online demonstrations (e.g., over zoom) of how to use common academic software.

In a personal computing setting, due to differences in the policies relating to digital content access and copyright, the participants reported fear of financial penalty, legal issues, and possible immigration complications (see §4.2). We suggest the universities organize seminars and workshops catering to the needs of international students. For instance, they can invite policy experts to the workshop to make the international students aware of copyright laws in the USA, and so on, to create a comfortable space for them to ask questions that they might be hesitant to ask anyone in a foreign land.

Our findings uncover the trust issues of international students around technology use due to their unfamiliarity, uncertainty, past experiences, and fear of scrutiny (see Sect. 4.2). In these contexts, the universities can organize a panel discussion with the tech experts to inform international students about the possible privacy and security risks in day-to-day technology use, which could be 'news' to many students as they relocate to the USA from their native country. We also encourage future research investigating the efficacy of customized phishing training, which should be designed focusing on the vulnerabilities relating to international students, e.g., scam calls exploiting the unfamiliarity of new international students with the U.S. government agencies.

5.2   Inclusive Design

Our study points to the significance of inclusive design for international students, which in turn, could ease their adaptation to the technology landscape in the USA. In these contexts, our results indicate that the unavailability of necessary resources for international pupils, including usable and understandable software and customized recommendations in the online crowd-sourced reviews could lead them to experience a sense of seclusion after relocating to the USA (see Sect. 4.1). Hence, in order to address these challenges, we recommend that researchers and industry practitioners involve international students in the pre-design and design phases of technology-focused systems through participatory design, and contextual inquiry-based studies.

We found that the challenges that result from the language barrier of international students, could impact their trust in the technology landscape in the USA, as well as to experience a sense of seclusion (see Sect. 4.1 and Sect. 4.2).

Thus, to cater to their needs and expectations, we recommend making the privacy notices available in multiple languages and letting the user choose one of the available options. We encourage future studies to investigate the usability, comprehension, and privacy implications of such privacy notices in further detail. In addition, customer services should consider having a multi-lingual support system to assist with technical issues as faced by non-native speakers, including international pupils.

6   Limitations and Future Work

We interviewed 26 participants in our study, where we followed the widely-used methods for qualitative research [7,11,12], focusing in depth on a small number of participants. We acknowledge the limitations of such a study that a different set of samples might yield varying results. Thus, we do not draw any quantitative, generalizable conclusion from our study, nor make a direct comparison between participants based on their country of origin and the USA state they currently live in. Our participants were young and university-educated. We encourage future research to focus on the older, and less-educated international population to understand their challenges to cope with the changes in technology use and policy practices after relocation to the USA.

We used snowball sampling for participant recruitment, where participants who have taken part in the study nominate people for recruitment whom they know well; thus, they may suffer from sampling bias. In addition, self-reported data might have limitations, like recall and observer bias.

There are diverse groups of the international population in the USA, who had relocated for a wide range of reasons [30,32]. In our qualitative study, we focused on a small group of the international population to understand their challenges in navigating through the technology landscape after relocation to the USA. All of our participants relocated to the USA to attain higher education, whose experiences, and challenges in technology use could be different from others, e.g., the ones who had relocated through a diversity visa program, or had experienced forced migration – a part of these populations might have started their educational career later in the USA – we did not capture them in our study. Hence, our findings are only applicable to the international population in the USA whose primary reason behind relocation was attaining higher education.

In our study, we unpacked the challenges of adaptation for international students, and shed light on their expectations from different U.S. institutions including their universities. In our future work, we would investigate through the lens of academic institutions to understand the role of Computing service and IT support, the Office of international education, and higher management of the universities in bridging the gap for international students to learn, understand and navigate through the technology landscape in a foreign country in a usable, secure, and privacy-preserving manner.

References

1. Al-Ameen, M.N., Kocabas, H., Nandy, S., Tamanna, T.: "We, three brothers have always known everything of each other": a cross-cultural study of sharing digital devices and online accounts. Proc. Privacy Enhan. Technol. **2021**(4), 203–224 (2021)
2. Al-Ameen, M.N., Tamanna, T., Nandy, S., Ahsan, M.M., Chandra, P., Ahmed, S.I.: We don't give a second thought before providing our information: Understanding users' perceptions of information collection by apps in urban bangladesh. In: Proceedings of the 3rd ACM SIGCAS Conference on Computing and Sustainable Societies, pp. 32–43 (2020)
3. Alsuhaibani, A., Cox, A., Hopfgartner, F., Zhao, X.: An investigation of the physical and digital transitions of saudi students coming to the uk. In: Proceedings of the Workshop on Life Transitions and Social Technologies: Research and Design for Times of Life Change (co-located with CSCW'20). Association for Computing Machinery (ACM) (2019)
4. Andrade, M.S.: International students in English-speaking universities: adjustment factors. J. Res. Int. Educ. **5**(2), 131–154 (2006)
5. Baker, D.M., et al.: Usa and asia hospitality & tourism students' perceptions and satisfaction with online learning versus traditional face-to-face instruction. E-J. Bus. Educ. Schol. Teach. **12**(2), 40–54 (2018)
6. Balali, S., Steinmacher, I., Annamalai, U., Sarma, A., Gerosa, M.A.: Newcomers' barriers... is that all? an analysis of mentors' and newcomers' barriers in OSS projects. Comput. Suppor. Cooperr.. Work (CSCW) **27**(3), 679–714 (2018)
7. Baxter, K., Courage, C., Caine, K.: Understanding Your Users: A Practical Guide to User Research Methods, 2nd edn. Morgan Kaufmann Publishers Inc., San Francisco (2015)
8. Beatty, P.C., Willis, G.B.: Research synthesis: the practice of cognitive interviewing. Public Opin. Q. **71**(2), 287–311 (2007)
9. Bhochhibhoya, A., Dong, Y., Branscum, P.: Sources of social support among international college students in the united states. J. Int. Stud. **7**(3), 671–686 (2017)
10. Bound, J., Braga, B., Khanna, G., Turner, S.: The globalization of postsecondary education: the role of international students in the us higher education system. J. Econ. Perspect. **35**(1), 163–84 (2021)
11. Boyatzis, R.E.:Transforming Qualitative Information: Thematic Analysis and Code Development. Sage, Thousand Oak (1998)
12. Braun, V., Clarke, V.: Using thematic analysis in psychology. Qual. Res. Psychol. **3**(2), 77–101 (2006)
13. Chang, S., Gomes, C.: Digital journeys: a perspective on understanding the digital experiences of international students. J. Int. Stud. **7**(2), 347–466 (2017)
14. Chang, S., Gomes, C., Platt, M., Trumpour, S., McKay, D., Alzougool, B.: Mapping the contours of digital journeys: a study of international students' social networks in Australian higher education. In: Higher Education Research & Development, pp. 1–17 (2021)
15. Chen, J., Paik, M., McCabe, K.: Exploring internet security perceptions and practices in urban china. In: 10th Symposium On Usable Privacy and Security (SOUPS 2014), pp. 129–142 (2014)
16. Cohney, S., et al.: Virtual classrooms and real harms: remote learning at us. universities. In: Seventeenth Symposium on Usable Privacy and Security (SOUPS 2021), pp. 653–674 (2021)

17. Collins, D.: Pretesting survey instruments: an overview of cognitive methods. Qual. Life Res. **12**(3), 229–238 (2003)
18. Cooper, J., Wight, J.: Implementing a buddy system in the workplace. Project Management Institute (2014)
19. Creary, S.J., Rothbard, N., Mariscal, E., Moore, O., Scruggs, J., Villarmán, N.: Evidence-based solutions for inclusion in the workplace: actions for middle managers (2020)
20. Emami-Naeini, P., Francisco, T., Kohno, T., Roesner, F.: Understanding privacy attitudes and concerns towards remote communications during the covid-19 pandemic. In: Seventeenth Symposium on Usable Privacy and Security (SOUPS 2021), pp. 695–714 (2021)
21. Fusilier, M., Durlabhji, S.: An exploration of student internet use in India: the technology acceptance model and the theory of planned behaviour. Campus-Wide Inf. Syst. **22**(4), 233–246 (2005)
22. Gunnarsson, J., Kulesza, W.J., Pettersson, A.: Teaching international students how to avoid plagiarism: librarians and faculty in collaboration. J. Acad. Librariansh. **40**(3–4), 413–417 (2014)
23. Haque, S.T., et al.: Privacy vulnerabilities in public digital service centers in Dhaka, Bangladesh. In: Proceedings of the 2020 International Conference on Information and Communication Technologies and Development, pp. 1–12 (2020)
24. IIE: Number of international students in the united states hits all-time high (November 2019), www.iie.org/Why-IIE/Announcements/2019/11/Number-of-International-Students-in-the-United-States-Hits-All-Time-High
25. Jackson, P.A.: Incoming international students and the library: a survey. Ref. Serv. Rev. **33**(2), 197–209(2005)
26. Khawaja, N.G., Stallman, H.M.: Understanding the coping strategies of international students: a qualitative approach. J. Psychol. Couns. Sch. **21**(2), 203–224 (2011)
27. Kocabas, H., Nandy, S., Tamanna, T., Al-Ameen, M.N.: Understanding user's behavior and protection strategy upon losing, or identifying unauthorized access to online account. In: International Conference on Human-Computer Interaction, pp. 310–325. Springer, Cham (2021)
28. Kriek, J., Coetzee, A.: Interaction between teacher and student beliefs when using different technology tools in a tertiary context. Int. J. Technol. Enhan. Learn. **13**(2), 121–138 (2021)
29. Lazem, S., Giglitto, D., Nkwo, M.S., Mthoko, H., Upani, J., Peters, A.: Challenges and paradoxes in decolonising hci: A critical discussion. Comput. Suppor. Cooper. Work (CSCW) **31**, 1–38 (2021)
30. Lebcir, R.M., Wells, H., Bond, A.: Factors affecting academic performance of international students in project management courses: a case study from a british post 92 university. Int. J. Project Manage. **26**(3), 268–274 (2008)
31. Li, J.: A cultural hybridization perspective: emerging academic subculture among international students from east Asia in us. Univ J. Educ.l Res. **4**(9), 2218–2228 (2016)
32. Molloy, R., Smith, C.L., Wozniak, A.: Internal migration in the united states. J. Econ. Perspect. **25**(3), 173–96 (2011)
33. Motahar, T., Jasim, M., Ahmed, S.I., Mahyar, N.: Exploring how international graduate students in the us seek support. In: Extended Abstracts of the 2020 CHI Conference on Human Factors in Computing Systems, pp. 1–8 (2020)

34. Natalie, R., Yuan, C.W., Wang, H.C.: Understanding information seeking behavior among international students for adaptation. In: Proceedings of the Sixth International Symposium of Chinese CHI, pp. 148–151 (2018)
35. O'Brien, J.: Employee onboarding: An analysis of best practice in employee onboarding and their implementation in the financial services industry in Ireland. Ph.D. thesis, Dublin, National College of Ireland (2013)
36. Oh, C.Y., Butler, B.S.: Newcomers from the other side of the globe: international students' local information seeking during adjustment. Proc. Assoc. Inf. Sci. Technol. **53**(1), 1–6 (2016)
37. Oleson, A., Solomon, M., Ko, A.J.: Computing students' learning difficulties in HCI education. In: Proceedings of the 2020 CHI Conference on Human Factors in Computing Systems, pp. 1–14 (2020)
38. Özturgut, O., Murphy, C.: Literature vs. practice: challenges for international students in the us. Int. J. Teach. Learn. Higher Educ. **22**(3), 374–385 (2009)
39. Pavlina, K.: Assessing best practices for the virtual onboarding of new hires in the technology industry. Pepperdine University (2020)
40. Phillips, L.S.: International students and academic libraries: initiatives for success. In: Jackson, P.A., Sullivan, P., (eds) Chicago: American Library Association, 2011. 234p. ALK. paper, $54.00 (ISBN 9780838985939). lc2011-040762. Coll. Res. Lib. **73**(3), 304-305 (2012)
41. Prasad, P., Maag, A., Redestowicz, M., Hoe, L.S.: Unfamiliar technology: reaction of international students to blended learning. Compu. Educ. **122**, 92–103 (2018)
42. Sabie, D., , et al.: Migration and mobility in HCI: Rethinking boundaries, methods, and impact. In: Extended Abstracts of the 2021 CHI Conference on Human Factors in Computing Systems, pp. 1–6 (2021)
43. Sambasivan, N., et al.:" Privacy is not for me, it's for those rich women": performative privacy practices on mobile phones by women in south Asia. In: Fourteenth Symposium on Usable Privacy and Security (SOUPS 2018), pp. 127–142 (2018)
44. Saw, G., Abbott, W., Donaghey, J., McDonald, C.: Social media for international students-it's not all about Facebook. Library Management (2013)
45. Steinmacher, I., Gerosa, M., Conte, T.U., Redmiles, D.F.: Overcoming social barriers when contributing to open source software projects. Comput. Suppor. Cooper Work (CSCW) **28**(1), 247–290 (2019)
46. Sultana, S., et al.: understanding the sensibility of social media use and privacy with bangladeshi facebook group users. In: Proceedings of the 3rd ACM SIGCAS Conference on Computing and Sustainable Societies (COMPASS'20). pp. 317–318. Association for Computing Machinery, New York, NY, USA (2020). doi: https://doi.org/10.1145/3378393.3402235
47. Thakkar, D., Sambasivan, N., Kulkarni, P., Kalenahalli Sudarshan, P., Toyama, K.: The unexpected entry and exodus of women in computing and HCI in India. In: Proceedings of the 2018 CHI Conference on Human Factors in Computing Systems, pp. 1–12 (2018)
48. Thompson, R.: A qualitative phenomenological study of emotional and cultural intelligence of international students in the united states of america. J. Int. Stud. **8**(2), 1220–1255 (2018)
49. Vashistha, A., Anderson, R., Mare, S.: Examining security and privacy research in developing regions. In: Proceedings of the 1st ACM SIGCAS Conference on Computing and Sustainable Societies (COMPASS'18). COMPASS'18, Association for Computing Machinery, New York, NY, USA (2018). https://doi.org/10.1145/3209811.3209818

50. Wut, T.M., Lee, S.W., Xu, J.: How do facilitating conditions influence student-to-student interaction within an online learning platform? a new typology of the serial mediation model. Educ. Sci. **12**(5), 337 (2022)
51. Yakunina, E.S., Weigold, I.K., McCarthy, A.S.: Group counseling with international students: practical, ethical, and cultural considerations. J. Coll. Stud. Psychother. **25**(1), 67–78 (2010)
52. Yarmand, M., Solyst, J., Klemmer, S., Weibel, N.: "it feels like i am talking into a void": Understanding interaction gaps in synchronous online classrooms. In: Proceedings of the 2021 CHI Conference on Human Factors in Computing Systems, pp. 1–9 (2021)
53. Yeh, C.J., Inose, M.: International students' reported English fluency, social support satisfaction, and social connectedness as predictors of acculturative stress. Couns. Psychol. Q. **16**(1), 15–28 (2003)
54. Yuan, C.W., Setlock, L.D., Fussell, S.R.: International students' use of Facebook vs. a home country site. In: CHI'14 Extended Abstracts on Human Factors in Computing Systems, pp. 2101–2106 (2014)
55. Zhang, Y., Mi, Y.: Another look at the language difficulties of international students. J. Stud. Int. Educ. **14**(4), 371–388 (2010)
56. Zhang, Y.L.: International students in transition: Voices of Chinese doctoral students in a us research university (2016)

The Impact of Strategic Agility on Innovation in Cross-Organization R&D Management

Yen Hsu[✉] [iD] and Jin-Chun Lai [iD]

The Graduate Institute of Design Science, Tatung University, Taipei, Taiwan
yhsu@gm.ttu.edu.tw

Abstract. Extensive attention has been paid to and much research has been carried out on strategic agility, a major means for business corporations to respond to external uncertainties in the management sector. Since the current studies fail to focus on small and medium-sized enterprises and product research and development (R&D) units within the organization structure, the dynamic changes and practical performance related to strategic agility still need to be studied. Therefore, by taking small and medium-sized manufacturing companies in the coastal areas of China as an example, this study, through the questionnaires and empirical analyses of 158 companies, identified the features of strategic agility in small and medium-sized enterprises that are different from those found in previous studies. On the basis of cluster analysis, enterprise organizations could be divided into four groups, including agile insight, effective resources, innovative management, and flexible responses. As the different strategy groups demonstrated distinctive features of product R&D, this study summarized different practices in the strategic implementation of the design of those groups. This finding provided new theoretical developments for innovation in R&D management and the exploration into strategic agility as well as practical references for small and medium-sized enterprises and practitioners.

Keywords: Strategic agility · R&D management · Product innovation · Design strategies · SMEs

1 Introduction

In the face of a business environment with increasing volatility, uncertainty, complexity, and ambiguity (VUCA), rapidly adapting to external changes and making high-quality decisions are increasingly important for corporate development. Currently, enterprise organizations have realized the importance of agility and are vigorously applying it to their actual activities, resulting in the concepts of manufacturing agility, organizational agility, and strategic agility. Specifically, strategic agility is attracting increasing attention from academic circles focusing on strategies and management (Doz & Kosonen 2008; Weber & Tarba 2014). In essence, the concept of strategic agility (Doz & Kosonen 2008) is within the theoretical aspect of strategic changes and human resource management and up-dates. The general assumption of strategic agility is that an existing large organization

© The Author(s), under exclusive license to Springer Nature Switzerland AG 2023
P.-L. P. Rau (Ed.): HCII 2023, LNCS 14022, pp. 221–235, 2023.
https://doi.org/10.1007/978-3-031-35936-1_16

can renew itself and inject creative ideas into its development to respond to external uncertainties and volatility while seeking new opportunities (Weber & Tarba 2014). Therefore, strategic agility is of practical significance for the renewal and innovation of constantly changing and uncertain organizations.

At present, most studies focus on transnational corporations and large organizations; little attention has been paid to small and medium-sized enterprises as well as start-up teams in different backgrounds (Parnel et al. 2012, Fourné, et al. 2014, Xing et al. 2019). Compared with transnational corporations and large organizations, start-up teams and small and medium-sized enterprises cannot predict and control environmental changes. The competitive strategy of small and medium-sized enterprises is to obtain maximum real-time returns and short-term ad-vantages based on limited resources (Eisenhardt 2013). The strategic management of such enterprises is a process of adaptation. They are required to adapt quickly to ever-changing environmental demands and formulate appropriate strategies to mitigate any possible threats (Jennings & Beaver 1997). In any organizational environment, studies on strategy and organization have demonstrated that a strategy is a linear, planned, or top-down process and a necessary but not sufficient condition to implement decisions (Xing et al. 2020).

As the world's largest exporter, more than 80% of enterprises in China can be classified as SMEs (Parnel et al. 2012), and in many ways, Chinese SMEs perform differently from the rest of the world in terms of management and decision-making choices (Parnel et al. 2015, Tang & Hull 2012). For example, Chinese executives tend to exhibit a high degree of uncertainty aversion (Hofstede 2003; Lockett 1988), organizational leaders place high priority on security, stability, and predictability. Moreover, when the environment is hostile and competitive, Chinese SMEs are unlikely to invest heavily in research and development (R&D) or establish strong brand names (Tsang 1996). When considered difficult to compete, Chinese entrepreneurs prefer to scale back or stay as is, avoiding risk-taking, innovative strategies as much as possible, in favor of safer marketing strategies (Lau & Busenitz 2001; Tang & Hull 2012).

Such characteristics and conditions reveal that Chinese SMEs are different from the existing research. Their success is of exploratory significance. Design organizations and teams are innately innovative, flexible, and market-oriented. Changes brought by agility, no doubt, is the company's new product development decision-making, play a key role in the organization and bring important driving force for the new product development performance (Luiz O. R et al. 2019; Claybaugh et al. 2015; Hauser & Urban 1993). A conceptual model based on start-up teams and strategic agility offers new perspectives for human re-source management. However, no studies have explored the strategic agility of design teams with innovative thinking (Xing et al. 2020).

On the basis of the preceding discussion, the main purposes of this study included: (1) incorporating the impact and innovation of strategic agility thinking on R&D management during the development of new products by business corporations in the chaotic and turbulent VUCA era; (2) exploring how Chinese small and medium-sized enterprises make responses and adjustments according to ex-ternal environmental changes during the actions of R&D management, and streamlining the corresponding leadership actions and strategies; and (3) discussing the difference in design strategies during practices under R&D management, especially the features of Chinese SMEs.

2 Literature Review

2.1 Strategic Agility

Many existing studies have investigated agility from the perspective of organizations and summarized strategic agility as an organizational capability. In particular, strategic agility is a capability for rapidly identifying and seizing opportunities, changing directions, and avoiding conflicts (McCann 2004). It is also an ability for predicting actions and initiating or exploiting changes in a rapid, decisive, and effective manner (Jamrog, Vickers & Bear 2006). Parallel to the organizational analysis study, different research fields emerged. These research fields examine agility in specific organizational environments, and knowledge-intensive companies and the manufacturing industry are the most commonly investigated environments. As some studies recognized the situation, early agility studies tended to emphasize agility and complicated technologies such as computer-integrated manufacturing (Sherehiy et al. 2007) for which those studies boast unique manufacturing agility.

Academics in the sector of human resource management are strongly interested in strategic agility and are exploring the major role of human resource management in strategic agility against the backdrop of different organizations and national environments (Doz 2020; Cumming et al. 2020; e Cunha et al. 2020; Xing et al. 2020; Khan et al. 2020). Strategic agility, which is a novel theoretical concept, still has many areas deserving to be developed, and follow-up studies can inspect the outstanding role of strategic agility in new places and environments. This study, based on the above viewpoints and starting from product R&D, probed into the significance and impact of strategic agility from the perspective of practices in product development.

Strategic agility evolves over time. Doz and Kosonen proposed three fundamental capabilities on how to maintain strategic agility, including strategic sensitivity, leadership unity, and resource fluidity. Only when these three capabilities are available at the same time can the strategies of companies be agile. Those capabilities are the coordinate axes in three dimensions and thus companies need to highlight each of them during decision making. If an organization only develops one brilliant capability while neglecting the others, the company's decisions will be suboptimal (Doz & Kosonen 2008). Thus, based on the statements of strategic agility, Doz and Kosonen (2008) put forward detailed matters of priority and a list of actions for leaders. They also developed three corresponding vectors from every perspective (strategic agility, leadership unity, and resource fluidity) and five suggestions for leadership behaviors. Each of those behaviors can promote and regulate the capability for updating the business models of companies.

Strategic commitments are long-term whereas agility changes rapidly. The inevitable contradiction between the two is a problem of strategic agility that cannot be eliminated. Every business corporation wants agility but not all of them can construct strategic agility. For leaders of those corporations, strategic agility may be the most rigorous leadership capability (project). The cultivation of strategic agility is a development goal of business corporations that needs to be listed at the highest level.

Relevant studies on business models driven by strategic agility have identified that leadership unity and resource fluidity seem to be the inherent capabilities of small and medium-sized enterprises because the status applies to them easily. Strategic agility is not prominent; nonetheless, it is essential (Arbussa, A., Bikfalvi, A., & Marquès, P. 2017). Arbussa, Bikfalvi and Marquès's research explored the key and particular capabilities of small and medium-sized enterprises through in-depth case studies based on the strategic agility of resourcefulness. Though the research had limitations due to targeting case studies, original points and research sites were provided for strategic agility in specific environments—for instance, the development of small and medium-sized enterprises.

2.2 Product R&D and Strategy

The relationship between innovation and enterprise survival has been studied in many existing papers, and different innovation indicators have been proposed. Some research has leveraged the occurrence or intensity of R&D, some have taken the occurrence or intensity measures of innovation output, and some have been related to the use of intellectual property rights. Based on the results of a literature review, Zhang and Mohnen (2022) summarized three types of innovation indicators for ease of comparison: R&D, innovation output (which is sometimes broken down into products, processes, organizations, and marketing innovation), and intellectual property rights (such as patents, trademarks, and copyrights). Among those studies, Zhang identified that for Chinese companies, enhancing R&D is a better way to ensure the survival of enterprises compared to launching innovative products. This finding can be explained by that innovation is risky, and excessive innovation or risk-taking innovation may be harmful to enterprise survival (Zhang & Mohnen 2013).

On the basis of a large-scale investigation and analysis on the samples of 730 Dutch companies, Heij, C. V. et al. (2020) identified that the management innovation of businesses can raise the effectiveness of corporate R&D being transformed into product innovation. In other words, focusing on R&D solely may fail to exert a positive impact on product innovation, particularly for companies with a low level of management innovation. For small and medium-sized enterprises, the emphasis of their effort is not on prediction and control over operating environments but rather on quickly adapting to environmental requirements that change constantly. In addition, proper strategies should be developed for minimizing the consequences brought about by any threatening change (Jennings & Beaver 1997).

Accordingly, effective management and decisions that are made rapidly and accurately can help small and medium-sized enterprises obtain competitive edges. From the perspective of R&D during the actual implementation of products, effective communication and resource management are extremely important. Strategic activities based on product R&D and production can therefore be referred to as the design strategies of products.

In terms of the definition of design strategies, there are miscellaneous definition methods in the academic circle, just as the emphasis on agility consideration is different for different corporate departments. For example, for advanced materials and technologies, design strategies represent the application of a specific material, during which approaches and ideas for innovation are proposed (Shi et al. 2018). From the perspective of semiology and art, design strategies can also be the design methods formulated for the appearance and packaging of products (Laura et al. 2020). At the same time, they can be development strategies (Hsu et al. 2013) for studying the emotional cognition of consumers and cultural factors so as to enhance companies' competitiveness during the launch of innovative products. The preceding discussion illustrates the intrinsic relation between design strategies and innovation—a major strategy for product innovation and R&D. In this study, the innovation role of design strategies at the beginning of product R&D was emphasized, as was the guiding significance for the R&D of new products. As a result, this study defined design strategies as the activities and practices related to product innovation and design.

3 Methodology

3.1 Research Measurement

The investigation of this study was based on quantitative research and utilized a questionnaire containing two parts. Prior to the collection of data, experienced CEOs in the sector and product development managers were invited to participate in the pretest using a draft of the questionnaire. Afterwards, the questionnaire was adjusted to eliminate semantic differences and conceptual deviations. In the first part, the questionnaire enquired about the innovation strategies for industrial design of the companies surveyed, and the relative importance of those strategies was assessed by a seven-point Likert scale. Through early case studies conducted by Chang and Hsu (2003, 2009), the current study summarized 20 innovation strategies for industrial design. Those strategies included cutting production costs; simplifying manufacturing processes and maintenance; satisfying security requirements, laws, and regulations; improving product quality; refining procedures for design and development; reinforcing the division of labor in the same industry; and developing unique products and product functions. They also included developing special forms and features of products; designing useful human-machine interfaces; enhancing the image of product design of the companies; strengthening technological cooperation; increasing R&D investment; introducing more product types; raising the promotion effectiveness; highlighting social and cultural performance; considering environmental design; developing new targeted markets; heightening the capabilities for collecting and adapting to marketing information; increasing the added value of products; and improving the image and popularity of products.

In the second part, the 15 leadership agendas for achieving strategic agility proposed by Doz and Kosonen were adapted and modified in this study. The agility of small and medium-sized enterprises may be different from those of large companies and transnational enterprises (Xing et al. 2019). The case study of Arbussa et al. (2016) found that overcoming limitations is the extra capability of small and medium-sized enterprises acquired during business operations. To have a further understanding of whether small and medium-sized enterprises have differentiated features, the current study adopted this capability of overcoming limitations to form a measurement scale for strategic agility. A seven-point Likert scale was employed for the proposed measurement scale.

3.2 Research Samples

This study was based on small and medium-sized manufacturing companies in the southeast coastal cities of China (Zhejiang, Fujian, and Guangdong). All of the investigated

Table 1. Sample Description

Descriptive features	Frequency	%		Frequency	%
Position					
Manager	59	37.3	Business	25	15.8
Department manager	55	34.8	Others	19	12.1
Type					
Consumer goods	34	21.5	Mechanical manufacturing	48	30.4
Electronics and appliances	30	19	Others	36	22.8
Furniture decorations	10	6.3			
Scale					
10–50	34	21.5	300–500	24	15.2
50–300	54	34.2	More than 500	46	29.1

companies were excellent manufacturers in the manufacturing of China. A total of 500 questionnaires were distributed from October 2022 to December 2022, and 300 questionnaires were collected. Upon quality screening and the removal of the questionnaires with incomplete answers, incorrect answers, and those coming from the same IP addresses, the number of valid questionnaires obtained reached 158, making up to 31.6% of the total polls (Table 1).

4 Results and Analysis

4.1 Features and Naming of Strategic Agility Groups

Through principal component analysis, a dimension reduction was conducted in this study for 18 specific leadership action agendas of strategic agility. Specifically, the factor composition was simplified and those factor clusters were interpreted. The results of the Bartlett sphericity test showed there was no relation among variables ($X^2 = 898.923$, df = 153, p < 0.001) while the KMO value was 0.809. Thus, the information was suitable for factor analysis (see Table 2).

Table 2. Results of the Bartlett Sphericity Test

KMO and Bartlett test		
Kaiser-Meyer-Olkin		.809
Bartlett's sphericity test	Approximate chi-square	898.923
	df	1953
	Statistical significance	.000

Five factors among the 18 strategic variables were extracted with the cumulative percentage of the total variance equal to 61.2%, indicating those factors could represent the original 18 variables. In order to simplify the factor structures and expound the four factors, Varimax rotation was selected for the explanation of these four factors (Lin 1992), and the eigenvalues of these four factors exceeded 1 (Robert & Wortzel 1979). Table 3 presents the results of the principal component analysis of strategic agility.

The observation of the structures of the variables shown in Table 3 revealed that the first factor involved five questions, with the content mainly related to the business models and practices of the companies. Thus, it was referred to as the factor of the innovation and management of business models. The second factor involved three questions mainly comprised of the responding methods when faced with changes. Thus, it was referred to as the factor of perceptual changes and teamwork. The third factor consisted of four

Table 3. Factor analysis of strategic agility (principal component analysis)

Rotated component matrix

	Component				
	1	2	3	4	5
SA5. Reframing	.800	.028	−.019	.195	.168
SA2. Experimenting	.707	.280	−.005	.219	−.045
SA9. Aligning	.642	.436	.135	−.035	.004
SA14. Switching	.619	.163	.524	−.231	−.024
SA4. Abstracting	.598	.033	.260	.182	.069
SA18. Economizing	.104	.761	.171	.048	.018
SA1. Anticipating	.393	.547	.001	.170	−.022
SA8. Integrating	.469	.528	−.122	.250	.166
SA11. Decoupling	.165	.014	.778	.145	.008
SA12. Modularizing	−.188	.211	.669	.275	.214
SA7. Revealing	.261	−.290	.529	.498	.163
SA13. Dissociating	.355	.292	.512	−.276	.273
SA6. Dialoguing	.168	.053	.097	.730	.176
SA3. Distancing	.183	.415	.200	.614	−.003
SA17. Leveraging strengths	.078	.189	−.044	.445	.679
SA10. Caring	−.026	−.204	.123	.103	.652
SA15. Grafting	.119	.494	.124	−.067	.569
SA16. Creative solving	.403	.204	.301	−.073	.437
Eigenvalue	5.306	1.895	1.534	1.273	1.008
Percentage of variance (%)	17.66	12.25	12.08	10.1	9.12
Cumulative variance (%)	17.67	29.92	42.0	52.1	61.23

questions related to the flexible use and coordination of resources. Thus, it was referred to as the factor of resource fluidity and flexible organization. The fourth factor contained two questions related to comprehensive opinions and uniform organization decisions. Thus, it was named the factor of collective commitments and rapid decision making. The fifth factor was comprised of four questions mainly related to team building, problem solving, and overcoming limitations; thus, it was referred to as the factor of overcoming limitations and team building.

4.2 Feature and Naming of Strategic Agility Groups

This study introduced cluster analysis based on the five common factors of companies to investigate whether the actual distribution and cognition of manufacturing enterprise organizations would have different factor analysis results and adopted two-stage cluster analysis (Anderberg 1973; Punj & Stewart 1983). First, the scores for the factors of each company were utilized for classification according to the Ward method. In the second stage, four clusters were selected among 158 observation materials, and K-means from non-hierarchical cluster analysis methods were adopted. The purpose was to probe into the features of leadership behaviors in manufacturing companies and their strategic agility. In the end, four new strategic agility groups were obtained.

Among the manufacturing companies surveyed, 27 strategies came from the first group (17.1%), 64 came from the second (40.5%), 31 came from the third (19.6%), and 36 came from the fourth (22.8%). In line with the average score of the strategy groups regarding each factor, the four groups were analyzed and confirmed (with reference to Table 4).

Table 4. Cluster analysis of the observation data

Observed data	Firms	%	Classification of groups
158	27	17.1	Group 1
	64	40.5	Group 2
	31	19.6	Group 3
	36	22.8	Group 4

As shown in Table 5, the differences among strategic agile groups were obvious, demonstrating that the business corporations in every strategy group possessed different features of strategic agility and strategic thinking. The first strategy group ranked first with regard to factors 2 and 4 but ranked third and fourth to factors 1 and 3, respectively. This result represented that the members of the group paid more attention to the insight into external environments, teamwork, and decision-making capabilities, and they tended to explore changes and make agile responses. As a result, the first strategy group was named the agile insight group.

The second strategy group ranked first in terms of factors 3 and 1, ranked second in factors 2 and 4, and ranked last in factor 5. This result demonstrated that the companies in the strategy group boasted outstanding capabilities for resource allocation and had flexible teams. In addition, the companies could make rapid responses to changes in external environments. Accordingly, this strategy group was referred to as the effective resource group.

The third strategy group ranked first concerning factors 1 and 5 but ranked fourth concerning factors 2 and 3. This result showed that the companies in the group emphasized the management capability and risk aversion of businesses and enjoyed explicit and rigorous organization structures, thus ensuring the stability of corporate operations. Therefore, this group was named the innovative management group.

The fourth strategy group ranked second in terms of factor 3 whereas the ranking regarding other factors was low. This result illustrated that the companies in the group underlined the flexible use of resources whereas the responses to corporate management and team decision making were negative. The strength of leadership had no impact on corporate operation, whereas the capabilities of employees were allowed to bring into full play. Thus, this strategy group was referred to as the flexible response group.

Table 5. ANOVA analysis of leadership actions regarding strategic agility

	G1	G2	G3	G4	F	P-value
F1: Innovation and management of business models	−1.206 (4)	0.359 (2)	0.906 (1)	−0.335 (3)	3.788	0.000 *
F2: Perceptual changes and teamwork	0.568 (1)	0.361 (2)	−0.812 (4)	−0.174 (3)	22.622	0.000 *
F3: Resource fluidity and flexible organization	−0.249 (3)	0.496 (1)	−0.895 (4)	−0.004 (2)	17.8	0.000 *
F4: Collective commitments and rapid decision making	0.518 (1)	0.289 (2)	0.266 (3)	−1.194 (4)	38.378	0.000 *
F5: Overcoming limitations and team building	0.336 (2)	−0.356 (4)	0.437 (1)	−0.011 (3)	6.071	0.001 *

* means that the significance was 0.001. The numbers in brackets refer to the rankings in the average value of clusters regarding each factor.

The results of the cluster analysis summarized above indicated that manufacturing enterprises in China boast different agile strategies and features. From the point of view of strategic agility, these manufacturing enterprises could be grouped into four independent strategic agility groups, and such capabilities could enable companies to respond to and survive in complicated and ever-changing business environments.

4.3 Case Study and Analysis

This study discussed the industrial design strategies of the strategic agility groups and learned about strategic approaches regarding product R&D and design through a questionnaire survey on manufacturing companies confronted with uncertain external environments. Moreover, it summarized the features of product R&D regarding different groups based on comparisons.

On the basis of the investigation scale of design strategies regarding product R&D, the scores of those strategies during specific implementation were acquired. Furthermore, by the division of strategic agility groups, the design strategies of manufacturing companies in different groups were inspected. The results are listed in Table 6. As shown in Table 6, different performances of 20 design strategies in different groups could be identified intuitively. The higher the score was, the more attention was paid to the strategy by the companies surveyed, and vice versa.

Table 6 indicates that in the agile insight group, the rankings of the scores for considering environmental design, intensifying the collection of market information and response capabilities, and increasing the added value of products were much higher than those for the other strategic agility groups. Such results demonstrated that the agile insight group conformed to the features of proactive exploration into the changes in external markets and adjustments to corporate strategies.

For the companies in the effective resource group, their performance in designing excellent human-computer interfaces and refining development procedures was better than the performance of the other strategic agility groups. This result represented that the effective resource group paid more attention to improvements in efficiency and product experience.

Compared with the other strategic agility groups, the innovative management group enjoyed advantages in developing new targeted markets, increasing the diversity of products, and strengthening technological cooperation. This result disclosed the special practices of companies in the group regarding strategic management and operation.

For the companies in the flexible response group, the rankings of the scores for improving the brand image of companies, strengthening promotion efficiency, investing more in R&D and design, and developing unique product appearances were much greater than those of the other strategic agility groups. This result indicated that the enterprise organizations in the flexible response group tended to develop their own uniqueness by acquiring novel features of products in order to increase organization competition in the market.

Lastly, according to the total score shown in Table 6, among the 20 design strategies, the practices which gained the most attention from the strategic agility groups were improving product quality, conforming to specifications and standards, improving the brand image of companies, making it easy for manufacturing and maintenance, and cutting the production costs of products. Most of these practices focused on product manufacturing itself, and such results were consistent with the general features of manufacturing. However, less attention was paid to strengthening technological cooperation, emphasizing social and cultural performance, developing unique product appearances, improving the design image of products, and strengthening the division of labor for R&D

Table 6. Scores of the approaches to design strategies in the strategic agile groups

Approaches to design strategies	G1	G2	G3	G4	Total
Improving product quality	184 (1)	389 (2)	201 (1)	152 (5)	926 (1)
Conforming to specifications and standards	181 (3)	390 (1)	195 (5)	155 (2)	921 (2)
Improving the brand image of companies	177 (4)	388 (3)	193 (7)	163 (1)	921 (3)
Making it easy for manufacturing and maintenance	176 (6)	376 (7)	194 (6)	152 (4)	898 (4)
Cutting the production costs of products	175 (7)	373 (9)	196 (4)	152 (3)	896 (5)
Considering environmental design	183 (2)	373 (11)	189 (9)	150 (7)	895 (6)
Developing new targeted markets	172 (12)	380 (4)	198 (3)	143 (15)	893 (7)
Increasing the diversity of products	171 (14)	379 (5)	201 (2)	136 (17)	887 (8)
Designing excellent human-machine interfaces	173 (9)	378 (6)	186 (13)	146 (12)	883 (9)
Strengthening promotion efficiency	166 (17)	373 (10)	189 (8)	151 (6)	879 (10)
Improving development procedures	172 (13)	376 (8)	186 (14)	145 (14)	879 (11)
Investing more in R&D design	173 (10)	369 (13)	185 (16)	149 (8)	876 (12)
Developing unique product functions	170 (15)	369 (12)	187 (10)	148 (9)	874 (13)
Intensifying the collection of market information and response capabilities	177 (5)	367 (14)	181 (17)	145 (13)	870 (14)
Increasing the added value of products	173 (8)	357 (19)	185 (15)	147 (11)	862 (15)
Strengthening the division of labor for R&D in the same industry	172 (11)	362 (17)	186 (11)	130 (20)	850 (16)
Improving the design image of products	169 (16)	366 (15)	179 (18)	135 (18)	849 (17)
Developing unique product appearances	165 (18)	358 (18)	176 (20)	147 (10)	846 (18)
Emphasizing social and cultural performance	162 (20)	363 (16)	178 (19)	140 (16)	843 (19)
Strengthening technological cooperation	163 (19)	350 (20)	186 (12)	132 (19)	831 (20)

[*] The numbers in brackets refer to the ranking concerning the total score of each design strategy in different groups. G1: Agile insight group; G2: Effective resources group; G3: Innovative management group; G4: Flexible responses group.

in the same industry. This result illustrated that manufacturing companies in China still need to invest more in technological and product innovation.

5   Conclusion

Through extensive investigations of small and medium-sized manufacturing companies in coastal China, this study explored the performance of strategic agility in R&D management in the chaotic and volatile VUCA era, and sorts out the differentiated features of products during the implementation of design strategies in different strategic agility groups. The main conclusions are shown below.

1. This study combined the viewpoints of strategic agility and R&D management innovation within two different frameworks and explored the role of strategic agility in small and medium-sized manufacturing companies. Strategic sensitivity, leadership unity, resource fluidity, and overcoming limitations all demonstrated different but excellent properties, which supported the standpoint of enterprises possessing different agility features (Xing et al. 2019; Arbussa et al. 2018). This finding also verified the perspective of dynamic capabilities found in the literature on strategic agility (Doz & Kosonen 2010; Eggers & Kaplan 2013; Helfat & Peteraf 2015).
2. Chinese SME companies have different responses and characteristics when faced with an uncertain external environment. From the perspective of strategic agility, the leadership decision making of manufacturing enterprises in the coastal areas of China can be grouped into five factors: innovation and management of business models; perceptual changes and teamwork; resource fluidity and flexible organization; collective commitments and rapid decision making; and overcoming limitations and team building. Furthermore, small and medium-sized manufacturing companies can be classified into four strategy groups: those with agile insight, effective resources, innovative management, and flexible responses.(see Table 7).
3. When inspecting strategic implementation from a more micro perspective, this study streamlined the practices of different strategic agility groups in product R&D and innovation. Additionally, it discussed the differences in design strategies and summarized the features of different strategy groups. This helped establish the macro and micro connections in strategic management (Eggers & Kaplan 2013), thus providing a further micro-experience for research on the dynamic capabilities of strategic agility.

At the same time, this study is significant to management and R&D innovation. From the perspective of strategies, the implementation of strategies was discussed in actual R&D activities. The viewpoints of design strategies were added, different from the concept of human resource management, of which, the addition of design strategies offered new theoretical concepts for the micro discussion about strategic agility. During the R&D management of teams, the flexible application of strategies and thinking on design perspectives can bring agility to teams and enterprises. Therefore, this study has practical significance. Moreover, this study summarized and streamlined the corresponding design strategies for agility, which could be used as a reference by practitioners.

Table 7. Strategic agility characteristics of small and medium-sized enterprises in China

leadership decision Factos	Innovation & management of business models	Perceptual changes & teamwork	Resource fluidity and flexible organization	Collective commitments & rapid decision making	Overcoming limitations & team building
Strategic agility group		(G1) Agile insight	(G2) Effective resources	(G3) Innovative management	(G4) Flexible responses
Design strategy		Considering environmental design	Designing excellent human-machine interfaces	Developing new targeted markets	Improving the brand image of companies
		Intensifying the collection of market information and response capabilities	Improving development procedures	Increasing the diversity of products	Strengthening promotion efficiency
		Increasing the added value of products		Strengthening technological cooperation	Investing more in R&D design
					Developing unique product appearances

References

Anderberg, M.: Cluster Analysis for Application. Academic Press, New York (1973)

Arbussa, A., Bikfalvi, A., Marquès, P.: Strategic agility-driven business model renewal: the case of an SME. Manage. Decision (2017)

Baron, R.M., Kenny, D.A.: The moderator–mediator variable distinction in social psychological research: conceptual, strategic, and statistical considerations. J. Pers. Soc. Psychol. 51(6), 1173 (1986)

Chang, W., Hsu, Y.: A study on the product design strategy Taiwan home appliance manufacturers adopted after Taiwan joined WTO. Journal of the Asian Design International Conference, University of Tsukuba Institute of Art and Design, Japan, CD title (2003)

Claybaugh, C.C., Ramamurthy, K., Haseman, W.D.: Assimilation of enterprise technology upgrades: a factor-based study. Enterp. Inform. Syst. 11(2), 250–283 (2015)

Cumming, D., Filatotchev, I., Reinecke, J., Wood, G.: New investor categories, agility and HRM: the case of Sovereign Wealth Funds. Hum. Resour. Manag. Rev. 30(1), 100694 (2020)

Doz, Y., Kosonen, M.: Embedding strategic agility: a leadership agenda for accelerating business model renewal. Long Range Plan. 43(2–3), 370–382 (2010)

Doz, Y., Kosonen, M.: The dynamics of strategic agility: nokia's rollercoaster experience. Calif. Manage. Rev. 50(3), 95–118 (2008)

Doz, Y.: Fostering strategic agility: how individual executives and human resource practices contribute. Hum. Resour. Manag. Rev. **30**(1), 100693 (2020)

Eggers, J.P., Kaplan, S.: Cognition and capabilities: a multi-level perspective. Acad. Manag. Ann. **7**(1), 295–340 (2013)

Eisenhardt, K.M.: Top management teams and the performance of entrepreneurial firms. Small Bus. Econ. **40**(4), 805–816 (2013). https://doi.org/10.1007/s11187-013-9473-0

e Cunha, M.P., et al.: Strategic agility through improvisational capabilities: implications for a paradox-sensitive HRM. Hum. Resource Manage. Rev. **30**(1), 100695 (2020)

Fourné, S.P., Jansen, J.J., Mom, T.J.: Strategic agility in MNEs: managing tensions to capture opportunities across emerging and established markets. Calif. Manage. Rev. **56**(3), 13–28 (2014)

Hauser, J.R., Urban, G.L., Weinberg, B.D.: How consumers allocate their time when searching for information. J. Mark. Res. **30**(4), 452–466 (1993)

Helfat, C.E., Peteraf, M.A.: Managerial cognitive capabilities and the microfoundations of dynamic capabilities. Strateg. Manag. J. **36**(6), 831–850 (2015)

Heij, C.V., Volberda, H.W., Van den Bosch, F.A., Hollen, R.M.: How to leverage the impact of R&D on product innovation? The moderating effect of management innovation. R&D Manage. **50**(2), 277–294 (2020)

Hofstede, G.: Culture's Consequences: Comparing Values, Behaviors, Institutions, and Organizations Across Nations. Sage, Thousand Oaks, CA (2003)

Hsu, C.H., Chang, S.H., Lin, R.: A design strategy for turning local culture into global market products. Int. J. Affect. Eng. **12**(2), 275–283 (2013)

Hsu, Y.: Exploring design innovation and performance: the roles of issue related to design strategy. J. Eng. Des. **20**(6), 555–569 (2009)

Jamrog, J., Vickers, M., Bear, D.: Building and sustaining a culture that supports innovation. People Strat. **29**(3), 9 (2006)

Jennings, P.L., Beaver, G.: The performance and competitive advantage of small firms: a management perspective. Int. Small Bus. J. **15**(2), 63–75 (1997)

Khan, Z., Soundararajan, V., Shoham, A.: Global post-merger agility, transactive memory systems and human resource management practices. Hum. Resour. Manag. Rev. **30**(1), 100697 (2020)

Lau, C., Busenitz, L.: growth intentions of entrepreneurs in a transitional economy: the People's Republic of China. Entrep. Theory Pract. **26**, 5–20 (2001)

Lin, C.: Statistics: psychology and education. Donhwa Book Press, Taipei (1992)

Lockett, M.: Culture and the problems of Chinese management. Organ. Stud. **9**(4), 475–496 (1988)

Luiz, O.R., de Souza, F.B., Luiz, J.V.R., Jugend, D., Salgado, M.H., da Silva, S.L.: Impact of critical chain project management and product portfolio management on new product development performance. .J. Bus. Indust. Market. **34**(8), 1692–1705. (2019)

McCann, J.: Organizational effectiveness: changing concepts for changing environments. People Strat. **27**(1), 42 (2004)

Oswald, L.R.: Doing Semiotics: A Research Guide for Marketers at the Edge of Culture. Oxford University Press (2020). https://doi.org/10.1093/oso/9780198822028.001.0001

Parnell, J.A., Lester, D.L., Long, Z., Köseoglu, M.A.: How environmental uncertainty affects the link between business strategy and performance in SMEs: evidence from China, Turkey, and the USA. Manage. Decision **50**(4), 546–568 (2012)

Parnell, J.A., Long, Z., Lester, D.: Competitive strategy, capabilities and uncertainty in small and medium sized enterprises (SMEs) in China and the United States. Manag. Decis. **53**(2), 402–431 (2015)

Punj, G., Stewart, D.: Cluster analysis in marketing research: review and suggestions for application. J. Mark. Res. **20**, 134–148 (1983)

Robert, M.L., Wortzel, L.H.: New life style determinants of women's food shopping behaviour. J. Mark. **43**(3), 28–29 (1979)

Sherehiy, B., Karwowski, W., Layer, J.K.: A review of enterprise agility: concepts, frameworks, and attributes. Int. J. Ind. Ergon. **37**(5), 445–460 (2007)

Shi, Y., et al.: A strategy for architecture design of crystalline perovskite light-emitting diodes with high performance. Adv. Mater. **30**(25), 1800251 (2018)

Tang, Z., Hull, C.: An investigation of entrepreneurial orientation, perceived environmental hostility, and strategy application among Chinese SMEs. J. Small Bus. Manage. **50**(1), 132–158 (2012)

Tsang, E..: In search of legitimacy: the private entrepreneur in China. Entrep. Theory Pract. **21**, 21–30 (1996)

Walsh, V., et al.: Winning by Design: Technology, Product Design, and International Competitiveness. Blackwell Business Publishing, Oxford (1992)

Weber, Y., Tarba, S.Y.: Strategic agility: a state of the art introduction to the special section on strategic agility. Calif. Manage. Rev. **56**(3), 5–12 (2014)

Xing, Y., Liu, Y., Boojihawon, D.K., Tarba, S.: Entrepreneurial team and strategic agility: a conceptual framework and research agenda. Hum. Resour. Manag. Rev. **30**(1), 1–10 (2020)

Zhang, M., Mohnen, P.: Innovation and survival of new firms in Chinese manufacturing, 2000–2006 (2013)

Zhang, M., Mohnen, P.: R&D, innovation and firm survival in Chinese manufacturing, 2000–2006. Eurasian Bus. Rev. **12**(1), 59–95 (2022)

Research on Future Digital Memorial Model Based on Interaction Ritual Chain Theory: A Case Study of the Design Scheme of "Remember Me"

Ping Li[1] , Jing Li[1] , Ruoyan Ji[2], and Lie Zhang[1]([⊠])

[1] Tsinghua University, Beijing 100084, China
{lip20,j-122}@mails.tsinghua.edu.cn, zhlie@tsinghua.edu.cn
[2] Century College, Beijing University of Posts and Telecommunications, Beijing 102101, China

Abstract. Rituals are indispensable activities in the history of human development to express values and connotations and are characterized by repeatability and regularity. Funeral rituals are not only a way to cherish the memory of the loved ones we lost, but also a channel for living relatives to maintain connections and deepen emotional bonds. The research, based on Collins' interaction ritual chain theory and combined with the design scheme of "remember me", aims to propose approaches and factors for interactive memorial rituals to exert the function of emotional connection and bereavement grief relief under the background of deepening digitization. It also studies the design of virtual service products for future digital memorial modes and the funeral industry amidst the normalization of COVID-19, cultural globalization, metaverse, and other technological developments.

Keywords: Interaction Ritual Chain · Future Design · Virtual Reality · Culture · Funeral Ritual

1 Introduction

As a typical research problem in anthropology, rituals are indispensable cultural activities for human beings to express values and connotations in the history of development. For individuals in whatever culture, death is an unbreakable physical limitation, but funeral rituals are changeable public events that connect not only the relatives of the dead and the community but also the two worlds of the dead and the living [1]. During the prevail of the COVID-19 pandemic, governments around the world introduced policies to restrict memorial rituals, not only breaking the memorial ritual customs of various cultures but also posing challenges to the traditional funeral industry. Although online virtual memorial rituals via teleconferencing or social platforms have been used as an alternative during the COVID-19 pandemic, it remains to be discussed whether they can take over traditional rituals in functions such as providing psychological role transformation, social role remodeling, and easing bereavement grief for relatives. This research,

P.-L. P. Rau (Ed.): HCII 2023, LNCS 14022, pp. 236–253, 2023.
https://doi.org/10.1007/978-3-031-35936-1_17

based on Collins' interaction ritual chain theory and combined with the design scheme of "remember me", aims to propose approaches and factors for interactive memorial rituals to exert the function of emotional connection and bereavement grief relief under the background of deepening digitization. It also studies the design of virtual service products for future digital memorial modes and the funeral industry amidst the normalization of COVID-19, cultural globalization, metaverse, and other technological developments.

1.1 Limitations on Traditional Ritual Culture by the COVID-19 Pandemic

As the most widespread human catastrophe after SARS, the COVID-19 pandemic has lasted for three years since 2019 and will continue to impact human production and life for a long time to come. COVID-19 is primarily airborne between people, thus governments of various countries introduced policies to avoid crowds and contact, which reduced human-to-human transmission of the virus to some extent. By maintaining physical distance between people according to their funeral customs, these policies are aimed to minimize human interaction to reduce the transmission of the disease [2]. Figure 1 shows the changes in policies on memorial rituals in some countries.

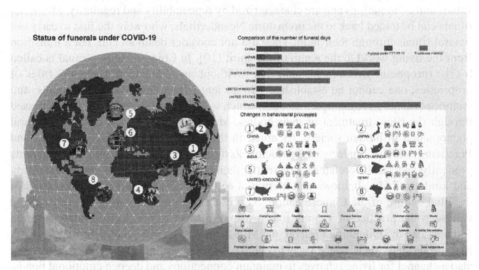

Fig. 1. Comparative analysis of policies on the number of days and forms of rituals since the pandemic in some countries. Source: Own elaboration. The authors

Here are some representative policies: *The COVID-19 INTERIM GUIDANCE FOR THE MANAGEMENT OF THE DEAD IN HUMANITARIAN SETTINGS* [3] jointly released by the IFRC, ICRC, and WHO in 2020 stated that "Support communities to modify traditional funeral practices to facilitate physical distancing and advise family members to refrain from kissing or touching the deceased." *The Guidelines on Disposal of Bodies of Pneumonia Patients Infected with COVID-19 (Trial)* [4] promulgated in 2020 by the National Health Commission of the People's Republic of China required that no final tributes and other forms of funeral activities should be held for the dead. In

November 2020, the NFDA of the United States proposed to hold small family funeral services online [5]. The Japanese government forbade visitations to dying COVID-19 patients [6]. As reported by NPR, relatives were not allowed to participate in the washing and burial rituals of the dead in Iraq; the duration of burial was restricted to 12 h in the Philippines [7]. Australia, the UK, the US, and Brazil required that mourners of a funeral should be limited to a maximum of 10 persons [8]; the number of mourners was also limited to 20 in India and they were not allowed to contact the body [9].

It can be seen that the outbreak of COVID-19 not only greatly affects people's living and production mode, but also directly or indirectly impacts human cultural activities and ways of cultural inheritance, emotional expression, and communication. The pandemic fundamentally changed funeral practices around the world from the very beginning [10]. Policy restrictions around the world disrupted the funeral industry with diverse cultural backgrounds on the one hand, and also brought about new challenges and opportunities for the development of funeral services in the future on the other hand.

1.2   Shared Significance of Funeral Rituals in Different Cultures

Rituals are indispensable activities in the history of human development to express values and connotations and are characterized by repeatability and regularity. Memorial rituals can be traced back to the prehistoric Neanderthals, who were the first to carry out funeral rituals through their faith. They did not consider death an end, but a transition from the living world to the realm of the spirit [10]. In Chinese culture, ritual is called li (礼) (proprieties). Confucius said that "Without an acquaintance with the rules of proprieties, one cannot be established." In ancient China, there were five rituals, and memorial rituals were inauspicious ones, which were to express respect for the deceased through the ritual treatment of their bodies. Memorial rituals are a common cultural phenomenon in human society. As noted in the chapter of "Xue Er" (Studying and Practicing) of The Analects of Confucius, Zeng Zi said, "Treat the funeral of parents prudently and recall forefathers reverently, then the people will resume the simplicity and kindness." [11] It shows that memorial action is also an important expression of the filial culture of the Chinese nation. At present, people celebrating Chinese culture still keep the practice of visiting tombs to pay respect to the dead in major reunion festivals like the Qingming Festival, the Mid-Autumn Festival, and the Spring Festival. Memorial rituals are not only a way to cherish the memory of the loved ones we lost, but also a channel for living relatives to maintain connections and deepen emotional bonds. Many Chinese minority cultures view memorial rituals as an important form of cultural inheritance, and they carry out various folk activities at important memorial days. The UN Intangible Cultural Heritage of Humanity list includes several cultural activities related to memorial rituals. For example, China's Grand song of the Dong ethnic group [12] was incorporated into the list in 2009, the mournful songs of which are sung at funerals; Gule Wamkulu [13], originating from Malawi, Mozambique, and Zambia, and listed as UN Intangible Cultural Heritage in 2008, is also to perform a gathering ritual by dressing up, singing, and dancing. Memorial rituals are ethnic and cultural behavior that can be found worldwide. They foster a scene where the bereaved people can switch roles in a particular time and space and relieve grief and alleviate traumatic stress disorder. Rituals and traditions about death and mourning exist in almost every society. They may vary by society or culture, but they have lasted for thousands of years [14]. Rituals provide vehicles for the expression and containment of strong emotions, and their repetition and regularity relieve anxiety and malaise [15]. Some believe that rituals, with their ability to provide structure and order, have a healing effect in times of chaos and disorder. People tend to visit tombs of deceased relatives or great people to pay respect in the case of difficulties in life or big anniversaries. For example, the Qingming festival has been on record for as long as 2,500 years since ancient China. During the festival, people would pay tribute to ancestors, get together, or go hiking. The underlying emotion and original purpose of the Qingming Festival is to commemorate the deceased ancestors. Standing before the tombs of our deceased ancestors, we tend to see their lives before us, making us think about the meaning of life [16].

Almost every nation in the world has its own unique memorial rituals. They serve as a cultural symbol representing the nation and constructing another world for the dead with national culture. These memorial rituals share formalized and materialized spiritual sustenance of human beings under the multicultural background. Memorial rituals are to recognize the life value of the dead in society, allow the co-existence of life and death, and redefine the meaning of life. It helps living relatives adjust their mental state and relieve emotional trauma [10].

1.3 Evolutionary Trend of Future-oriented Digital Memorial Services

Almost every large-scale public health event in history has triggered social and cultural changes. During 1347–1351, the Black Death swept through Europe, killing at least a third of the population of the continent. After that catastrophe, people began to review their beliefs and ways of life, the church declined in power gradually, and classical culture was restored and developed into a new cultural wave, leading to the Italian Renaissance [17]. Although the impact of COVID-19 will be gradually faded, the model of online working, learning, and living brought about by the pandemic will be preserved. People will increasingly accept their virtual identities, just as the birth of the modern public health system followed the Black Death. Restrictions for public health (physical distancing) forced families to give up traditional memorial rituals and turn to virtual ones [18]. In the digital age, communication technologies can make up for the geographical distance between people, and the place of mourning can be shifted from physical space to cyberspace that needs not a physical venue and is not rigidly stratified, providing future digital mourning with more technical support and creative designs. Research shows that digital memorials are preferred if the death involves suicide or the loss of a child [19]. In that way, bereaved people can access a memorial website at any time and contact people with similar experiences [20]. On-site funeral services may be restored later, but virtual funerals will no doubt continue to exist, because they have unexpected advantages, such as being able to reach more people and reducing the anxiety of being in close physical contact with others [21]. Many people who have lost loved ones are changing the traditional funeral customs with a virtual approach, asking for more ways of meaningful experiences in the grieving process [22]. Although virtual funerals cannot replace some elements of on-site funerals, such as physical contact, they can still be a meaningful experience, providing a sense of social connection to the grieving person [23]. Memorial websites offer a socially acceptable channel for people to keep in constant communication with the dead [24]. New technology-based healing methods for bereaved relatives are also being tried. For example, virtual reality exposure therapy (VRET) can be used to combat panic and pain [25]; the VR project "I met you" built a virtual scene of a familiar environment for the mother who lost her daughter to let her talk with the "daughter" in the virtual environment, which, to some extent, consoles the bereavement pain [26].

Over time, the impact of COVID-19 on human society will diminish, but the form of virtual rituals, virtual classes, and virtual gatherings will remain. With this pandemic, people are more willing to accept the lifestyle of online working and online communication and have a stronger sense of identity in virtual environments and virtual identity. In a society with increasingly diverse belief systems and developing information technology, the future development direction of digital memorial services is to provide more suitable caring models for people who lost loved ones to heal their grief.

2 Theoretical Framework

This theoretical research on future digital memorial models is based on the Interaction Ritual Chains theory of Randall Collins [27], an American sociologist, and focuses on the presentation pattern of interaction ritual chain and the operation mechanism of long-lasting emotional connection in memorial rituals. Memorial rituals not only provide basic ritual healing effects but also enable relatives to establish closer kinship and emotional ties. Therefore, this research, based on the design project of "remember me" and the Interaction Ritual Chains theory, aims to explore the ways of formation of emotional bonds and long-term maintenance of family emotion in future remote interpersonal interactions. Besides, digital commemoration has already been widely used on social platforms, indicating a clear need for bereaved people to release their grief on digital platforms [28]. However, the study of digital technology intervention's effect in relieving bereavement grief and healing pains and funeral services in conformity with future digital development is still in its preliminary stage, and there are few service design frameworks for reference.

2.1 Interaction Ritual Chains Theory and Memorial Rituals

The theory of interaction ritual chains integrates micro and macro social theories and studies the face-to-face interaction of a small group of people in an on-site ritual. Although Collins doubted the effect of interaction rituals launched online or remotely, he still put forward that, if electronic media in the future can be designed to stimulate human physiological properties, specially enhance the communication between present participants and remote participants, and establish a high level of focus of attention and emotional bond between present participants and remote participants, those interaction rituals can still work as they are expected [27]. Collins stressed that "A theory of interaction ritual (IR) and interaction ritual chains is above all a theory of situations. It is a theory of momentary encounters among human bodies charged up with emotions and consciousness because they have gone through chains of previous encounters [27]." "There are four prerequisite factors for interaction rituals to play a role:

1. Two or more people are physically assembled in the same place, so that they affect each other by their bodily presence, whether it is in the foreground of their conscious attention or not.
2. There are boundaries to outsiders so that participants have a sense of who is taking part and who is excluded.
3. People focus their attention upon a common object or activity, and by communicating this focus to each other become mutually aware of each other's focus of attention.
4. They share a common mood or emotional experience [27]."

The first prerequisite factor appears in the course of memorial rituals. Relatives and friends of the deceased gather for the memorial ritual, so that those who may have never met each other before are brought together by presenting at the ritual. As to the second factor, "outsiders" are no doubt easy to be excluded. Whatever the cultural context, participants gathering for funerals or memorial rituals are solemnly dressed up and carry gifts for close relatives of the deceased (flowers in the West, cash or wreaths in most parts of China). The third and fourth factors are the most important, that is, to share a common emotional experience with relatives. "As the persons become more tightly focused on their common activity, more aware of what each other is doing and feeling, and more aware of each other's awareness, they experience their shared emotion more intensely, as it comes to dominate their awareness [27]." During a funeral or memorial ritual, the shared memory and sadness of participating relatives and friends for the loss of the dead can be amplified and interacted through their communication and exchanges. With all these prerequisite factors present, an interaction ritual will come into play and the memorial ritual will build and strengthen the emotional bond between the participants.

The close connection between the factors of interaction rituals would lead to the following four results, as shown in Fig. 2.

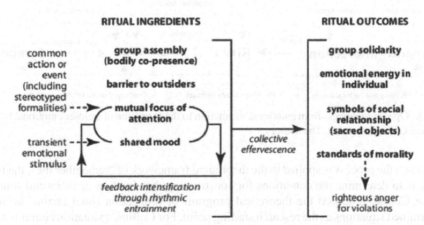

Fig. 2. Interaction ritual. Source: Collins R, Interaction Ritual Chains, Princeton: Princeton University Press, 2004. pp. 48

"There are four main outcomes of interaction rituals:

1. group solidarity, a feeling of membership;
2. emotional energy(EE)in the individual: a feeling of confidence, elation, strength, enthusiasm, and initiative in taking action;
3. symbols that represent the group: emblems or other representations (visual icons, words, gestures) that members feel are associated with themselves collectively; these are Durkheim's "sacred objects." Persons pumped up with feelings of group solidarity treat symbols with great respect and defend them against the disrespect of outsiders, and even more, of renegade insiders.
4. feelings of morality: the sense of rightness in adhering to the group, respecting its symbols, and defending both against transgressors. Along with this goes the sense of moral evil or impropriety in violating the group's solidarity and its symbolic representations [27]."

To sum up, the results of Collins' interaction rituals show that, first of all, they make participating individuals form a sense of participation; next, they keep participants in high spirits and enthusiastic; then, it forms unique symbols or representations within the group that allow individuals to integrate themselves into the group; last, they offer the feelings of morality, which makes participating individuals form a sense of collective honor and maintain the group. Individuals involve in memorial rituals out of their memory of the deceased and the influence of the situation gradually turns individual feelings into collective emotions. This regular or rhythmic form of interaction is preserved to contribute to the ritual state, and then form an emotional bond of shared remembrance for deceased relatives. Eventually, the time, situation, and emotion would be combined into a symbol, and individuals would spontaneously gather into groups for emotional interaction on subsequent anniversaries, so as to form a closer emotional bond. The operation process is shown in Fig. 3.

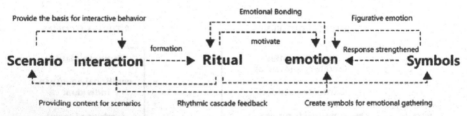

Fig. 3. Operation process from emotional interaction to the formation of a closer emotional bond. Source: Own elaboration. The authors

When the process is applied to the theoretical framework of "remember me", the first thing is to determine the conditions for constructing the situation of memorial rituals. When Collins proposed the theoretical program of interaction ritual chains, he first determined situations as the research starting point. For Collins, a situation contains a lot of meaning, and the individuals involved can also be a situation. But in general, a situation of a memorial ritual can be understood as the people gathering for the deceased and the atmosphere of the ritual, which is the basis for the interaction ritual chain to play a role.

That is, the project "remember me" needs to provide a separate space that blocks out other groups. The next comes interaction. The participants share the same strong emotions of sadness and memory, which would trigger fluctuations of collective emotion according to the content and process of traditional rituals. The interaction is not only between individuals but also includes the correlation and interaction between people and space, and people and relics. At this moment, the emotional response would automatically form a group emotional aggregation and obviously exclude other emotions. Then, with the aggregation of emotions, the memorial ritual forms an emblem with collective emotion, something like an emotional imprint with familial characteristics (memorial tablets for the dead in Chinese culture, and tombstones in Western culture), which would motivate the group to repeat the ritual regularly over a long period of time to cement the emotional bond.

2.2 Bereavement Grief and Ritual Healing

The earliest study of grief can be traced back to Freud's concept of "Trauerarbeit" [29], or grief work, while Bowlby's attachment theory [30] is the most famous study of bereavement. Bowlby proposed that attachment behavior is the most fundamental cause of grief, so when a person was separated from an attachment object due to death, grief occurs. Studies by psychologists and sociologists reveal that grief is a multi-dimensional experience of loss formed based on the cultural context of human beings [31]. By studying bereavement grief, researchers found that a ritual for the dead is usually a one-time event, but grief is a process that lasts for a long time [15]. That is, a funeral ritual is a one-time event, but grief is a long-time process. Therefore, the psychological healing of a bereaved family member cannot be accomplished by one single memorial ritual. The future digital care discussed in this research mainly focuses on potential long-term healing for bereavement grief under a certain cultural background and religious belief. Due to cultural differences, after a person died, relatives' behavior and what other people expect them to do significantly vary [32]. Although the eastern and western cultures have different interpretations of death, both recognize that mourning rituals are a means of releasing grieved emotions after the death of a loved one, as well as an approach for group communication to resolve grief. Bronna D. Romanoff, a professor of psychology, combined memorial rituals and grief resolution from the perspective of culture and psychological therapy and summarized the process of emotional transformation, transition, and connection in bereavement: "transformation, which occurs within the intrapsychic domain; transition, which occurs within the psychosocial domain; and connection, which occurs in the communal context and is sustained by both psychic life and social status [15]", as shown in Fig. 4.

Via social transformation through rituals, individuals would be separated from the previous social structure and try to accept a new identity in various states of dissociation before they rejoin the group after accepting the new identity. Conclusion: In summary, the project "remember me" mainly incorporates the following design elements.

1. **Situation:** It is a situational space for family relatives to gather as a group. The situation here has two forms. One is the real space at a physical venue where people can have face-to-face emotional exchange and grief healing. The other is the virtual

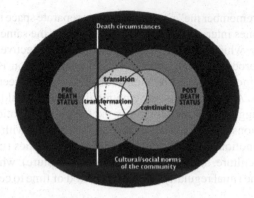

Fig. 4. The grieving process. Source: Romanoff, B. RITUALS AND THE GRIEVING PROCESS. Death Studies, 22(8), pp. 703. (1998).

space that could, when Collins' conditions are met, simulate the physical properties of interpersonal communication and establish a high level of emotional connection model between present and remote relatives. The virtual and physical spaces work together to create a situation for the bereaved to transform their psychological and social relationships.

2. **Interaction:** Communication and interaction can be carried out between relatives and between relatives and the deceased in the situation provided; it should conform with the flow of the interaction ritual and factors for a successful emotional connection as proposed by Collins.
3. **Ritual:** There are ritual patterns with fixed time cycles and ritual customs with family as a group to form a strong emotional bond and a unique emotional symbol between relatives.

3 Design Practice

This practice, based on the theoretical framework, starting from the demand, and relying on immersive technologies such as metaverse, is to design a multimedia interactive experience for the exhibition space of Yaoshan Talin Service Center in Guangxi, China.

3.1 Demand Survey

Questionnaire: An online questionnaire survey was conducted on the restrictions on memorial rituals in various parts of China imposed in response to the COVID-19 pandemic and people's degree of acceptance of digital memorial rituals. The questionnaire survey was hosted by wjx.cn, a questionnaire platform, and distributed by people involved in the design via their WeChat Moments. By December 2022, about 160 responses were received. The respondents are mainly aged from 25 to 50, and those who use mobile phones frequently, have a high acceptance of new technology products and do not strongly reject the topic of mourning were selected as the participants. The questionnaire content and data collected are shown in Fig. 5.

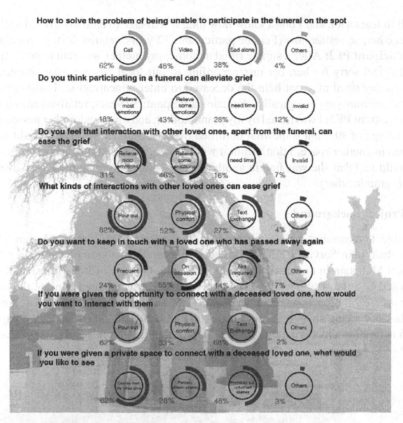

Fig. 5. Results of the online questionnaire survey on the acceptance degree of digital memorial rituals. Source: Own elaboration. The authors

The questionnaire survey found that: first, most of the participants would choose to participate in memorial rituals or family memorial activities through video calls or voice calls if they were unable to be present because most people believe that these rituals can ease their bereavement grief. Then, in terms of grief healing, participants believe that verbal or physical interactions between relatives could greatly ease bereavement grief. Moreover, a large proportion of participants believe that they are not averse to communicating with their dead relatives in a certain way, in a life scene they are both familiar with or a scene with lingering regrets, even a small talk or just sitting in silence can be a great way to ease their grief.

Offline interviews: After further sorting the data of questionnaire respondents, a number of participants who had recently lost a close relative were selected for interview. The interviews took place between March 2022 and December 2022, in the form of telephone calls and face-to-face talks.

1. **Participant PF1:** Due to the prevention and control measures for the COVID-19 pandemic and the different quarantine policies of different cities, I was not able to attend my grandmother's memorial ritual. And even now, three months later, I am

still in tears a lot, and I don't know how long it will take to ease my grief. I still want to see her, no matter how (Female participant; 32 years; relative lost: grandmother).

2. **Participant PF2:** After a simple ritual at home, my mother was sent to be cremated. I still feel sorry for her, because according to our local customs, the absence of a seven-day ritual may not help the deceased to enter reincarnation. It also gives me great pressure psychologically. (Female participant; 50 years; relative lost: mother).

3. **Participant PF3:** I was raised by my grandmother, and my grandmother passed away, at the age of 90. I am somewhat unruffled by her death. However, if I could see her again in another space, I don't think I would reject it. It would be a comfort to me if I could feel that she was fine in another place. (Male participant; 37 years; relative lost: grandmother).

3.2 Project Background

The project "remember me" originated from the space and multimedia design scheme of Yaoshan Talin Service Center. Located on the northwest side of the main peak of Yaoshan Mountain in the eastern suburbs of Guilin, Guangxi, China, Yaoshan Talin is composed of a forest of pagodas, a service center, and scenic areas. Inside the service center is an exhibition and experience space 12.58 m high and 14 m wide. The forest of pagodas, occupying an area of more than 400 mu, contains 36,564 Dadetong pagodas, each 5 m high, as a modern memorial product for families to offer and pass on blessings (Fig. 6).

Fig. 6. Rendering of Yaoshan Talin Service Center, Guangxi, China. Source: Guangxi Yaoshan Talin Ecological Garden Construction Co.

Yaoshan Talin Service Center is positioned to provide spiritual healing experience for bereaved families with emerging technologies, display and promote Chinese traditional family culture, and promote and sell funeral products. The Chinese nation values the root of ancestors, the traditional Chinese culture focuses on loyalty and filial piety, and the attitude towards nourishing parents and handling their funerals is one of the criteria to measure one's loyalty and filial piety [33]. Therefore, most parts of southern China still follow the tradition of clan memorial ceremonies.

3.3 Design of Functions and Structure

The product "remember me" combines offline and online approaches. For the online service, a mobile APP provides users with functions such as close relative communication, generation of virtual images, booking offline meeting places, and VR experience of remote ritual participation. The offline service provides immersive spaces with single and multi-person venues, which can be online booked on the APP. The product structure is shown in Fig. 7 and 8:

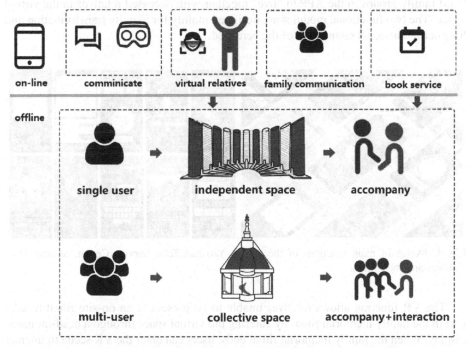

Fig. 7. Structure of the digital memorial products integrating online and offline services of Yaoshan Talin Service Center. Source: Own elaboration. The authors

The mobile app of Yaoshan Talin Service Center has three major functions, as shown in Fig. 8 and Fig. 9. The first function is the generation and use of digital images; the second is the communication between relatives; the third is to customize single or multi-person ritual space services from Yaoshan Talin. Users can upload photos of their deceased relatives to generate their virtual images, then they can make video calls and voice calls with this digital image of their deceased relatives through the APP or meet them in a virtual environment through a head-mounted display. Users can also

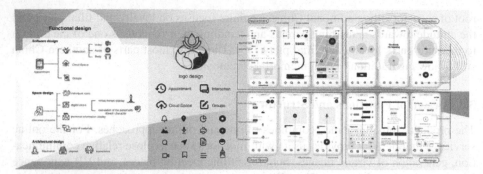

Fig. 8. Function of the digital memorial products integrating online and offline services of Yaoshan Talin Service Center. Source: Own elaboration. The authors

build family groups in the APP to "live" together with deceased relatives in the virtual space. The two functional modules are designed mainly for identity transformation and long-term emotional connection of the bereaved.

Fig. 9. Sketch of main functions of the app of Yaoshan Talin Service Center. Source: Own elaboration. The authors

The VR function allows relatives unable to be present at an on-site ritual to take part in the family memorial ritual by entering the virtual space through a head-mounted display. When the family memorial ritual ends, users can enter the VR scene to interact with the deceased relative virtually. Figures 10, and 11 shows the test scenario of the technology being developed for avatar action binding and face shaping.

The offline multimedia interactive space of Yaoshan Talin Service Center is planned and designed simultaneously with its external architectural structure (Fig. 12).

For the current conceptual design scheme of Yaoshan Talin multimedia interaction and display area, the space planning underlines the creation of atmosphere rather than on highlighting beliefs and religions. The plastic effect in the architectural design is used to create a sense of ritual atmosphere, keeping the main product of Yaoshan Talin in the tower structure. Italian architect Terragni attaches great importance to the atmosphere in architectural design, viewing that atmosphere and relevant references and emotions

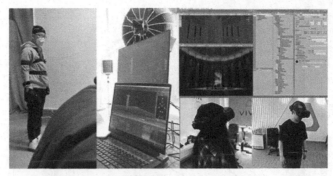

Fig. 10. VR system and action capture development testing. Source: Own elaboration. The authors

Fig. 11. Facial capture testing with cooperating group. Source: AiHuaShen Technology Beijing Co.

have the power to touch the heart [34]. The functional divisions of the overall space are roughly divided as follows: B1 is for product exhibition, F1 is for single-person experience, F2-3 is for communication, and F4 is for multi-person ritual and immersive experience, as shown in Fig. 13.

The first floor consists of separated columnar experience spaces. Users can customize single-person experience space service through the APP, and with the help of an interior LED screen, they can enter the space to have intelligent interaction with the virtual deceased in the APP. The middle area enclosed by the separated columnar spaces assumes the role of the exhibition hall, dynamically displaying the visual images of Talin products. The second and the third floors also adopt the same architectural style, using a columnar structure to create a sense of order, and combined with a transparent arch structure. The top of the atrium is installed with a circular LED screen, displaying images such as the sky, birds, and forests, so that people would feel calm, solemn, and hopeful when they look up. This floor is mainly used for the office area and equipment room; it is also the rest and communication space for relatives to communicate with each other. The fourth floor is a customizable immersive space that can accommodate multiple people to hold rituals.

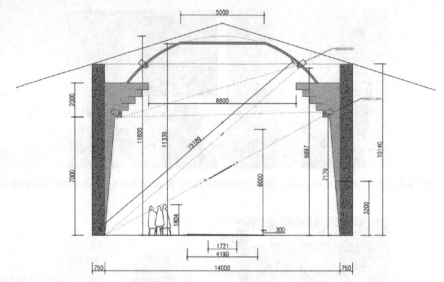

Fig. 12. CAD elevation of multimedia interactive area inside Yaoshan Talin Service Center. Source: Guangxi Yaoshan Talin Ecological Garden Construction Co.

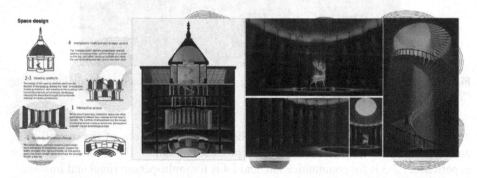

Fig. 13. Space design scheme of Yaoshan Talin Service Center's multimedia interaction and display area. Source: Own elaboration. The authors

4   Conclusion

This research, based on the approaches and factors for Collins' interaction ritual chain theory to play a role in memorial rituals and combined with the design scheme of "remember me", tries to explore the factors for memorial rituals to play the role of emotional connection, as well as ways of relieving bereavement grief under the background of digitalization. It also aims to explore the development direction of funeral products and services in the future from psychological and sociological perspectives. Although it is at the planning and preliminary development stage, the scheme is a bold tentative design for Chinese traditional funeral services. Based on the current design, the project will later be added with a variety of technical elements based on metaverse technology to make the product more compatible with the development direction of the funeral industry in the future. Product usability testing will be conducted when the project is put into operation. The follow-up user research will intensify the study of its active users and form a service blueprint. The function would be extended, for example, by adding the function suggested by questionnaire participants of generating the image of deceased pets.

As a new memorial pattern, the project "remember me" needs to be further studied based on users' feedback to evaluate its function of grief healing and family bonding. Admittedly, not all grief healing processes are the same. The length of grief is related to many factors such as religious beliefs and the cause of death of the relative. The study of both memorial rituals and bereavement grief should be based on relevant nations' cultural backgrounds. Different cultures and religions have different attitudes toward death, and so do people's behaviors and what others expect them to do after a relative died. Although people with different faiths have different expressions of grief, the feeling of grief is similar. The development of new technologies and cultural globalization will surely provide more ways to express traditional culture and promote the formation of diversified but universally recognized new commemorative methods.

Acknowledgment. This paper was funded by Program for Youth Project of Humanities and Social Sciences Sponsored by Ministry of Education in China, Grant 20YJC860018.The support from MOE is gratefully acknowledged.

References

1. Sun, P.: Funeral ritual and emotional expression: western discourse and Chinese experience. Si Xiang Zhan Xian **44**(5), 50–56 (2018)
2. Lotfi, M., Hamblin, M.R., Rezaei, N.: COVID-19: Transmission, prevention, and potential therapeutic opportunities. Clin. Chim. Acta **508**, 254–266 (2020)
3. International Federation of the Red Cross and Red Crescent Societies, International Committee of the Red Cross, World Health Organization. COVID-19 Interim guidance for the management of the dead in humanitarian settings. Geneva, 2020,
4. National Health Commission of the People's Republic of China, The Guidelines on Disposal of Bodies of Pneumonia Patients Infected with COVID-19 (Trial). 2020. http://www.nhc.gov.cn/yzygj/s7659/202002/163c26a24057489dbf64dba359c59a5f.shtml. Accessed 9 Feb 2023
5. National Funeral Directors Association.: Public Gathering Guidance (2020). https://nfda.org/covid-19/visitations-funerals. Accessed 9 Feb 2023
6. Japanese Society for Infection Prevention and Control. A guide to dealing with COVID-19 infections in medical institutions ver.3. Japanese Society for Infection Prevention and Control (2020). http://www.kankyokansen.org/uploads/uploads/files/jsipc/COVID-19_taioguide3.pdf. Accessed 9 Feb 2023
7. Frayer, L., Estrin, D., Arraf, J.: Coronavirus Is Changing the Rituals of Death for Many Religions (2020). https://www.npr.org/sections/goatsandsoda/2020/04/07/828317535/coronavirus-is-changing-the-rituals-of-death-for-many-religions. Accessed 9 Feb 2023
8. Watson, K.: Coronavirus: 'Undocumented explosion' spreads around Brazil (2020). https://www.bbc.com/news/world-latin-america-52307339. Accessed 9 Feb 2023
9. Government of India Ministry of Health & Family Welfare Directorate General of Health Services.: COVID-19: Guidelines on Dead Body Management (2020)

10. Júnior, J.G., Moreira, M.M., Rolim, M.L.: Silent cries, intensify the pain of the life that is ending: the COVID-19 is robbing families of the chance to say a final goodbye. Front. Psych. **11**, 570773 (2020)
11. Confucius, Yang, B., Yang, F.: The Analects of Confucius. pp.5.Changsha: Yue Lu Shu She (2011)
12. UNESCO Intangible Culture Heritage.: Grand song of the Dong ethnic group, https://ich.une sco.org/en/RL/grand-song-of-the-dong-ethnic-group-00202, last accessed 2023/02/09
13. UNESCO Intangible Culture Heritage.: Gule Wamkulu. https://ich.unesco.org/en/RL/gule-wamkulu-00142. Accessed 9 Feb 2023
14. Erbiçer, E.S., Metin, A., Doğan, T.: Grief and mourning in Covid-19 pandemic and delayed business as a new concept. Culture Psychol. (2022)
15. Romanoff, B.: Rituals and the grieving process. Death Stud. **22**(8), 697–711 (1998)
16. Chang, H.: Qingming Festival customs and humanistic spirit. Beijing Dangan **291**(03), 10–13 (2015)
17. Liu, J.: On the Multiple Origins of the New Culture of the European Renaissance. Journal of Northeast Normal University (Social Sciences) (02), 63–72 (1999)
18. Lockwood, M.: Families have options for funerals during pandemic. Superior Telegram (2020). https://www.superiortelegram.com/business/small-business/6459186-Fam ilies-have-options-for-funerals-during-pandemic. Accessed 9 Feb 2023
19. Chapple, A., Ziebland, S.: How the Internet is changing the experience of bereavement by suicide: a qualitative study in the UK. Health (London) **15**(2), 173–187 (2011)
20. Mitchell, L., Stephenson, P., Cadell, S., et al.: Death and grief on-line: virtual memorialization and changing concepts of childhood death and parental bereavement on the Internet. Health Sociol Rev **21**(4), 413–431 (2012)
21. Lowe, J., Rumbold, B., Aoun, S.M.: Memorialisation during COVID-19: Implications for the bereaved, service providers and policy makers. Palliative Care Soc. Pract. **14**, 1–9 (2020)
22. MacNeil, A., Findlay, B., Bimman, R., Hocking, T., Barclay, T., Ho, J.: Exploring the Use of Virtual Funerals during the COVID-19 Pandemic: A Scoping Review. OMEGA - Journal of Death and Dying (2021)
23. Bitusikova, A.: COVID-19 and funeral-by-Zoom. Urbanities-J. Urban Ethnography **10**(4), 51–55 (2020)
24. Walter, T., Hourizi, R., Moncur, W., Pitsillides, S.: Does the internet change how we die and mourn? Overview and analysis. OMEGA – J. Death Dying **64**(4), 275–302(2012)
25. Wechsler, T.F., Kümpers, F., Mühlberger, A.: Inferiority or even superiority of virtual reality exposure therapy in phobias? a systematic review and quantitative meta-analysis on randomized controlled trials specifically comparing the efficacy of virtual reality exposure to gold standard *in vivo* exposure in agoraphobia, specific phobia, and social phobia. Front. Psychol. **10**, 1758 (2019)
26. Pizzoli, S., Monzani, D., Vergani, L., Sanchini, V., Mazzocco, K.: From virtual to real healing: a critical overview of the therapeutic use of virtual reality to cope with mourning. Current Psychol. (New Brunswick, N.J.), 1–8 (2021)
27. Collins, R.: Interaction Ritual Chains, p. 3, 5, 48, 49, 64. Princeton University Press, Princeton (2004)
28. Roberts, P.: 2 people like this': mourning according to format. Bereavement Care **31**(2), 55–61 (2012)
29. Margaret, S., Henk, S.: The dual process model of coping with bereavement: rationale and description. Death Stud. **23**(3), 197–224 (1999)
30. Bowlby, J.: Attachment and Loss. Basic Books, New York (1980)

31. Bonanno, G.: Grief and emotion: comparing the grief work and social functional perspectives. In: Stroebe, M.S., Hansson, R.O., Stroebe, W., Shut, H. (eds.) Handbook of bereavement research: Consequences, Coping and Care, pp. 493–516. American Psychological Association Press, Washington, D.C. (2001)

32. Gire, J.: How death imitates life: cultural influences on conceptions of death and dying. Online Read. Psychol. Culture 6(2) (2014)

33. Chen, W.: Funerary culture of ancient south china minorities. J. Chin. Historic. Stud. (02), 142–151 (1996)

34. Lu, A.: The telling of a spatial allegory: the Danteum as narrative labyrinth. Archit. Res. Q. 14(3), 237–246 (2010)

Government Responses to Digital Workforce Shortages: A Study of the U.S., Germany, Japan, and China

Ziyang Li[✉]

China Academy of Industrial Internet, Beijing 100102, China
lisa_ziyangli@163.com

Abstract. An effective digital state requires a competent, empowered, and motivated workforce. The world is currently experiencing a digital workforce shortage. Policymakers are taking step to equip the workforce for Industry 4.0 and the digital age. In this study, we chose the U.S., China, Germany, and Japan as the top performers in digitalization and investigated their strategies for cultivating a digital workforce in the last three years. We found they all actively produced numerous plans and actions in scaling and upskilling the digital workforce, such as the US's National Strategy for Advanced Manufacturing, Germany's Data Strategy of the Federal German Government, Japan's Vision for a Digital Garden City Nation, and China's Action Outline for Improving Digital Literacy and Skills for All. Their strategies share common features: (1) enhancing digital skills among the populace to broaden the labor pool; (2) developing school education and social training in digital skills; (3) advancing the digital industries and workforce simultaneously; (4) attracting a global digital qualified workforce. Finally, suggestions were made concerning how global countries can increase the digital literacy of their workforce.

Keywords: Digitalization · Workforce shortage · Digital workforce

1 Introduction

In the age of the COVID-19 pandemic, digitalization has refined our living and working conditions, thereby facilitating the reconstruction of global order. For example, online chat and office platforms facilitate remote work. Internet of things (IoT), virtual reality, and artificial intelligence (AI) facilitate the reorganization of industrial production processes to respect safety measures and enable social distancing while additive manufacturing solutions help minimize the input shortage [1]. This novel human-machine paradigm calls for a fusion of new digital/technical competence and soft skills such as decision-making and problem-solving across the entire workforce. Workforce upskilling requires the joint efforts of individuals, organizations (for example, schools, universities, and companies), and governments. Among them, the government is in charge of strategy formulation, policy announcement, and direction guidance, which facilitate digital workforce improvement. An effective digital state requires a competent, empowered,

P.-L. P. Rau (Ed.): HCII 2023, LNCS 14022, pp. 254–267, 2023.
https://doi.org/10.1007/978-3-031-35936-1_18

and motivated workforce [2]. Consequently, centering work around humans can give governments a competitive advantage in the digital realm.

There is a pronounced disparity between countries in terms of digital development. United Nations in its Digital Economy Report 2021 illustrated that only 20% of people in the least developed countries of the digital economy use the Internet with low download speeds and high expense while those in the U.S. and China, with half the world's hyperscale data centers, 70% of the world's top AI researchers and some of the highest rates of 5G adoption in the world, performed best.[3]. An evaluation of digital economy development worldwide discovered that the United States, China, Germany, and Japan were the top four, leading the development of global digitalization. Thus, we chose the U.S., China, Germany, and Japan (covering North America, Asia, and Europe, the most developed digital economy regions), which are the top performers in digitalization for this study and investigated their strategies and efforts in cultivating the digital workforce. By reviewing the main digital workforce strategies of these four countries in the last three years, particularly during the COVID-19 pandemic, we can summarize their experience in scaling and upskilling the digital workforce, and provide suggestions for other countries and regions across the globe.

2 Literature Review

2.1 Digitalization and Industry 4.0

Digitalization is characterized by the integration of digital technologies into all aspects of our social life [4, 5]. For instance, phone applications and social media have changed how we interact, socialize, work, shop, and present ourselves; the industrial internet of things (IIoT) and industrial robots have increased operational efficiency and shifted the industrial paradigm. Digitalization is intrinsically linked to digital technologies, including mobile phones, social media, robotics, IoT, and online games. Digital technologies convert the information into digital (i.e., computer-readable) format, changing and re-building the world we live in. Some studies interpreted digitalization with a social-oriented focus. Musik and Bogner (2019) summarized three approaches to interpreting the relationship between digitalization and society: (1) social constructivism, (2) co-production, and (3) post-humanism, which were interconnected and interacted [5]. The social constructivism approach conceptualized digitalization as a product of society (for example, societal activities and negotiations [6]). The co-production approach focused on the alignment of digitalization and society and argued that digitalization is both social and technical [7]. The post-humanism approach perceived digitalization as a social actor with its own identity, such as an agency of non-human entities [8]. Moreover, some consulting companies and institutions tend to interpret digitalization with a business-oriented focus. Gartner defines digitalization as "the use of digital technologies to change a business model and provide new revenue and value-producing opportunities" [9]. Deloitte refers to digitalization as the adoption of digital technologies to transform services or businesses. This is achieved by replacing manual processes/outdated digital technologies with digital ones/upgraded digital technologies [10]. Forbes highlighted that all types of enterprises (for example, small businesses, large corporations, non-profits, and government agencies) are undergoing digital transformation and transforming digitalization into new processes, activities, and transactions [11]. Regardless of the definition of digitalization, it has become an integral part of our lives and work.

The fourth industrial revolution (Industry 4.0) describes the increasing digitalization of the entire value chain and the resulting interconnection of people, machines, and systems [12, 13], which is also considered equivalent to digitalization [14]. Industry 4.0 gathers attention from politicians and business leaders. The German government labeled the challenges and opportunities posed by the digitalization of manufacturing systems "Industry 4.0" [14]. This inspired initiatives and actions of other countries such as "Smart Manufacturing" in the United States, and "Industrial Internet" in Japan. Moreover, Industry IoT Consortium (IIC) founded in 2014 is a global nonprofit partnership of industries, governments, and academia, including contributing members Huawei and Microsoft. IIC has helped organizations leverage digital technologies and achieve positive outcomes. Their goal is to help members maximize the return on their IoT investment.

2.2 Global Digital Workforce Shortage

The world is currently facing a digital labor shortage. This shortage, on the surface, is insufficient in quantity, but in essence, it is a reflection of an unqualified workforce. Digitalization relies on a skilled digital workforce, rather than manpower. Historical evidence demonstrates that, apart from labor-intensive industries, such as agriculture, new technologies alter how the workforce operates rather than their share in the sectors. From 1850 to 2015, the change in total employment share in the US was −55.9% in agriculture (the lowest), −3.6% in manufacturing, +0.7% in telecommunications, + 5.0% in professional service, +12.8% in trade (the highest) [15]. History has proven that digitalization can create new job opportunities to offset traditional jobs. For instance, the adoption of automated guided vehicles (AGVs) reduced the number of porters but created new opportunities for AGV operators. Currently, despite over 2.7 million industrial robots (for example, fixed robotic arms, moving robots, and AGV) being used worldwide, human resources are still needed to interact, manage, and operate those machines for production.

The digital workforce shortage affects all areas of business worldwide.

Over half of the organizations believed the digital workforce gap impeded their digital transformation programs, leading to lost competitive advantages; additionally, more than half of the digital talents were likely to be attracted to organizations providing superior digital opportunities [16]. Failing to fill job vacancies and not possessing requisite skillsets in the workforce can detrimentally impact production levels and responsiveness to market opportunities at the corporate level. For example, Siemens disclosed that they had a shortage of skilled workers (for example, specialist and digital talents) and have an ongoing demand for highly skilled workers in the 2021 Fiscal Report. They believed their future success partly depended on their continued ability to identify, access, and hire digital talents. At a national level, digital transformation in manufacturing necessitates and fosters skills not possessed by the existing workforce. Without altering the employees' skill sets, US manufacturing is projected to have 2.1 million vacant positions by 2030, affecting productivity, innovation, competitiveness, and GDP [17]. In 2019, there were 7.8 million information and communication technology (ICT) specialists in the EU with an annual growth rate of 4.2%. This is far below the projected need of 20 million digital specialists by 2030. The shortage of a digitally skilled workforce is an obstacle to the investment of over 70% of businesses [18].

2.3 Upskilling Workforces in Digitalization

Digitalization requires a new set of human skills to ensure usability and efficiency for the application of digital technologies. There is a growing gap between existing and needed digital skills of the workforce to master the challenges of the digitalized future at work [19]. First, organizations should upskill their workforce to be able to solve these challenges. Digital workers in Industry 4.0 could handle management as well as production and use digital technologies namely big data, robot-assisted production, self-driving logistics vehicles, and augmented reality and additive manufacturing [20, 21]. Grzybowska and Łupicka (2017) explored eight managerial competencies of engineers and managers in Industry 4.0, including creativity, problem-solving, conflict-solving, and decision-making [13]. Mazurchenko and Maršíková (2019) highlighted an increasing number of jobs that required ICT and digital skills [22]. Siddoo et al. (2019) clustered digital workforce competencies into three categories and found that industries expected high competencies in the professional skills and IT knowledge category (including lifelong learning, personal attitudes, and dependability), followed by the IT technical category (including project management, and digital communication), and IT management and support category (including basic IT for works, database, and English for IT) [23]. Oberländer et al. (2020) identified and validated 25 dimensions of digital competencies for white-collar workers (for example, handling of hardware, programming, applications, effective usage, and communication) based on the perspective from research and practice. It was illustrated that no job position requires a maximum of 25 dimensions of digital competencies, though a subset of those are necessary for each job position.

Digitalization also leads to a change in education and training. The education and training sectors should update their programs develop and adapt their courses to meet the changing needs of digitalization [24]. Almeida et al. (2020) argued that digital courses should enhance specific skills in several areas and responses to social challenges (for example, interpersonal relationships) in the post-COVID-19 era. They also encouraged the development of vocational training and close collaboration between public and private employers by stimulating the diversification and specialization of the educational offer [25]. Li et al. (2021) investigated the cultivation of digital undergraduates from the perspective of IIoT academic-major. They found that IoT engineering, AI, data science, and Big Data technologies were relevant academic majors; but universities lacked sufficient digital resources (for example, course and practice bases) in digital undergraduate studies [26]. The European Commission launched a study to examine the penetration of digital technologies in workplaces. The study emphasized the importance of accounting for diversity in skills possessed by the workforce, noting that employers need digital skills (for example, types and levels) tailored to their industry, size, market, and country. Accordingly, tailored approaches are needed in addressing digital skills of the workforce [24].

3 National Actions

3.1 Strategies and Actions

Policymakers are taking action to upskill workforces for Industry 4.0 and the digital age. They proposed various policies for industries and the workforce to utilize and promote the opportunities offered by digitalization.

United States. Manufacturing is an engine of America's economic growth and national security. Implementation of digital technologies in advanced manufacturing requires a highly skilled and diverse workforce. One of three main goals of "National Strategy for Advanced Manufacturing" of the U.S. in 2022 was "Goal 3: grow the advanced manufacturing workforce". To achieve this goal, strategic objectives and recommendations were outlined for the next four years (see Table 1). It is clear that the U.S. conducts comprehensive investment from elementary school through post-graduate degrees, technical training programs with industry-recognized credentials, apprenticeships and internships, and leadership development programs. Moreover, the 2022 Manufacturing USA[1] Highlights Report summarized American innovations in digital workforce development [27]. In the fiscal year 2021, they engaged over 90,000 people with workforce knowledge and skills in advanced manufacturing and created training programs and courses to upskill the workforce (present and future), such as AIM Photonics' chip fabrication facility in Albany, flexible hybrid electronics workforce development programs at NextFlex in San Jose, and Additive Edge project to introduce high school students to additive manufacturing. Moreover, the U.S. released an updated list of Critical and Emerging Technologies (CET List) in 2022, which will serve to inform a forthcoming strategy on U.S. technological competitiveness and national security [28]. The CET List contains numerous digital technologies, such as AI, autonomous systems and robotics, communication and networking technologies, and quantum information technologies. The CET List was supposed to be a reference for hiring international talents.

Germany. Germany believes data to be the core element of the digital world, and that data is insufficiently used in present-day Germany and Europe. In 2021, the German government released the Data Strategy of the Federal German Government, aiming to increase innovative and responsible data provision and use in industries, science, civil society, and public administration. "Area 3: improving data skills and establishing a data culture" is one of the four areas of action of the Data Strategy. We summarized the sub-areas and contents of Area 3 to understand German actions (see Table 2). Besides, regarding globalization and digitalization, Germany announced the National Industrial Strategy 2030 in 2019, put forward by Federal Minister Peter Altmaier to strengthen the competitiveness of its industrial sector. The National Industrial Strategy 2030 specifies the measures concerning the workforce, including "making the labor market more flexible" and "mobilizing skilled labor" [30]. The previous approach highlighted the preservation of private-sector jobs in the long run, such as instituting a weekly cap on the maximum working hours. The latter focuses on training the domestic skilled workforce

---

[1] Manufacturing USA is a national network of public and private partnerships to secure U.S. global leadership in advanced manufacturing. The network includes 16 sponsored manufacturing innovation institutes and six other federal partner agencies.

Table 1. Strategic objects and recommendations for Goal 3 [29].

Goal	Objectives	Recommendations
Grow the advanced manufacturing workforce	Expand and diversify the advanced manufacturing talent pool	Promote awareness of advanced manufacturing careers
		Engage underrepresented communities
		Address social and structural barriers for underserved groups
	Develop, scale, and promote advanced manufacturing education and training	Incorporate advanced manufacturing into foundational STEM education
		Modernize career technical education for advanced manufacturing
		Expand and disseminate new learning technologies and practices
	Strengthen the connections between employers and educational organizations	Expand work-based learning and apprenticeships
		Establish industry-recognized credentials and certifications

(for example, skills needed in the digital workforce and dual vocational training in digitalization) and approaching foreign qualified professionals (for example, improvements in visa procedures and recognition of vocational qualifications obtained abroad).

Japan. In 2021, Prime Minister Kishida presented his 'Vision for a Digital Garden City Nation' (デジタル田園都市国家構想)[32], aiming to achieve rural-urban digital integration and transformation. Ten meetings of the council for the Realization of the Vision for a Digital Garden City Nation have been held, of which the first, eighth, and ninth meetings were headed by Prime Minister Kishida [33]. The Basic Policy of Vision for a Digital Garden City Nation was released in June 2022, which specifies four areas of action. "Area 3: develop and secure digital human resources", and "Area 4: leave no one behind" focus on the digital workforce (see Table 3). Japan plans to create an environment where anyone can master digital skills and ensure the entire workforce such as business architects and data scientists, are digitally literate and can use digital technologies. Japan currently has around one million digital talents and aims to increase them to 3.3 million in 2026 [34]. Moreover, the Japanese Ministry of Economy, Trade, and Industry released the Strategy for Semiconductors and the Digital Industry (SD Strategy), that stresses on semiconductors, data centers, and clouds being the foundation of the digital industry. The digital workforce is the prerequisite for the implementation of the SD Strategy. Thus, it is required to cultivate digital technology and management talents through cooperation of government, industries, and universities [35]. Moreover, the Japanese government

Table 2. Summary of area 3 [31]

Area	Sub-area	Contents
Improving data skills and establishing a data culture	Skilled society: self-determined and informed	*Status:* most citizens acquired digital skills on their own or with the help of family and friends; very few through basic and advanced training, etc
		Goal: strengthen the citizens' data skills; make excellent learning opportunities available to everyone based on their needs, etc
		Measures: a national digital educational campaign; a digital platform for further vocational training; continuous long-term monitoring of data skills, etc
	Improving data skills in education and vocational training	*Status:* data skills are not added to the curriculum or anchored in syllabuses in school education; no comprehensive subject-specific courses on data skills for university students, etc
		Goal: integrate data skills with a wide range of subjects; ensure everyone who completes vocational training or a degree course masters data skills of a minimum standard, etc
		Measures: update basic and further training regulations; teach sustainable skills for data-based empirical work; set up a doctoral program in data science
	Demand for and provision of data skills in the industry	*Status:* a shortage of 114,000 data experts in Germany in 2019; this number is predicted to increase to 126,000 in 2025, etc

(continued)

Table 2. (*continued*)

Area	Sub-area	Contents
		Goal: provide training for future data experts at the highest international level; help small and medium-sized enterprises (SMEs) access the potential of data-based value creation; support companies in training their employees in demand-based data skills etc
		Measures: "Go-Data" funding program (support SMEs); "Future centers" (AI) federal program (support SMEs and employees); "Innovative SMEs: research on products and services" funding (enable companies to develop new solutions for Industry 4.0), etc
	Data skills in civil organizations	***Status:*** a civil organization dedicated to transferring data skills to the public freely without government funding; they have to fulfill the legal requirement of data controllers, etc
		Goal: develop the data skills of civil organizations; make non-personal data records freely available to the public, etc
		Measures: promote non-financial assistance to civil organizations within the framework of statutory regulations; run "promoting digital sovereignty of senior citizens with AI technologies" project for older people, etc

formulated and released AI Strategy 2022 and Vision of Quantum Future Society in 2022, which emphasized the development and securing of digital human resources through public-private partnerships. These digital human resources could promote integration of the cutting-edge technologies (for example, AI, digital twin, and quantum) with fields in which Japan is strong, such as health and medical care, agriculture, infrastructure, disaster prevention, and manufacturing.

China. President Xi Jinping has stressed the efforts to implement the workforce development strategy in the new era and accelerated China's development as a major world

Table 3. Contents of Initiatives 2 and 4 of [34].

Area	Objectives	Measures
Develop and secure digital human resources	*Qualitative:* help university students and vocational training receivers acquire powerful digital skills *Quantitative:* train 450,000 personnel annually for the promotion of digitalization in local regions by the end of fiscal 2024, reaching a total of 2.3 million by 2026	Build a platform for digital human resource development,
		Place emphasis on the digital field of vocational training,
		Develop digital human resources at institutions of higher education, etc
		Encourage digital workforce back to local areas,
		Develop and secure female digital human resources,
		Other related important measures
Leave no one behind	*Qualitative:* establish a human-resource support system to promote and realize a digital society where no one is left behind *Quantitative:* start the human-resource support system in fiscal 2022, with more than 10,000 nationwide digitalization supporters	Support the implementation of digitalization
		Support for those who are concerned about implementing digitalization
		Host and disseminate activities that contribute to the realization of "leave no one behind"

center of talent and innovation at a central conference on talent-related work on Sept 27, 2021 [36]. China is a rapidly developing digital economy (including the industrialization of digital technologies and digitalization of various industries) and pays attention to the digital workforce. Action Outline for Improving Digital Literacy and Skills for All (提升全民数字素养与技能行动纲要, abbreviated to the "Action Outline") was published in 2021, aiming to bridge the digital gap and promote common prosperity for all [37]. The Action Outline listed seven main tasks and corresponding measures/actions (see Table 4). China proposed the development of the Industrial Internet in 2018 to face the challenges of Industry 4.0 and published the Action Plan for Innovation and Development of Industrial Internet (2021–2023) in 2021 [38], which proposed to expand the Industrial Internet workforce scale including cultivation of compound and innovative talents, high-level scientists, and industrial experts. Moreover, a national scientific research institution—China Academy of Industrial Internet, was established, which is responsible for the development of the Industrial Internet (for example, policy research, platform construction, and standard development) and talent cultivation (for example, educating, training, evaluation, and certification of the digital workforce).

Table 4. Brief summary of the Action Outline [37]

Goals	Main Tasks	Measures
Improve digital adaptability, competence, and creativity of the entire population by 2025, and the digital literacy and skills of the Chinese people to match that of those in developed countries	Enrich the supply of high-quality digital resources	Enrich the contents of digital education and training resources, promote the opening and sharing of digital resources, etc
	Improve high-quality digital life	Cultivate a new lifestyle of smart home, enrich new digital life scenes, digital actions to help the elderly and the disabled, etc
	Improve high-efficient digital work capabilities	Improve the digital skills of industrial workers, upgrade the digital skills of farmers and new occupational groups, etc
	Build a lifelong digital learning system	Improve the level of digital education in schools, improve vocational education and training systems on digital skills, etc
	Stimulate the vitality of digital innovation	Build digital competitiveness of enterprises, explore new paradigms of data-driven scientific research, etc
	Improve the capabilities of digital security protection	Improve network-security protection capabilities of the entire population, and strengthen the protection of personal information and privacy
	Strengthen the rule of law and ethics in the digital society	Guide the entire population to surf the Internet legally, and improve their Internet literacy

3.2 Common Features

Despite differing strategies, the four countries are unified in their goal of enlarging the scale and enhancing the quality of their digital workforce. Common features of those national strategies can be summarized in four directions (see Table 5). **(1) Enhancing digital skills for the whole people to expand the workforce base.** Germany, Japan, and China all launched national strategies to improve data skills of every citizen. Improving digital literacy and skills of citizens is the basis of expanding the digital workforce.

These countries strive to create a society where each person can master digital skills and ensure the entire workforce is digitally literate and use digital technologies. **(2) Developing school education and social training in digital skills.** School education and social training are direct and effective means of improving digital skills. In developing digital skills, school education emphasizes the provision of digital skills/courses in the curriculum, syllabuses, and university-majors; social training belonging to the lifelong education system provides service on digital skill development in all aspects of work and life. Thus, the power of schools and social organizations should be harnessed synergistically to develop and promote the digital skills of the present and future workforce. **(3) Advancing the digital industries and workforce simultaneously.** The development of digital technologies/industries in all the four countries is accompanied by digital workforce support policies, such as advanced manufacturing in the U.S., AI and Quantum in Japan, and Industrial Internet in China. A qualified digital workforce

Table 5. Common features of the aforementioned strategies

Features	Countries and representative strategies
Enhancing digital skills for the entire population	Germany: Data Strategy of the Federal German Government
	Japan: Vision for a Digital Garden City Nation
	China: Action Outline for Improving Digital Literacy and Skills for All
Advancing digital industries and workforce simultaneously	The U.S.: National Strategy for Advanced Manufacturing
	Germany: National Industrial Strategy 2030
	Japan: AI Strategy 2022, Vision of Quantum Future Society, Strategy for Semiconductors and the Digital Industry
	China: Action Plan for Innovation and Development of Industrial Internet (2021–2023)
Developing school education and social training in digital skills	The U.S.: 2022 Manufacturing USA Highlights Report
	Germany: Data Strategy of the Federal German Government
	Japan: Vision for a Digital Garden City Nation
	China: Action Outline for Improving Digital Literacy and Skills for All
Attracting a global digital qualified workforce	The U.S.: Updated List of Critical and Emerging Technologies
	Germany: National Industrial Strategy 2030
	Japan: AI Strategy 2022

has become the first resource for the development of digital industries and their development should be synchronized with training and upgrading the digital workforce. **(4) Attracting a digitally-qualified global workforce.** There is a global trend in the flow of digital workforce. Countries are vigorously cultivating domestic experts and introducing a high-level digital workforce, such as the U.S., Germany, and Japan. Compared with educating the local workforce, introducing a global workforce will help handle the digital workforce shortage more quickly and effectively.

Based on the above results, we propose some suggestions for upgrading the national or regional digital workforce. First, make efforts on strengthening the digital skills of the entire population. Moreover, digital upskilling of citizens is a national campaign where educational and social development opportunities (for example, courses and curriculum on data skills, work-based learning and apprenticeships) should be available and acquired by each person depending on their needs, to cultivate data competencies. Finally, cultivate digital industry experts and introduce outstanding digital talents simultaneously. The development of digital technology and industry relies on a digital workforce, including highly skilled craftsmen, top scientific research experts, and digital engineers. It requires both domestic cultivation and active participation from abroad.

4   Conclusions

The workforce is a fundamental driving factor in digitalization. The world is currently facing a digital workforce shortage which affects all areas of business worldwide. Governments that take effective actions in responding to the digital workforce shortage would gain an edge in digital competition. Thus, policymakers are taking action to upskill workforces in the digital age. In this study, we investigated and summarized the strategies of the U.S., China, Germany, and Japan (the top performers in digitalization) in scaling and upskilling the digital workforce. Four common features of strategies were identified: (1) enhancing digital skills for the entire population to expand the workforce base; (2) developing school education and social training in digital skills; (3) advancing the digital industries and workforce simultaneously; (4) attracting a digitally-qualified global workforce. Besides, suggestions were given for other global countries to address digital workforce shortages.

References

1. United Nations Industrial Development Organization: Industrial Development Report 2022: The Future of Industrialization in a Post-Pandemic World. United Nations (2022)
2. Bertrand, A., Bakshi, S., McQueen, J.: How government planning for a future-fit, digital workforce
3. United Nations: Digital Economy Report 2021-Cross-border data flows and development: For whom the data flow (2021)
4. Gray, J., Rumpe, B.: Models for digitalization (2015)
5. Musik, C., Bogner, A.: Book title: digitalization & society. Österreichische Zeitschrift für Soziologie **44**, 1–14 (2019)
6. MacKenzie, D., Wajcman, J.: The Social Shaping of Technology. Open University Press (1999)

7. Houben, D., Prietl, B.: Datengesellschaft: Einsichten in die Datafizierung des Sozialen. transcript Verlag (2018)
8. Li, Z., Rau, P.-L.P.: Talking with an IoT-CA: effects of the use of internet of things conversational agents on face-to-face conversations. Interact. Comput. **33**, 238–249 (2021)
9. Definition of Digitalization - Gartner Information Technology Glossary. https://www.gartner.com/en/information-technology/glossary/digitalization
10. Deloitte: What is digital economy?
11. Press, G.: A Very Short History of Digitization. https://www.forbes.com/sites/gilpress/2015/12/27/a-very-short-history-of-digitization/
12. Schwab, K.: The fourth industrial revolution. Currency (2017)
13. Grzybowska, K., \Lupicka, A.: Key competencies for Industry 4.0. Econ. Manage. Innov. **1**, 250–253 (2017)
14. Björkdahl, J.: Strategies for digitalization in manufacturing firms. Calif. Manage. Rev. **62**, 17–36 (2020)
15. McKinsey: What the future of work will mean for jobs, skills, and wages: Jobs lost, jobs gained (2017)
16. Capgemini Digital Transformation Institute: The digital talent gap: Are companies doing enough? Capgemini and LinkedIn, Paris, France (2017)
17. Wellener, P., Reyes, V., Ashton, H., Moutray, C.: Creating pathways for tomorrow's workforce today. https://www2.deloitte.com/us/en/insights/industry/manufacturing/manufacturing-industry-diversity.html
18. Commission, E.: 2030 Digital Compass: The European Way for the Digital Decade (2021)
19. Oberländer, M., Beinicke, A., Bipp, T.: Digital competencies: a review of the literature and applications in the workplace. Comput. Educ. **146**, 103752 (2020)
20. Nardo, M.D., Forino, D., Murino, T.: The evolution of man–machine interaction: the role of human in Industry 4.0 paradigm. Product. Manufac. Res. **8**, 20–34 (2020)
21. Galati, F., Bigliardi, B.: Industry 4.0: emerging themes and future research avenues using a text mining approach. Comput. Indust. **109**, 100–113 (2019)
22. Mazurchenko, A., Maršíková, K.: Digitally-powered human resource management: skills and roles in the digital era. Acta Informatica Pragensia. **8**, 72–87 (2019)
23. Siddoo, V., Sawattawee, J., Janchai, W., Thinnukool, O.: An exploratory study of digital workforce competency in Thailand. Heliyon. **5**, e01723 (2019)
24. Curtarelli, M., Gualtieri, V., Jannati, M.S., Donlevy, V.: ICT for work: digital skills in the workplace
25. Almeida, F., Santos, J.D., Monteiro, J.A.: The challenges and opportunities in the digitalization of companies in a post-COVID-19 World. IEEE Eng. Manage. Rev. **48**, 97–103 (2020)
26. Li, Z., Li, Z., Zhang, A.: Industrial internet talent cultivation in china from the perspective of undergraduate majors. In: Rau, P.-L. (ed.) HCII 2021. LNCS, vol. 12772, pp. 362–373. Springer, Cham (2021). https://doi.org/10.1007/978-3-030-77077-8_28
27. Brunner, Z.: Manufacturing USA Highlights Report 2022 (2022)
28. United States Releases Updated List of Critical and Emerging Technologies. https://www.state.gov/united-states-releases-updated-list-of-critical-and-emerging-technologies/
29. Subcommittee on Advanced Manufacturing Committee on Technology: National Strategy for Advanced Manufacturing (2022)
30. Action, B.-F.M. for E.A. and C.: National Industrial Strategy 2030. https://www.bmwk.de/Redaktion/EN/Publikationen/Industry/national-industry-strategy-2030.html
31. German Federal Government: Data Strategy of the Federal German Government
32. Vision for a Digital Garden City Nation: Achieving Rural-Urban Digital Integration and Transformation. https://www.japan.go.jp/kizuna/2022/01/vision_for_a_digital_garden_city_nation.html

33. Cabinet Secretariat: デジタル田園都市国家構想実現会議, https://www.cas.go.jp/jp/sei saku/digital_denen/index.html
34. Cabinet Secretariat: デジタル田園都市国家構想基本方針 (2022)
35. 経済産業省: 半導体・デジタル産業戦略 (2021)
36. Xi calls for accelerating building of world center for talent, innovation. http://english.www. gov.cn/news/topnews/202109/29/content_WS6153c339c6d0df57f98e108d.html
37. Office of the Central Cyberspace Affairs Commission, Cyberspace Administration of China: 提升全民数字素养与技能行动纲要 (20211–05)
38. 关于印发《工业互联网创新发展行动计划 (2021–2023年) 》的通知. http://www.gov.cn/ zhcngce/zhengceku/2021-01/13/content_5579519.htm

Touched by VR Storytelling: A Pilot Study of the Interactive Digital Narrative Evaluation Matrix for Shaping Values

Yanru Lyu[1], Zhouhengyi Yi[1], Tingxuan Hao[1], and Yaoyao Wu[2(✉)]

[1] Department of Digital Media Arts, School of Media and Design, Beijing Technology and Business University, Beijing 102248, China
[2] Academy of Arts and Design, Beijing City University, Beijing 100083, China
156268208@qq.com

Abstract. Interactive digital narrative (IDN) is a form of expression by a computer-based system with broad potential for virtual reality (VR) application. This study investigates the experience factors to clarify what it is like to shape the values of individuals and groups through VR storytelling. An IDN experience matrix is proposed for the design and evaluation of VR storytelling. This approach is based on the communication theory to map a bottom-to-up 3×3 structure, crossing the design process and perception level. Its usefulness was demonstrated by investigating 31 participants with a digital media background. The results show that the approach could be applied to understanding the cognitive experience of stories in VR and provides designers with an idea of how to improve the effect of shaping values. In addition, the matrix will be validated in more testing and evaluating of VR works in further study.

Keywords: VR Storytelling · Interactive Digital Narrative · Evaluation Matrix · Communication theory

1 Introduction

All kinds of languages, images, texts, and so on embody narration. In the trend of "digitalization", the way of storytelling is constantly changing as well content is constantly evolving. VR technology has been developed in the fast lane for decades, and its application can be found in fields as diverse as entertainment, marketing, education, medicine, and many others. Especially in recent years, various consumer-grade all-in-one (AIO) devices have been influx into the market (e.g., Oculus Quest, HTC Vive Focus, and PICO Neo), stimulating more need for producing VR content. At the same time, with the popularity of the concept of Metaverse, the experience in the virtual world has attracted more attention. As an effective storytelling medium, VR provides a narrative experience, which can transport the audience to a 3D virtual world connecting with a scenario that represents a story [1]. In the virtual world, the audience can be in any time and space generated by the computer and reconstruct the information under the drive of sensory stimulus and interactive action. Therefore, VR can help people today to dialogue with history and reflect on the present.

P.-L. P. Rau (Ed.): HCII 2023, LNCS 14022, pp. 268–279, 2023.
https://doi.org/10.1007/978-3-031-35936-1_19

As the main form of storytelling, novels, films, and drama are well known, and their common feature is that a core value is hidden in the form. With the advent of the digital era, DIN, as a form of expression at the intersection of different artistic approaches, is emerging in updated storytelling experience in both a traditional art medium and new media [2, 3]. Even in the VR environment, DIN is still continuous communication while being influenced by digital properties. From the communication theory perspective, the creator coding is based on the core value and hopes the audience can decode to accurately understand and identify the values [4, 5]. Values transfer, such as patriotism education, may achieve better effects from the VR experience.

Cognition of the story is a complex process involving multiple factors such as creator telling and audience traits. So far, few studies have examined story cognition and values perception influencing factors and the need for established frameworks for developing IDN systems by linking the design and evaluation process. Therefore, this paper aims to study factors affecting the story experience and values shaping in VR storytelling. Then, these factors are analyzed and discussed in order to establish an evaluation matrix to understand the perceptions of value during interactive digital narrative using the VR AIO headset. Figure 1 shows that this study could be divided into three sections. In Sect. 1, a literature review was made to explore the IDN evaluation matrix in VR for shaping values. In Sect. 2, ten experts with digital media backgrounds were invited to rank the items from the prepared list according to their experience in the sample of VR storytelling. And then, select the three most essential items in each factor, a total of 27 items, as the question to design the questionnaire. In the formal experiment, 31 participants were invited. Section 3, the data were collected for analysis and discussion. Finally, the conclusions of this study were given.

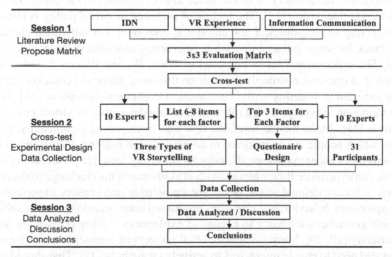

Fig. 1. The procedures for this study: the horizontal line divides three sessions, and the arrows indicate the direction of functions and processes.

2 Literature Review

2.1 Experience Dimensions of IDN in VR

In the digital experience environment, IDN is a merging form of a narrative by a computer-based system in which the audience can participate and influence the narrative progression [6]. It dissolves the division and builds the bridge between the active creator and passive audience to form a ternary relationship between creators, dynamic narrative artifacts, and audiences as participants [3]. Janet Murray provided broad categories to describe the user experience in IDN, which involves agency, immersion, and transformation as the main aspects of experiential qualities [7]. As a further evaluation study, Roth, C., and Koenitz, H. map Murray's influential theoretical framework to empirical dimensions and thus connect an analytical framework to empirical research [2, 3]. Their works describe 12 experience dimensions in more detail, including usability, effectance, autonomy, flow, presence, role-identification, curiosity, suspense, believability, eudaimonic appreciation, affect, and enjoyment.

As a typical IDN medium, VR is a computer-generated experience that is usually used as a medium to deliver a story. The defining characteristic of VR is its ability to provide immersion [8], induce a feeling of presence in the computer-generated world [9] and arousal of affection. Presence is a subjective sensation of being in an environment and is considered a state of consciousness affected by the experience of surroundings [10]. VR can simulate physical presence in real or imagined environments where users feel like being there [1, 11]. The mode of presenting information may affect how much presence is experienced. Most information the attention we usually focus on comes from visual channels, so the visual information may strongly affect the sense of presence. In addition, the auditory or tactile mode also contributes to the experience, but it has less weight than vision [12]. The feeling of presence in virtual reality is also linked to the triggering of physiological and emotional responses. For individual characteristics, feedback for sense and usability while interacting also affects the presence in VR [13, 14]. The experimental result proposed by Shin, D., and Biocca, F. indicates that the meaning of immersion strongly depends on the users' traits and contexts [2]. In any medium experience, usability is the fundamental evaluation dimension [15]. In addition, participation also plays a vital role in enhancing the quality of virtual environment experiences [16]. At the mental level, the flow can be improved significantly, which is a state in which people are so involved in an activity that nothing else seems to matter [17]. Focus and concentration are the keys to achieving flow [18]. According to flow theory, we can experience flow when individual skills match the challenge of the activity. Curiosity, generally defined as the desire for knowledge and sensory experiences that sparks exploratory behavior, is a transitory emotional state occasioned when subjective uncertainty generates a tendency to engage in exploratory solving or partially mitigate the uncertainty [19, 20]. Murray suggested that creators of interactive narrative experiences instead need to enable interactors to actively create belief [7]. That should involve character and story believability, and a series of complex perceptions will eventually connect emotion.

2.2 Information Communication Mechanism

Regarding the theory of information communication, one of the views regards communication as the process of information transmission and is concerned with how information is transformed between the addresser and the addressee. The basis of communication theory, a successful information transmission should achieve three levels: technical, semantic, and effectiveness—the technical level should be seeing, hearing, touching, or even feeling. The semantic level is also regarded as the cognitive level, which requires letting the addressee understand the message's meaning without misinterpreting, misunderstanding, or not understanding it at all. The effectiveness level concerns letting the addressee reflect and then take the right action matching the original coding intention [4, 5]. The data-information-knowledge-wisdom (DIKW) model is often used to explain the human's understanding in the perceptual and cognitive space [21]. Zeleny [22] described the component of the DIKW model according to their different purposes as know-nothing (data), know-what (information), know-how (knowledge), and know-why (wisdom). According to this model, if VR storytelling is regarded as releasing information, only when the audience understands how and why can they shape their wisdom.

From the perspective of product emotional design, Norman [23] put forward the design of three layers (i.e., visceral layer, behavioral layer, and reflective layer). In order to design a story experience in the interactive digital environment, Lyu et al. [21] used a story-scenario approach to code the work of big data storytelling, which involved setting a scenario, telling a story, writing a script, and visualization. For the design scenario in a virtual environment, from the attraction (technical level) to cognition (semantic level) to feeling (effectiveness level), they are related to the sense attraction (e.g., see and hear), realness (e.g., same as reality) and presence (feeling be there). In writing a script, the main work is to focus on how to guide the narrative through interactive activities. Therefore, beyond the usability is the sense of flow during deep participation with story components. When the audience stands in the scenario, telling a fantastic story aims to arouse their affection. As the starting point of storytelling and the end point of experience, values are abstract. This study aims to explore how to accurately shape audience values by integrating the communication theory into VR storytelling.

2.3 Research Framework

Based on previous studies [4, 5, 21], a research framework combining communication theory with experience dimensions of IDN in VR was proposed to explore the issue of an evaluation matrix for shaping values, as shown in Fig. 2.

For evaluating the IDN experience in VR for shaping values, the designer involves three key stages to transfer values through interactive digital experience: set a scenario, write a script, and tell a story. For the audience, there are three sections to receive the information of the story: scenario experience, interactive experience, and emotional experience. For each section, the decoding is a bottom-to-up process from the attractive level to the cognitive level to the affection level.

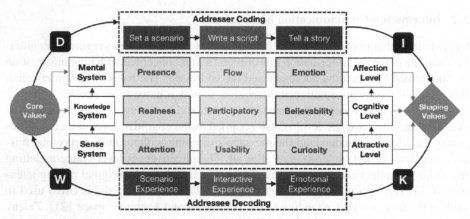

Fig. 2. The IDN evaluation matrix in VR for shaping values. The original name of "D" is "Data", "I" is "Information", "K" is "Knowledge", and "W" is "Wisdom".

3 Methods

3.1 Cross-Test

Crosse-test involved using questionnaire interviews to derive the predicted variable that affects evaluating VR storytelling. Twenty professional designers of digital media were divided into groups A and B. At first, group A was asked to describe in their own words any item that would influence the experience of nine factors (i.e., Attention, Realness, Presence, Usability, Participatory, Flow, Curiosity, Memory, Affection). And then, the descriptions were summarized and listed 5–8 items in each factor. Secondly, group B was requested to rate each item by its importance to the audience on a rating scale from 1 to 7. These rating data were used to determine the statistically important attributes for evaluating VR storytelling. Three critical items were selected for each factor, as shown in Table 1.

3.2 Stimuli

This study selected three types of VR storytelling as samples, illustrated in Fig. 3. All three samples tell the story of the Chinese red army in the war years. *Red Army Climbing Snow Mountain* belongs to the scenario type with a great snowy mountain scene. *Flying to Luding Bridge* is an interactive type full of more game-like interaction, such as shooting. As the narrative type, *Red Army Crossed the Grassland* has more content modules and narration duration.

3.3 Participants

Thirty-one students with digital media arts from Beijing Technology and Business University (BTBU) participated in the experiment. The subjects consisted of 16 females and 15 males between 19–27 years (M = 22.65; SD = 2.01). Participants are without a

Table 1. The key factors for evaluating VR storytelling.

IDN Design Coding			
	Set a scenario	**Write a script**	**Tell a story**	
Design Dimension C	CP-1: Feel be part of there	CF-1: Focus on the storytelling	CE-1: Emotional resonance	**Affection Level**
	CP-2: Sense of being there	CF-2: Time ignored	CE-2: Touched by the story	
	CP-3: Attracted be there	CF-3: Block out any external input	CE-3: Impressed by the story	
Design Dimension B	CR-1: Freedom of movement	CP-1: Role of promote narration	CB-1: Highly authentic story	**Cognitive Level**
	CR-2: Feedback to action	CP-2: Interact with virtual props	CB2:Smooth plot	
	CR-3: Scene be real	CP-3:Autonomous interaction	CB-3: easy-to-understand plot	
Design Dimension A	CA-1: Visual quality	CU-1: Accurate interaction	CC-1: Attracted by the story	**Abstractive Level**
	CA-2: Auditory quality	CU-2: Easy interaction	CC-2: Interested to explore	
	CA-3: Touch reality	CU-3:Innovative interaction	CC-3: Unexpected narration	
	Scenario Experience	**Interactive Experience**	**Emotional Experience**	
Experience Decoding				

Fig. 3. War story with HMD VR. The screenshot on the left is "Red Army Climbing Snow Mountain", the middle one is "Flying to Luding Bridge", and the right is "Red Army Crossed the Grassland".

history of neurological disease, head injury, and other psychological or emotional problems. After a short introduction, students experienced three VR storytelling randomly by wearing PICO G2, a Helmet Mounted Display (HMD), as shown in Fig. 4.

3.4 Questionnaire Design

The questionnaire consists of three parts: The first part is the basic information, including gender, age, and familiarity with VR experience; the second part is a questionnaire on experience, which had 27 validated 5-point Likert scales based on the 3 × 3 evaluation matrix of VR storytelling (see Table 1). Each question was evaluated with 1 point (strongly disagree), 2 points (disagree), 3 points (fair), 4 points (agree), or 5 points

Fig. 4. An interviewee is watching and interacting with VR.

(strongly agree). The third part was to evaluate the overall feeling of value reshaping with 1 to 5 score, involved three questions: "Trigger the memory of historical heroes", "Trigger the cherishing of the present life", and "Trigger the action for a better future".

3.5 Experiment Procedure

The researchers introduced the process to the subjects and invited everyone to experience three VR storytelling in random order. There is a ten minutes break for rest. In the experiment, subjects used PICO G2, an AIO HMD VR, to view the VR content. This experiment did not set a time limitation for viewing. Hence, the participants could decide how long to spend appreciating each painting after filling out the questionnaire. The average time to experience one VR is about 3 min (M = 181.47 s SD = 97.33).

4 Results and Discussion

4.1 Results of Descriptive Statistics

This study aimed to determine whether the matrix can evaluate the experience of VR storytelling. According to the results of variation analysis in Table 2, although they displayed no significant difference in their feelings in the three samples, each type of work got higher scores on its corresponding attributes than others. This result indicates that the evaluation matrix can be adapted to the needs and priorities of the different types of VR storytelling and explore the experience from a multi-dimensional. The Narrative type sample, Red Army Crossed the Grassland, has the highest score on "Memory of historical heroes", "Cherishing of the present life", and "Action for a better future". It shows that the experience of narrative-type VR content is more effective in shaping participants' values.

Table 2. Results of descriptive statistics.

Subjective Questionnaire (1-5 points)	Three types of VR storytelling		
	Scenario type	Interactive type	Narrative type
1. Attention	3.37±1.27	3.44±1.17	3.40±1.15
2. Realness	3.38±1.27	3.24±1.22	3.39±1.25
3.Presence	3.61±1.22	3.59±1.14	3.25±1.06
4.Usability	3.48±1.23	4.01±1.12	3.78±1.13
5.Participatory	3.22±1.33	3.53±1.26	3.25±1.27
6.Flow	3.74±1.11	3.75±1.12	3.67±1.16
7. Curiosity	3.15±1.24	3.30±1.31	3.29±1.24
8. Believability	4.11±0.85	4.18±1.00	4.18±0.95
9.Emotion	3.29±1.13	3.29±1.12	3.46+1.08
Memory of historical heroes	3.87±1.12	3.68±1.28	4.06±0.96
Cherishing of the present life	3.87±1.26	3.48±1.29	3.90±1.22
Action for a better future	3.61±1.23	3.42±1.36	3.68±1.25

4.2 Relationship Between User Trait and Experience

The results of ANOVA analysis on gender, VR play times, and preference show that only familiarity with VR significantly differs from the three samples' experience. The more VR play, the lower the experience score for the three samples. Table 3 shows only items with significant differences. It is worth noting that the interactive style sample has the most items with a significant difference, mainly in attention, realness, and participation. Combined with the interview results, users with rich VR experience have experienced more high-quality content, so their evaluation standards are higher than others. In contrast, they felt that the experimental samples need more quantity in visual quality and interactivity.

4.3 Correlations Between Experience and Values Shaping

This study used correlation analysis to understand further the relationship between scenario experience (Attention, Realness, Presence), interactive experience (Usability, Participatory, Flow), emotional experience (Curiosity, Believability, Emotion), and values shaping aspects (Memory of historical heroes, Cherishing of the present life, Action for

Table 3. The relationship between VR play times and experience in matrix.

Subjective Questionnaire (1–5 points)	0 Time (n = 5)	1–5 Times (n = 18)	5–10 Times (n = 3)	More than 10 times (n = 5)	Sig
Scenario type					
CR-1: Freedom of movement	4.60 ± 0.55	3.33 ± 1.08	1.67 ± 1.15	2.20 ± 1.79	**
CR-2: Feedback to action	4.60 ± 0.89	3.56 ± 0.92	3.00 ± 1.00	2.60 ± 1.67	*
CP-2: Interact with virtual props	4.60 ± 0.55	3.50 ± 1.10	3.00 ± 1.73	2.20 ± 1.30	*
CC-1: Attracted by the story	3.20 ± 1.10	3.61 ± 0.85	3.00 ± 1.00	2.00 ± 1.22	*
CE-1: Emotional resonance	3.00 ± 1.22	3.56 ± 0.98	2.67 ± 1.53	1.80 ± 0.84	*
CE-2: Touched by the story	3.20 ± 1.30	3.67 ± 0.84	2.33 ± 1.15	2.20 ± 0.84	*
Interactive type					
CA-1: Visual quality	3.80 ± 1.10	3.72 ± 0.89	3.33 ± 0.58	2.20 ± 1.30	*
CA-3: Touch reality	3.40 ± 1.52	3.39 ± 0.85	2.00 ± 1.00	1.60 ± 0.89	**
CR-1: Freedom of movement	3.60 ± 1.34	3.33 ± 1.14	2.33 ± 1.15	1.40 ± 0.89	*
CR-2: Feedback to action	3.80 ± 0.84	3.78 ± 0.88	4.00 ± 0.00	2.20 ± 1.10	**
CP-2: Interact with virtual props	4.60 ± 0.89	4.06 ± 0.94	3.00 ± 1.00	2.60 ± 1.34	*
CP-3:Autonomous interaction	3.80 ± 0.84	3.33 ± 1.14	2.67 ± 1.53	1.40 ± 0.89	**
CC-1: Attracted by the story	3.40 ± 1.52	3.67 ± 1.03	3.33 ± 2.08	1.80 ± 1.10	*
CE-1: Emotional resonance	3.60 ± 1.52	3.61 ± 0.98	2.00 ± 1.00	1.80 ± 0.84	**
Narrative type					
CR-1: Freedom of movement	4.00 ± 1.41	3.61 ± 0.92	1.67 ± 0.58	2.40 ± 1.95	*
CP-3:Autonomous interaction	3.80 ± 1.64	3.33 ± 1.08	1.67 ± 0.58	1.80 ± 0.84	**

a better future). The correlation analysis is shown in Fig. 5. This figure shows the significant relevance between every two variables ($p < 0.05$), and the relevance should be improved for better value shaping. A significant positive correlation is observed in all factors of the matrix. Among, arousal emotion has the highest correlation with influencing values.

4.4 Preference Analysis of VR Storytelling

Figure 6 shows the proportion of people selecting their favorite type among all the participants. The top favorite sample was the interactive type (55.84%), higher than the other two types. Although interactive samples perform poorly in arousing emotions, strong interactive characteristics are more attractive to participants. Therefore, the experience interest of the audience can be stimulated by adding high-quality interaction.

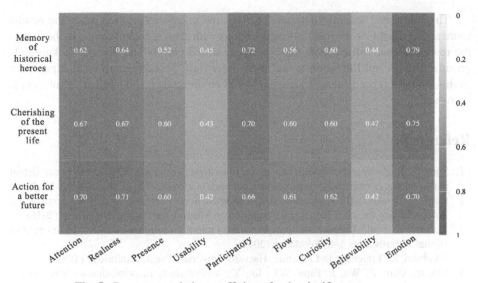

Fig. 5. Pearson correlation coefficients for the significant measures.

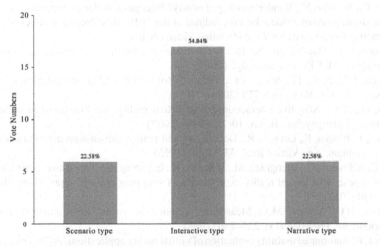

Fig. 6. Proportion of each type being selected as a favorite.

5   Conclusions

The pilot studies were conducted to explore the perception differences of three VR story samples based on the IDN evaluation matrix, understanding how an audience evaluates the experience of a story and the effect of their value shaping. According to the experiment results, the experience of VR storytelling is a bottom-to-up procedure with also affected by user traits, such as media familiarity. This study used an experience matrix as a technique for evaluating VR storytelling. This approach can be validated in more testing and evaluating of IDN in further study.

This study had several limitations. Firstly, the narrow age group made the results more applicable to 19–27 year old healthy adults with artistic backgrounds. In the future, the research team will evaluate the experience of the elderly and diverse backgrounds groups. The second limitation is that there were only 31 subjects in each experiment in this study. A more general conclusion could be obtained if the number of subjects is increased.

References

1. Shin, D.: Empathy and embodied experience in virtual environment: to what extent can virtual reality stimulate empathy and embodied experience? Comput. Hum. Behav. **78**, 64–73 (2018)
2. Roth, C., Koenitz, H.: Evaluating the user experience of interactive digital narrative. In: Proceedings of the 1st International Workshop on Multimedia Alternate Realities (2016)
3. Koenitz, H., et al.: Introduction: perspectives on interactive digital narrative. In: Interactive Digital Narrative, pp. 1–8. Routledge (2015)
4. Jakobson, R.: Language in Literature. Harvard University Press, Cambridge (1987)
5. Lin, R., Qian, F., Wu, J., Fang, WT., Jin, Y.: A pilot study of communication matrix for evaluating artworks. In: Rau, PL. (eds.) CCD 2017. LNCS, vol. 10281, pp. 356–368. Springer, Cham (2017). https://doi.org/10.1007/978-3-319-57931-3_29
6. Roth, C., Koenitz, H.: Bandersnatch, yea or nay? Reception and user experience of an interactive digital narrative video. In: Proceedings of the 2019 ACM International Conference on Interactive Experiences for TV and Online Video (2019)
7. Murray, J.H.: Hamlet on the Holodeck, updated edition: The Future of Narrative in Cyberspace. MIT Press, Cambridge (2017)
8. Steffen, J.H., et al.: Framework of affordances for virtual reality and augmented reality. J. Manag. Inf. Syst. **36**(3), 683–729 (2019)
9. Riva, G., et al.: Affective interactions using virtual reality: the link between presence and emotions. Cyberpsychol. Behav. **10**(1), 45–56 (2007)
10. Steuer, J., Biocca, F., Levy, M.R.: Defining virtual reality: dimensions determining telepresence. Commun. Age Virtual Real. **33**, 37–39 (1995)
11. Van Kerrebroeck, H., Brengman, M., Willems, K.: Escaping the crowd: an experimental study on the impact of a virtual reality experience in a shopping mall. Comput. Hum. Behav. **77**, 437–450 (2017)
12. Witmer, B.G., Singer, M.J.: Measuring presence in virtual environments: a presence questionnaire. Presence **7**(3), 225–240 (1998)
13. Harms, P.: Automated usability evaluation of virtual reality applications. ACM Trans. Comput. Hum. Interact. (TOCHI) **26**(3), 1–36 (2019)
14. Ma, R., Kaber, D.B.: Presence, workload and performance effects of synthetic environment design factors. Int. J. Hum. Comput. Stud. **64**(6), 541–552 (2006)
15. Jordan, P.W.: An Introduction to Usability. CRC Press, Boca Raton (2020)
16. Baradaran Rahimi, F., Boyd, J.E., Eiserman, J.R., Levy, R.M., Kim, B.: Museum beyond physical walls: an exploration of virtual reality-enhanced experience in an exhibition-like space. Virtual Real. **26**(4), 1471–1488 (2022). https://doi.org/10.1007/s10055-022-00643-5
17. Csikszentmihalyi, M., et al.: Flow and the Foundations of Positive Psychology: The Collected Works of Mihaly Csikszentmihalyi, pp. 227–238. Springer, Dordrecht (2014). https://doi.org/10.1007/978-94-017-9088-8
18. Csikszentmihalyi, M.: Flow and the Psychology of Discovery and Invention, vol. 39, pp. 1–16. HarperPerennial, New York (1997)
19. Roth, C.: Experiencing interactive storytelling. Vrije Universiteit 24 (2016)

20. Berlyne, D.E.: Curiosity and learning. Motiv. Emot. **2**, 97–175 (1978)
21. Lyu, Y., Cheng, T.F., Lin, R.: Visual data storytelling: a case study of turning big data into Chinese painting. In: Rau, PL. (eds.) HCII 2020. LNCS, Part II, vol. 12193, pp. 526–535. Springer, Cham (2020). https://doi.org/10.1007/978-3-030-49913-6_43
22. Zeleny, M.: Human Systems Management: Integrating Knowledge, Management and Systems. World Scientific (2005)
23. Norman, D.A.: Emotional Design: Why We Love (Or Hate) Everyday Things. Civitas Books (2004)

The Impact of Visual Design on a Social Movement - A Case Study of the Taipei Natural Foot Association

Ying-Hsuehe Shih[✉]

Graduate School of Creative Industry Design, National Taiwan University of Arts, Daguan Road, Banqiao District, New Taipei City 22058, Taiwan
megshih2@gmail.com

Abstract. Before the 19th century, foot-binding was a taboo subject. While foot-binding was listed in the early period of the Japanese colonial rule as one of three depraved customs, along with opium smoking and hair plaiting, foot-binding was the one that had a direct impact upon the rights and interests of women.

The advocacy of foot-binding abolishment as a social movement in Taiwan was pushed by the Japanese government. In 1899, the Taipei Natural Foot Association (the Association) was founded by the local intelligentsia, this marked the start of the foot-binding abolishment campaign. The Association was officially up and running in February 1900 and went on to instigate a series of advocacy activities until 1910. Next, numerous foot-binding abolishment organizations led by female elites emerged and followed suit. As a result, women became a contributing force to society as human resources.

This study shows the design of a mark or emblem of the Taipei Natural Foot Association to enable visual transmission. The Association's emblem is considered one of the factors that contributed to the success of the movement. It was a mark that represented and established a clear identification with foot-binding abolishment. The design of this mark, together with the information that it transmitted, exerted an incremental impact on society and cannot be overlooked. The Association emblem is also the only concrete symbol that has been passed on to this day and sufficiently represents this critical social movement. This study will present an analysis of the success factors behind the Association emblem and explore the impact that modern visual design has on a social movement.

Keywords: Cultural and Creative Industry · Foot-binding · Natural Foot

1 Introduction

1.1 Research Motivation and Background

Before the 19th century, foot-binding was a taboo subject. In the early period of Japanese colonial rule, foot-binding was listed as one of the three depraved customs along with opium smoking and hair plaiting. Foot-binding impacted a woman's role, status, and marriage.

P.-L. P. Rau (Ed.): HCII 2023, LNCS 14022, pp. 280–296, 2023.
https://doi.org/10.1007/978-3-031-35936-1_20

The Japanese government played a decisive role in the advocacy of the foot-binding abolishment campaign, and accelerate abolishment by stipulating specific policies. In 1899, the local intelligentsia set up the Taipei Natural Foot Association which officially started running in February 1900 and in the short span of 10 years (1900–1910) successfully dismantled the traditional feudal authority's control over women's bodies by launching a series of promotional events. Women were then able to function as a contributing force to society.

This findings of this study show that the Association's efforts and results of advocating the natural foot concept may seem less than pronounced on the surface. However, throughout the entire abolishment campaign, it was the Association in the role of a traditional authority that kick-started the social movement that catalyzed the emergence of women-led foot-binding abolishment organizations that put women in the leading position of this social movement. Eventually the depraved custom of foot-binding was eradicated when it was incorporated and regulated in the Pao-Chia System (a community-based system of law enforcement and civil control). In this light, the Association had exerted a major incremental impact upon society of that time that cannot be overlooked. During the process of transmitting ideas, these steps and methods were followed: assimilating ideas, establishing organization guidelines, hosting rituals and events, solidifying a sense of identity, and dissipation. In the ten years after the Association was established (1900–1910), against the backdrop of the Japanese colonial culture, the value and impact generated by the Association deserve a considerable amount of analysis and deconstruction.

The Association emblem is the only concrete symbol that has been passed on to this day and sufficiently represents this important social movement. This physical emblem, gave Association members a sense of honor while also amplifying their social status. The visual design of the emblem tacitly demonstrates the advocacy of the natural foot concept and the ethos of this social movement. How this emblem invigorated the movement with a non-verbal visual message is well worth academic research.

1.2 Research Objectives

Based on news coverage of the Association "inauguration ceremony" in the Natural Foot Association Newsletter and the Taiwan Daily News and supplemented with events as documented in literature, as well as the reward items generated from this social movement, the study aims to achieve the following research objectives:

1. A literature survey helped with the interpretation of the social movement that took place a century ago and an analysis of the advocacy strategies of the natural foot concept association.
2. The analysis focuses on the design elements of the Association emblem as a visual symbol, the Lotus "Flower Badge", that still exists today and whether it could achieve the goal of advancing this social movement.

1.3   Analysis of the Association's Advocacy Strategies for Foot-Binding Abolishment

The Association was founded by Mr Huang Yu-Chieh along with about 40 members of the local intelligentsia and businessmen in 1899. It was registered in Taipei County, advocating the two advanced ideas of "Keeping feet unbound" and "Abolishing foot-binding". The Association's inauguration ceremony was held in the "Puyuanshe Lecture Hall" on Ri-Xin Street in Dadaocheng in 1900. *The Natural Foot Association Newsletter* was launched in the same year and covered the Association's founding mission, organization members, attending guests, lists of members in various categories, donation amounts, the timeline of development of the Association and various historical events. In this study an analysis of the Association's advocacy strategies covers all aspects of the foot-binding abolishment campaign: the establishment of an awareness of subjectivity, achievement of consensus within the society, the taking of consistent action through organization guidelines, the activation of rituals to confer a sense of honor upon participants, the application of visual design to enhance participants' identification with the cause, the generation of dissipation effects and ultimate termination of the social practice of foot-binding through the Pao-Chia System. The image below illustrates and analyzes the movement's advocacy strategies:

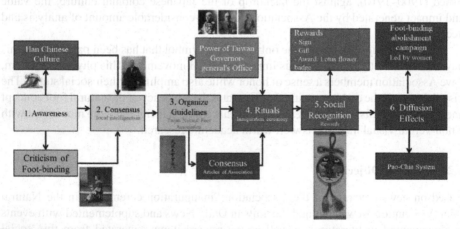

Fig. 1. The analysis structure of the Taipei Natural Foot Association's advocacy of the natural foot concept.

The foot-binding abolishment campaign, as shown in Fig. 1, has been examined as an historical social event by a review of the six steps that had been undertaken by the movement: establishment of an awareness of subjectivity (Awareness) the achievement of a consensus (Consensus), Organize guidelines, the hosting of rituals (Rituals), solidifying social recognition (Social Recognition), and the activation of diffusion effects (Diffusion Effects).

Establishment of an awareness of subjectivity. Legend has it that foot-binding may have originated in the upper social class of 10th-century China during the Five Dynasties period. Li Yu, also known as Li Houzhu (meaning "Last Ruler Li") of the Southern Tang state was known to have a particular fondness for the golden lotus dance performed by his consort on bound feet. The consort's bound feet then became the new trend to imitate, hence giving rise to the term "Three-Inch Golden Lotus". The earliest written record of foot-binding was penned by the Song-dynasty scholar, Zhang Bang-Qi, who is later frequently quoted. It is estimated that foot-binding originated no earlier than the 12th century [6].

Over the centuries, women were deeply influenced by Confucian thoughts and were required by the patriarchic society to comply with the "customs of courtesy" and follow the cultural practice of "foot-binding". The foot-binding abolishment campaign brought together a collective social awareness that foot-binding was barbaric, unproductive and embarrassing. The practice also actively reversed civilization for women, their identity and economic status [15]. Therefore, a high level of social recognition was required, both conceptual and actual, for natural foot preservation and for the abolishment of foot-binding advocacy to succeed.

Achievement of a Consensus: By Placing Local Intelligentsia in Leading Positions in the Foot-Binding Abolishment Campaign. Starting in 1895, the Japanese Taiwan Governor-General's Office constantly invited the intelligentsia from all over Taiwan to visit and tour Japan, to observe life there and to communicate new concepts to them so that they would start promoting the natural foot campaign once they returned to Taiwan. For instance, in 1896, Li Chun-Sheng, a wealthy merchant in Dadaocheng visited Japan with his entire family at the invitation of Kabayama Sukenori, the Japanese Governor-General of Taiwan, and wrote *A Journal of Sixty-four Days Trip to the East* [10] upon his return to Taiwan. This documented, in the form of a journal, his trips and experiences in Japan. The intention behind the invitation by the Taiwan Governor-General's Office was clear. As Taiwan was a patriarchal society under Japanese colonial rule, the Japanese government at the time strategically encouraged the local intelligentsia to take the initiative of advocating the natural foot concept as part of Japan's incremental governance.

The Association advocated that the foot-binding custom deprived women of opportunities to receive education and skills training and that women with bound feet were not able to do housework properly either. This shows that the aim, from the perspective of the colonial Japanese government at the time, was to unleash a female labor and economic force [15].

Organize Guidelines. At the end of 1899, Huang Yu-Chieh called on famous personalities across all regions to organize and establish the Association and registered it in the Taipei County. Up to 40 people signed up as the initiators, all Taiwanese, mostly men and Dadaocheng merchants. They were all from various professions: Chinese herbal medicine, western medicine, business, and politics. The Association membership list shows it took a decidedly male stance in its advocacy of the natural foot concept. Membership doubled before the organization registration was affirmed and this showed that the vision and mission of the Association had won the recognition and respect of the people. There were four categories of membership: official members, governing members, sponsoring members, and root members. Members held each other to this agreement: never marry a woman with bound feet and never impose foot-binding on their daughters.

Host Initiation Rituals: Inauguration Ceremony. The Association's inauguration ceremony was held in the "Puyuanshe Lecture Hall" and more than 250 people attended, including all the Association founders and members. Numerous dignitaries present at the ceremony included Kodama Gentaro, the Governor-General of Taiwan, Gotō Shinpei, the head of civilian affairs, Murakami Yoshio, the Taipei County governor, all department chiefs of the Taipei city government, and the Taiwan Local Red Cross Branch representatives of the Japanese Red Cross Society. Additionally, the Taiwan Governor-General' Office invited more than 70 renowned scholars from the Yangwen Group all across Taiwan to the ceremony. The large turnout resulted in many of them later becoming a helping force that set up other foot-binding abolishment organizations all over Taiwan [5]. As described above, the convergence of politicians, merchants, intelligentsia, and literary scholars at the ceremony contributed to the forming and dissipation of public opinion and made a very declarative statement.

Achievement of a Sense of Identification: Reward Measures. Three types of rewards were stipulated by the Association to expand its membership and to encourage members to proactively release bound feet or keep feet unbound [14]:

Sign. Hang up a sign on the members' house gates to mark and honor them as a former household that had bound feet.

Gift. Gift those terminating the foot-binding practice with a pair of embroidered shoes.

Award. Award them with the lotus flower badge embroidered with "Daijishō" (the official emblem of Taiwan under Japanese rule) to those terminating the foot-binding practice, or for keeping feet unbound. The badge was seen as an honor and a distinction from the servants [2]. Those who released bound feet or kept feet unbound were conferred with a blue or red ribbon emblem. In commemoration of the deed, they were also gifted with a figure-eight scarf embroidered with the inscription, "Not harming one's body is the first step to performing one's filial piety" by Kodama Gentaro, the Governor-General of Taiwan [13]. Only the physical Association emblems were found in a search for items that symbolized the movement, none of the others could be found (Figs. 2 and 3).

Diffusion Effects. The key events in the timeline of the foot-binding abolishment campaign indicate that the Association was led by men, while the major diffusion effects of the change were led by women. The foot-binding custom was finally abolished when it was incorporated and regulated in the Pao-Chia System.

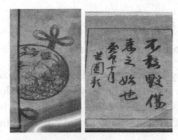

Fig. 2. A figure-of-eight scarf embroidered with the inscription, "Not harming one's body is the first step to performing one's filial piety" by Kodama Gentaro, the Governor-General of Taiwan (in the permanent collection of the National Taiwan Museum).

Fig. 3. Taipei Natural Foot Association emblem, "Flower Badge" (housed with the collection of the Taipei Supreme Kindness Hall Foundation).

In 1899, Huang Yu-Chieh and the local intelligentsia jointly initiated and founded the "Taipei Natural Foot Association", Taiwan's first organization to advocate natural feet and the abolishment of foot-binding.

In 1900, the inauguration ceremony of the "Taipei Natural Foot Association" was held in "Puyuanshe Lecture Hall" on Rixin Street in Dadaocheng. In the following three years, seven related organizations were established.

In 1911, other foot-binding abolishment organizations were set up one after another in a very short period of time and were led by women, not men.

In 1915, in the name of celebrating the 20-year governance in Taiwan, the Japanese Taiwan Governor-General's Office had foot-binding regulated by the Pao-Chia System and issued an executive order that made the practice of foot-binding a punishable offence.

Taiwan's foot-binding population went down from 800,000 in 1905 to about 280,000 in 1915. Following the termination of hair plaiting, foot-binding was eradicated by the Pao-Chia System. The foot-binding cloth officially became a thing of the past.

2 Literature Review

2.1 Visual Communication Related Research

The design of each campaign needed to be further visualized to be perceived by the consumer and so the Taipei Natural Foot Association emblem was carefully analyzed for perception by the recipients. According to Jacobson [4], a successful language communication model must have six elements and six functions, which are:

Addresser. The Addresser encodes and transmits the message to the Addressee in the transmission process.

Addressee. The Addressee is the target or specific audience to which the message is sent.

Context. The message must be framed in a reference context in order to form a specific meaning.

Message. Message is composed of a linguistic gene of symbolic representation, which encodes information according to a specific symbolic structure, and then generates meaning and understanding through the decoding process of the addressee.

Contact. Also known as a conduit or medium, is a physical device or tool for transmitting a message and is used to establish a relationship between the sender and the receiver.

Code. Code is an organized and understandable information system, and the Addresser and Addressee must share a common code system to enable understanding and to proceed.

Norman [11] pointed out three levels of the design process; visceral, behavioral, and reflective. First, to ascertain if the Addressee sees and produces sensory impressions of shape perception; second, if the Addressee understands the thought process of meaning recognition; and finally, if it resonates with the Addressee, who realizes the mental activity of inner feelings [9]. By integrating Norman's three mental cognitive psychology models and the concept of emotional design, the addresser (designer) converts the design into cultural symbols or elements, includes them in the design, and transmits them to the addressee as a message. The received messages are interpreted and the information has an effect on the addressee which causes behavioral changes. By integrating the above two theoretical concepts, the following analytical model for the design of the Taipei Natural Foot Association emblem was developed, and an interpretation of whether the design elements of the emblem could accomplish the message of "Unbinding to protect the natural foot" was conducted (Fig. 4).

2.2 Metaphorical Design-Related Research

The term metaphor refers to the explanation of one thing through the perception of another thing. Cultural and creative design uses metaphors to transform concepts into products. From a Western point of view, Lakeoff & Jonson [7] explain in their book *Metaphors We Live By* that metaphors are abundant in human life, not only in language

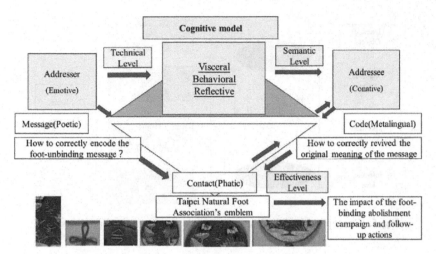

Fig. 4. The cognitive communication model of cultural and creative material [10].

but also in actions and thoughts. Ernst Cassirer [1] further suggests that metaphors are unavoidable in normal speech. There are two classes of metaphor: the subject is the abstract concept that we want to express, and the carrier is the symbol that carries the abstract concept. In life, the characteristics of the carrier are often transferred to the subject, and the subject and carrier are interactive. [12].

From an Oriental point of view, the connection between metaphors and rhetoric can be seen in Liu Xie's "*The Literary Mind and the Carving of Dragons - Bi-Xing*" [3]. *Bi* explains things according to their similarities; *Xing* expresses feelings according to the subtleties of things. The form of analogy: "The meaning of analogy is not always the same; it is either association via homonym; formed via similitude; created via empathy; or invented via analogy" The material of metaphor comes from sounds such as homophones (Association via Homonym), or appearance imitating the form of birds, animals, and people (Formed via Similitude), from intangible thoughts such as rituals and rules (Creation via Empathy), and from analogies to storylines or historical events and myths, as an analogy for what is meant beyond words (Invented via Analogy) [8]. By combining the Chinese and Western perspectives, the conceptual model of metaphorical design for cultural products was formed, see (Fig. 5).

When designers transform symbols, it is more pivotal to grasp the extended meanings that they can provide, in addition to the original meaning of the carrier itself. By considering the product as a symbolic system, the symbolic qualities of the product are studied and the knowledge is applied to the product design. Art is a combination of cultural symbols, and the connotation carried by the symbols and their denotation are symbiotic concepts. Therefore, in this study the above framework was leveraged to explain the connotation of the six design elements of the Association emblem, to understand how well the coders could convey their meaning to the decoders, so that an understanding of the decoding ability of the emblem in this social movement could be achieved.

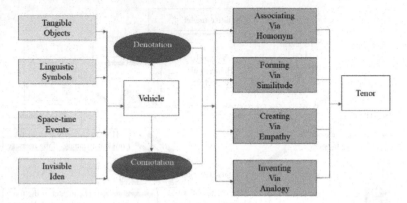

Fig. 5. Conceptual model of metaphorical design for cultural products [8].

3 Research Methodology

The Taipei Natural Foot Association emblem, which represents the foot-unbinding social movement, was divided into six design elements, including the swastika knot, Daijisho, flower badge, medallion, lotus badge, swallow badge, and water motif. The cognitive model of metaphorical design concept and communication of cultural products was used to analyze the six elements of the emblem, and the design power of the technical, semantic, and effect levels of the cognitive model was set as the basis for the study and analysis. A total of 116 valid questionnaires were collected in a social network survey, and a perception map was created using Multidimensional Scaling (MDS) and multiple regression analysis to understand the association between the design elements and attributes.

3.1 Analysis of the Totems and Design of the Taipei Natural Foot Association Emblem

The founder of the Association, Huang Yu-Chieh, was the district head of the Dadaocheng District and Dalongdong District, and was the first in the lineage of local gentry in Taiwan. He was also the first Taiwanese to obtain an official Chinese Traditional Medicine license from the colonial Japanese authorities. Huang leveraged his political and local connections to promote important contemporary social movements. "Flower Badge", the most important surviving artifact in the context of the six design elements of the social movement, is analyzed in the following illustration (Table 1):

The design elements and concepts used in the badge of the Taipei Natural Foot Association are clearly described in the *Taiwan Kanshu Kiji* (Taiwan Customary Records): "The badge used by the members of the association is shaped like the gentleman's badge of the islanders, with "Daijisho" inscribed in the middle of the lotus flower, blue for those who have unbound their feet, and red for those who maintain natural foot.". In this paper, the metaphorical design concept of a cultural product to has been used to explain the representation and influence of the Taipei Natural Foot Association emblem on the

Table 1. The Taipei Natural Foot Association emblem "Flower Badge" and six design elements

Swastika Knot	Daijisho
Flower Badge	Lotus Flower
Swallow	Water Motif.

social movement of foot-binding by integrating the records of the *Taiwan Kanshu Kiji* with extended semantics.

Swastika Knot. The symbol of the "Swastika Knot" is used as the beginning of the badge emblem, signifying the auspicious symbol of all things going well. The Swastika is a common Buddhist symbol and the knot can be extended in all four directions. In practice it can be attached to the chest button of the shirt using its clasp, which expresses the honor of wearing the badge as a member of the Taipei Natural Foot Association.

Daijisho. Observation of the artifact, shows the embroidered pattern to be the "Daijisho" with a front and an inverted triangle embroidered in gold thread, which was recorded in the *Civil Service System of the Government-General of Taiwan* in 1920 as a badge representing the Government-General of Taiwan. In 1900, the Taipei Natural Foot Association was registered by the Government-General of Taiwan, and as an extension unit of the Government-General of Taiwan. Therefore, the Association was able to use the "Daijisho" badge as part of the emblem of the Taipei Natural Foot Association.

Flower Badge. The "Taipei Natural Foot Association Historical Income and Expenditure Accounts and Inventory", in the collection of the Taipei City Zhishantang Foundation, lists the expenses of the Flower Badge. In Buddhist scriptures the lotus flower represents many meanings and there is extensive use of lotus flower imagery. In the Taiwan Daily News, the Flower Badge is depicted as "three characters inscribed in the center of the lotus flower". Therefore, it can be inferred that "Flower Badge" also means "Lotus Badge".

Lotus Flower. Two lotus flowers embroidered with gold threads can be found on the Flower Badge. The left side of the lotus flower is shown from the front, with the pistil visible in the middle and the lotus seedpod embroidered on it, symbolizing the concept of a mother passing the concept of natural feet to her daughter to liberate the female body. It was recorded in the Taiwan Daily News and the *Taiwan Kanshu Kiji* that the lotus flower is embroidered with gold thread, to signify the golden lotus. The golden lotus in full bloom infers to liberation of the "Three-Inch Golden Lotus".

Swallow. The swallow is a symbol of good luck in Chinese iconography. Its wings appear to be open. The author deduces that the swallow flying into the sky represents the freedom of the body.

Water Motif. Water motifs are widely used in Chinese art, representing auspiciousness and the imagination of good things. Water nourishes all things, so it is also means generous virtue and tolerance of all. The water motif in the Flower Badge nourishes the lotus flower, as Chou, Tun-I of the Song dynasty describes "emerges from the mud without a speck of dirt, and washes the mud without becoming a demon", describing the lotus flower washed by water without appearing demonic, to imply the owner of this badge is of high moral integrity.

3.2 Multidimensional Scaling (MDS)

The emblem of the Taipei Natural Foot Association was divided into the above six graphic elements and a survey with a questionnaire was conducted to explain the perception of the six graphic designs on the medallion. Two questions were designated for each: the technical layer (precision of visual design and sophistication of craftsmanship), the semantic layer (aesthetic expression and symbolic meaning), and the effect layer (cultural connotation and creative expression). A total of 116 questionnaires were collected by random sampling, and after MDS analysis, the stress index $= 0.06743$ and the suitability (RSQ) $= .98559$, which can reasonably explain the relationship between the six attributes and the six images. The following table indicates the mean scores of the overall attributes of each image of the Flower Badge work (Table 2).

Table 2. Average scores for the overall attributes of the Taipei Natural Foot Association emblem

	p1	p2	p3	p4	p5	P6
q1 precision of visual design	3.15	3.11	3.28	3.38	3.42	3.47
q2 sophistication of craftsmanship	3.22	2.96	3.42	3.66	3.35	3.61
q3 aesthetic expression	3.24	2.85	3.32	3.52	3.22	3.60
q4 symbolic meaning	3.26	3.28	3.39	3.36	3.47	3.44
q5 cultural connotation	3.51	3.34	3.45	3.65	3.53	3.52
q6 creative expression	3.15	3.13	3.15	3.52	3.50	3.52

Among the six attributes, it can be clearly seen that the attributes with higher scores are figurative images, the lotus, swallow, and water motifs, indicating that the figurative images were more easily interpreted by the addressee than the textual designs (Swastika, Daijisho, Flower Badge). A look at the scores for the six attributes in the image from a horizontal perspective showed: the image with the highest design accuracy score was the water motif; sophistication of craftsmanship, the lotus; aesthetic expression, the water motif; symbolic meaning; the swallow; cultural connotation; the lotus; and creative expression, the lotus and the water motif together. The lotus flower had the three highest attribute scores, for craft sophistication, cultural connotation, and creative expression. The water motif had the highest scores for design precision, aesthetic expression, and creative expression. The swallow had the highest score in the symbolic meaning attribute.

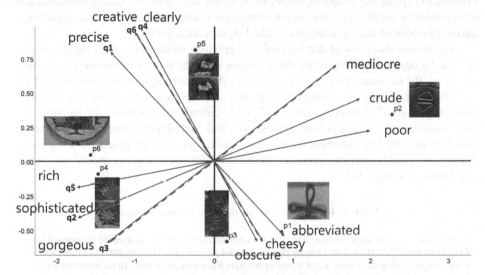

Fig. 6. MDS analysis of the attributes of the "Flower Badge".

As shown in Fig. 6, the two least relevant attributes are modified into new x-axis and y-axis (see the blue line in Fig. 6), forming four quadrants.

First Quadrant: Swallow, where the attributes are clear.

Second Quadrant: water motif and lotus, whose attributes are creative, precise, rich, sophisticated, and gorgeous.

Third Quadrant: the Flower Badge, whose attributes are obscure.

Fourth Quadrant: the Swastika Knot and the Daijisho, where the attributes are abbreviated, poor, crude, and mediocre.

Among them, the swallows, water motif and lotus flowers in the first and second quadrants are figurative images with high scores. The third and fourth quadrants of the Flower Badge, the Swastika Knot, and Daijisho are icons converted from words. It is clear that that metaphors, the conversion of physical images into semantic meanings, are more persuasive than direct expressions in words.

It is worth noting that, for example, the abbreviated, poor, crude, mediocre, and obscure are contrasted with the creative, precise, rich, refined, and gorgeous, which seem to be negative narrative but are actually only descriptions of phenomena. For example, the contrast of Daijisho with the fine embroidery of the lotus flower is naturally described as abbreviated.

3.3 Regression Analysis Results

Based on the above analysis, the three images with higher mean scores (lotus flower, swallow, and water motifs) were selected and the results of the regression analysis were utilized to explain the design ingenuity of these six attributes, the results indicated that the correlation coefficient r, the overall correlation coefficient R, the explained variance, and the F-value of the three images reached significant levels.

The results also showed that the overall regression model was useful for the prediction of the design ingenuity of the three images using by the six independent variables, However, the important predictive variables for the three images were all slightly different: "design precision", "cultural connotation", and "aesthetic expression" for the lotus; "design precision", "creative expression", and "cultural connotation" for the swallow; and "design precision", "aesthetic expression", and "cultural connotation" for the water motif. While the key variables for the water motif are "design precision", "aesthetic expression", and "cultural connotation". For the results of the regression analysis, please see Tables 3, 4 and 5 below.

Table 3. Regression analysis table for the lotus imagery

Question: Do you think the lotus flower on the emblem interprets "the concept of the natural foot being liberated from the female body by the mother and passed on to the daughter. The lotus flower embroidered with gold thread in full bloom symbolizes liberation from the "Three-Inch Golden Lotus", just like the lotus flower in full bloom.

independent variable	Predicted variable	B	r	β	t
Design ingenuity	Precision of design	.47 1	.755***	.381	3.927***
	Exquisite craftsmanship	.22 8	.567***	.176	1.650
	Aesthetic expression	-.326	.460***	-.272	-2.697**
	Symbolic meaning	.17 3	.673***	.155	1.852
	Cultural connotation	.47 1	.751***	.367	4.159***
	Creative expression	.12 5	.589***	.095	1.160
R=.836			R2=.682		F=40.991***

*p <0.05   **p <0.01   ***p <0.001

Table 4. Swallow image regression analysis table

Question: Do you think the swallow on the emblem is a "metaphor for the swallow that flies into the sky after a woman's feet are unbound, representing the freedom that comes from physical autonomy?

Independent variable	Predicted variable	B	r	β	t
Design ingenuity	Exquisite craftsmanship	.031	.650***	.032	3.798
	Symbolic meaning	.119	.708***	.125	-.817
	Creative expression	.248	.735***	.246	2.108*
	R=.821		R2=.675	F=37.683***	

*p <0.05 **p <0.01 ***p <0.001

Table 5. Regression analysis table for the water motif

Question: Do you think the water motif can interpret the meaning of "being an auspicious symbol, that represents the ability of water to nourish all things, and through the clean and implying thar the wearer of this badge has a high moral character by virtue of the water motif"?

Independent variable	Predicted variable	B	r	β	t
Design ingenuity	Exquisite craftsmanship	-.156	.650***	-.135	-1.461
	Symbolic meaning	.071	.713***	.066	.680
	Creative expression	.085	.696***	.077	.875
	R=.851		R2=.725	F=47.860***	

*p <0.05 **p <0.01 ***p <0.001

4 Research Results/Conclusions and Recommendations

The metaphorical design and communication cognitive model were combined with the results of multidimensional scaling analysis and regression analysis to analyze the visual design communication effect of the Taipei Natural Foot Association's emblem by using the design attributes of three specific images: lotus, swallow, and water motifs. The findings suggest that the three elements in the metaphorical design are all tangible objects that are transformed by "similitude" and "analogy", and the original context is transformed into an extended meaning, as follows:

1. The Lotus flower

Image	Vehicle	Element Attribute	Denotation	Connotation	conversion /metaphor	Tenor	Design Elements	Cognitive level
	Lotus flower	Tangible Objects	Flower	1. Lotus feet. 2. The lotus grows out of the mud but not stained 3. A metaphor for foot-unbinding is like a lotus flower blooming	Forming Via Similitude and Inventing Via Analogy	Women's social status and character	Precision of visual design Aesthetic expression Cultural connotation	Technical level Semantic level Effectiveness level

The Taipei Natural Foot Association emblem leverages the tangible object in the form of a lotus flower to transform the connotation of foot-binding (lotus feet), the unstained mud and the unbound foot conveys a meaning of social status and character in women. The multidimensional scaling analysis and regression analyses show that, in terms of communication and cognition, there is an attribute of precision, aesthetic expression and cultural connotation, in the technical, semantic, and effect layers that illustrate the ingenuity of the lotus flower design.

2. The Swallo

Image	Vehicle	Element Attribute	Denotation	Connotation	conversion /metaphor	Tenor	Design Elements	Cognitive level
	Swallow	Tangible Objects	Bird	Fly, Freedom	Forming Via Similitude and Inventing Via Analogy	Freedom from footbinding and liberation of the body	Precision of visual design Creative expression Cultural connotation	Technical level Effectiveness level Effectiveness level

The concept of transforming freedom with a tangible swallow conveys the meaning of freedom from foot-binding and liberation of the body. The multidimensional scaling analysis and regression analysis showed that the technical layer was based on design precision, while the effect layer was based on two attributes: creative expression and cultural connotation, which serves to explain the design ingenuity of the swallow.

3. The Water motif

Image	Vehicle	Element Attribute	Denotation	Connotation	conversion/ metaphor	Tenor	Design Elements	Cognitive level
	Water motif	Tangible Objects	Water	The water motif is used as a metaphor for a woman's noble character and innocence as water	Forming Via Similitude and Inventing Via Analogy	Noble character and immaculate bearing	Precision of visual design Aesthetic expression Cultural connotation	Technical level Semantic level Effectiveness level

The water motif was used as a metaphor for the noble character of women and innocence. Water implies noble character and immaculate bearing. Multidimensional scaling and regression analyses showed the technical layer was based on design precision, the semantic layer on aesthetic expression, and the effect layer on cultural connotation, which together account for the ingenuity of the design.

In summary, the Taipei Natural Foot Association emblem utilizes figurative iconography and metaphorical design transformation to convey the social movement idea of unbinding the feet and the protection of natural feet, which is more convincing than the use of words to convey the same idea. As shown in the table above, the four design elements of design precision, cultural connotation, aesthetic expression, and creative expression have stronger explanatory power than the others. Among the explanatory factors at the cognitive level, the lotus flower, the swallow, and the water motifs all appear in the precise design (technical layer) and cultural connotation (effect layer), while the aesthetic expression (semantic layer) appears in the lotus flower and the water motif. The above findings clearly show that the sophistication of craftsmanship and cultural connotation play an indispensable role in the message of the work. The craftsmanship enhances the aesthetic performance, while culture increases the design connotation of the cultural material, which together complete communication of the cognitive concept of the social movement of the Taipei Natural Foot Association emblem and prompts the addressees to take action.

References

1. Cassirer, E.: Symbol, Myth, and Culture. Yale University Press, London (1979)
2. Chang, S.-W.: A study of the anti foot-binding movement in Taiwan during the Japanese colonial period, Master's thesis, Department of Cultural Heritage Conservation, National Yunlin University of Science and Technology (2008)
3. Fan, W.-L.: The Literary Mind and the Carving of Dragons Taipei: Taiwan Kai Ming Book Co. Ltd. (1975)
4. Jakobson, R.: Language in Literature. Harvard University Press, Cambridge (1987)
5. Jao, J.-C.: The Taipei Natural Foot Association Journal, Taipei, Dadaocheng Rixin Street Natural Foot Association Publishing House (1900)
6. Ko, Y.-I.: Defining Foot-binding: Ciderella's Sisters: A Revisionist History of Footbinding Taipei, Rive Gauche, June 2007, p.188 (2007)

7. Lakoff, G., Johnson, M.: Metaphor We Live By. University of Chicago Press, Chicago (1980)
8. Lin, P.-H., Yeh, M.-L.: Representing traditional culture–applying ho lo culture elements on creative product design. In: Proceedings of the Tenth Hoklo Culture Symposium: Hoklo Culture and Taiwan Culture, pp. 579–588. Henan People's Publishing House (2011)
9. Lin, R., Lee, S.: Poetry and Painting - Experience Sharing of the Beauty of Xian Yun's Works New Taipei City: National Taiwan University of Arts (2015)
10. Lin, S.-H.: Women's movement to untie their feet and its cultural significance in Taiwan during the Japanese rule. Natl. Central Libr. Bull. **10**(2), 76–93 (2004)
11. Norman, D.A.: The Design of Everyday Things. Basic Books, New York (2002)
12. Richards, I.A.: The Philosophy of Rhetoric. Oxford University Press, Oxford (1965). Levi-Strauss, C. (1963). Structural and anthropology. C. Jacobson & B. G. Schoepf (Trans.). NY: Basic Books (1965)
13. Taiwan Daily News: Awarding Ceremony of the Taipei Natural Foot Association's Lotus Badge, Taiwan Daily News, p. 2, 1 November 1903
14. Taiwan Kanshū kenkyūkai: Taiwan Kanshu Kiji , vol. 1, no. 5. Taiwan Memory System, National Central Library (1901). https://tm.ncl.edu.tw/
15. Taiwan Kanshū kenkyūkai: Taiwan Kanshu Kiji, vol. 3, no. 12. Taiwan Memory System of National Central Library (1903). https://tm.ncl.edu.tw/
16. Miao, Y.-W.: From "natural feet societies" to "footbinding liberation societies": the politics of female body in early colonial Taiwan (1900–1915). Taiwan A Radic. Q. Soc. Stud. **91**, 125–174 (2013)

The Impact of HCI on the Protection of the Rights and Interests of Minors in China and Legal Responses

Huiqing Wen[✉]

Beijing Youth Politics College, Beijing 100102, China
rucwenhuiqing@aliyun.com

Abstract. Human-computer interaction (HCI) has become the main growth space for minors in contemporary China. The human-computer interaction methods of minors are mainly reflected in the interaction with social networks and social media, the acceptance and analysis of digital social information, and the decision-making and feedback of digital information. Due to the popularization of human-computer interaction, the protection of minors' rights and interests has also undergone tremendous changes, including: minors' privacy and personal information have become an important part of the protection of rights and interests, crimes against minors have appeared networked characteristics, bullies use social networks to bully minors in school, and online consumer disputes between minors and businesses have increased greatly. In response to this, China has established a legislative system for the online protection of minors. The practice of protecting minors' online security through civil legal means is very common and effective. For example, provisions and judicial practices in areas such as online guardianship of minors, the validity of contractual acts in online transactions for minors, and the protection of minors' personal information have effectively protected the legitimate rights and interests of minors.

Keywords: HCI · Minors · Network Protection · Judicial Practice

1 Introduction

China's digitalization process is reshaping today's economy and society and will directly affect the direction of the future. As a generation born after the 21st century, Chinese minors are veritable digital natives. The key point of the digital society is human-computer interaction. The so-called human-computer interaction refers to the information exchange process between people and computers using a certain dialogue language in a certain interactive way to complete the determined task. Human-computer interaction focuses on the design and use of computer technology and the interaction between people (users) and computers. Minors in the digital age rely on human-computer interaction in all aspects of their lives, studies, socialization, entertainment and so on.

Although human-computer interaction belongs to the category of computer science, because China has formed a digital social governance model based on human-computer

P.-L. P. Rau (Ed.): HCII 2023, LNCS 14022, pp. 297–305, 2023.
https://doi.org/10.1007/978-3-031-35936-1_21

interaction, human-computer interaction has become the basic background of social science research. Similarly, compared with the traditional era, the protection of the rights and interests of minors has also been deeply affected by the digital society - profound changes have taken place in the subject, object and content of rights and interests protection. Therefore, the protection of the rights and interests of minors in China in the new era will also take "human-computer interaction" as the research background. When protecting the legitimate rights and interests of minors, we must deeply consider this change and respond positively.

2 The Way Minors Interact with Computer Networks

2.1 Computer Network Usage by Minors in China

According to the "2021 National Research Report on Internet Use by Minors" jointly released by the Department for Safeguarding Youth Rights and Interests of the Central Committee of the Communist Youth League and the China Internet Network Information Center in 2022, since 2018, the scale of Chinese juvenile Internet users has maintained an increase trend for four consecutive years. In 2021, it reached 191 million, and the Internet penetration rate of minors was 96.8%, an increase of 1.9% points over 2020 (94.9%) [1]. This huge group mainly connects to the Internet through internet devices such as smart phones, desktop computers, laptops, tablet computers, smart watches, smart desk lamps, smart speakers, dictionary pens, etc., in order to carry out human-computer interaction, so as to meet the needs of life and learning. Among them, the use of smart devices better reflects the characteristics of human-computer interaction among minors.

2.2 Ways in Which Minors Interact with Computer Networks

Minors interact with computer networks in a variety of ways. In a nutshell, they can be divided into the following three categories.

The first way is the minor's interaction with social networks and social media. With the "ubiquitous interconnection" of the mobile Internet space, all social individuals, including minors, are wrapped in social networks and social media. Their social behavior is undoubtedly influenced by social networks and social media. Moreover, the interactivity of the Internet accelerates the process of socialization of minors. As minors grow older, online social interaction increases, and older minors use the Internet as an important channel for making friends - building social relationships through the Internet. In fact, Internet interpersonal communication belongs to the interpersonal communication in the virtual network society. On the one hand, it has the advantages of vitality, speed and openness [2]; on the other hand, due to the virtualization, diversification, and complexity of Internet social networking and the indirectness and abstraction of communication methods [3], it has also led to the increased danger of minors' online social networking.

The second way is the acceptance and analysis of digital social information by individual minors. With the acceleration of the digital age, the impact of human computer interaction technology on the learning and life of minors is becoming more and more deep. The popularity of digital devices among minors has made minors wrapped in digital social information. In the face of the same information, different minors and their guardians have different ability to process and analyze it. This is closely related to the effective social freedoms available to them and their guardians, expectations of future development, and the possibility of vested interests. At the same time, the information accepted and analyzed by minors and the data related to the information they receive have also become the privacy of minors and need to be protected by law.

The third way is individual minors' decision-making and feedback on digital information. The minor's learning and life are wrapped in digital information, and after acceptance and analysis, feedback will also be made through self-decision-making. This is an important step in human-computer interaction. Minors and their guardians make different decisions and feedback on social information in a human-computer interaction environment based on their own social network system and ability to process information. For example, after receiving an invitation to make an offer from an online shopping platform, some minors will make an expression of whether to "place an order" or not, that is, feedback, based on self-knowledge. For another example, some minors decide whether to "tip" after receiving information from the webcast. It is also a kind of decision-making and feedback on digital information.

3 The Impact of Human-Computer Interaction on the Protection of the Rights and Interests of Minors

In today's Chinese society, human-computer interaction design is ubiquitous, but it is difficult to make people deliberately notice. Compared with the traditional era, the rights and interests of minors in the era of human-computer interaction have undergone earth-shaking changes.

3.1 The Privacy and Personal Information of Minors Have Become an Important Part of the Protection of Rights and Interests

Minors and their guardians are surrounded by social networks and social media, and their personal privacy and personal information are far more likely to be leaked. The Civil Code of China, the Law on the Protection of Minors, and the Personal Information Protection Law all provide corresponding provisions.

3.2 Crimes Against Minors Appear Networked

Criminals use computer networks and various programs as a medium to commit crimes such as violence, fraud, rape and other crimes against minors. It is worth noting that the "generational barrier" of minors and adult cyberspace has increased, with minors managing to keep their social information out of their parents; Moreover, the social platforms used by minors and adults are diverging. This barrier objectively reflects the online culture of different ages, but due to the lack of guardian supervision, it also increases the possibility of minors being at risk. For example, minors in China widely use QQ space, while adults are more popular to use WeChat, and criminals take advantage of this phenomenon to infringe on the legitimate rights and interests of minors in QQ space. For another example, criminals use the Internet to lure underage girls, gain trust, and rape offline.

3.3 Bullies Use Social Networks to Bully Minors in School

At present, due to the influence of social and individual aberrations, especially the influence of the younger age and addiction of internet and mobile phone use, cyberbullying incidents are frequent, seriously affecting the physical and mental health of minors with weak self-control and endurance, and causing many social problems [4]. According to the 2021 National Research Report on Internet Use by Minors, the proportion of underage netizens who were ridiculed or abused online was 16.6%; 7.0% of people or their relatives and friends were maliciously harassed online; The percentage of personal information that was disclosed online without permission was 6.1%. In the era of human-computer interaction, minors' personal life learning and social networks have shifted from offline to online, and bullying has also evolved from direct infringement to cyberbullying and direct reality bullying. The main forms of cyberbullying are harassment, defamation, online polemics, theft of other people's information, dissemination of other people's private information, online stalking, etc.

3.4 Online Consumer Disputes Between Minors and Merchants Have Increased Significantly

In the human-computer interaction environment, e-commerce is developed, online consumption is convenient, payment methods are diverse. Minors use smart terminals to purchase items, purchase network services, and recharge online games without authorization. These minors have become an army of online consumers and are caught in a series of consumer disputes.

4 China's Legislative System for the Protection of the Rights and Interests of Minors Based on Human-Computer Interaction

The protection of minors' rights and interests based on human-computer interaction is mainly reflected in the protection of minors' networks. At present, China has issued more than 50 normative documents at the national level concerning the protection of minors' online rights and interests. Their sources (i.e., legal forms) include laws, administrative regulations, judicial interpretations, departmental rules and industry regulations. Among them, more than ten are special normative documents, mainly manifested as administrative regulations and departmental rules [5]. At the same time, all localities have also formulated relevant normative documents in accordance with higher-level laws in light of local actual conditions, so as to more effectively protect the legitimate rights and interests of minors online.

From the perspective of the scope of the concept, the online protection of minors belongs to the subordinate concept of the protection of minors, so the first thing to discuss the legal norms of the online protection of minors is the Law of the People's Republic of China on the Protection of Minors. The Act was passed in 1991. On June 2021, on International Children's Day, the newly revised Law on the Protection of Minors was officially implemented. The new law is hailed as "the biggest holiday gift for Chinese children" - this newly revised law has created a special chapter on "network protection", based on the five themes of online literacy education, online information management, online addiction prevention, personal information protection, and cyberbullying prevention and control, and based on the four responsible subjects of the state, society, school and family, forming a scientific, systematic and holistic online protection system for minors, complementing the traditional protection system, so as to achieve all-round online and offline protection for minors. This practice has attracted the attention of the whole Chinese society.

In addition to the Law of the People's Republic of China on the Protection of Minors, laws and regulations such as the Civil Code of the People's Republic of China, the Personal Information Protection Law of the People's Republic of China, and the Cybersecurity Law of the People's Republic of China also provide for the cybersecurity of minors.

5 Civil Legal Norms and Judicial Practices for the Online Protection of Minors in the Era of Human-Computer Interaction

The impact of human-computer interaction on minors has been discussed earlier. This impact is a challenge to the traditional protection of the rights and interests of minors - due to the influence of technology, the rights infringement or danger suffered by minors are diverse, limited and complex. Therefore, in the era of human-computer interaction, the ways of online protection of minors should be diversified. Civil law, as the most important legal system in people's social life, plays a vital role in the protection of minors online. In other words, the current practice of adjusting relevant legal relationships through civil legal means to protect the online security of minors is very common and effective.

5.1 Online Guardianship of Minors in the Era of Human-Computer Interaction

Articles 34 and 35 of the Civil Code of the People's Republic of China stipulate the guardianship duties of guardians: to carry out civil legal acts on behalf of the ward, and to protect the ward's personal rights, property rights and other lawful rights and interests. The Law of the People's Republic of China on the Protection of Minors further refines the guardianship responsibilities of guardians on the basis of the Civil Code. This includes network guardianship duties. The law stipulates that parents or other guardians of minors shall strengthen guidance and supervision of minors' use of the internet; minors must not be allowed to indulge in the Internet and come into contact with books, newspapers and periodicals, movies, radio and television programs, audio-visual products, electronic publications, and online information that harm or may affect their physical and mental health. Require guardians to avoid minors' exposure to network information that harms or may affect their physical and mental health by installing network protection software for minors on smart terminal products, selecting service models and management functions suitable for minors, and so forth; Reasonably arrange the time minors spend using the Internet, effectively preventing minors from indulging in the Internet.

In judicial practice, the courts issue a Family Education Guidance Order to minors who neglect to exercise their online guardianship duties, mainly in accordance with the provisions of the Family Education Promotion Law of the People's Republic of

China, to reprimand the above-mentioned guardians and order them to accept family education guidance. The so-called family education guidance order is a legal document. Generally speaking, its content is a negative evaluation of the behavior of the party who has not fulfilled the obligation of support and education. For example, The plaintiff is a primary school student. His mother gave her personal mobile phone to the plaintiff for use without installing online protection software for minors, choosing service models and management functions suitable for minors, and failing to take effective consumption management measures, so that the plaintiff registered a live streaming platform account in the name of his mother and recharged and rewarded more than 10,000 RMB. The plaintiff's guardian found out and sued the court, requesting the court to order the live streaming platform to refund the full amount of the tip. In the course of hearing the case, the court found that the plaintiff's parents, as guardians, gave their personal mobile phones to their minor children for use, but did not pay attention to the time and content of use, and did not properly keep their personal payment accounts, and did not perform their online guardianship duties in accordance with the law, resulting in the plaintiff being addicted to the Internet to a certain extent. The court then issued a Family Education Guidance Order to the plaintiff's parents, requiring them to educate and guide their children to surf the Internet healthily, strengthen parent-child companionship, prevent minors from becoming addicted to the internet, and receive family education guidance on the court's online family education platform, learn and master the "youth mode" user guide of the main live broadcast platform, and improve parents' Internet literacy and children's self-management ability related courses [6].

In addition to the above circumstances, there is also a more serious situation - if the parents or other guardians of minors neglect to perform their guardianship duties, or are unable to perform guardianship duties and refuse to entrust part or all of their guardianship duties to others, resulting in the minors being in a state of distress, according to the provisions of the Civil Code of the People's Republic of China, the court will revoke his guardianship qualifications according to the application of the relevant individual or organization, and arrange necessary temporary guardianship measures. And appoint new guardians in accordance with the law in accordance with the principle of the best interests of the ward.

5.2 The Validity of Contracts Signed by Minors in the Era of Human-Computer Interaction

In recent years, with the development of online games and online live broadcast platforms, game recharge, tips and other behaviors have become the main reasons for some minors' online consumption. However, while some minors empty their parents' wallets and aggravate their internet addiction, they may also breed bad thoughts, such as money worship and vanity. Even their outlook on life and values are alienated and distorted. According to recent statistics from the judicial department, the number of online dispute cases involving minors is the largest, and the proportion of cases involving recharge and tipping is the highest.

According to the provisions of the Civil Code of the People's Republic of China, a natural person aged 0–8 is a person without civil capacity, and his legal representative concludes a contract on his behalf, and the validity of the contract concluded by him alone is invalid. Natural persons over the age of 8 but under the age of 18 who are persons with limited capacity for civil conduct shall also be represented by their legally-designated representatives in the case of carrying out civil legal acts that are purely beneficial or civil legal acts appropriate to their age and intelligence. If he exercises a civil act alone, the attribution of effects of that act is pending; If it is later recognized by the legal guardian, the act is valid, and vice versa. For example, China's Supreme People's Court recently released a typical case. The 14-year-old plaintiff, without the knowledge of his parents, purchased hundreds of game accounts from the defendant's online store seven times through a platform, paying a total of more than RMB 30,000. After the plaintiff's parents discovered it the next day, they promptly contacted the customer service staff of the defendant's online store, saying that they would not recognize the plaintiff's purchase of the game account and payment, and asked the defendant for a refund. But the defendant did not agree to a full refund. After hearing, the court held that the plaintiff was a minor, a person with limited civil capacity, and the purchase of a game account was obviously incompatible with his age and intelligence, and his guardian, that is, the legal representative, also clearly stated that he would not recognize the act, so the purchase act implemented by the plaintiff was invalid, and ordered the defendant to return the full amount of the purchase of the game account to the plaintiff.

5.3 Protection of Minors' Personal Information in the Era of Human-Computer Interaction

The Civil Code of the People's Republic of China stipulates that the personal information of natural persons is protected by law. In November 2021, the Personal Information Protection Law of the People's Republic of China was officially implemented. The law specifically stipulates the personal information of minors and its protection: the personal information of minors under the age of 14 is sensitive personal information. Personal information processors may process sensitive personal information only if they have a specific purpose and sufficient necessity and take strict protection measures. The handling of sensitive personal information shall obtain the consent of the minor's guardian. The above provisions establish the principle of minimum necessity for the protection of minors' personal information, the principle of guardian consent, and the principle of special trial of industries involving minors. In judicial practice, if the private information in the personal information of minors is infringed, the legal provisions on privacy shall apply; If there are no provisions, the laws and regulations on the protection of personal information shall apply.

In addition to the above two laws, the Cyberspace Administration of China issued the Provisions on the Online Protection of Children's Personal Information in August 2019. This legal document specifically regulates the collection, storage, use, transfer and disclosure of personal information of children under the age of 14 through the Internet in the People's Republic of China.

For example, China's first civil public interest lawsuit on the protection of minors' online protection was a case concerning the protection of minors' personal information. In recent years, several criminal cases in a certain city have pointed to apps developed and operated by a certain company. During the operation of the App, without informing and obtaining the valid and explicit consent of the child's guardian in a conspicuous and clear manner, the App is allowed to register a child's account, collect and store children's personal information without authorization, and directly push short videos containing children's personal information to users with relevant browsing preferences. In addition, no technical means have been taken to specifically protect children's information. The behavior of the company not only violates the law, but also poses potential risks to the personal safety and tranquility of unspecified minors, and even causes damage consequences after the personal information of several minors is used by criminals. Therefore, the local people's procuratorate filed a civil public interest lawsuit with the local court in accordance with the law, requesting that a company be ordered to immediately stop the infringement of children's personal information by using the company's App, apologize, eliminate the impact, compensate for losses, and hand over the money to the relevant child protection public interest organization, specifically for children's personal information protection public interest matters [7].

Ensuring the legal, safe and healthy use of the Internet by minors in China is both the aspiration and the shared responsibility of the state and thousands of families. To this end, China will continue to work hard to abide by the "principle of the best interests of minors" and support a clear online sky for Chinese children.

6 Conclusion

Human-computer interaction has had a profound impact on the protection of the rights and interests of minors. In order to protect the lawful rights and interests of minors in the era of human-computer interaction, Chinese law stipulates the online guardianship duties of guardians, and also stipulates the effect of restricting persons with civil capacity from participating in online transactions such as online paid games or online live streaming platform "tips". In dealing with children's right to information, the personal information of minors under the age of 14 is specifically identified as sensitive information, and the consent of the minors' parents or other guardians shall be obtained for the handling of such information.

In short, based on human-computer interaction, China has built and is working hard to improve the legal system for the protection of minors online. This system is a combination of empowerment and protection, aiming to safeguard the legitimate rights and interests of minors. This means that, on the one hand, China's laws on the online protection of minors help minors protect their legitimate rights and interests from infringement; on the other hand, China also attaches great importance to the cultivation of minors' digital literacy, so that minors will get along with technology correctly. We believe that with the further development of human-computer interaction technology, human life will be better.

References

1. Ministry of Safeguarding Youth Rights and Interests of the Central Committee of the Communist Youth League, China Internet Network Information Center: 2021 National Research Report on Internet Use by Minors, November 2022

2. Li, H.: Comparison of "virtual world" and "real world" interpersonal communication. China Sci. Technol. Inf. **1**, 121–122+125 (2008)
3. Lu, Q., Lei, Y., Ma, X., Zhang, G., Liu, K., Geng, J.: Research on the Social Development of Professional School Students. Social Sciences Academic Press (2021)
4. Mo, M.: Exploration and thinking on the governance of cyberbullying among minors. People's Forum **36**, 82–85 (2021)
5. Wang, J., Sun, Y., Kang, L.: Legislative practice and interpretation: minors network protection system. Juv. Delinq. Prev. Res. **1**, 20–27 (2021)
6. Beijing Internet Court Releases Typical Cases on Online Judicial Protection of Minors. https://baijiahao.baidu.com/s?id=1733945713544073308&wfr=spider&for=pc. Accessed 9 Feb 2023
7. Official website of the Supreme People's Procuratorate. https://www.spp.gov.cn/spp/zdgz/202 103/t20210317_512919.shtml. Accessed 9 Feb 2023

Exploring the Empowerment of Chinese Women's Discourse in Tik Tok

Qian Wu[1]([✉]), Hang Jiang[2], and Wenyan Lu[1]

[1] Fuzhou University of International Studies and Trade, 28, Yuhuan Road, Shouzhan New District, Changle District , Fuzhou 350202, Fujian, China
278376200@qq.com
[2] Fuzhou Polytechnic, No. 8, Lianrong Road, Fuzhou 350102, Fujian, China

Abstract. In the new media environment, women are no longer the recipients of information, but rather the producers and consumers of information. The media image of women has become more diverse. Tik Tok is a product of the rapid development of new media, where women are empowered in many aspects of production, performance, distribution and reception. In many Tik Tok videos, women express themselves, with topics ranging from beauty and dressing to work and even gender relations. While this is a somewhat new look compared to the past, Chinese women are still influenced by traditional culture and there is still a hidden power manipulation behind it. The study of Tik Tok is relevant to the construction of equal gender relations in Tik Tok and other short social videos. At the same time, as the age group of Tik Tok users is young, it helps us to understand the contemporary media position of women in the social video sphere. This study collects the participation of some active female users in Tik Tok on public issues, analyses the most popular female short videos posted by female users in Tik Tok, and examines the media image of female users in Tik Tok platform using a qualitative research approach, supplemented by quantitative research. In this way, we analyze whether women's right to express themselves is being realized unconsciously and whether there is a qualitative improvement in the expression of women's voices compared to the traditional media era.

Keywords: Tik Tok · Media Images of Women · Female Empowerment

1 First Section Introduction

1.1 Research Background

As we enter the 21st century, the communications landscape is changing significantly and access to information is no longer limited to traditional media such as newspapers, radio and television. The rapid growth of the mobile internet is being driven by new iterations of communication technologies that are changing the way people live and play [1]. The 3 Generation mobile communication technology period was dominated by graphic-based social applications, which could not yet support a good video experience. The fourth generation of mobile communication technology has seen a significant increase in speed, driving the rapid development of video applications. The

P.-L. P. Rau (Ed.): HCII 2023, LNCS 14022, pp. 306–316, 2023.
https://doi.org/10.1007/978-3-031-35936-1_22

fifth-generation mobile communication technology is a new type of mobile communication network that not only solves the problem of human-to-human communication, but also provides users with a more immersive and extreme service experience such as augmented reality, virtual reality and ultra-high definition (3D) video, bringing them the ultimate entertainment experience. Various new media have entered people's daily lives. The boundaries between online and offline are becoming increasingly blurred, with various e-commerce, entertainment and tool apps coming into being, allowing people to meet their daily needs without having to leave home. According to the 5G Personal Application Development Research Report 2021 released by Ariadne, the number of 5G package subscribers of the three major operators reached 452 million by May 2021, a net increase of 129 million compared to the end of 2020 [2]. Meanwhile, the penetration rate of 5G packages also increased from 20.2% at the end of 2020 to 28.0% in May 2021.

With the popularity and maturity of mobile Internet, consumers' Internet-based content consumption and online social networking needs are increasing. The original graphic consumption can no longer meet users' needs, and video has become more preferred content. Short videos have currently become an important development direction for current information dissemination due to their low creation threshold, social attributes and strong interactivity, fragmented consumption and dissemination. Considered by the industry as a windfall in the Internet field, talents and funds are entering on a large scale. Tencent, Sina, Ali, Baidu and other major Internet giants have laid out to seize the high ground in the short video industry, relying on platforms and content. The number of short video users began to grow explosively as a result of the introduction of various short video APPs, such as Racer, Secapai and Xiaogaxiu. On 27 August 2021, China Internet Network Information Centre (CNNIC) released the 48th Statistical Report on the Development Status of the Internet in China. The report pointed out that as of June 2021, the size of Chinese short video users was 888 million, accounting for 87.8% of Internet users overall. The growth of short-form video has become the biggest bonus cake of the moment.

Since its launch in September 2016, Tik Tok has grown rapidly, attracting a large number of users in a short period of time [3]. Although it was not well known in its early stages, in just nine months it has grown exponentially with over 100 million users and one billion daily plays. In the Spring Festival of 2018, Tik Tok's daily activity reached 65 million and even surpassed Alipay in the App Store download ranking at one point, becoming a phenomenon sought after by the post-90s and post-00s [4]. The Mobile APP Index provided by Ariadata shows that as of November 2018, Tik Tok's monthly unique device downloads have reached 293.47 million units, successfully catching up with Racer and becoming the industry giant of short video APPs. According to The Economist, TikTok has become an indispensable companion for teenagers around the world when they are forced to stay home from school because of the epidemic [5]. As of March 2020, TikTok has been downloaded 115 million times and has over 1 billion users. And among the large group of users, female users have become the mainstay. Quest Mobile has released the "2020 China Mobile Internet Spring Report". The report states that the size of Tik Tok users in China reached 518 million, with female users accounting for 57% of the total [6].

With the changing times and technological innovations, the media structure in China has undergone a radical change. Traditional media are in decline and new media are flourishing. Women have also changed dramatically in this media revolution, with female communicators no longer confined to professional women in media organizations. The birth of the Internet has lowered the threshold of communication. Women are no longer passive recipients of information, but active producers and consumers of information, and the relationship between communicator and audience has gradually become blurred. In the new media environment, the image of women has also become more diverse. As a result, some scholars have begun to look to the new media and have begun to analyses the image of women, women's discourse and the field of women's discourse in the new media environment. The widespread use of new media offers instrumental possibilities for the expression and widespread dissemination of women's discourse, which means that new media offers a form of 'technological empowerment' or new media empowerment for the new practices of women's discourse today [7].

The mass and lifestyle nature of short videos, as well as their interactive, consumable and audiovisual nature, offers the possibility for women to participate fully, empowering them in a number of ways, including production, performance, distribution and reception. Tik Tok is a product of the rapid development of visual culture and belongs to the field of visual communication. The issues that arise in the field of visual communication are not only a focus of attention in the field of communication, but also a growing concern for feminist scholars. In many Tik Tok videos, women express themselves, portraying more than just beauty or dependence on men in the traditional sense, with themes ranging from beauty and fashion to work and even gender relations. The body itself becomes not only a vehicle for short video narratives, but also one of the most important forms of narrative. Although this takes on a somewhat new look compared to the past, women are still influenced by traditional culture and there is still a hidden manipulation of power behind it.

1.2 Problem Statement

The study of women and the media in China began at the World Conference on Women in Beijing in 1995 and is of great importance to Chinese academics. Women and media studies is not only an important branch of feminist studies, but also an important school of communication studies, and an important research area in China and the world [8]. After many years of development, women and media studies has achieved many important research results in China [9]. However, compared to the West, relatively few Chinese scholars have focused on this area, and women and media studies are a relatively marginal discipline in the field of communication in China [10]. Through a collection of relevant academic results, it is found that most of the research on women and media in China focuses on traditional media, with few studies involving the field of new media, and most of them are only macro studies, lacking targeted case studies. In addition, the output of women and media studies in the field of new media has failed to keep pace with the development of the new media industry, with most scholars currently focusing on new media platforms such as blogs, microblogs and live streaming, and lacking corresponding attention to the current short-form video boom. In 2017, the short video industry witnessed explosive growth, with the influx of major giants in the Internet industry and the emergence of various short video APPs, but as short video is an emerging thing that has only emerged in recent years, there is not much research on short video in academia yet. An internet search using the keyword "short video" revealed only 1,400 academic papers on short video, and only 300 academic papers on "Tik Tok". Most of these studies are rather one-sided and lack an overall understanding of the female population in the short-form video field [11].

The imbalance in the gender power structure of the traditional media era has been broken, providing an opportunity for the advancement of women's voices. The birth of short videos have further lowered the barriers to entry and provided a platform for women to express themselves [12]. Tik Tok, the leading social short video, has attracted many female users and created many female celebrities. Short videos have a distinctly female participatory character. According to statistics, as producers and distributors, most of the people who upload short videos are post-00s, women. As an audience, women are more inclined to video. According to the survey, men are more inclined to use news and game apps, while women are more inclined to use consumer and video apps, so short videos are predominantly female at both the production-publishing and viewing-sharing ends, making them an important area for online feminist research [13]. This situation is related to the lived-in nature of short videos. As short videos move from private to public space and from folk culture to public communication, their cultural tone is 'lived-in', which matches the strengths of women in related fields, thus making women highly compatible with short videos and forming a set of narrative and cultural mechanisms that effectively contribute to the construction and dissemination of short videos. These characteristics also make the female participation and empowerment approach of short videos different from, for example, women's literature and other women's literary arts [14]. However, Woolf's vision of autonomous female expression has not been fully realized on the Tik Tok platform. For female users, the limited scope of discourse and lack of self-expression persists, and the logic of 'beauty is justice' still prevails. The study of Tik Tok will not only enrich the findings of women and media studies in the field of new media, but will also have implications for the construction of equal gender.

1.3 Research Objective

The 'narrative' of the short video is in line with the little narratives of the French philosopher Jean-François Lyotard in that it does not attempt to answer all social questions or play a decisive role in the organization of society, but rather encourages fragmented knowledge and the parody of grand narratives [15]. It encourages fragmented knowledge and the parody, appropriation and deconstruction of grand narratives, but also gives full play to individual creativity in an attempt to construct more egalitarian and richly diverse social connections, creating a real society that is interconnected, contradictory and mutually diverse. It is through such small, personal narratives that women give power to short videos. The author intends to analyses the content and statistics of Tik Tok short videos, as well as the number of most popular Tik Tok female videos in ten genres, in an attempt to summarize women's participation and empowerment strategies in short videos, and also to draw attention to and discuss related issues. At the same time, this study explores the basic paths of women's full participation and empowerment in short video applications, from Mead's symbolic interaction theory, to Collins' ritual interaction theory, to Marcovitz's media scenario theory. We aim to construct three dimensions of women's empowerment strategies in short videos, mainly body narratives, relational narratives and situational narratives, which embody individual, group and social models respectively.

1.4 Significance of This Study

In today's self-media platforms, "women's discourse" is no longer a term exclusive to academics, but is increasingly referred to by netizens. The rapid development of self-media has provided a platform for women's discourse to be fully expressed. From a theoretical point of view, most studies of women's discourse in China have been conducted at the level of cultural institutions, analyzing women's discourse from the perspective of female images in literature, film and television works and traditional media. Therefore, this study will analyze the female discourse behind female short videos on the Tik Tok platform in the age of self-media, using a combination of communication perspective and literary theory to provide a new perspective for the study of female discourse, which on the one hand can complement the relevant feminist theories. On the other hand, it is hoped that the study of women's discourse on the Tik Tok platform will bring inspiration to relevant women's movements and theories in reality [16].

From a practical point of view, most women in China aspire to have equal social status and voice with men. However, as feminist research in China started far behind the West, there is no complete theoretical system to support it, and no concrete practical experience to draw on. Therefore, this study analyses the phenomenon and current dilemma of women's discourse on the Tik Tok short video platform in the context of the self-media era, so that more people can pay attention to and understand the current situation of women's discourse in China and arouse women's sensitivity to Chinese women's discourse. Rather than laying the groundwork for women's discourse by weakening or devaluing men's legitimate right to discourse, it effectively alleviates the strong antagonism in the current online environment through the identification of hyper-gender consciousness, realizes the true meaning of transgender identity, promotes every individual in the current society to face women squarely again, respects women's right to discourse expression, and provides feasible reference significance for women's discourse research.

2   First Section Introduction

A study of the most popular female video numbers in each genre through Shake Chat data reveals some patterns. Each blogger posts thousands of short videos featuring herself in a video number, mostly following the same narrative strategy and maintaining an overall consistent narrative style. Generally, three narrative styles are used or overlaid: physical narrative, relationship narrative and scene narrative. These three narrative styles embody the individual, the group and the community respectively.

2.1 Body Narrative

The body narrative uses the body as a vehicle. Subject and object are intertwined through the medium of the body. The body is both the subject of the act and the narrative, and is also subject to the perceptions of the maker and performer and the scrutiny of the receiver, completing the narrative and the feedback of the meaning it carries in the process of being viewed. The interaction between women's 'body theory' and the media began in the 1970s, when it quickly became an effective form of symbolic coding in the mass media or cultural landscape. Today, women in short videos are expanding the expressive power of the body, using it as a vehicle to complete gender narratives, to fully explain the bodily concerns, identities or other subjective intentions of both genders, and to empower short videos through body narratives [17].

Firstly, women have a freer reign over their bodies and a richer range of physical expressions, which has led to more women's bodies being 'shown' rather than 'covered', resulting in more diverse images of women in the media. Unlike male culture, where the state of the body is determined by the needs of men, the state of the body is more often determined by oneself or the female audience, as the producers are also women, and the shots of female performers are less focused on the gendered breasts and buttocks, and more on the female face and the panoramic view of the female pose. Female audiences also prefer to see face make-up and full body wear, in line with the aesthetics of female producers and performers. Beauty bloggers are more typical in that they focus on the relationship between their own bodies and the bodies of their female audience, resorting to their own quest for beautiful bodies in an effort to make their female audience improve their image and reinvent themselves, guiding their female audience into hallucinatory projections of her body, realizing the I- deal-ego and the 'ego-ideal' according to Lacan's theory of mirroring and gazing "The projection of i- deal-ego and ego-ideal is based on Lacan's theory of mirroring and gaze.

Secondly, women are returning to the focus on the essence of women's lives, exploring them subjectivity and looking at their bodies from more angles. For example, female bloggers in the knowledge and sports categories show the intellectuality and health of women; bloggers in the food and family life categories, represented by "Li Zi qi", highlight the poetry and practicality of women through their dress and body language; and "Grandma Wang, who only wears high heels "She wears exaggerated pearl earrings, a long pearl necklace, a hat and high heels in every appearance, showing her chicness and sophistication in defiance of her age through her clothes and temperament (Table 1).

Table 1. An example of Top Female User Accounts From a Tik Tok.

Name	Number of works	Number of likes	Number of fans
Ah huai	170	9,295,000	1,358,000
Yi Zhinannan	385	25,345,000	2,823.000
Li Ziqi	772	220,000.000	52,966,000

Finally, women achieve absolute control over their own bodies in short videos and have the right to transform their bodies at will. Through case studies, I found that 'cross-dressing' is the most important tool in the narrative of women's bodies, i.e., the process of transforming the body from ugly (or ordinary) to beautiful by means of make-up, changing clothes and accessories. For example, "Little Orange", one of the top online beauty bloggers in terms of number of followers, has adopted the strategy of "national style cross-dressing", and its "Daji cross-dressing" video released on 11 October 2020 has received 4.055 million likes. The video "Daji in disguise", released on 11 October 2020, has received 405.5 million likes. The drama blogger "Xin Jiu'er" has adopted a dramatic "Chinese costume cross-dressing" direction. The blogger "Huang Sanqin" has also gained a lot of fans by combining "drama + beauty" and transforming herself from an ordinary passerby into a beautiful and sophisticated female boss. The "cross-dressing" narrative is also a common tactic among beauty bloggers. "The 'cross-dressing' video content is very popular with female audiences. The "drag" body narrative in short videos highlights the importance women place on their bodies and their confidence in them, but more importantly, the contrast between a woman's delicate make-up and her before and after body, with strong memorable music and simple gestures, pleases the female audience, allowing them to see their ideal female image and to have a It is a visual and aesthetic pleasure to learn how to make themselves beautiful and to provoke their own latent physical and psychological desires. It is all about sensuality and meeting the needs of the female audience through emotion.

2.2 Relational Narratives

Sisterhood, an important theme in Western women's literature. It originally referred to the bond between women as a weapon to unite them against racial discrimination and class exploitation, to confront patriarchal culture and to build a female identity. As historical conditions and the situation of women in different social forms have changed, there is now less talk of solidarity and more of support. Support can mean agreeing with what someone thinks is right, or defending it. It also means acting as a support or foundation for weaker structures.

However, traditionally the most common sisterly relationships presented in our film and literature have been either adversarial, or "plastic sisterhoods" in which false feelings can be dismantled by interests. In short videos, however, women are more often presented with a new narrative strategy based on supportive relationships. For example, the hilarious blogger "Crazy Sisters", which revolves around Zhang Xiaohua and Shao Yuxuan's daily routines of hilarity, eating and drinking among their girlfriends, uses Shao Yuxuan's first point of view to show them friendship as women who support each other despite their hijinks. As can be seen, there are two main ways of presenting the narrative strategy of the "supportive" relationship between the sisters. The first is that the protagonist is usually a strong, independent woman, i.e., the "big female protagonist" persona, who gives support to the relatively weak women. "The emergence of the female protagonist as a medium signifies the movement of women from a marginalized 'Second nature' to the center. Such a persona and storyline can satisfy the female audience's sense of self-worth in terms of gender, allowing them to experience a sense of release and comfort along with the storyline. Many people don't understand why the video is 'out of the loop', but it is actually influenced by the famous American sitcom 'The Broker Sisters', which portrays a very grounded, realistic, superficially mean but confident relationship with each other, full of equal love for women. Similarly, the drama blogger 'Wan'er's Treasure Sister' uses the daily routine of sharing a house as a creative point of reference, showing the relationships between multiple women with different personalities through a progressive 'break-in' model, exploring what true female friendship is. The premise of this narrative strategy is that the female subjects must have a strong relationship or emotional foundation with each other, and that each individual has a certain degree of independence.

The new mother-daughter relationships of today also follow this narrative strategy. For example, the hilarious blogger "Wen Jingling" is famous for her "100 ways to imitate your mother" and "100 ways to piss her off". She calls her mother "Sister Rong" and "Ms. Rong", and while Ms. Rong apparently "dislikes her daughter", mother and daughter are more like a pair of girlfriends who "dislike" each other. The mother and daughter are more like girlfriends who "dislike" each other. The daughter is not only on an equal footing with her mother, but she can even tease her mother in turn. Through the superficial teasing, the audience sees a very strong and deep bond between the women behind the scenes, who understand and support each other fully, and are a source of joy and emotional support for each other. It can be seen that female relationships have changed from the traditional narrative strategy of hostility to a relationship narrative strategy based on sisterly "support" in the short video; from the independent party supporting the weaker party, to both parties being independent and supporting each other, to the superficial "dislike" and even teasing of each other We see this in the short videos of women who are not only independent and supportive of each other, but are also superficially "disliking" each other and even teasing each other, but are also confident in their relationships. We see a new presentation of women's same-sex relationships in short videos, and we also see a growing trust between women, even across age, generation and class, and the possibility of genuine friendship.

In addition to sisterhood, there are also relationships between female bloggers and members of the opposite sex in short videos, such as brother and sister, father and daughter, mother and son, husband and wife, and couples. These are grouped together and discussed together because they share a similar narrative strategy in that women are dominant in these relationships and are at the center of the narrative. For example, the hottest video in this genre, "Big Wolf Dog Zheng Jianpeng & Yan Zhen Couple", creates a relationship between a husband and a wife by contrasting the image of a scruffy landlord and an exquisite landlady, creating a huge contrast between the husband and the wife, reflecting the family relationship of a strong woman and a weak man. Even the eldest daughter has a higher status than the husband. "Tall, short, fat and thin" is a female blogger from a middle-class family in Hong Kong. She is also the absolute center of the family, often coming up with ideas to keep the whole family busy. The hottest blogger in the male cross-dressing category, "Superfluous and Mao Mao", has also borrowed this narrative strategy, with one person playing two roles, the female Mao Mao and the male Superfluous being the couple, but Mao Mao being the absolute subject of the video content. The video's main content is based on a small theatre that imitates women's mental activities and body language, giving voice to women and showing their charm.

In this way we also see the respect, understanding and support of the male community for women, which marks a more equal and diverse society.

2.3 Scene Narrative

Joshua Meyerowitz, a communication scholar, based on the media theories of Innes and McLuhan and Goffman's mimesis, introduced the concept of situation as a way to study the behavioral and psychological impact of "media scenes" on people. Situation has also become one of the characteristics of short videos. As mentioned earlier, the cultural underpinning of short videos is life, and most of the short videos produced are based on life scenes. Therefore, nature, home, school and workplace are the most popular settings for women's short videos, and accordingly, fields, scenic spots, living rooms, classrooms and offices are also the most popular scenes. Scene narratives have become an important dimension in the narratives of women in short videos. Scene narratives are more often used in the categories of food, travel, family life, drama, and funny. The most notable example is the short videos of women in the food category, represented by "Li Zi qi". In the same category, there are also "Peach Sister in Shu", "Pan Lou Lou", "Nostalgia" and "Chuan Xiang Qiu Yue". Whether they are set in the southwest of Shu, in the Dabie Mountains or at the foot of the Wuyi Mountains, the idyllic scenes of nature become an important strategy in the narrative, whether it is the pastoral style of the village or the unadorned earthen houses and stoves, they all present an original and authentic rural life. Every scene, including the mountains, streams, courtyards, lotus ponds and rice paddies, is imbued with a sense of life.

In addition, the city's "Aya Kitchen", which cooks breakfast for children, and "Pupu Kiki", which cooks food for the husband, are often set in the kitchen or living room of their homes, with all kinds of soft furnishings, tables, kitchen utensils, tableware and packaging items, all warm and lovely, seemingly They look like they are making food, but in fact they are showing an ideal state of 'home' through their scenes. The office is also a common scene in the city, and women give it a meaning outside of work, such as "Office Ono" making food in the office, conveying the idea that it's important to go to work and enjoy life first. In the above video, the scene is the main narrative, and through the scene narrative, the food becomes a poetic and pictorial picture of life, and the steaming meal carries the life, conveying a simple and moving, back-to-basics lifestyle and philosophy of life. The same narrative strategy is also found in almost all female travel bloggers. In a place with picturesque natural scenery and breathtaking human beauty, bloggers are conveying a philosophy and lifestyle through the narrative of scenes. One can find that the use of everyday, warm, beautiful and comfortable life scenes has become an important narrative dimension of female empowerment in short videos. The scenes and life are infused with each other, and the scenes reflect the quality of life and the concept of life, making short videos the best tool for women to "record the good life"; in turn, the rich life gives women unlimited sources of expression and materials, promoting the further practice of short videos for women. Of course, the above conclusions are drawn by looking at popular videos, and there may be some short videos that use other narrative dimensions, but because they are not popular and belong to a niche area, they are not studied. However, it can be said that narrative approaches based on bodies, relationships and scenes have become a fundamental strategy for female empowerment in short videos.

3 Conclusion

In summary, through the exploration of the issue of female participation and empowerment in short videos, it can be found that short videos have brought new space for women's full participation. Narrative is an important means of processing information, carrying expression and establishing communication in online society, and it is also a basic path for women's full participation and empowerment in short video applications. The main strategies for female empowerment in short video are body narratives, relationship narratives and scene narratives, which embody the three dimensions of the individual, the group and the society, or the close object, the close person and the distant view respectively. In short videos, women express themselves through narratives based on their bodies, relationships and scenes, creating a more diverse image of women in a 'small narrative', and a more harmonious relationship with their same-sex counterparts, supported and understood by men, and even dominant in both genders.

At the same time, although the images of women in women's videos have become richer, they are not exactly real-life images of women, but rather images that meet women's needs and are 'liked' by them. There is also a focus on real, vulnerable women in women's videos, but these videos are hardly ever on the top of the list of women's public view. Women don't seem to want to see real women who are really vulnerable and in pain, they want to see ideal women who carry women's dreams and emotions. Or rather, the image of women in the medium is constructed by women, who do not construct real women in their lives, but rather the ideal image.

We have to acknowledge that while women are presenting a certain new face in short videos, the consciousness of women, especially the female audience, is still strongly influenced by traditional culture, and the long history of power manipulation exists in a more hidden way, where women's self-worth is reflected, and there is still a long way to go to explore the mechanisms of participation and empowerment, and even dissemination and sharing of short videos by Chinese women.

References

1. Hua, J., Shaw, R.: 5G and its implication to communication in China. In: Hua, J., Adu Gyamfi, B., Shaw, R. (eds.) Considerations for a Post-COVID-19 Technology and Innovation Ecosystem in China. DRR, pp. 127–143. Springer, Singapore (2022). https://doi.org/10.1007/978-981-16-6959-0_9
2. Wu, H., et al.: How does internet development affect energy-saving and emission reduction? Evidence from China. Energy Econ. **103**, 105577 (2021)
3. Wang, Y.-H., Gu, T.-J., Wang, S.-Y.: Causes and characteristics of short video platform internet community taking the TikTok short video application as an example. In: 2019 IEEE International Conference on Consumer Electronics-Taiwan (ICCE-TW). IEEE (2019)
4. Unni, Z., Weinstein, E.: Shelter in place, connect online: trending TikTok content during the early days of the US Covid-19 pandemic. J. Adolesc. Health **68**(5), 863–868 (2021)
5. Zhang, Z.: Infrastructuralization of Tik Tok: transformation, power relationships, and platformization of video entertainment in China. Media Cult. Soc. **43**(2), 219–236 (2021)
6. Gan, S.: Short video applications by key opinion leaders as online marketing on social media (2020)

7. Döring, N.: Feminist views of cybersex: victimization, liberation, and empowerment. Cyberpsychol. Behav. **3**(5), 863–884 (2000)
8. Mao, C.: Feminist activism via social media in China. Asian J. Women's Stud. **26**(2), 245–258 (2020)
9. Yunjuan, L., Xiaoming, H.: Media portrayal of women and social change: a case study of women of China. Fem. Media Stud. **7**(3), 281–298 (2007)
10. Peng, A.Y.: Neoliberal feminism, gender relations, and a feminized male ideal in China: a critical discourse analysis of Mimeng's WeChat posts. Fem. Media Stud. **21**(1), 115–131 (2021)
11. Chang, J., Tian, H.: Girl power in boy love: Yaoi, online female counterculture, and digital feminism in China. Fem. Media Stud. **21**(4), 604–620 (2021)
12. Yang, F.: Post-feminism and chick flicks in China: subjects, discursive origin and new gender norms. Fem. Media Stud., 1–16 (2020)
13. Yang, J.: Women in China moving forward: progress, challenges and reflections. Soc. Incl. **8**(2), 23–35 (2020)
14. Shata, A., Seelig, M.I.: The dragonfly effect: analysis of the social media women's empowerment campaign. J. Creat. Commun. **16**(3), 331–346 (2021)
15. Lyotard, J.-F.: Excerpts from the postmodern condition: a report on knowledge. In: A Postmodern Reader, pp. 71–90 (1993)
16. Yuqing, C., Xiaoyue, D., Liping, Y.: Research on the priority of China's internet development. Phys. Procedia **24**, 1595–1600 (2012)
17. Lu, W., et al.: Internet development in China. J. Inf. Sci. **28**(3), 207–223 (2002)

Between Institutioning and Commoning: Grassroots Co-creation in Web3 Communities

Man Zhang[1]([⊠]), Jing Wang[2] [iD], and Danwen Ji[1]

[1] Tongji University, No. 1239, Siping Road, Shanghai, China
{zhangman99,danwen_ji}@tongji.edu.cn
[2] Tsinghua University, Hai Dian District, Beijing, China
wangjing21@mails.tsinghua.edu.cn

Abstract. A growing body of research is focusing on how to co-design with grassroots communities. Particularly within the vision of design for social innovation, the role of designers is shifting from traditional design leads to supporters of collaborative design. The potential ethic of co-creation with grassroots communities is to support more bottom-up innovation, thereby stimulating the potential for distributed social innovation. Grassroots innovation is often inseparable from collaboration with institutions, and recent design research has begun to focus on the role of designers as intermediaries between grassroots communities and institutions to help co-creation activities achieve a balance of commoning and institutioning. With the development of blockchain technology, a new type of organizational design, DAO (decentralized autonomous organization), on which web3 practice is based, provides some new insights and opportunities for a more broadly participatory grassroots co-creation. In this paper, we use a theoretical framework and thematic analysis based on six DAO samples to explain and analyze the ambiguity and complexity of web3 communities in both commoning and institutioning dimensions, inspiring new types of grassroots co-creation.

Keywords: Grassroots · Co-creation · Social innovation · Web3 · Institutioning · Commoning

1 Introduction

With the conceptual expansion of participation, Co-design with communities has gradually become the focus of participatory design. Still, design with communities is often extremely challenging due to the complexity of the communities themselves and the intricate interests within them [1–3]. The word community itself has multiple concepts, and in the design context, it can be divided into the following categories according to the different focuses of communities [4]: communities of place, where people are connected due to the same geographical location and form communities with distinct geographical characteristics under the influence of geo-based social interactions and cultural practices [5]; communities of interest, where people come together due to common concern and interest, thus transcending mere geopolitical constraints, but such communities often disintegrate with the achievement of common goals, making it difficult to maintain

P.-L. P. Rau (Ed.): HCII 2023, LNCS 14022, pp. 317–329, 2023.
https://doi.org/10.1007/978-3-031-35936-1_23

long-term relationships [6]; communities of practice, where people come together due to common experiences, occupations, hobbies, etc., are a more liberal, lower-threshold association of social relations [7, 8]; grassroots communities, people in which share the same position of relative autonomy in relation to constituted powers [9, 10]. Classifying communities does not imply that they are entirely isolated; in fact, in design practice, a community may have the characteristics of multiple communities at the same time [4]. However, focusing on the elements of different communities can help designers develop appropriate tools and methods for more efficient co-design with communities.

Among the many community types, grassroots communities are the more emerging design co-creators, which originate from the grassroots innovation movement, which seeks innovation processes that are socially inclusive towards local communities in terms of the knowledge, processes and outcomes involved [11]. The existence of grassroots communities means that grassroots innovation can be structured in organizational forms that differ from centralized power systems, providing a more diverse and inclusive innovation space for policy development, product development, and knowledge creation. This connotation coincides with participatory design, which is centered on democracy and empowerment [12], and the tendency to focus on grassroots innovation is becoming more and more evident as participatory design gradually expands from the field of work to a common design approach in all areas. This principle is not only reflected in the design process of decision-making in citizen politics [3, 9] but also internalized as a fundamental principle in co-creation. Therefore, when designing with communities, the potentially right choice for designers is to give as much design autonomy as possible to grassroots members and help communities have the capabilities needed for self-determination [10, 13].

However, supporting any bottom-up emergent practice is challenging, and the difficulties encountered in co-creation with grassroots communities stem from, on the one hand, the fragmented distribution of power and the complex social relations among their members and, on the other, the confrontation between grassroots communities and the existing centralized power system [14]. Indeed, co-designing with grassroots communities frequently entails collaboration with institutions, particularly when dealing with civic and political issues [15, 16]. Both grassroots and institutions play for their own interests in the design process, representing two different political tendencies, the former implying decentered public participation and democratic expansion, known as commoning, and the latter implying centralized power and difference reduction, known as institutioning, which also creates the possibility of fundamental contradictions in the co-creation process [4]. As a result, designers frequently serve as a bridge between grassroots communities and institutions, assisting both parties in identifying points of common interest that lead to collaboration [13, 17].

The intermediary role implies a shift in the designer's role from user-centered design to collaborative design. The designer shifts from being the dominant agent in the design process to the enabling agent [18, 19]. Instead of serving as the "central translator between invention and use," the designer takes on a more facilitative and coordinating role [20–22], aiming to increase participants' willingness and ability to integrate and sustain collaborative design. The designer's primary task, especially in the context of social innovation design with openness and participation at its core, is to become a bridge between participants, and the core issue is how to organize various social relationships and build a collaborative network of social innovation design, in order to stimulate more bottom-up grassroots innovation. Many scholars refer to this relational construction as infrastructure [23–28], implying an ongoing process in which different participants resolve conflicts of interest to build good collaborative relationships. Infrastructure goes beyond project-based participatory design by focusing on potential interpersonal relationships before a given design project begins and long-term relational interactions after it concludes, thereby shaping a more participatory and sustainable social change by constructing a relational collaborative network that connects multiple individuals and organizations [24, 29, 30]. The designer acting as an intermediation is shaping a series of infrastructures for co-design with grassroots communities and institutions, striking a delicate balance between commoning and institutioning.

The new organizational design on which the web3 practice is based offers some new insights and possibilities regarding infrastructure. DAOs (decentralized autonomous organizations) of all kinds have emerged as a hub for grassroots innovation, and these DAOs operate autonomously on the blockchain using smart contracts. For DAOs, democracy is a belief and principle that easily resonates, which confirms web3's tone of breaking down barriers and respecting individual freedom. However, as DAO has evolved, some pathologies common in traditional institutions have gradually emerged, making DAO contradictory in terms of commoning and institutioning, as well as raising concerns about DAO's feasibility and doubts about its grassroots nature [31–33]. So, is there an antagonistic relationship between commoning and institutionalizing in web3 co-creation activities? If it exists, what role does the DAO mechanism play as an infrastructure in shaping and coordinating this antagonistic relationship?

2 Institutioning and Commoning

2.1 Institutioning: Design with Institutions

Although participatory design, born in the late 20th century, began by working with large institutions. As democratization and liberal economies developed, designers gradually and deliberately moved away from institutions and toward professional groups or small-scale civic collaborations. In fact, design with institutions has a long history, but the details of the collaboration are often not disclosed so as not to scare off the other participants with these cumbersome, archaic, and uninteresting parts, so the part of the collaboration with institutions is often called the back office of design. However, these intentionally overlooked details frequently determine the success or failure of collaborative design, particularly in the context of increasing collaboration with institutions, and design researchers must rediscover these details. Institutioning is the process by which design produces mutual shaping with existing or new institutions, specifically how design responds to, abolishes, or transforms institutional framing [4].

Scholars have commonly introduced the concept of institutional framing in understanding the action of institutions. According to Schön and Rein [35], 'framing' is 'an operation of selectivity and organization' when dealing with complex information, and institutional framing includes formal written documents, talks, etc., and informal communication. Building on framing, Castell [36] further elaborated institutional framing by dividing the institution's action guidelines into 'metacultural frames,' which describe the institution's cultural goals and conceptual principles, 'institutional action frames,' which represent the behavioral characteristics of the institution as an organization; and 'policy frames,' which describe how the institution defines itself in specific actions. Institutional framing provides insight for designers to understand and co-design with institutions. Huybrechts et al. [34] specifically suggest focusing on the relationship between design goals and institutional framing in the co-design process, where consistency in the relationship helps the process run smoothly, but inconsistency in the relationship also has the potential to drive institutional transformation. On the other hand, Lodato and Disalvo [37] introduced the concept of institutional constraints to refer to the interplay between PD practice and institutional framing. They classified institutional constraints as 'sandbox,' limited experimental space; 'administration Gap,' lack of resource support for sustainability; 'ideological mismatch,' overly sensitive conflict of values and beliefs.

The complexity of institutions leads designers to take a deliberate approach to co-creation with them, especially in participatory design, where the potential goal of designers is to consciously provoke change in institutions and thus contribute to the re-politicization of the design process [34]. Thus, Teil et al. [13] distinguish between 'co-optation' and 'intermediation' as the interaction mechanisms between design and institutions. The former describes institutions acting strategically and assimilating PD processes with a potential loss of their emancipatory qualities; the latter occurs when design researchers act strategically, aiming to trigger institutional transformation. The interaction of these two mechanisms influences the degree to which participatory design is politicized.

2.2 Commoning: Design with Grassroots Communities

Grassroots communities are very different from institutions. In contrast to the power structures implemented by traditional top-down organizations, grassroots activism is often spontaneous, nonhierarchical, and volunteer-driven. Consequently, grassroots communities face unique challenges, risks, and constraints, which shape designs and appropriations of interactive systems [10]. Because co-creation with grassroots communities is frequently inextricably linked to institutional support, the related literature strongly emphasizes the designers' mediating role. Cibin et al. [38] examined the challenges and opportunities that designers face when co-designing with grassroots and institutional organizations, arguing that designers can reconcile differences between grassroots and institutional organizations by enlisting the assistance of other people or organizations. Cibin et al. [39] further focus on the role of intermediaries in social innovation design, arguing that designers should pay attention to the interests and goals represented by the intermediaries themselves to avoid the intermediaries' dynamics from adversely affecting collaborative design. In their subsequent paper [4], they expand on the significance of the intermediary role in co-design, arguing that the designer primarily serves as a 'cultural intermediary,' as Bourdieu defines it. Different organizations have their own logic and structure when designing with grassroots communities and institutions. Still, collaborative design often constructs "designerly spaces" through various design activities and tools and therefore requires intermediary roles to translate.

The design process for collective ownership has been described as commoning, a partnership that embodies broader social relationships and more diverse forms of participation than institutioning [40]. In contrast to institutioning, Teil [13] describes the mechanisms of interaction between design and grassroots as 'the formation of publics' and 'entanglements.' The former can be understood as a 'particular configuration of individuals bound by common cause in confronting a shared issue [41],' a term that implies that in design, the consensus is not a smooth process but is often accompanied by argument and conflict. The designer's goal is not to eliminate dissenting voices but to provide a space where all voices can be heard. The latter means the particular connections between critical perspectives and design practices [42], which has been explored as a 'politics of mattering' to account for 'the design process as an always relational becoming and its practices as already-political[43].' Here are the relationships of institutioning and commoning (see Fig. 1).

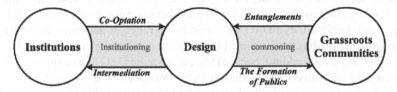

Fig. 1. Design as intermediation between institutioning and commoning

Remark 1. Design serves as intermediation between institutions and grassroots communities. The interactive mechanisms are known as institutioning with elements of 'co-optation' and 'intermediation,' and commoning with 'the formation of publics' and 'entanglements.'

3   Methodology

3.1   Thematic Analysis

This paper is an exploratory empirical study that investigates the relationship between institutioning and commoning in DAO using existing theories and textual data and thus employs the research method of thematic analysis, a qualitative data-driven research method. Thematic analysis, according to Braun and Clarke [44], is a method for identifying, analyzing, and reporting patterns (themes) within data. It minimally organizes and describes data in great detail. However, frequently it goes further than this and interprets various aspects of the research topic. This method involves three key terms: 'code', a data segment descriptor that assigns meaning; 'category,' which is derived from codes and more conceptual and abstract; 'Theme,' the theoretical construct that explains similarities or variations across codes. The thematic analysis comprises six stages: familiarizing yourself with your data, generating initial codes, generating themes, reviewing potential themes, defining and naming themes, and producing the report.

3.2 Data

Because co-creation activities in web3 are primarily based on DAOs as organizational forms, this paper has chosen six DAOs as case studies. In co-creation involving grassroots communities, institutions, and designers, designers play the role of intermediaries, generating interaction mechanisms with grassroots communities and institutions, respectively. However, in the DAO, the designer's role disappears, and the blockchain-based smart contract takes its place as a third party that coordinates social relationships. Although different DAOs write different meta-rules in smart contracts, this paper attempts to step outside the cases by reducing these meta-rules to codes with general meaning through thematic analysis. Furthermore, this paper employs a deductive approach to data coding based on the theoretical framework of institutioning and commoning.

This paper selects six DAOs of different types and high impact from around the world. They are: BitDAO, as the investment DAO is responsible for controlling the funds in the DAO vault and using them to initiate and manage investments whose primary purpose is to generate profits for its members, similar to a private equity fund or hedge fund; SeeDAO, as a DAO incubator, has a range of activities including web3 education, quality media content, thought-provoking networking events and offline gatherings, and community building; banlessDAO, as a Media DAO aims to reinvent the way content creators, consumers and media interact; FWB DAO, as a Social DAO is a global community of culture creators, thinkers and builders; Gitcoin DAO, as a cause-based DAO whose vision is to support all kinds of open source projects and free developers of open source projects through the blockchain; The Party DAO, as a community-driven DAO, is a NFT bidding service platform where any individual can create crowdfunding through its official website, participate in or initiate designated NFT auctions, in order

Table 1. Results of thematic analysis

Theme	Institutioning		Commoning	
Sub-theme	Co-optation	Intermediation	Entanglements	Formation of publics
Workflow	Long-term project system	Trade Union System	Short-term project system	Collective Resolution
Organizational structure	Not fully decentralized, with core membership or proxy delegation	Combination of top-down and bottom-up, tiered governance		Fully decentralized
Consensus mechanism	Proxy Voting		Non-equal weighted voting	Equal weighted voting
Incentive model	Governance rights can be freely bought and sold			Governance rights can't be freely bought and sold

to significantly lower the threshold for ordinary users to participate in buying quality NFT assets.

Based on publicly published meta-rules and participatory observations, this paper reviews the above six DAOs in four aspects: workflow, organizational structure, consensus mechanism, and incentive model. The results of the thematic analysis are shown in Table 1.

4 Result

4.1 Institutioning in DAO

(1) Co-optation. DAO's metacultural framing is generally well-set and distinctive. Most DAOs develop long-term programs, such as periodic events or incubators, to ensure the overall unity of DAO principles and the path forward. Although DAOs are more tolerant of member proposals, it is the long-term projects that represent the attributes and beliefs of a DAO with the highest priority. As a result, a solid metacultural framing severely limits co-creation both within and outside the DAO. However, due to the warnings of the tragedy of the commons and the plague of inefficiency, not all DAOs have achieved complete decentralization. Some DAOs still intentionally retain core power groups or refer to representative democracy to allow members to delegate their proxies. This also leads to the plague of power concentration in the actual governance process, especially when DAOs allow members to delegate their voting power to other representatives, prone to the phenomenon of large token holders manipulating their votes and thus leading to unfair consensus results. And once the token can be freely bought and sold outside the DAO, the ownership of the DAO is marketed, essentially conforming to private ownership, which is more likely to exacerbate the contradictions mentioned above and thus not conducive to the politicization of co-creation.

(2) Intermediation. Unions initially emerged as progressive products of workplace democratization and, over time, developed five main functions: a service function; a representation function; a regulatory function; a government function; and a public administration function [45]. DAOs generally adopt unionization, which revolutionizes the hierarchical organization of traditional organizations into a network of connected unions, shaping a flatter power distribution model and revolutionizing the operational framework of traditional institutions. However, unionization does not represent complete decentralization. It is more common in DAOs to have a higher level of governance above the unions, combining bottom-up and top-down with hierarchical governance. Although not completely decentralized, this model of power distribution suggests a compromise in transition.

4.2 Commoning in DAO

(1) Entanglements. Following the principles of bottom-up and autonomy, it is common practice for DAOs to encourage members to make their own proposals and bring interested members together to accomplish co-creation. Because DAOs have fewer restrictions on membership and lower barriers to entry than traditional organizations,

some proposals have a clear values orientation and may violate the DAO metacultural framework in the absence of supervision. These proposals enrich the practice of co-creation within DAOs and inadvertently influence the metacultural framework of the entire organization. On the other hand, some DAOs set the weight of voting rights, and different ways of determining the weight also imply different values, which affect the process and results of co-creation.

(2) Formation of publics. Collective resolution is one of the core manifestations of decentralization, and any decision of DAO requires the participation of multiple consensus nodes, i.e., it allows all participants to reach a unified opinion on a specific issue and take relevant measures without prior trust. It can be said that the consensus mechanism of blockchain is designed to reach an optimal solution by creating a game mechanism in which various stakeholders deepen their concerns about the same issue in order to maintain their interests and reach a dynamic consensus in an open and transparent debate. On the other hand, some DAOs directly adopt a completely decentralized organizational structure and a consensus mechanism of equal-weight voting, which theoretically achieves complete equality in power distribution. Still, completely flat management is also prone to disadvantages such as inefficiency and poor decision-making. In addition, some DAOs explicitly state that tokens cannot be freely traded outside the DAO, and they regard governance as an essential part of collective ownership, which helps to avoid the emergence of an oligarchy.

5 Discussion

The distribution of decision-making power is the primary distinction between DAOs and traditional organizations. While traditional organizational structures (such as corporations and nonprofits) provide mechanisms such as shareholder proposals and board elections that allow stakeholders to contribute to decision-making, due to their structure and lack of effective tools, they are frequently far from equitable governance participation. DAOs, on the other hand, use blockchain technology to enable equitable decentralized governance while also ensuring transparency and auditability of critical decisions through processes such as on-chain voting. DAOs are network organizations, which distinguishes them from traditional organizations in terms of organization type. Powell [46] distinguishes three types of organizations: market-based organizations that regulate behavior and thus exchange commercial benefits through contracts, hierarchical organizations that constrain social relations through power, and network-based organizations formed by networks of individuals engaged in reciprocal, preferential, mutually supportive actions. In contrast to traditional organizations, DAOs impose few constraints on their members and are often subject to informal social control, with few norms of coercive effect established. On the one hand, decentralization implies that a DAO has no absolute center of power and that all members have equal status and power distribution. This is consistent with the participatory design vision, which states that any decision made during the co-creation process should not represent only a subset of the group but should allow for consensus decisions formed by the participants after full expression, understanding, and communication [47]. Blockchain technology, on the other hand, ensures a fully open and transparent action footprint, eliminating the higher exclusivity qualities of traditional organizations.

While sociology views a network as a group of people linked by relatively loose social ties or relationships, more scholars want to unify broad social forms into networks through a lens that extends beyond organizations and communities. Grassroots innovations are typically formed by relatively informal social ties that form loose social structures. As these interactions continue, they take on more recognizable characteristics [48], such as community [49] or more formal organizations. DAO is in this transition period and demonstrates a tendency to move from community to institution, which has led to a very vague definition and conceptualization of DAO and invites doubts about its initial utopian philosophy. The results of the thematic analysis indicate that the workflow, organizational structure, consensus mechanism, and incentive model of extant DAOs extend in both dimensions, which illustrates the ambiguity and complexity of DAOs in both institutioning and commoning (see Fig. 2), and the need for DAO governance to consider these two dimensions in an integrated manner. Given the diversity of goals and structures of DAOs, there is no one perfect governance approach. However, the framework of institutioning and commoning used in this paper can provide insight into understanding and explaining the tendencies of DAOs in co-creation. In fact, many scholars have focused on the contradictions that exist in DAOs themselves [50, 51], such as decision efficiency versus decision equity, voter apathy versus governance costs, and information security versus technological beliefs. These contradictions exist not only in DAOs, but other grassroots communities may also face similar situations in the development process, thus increasing the difficulty of bottom-up social innovation. Referring to Teil et al.'s suggestion [4], an effective way to do this is to clarify the balance between these two dimensions, take various measures to achieve it, and pay attention to the power dynamics in co-creation.

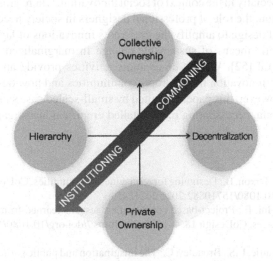

Fig. 2. Institutioning and communing in DAO

Remark 2. This paper categorizes DAO meta-rules into four groups based on their tendencies. The horizontal axis in this figure represents hierarchy versus decentralization, with the closer to hierarchy representing institutioning and the closer to decentralization representing commoning. The vertical axis contrasts private ownership versus collective ownership, with the closer to private ownership representing institutioning and the closer to collective ownership representing commoning.

6 Conclusion

Communities have become increasingly important partners in collaborative design, with grassroots communities receiving widespread interest in the wave of social innovation, but many problems still exist. Academics' call to re-politicize participatory design is, in fact, a nod to the rise of grassroots innovation, bringing the concept of institutioning versus commoning into the design debate. Based on the theoretical framework of this group of antagonistic relations, this paper adopts the thematic analysis method to examine the emerging web3 grassroots co-creation activities to reveal the complex power dynamics of DAO, a new type of grassroots community, and provide further inspiration for contemporary design. Looking back at the history of design, design research has shifted from user-centered design to collaborative design, a shift that has changed the roles of designers, researchers, and those formerly known as users, while also signaling the entry of design into the realm of shaping collective creativity. The practice of collaborative design is gradually changing the ways, objects, and groups of people who act as designers, and new collaborative design languages that support and facilitate a variety of cross-cultural, organizational, and disciplinary approaches are receiving increasing attention [22]. Especially in the context of social innovation, where grassroots innovation plays a vast potential, the role of professional designers in society needs to be redefined. Using professional design to amplify the grassroots innovations of lay designers should become an authentic means of sustainable change in marginalized communities and the world in general [52]. Web3's co-creation activities provide an emerging insight into understanding innovation in grassroots communities and how designers can play a mediating role. However, this paper is limited by small-scaled case samples and requires more qualitative data, necessitating more detailed empirical investigations.

References

1. McHattie, L.-S., Dixon, B.: Designing for reimagined communities. CoDesign **18**, 1–3 (2022). https://doi.org/10.1080/15710882.2021.2021245
2. Fassi, D., Manzini, E.: Project-based communities: lessons learned from collaborative city-making experiences. CoDesign **18**, 4–15 (2022). https://doi.org/10.1080/15710882.2021.2001535
3. Dixon, B., McHattie, L.S., Broadley, C.: The imagination and public participation: a Deweyan perspective on the potential of design innovation and participatory design in policy-making. CoDesign **18**, 151–163 (2022). https://doi.org/10.1080/15710882.2021.1979588
4. Teli, M., McQueenie, J., Cibin, R., Foth, M.: Intermediation in design as a practice of institutioning and commoning. Des. Stud. **82**, 101132 (2022). https://doi.org/10.1016/j.destud.2022.101132

5. Foth, M.: Connectivity does not ensure community: on social capital, networks and communities of place. In: Proceedings of the 5th International Information Technology in Regional Areas (ITiRA) Conference 2003, pp. 31–39. ITiRA 2003 Conference Committee/Central Qld University Press (2003)
6. Fischer, G.: Communities of interest: learning through the interaction of multiple knowledge systems. In: Proceedings of the 24th IRIS Conference, pp. 1–13. Department of Information Science, Bergen (2001)
7. Wenger, E.: Communities of Practice: Learning, Meaning, and Identity. Cambridge University Press (1998). https://doi.org/10.1017/CBO9780511803932
8. Wenger, E.: Communities of practice and social learning systems. Organization 7, 225–246 (2000). https://doi.org/10.1177/135050840072002
9. Foth, M., Tomitsch, M., Satchell, C., Haeusler, M.H.: From users to citizens: some thoughts on designing for polity and civics. In: Proceedings of the Annual Meeting of the Australian Special Interest Group for Computer Human Interaction, Parkville, VIC, Australia, pp. 623–633. ACM (2015). https://doi.org/10.1145/2838739.2838769
10. Kuznetsov, S., et al.: HCI, politics and the city: engaging with urban grassroots movements for reflection and action. In: Proceedings of the 2011 Annual Conference Extended Abstracts on Human Factors in Computing Systems - CHI EA 2011, Vancouver, BC, Canada, p. 2409. ACM Press (2011). https://doi.org/10.1145/1979742.1979568
11. Smith, A., Fressoli, M., Thomas, H.: Grassroots innovation movements: challenges and contributions. J. Clean. Prod. 63, 114–124 (2014). https://doi.org/10.1016/j.jclepro.2012.12.025
12. Correia, A.-P., Yusop, F.D.: "I don't want to be empowered": the challenge of involving real-world clients in instructional design experiences. In: PDC, pp. 214–216 (2008)
13. Teli, M., Foth, M., Sciannamblo, M., Anastasiu, I., Lyle, P.: Tales of institutioning and commoning: participatory design processes with a strategic and tactical perspective. In: Proceedings of the 16th Participatory Design Conference 2020 - Participation(s) Otherwise - Volume 1, Manizales, Colombia, pp. 159–171. ACM (2020). https://doi.org/10.1145/3385010.3385020
14. Dow, A., Comber, R., Vines, J.: Between grassroots and the hierarchy: lessons learned from the design of a public services directory. In: Proceedings of the 2018 CHI Conference on Human Factors in Computing Systems, Montreal, QC, Canada, pp. 1–13. ACM (2018). https://doi.org/10.1145/3173574.3174016
15. DiSalvo, C.: Design and the construction of publics. Des. Issues 25, 48–63 (2009). https://doi.org/10.1162/desi.2009.25.1.48
16. Helmke, G., Levitsky, S.: Informal institutions and comparative politics: a research agenda. Perspect. Polit. 2, 725–740 (2004). https://doi.org/10.1017/S1537592704040472
17. Dow, A., Comber, R., Vines, J.: Communities to the left of me, bureaucrats to the right…here I am, stuck in the middle. Interactions 26, 26–33 (2019). https://doi.org/10.1145/3351735
18. Manzini, E., Coad, R.: Design, When Everybody Designs: An Introduction to Design for Social Innovation. The MIT Press, Cambridge (2015)
19. Manzini, E.: Making things happen: social innovation and design. Des. Issues 30, 57–66 (2014). https://doi.org/10.1162/DESI_a_00248
20. Catoir-Brisson, M.-J., Vial, S., Deni, M., Watkin, T.: From the specificity of the project in design to social innovation by design: a contribution. Presented at the Design Research Society Conference, 25 June 2016 (2016). University of Nîmes. https://doi.org/10.21606/drs.2016.143
21. Cairns, G.: Can design inform effective social innovation? Des. J. 20, 725–734 (2017). https://doi.org/10.1080/14606925.2017.1370658
22. Sanders, E.B.-N., Stappers, P.J.: Co-creation and the new landscapes of design. CoDesign 4, 5–18 (2008). https://doi.org/10.1080/15710880701875068

23. Bødker, S., Dindler, C., Iversen, O.S.: Tying knots: participatory infrastructuring at work. Comput. Support. Coop. Work (CSCW) **26**(1–2), 245–273 (2017). https://doi.org/10.1007/s10606-017-9268-y
24. Hillgren, P.-A., Seravalli, A., Emilson, A.: Prototyping and infrastructuring in design for social innovation. CoDesign **7**, 169–183 (2011). https://doi.org/10.1080/15710882.2011.630474
25. Karasti, H.: Infrastructuring in participatory design. In: Proceedings of the 13th Participatory Design Conference on Research Papers - PDC 2014, Windhoek, Namibia, pp. 141–150. ACM Press (2014). https://doi.org/10.1145/2661435.2661450
26. Seravalli, A., Agger Eriksen, M., Hillgren, P.-A.: Co-design in co-production processes: jointly articulating and appropriating infrastructuring and commoning with civil servants. CoDesign **13**, 187–201 (2017). https://doi.org/10.1080/15710882.2017.1355004
27. Simonsen, J., Karasti, H., Hertzum, M.: Infrastructuring and participatory design: exploring infrastructural inversion as analytic, empirical and generative. Comput. Support. Coop. Work (CSCW) **29**(1–2), 115–151 (2019). https://doi.org/10.1007/s10606-019-09365-w
28. Björgvinsson, E., Ehn, P., Hillgren, P.-A.: Agonistic participatory design: working with marginalised social movements. CoDesign **8**, 127–144 (2012). https://doi.org/10.1080/15710882.2012.672577
29. Petrella, V., Yee, J., Clarke, R.E.: Mutuality and reciprocity: foregrounding relationships in design and social innovation. Presented at the Design Research Society Conference, 10 September 2020 (2020). Northumbria University, Newcastle upon Tyne, UK. https://doi.org/10.21606/drs.2020.177
30. Tjahja, C., Yee, J.: Being a sociable designer: reimagining the role of designers in social innovation. CoDesign **18**, 135–150 (2022). https://doi.org/10.1080/15710882.2021.2021244
31. Valiente, M.-C., Rozas, D.: Integration of ontologies with decentralized autonomous organizations development: a systematic literature review. In: Garoufallou, E., Ovalle-Perandones, M.-A., Vlachidis, A. (eds.) MTSR 2021. CCIS, vol. 1537, pp. 171–184. Springer, Cham (2022). https://doi.org/10.1007/978-3-030-98876-0_15
32. Chohan, U.W.: The decentralized autonomous organization and governance issues. SSRN J. (2017). https://doi.org/10.2139/ssrn.3082055
33. Bellavitis, C., Fisch, C., Momtaz, P.P.: The rise of decentralized autonomous organizations (DAOs): a first empirical glimpse. Venture Cap., 1–17 (2022). https://doi.org/10.1080/13691066.2022.2116797
34. Huybrechts, L., Benesch, H., Geib, J.: Institutioning: participatory design, co-design and the public realm. CoDesign **13**, 148–159 (2017). https://doi.org/10.1080/15710882.2017.1355006
35. Meyer, P.B.: Frame reflection: toward the resolution of intractable policy controversies. J. Econ. Issues **29**, 965–968 (1995). https://doi.org/10.1080/00213624.1995.11505729
36. Castell, P.: Institutional framing of citizen initiatives: a challenge for advancing public participation in Sweden. Int. Plan. Stud. **21**, 305–316 (2016). https://doi.org/10.1080/13563475.2015.1124756
37. Lodato, T., DiSalvo, C.: Institutional constraints: the forms and limits of participatory design in the public realm. In: Proceedings of the 15th Participatory Design Conference: Full Papers - Volume 1, Hasselt, Genk, Belgium, pp. 1–12. ACM (2018). https://doi.org/10.1145/3210586.3210595
38. Cibin, R., Teli, M., Robinson, S.: Institutioning and Community Radio. A comparative perspective. In: Proceedings of the 9th International Conference on Communities & Technologies - Transforming Communities, Vienna, Austria, pp. 143–154. ACM (2019). https://doi.org/10.1145/3328320.3328392

39. Cibin, R., Robinson, S., Teli, M., Linehan, C., Maye, L., Csíkszentmihályi, C.: Shaping social innovation in local communities: the contribution of intermediaries. In: Proceedings of the 11th Nordic Conference on Human-Computer Interaction: Shaping Experiences, Shaping Society, Tallinn, Estonia, pp. 1–12. ACM (2020). https://doi.org/10.1145/3419249.3420178

40. Simonsen, J., Robertson, T. (eds.): Communities: participatory design for, with and by communities. In: Routledge International Handbook of Participatory Design, pp. 202–230. Routledge (2012). https://doi.org/10.4324/9780203108543-15

41. Dantec, C.A.L., DiSalvo, C.: Infrastructuring and the formation of publics in participatory design. Soc. Stud. Sci. **43**, 241–264 (2013). https://doi.org/10.1177/0306312712471581

42. Sciannamblo, M., Lyle, P., Teli, M.: Fostering commonfare. Entanglements between participatory design and feminism. Presented at the Design Research Society Conference, 28 June 2018 (2018). Madeira Interactive Technologies Institute. https://doi.org/10.21606/drs.2018.557

43. Pihkala, S., Karasti, H.: Politics of mattering in the practices of participatory design. In: Proceedings of the 15th Participatory Design Conference: Short Papers, Situated Actions, Workshops and Tutorial - Volume 2, Hasselt, Genk, Belgium, pp. 1–5. ACM (2018). https://doi.org/10.1145/3210604.3210616

44. Braun, V., Clarke, V.: Using thematic analysis in psychology. Qual. Res. Psychol. **3**, 77–101 (2006). https://doi.org/10.1191/1478088706qp063oa

45. Ewing, K.D.: The function of trade unions. Ind. Law J. **34**, 1–22 (2005). https://doi.org/10.1093/ilj/34.1.1

46. Powell, W., et al.: Neither market nor hierarchy. Sociol. Organ. Class. Contemp. Crit. Read. **315**, 104–117 (2003)

47. Bratteteig, T., Wagner, I.: Disentangling power and decision-making in participatory design. In: Proceedings of the 12th Participatory Design Conference on Research Papers: Volume 1 - PDC 2012, Roskilde, Denmark, p. 41. ACM Press (2012). https://doi.org/10.1145/2347635.2347642

48. Wasserman, S., Faust, K.: Social network analysis in the social and behavioral sciences. Soc. Netw. Anal. Methods Appl. **1994**, 1–27 (1994)

49. Bauman, Z.: Community: Seeking Safety in An Insecure World. Wiley, Hoboken (2013)

50. Zargham, M., Nabben, K.: Aligning 'decentralized autonomous organization' to precedents in cybernetics. SSRN J. (2022). https://doi.org/10.2139/ssrn.4077358

51. Rikken, O., Janssen, M., Kwee, Z.: Governance challenges of blockchain and decentralized autonomous organizations. IP **24**, 397–417 (2019). https://doi.org/10.3233/IP-190154

52. Campbell, A.D.: Lay designers: grassroots innovation for appropriate change. Des. Issues **33**, 30–47 (2017). https://doi.org/10.1162/DESI_a_00424

Sustainable Design Methods and Practices

Constructing Cultural Branding
for Sustainability: A Case Study of Designing
'Traditional Circular' into 'Modern Product'

Jing Cao[1,2]([✉]), Po-Hsien Lin[2], and Rungtai Lin[2]

[1] School of Media and Design, Hangzhou Dianzi University, Hangzhou, People's Republic of China
872027708@QQ.com

[2] Graduate School of Creative Industry Design, National Taiwan University of Arts, New Taipei City, Taiwan
{t0131,rtlin}@ntua.edu.tw

Abstract. The fusion of creativity and cultural elements is one of the topics that researchers have discussed for a long time. In addition to being able to integrate with innovation, the cultural elements are not only a carrier that highlights local culture and global design value, but also the basis for shaping cultural brands. This research takes cultural element "Circular" as the starting point, combined with corresponding academic theories, and explores the value of transforming "cultural elements" into "commercial connotation". Finally, taking the wedding custom of "Ten-Mile Red Dowry" in eastern Zhejiang of China as a research case, the paper is to analyze the reasons for the emergence and decline of the concept of "Circle" in traditional wedding custom relics. Continuing, the concept of interaction between culture and human factors engineering is used to carry out innovative design practice and build a model of sustainable development of cultural elements. It is hoped that this research will respond to the sustainable development of cultural elements through design practice and show the value of cultural and creative industries.

Keywords: Cultural elements · Cultural branding · Sustainability · Designing "Circular" · Creative product

1 Introduction

In recent years, more and more researchers are attempting to find out ways to shape national identity through cultural creativity and contribute to the sustainable development of national culture [1–3]. Circles are a visual symbol that can guide the cultural orientation in Eastern and Western cultures. Since ancient times, the Chinese have hoped to express a beautiful vision by adding circles to ritual scenes or artificial designs. In Chinese culture, a circle represents joy, harmony and completeness. Up to this day, most of China's excellent ideas based on the "circles" are preserved in museums or historical books, and are becoming less and less popular.

© The Author(s), under exclusive license to Springer Nature Switzerland AG 2023
P.-L. P. Rau (Ed.): HCII 2023, LNCS 14022, pp. 333–346, 2023.
https://doi.org/10.1007/978-3-031-35936-1_24

At the end of 20th century, the "Girotondo" series designed and produced by Alessi was inspired by a cluster of silhouettes of little people who appeared to be dancing in a circular. Subsequently, these lovely little people appeared in many Alessi daily necessities [4], becoming one of Alessi's most recognizable product series. The success of the "Girotondo" series provoked the thought that, compared to other designs with the concept of a circle, why these "standing little people" continue to arouse the inner joys and emotions of users by use of the signs of emotional features and cultural features? Why would there be lasting economic and cultural benefits from a deceptively simple concept?

With the rise of the experience-based economy and the transformation of consumption patterns, the cultural aesthetics has also changed from the pursuit of high-tech quality to the hi-touch taste [5]. The Chinese ancestors so admired the status of the circle. By analyzing the performance of the circle in cultural innovation, it is worth further research to explore how to inherit and carry forward this national cultural spirit and shape modern products with national character. Therefore, this study starts with the circle as cultural element, takes the marriage custom of Ten-Mile Red Dowry in eastern Zhejiang Province as the example to discuss the relationship among ritual, form and creativity, and finally summarizes the model of sustainable development of cultural creativity by using cultural elements. Its main purposes include:

1. To explore how to apply cultural features in daily life to highlight the value of local design in global market.
2. To construct a model that is inspiration from culture, ideation with product, implementation for life, and completion in branding, for the sustainability of culture.

2   Literature Discussion

2.1   Cultural Meaning: The Application of Circular in the Form and Ritual

Circles are generally believed to be the shape of a ritual scene, and the resulting various forms of circular dance are a common cultural expression in countries around the world. Therefore, at carnivals, sacrifices or celebrations, people dance naturally in a circular, forming a space and spiritual center and symbolizing joyful emotions, which are common in ancient and modern China and abroad [6]. Circular dances are profound in formal and ritual characteristics and evoke great collective enthusiasm. For example, as shown in Fig. 1, picture A shows the Aboriginal Harvest Festival of Taiwan [7], the people in a tribe surrounds the campfire in a circular with hands in hands, to officially launch the singing and dancing ceremony of the Ying Ling Festival (Greeting the souls festival). It is a comprehensive carnival ceremony that combines festival, celebration and joy [8, 9]. Picture B shows the nine muses in Greek mythology are the embodiment of happiness and harmony. They sing and dance together to encourage people to eliminate troubles and forget pain. Their cheerful scenes are the source of inspiration for artistic creation [10]. Clive Bell (1914) proposed that people attach importance to the form with meaning to evoke a certain aesthetic emotion of human beings, and the circular is also abstracted, symbolized and introduced into various artistic creations [11]. This indicates that the ancestors used the tools in life to show the cultural meaning, which was the source of artistic creation. The circle is an important symbol in culture. Whether it is in nature or in art, the circle has a formal beauty that reminds people of harmony, joy and satisfaction [12].

Fig. 1. The scene of a circular dance at the Aboriginal Harvest Festival. Figure 2. Baldassare Peruzzi (1481–1537), Muses Dancing with Apollo.

2.2 Cultural Sustainability: From Culture Meaning to Business Model

Culture plays an important role in designing and is called the way of life of the whole society [13]. Integrating cultural elements into business is another means of promoting cultural sustainability [14]. In addition to cultural connotations, if the commodities ideated with culture have the characteristics that can resonate in the minds of consumers, then this aesthetic economy rising with culture and design will certainly lead the global trend, and commodities with cultural meaning circulated worldwide are the best carrier for promoting the culture. For example, the "Girotondo" trays designed and produced by Alessi feature a series of silhouettes of little people. The silhouettes at the edge of the product are like a group of children dancing happily to a nursery rhyme in a circular. These seemingly simple products were a huge success when they hit the market at the end of last century.

The driving force of creativity lies in that the designer extracts the symbolic meaning of a specific lifestyle, transforms the symbolic meaning into visual consumption symbols, and then design these consumption symbols into creative life products [15]. Figure 2 summarizes the relationship between Alessi's "Girotondo" series of products and creative symbols. Lin believes that style design can be generalized into three levels, namely form, function, and significance [16, 17], which respectively represent that: (1) design focuses on the product appearance, aiming to transform its form, texture and pattern into a new product. (2) design focuses on the use, function, performance, and usability of a cultural object. (3) design involves feelings, emotions, and cognitions generated from experiencing of a cultural object. It can be found that the instinctive design, behavioral design and reflective design reflected in a product [18] as proposed by Norman echo respectively with the form, function and significance. The "Girotondo" series of products conveys a life attitude and way of life through the relationship between people and cultural symbols.

Subsequently, these cute little people appeared in many Alessi daily products, and the product type extended from the initial trays to the entire kitchen product system, and then to the office and even jewelry fashion field. Product materials include metals and plastics. By use of cultural symbols, the "Girotondo" series has captured the meaning of "interest"

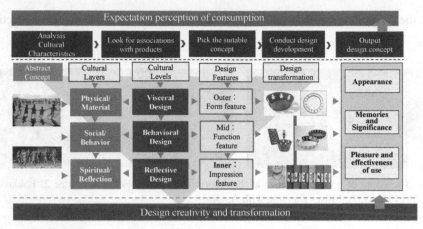

Fig. 2. Relationship between "Girotondo" series product modeling and culture. (source: this study).

and "emotion" in products [4], and has achieved a classic series ranging from culture to sustainable management, as shown in Fig. 3. This case has practical implications for creating a beautiful and meaningful life. As can be seen from the Fig. 3, culture is a kind of lifestyle. The formation of culture requires a group of people's life claims to form a kind of life taste, and finally gains the recognition of more people and becomes a reaction of lifestyle. As more and more people adopt and apply, it gradually forms a lifestyle. The driving force for design innovation is that the designer refines the symbolic meaning of a specific lifestyle, transforms the meaning of the symbol into a visual consumption symbol, and then designs these consumer symbols into living products and creative commodities. Industry is the medium to realize cultural creativity. It mainly shows a certain life proposition, to form a brand, to promotes living taste through brand marketing, and finally, to meet consumers of a certain lifestyle with creative products, continue to promote and expand implementation to create cultural and creative industries [21]. Therefore, the commercial connotation of cultural and creative industries can be simplified as "inspiration from culture, ideation with product, implementation for life, and completion in branding" [21, 22].

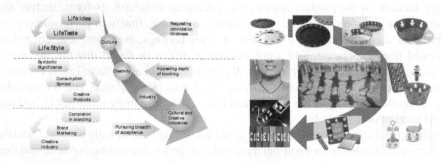

Fig. 3. From cultural features to cultural industries. (Adapted from [21]. Copyright 2011 Lin.).

2.3 Creative Model: Framework for Designing Cultural Product

Traditional culture has continuous and extensive influence on the design of future generations of products. Similarly, the development mode of cultural products will also change with the development of lifestyle. In the past few decades, people have been discussing for a long period of time to understand HCI (human-computer interaction), and the interaction between human and culture is a problem that needs to be solved in the future innovative design. As shown in Fig. 7, taking the series of Dou trays (grain serving vessel) designed and produced by JIA brand as an example, Dou tray was a very important food vessel and ritual vessel in China's pre-Qin period [23]. Chinese people attach great importance to gathering. The design group first analyzes the living conditions of people at that time and extract information. Then designers analyzed the venues where the vessels circulated according to the data. Through creative thinking, designers sampled the disc and high-footed shape of the Dou tray, and designed a contemporary *Dou* tray [24]. This design well interprets the relationship between cultural symbols and design. It not only retains the temperament of the old cultural relics, but also it is endowed with good meaning according to the ritual emotions, which meets the needs of the modern market.

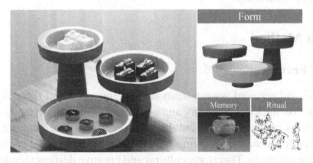

Fig. 4. *Dou* Tray (grain serving vessel). Chinese people are very particular about all kinds of utensils for banquets and sacrifices. The upper part of the Dou is disc-shaped, and the high-footed design is suitable for holding it. It is also in line with the custom of the ancient nobles to kneel and sit.

Based on Norman's previous research into definition of conceptual prototype of mental model, combined with the conceptual model of Lin [25], this study proposes a cultural concept interaction model to study the ways of cross-cultural communication between users and designers, as well as the cultural aspects of interaction and user experience in the design process. From the summary in Fig. 8, it can be clearly seen that the cultural concept model is formed at three stages: information bonus, knowledge bonus and creativity bonus. The semantic level of the final product is reflected in the product significance. In the design model, the most important thing for designers at the design level is to find how to convey cultural information. The user model is formed through the interaction between users and cultural products. Based on the cultural context, designers expect the user model to be consistent with the design model through the cultural level of interaction design.

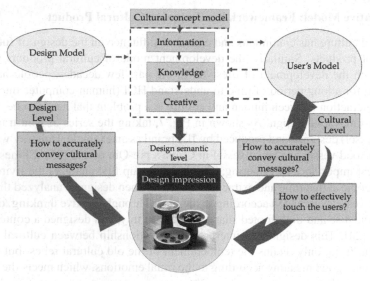

Fig. 5. The Design and Dissemination Process of Cultural and Creative Products. (Adapt from [25]. Copyright 2018 Gao et al.)

3 Research Method

3.1 Research Framework

Various national and regional governments are paying more and more attention to the impact of culture on the local economy and environment, but there are also some problems in the process of transforming culture into creativity. For example, the abuse of cultural elements or mechanical copying leads to serious homogeneity of products and lack of design connotations. Therefore, cultural and creative designs should be translated in a systematic thinking process. Based on this situation, this study chosen the marriage custom of "Ten-Mile Red Dowry" in Zhejiang Province of China is selected as a study case. Constructing theories from case study is a research strategy. The case study method is suitable for analyzing cases with authenticity and complexity, and often establishes some interesting theories [26].

The current concept of product design has gradually changed from form follows function to form follows emotion. Form (shaping) is the final result of product innovation and design activities. Form is the best combination of function and aesthetics, while ritual is the overall performance of technology and human nature. A complex mental stage is necessary for product design. Lin and Kreifeldt believe that integrating culture into products should be the trend of human factors engineering, and the interaction between human and culture will be the direction of future experience design research. They proposed a model of cultural human factors engineering, which could be applied to the design of cross-cultural products [27, 28]. Based on the research model proposed by Lin and Kreifeldt [28] and the literature review, this study proposes a conceptual model for itself. As shown in Fig. 6, design activities are conducted in three steps: analysis and conclusion, gift of meaning, and flexible application. Finally, the ideal product aesthetic interface is achieved. According to the research framework, this study conducts experiments on the design application of cultural and creative products, verifies the feasibility of these three bonus activities in the application model of future cultural and creative design, and provide relevant research references.

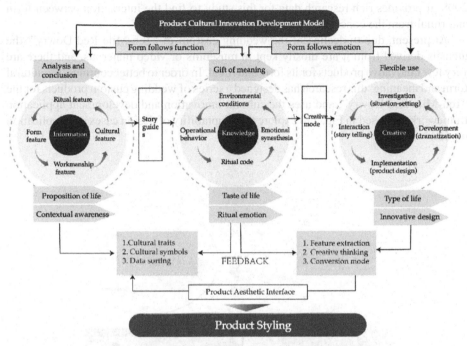

Fig. 6. Roduct Cultural Innovation Development Model ((Adapt from [28]. Copyright 2016 Krcifcldt et al.)

3.2 Overview of the Case

Wedding custom is a marriage custom formed by a nation in the long-term historical evolution. Marriage is one of the most important life etiquette activities for Chinese people. In China, wedding rituals are very diverse, and its ultimate purpose is to hope that the new couple can be fulfilled and happy in their marriage life. Marriage products are a symbol of marriage culture and ritual materialization. Therefore, the ceremonies or products related to wedding customs will adopt rounded shapes in appearance, and the products imply the concept of perfection. The "Ten-Mile Red Dowry" wedding custom took place on the eastern coast of Zhejiang Province, China. Since the Southern Song Dynasty, rich or common families preferred to show ostentation when marrying off a daughter. Therefore, wealthy families spared no expense to send dowry stretching for dozens of miles. This custom was gradually spread, shaping the locally unique spectacular scene of dowry, and forming the wedding custom of "Ten-Mile Red Dowry" [29]. The following Fig. 7 shows the location of the "Ten-Mile Red Dowry" wedding custom and the dowry to be given. Affected by the openness of Chinese society and western marriage etiquette, the wedding custom of "Ten-Mile Red Dowry" is no longer popular, but this scene expresses the love of parents on the one hand, and also hopes that the daughter can live a perfect and happy life after marriage [29]. The wedding custom of "Ten-Mile Red Dowry" was included in the national intangible cultural heritage in 2008. It provides rich research data for this study to find the interaction between form and ritual from the concept of Circular.

At present, due to decline of the wedding custom of "Ten-Mile Red Dowry", the utensils derived from it are mostly kept in museums or video materials, and there are very few innovative products for its form and ritual. In order to better continue the cultural form and meaning, this research has designed a series of wedding custom products for the "Ten-Mile Red Dowry", and uses the cultural innovation and development application framework proposed in Fig. 7 to explore the adaptability of design cases and application modes.

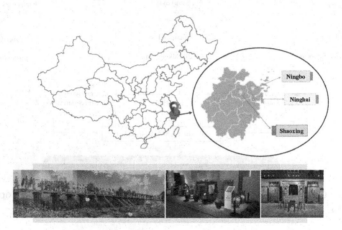

Fig. 7. The location where the wedding custom of Ten-Mile Red Dowry occurred and the scene of the dowry delivery. (Source: this study).

4　Case Study and Discussions

4.1　Case Study I

In order to bridge the gap between people and products, this study designed a set of combs through the modeling of The Ten-Mile Red Dowry representative objects, as shown in the Fig. 8. There are three combs in this design, and each comb is one pair that can be separated and used as both or put together. When assembled, both combs form a circle and have a full motif at the same time. The designs are representative of The Ten-Mile Red Dowry: *Wangong* sedan(sedan), *Qiangong* bed (bed) and *Nver* altar (wine altar). In China, the comb stands for the sense of perfection. In China, there is a saying that "a comb till the hair is white", a comb as a wedding gift is a relatively common phenomenon. This design group through the extraction of the image modelling cultural relics, for comb design to increase creativity and design connotation, to express people's aspiration for a happy life. We can say that the design keeps the concept and the symbolism of the circle.

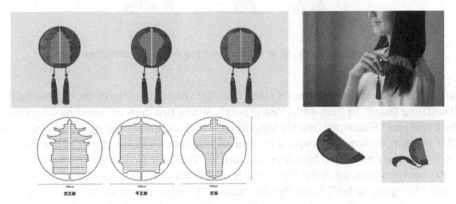

Fig. 8. A series of comb designs based on the Ten-mile red dowry. (Source: this study).

4.2   Case Study II

Lighting a candlestick was an essential ritual in ancient Chinese weddings. During the wedding ceremony, the husband and wife light the menorah to symbolize the continuation of future generations and the beginning of a better life for the newlyweds. Candles are rarely used in modern weddings, but people's desire for a better life with light has not changed. In this design, as shown in Fig. 9, in order to transform cultural relics into products that meet the needs of the modern market, while retaining a solemn sense of ceremony, the designer designed a pair of lamps. Based on the concept of bionic design, the lamps use the images of the couple as inspiration, one high and the other low, just like the bride and groom. Through the analysis of The Ten- Mile Red Dowry traditional wedding dress, the designer simplified and abstracted the traditional wedding dress and wedding accessories. Designers abandoned the cumbersome decoration, and only retain the original basic form used in the lamp design. The design conveys feelings of joy and sweetness by surrounding light, which symbolizes light and hope.

4.3   Case Study III

In the wedding custom of Ten-Mile Red Dowry, there was a tea serving ceremony. This ritual is also a kind of ceremony that has been used in China for thousands of years. On the wedding day, the bride's family will prepare tea in advance. The bride and groom offer tea to their parents and elders to show their respect. The tea serving ceremony requires the use of pairs of cups, and this piece of work is called "Love Cups", as shown in Fig. 10. The type of this product is taken from the implication of round sky and square

Fig. 9. Lamp design based on the Ten-mile red dowry. (Source: this study).

earth. The top element of the cup is taken from the shape of the top of the representative "*WanGong* sedan" in "Ten-Mile Red Dowry". When two cups are combined together, there will be a "Shuangxi" (double happiness), which means two happy events come one after another, wishing the couple a lifetime of happiness. The small tray below the cup takes the square round and fan-shaped pattern in "Ten-Mile Red Dowry". The large tray at the bottom stands up at the four corners, and is taken from the shape of the bottom of the "*Wangong* sedan". From the perspective of design function, the cups are a pair, including the cups, the cup bases and the tray. The cup base can be used separately to match with a cup, and the base can be placed in the bottom, which is in line with the use situation and function. Based on the graphic elements of the cup base, this design also developed a series of cultural and creative products, including silk scarves, key chains and red envelopes. From the perspective of design reflection, this product combines traditional customs with product forms through tea serving ceremony, and retains the spiritual culture of circle. In addition, the development of the serialization of cultural and creative products has increased the application scope of design imagery, increased the pleasure of consumer selection, and created a modern attitude towards design and life.

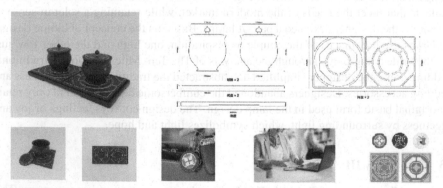

Fig. 10. Love Cups - Series design based on Ten-mile red dowry. (Source: this study).

4.4   Discussion and Enlightenment

This study shows that after analysis and understanding of the circular concept in Chinese culture, the design group found that most of the cultural resources are intangible. For example, the tao, state and beauty of circular derived from circular are a kind of cultural spirit, and need to be spread through a medium or entity. Therefore, this study selects tangible entities that have entered the museum to verify the innovative devel-opment model of product culture proposed above. The design group chooses to redesign the copper coins that no longer exist and wedding supplies for The Ten-Mile Red Dowry, and the redesigned products can express cultural value. Through the practice of three design cases, it is found in this study that:

- Theoretical Implications: This study proposed a conceptual model based on the rela-tionship between circle and culture to provide implementation methods and basis for the sustainable development of cultural assets. Only on the basis of under-standing can the public become the media of cultural dissemination. Culture is the essential characteristic that identify a nation, and a sign that distinguishes a nation from other nations. It can be said that culture, with its rich materiality, deep-rooted cultural iden-tity and intrinsic value, echoes the style of people's daily life in different countries and regions. Thus, the core question is how we can help ordinary people have a cultural understanding and experience, so as to participate in the cultural dissemination. This study though circle provides an channel.
- Practical Implications: This study is intended to bridge the gap between theory and practice through design cases. Cultural product design is an adaptative process of reexamining, rethinking, redefining and redesigning culture. Bruner (1966) argued that the personal growth is achieved through a process of internalizing behavioral, imaginative, and symbolic modes that exist in their culture. Such modes may enhance human strength [30]. The design group noted the importance of linking products with local cultural characteristics to enhance product value. So, the design group applied design framework to the design of cultural products, emphasizing the analysis and application of culture. This systematic research structure can help designers better understand the meaning of culture in the design process, and use this understanding to design and evaluate products, so that the public can recognize the value of culture.
- Social Implications: Integrating cultural elements into business is another means of promoting cultural sustainability. Cultural institutions and cultural decision makers usually address cultural sustainability issues by cooperating in and producing new service products. For example, the JIA brand mentioned above has been established based on the concept of Chinese culture and family warmth, and has built brand effects for the sustainable development of cultural spirit. Based on the cultural spirit of the circle, this study can construct the concept of a cultural brand with harmonious, perfection, motion. The realization of cultural sustainability also includes public participation and judgment on cultural design. Only after the public have a high understanding of the essence of traditional culture and national culture can a virtuous circular of development of culture and commerce be formed. Successful commercial applications indicate that traditional cultures can also contribute to market-oriented

goals in modern times, such as adapting to the needs of new audiences and developing collective creativity to enable innovation.

If the Sustainable Development Goals (SDGs) take the economy, society and environment as the three pillars, then culture and creativity make important contributions to each pillar horizontally and are the internal driving force of sustainable construction [2]. Based on the model constructed in this study, cultural elements, innovative thinking and brand effect are examined in relation to sustainable development. It is found that the sustainable development of culture can be realized through the cycle of cultural industrialization to industry culturalization. The relationship of all parts is shown in Fig. 11. The significance of this model is to provide a cultural innovation and sustainable development idea that is inspired from culture, ideated in products, implemented for life, and completed in branding. Through creative design, the cultural genes in cultural assets are transformed into business ideas, so as to realize the sustainable development of the cultural industry. Through examples of design practice, this study verifies the effectiveness of model construction.

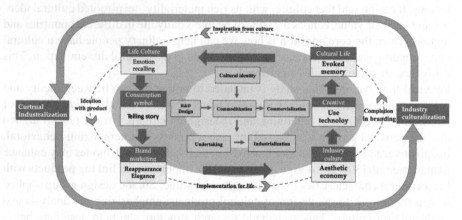

Fig. 11. Sustainable development model of cultural creativity. (Source: this study).

5   Research Results and Discussion

This study starts from a "Circular" shape, and uses cultural heritage as the carrier to discuss how traditional cultural elements continue and enrich their contemporary values, and promote the sustainable development of excellent culture. Taking this as an idea, this study has chosen the Chinese wedding custom of "Ten-Mile Red Dowry" that is no longer popular in modern society as the research case. From the perspective of cultural human factors, discuss how designers should explore the potential ceremony and stories of cultural elements in modern life through the external forms of cultural elements, and reproduce the cultural connotation of "Circle" in life, and through cultural and creative products, make ordinary people feel the charm of traditional cultural elements.

The purpose of this study is to provide a conceptual research framework. From the perspective of the life cycle of cultural elements, it emphasizes the interconnection between sustainability and product innovation design. In this context, the three products designed in this study can reflect the core value of Circle in traditional culture, and the designed products are in line with the lifestyle of modern people. Based on the analysis of the above three cases and the contemporary aesthetic economic thinking, this study proposes the cultural creativity sustainable development model shown in Fig. 11. However, due to the limitation of objective conditions, only 3 cases were designed in this study. Whether the 3 cases can well interpret the intention of this study needs to be demonstrated in subsequent research. However, in this article, the focus of this study is how to realize the cultural element "thinking of the ancient times and reproducing the glory and charm", which can be used as preliminary research for subsequent studies. In addition, although the "Ten-Mile Red Dowry" is the culture of the Chinese world, the model of thinking constructed by this research can be adopted by other countries or regions. Whether this model is applicable to the sustainable development of other countries or national cultures in the world needs further verification.

Funding. The authors gratefully acknowledge the support for this research provided by the General Research Project of Education Department of Zhejiang Province, No. Y202044449.

References

1. Kagan, S.: Culture and the Arts in Sustainable Development: Rethinking Sustainability Research. In Cultural Sustainability, 1st edn. Routledge, London (2018)
2. Culture: the core of the Sustainable Development Goals. https://zh.unesco.org/courier/april-june-2017/wen-hua-ke-chi-xu-fa-zhan-mu-biao-he-xin. Accessed 4 Nov 2017
3. Soini, K., Dessein, J.: Culture-sustainability relation: towards a conceptual framework. Sustainability **8**(2), 167 (2016)
4. Alessi, A.: The Dream Factory: Alessi Since 1921. Rizzoli, Milan Italy (2016)
5. Lin, R.: A framework for human-culture interaction design–beyond human-computer interaction. In International Symposium for Emotion and Sensibility. **1**, 27–29 (2008)
6. Liu, Z.: Etiquette and primitive dance. Natl. Arts, **4**, 101–110 (1998)
7. Festival. https://zh.m.wikipedia.org/zh/%E8%B1%90%E5%B9%B4%E7%A5%AD. Accessed 15 June 2022
8. Leo, L.: Corposcopio: an interactive installation performance in the intersection of ritual, dance and new technologies. Technoetic. Arts **5**(2), 113–117 (2007)
9. Shannon, L.; UK, D.D.: Living ritual dance: dreaming the past, dancing the future. In: American Dance Therapy Association 28th Annual Conference Proceedings, Atlanta, GA, USA (1993)
10. The Muses of Ancient Greece. https://discover.hubpages.com/education/The-Muses-of-Ancient-Greece. Accessed 08 Jan 2015
11. Bell, C.: Art as significant form. In: Dickie, G., Sclafani, R., Roblin, R. (eds.) Aesthetics, a Critical Anthology, pp. 73–83. St. Martin's Press, New York (2014)
12. Wu, C.: The cultural mentality of "cicular." J. Jianghan Univ. (Social Sciences Edition) **1**, 77–80 (1989)
13. Leong, D., Clark, H.: Culture-based knowledge towards new design thinking and practice: a dialogue. Des. Issues **19**(3), 48–58 (2003)

14. Luisa, E., Roberto, M.: Leveraging smart open innovation for achieving cultural sustainability: learning from a new city museum project. Sustainability **10**, 1964 (2018)
15. Wu, J., Ju, L.H., Lin, P.H., Lyu, Y.: The relationship between form and ritual in cultural sustainability. Sustainability **14**(15), 9157 (2022)
16. Lin, R.: A study of visual features for icon design. Des. Stud. **15**(2), 185–197 (1996)
17. Wu, J., Sun, Y., Lin, R.T.: Less is more: audience cognition of comic simplification in the characters of Peking opera. Science **4**(1), 2 (2022)
18. Norman, D.: Emotional Design: Why We Love (or Hate) Everyday Things. Basic Books, New York (2004)
19. Ashby, M., Johnson, K.: The art of materials selection. Mater. Today **6**(12), 24–35 (2003)
20. Evans, J.R.; Lindsay, W.M.: The Management and Control of Quality. 4th edn. South-Western, New York, (1999)
21. Lin, R.: Preface - The essence and research of cultural and creative industry. J. Des., **16**(4) (2011)
22. Chiang, I.Y., Lin, P.H., Kreifeldt, J.G., Lin, R.: From theory to practice: an adaptive development of design education. Educ. Sci. **11**(11), 673 (2021)
23. Chinese ritual vessels. https://zh.wikipedia.org/zh-tw/%E4%B8%AD%E5%9C%8B%E7%A6%AE%E5%99%A8. Accessed 16 May 2019
24. Get together— *"DOU"* dish. Available online: https://www.jia-inc.com/our-products/p/ftdp05fy6pxcbdzgsmjkx9v7orqn80, Accessed 21 Jan 2017
25. Gao, Y.J., Chang, W., Fang, W., Lin, R.: Acculturation in human culture interaction—a case study of culture meaning in cultural product design. Ergon. Int. J. **2**, 1–10 (2018)
26. Eisenhardt, K.M., Graebner, M.E.: Theory building from cases: opportunities and challenges. Acad. Manag. J. **50**(1), 25–32 (2007)
27. Lin, R., Kreifeldt, J.: Do Not Touch – A Conversation Between Technology to Humart. NTUA, New Taipei City (2014)
28. Kreifeldt, J.; Taru, Y.; Sun, M.X.; Lin, R.: Cultural ergonomics beyond culture-the collector as consumer in cultural product design. In International Conference on Cross-Cultural Design; Springer: Cham, Switzerland (2016)
29. Fan, P.L.: Ten-mile red dowry – A Study on folk dowry ware in Eastern Zhejiang, 1st edn. Cultural Relics Publishing House, Hangzhou (2012)
30. Bruner, J.S., Olver, R.R., Greenfield, P.M.: Studies in Cognitive Growth. Wiley, New York (1966)

Development and Verification of Sustainable Design Thinking Model — Case Study of Dehua Ceramics

Hao Chen[1](✉), Zhou-Bin Zen[1], Chao Liu[2], and Wen-Ko Chiou[3]

[1] School of Film Television and Communication, Xiamen University of Technology, Xiamen, China
haochen19606@163.com, 1063457538@qq.com
[2] School of Journalism and Communication, Hua Qiao University, Xiamen 361021, China
[3] Department of Industrial Design, Chang Gung University, Taoyuan City, Taiwan
wkchiu@mail.cgu.edu.tw

Abstract. This study uses the qualitative research method of grounded theory to organically integrate the innovation-driven theory, the design thinking theory, the sustainable development theory and the transitional design theory, to develop and put forward the sustainable design thinking model, which serves the innovative design of enterprises in Fujian Province and the "14th Five-Year Plan" scientific and technological innovation development plan. The sustainable design thinking model is composed of three double diamond models, which are analyzed from three dimensions: social economy, technological development and product service design. Potential opportunity gaps at key nodes are identified through divergent and convergent thinking processes. After that, Dehua ceramic industry in Fujian Province is taken as a case study and the sustainable design thinking model is used for case study. This paper analyzes the ceramic industry in Dehua from the macroscopic industrial level and the microscopic product design level respectively, and puts forward the existing problems and solutions. The results show that sustainable design thinking mode can strengthen the team's user-oriented concept, increase the team creativity, and effectively improve the maturity and clarity of product concept. Sustainable design mindsets positively influence communication, design learning, consensus and thinking among team members in cross-domain collaborative design, thereby enhancing team innovation and creativity, and reinforcing user-oriented concepts and sustainable development goals.

Keywords: Innovation-driven development strategy · Sustainability · Design Thinking · Transition design · Dehua Ceramics

1 Introduction

The innovation-driven development strategy is a major national development strategy of China [1]. As Fujian is at the core of the Belt and Road Maritime Silk Road, innovation-driven development is more urgent, and the industrial innovation design needs the guidance of methodology [2]. Silicon Valley is known as the global center of technological innovation. Among the many methodologies pioneered in Silicon Valley, the most

P.-L. P. Rau (Ed.): HCII 2023, LNCS 14022, pp. 347–358, 2023.
https://doi.org/10.1007/978-3-031-35936-1_25

famous is Design Thinking, a theory from Stanford University's d. school [3]. In this study, design thinking and transitional design theory are combined and integrated into the innovation practice in Fujian, and the sustainable design thinking model is built to serve the innovative design of Fujian enterprises and the scientific and technological innovation development plan.

With the promotion of innovation-driven development strategy, many relevant researches on the promotion of industrial development by innovative design have emerged in Fujian in recent years [4]. These studies compared comprehensively presents the current situation of Fujian innovative design development, trend and main problems, from the design discipline, innovation mechanism, talent cultivation, promote transformation and upgrading of industries, such as macro level puts forward a new countermeasure and implementation path, but ignores the micro-level enterprises in innovation, organization should follow how the specific methodology guidance [5]. The theory of design-driven innovation holds that the meaning of innovation generated by design drives the innovation behavior, and the value appeal of the meaning of innovation can be grasped through a deep understanding of the development trend of society, economy and technology [6]. Design-driven innovation transcends market demand and technological change and is a more essential innovation theory.

Design thinking is a people-oriented innovative design methodology that integrates human needs, technological possibilities and elements of business success to seek innovative solutions for a variety of complex issues [7]. Design thinking follows the innovative design methodology of "design-driven innovation" [8]. Through in-depth analysis of potential opportunities at social, economic and technological levels, design thinking can grasp the core value proposition of users and guide innovation practice [9]. However, the theoretical model of design thinking still only focuses on users [10]. Although it integrates technical and business factors, it fails to consider the system as a whole and include all stakeholders in the model, and fails to provide long-term solutions to achieve the goal of sustainable development [11]. Therefore, this study combines transitional design theory with design thinking and proposes a new innovative design methodology.

Transition design theory focuses on the process of transition from traditional society to the sustainable development in the future, the design for the social role, promoting society to a more sustainable and more ideal future transformation, to deal with complex solution resistance problems facing society, as well as the catalysis and promote the society to a more sustainable and preferable to long-term development in the future [12]. The user-centered design approach of design thinking does not broaden the focus to all affected stakeholder groups and rarely studies their common beliefs, assumptions, and cultural norms [13]. Transition design focuses on the process of innovation in production and consumption systems, especially the relationship between product strategy and environmental policy in a sustainable development perspective [14]. Transition design seeks solutions for sustainable development.

To sum up, the sustainable design thinking should: (1) not only focus on users, but also understand the overall complexity of the system and the interdependence of variables; (2) Integrate the shared beliefs of all stakeholders into design frameworks and interventions to provide long-term sustainable facilitation programs; (3) Based on the innovation practice in Fujian, a new methodology suitable for local enterprises in

Fujian is proposed. The goal of this study is to integrate design thinking and transitional design theory, based on the development status and trend of innovative design practice in Fujian Province, take Fujian Dehua ceramics as a case study, and put forward a sustainable design thinking model.

2   Sustainable Design Thinking Model

According to the research framework of "theoretical research - empirical analysis - practical application", and the research logic from divergence to convergence. This study used grounded theory to conduct in-depth analysis and collation of literature. In addition, relevant concepts, theories and models are analyzed, disassembled and reorganized, and the analytical methods of deduction and induction are used to find the internal relations between them.

Three double-diamond models were used to analyze and discuss from three aspects: socio-economic form, technological development trend, and product and service design (as shown in Fig. 1), and the prototype of sustainable design thinking model was constructed.

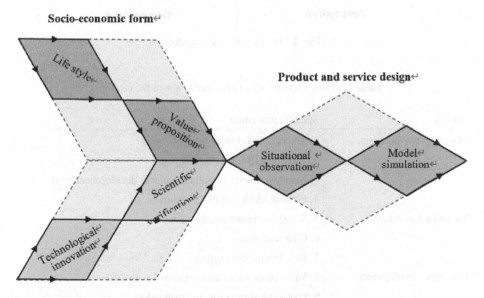

Fig. 1. The structural relationships of three double-diamond models

Each double-diamond model has gone through two processes of convergence and divergence of thinking [15]. First, analyze the driving factors in the fields of society economy and technology (S.E.T.) from a macro perspective, and get the potential opportunity gap (POG) [16]. Then analyze the user's usage scenarios from a micro perspective, so as to get the key themes and value propositions to be solved [17]. Finally, comprehensively propose the prototype concept and business model canvas of the product [18]. The steps of the double-diamond model method are shown in Table 1 and Fig. 2.

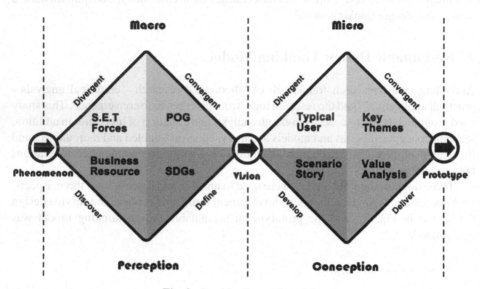

Fig. 2. Double-diamond models

Table 1. Table captions should be placed above the tables.

Section	Specific procedure
Macro factors analysis	1. Macro S.E.T. forces brainstorming
	2. S.E.T. top10 forces converging
	3. Business resources and sustainable development goals
	4. Product ideas and POG statement
Micro factors analysis	5. Scenario brainstorming sketch
	6. Character map
	7. Key themes converging
Prototype development	8. Value proposition and opportunity analysis
	9. Prototype simulation and evaluation
	10. Business model generation

Based on the full reference and absorption of domestic and foreign relevant research achievements, this study takes design and management as the main discipline background, and design psychology as the assistance, to conduct a comprehensive interdisciplinary research. In-depth analysis of relevant research results in Chinese and foreign academic circles, mainly using grounded theory and inductive and deductive analysis

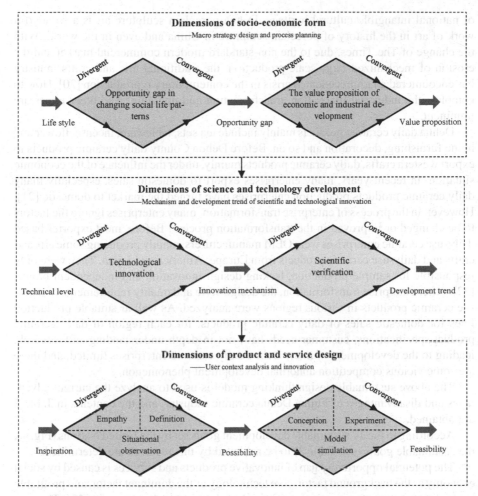

Fig. 3. Three double-diamond structures of sustainable design thinking model

methods, to analyze, disassemble and restructure related concepts, theories and models, laying a solid theoretical foundation for the construction of the sustainable design thinking model (see Fig. 3).

3   Case Study of Dehua Ceramics

Dehua, Fujian Province, is an important white porcelain production area in China, and also the starting point of the Maritime Silk Road. Dehua's ceramic industry has a long history and profound ceramic culture. It integrates Marine culture, religious culture, folk culture and foreign cultures introduced along the "Maritime Silk Road" and other multi-cultures, and is a representative traditional arts and crafts industry in southern Fujian [19]. Dehua porcelain firing technique has been selected as one of the first batch of national intangible cultural heritage. Dehua porcelain sculpture art is a wonderful work of art in the history of porcelain sculpture in China and even in the world. With the change of The Times, due to the non-standard modern commercial market and the erosion of mechanized large-scale production, the traditional arts and crafts industry has encountered an unprecedented crisis in the contemporary reproduction [20]. How to complete the industrial innovation, transformation and upgrading and other issues are imminent.

Dehua daily ceramic products mainly include tea sets, tableware, incense, flower and home furnishing, decoration and so on. Before Dehua County daily ceramic products to export western crafts, daily ceramic products mainly, under the influence of the economic situation, in recent years, many enterprises export to domestic sales, especially many daily ceramic products production enterprises have turned the market to domestic [21]. However, in the process of enterprise transformation, many enterprises ignore the factors to be changed or improved in the transformation process: Before, most exporter-based daily-use ceramic enterprises were OEM manufacturers, mainly producing some arts and crafts and daily-use ceramic products from Europe, America and Japan. They were only responsible for sample production, lacking design innovation and independent brands [22]. After enterprise transformation, the design style and quality requirements of daily-use ceramic products in various regions were analyzed. As well as suitable production lines for domestic sales of daily ceramic products, for each region of daily ceramic product specifications, customer needs have not in-depth understanding and research, leading to the development of many Dehua daily ceramic enterprises limited, and there are some vicious competition abnormal development phenomenon.

The above sustainable design thinking model is used to analyze the current advantages and disadvantages of Fujian Dehua ceramic industry, and the contents in Table 2 are obtained.

According to the 17 sustainable development goals set by the United Nations (Fig. 4), the sustainable goals (see Table 3) to be achieved by this research are determined.

The potential opportunity gap of innovative products and services is caused by social economy as the background factor, core technology as the dominant factor, and profitable business resources of enterprises as the goal of sustainable development [23]. Through the brainstorming of cross-field expert team members, divergent thinking and ideas can be found from the perspectives of society, economy and technology to find as many macro influences and driving factors as possible [24].

From the macroscopic analysis of society and economy, the important phenomena, the obvious trends, and the driving forces behind them were obtained [25]. Then analyze the possibility of solving these problems under the existing technical conditions, so as to get the potential opportunity gap statement (Table 3). Combining with the commercial resources we have and the sustainable development goals that want to achieve, there have a clearer concept and idea for the product to be designed [26].

Based on the above macro-level analysis, we finally point out the problems existing in the design of Dehua ceramics and give corresponding suggestions (Table 4).

Table 2. The advantages and disadvantages of Dehua ceramic industry

The advantages of Dehua ceramics industry
1. Diversification of materials
2. Dehua white porcelain is well known at home and abroad
3. Dehua regional brand effect is obvious
4. It has a long history and rich culture
5. The government policy system is relatively complete
6. A supporting service network has taken shape
The disadvantages of Dehua ceramic industry
1. There is less collaboration among enterprises in industrial clusters
2. Trade associations play a limited role
3. The equipment is old and the production technology is backward
4. The variety of products is diversified, and the enterprise does not specialize in production
5. The level of enterprise management needs to be improved
6. Brand building is immature

Fig. 4. 17 sustainable development goals set by the United Nations

Table 3. Potential opportunity gap statement

Business	Society and economy
• Enhance the regional brand of Dehua ceramics	• Building "strategic Alliance" of industrial clusters
• Promote enterprise and product brand building	• Enhance the independent innovation capacity of industrial clusters
• Innovate the mode of operation and management	• Improve the functions of trade associations
	• Give full play to the macro-guidance role of the government
Sustainable development goals	**Technology**
• Decent work and economic growth	• Silicone mold transfer
• Industry, innovation, and infrastructure	• Ceramic self-releasing glaze
• Responsible consumption and production	• Microwave drying and microwave firing
• Partnerships to achieve the goal	• Digital molding and 3D printing
	• Intelligent carving

Table 4. Problems and improvement methods in the design of Dehua ceramic products

Problems existing in Dehua daily ceramic product design
1. Product modeling is seriously homogenized
2. Product value is low, profit margin is low
3. The product is more form than function
4. Product sales market is relatively single
5. The design lacks cultural connotation
Design method to improve the value of Dehua ceramic products
1. Innovative design method, break through the homogeneity of modeling
2. Improve product functional utility through formal design
3. Improve product function and utility through material innovation
4. Increase the cultural connotation and integrate the cultural factors of southern Fujian into the design
5. Raise the awareness of product intellectual property protection, strengthen brand construction

4 Discussion

With the popularization of ceramic products, as well as the development of science and technology level, production mechanization, more diverse production of raw materials, modern ceramic products generally lack of delicacy, product safety and environmental protection considerations, more by the production process and use of function constrained and replaced. In fact, in today's material life with great satisfaction, people pay more attention to and pursue the quality of life than in the past, while many modern ceramic products lose their original exquisite beauty, and products produced in mechanized mass production ignore the quality of products because of the pursuit of quantification [27]. Therefore, in the innovation process of modern ceramic products, we cannot ignore the quality that has been pursued in the inheritance of Chinese ceramic culture for thousands of years, so that industrial production has changed the exquisite and delicate nature of ceramic products. Instead, we should combine modern production means and design methods with traditional ceramic culture to better carry forward and inherit Chinese ceramic culture.

Many ceramic enterprises in Dehua do not have the ability of independent design. Many ceramic enterprises in Dehua are disconnected from design to production. Designers do not understand production, and production personnel do not understand the design intention. Ceramic in the earliest ancient human invention it is closely combined with manual, even now the degree of mechanization is much higher than in the past, but there are still some manual completion of the process, and in the production process of ceramic may appear changes and problems can't be seen in the textbook, are the summary of the experience of workers. Therefore, if the designer is separated from the production, then most of the time the work will be in vain, and can't really understand the essence of ceramic products. Design innovation is the only way of enterprise transformation. Dehua ceramic enterprises should get rid of the traditional OEM mode and attach importance to the power of design innovation. In the beginning of the design part of the enterprise, the resident designer is hired to let the designer down to the production line to understand the production process, and even learn the production process of each link in person [28]. Only in this way can the designer truly understand the connotation of ceramic production, improve the efficiency of product design, and the enterprise can truly have the ability of product research and development.

According to the current development status of the ceramic industry in Dehua, it is necessary to get rid of the existing development mode of taking advantage of current benefits and consuming resources, take design innovation as the driving force of the ceramic industry, encourage enterprises to pay attention to design innovation, improve their ability to independently develop products, and form a benign development atmosphere by referring to Jingdezhen and other cities that do well in design innovation. Design innovation is also an effective way to help products form regional characteristics, so as to form product differentiation design and enhance product market competitiveness. Product differentiation is not only in the appearance of the style of differentiation design, in modern, but also includes the production technology, material engineering, performance and other aspects of differentiation design [29]. The ceramic product design of

Dehua should also integrate regional cultural characteristics into technological innovation, material innovation, technological innovation and appearance design in the process of design innovation, so as to form product design with Dehua characteristics.

Dehua has been rated as the "Ceramic Capital of the World", which means that Dehua will undertake more responsibilities for the inheritance and development of ceramics. For ceramic culture, we not only need to inherit, but also need innovation, so that it can have corresponding development in each era, so that it can adapt to the needs of The Times, and get better inheritance.

5 Conclusion

This study uses the sustainable design thinking model to analyze the case of Dehua ceramic design, to find out the potential product value opportunity gap and achieve the goal of sustainable development. Design approaches to achieving the SDGS can be advanced by:(1) working with and learning from those experienced in creative design approaches; (2) Create opportunities for exploration and insight; (3) Apply design methods to the Sustainable Development Goals and share results and processes. To sum up, the sustainable design thinking model can effectively bridge the differences in cross-domain communication, provide a common orientation, user-centered, comprehensive consideration of all stakeholders, and establish a common goal of sustainable development. The results of the case study found that the sustainable design thinking model can strengthen the team's user-oriented concept, increase the team creativity, and effectively improve the maturity and clarity of the product concept. The sustainable design thinking model positively influences communication, design learning, consensus and thinking among team members in cross-domain collaborative design, thereby enhancing team innovation and creativity, and reinforcing user-oriented conceptuality and sustainable development goals.

Funding. This research was supported by Social Science Fund of Fujian Province (No. FJ2022BF058).

References

1. Cao, W.B., Zhang, Y., Qian, P.: The effect of innovation-driven strategy on green economic development in China-An Empirical Study of Smart Cities. Int. J. Environ. Res. Public Health **16**(9), (2019)
2. Xiao, W,S,. Kong, H.J., Shi, L.F., Boamah, V., Tang, D.C.: The impact of innovation-driven strategy on high-quality economic development: evidence from China. Sustainability **14**(7), (2022)
3. Liedtka, J.: Perspective: linking design thinking with innovation outcomes through cognitive bias reduction. J. Prod. Innov. Manag. **32**(6), 925–938 (2015)
4. Chen, G., Mao, L.L., Pifer, N.D., Zhang, J.J.: Innovation-driven development strategy and research development investment: a case study of Chinese sport firms. Asia Pac. J. Mark. Logist. **33**(7), 1578–1595 (2021)
5. Song, Y.Q.: Boosting the strategy of innovation-driven development: intellectual property services in China's Universities. Ser. Rev. **47**(3–4), 215–223 (2021)

6. Xu, S., Yue, Q.D., Lu, B.B.: Grey correlation analysis on the synergistic development between innovation-driven strategy and marine industrial agglomeration: based on China's coastal provinces. Grey Sys.-Theory Appl. **12**(1), 269–289 (2022)
7. Brown, T.: Design thinking. Harvard Bus. Rev. **86**(6), 84-+ (2008)
8. Beckman, S.L., Barry, M.: Innovation as a learning process: embedding design thinking. Calif. Manag. Rev. **50**(1), 25-+ (2007)
9. Dorst, K.: The core of "design thinking" and its application. Des. Stud. **32**(6), 521–532 (2011)
10. Johansson-Skoldberg, U., Woodilla, J., Cetinkaya, M.: Design thinking: past, present and possible futures. Creat. Innov. Manag. **22**(2), 121–146 (2013)
11. Razzouk, R., Shute, V.: What Is design thinking and why is it important? Rev. Educ. Res. **82**(3), 330–348 (2012)
12. Irwin, T.J.D.: Culture. Transition design: a proposal for a new area of design practice, study, and research. Des. Cult **7**(2), 229–246 (2015)
13. Irwin, T., Tonkinwise, C., Kossoff, G.: Transition design: An educational framework for advancing the study and design of sustainable transitions. Cuadernos del Centro de Estudios de Diseño y Comunicación**105**, 31–72 (2022)
14. Gaziulusoy, I., Erdoğan Öztekin, E.J.S.: Design for sustainability transitions: origins, attitudes and future directions. Sustainability **11**(13), 3601 (2019)
15. Chiou, W.-K., et al.: ISDT case study of We'll App for postpartum depression women. In: 23rd HCI International Conference, pp. 119–137. Springer, Virtual Event (2021)
16. Liu, C., Chen, H., Liang, Y.-C, Lin, R., Chiou, W.-K.: ISDT case study of loving kindness meditation for flight attendants. In: 23rd HCI International Conference, pp. 201–216. Springer, Virtual Event (2021)
17. Pyykkoe, H., Suoheimo, M., Walter, S.: approaching sustainability transition in supply chains as a wicked problem: systematic literature review in light of the evolved double diamond design process model. Processes **9**(12), (2021)
18. Chen, H., Liu, C., Liang, Y.-C., Lin, R., Chiou, W.-K.: ISDT Case study of cultivation of employees' creativity in cultural and creative industries. In: 23rd HCI International Conference, pp. 18–30. Springer, Virtual Event (2021)
19. Yu, G., Jin, Z.Y., Chen, L.F., Wang, F., Wang, X.R., Wu, X.T., et al.: Analyzing the earliest Chinese proto-porcelain: Study on the materials from Liaotianjianshan kiln sites, Dehua County, Fujian Province (China). Ceram. Int. **44**(17), 21648–21655 (2018)
20. Xu, W.P., Yang, Z.L., Chen, L.F., Cui, J.F.: Dussubieux, L., Wang, W.J.: Compositional analysis below the production region level: a case study of porcelain production at Dehua, Fujian, China. J, Archaeol. Sci. **135**((2021)
21. Lian, X.B., Qiu, G.P., Chen, Z.H., Wang, T., Yuan, B.L., Zhang, Z.J.: Effect of green products advertising design demand on environment awareness and consumers' purchase intention - case on Dehua ceramic tea sets. J. Environ. Prot. Ecol. **22**(2), 706–713 (2021)
22. Ni, P., et al.: Geology, ore-forming fluid and genesis of the Qiucun gold deposit: Implication for mineral exploration at Dehua prospecting region, SE China. J. Geochem. Explor. **195** (3–15 (2018)
23. D'Agostino, L.M., Santangelo, G.D.: Do overseas R&D laboratories in emerging markets contribute to home knowledge creation? An extension of the double diamond model. Manag. Int. Rev. **52**(2), 251–273 (2012)
24. Morgan, S.L.: A double-diamond retrospective on modeling change in attitudes and opinions. Soc. Sci. Res. **109** ((2023)
25. Nail, P.R., Di Domenico, S.I., MacDonald, G.: Proposal of a double diamond model of social response. Rev. Gen. Psychol. **17**(1), 1–19 (2013)
26. Liang, Y.-C., Liu, C., Chen, H., Huang, D.-H., Chiou, W.-K.: The core values and methodology of cross-cultural i-sustainability design thinking. In: 23rd HCI International Conference, pp. 100–114. Springer, Virtual Event (2021)

27. Li, W.D., Luo, H.J., Li, J.A., Lu, X.K., Guo, J.K.: The white porcelains from Dehua kiln site of China. Part II: Microstructure and its physicochemical basis. Ceramics Int. **37**(2), 651–658 (2011)

28. Li, W.D., Luo, H.J., L., J.N., Lu, X.K., Guo, J.K.: The white porcelains from Dehua kiln site of China: Part I. Chemical compositions and the evolution regularity. Ceramics Int. **37**(1), 355–361 (2011)

29. Wu, J., Hou, T.J., Zhang, M.L., Li, Q.J., Wu, J.M., Li, J.Z., et al.: A technical comparison of three Chinese white porcelains: Ding, Shufu, and Dehua. Stud. Conserv. **59**(5), 341–349 (2014)

The Design of Information Visualization on the Service Evaluation Interface of an Online Car-Hailing Applet

Qiao Feng and Meng-Xi Chen(✉) (iD)

Shantou University, Shantou 515063, Guangdong, China
cmx12677@gmail.com

Abstract. Online car-hailing is progressively becoming the preferred mode of transportation for the younger population, and the related products and services are gaining traction. This study mainly explored car-hailing users' task performance and experiences among different information visualization designs on the service evaluation interfaces. This experiment adopted a single-factor, between-subjects design. Participants were required to complete two evaluation tasks using an online car-hailing applet. Subjective feelings about the service evaluation interface were investigated through post-experimental questionnaires and interviews. After analyzing the collected data, the results show that (1) Information architecture can affect user performance. Service evaluation information organized by the type of content is significantly more efficient than information organized by the level of overall experience. (2) Using emoticons separately in detailed information can reduce efficiency. (3) Colors and icons on the service evaluation interface may have a positive impact on users' subjective feelings.

Keywords: Information visualization · Evaluation interface · User experience

1 Introduction

As a result of the rapid expansion of the internet economy, the internet service and related sectors have grown incredibly fast in the years. From a single trip-sharing system to efficient and diverse online car-hailing services, the major online car-hailing platforms have amassed large numbers of users. The car-hailing platforms even taking the advantages of applets, a lightweight carrier, to provide users with ease and convenience of use. At the same time, interaction experience between people and interfaces on the mobile platforms has broken through the single behavior of touch, depending more on the comprehensive experience of visual and aural elements. Except for the internal and invisible operation part of a product, the design of other parts, such as buttons, layout and text, are directly perceived by users, are determined by users' psychological feelings and behaviors [1], but not by the functions. Therefore, users' emotional experience should be factored into the visual design of the application interfaces, as well as the creation and iteration of the interface features. When using any interface, users rely on their

P.-L. P. Rau (Ed.): HCII 2023, LNCS 14022, pp. 359–368, 2023.
https://doi.org/10.1007/978-3-031-35936-1_26

intuition. As a result, if the interface design fits users' mental model, it can provide a positive user experience. The service evaluation interface of an online car-hailing applet serves as a function-driven interface, whether the information provided to users is fair and understandable is an important aspect of the design of information visualization, which influences the interaction experience to some extent.

This study focused on two aspects of the information visualization designs on the service evaluation interface: information architecture and visual presentation. User experience was examined through experiments using a car-hailing applet. We combined current theories as the foundation of the study, which included cognitive psychology, emotional design theory, human-computer interaction interface design principles, and other theoretical support. After reviewing previous studies on car-hailing products and services, we investigated the effects of information structure and visual presentation on user performance and experiences in order to give some advices on information visualization designs on the service evaluation interface.

1.1 Car-Hailing Service Evaluation

With the development of internet, there are numerous car-hailing platforms. However, there have also been certain service quality issues that have negatively impacted customers' experiences. Therefore, it is necessary to improve the service quality of the car-hailing platforms. Previous studies have investigated the user experience of the brick-and-mortar taxi industry. However, there is a lack of research on the current state of the user experience of the expanding online car-hailing platform. On the one hand, some researchers upgraded 22 indicators in 5 dimensions of the SERVPERF scale to produce 20 indicators encompassing 6 aspects of safety, dependability, efficiency, integrity, facilities, and service to assess the quality of online car-hailing service [2]. However, none of these studies involve users' interaction experience of the car-hailing service evaluation interface. For the time being, smartphone applications and applets are the primary platforms for online car-hailing. As a result, the interaction and interface design become more direct measurements that influence the user experience and overall service assessment of the online car-hailing platform. On the other hand, a prior study indicated that the influencing factors of service quality include five aspects: passengers' personal characteristics, the characteristics of car-hailing platform and drivers, the factors of mobile client technology and external environment special detection, from the perspective of user trust [3]. This is one of the few studies to consider the impact of users' perception and the design of applications on users' experience. Based on this, it's worthwhile to further investigate the relationship between visual design, information design, user cognitive models and emotional experience of the service evaluation interfaces.

1.2 Cognitive Psychology and Emotional Design

Cognitive psychology is the study of how people observe, understand and process information in the processes of knowing the world [4]. The internal mental process connecting visual input to behavioral output is the core of visual cognition. To ensure the comprehensibility of visual cognition, visual representation should adhere to the rules visual cognition such as Gestalt psychology. The followings are the particular principles of interface design according to Gestalt psychology [5]:

1) The principle of closeness. To separate different content blocks into distinct regions according to their functions. Content blocks with the same functions are grouped together and segregated from the others. Spatial location can be the prime criterion for information classification.
2) The principle of similarity. Information in the same level or blocks in the same should be presented in a comparable visual style, such as both using text or similar colors. Visual presentation can be utilized as a secondary criterion for information classification.

Furthermore, a practical product may be transformed into a memorable and enduring emotional experience for users through emotional design. According to the emotional design theory at three levels: instinctual, behavioral, and reflexive, images have a greater emotional impact on users in the overall interface design, and information in the image-dominated region is more likely to be perceived by users, so this portion of the information may be profoundly digested by the brain [6]. As a result, replacing textual information with attractive visual features on the interface might improve users' emotional experience on both instinctual and behavioral levels. Therefore, this study investigated the effects of information structure and visual expression on user experience.

1.3 Information Visualization Designs on the Service Evaluation Interface

Users will be distracted by the dense and cluttered interface, so designers should think more about human psychology and cognitive characteristics in order to improve the usability of interfaces. Some scholars investigated the directness and symbolic nature of icon representation based on the cognitive characteristics of icons on the interfaces so that users can easily learn to operate them in the process of using them, to explore the principles of visual friendly human-computer interface design [7]. Another research studied shape coding for improving visual order and user performance, and suggested that menu icon design utilizing diverse combinations of shapes with varying degrees of complexity can increase visual search efficiency. A previous study suggested that the salience of the target shape on interfaces can be increased by increasing the contrast of properties and form characteristics to improve cognitive efficiency [8]. An empirical study found that different designs of icons on an interactive map can significantly affect user performance [9]. Based on the above-mentioned theories of visual properties on interaction interfaces, this study aimed to improve the design of the information visualization on the service evaluation interfaces of car-hailing platforms.

At present, the layout of the car-hailing service evaluation interface is mostly based on the types of submodule layout and squared up layout, which make the evaluation function clear and succinct. Generally speaking, a general comment about the overall experience will be made first, followed by the comments on the car, the driver and the route, which is how the information in service evaluation interface is structured. The evaluation contents are primarily presented using undifferentiated text descriptions, which may increase the challenges of understanding the information in the interface. In this study, we redesigned the common information architecture and visual presentation on the car-hailing service evaluation interfaces, and conducted experiments to compare different information visualization designs.

2 Methods

2.1 Participants

A total of 25 participants were invited to take part in the experiment via convenience sampling method. Their ages ranged between 20 and 30 years old. All the participants have the experience of using car-hailing applets. A single-factor, between-subjects experimental design was adopted. Participants were randomly assigned to one group and each participant operated one experimental sample.

2.2 Materials and Apparatus

The prototype of the car-hailing applet was created with the Photoshop software. The experiment was conducted on an iPhone 6 Plus smartphone using the iOS 10.3.2 operating system. It is equipped with a 5.5-inch screen.

In this study, four types of information visualization designs on the service evaluation interface were designed based on the research variables in Table1. Two kinds of information architecture included service evaluation information organized by the level of overall experience (sample 1) and information organized by the type of content (sample 2). The visual presentation styles included text (sample 1 and sample2), text with color coding (sample 3) and text with emoticons (sample 4). The service evaluation interfaces of four experimental samples are shown in Fig. 1.

Table 1. Descriptive of four experimental samples.

	Information architecture	Visual presentation
Sample 1	Organized by the level of overall experience	Text
Sample 2	Organized by the type of content	Text
Sample 3	Organized by the type of content	Text and Color Coding
Sample 4	Organized by the type of content	Text and Emoticons

2.3 Experiment Procedure

Participants were asked to interact with the service evaluation interfaces to test user performance and experiences. According to the independent variables, participants were divided into five groups.

There were two evaluation tasks adopted in this study. In order to compare the interface designs of sample 1 and sample 2, the first task was to select "License number does

Fig. 1. The service evaluation interfaces of four experimental samples. 评价: comment; 很糟糕: Terrible; 一般般: Normal; 太赞了: Wonderful; 车辆: Car; 司机: Driver; 线路: Route; z z提交: Submit anonymously; 车牌号不符: License number does not match; 安全带不可用: Seatbelt not available.

not match" and "More patient service", and then click the "Submit anonymously" button. In order to compare the interface designs of sample 2, sample 3 and sample 4, the second task was to select "Seatbelt not available (or a bad rating for seatbelt perfection)", "more precise pick-up location (or an outstanding pick-up location)", and "smooth driving (or outstanding smooth driving)", and then click the "Submit anonymously" button. The task completion time of each sample was recorded to analyze users' performance.

In addition, participants were asked to complete a questionnaire regarding their overall satisfaction. The questionnaire was designed based on a 7-point Likert scale anchored by 1: less satisfied and 7: much satisfied. After that participants were asked to do an interview to investigate their subjective feelings about the service evaluation interface.

3 Results

3.1 Analysis of Task Completion Time

All participants finished the tasks successfully, and the collected data were analyzed by the IBM Statistical Package for the Social Sciences (SPSS) software.

The first task was to compare two kinds of information architecture. The results generated from the descriptive statistics and one sample T-test of task 1 completion time are shown in Table 2. The results indicated that there was a significant effect of information architecture regarding the task 1 completion time ($F = 6.855$, $p = 0.031 < 0.05$). The task 1 completion time for sample 2 ($M = 21.464$, $Sd = 11.045$) was significantly shorter than that for sample 1 ($M = 42.794$, $Sd = 4.847$).

Table 2. Descriptive statistics and one sample T-test of Task 1 completion time.

	M	SD	N	F	P
Sample 1	42.794	4.847	5	6.855	*0.031
Sample 2	21.464	11.045	5		

$\alpha = 0.05$, *$p < 0.05$.

The second task was to know the influence of visual presentation styles. The results generated from the descriptive statistics and one-way analysis of variance (ANOVA) of task 2 completion time are shown in Table 3. The results indicated that there was a significant effect of visual presentation regarding the task 2 completion time ($F = 4.307$, $p = 0.039 < 0.05$). The post-hoc comparison indicated a significant difference between sample 2 and sample 4 ($p = 0.017 < 0.05$) and sample 3 and sample 4 ($p = 0.0457 < 0.05$) (Table 4). The task 2 completion time for sample 2 ($M = 29.406$, $Sd = 7.322$) and sample 3 ($M = 32.492$, $Sd = 10.81$) were both significantly shorter than that for sample 4 ($M = 45.780$, $Sd = 9.646$). However, no significant difference was observed between sample 2 and sample 3 ($p = 0.612 > 0.05$).

Table 3. Descriptive statistics and one-way ANOVA of Task 2 completion time.

	M	SD	N	F	P
Sample 2	29.406	7.322	5	4.307	*0.039
Sample 3	32.492	10.81	5		
Sample 4	45.780	9.646	5		

$\alpha = 0.05$, *$p < 0.05$.

Table 4. Post hoc multiple comparison of Task 2 completion time.

	Sample 2	Sample 3	Sample 4
Sample 2		0.612	0.017*
Sample 3			0.045*
Sample 4			

$\alpha = 0.05$, *$p < 0.05$.

3.2 Analysis of Subjective Satisfaction

The data of subjective satisfaction were analyzed to find out which kind of information visualization design offered most positive feelings. The results regarding subjective satisfaction reveals no significant difference between sample 1 and sample 2 ($F = 0.667$, $P = 0.438 > 0.05$). No significant difference was found between samples 2 and sample 3 ($P = 0.711 > 0.05$), sample 2 and sample 4 ($P = 0.146$) and sample 3 and sample 4 ($P = 0.263$). Moreover, as shown in Fig. 2, the subjective satisfaction of the four samples is increasing.

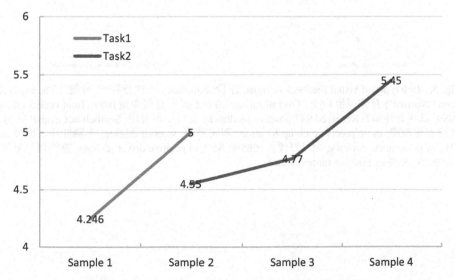

Fig. 2. Results of the assessment on subjective satisfaction.

3.3 Qualitative Results

Besides the quantitative results, we also collected qualitative data from post interviews. Thirteen participants mentioned that the contents on the service evaluation interface doesn't match the content in their mind, hence they require a manual input feature. "After finishing the tasks, I want to see the total results of service evaluations on the interface, not just the feedback for current evaluation," commented 15 participants. The interviews revealed that 80% of the participants preferred the feedback interface showing the total evaluation results with colors and icons than the description of current evaluation (Fig. 3).

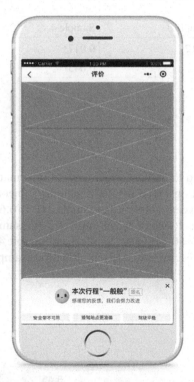 

Fig. 3. Two types of visual feedback designs. 评价: comment; 本次行程"一般般": The trip has been "Normal"; 总体评价4.6分: Overall rating 4.6 out of 5; 总接单量1089: Total orders taken 1089; 获得好评947: Received 947 positive feedback; 安全带不可用: Seatbelt not available; 接驾地点更准确: more precise pick-up location; 驾驶平稳: smooth driving; 车辆好评占比53%: 53% of positive car reviews; 司机好评占比85%: 85% of positive driver reviews; 路线规划好评占比85%: 85% of positive route reviews

4 Discussion

The analysis of task completion time revealed that information architecture and visual presentation make significant differences in user performance. The service evaluation information organized by the type of content (sample 2) was significantly more efficient than information organized by the level of overall experience (sample 1). This might because users usually make a production evaluation about the car, driver, and route before giving an overall rating. The service evaluation information organized by the level of overall experience is the inverse of the real-world user experience.

The visual presentation styles using text (sample2) and text with color coding (sample 3) were significantly more efficient than using text with emoticons (sample 4). Perhaps emoticons increased the complexity of information visualization. Even simple visual elements on the interface can influence the way of people to process visual information. However, using color coding (sample 3) and emoticons (sample 4) to indicate the hierarchy of the textual information supplied on the interface may improve users' satisfaction.

5 Conclusion

The purpose of this research was in order to explore the effects of information visualization designs on car-hailing users' task performance and experiences using the service evaluation interfaces. Firstly, our results suggest that information architecture can affect user performance. Service evaluation information organized by the type of content is significantly more efficient than information organized by the level of overall experience. We recommend that designers organize the information according to users' cognitive process. Secondly, using emoticons separately in detailed information can reduce efficiency. Finally, colors and icons on the service evaluation interface may have a positive impact on users' subjective feelings.

The findings imply that, in addition to the essential functional and aesthetic criteria of interactive interfaces, designers should consider the use of clear and easy-understand icons on the service evaluation interface to increase users' experience. Further research into the design of service evaluation interface is suggested, which includes a larger variety of complex icons features such as shape, scale, complexity, and so on.

Acknowledgements. This work was funded by Philosophy and Social Science Planning Project of Guangdong Province [GD22XYS31], and STU Scientific Research Initiation Grant [STF22003].

References

1. Jesse, J.G., Fan, X.Y.(translated).: The Element of User Experience: User-Centered Design for the Web and Beyond. 2nd edu. China Machine Press, Beijing (2019). (in Chinese)
2. Li, J., Jiang, Y.D., Gu, T.Q.: Evaluating quality of online ride-hailing service based on users. Urban Transp. China **19**(2), 103–111 (2021). (in Chinese)
3. Zheng, Y.Y.: Research on the evaluation of passenger trust on car-hailing service. MS thesis. Wuhan University of Technology (2018). (in Chinese)

4. Du, S.Y.: Principles of visual communication design. Augmented Edu. Shanghai People's Fine Arts Publishing House, Shanghai (2009). (in Chinese)
5. Jing, H.F.: Research on the interface interaction design of intelligent TV based on visual cognition. Indust. Des. 57–58 (2020). (in Chinese)
6. Liu, X., Lyu, J., Yu, J.: User visual cognition difference based on interface designated task. Pack. Eng. 39(22), 97–103 (2018). (in Chinese)
7. Zeng, Y., Liang, T.: A study of the visuo-cognitive characteristics of human-computer interaction interface icons. Art Panorama 8, 143 (2014). (in Chinese)
8. Li, J., Yu, S.L., Wu, X.L.: Effects of shape character encodings in the human-computer interface on visual cognitive performance. J. Comput.-Aid. Des. Comput. Graph. 30(1), 163–172 (2018). (in Chinese)
9. Chen, C.H., Chen, M.X.: Wayfinding in virtual environments with landmarks on overview maps. Interact. Comput. 32(3), 316–329 (2020)

The Study of Sustainable Design for Child-Friendly Urban Public Spaces

Xing Ji[1,2,3](✉), YaLin Yang[4](✉), and Jie Tang[1,2](✉)

[1] Beijing Technology Institute, Zhuhai, Zhuhai 519088, People's Republic of China
54619184@qq.com, 4448286@qq.com
[2] Studying School for Doctor's Degree, Bangkokthonburi University, Bangkok 10170, Thailand
[3] Institute of Innovation Design for Well-Being, Zhuhai 519088, People's Republic of China
[4] Guangdong Polytechnic of Science and Technology, Guang Zhou, People's Republic of China
Linyayang@126.com

Abstract. Children's activity space is one of the important components in urban public space. With the acceleration of urbanisation, children's activity sites in urban public spaces are subjected to a number of factors such as economic and environmental constraints, so children's activity spaces have not been given much attention, which leads to the neglect of the environment for children's growth. In many cities in China, public spaces are unreasonably designed, making the urban public spaces available for activities near residential areas completely inadequate to meet the daily needs of the people, let alone spaces specifically designed for children's activities.

Creating an age-appropriate space for children in urban public spaces is not just about creating space, but more importantly about getting into the hearts of children. What is needed in today's urban public spaces is a safe, fun and vibrant space for children's activities. The question of how to make urban public spaces that meet the needs of contemporary children's activities is a constant concern for us in the future. What kind of activity space can be beneficial to children's development and health? What kind of space design can meet the needs of children's activities? How can we create an urban public space that is suitable for children's growth, so as to promote their overall healthy development and achieve real sustainable development?

This paper investigates the design of children's public outdoor activity spaces; studies advanced research results at home and abroad; analyses the situation of children's activities in the outdoors; finds shortcomings in the design of outdoor children's activity spaces; discusses the design of outdoor children's public activity spaces from the direction of design science, so as to put forward suggestions that are more suitable for the design of children's activity spaces in China; provides a reasonable theoretical basis for the design of children's public outdoor activity spaces; makes the theoretical system of the design of children's public activity spaces in China more perfect, and designs outdoor activity spaces that are more in line with children's activities in China in the future, so that people's quality of life can improve their lives.

Keywords: Children-friendly · Urban Public Space · Sustainable design

P.-L. P. Rau (Ed.): HCII 2023, LNCS 14022, pp. 369–379, 2023.
https://doi.org/10.1007/978-3-031-35936-1_27

1 Theoretical Research Progress of Child-Friendly Cities in the World

1.1 Concept of Child-Friendly City

The concept of child-friendly city was put forward by UNICEF. By creating a material and social environment that can improve child-friendliness, the various behavioral needs of children living in the city can be met [1].To build a child-friendly city, it is necessary not only in terms of urban planning, reconstruction and design, but also in a reasonable way to redesign and slightly update various activity facilities, urban streets and public Spaces, so that the special needs and interests of children can be taken care of. If a city is friendly to children, it tends to be friendly to special groups such as the elderly and the disabled. It is a city that takes care of everyone. So child-friendly cities can make cities more vibrant, livable and inclusive.

The so-called child-friendly urban space is not to build a child-dominated block or city, but to improve the child-friendly degree of the existing block or city through certain measures. In other words, the child-friendly urban space should be built on the basis of the existing city, and the following spatial rights of children should be protected: (1) to walk safely alone on the street; (2) Meet and play with friends; (3) Live in an unpolluted environment with green space.

The purpose of sustainable development is to leave room for future human existence. However, in reality, they frantically plunder the resources of human beings in the future, ignoring and abandoning the present "future" with rhetoric. Little does it realize that the development of children is the key and foundation of all sustainable development. Caring for the healthy growth of children is the real sustainable development.

1.2 Research Progress of Child-Friendly Cities

Since 1996, many countries and regions have been striving to build child-friendly cities by incorporating the needs and rights of children into their policies, especially at the core of urban planning policies.Child-friendly cities include London, Buenos Aires, Munich and other cities in France and Italy. Child-friendly cities include London, Buenos Aires, Munich and other cities in France and Italy. The strategy of London, a member of the Programme, is to promote an inclusive, fair and healthy city, a London that provides a safe, happy and secure environment for its young people to grow up, to benefit from a vibrant and cohesive society, to enjoy the city's healthy built and natural environment, To pay attention to the voices of children and young people in this city, respect their rights and interests, and cultivate, recognize and realize their unique contributions and potential. In addition, many cities in the world are making efforts in these aspects, hoping to achieve the standard of "child-friendly city" through the construction of child-friendly city space, and realize the sustainable development of the city itself. For example, New York rebuilt and strengthened the children's playground in Central Park, trying to form a new attraction and create a more family-oriented Central Park. At the same time, the construction of child-friendly urban space is also applicable to a variety of blocks or cities with different basic conditions. For example, considering income, in high-income areas, the focus is on urban planning, safe space and green environment. In low - and middle-income regions, more emphasis is placed on healthy environments and child safety. In addition, neighborhoods or cities can also develop suitable spatial planning for child-friendly cities according to their own characteristics. For example, Bendigo, a small mining town near Melbourne, Australia, is often hit by tornadoes and droughts. In its spatial planning for children, the principle of keeping away from disasters is particularly emphasized. The Portland government of the United States has expressed concern for children's rights and interests in the process of promoting the construction of a child-friendly city [2]. Planning policies formulated by the government clearly propose to build a child-friendly urban environment, including child-friendly design of major places for children's outdoor activities such as neighborhood parks, streets and courtyards. Finland focuses on children's public participation and protection of children's rights and interests, and proposes to include children's participation in the planning and development of public space [3].

Although the specific forms of expression vary, the spatial concept of child-friendly cities is very clear and unified, which focuses on the protection of children's rights, namely, "non-discrimination against children, the best interests of the child, the protection of the child's right to survival and maximum development, and respect for the child's point of view" (the four principles set forth in the Convention on the Rights of the Child). Children's rights to survival, development, protection and participation should be fully protected in neighborhoods or cities. Therefore, a child-friendly city is a city that can provide a safe, happy and reliable environment for children to grow up, a city that gives priority to the interests and growth of children, and a city full of warmth, vitality and human care.

The research on child-friendly cities in China began in the 1950s and began to develop in the 1980s.Zhang Shouyi et al. [3] pay attention to the relationship between children and residential environment, identify children's spatial cognition, spatial preference and the impact of living environment on children by using questionnaires, children's drawings and other methods, and point out that special attention should be paid to the impact of high-rise housing on children's growth in the process of urban construction.In terms of works, Fang Xianfu [4, 5] wrote books such as Planning and Design of Children's Playgrounds in Residential Areas and Design and Examples of Children's Playgrounds. He proposed to design diversified children's playgrounds by groups of children of different ages, and provided a solid foundation for the study of children's playgrounds design in China from the aspects of overall layout, site design, greening design and facility design. In recent years, the number of empirical studies on children's play space in residential areas has increased, including the influence on the current situation, design, safety and characteristics of children's play behavior [6]. Zeng Peng et al. [7] put forward the planning and design concept of safe block and children's travel path in line with China's national conditions through the analysis of Woonerf and Kindlint cases. Huang Junlin et al. [8] paid attention to the "inclusiveness" of children in urban planning, and explored the whole-process participation planning method for children by institution-guided method transformation and case-based action. Governments are also increasingly concerned about children's Spaces,

In a word, child-friendly urban design in China has had a preliminary germination and development in the three spatial scales of "home, community and city". However, compared with developed countries, the empirical research on relevant theories started late, and most of the research focused on specific children's activity places in residential areas, especially the research on child-friendly design of community public space is insufficient. The practice model of different places also needs to be summarized and optimized.

2 Current Situation of Urban Children's Public Space in China

2.1 Children's Activity Space Planned by the State

The attention on children's public space in urban planning in China can be traced back to 1980, when Beijing included the construction of children's activity space into the unified construction of residential areas, and the following residential areas included children's activity space into the construction project. In 2004, the Ministry of Construction issued "Residential Environment Landscape Design Guidelines", which further standardized the children's activity site in more detail. Such a planning idea is deeply influenced by the "neighborhood unit" proposed by Perry in the 1920s, which holds that the children's activity space concerned in urban planning is concentrated in sports grounds and parks, so the corresponding activity space will be reserved in each community unit. For example, it is clearly pointed out in the code for planning and design of urban residential areas in China that residential areas should be set up public green Spaces at the residential district level, district level and group level, as well as children's playgrounds and other public green Spaces according to different levels of planning and organization structure. But in the actual construction, the nature of playground and park has greatly limited the shaping of children's activity space, coupled with rough construction, most of the children's activity space finally turned into a perfunctory form, only soft paving and a pile of sliding or climbing instruments.

2.2 Market Developed Children's Activity Space

From the perspective of scale, children's activity venues stipulated from top to bottom at the national level are generally limited to communities, and the scale is small. As children's issues have attracted more and more attention from the whole society, in recent years, bottom-up projects with children as the main audience have gradually increased, and the scale is large. From the functional form of children's public space has made a certain complement, but due to the backward concept, the lack of effective restraint management, quality is worrying. It can be roughly divided into two categories:

1. Theme children's parks, this kind of space often abandon natural elements, extremely artificial. Excessive pursuit of visual stimulation, full of all kinds of fresh challenges of large-scale amusement facilities, children's activities are simply equal to children's amusement, and there are common safety risks.
2. An entertainment and education base for children with intellectual development as its selling point. This kind of space is often chosen indoors, where the air is dirty. The rigid simulated scene setting cannot replace the real life experience, and greatly destroys children's creativity. Over-indoctrination of the upbringing of children is

contrary to their natural development nature. In general, the children's public space in Chinese cities is still in its infancy. The psychological and physiological needs of children in special stages have not been paid attention to in the urban public space, and children's curiosity and energy cannot be released reasonably.

3 Public Space Needs Based on Children's Behavioral Psychology

3.1 Children's Behavioral Psychology and Public Space

1) **Thrill seeking**. Strong curiosity makes children tend to find hidden things in the site, such as pebbles, branches, and like to play with the plastic sand, soil, etc. At the same time, they are also very adventurous, the pursuit of excitement, fantasy that they are a great explorer, weed sentient beings, unattended, with a certain mysterious place are the children like to patronize the place.

2) **Seek partners**. It is common to see that when some children start playing in a particular space, other children will show a clear tendency to participate and often join in the game. When children see other children playing, they want to participate and join the game. As soon as one child starts skating in the square, more and more children will join.

3) **Seek success and win**. Children often play for pleasure, so play is a kind of active behavior. Any new discovery, freedom of action, or successful experience in the game brings joy to them. This makes them constantly try, discover, practice and perform in games, express their will, vent their emotions and show their abilities.

4) **Imitation**. Children have strong imitation ability, and their imitation objects are also rich, such as adults, elderly children or animals, sculpture forms and so on. Children learn more and more activities in imitation, such as hide-and-seek, skipping rope and so on. In the process of imitation, children add their own innovation at the same time, which makes the activity more colorful.

5) **Egotism**. When children are engaged in activities, they tend to be too focused and self-centered, while ignoring the stimulation of the surrounding environment. In the activities, they focus on one point, showing a kind of "self-centered" thinking state that does not pay attention to the surrounding environment of children. Once invested in the game, they will forget themselves and ignore the potential safety risks [9].

3.2 Age Differences in Children's Activities

Children are a special group, with physical, psychological and behavioral characteristics, and with the growth of age, its physical, psychological and behavioral characteristics are also changing. Children at different ages are in different stages of growth and development, and there are differences in physical, psychological and physical strength, and they will show different experience characteristics. Therefore, age is the basis for children's group activities, and the activities of children of different ages are not the same. The design roughly divides children's growth into three important stages, which is similar to Piaget's division of the stages of thinking development.

   1) **Activity characteristics of infants (0–3 years old)**

Activity Nearby. Children aged between 0 and 3 years old are always accompanied by their guardians in their activities. They travel to some easily accessible places near their residential areas and do not go far to the playground. One of the reasons is that children's physical strength and incomplete behavioral ability do not have long time, long distance outside activities; Second, when children's guardians accompany their children out for activities, the longer the distance, the more nursing supplies they need to carry, and the more unpredictable situations may occur. Therefore, the activity area of infants and young children is relatively simple, and the site is generally chosen near the residential area.

Like to Get Close to Nature. In this period, children's activity ability is still limited and they will not use too complex activity facilities. They have simple requirements for activity equipment. They often choose natural ways to play, such as trotting, jumping, crawling, splashing, observing animals and so on. They are naturally curious about nature and explore the spirit, at this stage to provide children with some natural activity environment is most loved by them, and can improve children's cognitive ability.

Paternity. Most of the time, children in this period are accompanied by their parents to do activities, some are pushed out by their parents to bask in the sun, some play with their parents on the slides, some are held by adults to walk and talk in the living area, some are taken by their parents to play with other children. Parent-child is an obvious feature of children's activities in this period. Children can not be separated from their parents' independent activities, and parents can enhance their feelings when accompanying their children. Parent-child activities need the timely participation of parents, so that parents and children form a common communication.

Time and Seasonality. According to statistics, infants aged 0–3 years old are sent to the nursery or taken care of at home by their parents from 8 a.m. to 4:30 p.m. At 4:30 p.m., they have intensive outdoor activities, with an average of about 1.5 h of outdoor play time every day. Infants and toddlers are vulnerable to various seasonal diseases due to poor physical immunity, and their guardians will reduce the children's outdoor activities when the weather conditions are not ideal.

2) Activity characteristics of preschool children (3–6 years old)

Activities Require a Better Environment. Preschool children have higher requirements on the environment than infants. With the growth of age and the enhancement of activity ability, the transformation from simple activities to group and complex activities will put forward higher requirements on the outdoor space environment. Preschool children like group activities, which require a larger field and more varied space. In such activities, children learn to get along with others, understand interpersonal communication and cooperation.

Peer Aggregation. In this period, children tend to gather together at the same age, and generally can move freely in the residential area without the supervision of parents, and the improvement of activity ability enables them to carry out activities in a wider area of the residential area. Many friends gather together to form a certain scale of communication circle, small groups sometimes appear as small partners become close and distant.

Time and Seasonality. Preschoolers are not restricted by school schedules and have improved physical fitness compared to infancy, so their outdoor activities are least affected by time and season. They are allowed to participate in activities when their guardians allow and they have the energy. They are the most frequent users of activity venues in residential areas.

Perception and Intelligence. Children aged 3–6 are at a critical stage of cognitive development, with varied activities and enhanced texture and color perception of the environment. Activities that can promote children's cognition are more popular among children at this stage.

3) Activity characteristics of preschool children (3–6 years old)

Range Extension. School-age children in physical quality, energy and physical strength than the first two stages have been greatly improved, and can carry out strong physical activity, independent activity ability has been greatly enhanced; In terms of intelligence, they have the initial ability of abstract logical thinking and independent thinking, and do not like to be limited by a fixed pattern. They like to go to places where there is no clear information to guide them, and even places that seem dangerous and mysterious are more attractive to them. Outdoor activity space is an indispensable complement and extension of their school.

The Content of the Event is Complex and Unpredictable. In this period, children have been able to play a variety of games, and the children's game facilities in the residential area are no longer favored by them, so they usually choose open places for activities. As their cognitive abilities improve, certain fixed content game facilities are unable to meet their complex activity requirements. Often these children come from home to the outdoor playground in the residential area already prepared, such as which peers to play with, what to play with and what supplies to bring, but when the activity goes on for a period of time, there may be other discoveries that will make the content of the activity change. So the limited space on the doorstep can't accommodate these unpredictable activities.

Security. School-age children travel more distance, enhance the ability of activity, generally can be free to move without guardian. Because of these factors, the security of their activities is more difficult to guarantee. Some dangerous activities and environments are interesting to them. How to satisfy their exploration and curiosity while ensuring safety is a problem to be considered in open space.

Be Self-directed and Creative. They have independent behavior and thinking ability, do not want to be limited by the inherent form or content, so outdoor activities only need to be given the corresponding venue, let them to arrange the content of activities, time and how to use the venue. The autonomy of outdoor activities also helps children relieve the pressure of learning and balance the constraints of discipline. It is best for children to develop their creativity and induce them to think independently when they are free to act in accordance with their nature.

Sociality. In the activities of children's community groups, because the partners are familiar with each other, it is easy to form a good group relationship, which is conducive to children's learning of social communication and social life skills. Children from different families with different habits and ways of thinking have differences and frictions in group activities, so that children can learn the diversity and inclusiveness of society at an early date. In the space of community group communication, the quality of game activities should be improved as far as possible to help achieve the goal [10].

Psychological research shows that children tend to engage in individual activities close to their age, because their perception of the environment is similar to their requirements for the activity site. Therefore, in the design of children's activity space, attention should be paid to the characteristics of children of different ages to carry out diversified and flexible space layout.

3.3 Behavioral Characteristics of Children's Activities

1) Peer aggregation

Children at different ages have different ways and contents of activities, which are often divided into small groups for different ages. Children of the same age have similar perceptions of space and environment, and similar ways of thinking and expression. Therefore, children of the same age are more likely to form an activity group, which has a considerable degree of commonality, and each individual can experience the corresponding pleasure from the activity.

2) Affected by the season

For the human body, the comfortable temperature range is from 20 °C in winter to 26 °C in summer, the comfortable relative humidity should be kept below 20% all year round, and the comfortable airflow velocity range is approximately 0.1 m/s to 0.3 m/s (airflow from 0.3 m/s to 1m/s is noticeable, But it is acceptable in some active states). Therefore, children's activities are mainly concentrated in the spring and autumn when the climate is pleasant, while in the extreme hot and cold winter and summer, children's outdoor activities are relatively less frequent.

3) Affected by time

Because of climate change and light and sleep schedules, children's activity rates are basically pendulum-shaped throughout the day. It is mainly preschoolers who spend the day outdoors. After school, after lunch and before and after dinner are the main times for outdoor activities for children of all ages. On Sunday, festival, summer and cold holidays, the number of children's activities increased, the activity time is concentrated in the morning 9 to 11, 3 to 5 p.m. In summer, the indoor temperature is high, and many children enjoy outdoor activities after dark.

4) Random and variable activity content

Human movement has its track, many people move in the same direction, forming the space of tendency. Trajectory is the record of continuous events occurring in a period of time. Activities of different purposes, properties, subjects and modes correspond to different characteristics of the route. In the open space of the city, children are used to wandering in the things that arouse their interest. For example, influenced by landscape sketches and activities of various people, children's activity track shows an obvious curve.

The curious and active characteristics of children's activities are neither fixed time nor fixed point, not only in the designated field (children's playground equipped with traditional equipment), but also may reach the attractive potential field of activity, and stay for a longer time. Children's activities are variable and random. Their activities are undefined. Children not only play in the facilities or designated field, almost all children can find and reach a playground, children may be playing hide-and-seek one minute, the next minute may become a hawk to catch chickens. Therefore, the site of children's activities should have a certain degree of flexibility, which can allow a variety of activities, but also pay attention to the combination with other surrounding sites.

4 Child-Friendly Oriented Ecological Community Public Space Design Strategy

Combined with the behavioral and psychological characteristics of children of different ages mentioned above, the form of public space suitable for children's activity needs is proposed. Match different types of public space forms with public space types of ecological communities such as parks, green Spaces, squares and streets; In addition, the evaluation system of public space proposed by UN-Habitat is evolved into a five-part integrated public space design strategy system of "ecology, applicability, accessibility, comfort and safety"), the design method of public space is combed out, and a child-friendly ecological community public space design strategy is constructed.

Ecology means that public space should be guided by the idea of eco-city design to create a public space environment that is conducive to the health of the ecosystem and the physical and mental health of children and adults. The public space represented by the community park green space is the main place for children to contact the natural environment in their daily life. On the one hand, green space in parks can regulate microclimate, participate in carbon and oxygen cycle, and eliminate noise, so as to provide a good ecological environment for children [11] On the other hand, reasonable green design and rich plant species can ease children's mood and arouse children's curiosity and closeness to the natural environment.

Applicability refers to that all kinds of public space and internal facilities are suitable for children's use preferences and can meet children's needs for various activities in public space. Corresponding design techniques include: 1) **Functional type friendly**. The forms of games and activities conducted by children in community public space include single-player and multi-player activities, characteristic and random activities, etc. Children are in the stage of rapid growth and development of physiology and psychology, and the preferred forms of activities of children at different ages vary greatly. Therefore, the functional design of public space should incorporate the use needs and behavioral characteristics of children with inclusive activities. To meet the activity needs of different groups. 2) **Friendly group interaction**. Group activities include children's interaction with peer groups and intergenerational interaction with parents. 3) **Friendly design of public art display**. In the cultural and artistic theme of landscape sketch or public art display area, to increase the benefit of children's intellectual inspiration facilities, in order to achieve in the process of recreation to enhance scientific cognition, satisfy curiosity, inspire creativity and stimulate group interaction.

Accessibility refers to the convenience of children's access to all kinds of public Spaces, including the design of spatial layout, connection mode, connection path, namely street. Space design with high accessibility can effectively promote children's access to public Spaces and activities. Design techniques to improve accessibility include: **1) Friendly entrance and exit design**. If public Spaces such as squares and parks in communities are close to kindergartens, schools, art training institutions and residential areas where children gather, separate entrances and exits should be considered for public Spaces; If the school playground can have an entrance and exit facing the park, it can avoid the traffic congestion caused by the gathering of parents who pick up children at the school entrance and exit near the city road. It can also encourage children to have group recreational activities in the park after school. **2) Friendly path design**. Community roads connecting schools and kindergartens should consider designing independent bicycle lanes and skateboard lanes for children to add fun to children's commuting. On both sides of the community road leading to the park green space is enriched through street shops, weekend markets and other forms to enhance the attraction of public space.

Comfort means that the form, site design and service facility configuration design of public space can adapt to children's psychological behavior characteristics and physiological characteristics, and carry out customized design different from adults, so as to enhance children's comfortable experience in public space. Possible approaches to public space design include: **1) Visual communication friendliness**. The logo system of public space is designed with graphics and symbols that can be easily recognized by children. In areas where children's activities are concentrated, children's behaviors are appropriately guided by the logo system. **2) Friendly service facilities**. Facilities in public space are often designed according to the physiological characteristics of adults. Child-friendly public space should ensure the convenience of children's travel and comfort of children's activities.

Safety means that the facilities in the public space can guarantee the normal and orderly conduct of children's activities and avoid the potential risks of damaging children's physical and mental health. Children's ability to predict risk sources and protect their own safety is weak, so supporting construction of children's activities should be strengthened in public space. The design methods that can be adopted include: **1) Walking is safe and friendly**. Ensure dedicated, safe and convenient space for children to walk slowly. **2) Friendly safety tips**. In potentially dangerous environments for children, information boards and signs that children can understand should be set up to regulate children's behavior. **3) Friendly security partition**. Children's activities in public space are unstable and lack of crisis prediction ability makes them vulnerable. Therefore, it is advisable to isolate children from potential risks through safe zoning. For example, the child-friendly slow traffic space should be separated from the pedestrian space and the non-motor vehicle space through hedges and height differences. Outdoor public play areas where adults engage in vigorous physical activity, such as basketball courts and running tracks, should also be separated from children's play areas.

5 Conclusion

The process of children's growth is actually a process of "perceiving the world and knowing the world", and many of these processes are inadvertently completed in outdoor games, which shows the importance of child-friendly activity venues in urban public Spaces for children's growth.

Children are the future of the development of human society, and child-friendly public space design is an inevitable requirement for the humanized development of urban design. Urban planners should have humanistic quality and professional quality to conduct urban planning and space design from the perspective of caring for children. Based on children's behavioral psychological characteristics, this paper analyzes the design elements of public space that meet children's needs. Starting from the perspective of "ecology -- applicability -- accessibility -- comfort -- safety", it constructs a child-friendly ecological community public space design strategy system, hoping to provide new ideas and design methods for the construction of ecological communities and child-friendly cities in China. To some extent, it makes up for the lack of attention paid to the interests of children in China's urban planning field.

The establishment of child-friendly cities is by no means overnight. In addition to paying attention to the control of the above elements in the field of space design, children's basic rights and interests in urban space should also be clarified from the perspective of institutional management.

References

1. UNICEF. The child-friendly city initiative in Finland [EB/OL]. (2017-02-24) [2020-02-20]. https://s25924.pcdn.co/wpcontent/uploads/2017/10/CFCICase-Study-Finland.pdf
2. Liefaard, T., Doek, J.E.: Litigating the Rights of the Child. Springer, New York (2016)
3. Zhang, S.: Children and living environment. Archit. J. **12**, 403–413 (1990)
4. Xianfu, F.A.N.G., Quande, W.A.N.G., Xiongfei, L.I.: Planning and Design of Children's Playground in Residential Area. Tianjin Science and Technology Press, Tianjin (1986)
5. Xianfu, F.A.N.G.: Children's Playground Design and Examples. Tianjin Science and Technology Press, Tianjin (1992)
6. Baoxin, Z.H.A.I., Wei, Z.H.U.: Research on the evaluation of the built environment to promote children's outdoor activities in Shanghai. Shanghai Urban Plann. Rev. **1**, 90–94 (2018)
7. Zeng, P., Cai, L.: Safe block and children's travel route (Kindlint) planning under the concept of child-friendly city: a case study of Holland. City Plan. Rev. **42**(11), 103-110 (2018)
8. Huang, J., Li, Z., Zeng, Y., et al.: Child friendly planning practice towards communicative action, Changsha. Plann. **35**(1), 77–81, 87 (2019)
9. Gao, Y., Zhang, H.: Infant Psychology. Zhejiang Education Press, Zhejiang, vol. 11, pp. 57–66 (1993)
10. Xiangma, Y.: Environmental Psychology. Beijing: China Architecture and Building Press, pp. 25–33 (1986)
11. Chen, T., Zang, X., Wang, Q.: Research on urban design strategies for green blocks in ecocity. City Plann. Rev. **39**(7), 63–69, 76 (2015)
12. Flouri, E., MIdouhas, E., Joshi, H.: The role of urban neighbourhood green space in children's emotional and behavioural resilience. J. Environ. Psychol. **40**, 179–186 (2014)

Analysis and Exploration of Sustainable Design of Packaging Structure Based on Pentaward and Dieline Award-Winning Cases

Ou -Yang Li[✉][ID], Xiansi Zeng, Yue Zhao, and Han Li

Guangzhou Academy of Fine Arts, Guangzhou, Guangdong, China
oylee@163.com

Abstract. This study uses content analysis to analyze 84 winning cases of sustainable packaging in Pentaward and Dieline 2021–2022 competitions. The analysis is carried out from three aspects of the container's modeling type, structural elements, and materials. Find the shape type of the container: Among the 54 award-winning works in the Pentaward, there are more bottle structures, with a total of 19 (35%) works, and 12 pieces (22%) of the box structure; 30 types of packaging in the Dieline competition Among the products, there are ten kinds of products with box structure design (33%), and other special-shaped structures (8 pieces, 27%). Structural elements: Recyclable packaging is a necessary structural element in award-winning works. "Detachable, easy to compress, self-sealing folding packaging" and "design standardized, modular, serialized packaging" are the directions that researchers are focusing on. Materials: The more widely used materials are paper (41%) and glass (20%), and the paper and printing inks used on glass are mostly degradable and plant-based. From the analysis of the award-winning works of Pentaward awards and Dieline awards, it can be found that the judges are very concerned about whether the products' raw materials are natural and whether the brand has a sense of sustainability. The sustainable packaging brand that merchants, designers, and consumers participate in the building should be the future design trend.

Keywords: Sustainable design of packaging structure · Pentaward · Dieline · analysis and exploration

1 Introduction

In June 1972, the United Nations Conference on the Human Environment adopted the "United Nations Declaration on the Environment and Mankind," calling on governments and peoples of all countries to work together to maintain and improve the human environment for the benefit of future generations. The green packaging "Green Dot" logo launched by Germany has led developed countries in Europe and the United States to set off a wave of green design. In 2004, Japan proposed the "3R Initiative" at the "G8 Summit" to enhance the effective use of resources. China incorporated the sustainable development goals into the national economic and social development plans of the 13th and 14th five-year plans and translated the sustainable development goals into specific tasks in the economy, society, and environment. Sustainability enters our

P.-L. P. Rau (Ed.): HCII 2023, LNCS 14022, pp. 380–391, 2023.
https://doi.org/10.1007/978-3-031-35936-1_28

lives as a task of national development. The "13th Five-Year Plan" development plan of China's packaging industry points out that to accelerate the pace of my country's packaging transformation and development, comprehensively promote sustainable packaging development. In the just-concluded 20th National Congress of the Communist Party of China, green development and sustainability are the trends and keys of social development. Promoting green development, promoting the harmonious coexistence between man and nature, accelerating the transformation of development methods, and promoting green and low-carbon economic and social development are the critical links to achieving high-quality development. Accelerate the research and development, popularization, and application of advanced energy-saving and carbon-reducing technologies, advocate green consumption, and promote the formation of green and low-carbon production methods and lifestyles. We will follow the trend in packaging design and promote green packaging and sustainable packaging design.

2 Literature Review

2.1 Sustainable Packaging Design

Definition and Related Research of Sustainable Packaging. There needs to be a clear definition of sustainable packaging in China. Concepts such as green packaging, environmentally friendly packaging, ecological packaging, and eco-friendly packaging are often used interchangeably with sustainable packaging. Green packaging is a sustainable packaging design concept recognized by domestic designers. "In 1993, China's packaging industry adopted the meaning of environmental protection and collectively referred to pollution-free packaging or environmentally friendly packaging as green packaging. Green packaging has four connotations (3R + 1D principles): reduced packaging (Reduce), easy Reuse (Reuse) or easy recycling (Recycle), degradable (Degradable)" [1]. Researchers use this principle to expand the research direction of green design. Zhang Ming [2] proposed that the concept of "Refuse" should be added to promote environmentally conscious packaging. Zhang Qin [3] proposed that "Recover" packaging can obtain new value and use incineration to obtain energy and fuel. Yao Xinchao [4] suggested that export packaging should establish a recovery (Recovery) system, and actively conduct research on materials, technologies, and methods (Research). Yang Guang & E [5] suggested that energy should be saved (Resource), in all aspects of the entire packaging life cycle Focus on energy conservation and try to avoid waste of resources.

Under the principle of 3R + 1D, when designing the packaging, the designer also makes various attempts at sustainable packaging design in terms of materials, technology, structure, life cycle, and product circulation. For example, from the perspective of packaging raw materials: recyclable materials, degradable and edible materials [6, 7], use sustainable printing for recycling; reduce packaging costs from the perspective of reducing the number of packaging materials: original ecology [8], reduced design or integrated design [9, 10]; from the perspective of reducing the weight of packaging: lightweight design and small-scale design; from the perspective of extending packaging From the perspective of the life cycle: for example, transforming packaging into reusable or multifunctional products [11, 12]; from the perspective of green and environmentally friendly product circulation: simple structure, flattened, reusable Disassembly design, etc.

To sum up, sustainable design has been initiated by the United Nations since 1972, and the legislation of many countries has formulated guidelines for packaging design. Sustainable design has become a problem that designers must consider and a duty-bound responsibility.

Types of Container Shapes for Sustainable Packaging. Yan Chen et al. [13] divided the structure types of packaging containers into "box structure, barrel structure, bottle structure, bag structure, tube structure, blister structure, and other special-shaped structures. Structure, etc. Common packaging cover design types include threaded rotary type, embossed type, friction type, machine-rail type, twist-off type, tear-off type, easy-open type, crown-cap type, barrier type, etc.". This article mainly refers to the above content to analyze the award-winning works.

Purpose and Function Type of Sustainable Packaging Structure Design. Packaging design involves technical issues in packaging materials, technology, and structure. The packaging structure needs to have "three functions, such as protection function, use function, and promotion function. In addition, it needs to have good processing performance, easy molding, and easy recycling, and the molding and filling process is easy to realize mechanization, automation, and high speed [14]". Yan Chen et al. [13] according to the design purpose and function, the suggestions can be divided into lightweight structural design, multi-functional structural design, cycle-friendly structural design, standard structural design, and anti-scattering structural design.

The Table 1 below summarizes the structural elements of sustainable packaging design.

2.2 Pentaward and Dieline Competition

Pentaward and Dieline packaging design competitions are two top design competitions in the packaging profession. The two top awards have made significant contributions and professional guidance to society and the industry regarding sustainable environmental protection design. As the world's most authoritative international competition that only focuses on packaging design, Pen awards has been successfully held for 15 sessions. In 2021, the category of "Sustainable Design" will be added according to market trends and needs to commend outstanding packaging design works worldwide and promote progress and shared prosperity in the packaging design industry; Dieline awards The award was founded by Andrew Gibbs in 2007. As a global design award focusing on packaging design, it is committed to discovering the world's most outstanding packaging design works, commending and promoting them, to improve people's Awareness of consumer product packaging design and brand value.

Chinese researchers have been paying attention to the award-winning works of the Pen awards competition since 2010. Researchers have used the method of case analysis to sort out the works of previous years. The technology and other aspects analyzed the award-winning works from 2007 to 2014. Li et al. [18] analyzed the award-winning works from 2010 to 2016 from visual creativity, color, text, and packaging materials; they also analyzed the design of the award-winning works over the years. Style, material, and technology are used to think about how the traditional Chinese language can innovate [19]

Table 1. The structural elements of sustainable packaging design.

Structure	Aim of design	Researcher
Slid all-in-one design	**Protection function:** reduce foam, foaming, and other fillers; reduce secondary packaging	Zhang Junjie [15]
Hollow-carved design	**Display function:** increase the beauty	Zhang Junjie [15]
Detachable, easy to compress, self-sealing folding packaging design	**Reduce resource waste (recycling-friendly design):** reduce the use of tapes and glues, and facilitate transportation and recycling	Zhang Junjie, Yang Guoxin & Yang, [15, 16]
Recycled Packaging	**Reduction of waste of resources (recycling-friendly design):** recycling	Zhang Junjie [15]
Standardized, modularized, serialized packaging	**Reduced costs (standard version):** Save space in transport	Yan & Li. [13]
Multifunctional packaging (combined with daily necessities, combined with handicrafts, and decorations, combined to become new products and become supporting products)	**Multiple use functions (multi-function type):** have essential functions and can be used for other purposes	Yang Guang & E, Shi & Yu [5, 17]
Ready-to-shelf packaging	**Protection and promotion functions:** meet the most basic logistics protection functions of packaging and are easy to identify, easy to open, and easy to put on shelves	Yang Guang & E [5]

(Wang, 2022). More researchers will appreciate and analyze the award-winning works of a single year [20–26]. Research is carried out from a single category, such as food [18, 27]. Start research from the perspective of design techniques, such as bionic design [28], flat design [29], symbol design [30], and other design methods. The Pen awards competition will open sustainable packaging design categories in 2021, including six categories: beverages, food, health and beauty, home leisure and other markets, luxury goods, brands, and customers.

The winners of the Dieline awards provided excellent innovative designs and a good reference for the development direction of the packaging industry in terms of using plastic-free materials and emphasizing environmental protection. However, the Dieline awards have received relatively little attention in China, and it is necessary to conduct relevant research on them. In 2019, the Dieline Awards partnered with A Plastic Planet to launch the world's first plastic-free awards for sustainable packaging. A total of 4 winners will be recognized. The Dieline awards also began to separate the sustainable design into a design category in 2021, including six categories: beverages, food, health and beauty, home leisure and other markets, luxury goods, and concepts. However, in 2022, Two categories, Luxury and Concept, were removed from the awards category.

The works in the above competitions are primarily compared or appreciated from packaging graphics, colors, materials, and design styles. There are few studies on packaging design from the two aspects of sustainable packaging and structure. Research and analysis on the structure of sustainable packaging in the two competitions of Pen awards and Dieline can provide a particular theory for sustainable packaging design research support.

3 Research Methods

This study hopes to explore the trend of structural design in sustainable packaging design through the analysis of the winning entries in the sustainable design category of Pen prizes and Dieline packaging design competitions during 2021–2022.

The winning entries in the "Sustainable Design" category of the Pen awards and Dieline packaging design competitions were used as research objects. Using Excel tool to analyze a total of 84 sustainable design award-winning design works, analyzing how designers from various countries design packaging from the perspective of sustainable design from the three aspects of container shape type, structure, elements, and materials. Content analysis methods analysis, the classification, comparison of sustainable packaging design structure, and the study of design methods are carried out.

In order to prevent the subjective judgment of the researchers, the analysis invited five experts in the field of packaging design (designers who have worked in the industry for more than ten years) to make a joint judgment, and the analysis results are based on the majority judgment.

4 Results and Discussion

4.1 The Number of Award-Winning Works on Sustainable Packaging.

There is an award-winning works in the sustainable category in the Pen awards and Dieline awards, of which 54 works from the Pen awards and 30 works from the Dieline awards.

The Pentaward Diamond Award selects the best award-winning work from the award-winning works. Gold, silver, and bronze award-winning works are not fixed in the six categories, but there is a particular proportional relationship. There are 1–2 gold awards and silver awards. In 2022 Most of the bronze medals were 3.

Dieline awards are divided into three levels. Each level is an award. In the two years, there were six gold, silver, and bronze awards in each of the four categories of beverage, food, health and beauty, home leisure, and other markets, and three gold, silver, and bronze awards in the luxury and concept categories (Table 2).

Table 2. Pentaward 2021-2022 Number of Awards Note. The above data comes from the official website of Pentawards, and the author of this article compiled the above table. Pentawards (Ed.) (2023). The: winners. https://pentawards.com/directory/en/page/the-winners

2021				
Award category	Awards (items)	Awards (items)	Awards (items)	Awards (items)
Total(items)	1	5	8	6
Beverages		1	1	2
Food			2	1
Body, skin, health, and beauty		1	2	1
Home, leisure & other markets	1	1		1
Luxury goods		1	1	
Branding & consumer		1	2	1
2022				
Total(items)	1	8	9	16
Beverages			1	3
Food		2	1	3
Body, skin, health, and beauty		2	4	3
Home, leisure & other markets		1	1	3
Luxury goods		2	1	1
Branding & consumer	1	1	1	3

4.2 Shape Types of Recyclable Packaging Containers

According to Yan & Li [13], the classification of packaging container shape characteristics (box structure, barrel structure, bottle structure, bag structure, tube structure, blister structure, other special-shaped structures, etc.) Analyze the packaging container shape of the two competitions. After research, it was found that neither of the two competitions had a blister structure. Among the 54 award-winning works in Pentaward 2021–2022, most of the 54 winning works used the bottle structure, a total of 19 (35%) pieces of works, and 12 pieces of the box structure (22%), other special-shaped structures (9 pieces, 17%), tubular structures (7 pieces, 13%) and pocket structures (5 pieces, 9%) accounted for similar proportions, barrel structures (2 pieces, 4%) less. Among the 30 packaging products in the Dieline 2021–2022 competition, there are ten products with box structure design (33%), other special-shaped structures (8 pieces, 27%), barrel structures (5 pieces, 17%), bottle structure (5 pieces, 17%), bag type and tube structure both one piece (3%). Of the 84 award-winning works in the two competitions, bottle-type structures (24 pieces, 29%), box-type structures (22 pieces, 26%), and other special-shaped structures (20%) accounted for the most. The reason is that each category of the Pentaward competition has a bottle structure. In contrast, in the Dieline competition, except for the beverage category, there is no bottle structure, and the extension of the beverage packaging in the Dieline competition is more extensive, including water purification systems and portable packaging for beverages. In food container structure packaging, the P awards competition mainly uses bag and barrel structures, and Dieline mainly uses box and barrel structures. The Pentaward competition mainly uses bottle and box structures in the container structure of beauty cosmetics, while Dieline has various structure styles. In the container structure packaging of the household category, both the Pentaward and Dieline competitions are dominated by box structures. In the container structure packaging of luxury goods, the two competitors are mostly of special-shaped structures (Figs. 1 and 2).

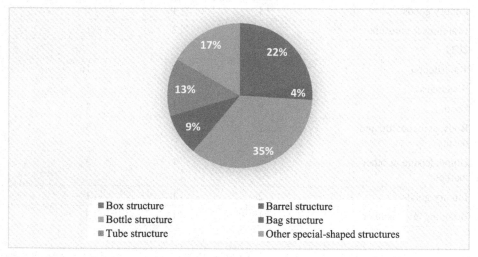

Fig. 1. The packaging container shape type of the award-winning works in Pentaward. Source: The above data comes from the official website of Pentawards, and the author of this article compiled the above table. Pentawards (Ed.)(2023). The: winners. https://pentawards.com/direct ory/en/page/the-winners.

To sum up, the bottle structure and the box structure are the more commonly used container structure methods in packaging design competitions, with relatively simple shapes and a wide range of applications. The styling features of each type of Pentawards competition focus on standardized design, and special-shaped structures are primarily used in luxury design. The Dieline competition has relatively many heterogeneous structures and appears in various categories. The participants in the Dieline competition are more creative, and their research is more exploratory.

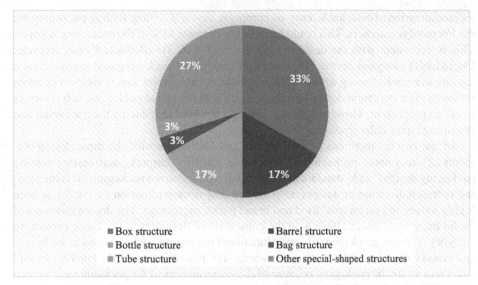

Fig. 2. The packaging container shape type of the award-winning works in Dieline. Source: The above data comes from the official website of Pentawards, and the author of this article compiled the above table. Pentawards (Ed.)(2023). The: winners. https://pentawards.com/directory/en/page/the-winners.

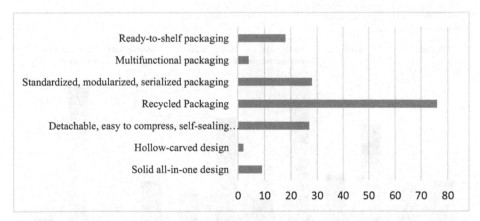

Fig. 3. Structural elements of sustainable packaging. Source: The above data comes from the official website of Pentawards, and the author of this article compiled the above table. Pentawards (Ed.)(2023). The: winners. https://pentawards.com/directory/en/page/the-winners.

4.3 Structural Elements of Sustainable Packaging

The structural elements of the two races are classified according to the classification of the structural elements. The data are shown in the table below (Fig. 3).

It can be seen from the figure that recyclable packaging is a necessary structural element in award-winning works, and the design and standardization, modularization, and serialization of detachable, easy-to-compress, and self-sealing folding packaging are the Focus of researchers. This could be possible because 41% of the packaging is paper. This is consistent with the design principles of 3 R + 1D (Reduce, Reuse, Recycle, Degradable) analyzed above. However, multifunctional packaging and hollow design are rare in award-winning works, and the decorative and display functions must be taken seriously. The structural design of easy-to-shelf and integrated packaging still occupies a certain proportion. These two design elements are vital in reducing the packaging and providing a particular display function.

In the two competitions of Pen awards and Dieline awards, the three design elements of "recyclable packaging," "detachable, easy-to-compress, self-sealing folding packaging design," and "standardized, modularized, serialized packaging" It is the leading research direction of designers. "Package that is easy to put on shelves" has been highly valued in Pen awards' food and brand packaging design. The design elements of "solid integrated design" have won the consensus of designers in the home furnishing category. The design element of "multifunctional packaging" only appears in the luxury and brand categories of the Pentaward awards. The reason is that the designer hopes that users will retain the packaging because of the exquisiteness of the packaging and reduce waste. The actual cases of "hollow design" are all food packaging. The designer hopes that through the packaging, consumers can quickly see the quality of the food (Fig. 4).

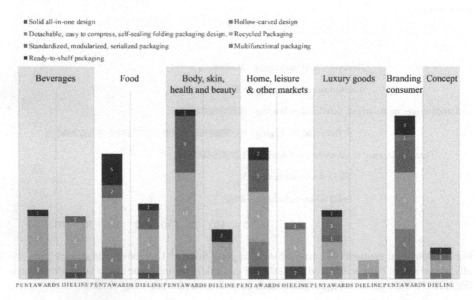

Fig. 4. Comparison chart of the number of structural elements of different categories in Pentaward and Dieline award-winning works. Source: The above data comes from the official website of Pentawards, and the author of this article compiled the above table. Pentawards (Ed.)(2023). The: winners. https://pentawards.com/directory/en/page/the-winners.

4.4 Material Elements of Sustainable Packaging

In the two competitions, the most widely used materials are paper (41%) and glass (20%), and most of the paper and printing inks used on glass are biodegradable and plant-based. Plastic (15%) and metal (7%) are used similarly, mainly as reusable outer packaging with refillable goods inside, so the materials are sustainable. Plastic materials also use discarded plastics for recycling to reduce plastic pollution to the earth. Organic materials (10%), renewable materials (3%), and degradable materials (1%) are also gradually gaining the attention of designers, although the numbers still need to be optimistic. Ceramic (3%) materials are mainly used as food bearing functions (Fig. 5).

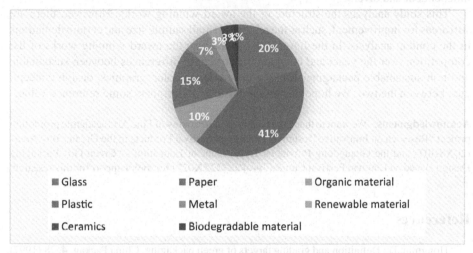

Fig. 5. Number of materials for Pentaward and Dieline winning entries. Source: The above data comes from the official website of Pentawards, and the author of this article compiled the above table. Pentawards(Ed.)(2023).The:winncrs. https.//pentawards.com/directory/en/page/the-winners.

5 Conclusion

Pentawards awards and Dieline awards, the recyclability of packaging is one of the vital judging criteria. In addition, the judges are very concerned about whether the products' raw materials are natural and whether the brand has a sense of sustainability. It should not only be the responsibility of designers to pay attention to sustainable design. Sustainable packaging design should be a full-process work involving the participation of merchants, designers, and consumers.

Different types of product categories have different emphases when designing structural elements. The beverage category focuses on recyclable, recyclable, or compostable solutions using glass or paper materials. Food packaging is mostly food containers, and the design concept of reusable utensils is still the mainstream design direction. However, new materials that can be thoroughly degraded have entered the designer's field of vision and become the trend of future design. Beauty packaging, in addition to the complementary design structure, also pays great attention to the quality of the packaging to improve the Style of consumers, such as using high-quality aluminum products, new biological mycelium packaging, and plastic outer packaging with fashionable colors Wait.

They are degradable and recyclable. The shape is relatively simple, and the box structure of the paper is mainly used. The luxury category pays more attention to the consumer's sense of experience and uses recyclable packaging with more technological characteristics to make the packaging a collection of consumers. Brand packaging will pay more attention to the brand's environmental protection concept, brand image, and personality quality, so the structural elements of sustainable packaging will be more independent and diverse.

This study analyzes the structure of the award-winning works. However, there are still areas for improvement, such as the relatively small sample size and certain deviations in the content analysis. In the future, we can analyze the award-winning works of the competition over the years and compare the structural differences between sustainable and non-sustainable packaging. And the difference in color, graphics, design concept, etc., between the two. We hope this research can give designers some reference value.

Acknowledgments. We want to thank the Guangzhou Academy of Fine Arts academic promotion project "Research on Innovative Design of Traditional Festival Products in the Greater Bay Area" (20XSB07) and the Guangdong Provincial Department of Education's "Green Gift Packaging Design Based on Lingnan Festival Culture" project (22ZX027) for their support for this research.

References

1. Hongmin, D.: Definition and grading targets of green packaging. China Packag. **4**, 28 (1997)
2. Zhang, M.: "Zero Packaging": the existence and development of packaging design. Decoration. **2**, 37–41 (2018). https://doi.org/10.16272/j.cnki.cn11-1392/j.2018.02.009
3. Zhang, Q.: Application research of green efficiency in packaging design. Packag. Eng. **32**(24), 95–97+101 (2011). https://doi.org/10.19554/j.cnki.1001-3563.2011.24.027
4. Yao, X.: Concepts and principles of green packaging design for export commodities. Foreign Econ. Trade Pract. **7**, 14–15 (1997)
5. Guang, Y., Yuping, E.: Packaging design in the low carbon era. Packag. Eng. **32**(4), 81–83 (2011). https://doi.org/10.19554/j.cnki.1001-3563.2011.04.024
6. Zhou, Z.: Research on moon cake packaging design under the concept of low-carbon design. Packag. Eng. **35**(24), 95–98 (2014). https://doi.org/10.19554/j.cnki.1001-3563.2014.24.024
7. Xiong, X., Shen, L.: On the material selection and application of innovative packaging for moon cakes in a low-carbon economic environment. Packag. Eng. **31**(24), 90–92+95 (2010). https://doi.org/10.19554/j.cnki.1001-3563.2010.24.025
8. Liu, W.: Low carbon: the revival of original ecological packaging. J. Nanjing Univ. Arts (Art Des Edn.). **1**, 168–172 (2012)
9. Yu, C., Liu, G.: Research the simple design of product packaging under the concept of low carbon. Packag. Eng. **36**(18), 37–40 (2015). https://doi.org/10.19554/j.cnki.1001-3563.2015.18.008
10. Zhou, J., Liu, A.: Research on development countermeasures of the packaging industry under the concept of circular development. Packag. Eng. **38**(17), 227–232 (2017). https://doi.org/10.19554/j.cnki.1001-3563.2017.17.048

11. Zhou, B.: The enlightenment of green design trends on product packaging design. Packag. Eng. **32**(2), 99–101+105 (2011). https://doi.org/10.19554/j.cnki.1001-3563.2011.02.028
12. Tang, H., Zang, Y., Liu, Y.: Research on innovative design of green packaging with multiple functions. Packag. Eng. **32**(24), 91–94 (2011). https://doi.org/10.19554/j.cnki.1001-3563. 2011.24.026
13. Yan, C., Li, Y.: Saving Packaging Design (1st ed.). Tsinghua University Press (2018)
14. Yin, X., Sun, C.: Constructing green packaging under the green logistics system. Packag. Eng. **4**, 104–105+111 (2006)
15. Zhang, J.: Solutions for express environmental protection packaging in the era of online shopping. Packag. Eng. **36**(20), 96–99 (2015). https://doi.org/10.19554/j.cnki.1001-3563.2015. 20.023
16. Yang, G., Yang, P.: Analysis of green packaging design. Packag. Eng.**3**, 240–241 (2006)
17. Shi, A., Yu, J.: "Zero Waste" packaging theory research. Packag. Eng. **34**(11), 126–130 (2013). https://doi.org/10.19554/j.cnki.1001-3563.2013.11.030
18. Li, L., Chen, H.: Global food packaging design creative trends viewed from "PENTAWARDS" award-winning works. Food Mach. **33**(2), 98–105 (2017). https://doi.org/10.13652/j.issn. 1003-5788.2017.02.022
19. Wang, H.: Research on winning works of Pentawards Packaging Design Competition [Master, Xihua University] (2022). https://kns.cnki.net/KCMS/detail/detail.aspx?dbcode=CMFD& dbname=CMFDTEMP&filename=1022693284.nh&v=
20. Caca: Pentawards packaging design awards. Design. **12**, 94 (2010)
21. Emma: Pentawards 2016: the world's most beautiful packaging design. Design, **22**, 94–99 (2016)
22. Ye: Pentawards packaging design awards. Design. **4**, 98–105 (2016)
23. Hao, F.: Appreciation of winning works of Pentawards international packaging design award 2009. Printing Technol. **6**, 65–67 (2010)
24. Hao, F.: Appreciation of 2010 Pentawards international packaging design award winning works. Printing Technol. **22**, 45–47 (2011)
25. Hao, F.: Appreciation of some award-winning works of Pentawards international packaging design award in 2011. Printing Technol. **4**, 68–71 (2012)
26. Hao, F.: Appreciation of some award-winning works of Pentawards international packaging design award in 2012. Printing Technol. **10**, 43–46 (2013)
27. Hu, J.: Application of biomimetic shape design of food packaging from Pentawards awards. J. Wuhan Univ. Light Indus. **40**(2), 97–103 (2021)
28. Tan, J.: Application research of bionic design in packaging design——taking Pentawards award-winning works as an example. Popul. Lit. Art. **13**, 74–75 (2019)
29. Tao, W.: The application of flat visual elements in packaging design from Pentawards awards. Food Mach. **34**(4), 132–135 (2018). https://doi.org/10.13652/j.issn.1003-5788.2018.04.027
30. Zeng, X.: Research on Packaging Design Techniques Based on Design Rhetoric Theory [Master, Beijing Jiaotong University] (2020). https://kns.cnki.net/KCMS/detail/detail.aspx? dbcode=CMFD&dbname=CMFD202101&filename=1020443656.nh&v=

Twitter Sentiment Analysis of Cross-Cultural Perspectives on Climate Change

Misha Mirza[✉], Stephan Lukosch, and Heide Lukosch

HIT Lab NZ, University of Canterbury, Canterbury, New Zealand
misha.mirza@pg.canterbury.ac.nz

Abstract. This study investigates the response of residents from different cultures to climate change and opinions about related activities on social media. The deep Long Short-Term Memory (LSTM) model is used for estimating sentiment polarity found in the social media posts. Cross-cultural polarity measurement using sentiment analysis refers to the use of sentiment analysis techniques to measure the emotional tone or sentiment of text in multiple languages or cultures. This can be used to compare and contrast the sentiments expressed in different cultures or to identify cultural-specific sentiment patterns. This research examines the sentiments of people living in Lahore, Pakistan and Christchurch, New Zealand related to climate change and possible actions. Both Lahore and Christchurch, located on opposite hemispheres, have diverse populations comprising a mix of different ethnic and religious groups. The analysis shows that the risk perceptions of people with regard to a global issue as climate change during the Covid-19 pandemic have created polarity in opinions posted on Twitter. The study finds that while the percentage of positive sentiments outweighs the negative ones in both countries, the negative sentiment values are still relatively high. Negative sentiments towards climate change can arise due to feelings of hopelessness, frustration, anger or despair in the face of overwhelming environmental challenges. This can lead to decreased motivation and engagement in actions to address climate change.

Keywords: Sentiment analysis · cross-cultural · climate change

1 Introduction

1.1 Analyzing Public Opinion Through Social Media Sentiment Analysis

Sentiment analysis is a method of using natural language processing, text analysis, and computational linguistics to identify and extract subjective information from source materials. It is often used to determine the emotional tone or sentiment of a piece of text, such as a sentence, paragraph, or entire document (Baccianella et al. 2010; Liu 2012).

However, while sentiment analysis is a powerful tool, it is important to keep in mind that it is not always possible to determine the sentiment of a piece of text with 100% accuracy, especially when working with cross-cultural text (Mohammad et al. 2013; Saif et al. 2016). Previous studies have shown that cross-cultural sentiment analysis can be challenging due to the cultural context, idiomatic expressions, and other cultural

© The Author(s), under exclusive license to Springer Nature Switzerland AG 2023
P.-L. P. Rau (Ed.): HCII 2023, LNCS 14022, pp. 392–406, 2023.
https://doi.org/10.1007/978-3-031-35936-1_29

specificities that might not be accurately captured by pre-trained models (Popescu and Pennacchiotti 2010). These difficulties can be overcome through the use of techniques such as fine-tuning pre-trained models, using parallel corpora for training and cross-lingual sentiment analysis (Popescu and Pennacchiotti 2010).

The COVID-19 pandemic has had a complex impact on people's opinions towards climate change, shifting public priorities and attention towards immediate health and economic concerns, while also increasing awareness of the need for environmental protection and sustainability. Such global crises have a direct impact on our social behavior; in any case, not all societies respond and react similarly given an emergency. Research has shown that people from different cultures tend to have different reasoning patterns, even in normal situations (Lee and Johnson-Laird n.d.). Nisbett (2004) states that East Asians (in general) tend to think rationalistically and comprehensively, while Westerners (in general) think consistently, conceptually, and systematically based on their respective experiences.

The traditional approach of measuring public opinion about climate change is through surveys. However, in recent years, online media and microblogging sites such as Twitter have become increasingly popular conversation platforms for many people around the world. Social scientists have used this newly discovered dataset to analyze public opinion and risk perception on climate change. For example, researchers have used Twitter data to study public opinions on Hurricane Irene and its potential impact on political decision-making (Mandel et al. 2012). In this way, Twitter can provide valuable insights into public opinion and perceptions of climate change.

There are various ways to study and quantify public opinion on climate change. For example, Van der Linden (2017) discusses the different factors that influence perceptions of climate change risk, including the impact of social networks on the development of these perceptions.

Therefore, this study will focus on exploring the collective reactions to events expressed in social media, with specific emphasis on analyzing people's reactions to climate change events on Twitter. This is because of Twitter's widespread popularity and ease of access through its API.

1.2 Related Work

A study by Dahal et al. (2019) used topic modeling and sentiment analysis to examine global climate change tweets on Twitter from both geospatial and temporal perspectives. The study found that tweets from the USA were more polarized in terms of climate or political events compared to tweets from other nations. This difference was likely the result of the significant 2017 hurricane season and the change in political administration in the USA (Dahal et al. 2019).

A case study on climate change used a LSTM deep learning model to analyze 278,264 tweets posted by the environmental activist Greta Thunberg and her followers between July 20th, 2019 and October 30th, 2020. The study looked at Greta's emotions over time, followers' reactions and location-based sentiment analysis to understand public opinion on climate change in different regions of the world. The results showed that the predominant emotions expressed in Greta's tweets were anger (43.7%), followed by joy (38.1%), and inspiration (17.4%). The study also found interesting results when analyzing location-based sentiment analysis of followers' replies, showing that culture can play an important role in shaping public opinion (El Barachi et al. 2021).

Another study was done to examine the reaction of individuals from various cultural backgrounds to the COVID-19 pandemic and their sentiments towards the measures taken by different countries. The study suggests that NLP-based sentiment analysis has the potential to provide cultural and emotional insight, although the number of tweets from non-English speaking countries may not be sufficient for conclusive results. The findings indicate a strong correlation between sentiments expressed by neighboring countries within a region, with both positive and negative emotions being observed in regards to the #lockdown hashtag. The study also suggests that NLP-based sentiment analysis can accurately link actual events to emotions expressed on social media, even in the face of socio-economic and cultural differences. (Imran et al. 2020).

Previous studies have also shown that social media can be a powerful tool for raising awareness about environmental issues and encouraging pro-environmental behavior (Darnoff, 2014; Leiserowitz et al. 2015; Stankiewicz and Roszkowski 2017). For example, a study by Khan et al. (2020) found that social media platforms like Twitter have been used extensively in Pakistan to raise awareness and mobilize actions on environmental issues such as air pollution. The study found that social media platforms are providing citizens with a platform to voice their concerns, share information, and mobilize actions against air pollution in Pakistan.

Additionally, research has also shown that people who are more aware of environmental issues are more likely to act to address them (Darnoff 2014; Leiserowitz et al. 2015). For example, a study by Ali et al. (2020) found that people in Pakistan who were more aware of the health impacts of air pollution were more likely to support policies aimed at reducing air pollution.

Earlier studies have shown that the media plays a crucial role in shaping public opinion and understanding of environmental issues, including climate change (Boykoff 2007; Cook et al. 2016; Prokopy et al., 2016). For example, a study by Cook and colleagues (2016) found that news media coverage of climate change was positively associated with public concern about the issue.

2 Study Design

2.1 Study Objectives and Research Questions

The primary objective of our study is to gain a deeper understanding of how various cultures respond and react to a global crisis, such as climate change. By examining cultural differences as a socio-technical system, the study provides valuable insights into the attitudes, behaviors, and emotional tendencies of society. This information can be used to better predict and respond to future crises and to understand how different cultures navigate the challenges of a global crisis. Furthermore, by investigating cultural behavior in times of crisis, the study aims to promote a better understanding of the complex dynamics that exist within and across different cultures, and to foster a greater sense of interconnectedness and empathy among individuals from diverse backgrounds.

Our study looks at these for the two countries the authors are residing at, namely New Zealand and Pakistan. This leads to the following research questions:

RQ1: To what extent are sentiments regarding climate change similar or different within and in Pakistan and New Zealand?

RQ2: What is the risk perception of people in these countries, expressed on Twitter, regarding a global issue as climate change during the Covid-19 pandemic?

The study employs a quantitative (experimental) research methodology to analyze tweets posted on climate change during the Covid-19 crisis. To conduct the analysis, tweets were searched using keywords related to climate change from users in Lahore, Pakistan and Christchurch, New Zealand. Containing trending keywords #smog, #energy, #carbonfootprint, #climatechange, fossil energy, carbon footprint and emissions. The keywords were chosen based on the trending keywords during that period.

2.2 Study Dimensions

The following dimensions are used for the interpretation of the results:

a) *Demography*: country/region under study. This study focuses on two opposite countries in the hemisphere, Pakistan and New Zealand
b) *Timeline*: One week from June 20th, 2021 to June 27th, 2021
c) *Culture*: East (South-East Asia) vs. West (Australasia)
d) *Polarity*: Sentiment classified as either positive or negative

2.3 Motivations for the Dimensions:

The motivation behind understanding the sentiments of people around climate change from the East and West is to gain insights into public perception and attitudes, inform effective communication and engagement strategies, and build greater public support for addressing the issue.

As far as vulnerability and readiness to climate change, Pakistan is a country with a high degree of vulnerability to environmental change but a low degree of readiness. Pakistan has a significant need for investment and development to improve its status and a great urgency for transformative action. On the other hand, New Zealand is a country with a low degree of vulnerability to environmental change and a high degree of readiness. It is well-positioned to adapt to climate change, but it still faces some variation challenges (Notre Dame Research, 2021).

Hofstede's Cultural Dimensions Theory, developed by Geert Hofstede, is a system used to identify distinct national cultures, the elements of culture, and evaluate their effect on a business setting. (Hofstede et al. 1984) Using the same framework, our study aims to determine the dimensions in which cultures vary. Hofstede identified six categories that can be used to analyze and differentiate different cultural groups. According to Hofstede's country comparison survey tool, the graph below shows a cross-cultural comparison of Pakistan and New Zealand. The six categories are power distance, individualism, masculinity, uncertainty avoidance, long term orientation and indulgence respectively. Power Distance reflects unequal power distribution and acceptance among less powerful members of institutions and organizations. Individualist societies prioritize self and direct family, while Collectivist societies value group loyalty and mutual support. Masculine societies prioritize competition, achievement, and success, while Feminine societies value caring for others and quality of life. The score on Uncertainty Avoidance reflects a culture's avoidance of ambiguous or unknown situations, Long term orientation balances past links and present/future challenges, and control of desires and impulses is either Indulgence (weak) or Restraint (strong) (Fig. 1).

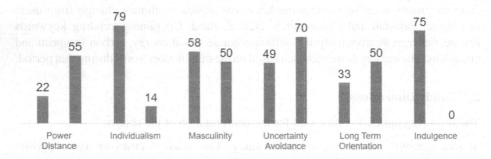

Fig. 1. Country comparison chart Pakistan (purple) – New Zealand (blue)

New Zealand is a low-power distance (22), high individualist (79), masculine (58), intermediate uncertainty avoidance (49), low long-term orientation (33), and high indulgence (75) culture, according to the 6-D Model©. It is characterized by a loosely-knit society, a focus on competition, achievement, and success, a preference for traditions over change, and a willingness to realize impulses and desires.

Pakistan on the other hand is a collectivist society with a low score of 14 on individualism. It has a high preference for avoiding uncertainty with a score of 70 on the uncertainty avoidance dimension. The culture of Pakistan cannot be said to indicate a preference for power distance or long-term orientation with intermediate scores of 55 and 50 respectively. It is a very restrained society with an extremely low score of 0 on indulgence. Understanding cultural differences through frameworks like Hofstede's cultural comparison is crucial for sentiment analysis because it helps to consider the cultural context in which the sentiment is expressed.

3 Data Collection

3.1 Data Collection Procedure

This study uses Python scripts to query the Tweepy, Twitter API to fetch users' tweets and extract a feature set for cataloging. The Natural Language Toolkit (NLTK) is used to preprocess the retrieved tweets. NLP-based deep learning models are used to predict sentiment polarity as a back-end deep learning engine. Visualization and LSTM model prediction are used as instruments to analyze the results. The results of sentiment are validated through an approach that utilizes keywords extracted from the tweets, which is a widely accepted feature of expressing one's feelings.

Only tweets in English for a given region were cataloged for further processing, containing Tweet ID, text, user name, time, and location.

The dataset of 3244 tweets was collected. Each geotagged tweet has a longitude and latitude pair associated with the location the user was in when the tweet was posted. The data for each tweet has the following relevant variables: tweetid (the unique code given to the tweet), userid (the Twitter code of the user that posted that tweet), postdate (the time and day the tweet was posted), latitude, longitude, and message (the body of the tweet).

The main step in data preparation is reverse geocoding, which is the process of obtaining a readable place name or address from a latitude/longitude point. This facilitates the process of pulling every tweet from a particular region at once, which is important when, for example, comparing the volume of tweets posted between countries. Reverse geocoding is performed by associating each tweet with the nearest city from the tweet's latitude/longitude values. This is done using the reverse geocoder Python library (Thampi 2016).

3.2 Model for Sentiment Analysis

The sentiments in the tweets were analyzed using the VADER (Valence Aware Dictionary and Sentiment Reasoner) model, the text is first tokenized into individual words and punctuation marks. Then, the sentiment scores of each word and punctuation mark are looked up in the VADER lexicon, which is a pre-defined list of words and their associated sentiment scores. Finally, the sentiment scores of all the tokens are combined to arrive at a composite sentiment score for the entire tweet. This score is then used to classify the tweet as positive, negative, or neutral in sentiment. This model is used for text sentiment analysis that is sensitive to both polarity (positive/negative) and intensity (strength) of emotion (Aditya Beri, 2020). The model analyzes the lexical highlights of a record, i.e., the words that appear, to decide a fundamental feeling score and then applies five unique standards dependent on broad syntactic and linguistic shows to alter that score, with the last score falling between − 1 (firmly negative) and 1 (unequivocally good). For instance, the principles treat exclamation points and capitalization as opinion enhancers, scaling the positive or negative feeling of an archive.

3.3 Data Preparation

The first step in order to analyze sentiments in tweets is filtering of tweets. The process is adopted to query climate change-related tweets and to filter out irrelevant ones. The following pre-processing steps are applied to clean the retrieved tweets:

1. **Removal of mentions and colons**: Mentions and colons are often used in social media text and may not carry any sentiment information. By removing them, the text data becomes more focused on the actual content of the tweet, which is more relevant for sentiment analysis.
2. **Removal of re-tweets**: Re-tweets are duplicate tweets that are reposted by other users. Removing them reduces the size of the dataset and ensures that each tweet is unique.

3. **Tokenization of tweets**: Tokenization is the process of breaking down a piece of text into smaller units, called tokens, usually words or phrases. This step prepares the text for further processing by converting it into a list of tokens that can be analyzed individually.
4. **Removal of stop-words and punctuation**: Stop-words are common words, such as "a", "and", "the", etc., that carry little meaning. Removing them reduces the noise in the data and makes the analysis more focused on the meaningful words. Punctuation is also removed because it does not carry any sentiment information.
5. **Tokens are appended**: After removing stop-words and punctuation, the remaining tokens are combined to form the cleaned tweet text. This step ensures that the cleaned text is ready for sentiment analysis by a machine learning algorithm.

4 Results

The results of this study are used to gain insights into public opinion on climate change in Lahore, Pakistan and Christchurch, New Zealand. Figure 2 indicates that a majority of the tweets from Lahore had a neutral sentiment, but a significant number of tweets were classified as negative. This could suggest that there is a level of concern or dissatisfaction among Twitter users in Lahore, Pakistan regarding climate change.

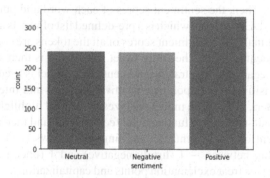

Fig. 2. Sentiment analysis of Lahore

The polarity index of the words in the tweets analyzed in this study shows that the majority of sentiments expressed by people with regard to smog and climate change are neutral. However, there is also a significant population of people who have positive sentiments toward these issues. This could indicate that while a portion of the population is concerned about the effects of smog and climate change, there is also a group of individuals who are taking a proactive stance and expressing positive sentiments toward finding solutions to these issues (Fig. 3).

The Figs. 4, 5, 6 show the use of neutral, positive and negative words in the tweets that were extracted. The word smog is most commonly used in all the tweets and words like unhealthy are linked to the environment.

The use of words such as "smog," "air pollution," and "unhealthy" in tweets from people in Pakistan can suggest a high level of awareness about the issue of air pollution in

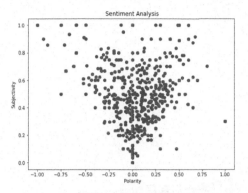

Fig. 3. Polarity graph of Lahore

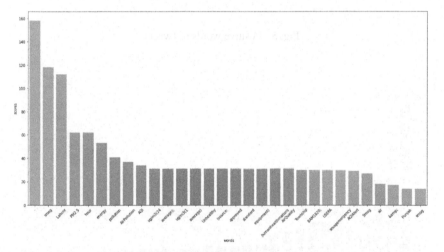

Fig. 4. Neutral words in tweets

the country. These words indicate that individuals are actively discussing and engaging with this topic on social media, which implies that air pollution is a significant concern for many people in Pakistan.

The presence of the word "news" in tweets discussing climate change likely indicates that individuals are getting their information about this issue from news sources and that their opinions and perceptions of the issue may be shaped by the way it is presented in the media.

A total of 44 tweets were pulled out from Christchurch, New Zealand. Out of them, 20 were positive, 12 were negative and 12 were neutral. A reason for the low number of tweets extracted from Christchurch could be the limited availability of geotagged tweets as not all tweets are geotagged and some users choose not to share their location information.

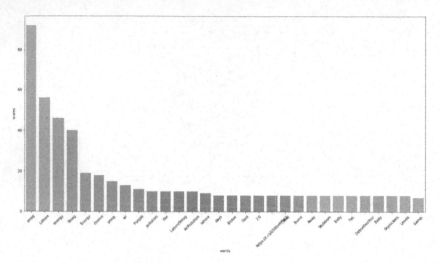

Fig. 5. Positive words in tweets

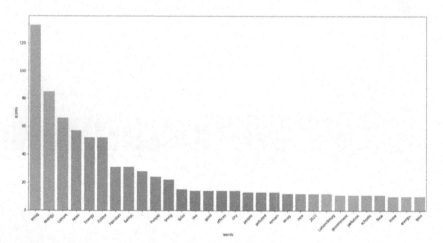

Fig. 6. Negative words in tweets

This study shows that the majority of the tweets from Christchurch, New Zealand had positive sentiment. However, it's also important to note that a relatively large number of tweets were classified as neutral which could mean that the tweets were not expressing any strong sentiment or that the tweets were not clear in expressing the sentiment.

Figure 7 represents the sentiments of people in Christchurch, New Zealand to climate change whereas Fig. 8 represents the same in a polarity/subjectivity graph. Figures 9, 10 and 11 represent the positive, negative and neutral words used in the tweets.

The use of words such as "climate change," "energy," and "Kyoto" in tweets from people in New Zealand can suggest a high level of awareness and concern about these

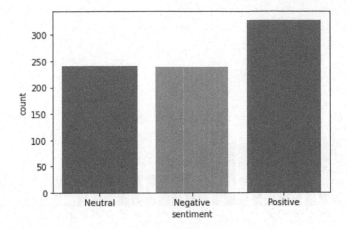

Fig. 7. Sentiment analysis of tweets from Christchurch, New Zealand

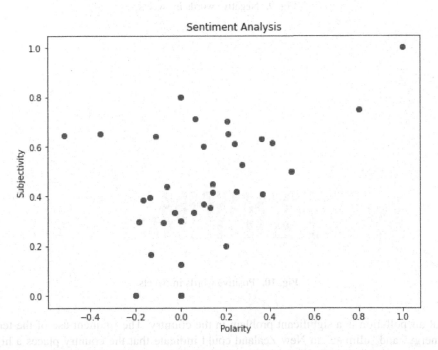

Fig. 8. Polarity index of the tweets from Christchurch, New Zealand

issues among the population, as well as a willingness to act to address climate change (Fig. 12).

The word clouds were developed in Python using the word cloud library. The importance of word clouds is that they provide a quick and easy way to visualize the most frequent words in a dataset. The use of the word "smog" in Pakistan likely suggests

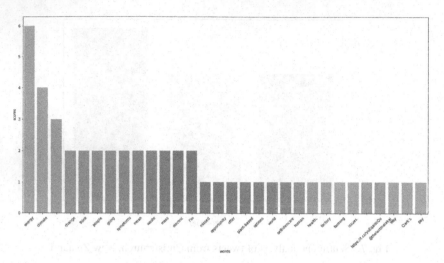

Fig. 9. Negative words in tweets

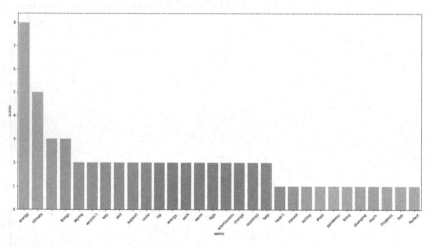

Fig. 10. Positive words in tweets

that air pollution is a significant problem in the country. The frequent use of the term "energy" and "climate" in New Zealand could indicate that the country places a high importance on renewable energy and reducing its carbon footprint.

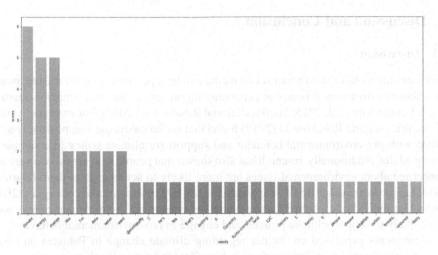

Fig. 11. Neutral words in tweets

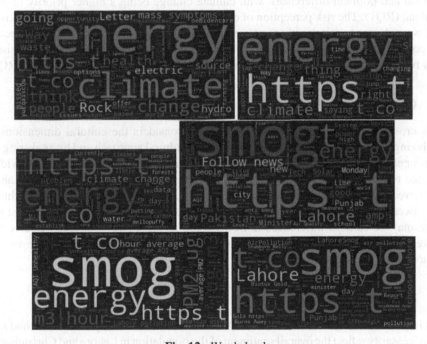

Fig. 12. Word cloud

5 Discussion and Conclusion

5.1 Discussion

Previous studies have shown that social media can be a powerful tool for raising awareness about environmental issues and encouraging pro-environmental behavior (Darnoff 2014; Leiserowitz et al. 2015; Stankiewicz and Roszkowski 2017). For example, a study by Stankiewicz and Roszkowski (2017) found that social media use was positively associated with pro-environmental behavior and support for climate policy in a sample of young adults. Additionally, research has also shown that people who are more aware and concerned about environmental issues are more likely to act to address them (Darnoff, 2014; Leiserowitz et al. 2015). For example, a study by Leiserowitz and colleagues (2015) found that individuals who were more aware and concerned about climate change were more likely to support climate policies and engage in pro-environmental behaviors.

Sentiments expressed on Twitter regarding climate change in Pakistan and New Zealand are diverse, with Twitter users in New Zealand generally showing greater concern and activism on the issue compared to Pakistan. This variability reflects broader societal and political differences, with climate change being a higher priority in New Zealand (RQ1). The risk perception of climate change expressed on Twitter in Pakistan and New Zealand varies, with greater concern and urgency in New Zealand reflecting the country's political priorities and wider public discourse, while in Pakistan the issue may receive less attention due to other pressing economic and security concerns (RQ2).

5.2 Conclusion

This cross-cultural approach to risk perception considers the cultural dimensions of analyzing uncertainty avoidance from Hofstede's cultural approach and by analyzing the sentiments of people from Lahore, Pakistan and Christchurch, New Zealand, it is evident that the two countries have a high uncertainty avoidance index. The people of Lahore have tweeted about the air quality being unhealthy, whereas the people of Christchurch have tweeted about carbon footprint and energy emissions. These findings suggest that there may be cultural differences in how people in these two countries perceive and express their concerns about climate change. This also shows the awareness level with regards to different types of problems.

5.3 Limitations and Future Research Directions

It is important to note that these results are based on a limited sample of tweets and may not necessarily reflect the overall sentiment of the population in Lahore and Christchurch.

The current limitations of this study include the number of tweet extraction limit using Tweepy. Another limitation was the extraction of historical data using the Twitter API. The academic research tool provided to the Twitter developer account holder allows researchers to analyze past data from tweets, however, the code was recently developed and was not yet incorporated into Python, so a limited amount of data could be extracted for the research. This means that the data used in this study may not represent the full picture of public opinion on climate change in Lahore, Pakistan. It is important to note that these limitations could affect the generalizability of the results, and therefore, further research with more tweets and a longer time frame should be conducted to gain a more comprehensive understanding of public opinion on climate change.

It should also be noted that as of 2021, the population of Lahore, Pakistan is approximately 11.13 million people according to the Pakistan Bureau of Statistics. Christchurch, New Zealand, on the other hand, has a population of approximately 392,700 people according to the New Zealand census of 2018. So, Lahore is significantly more populous than Christchurch, a difference that is reflected in the number of tweets extracted.

Future research could analyze global issues with a cultural comparison of neighboring countries and countries on opposing hemispheres. The expected result of analyzing global issues with a cultural comparison of neighboring countries on opposing hemispheres would be a deeper understanding of these issues and the ways in which they are shaped by cultural differences and the promotion of greater collaboration and cross-cultural understanding. The research can also be advanced by incorporating a focus on emoticons and by using a larger dataset to increase the sample size. Additionally, it is important to consider that the keywords used to filter the tweets also play a role in determining the sentiment of the tweets as they could have been filtered based on certain topics or events that might have skewed the results.

References

Hofstede, G., Bond, M.H.: Hofstede's culture dimensions: an independent validation using Rokeach's value survey. J. Cross Cult. Psychol. **15**(4), 417–433 (1984)

Dahal, B., Kumar, S.A.P., Li, Z.: Topic modeling and sentiment analysis of global climate change tweets. Soc. Netw. Anal. Min. **9**(1), 1–20 (2019). https://doi.org/10.1007/s13278-019-0568-8

El Barachi, M., AlKhatib, M., Mathew, S., Oroumchian, F.: A novel sentiment analysis framework for monitoring the evolving public opinion in real-time: Case study on climate change. J. Clean. Prod. **312**, 127820 (2021). https://doi.org/10.1016/j.jclepro.2021.127820

Hofstede's Cultural Dimensions Theory. (2015). Corporate Finance Institute. https://corporatefin anceinstitute.com/resources/knowledge/other/hofstedes-cultural-dimensions-theory/

Imran, A.S., Daudpota, S.M., Kastrati, Z., Batra, R.: Cross-cultural polarity and emotion detection using sentiment analysis and deep learning on COVID-19 related Tweets. IEEE Access **8**, 181074–181090 (2020). https://doi.org/10.1109/ACCESS.2020.3027350

Lee, N.Y.L., Johnson-Laird, P.N.: Are There Cross-Cultural Differences in Reasoning? http://mod eltheory.org/papers/2006xcultural.pdf

Mandel, B., Culotta, A., Boulahanis, J., Stark, D., Lewis, B., Rodrigue, J.: A demographic analysis of online sentiment during Hurricane Irene. In: Proceedings of the Second Workshop on Language in Social Media, 27–36 (2012).. https://aclanthology.org/W12-2104

Nisbett, R.: The Geography of Thought: How Asians and Westerners Think Differently...and Why. Simon and Schuster (2004)

SENTIMENTAL ANALYSIS USING VADER. interpretation and classification of... I by Aditya Beri I Towards Data Science. (n.d.). https://towardsdatascience.com/sentimental-analysis-using-vader-a3415fef7664. Accessed 27 Nov 2022

Baccianella, S., Esuli, A., Sebastiani, F.: SentiWordNet 3.0: an enhanced lexical resource for sentiment analysis and opinion mining. In: LREC, pp. 2200–2204 (2010)

Liu, B.: Sentiment analysis and opinion mining. Synth. Lect. Human Lang. Technol. **5**(1), 1–167 (2012)

Mohammad, S., Kiritchenko, S., Sobhani, P.: Emotions in text: a study of sentiment and emotion annotation schemes. In: Proceedings of the 1st international workshop on emotion representation, analysis, and synthesis in continuous time series, pp. 1–8, October 2013

Saif, H., He, Y., Al-Smadi, M., Liu, B.: Sentiment analysis of twitter data: a review of methods and applications. In: 2016 International Conference on Social Computing, Behavioral-Cultural Modeling, & Prediction and Behavior Representation in Modeling & Simulation (SBP-BRiMS), pp. 1–8, May 2016

Popescu, A.-M., Pennacchiotti, M.: Opinion extraction from comparative sentences. In: Proceedings of the 48th Annual Meeting of the Association for Computational Linguistics, pp. 1291–1299, May 2010

Leiserowitz, A., Feinberg, G., Maibach, E.: American risk perceptions: is climate change dangerous? Risk Anal. 35(2), 1–11 (2015)

Stankiewicz, M., Roszkowski, P.: Social media and pro-environmental behaviour: an analysis of the role of media use and political orientation. J. Environ. Psychol. 51, 1–11 (2017)

Discussion on the User Experience of Intelligent Travel Applications for Electric Bicycles

Qi Wang, Meng-Xi Chen(✉) ⓘ, and Haoyu Li

Shantou University, Shantou 515063, China
cmx12677@gmail.com

Abstract. This research mainly discussed the influence of interface design on the user experience of intelligent travel applications for electric bicycles. Three representative electric bicycle applications were selected as the experimental samples. Thirty subjects were asked to complete three tasks, including locking and unlocking an electric bicycle, finding the functions of authorizing others to use the electric bicycle and contacting for maintenance. The operation time of each task was measured. Participants were also required to fill out system usability scale (SUS) questionnaire to collect subjective data. The research results can be summarized as follows: (1) Using a sliding button to lock and unlock an electric bicycle can improve users' subjective evaluations of usability and their efficiency. (2) The main functional icons need to be integrated into a clear interface and have good affordance to improve users' efficiency. (3) It is recommended to use fewer colors on the interfaces of intelligent travel applications.

Keywords: Electric bicycle · Interface design · Usability · User experience

1 Introduction

With the development of social economy, while promoting the development of car ownership, it also aggravates the urban traffic congestion and reduces the quality of life of the city. Nowadays, China is promoting a green, low-carbon way of life and production, and encourage public to use of pollution-free tools for getting around. Many transportation vehicles based on the concept of green and low-carbon travel have emerged in China. The concept of convenience, efficiency, green and environmental protection has been deeply rooted in people's mind. Benefiting from ever-growing demand, the development of the electric bicycle has maintained strong growth momentum. Many of the travel companies have already been involved in shared electric bicycles business, such as Didi Chuxing, Hello Global, Aima and so on. However, homogenization is the main pain point for China's electric bicycle industry [1]. There's a great challenge of how to significantly enhance user experience in the homogeneous industry.

According to the intelligent travel applications for electric bicycles, the layout, visual presentation styles and interaction process may have impacts on users' subjective feelings about usability and ease of use. Therefore, it is necessary to discuss the effects of interface design on the user experience of intelligent travel applications for electric bicycles.

P.-L. P. Rau (Ed.): HCII 2023, LNCS 14022, pp. 407–416, 2023.
https://doi.org/10.1007/978-3-031-35936-1_30

2 Background

The well-known traditional electric bicycle manufacturers in China were basically established around 2000. These enterprises have complied with the development of battery technology, China's urbanization process and people's attention to environmental protection travel, so they have achieved considerable development. Among them, Aima was founded in 2004, and its predecessor was mainly engaged in bicycles. In that same year, the new Road Traffic Safety Law officially clarified that electric bicycles were included in the management of non-motor vehicles, and electric bicycles quickly became the best way for people to travel. Aima has successfully stepped into the industry tide by seizing the opportunity of industrial transformation. At present, Aima, based in Tianjin, has manufacturing bases in Wuxi, Shangqiu, Dongguan and Taizhou, forming a certain industrial cluster [2]. The more traditional electric bicycle manufacturers represent the leading edge of local electric bicycle technology and have considerable industrial influence.

We have been seeing electronic lock technology advance in recent years. The hassle of manually operating a switch is replaced by a smart technique which involves operating the switches using the web browser present in mobile phones, laptops or any other electronic gadgets [3]. The electronic lock has realized the function of networking with business servers by adopting NB-IoT (Narrow Band Internet of Things) technology. This mode is currently mainly used in electronic locks such as access control and vehicle control. Compared with the non-networking mode of the electronic lock, the networking mode of the electronic lock can query or monitor the status of the electronic lock in real time through the NB-IoT network because it is connected with the business server. In addition, the electronic lock networking mode can also directly issue the dynamic unlock password according to the demand scenario, which greatly increases the security [4, 5].

These promising technologies bring a new experience and strengthen the efficiency of using electric bicycles. However, the application of new technology can also bring new challenges to the development of intelligent travel applications. The applications not only need to realize all necessary functions, but also need to meet the principles of interaction design: visibility, feedback, constraints, layout, unity of interface, availability, flexibility, efficiency and beauty. And on this basis, the applications should have the brand personality of the travel companies and provide better user experiences in the process of using the electric bicycles.

User experience is playing a major role in our modern life. Human-computer interaction (HCI) is the study of communication between humans and machines, and as the term suggests, the user is essential to this field [6]. We must consider users first in the design of interfaces for communicating with the computer system. User interface consists of guidelines, workflows, color system, design process, etc., which help users to interact with a product [7]. The goals of interface design are to improve user performance, decrease errors and increase user satisfaction [8].

3 Methods

3.1 Participants

A total of 30 participants (9 men and 21 women) were invited to take part in the experiment based on convenience sampling method. They are between 18 and 30 years old and have the experience of operating smart phones. Thus problems in basic operation during the experiment can be prevented. Each group contained 10 participants. All participants finished tasks successfully and then answered a questionnaire about gender, occupation, age, the experience of intelligent travel, user needs, subjective evaluations and so on.

60% of the participants have not used intelligent travel applications. 88.9% of the participants hope to use intelligent travel applications if they have electric bicycles. 90% of the participants would like to control their electric bicycles through an application. It can be seen that the switch lock is one of the most important functions. However, 93.3% of the participants worry that the applications may fail to lock their electric bicycles. In addition, more than half of the participants need the function of authorizing others to use the electric bicycle. 83.3% of the participants need the function of after-sales service.

3.2 Materials and Apparatus

This experiment was conducted on an iPhone XR, with screen size of 6.1-inch, resolution of 1792 × 828 pixels, and iOS 12.3 operating system. Three selected intelligent travel applications have been downloaded onto the phone before the experiment.

The interfaces of software A use strong and contrasting colors, two separate switch lock icons and many other scattered icons (see Fig. 1). The interfaces of software B use strong colors with fewer centralized icons, and the same button is used for locking and unlocking the electric bicycle (see Fig. 2). The interfaces of software C use fewer colors, fewer icons and a unified icon with sliding mode of locking or unlocking the electric bicycle (see Fig. 3).

3.3 Experimental Procedure

The participants were randomly assigned to three groups, and each participant tested only one kind of interface. Participants were provided a briefing on the study. Participants were asked to conduct three tasks with the intelligent travel applications. Task 1: Please find the switch lock icon and perform the operation of unlocking and then locking the electric bicycle; Task 2: Please find the function of authorizing others to use the electric bicycle and click to operate; Task 3: Please find the function that you think can be contacted for on-site maintenance and click. The performance was measured by task operation time.

After completing all the tasks, each participant was required to complete a questionnaire to gather data regarding their subjective evaluations. The System Usability Scale (SUS) [9] was used to assess the usability of interfaces. The SUS consists of ten positive and negative statements. Each statement in the SUS questionnaire was scored using a five-point Likert scale anchored by 1: strongly disagree and 5: strongly agree. The higher the scores of SUS, the better usability of the application.

Fig. 1. The interface design of software A. 剩余电量: Remaining power; 已锁车: Locked; 鸣笛寻车: Press the beep to find the vehicle; 多人用车: The vehicle can be used by more than one person; 骑行导航: Cycling navigation; 启动: start-up; 锁车: locking; 历史轨迹: Historical track; 更多: More.

Fig. 2. The interface design of software B. 开锁: Unlock; 设防: Fortification; 自检: Self-inspection; 打开坐垫: Open the cushion.

Fig. 3. The interface design of software C. 右滑启动车辆: Slide right to start the vehicle; 爱车: Your beloved vehicle; 服务: Service; 我的: My.

4　Results

4.1　Analysis of SUS

The collected data were analyzed by the IBM Statistical Package for the Social Sciences (SPSS) software. The generated results of the SUS questionnaire are shown in Table 1. The one-way analysis of variance (ANOVA) results point out that there was a significant difference in the usability of the three samples ($P = 0.004 < 0.05$).

The results of post-hoc multiple comparison of SUS are shown in Table 2. There is a significant difference between software B and software C ($P = 0.01 < 0.05$). Participants using software C (M = 74.25, Sd = 6.877) gave significantly higher SUS scores than those using the software B (M = 57.7, Sd = 11.989). However, no significant difference

Table 1. Descriptive statistics and one-way ANOVA of SUS

A	B	C	F	P
66.47 (10.664)	57.7 (11.989)	74.25 (6.877)	6.749	0.004*

$\alpha = 0.05$, *P < 0.05

was observed between software A and software B (P = 0.062 > 0.05) and software A and software C (P = 0.069 > 0.05).

Systems with a SUS score of less than 60 are generally considered as products with poor usability. It can be seen that according to the usability of the three samples, there is still room for improvement. The SUS score of software B is the lowest and the SUS score of software C is the highest of the three samples. The usability of software C was good and the interface was easy to use for participants.

Table 2. Post-hoc multiple comparison of SUS

	A	B	C
A		0.062	0.069
B			0.01*
C			

$\alpha = 0.05$, *P < 0.05

4.2 Analysis of Task Operation Time

The results generated from the descriptive statistics and one-way ANOVA of task operation time are shown in Table 3. The results indicated that there was a significant difference in the task operation time of the three samples (P = 0.000 < 0.05).

Table 3. Descriptive statistics and one-way ANOVA of task operation time

	A	B	C	F	P
Task 1	12.186 (3.466)	7.164 (1.916)	5.349 (1.603)	20.617	.000*
Task 2	5.556 (3.491)	56.788 (26.800)	24.176 (8.354)	25.212	.000*
Task 3	6.93 (2.499)	36.682 (14.242)	8.96 (4.419)	36.258	.000*

$\alpha = 0.05$, *P < 0.05

The first task was to lock and unlock an electric bicycle. The results of post-hoc multiple comparison of task 1 operation time are shown in Table 4. There is a significant difference between software A and software B (P = 0.000 < 0.05) and software A and software C (P = 0.000 < 0.05). The task 1 operation time for software B (M = 7.164, Sd = 1.916) and software C (M = 5.349, Sd = 1.603) were both significantly shorter than that for software A (M = 12.186, Sd = 3.466). However, no significant difference was observed between software B and software C (P = 0.111 > 0.05).

Table 4. Post-hoc multiple comparison of task 1 operation time

	A	B	C
A		.000*	.000*
B			0.111
C			

$\alpha = 0.05$, *P < 0.05

The second task was a more difficult task in which participants needed to find the function of authorizing others to use the electric bicycle. The results of post-hoc multiple comparison of task 2 operation time are shown in Table 5. There is a significant difference between software A and software B (P = 0.000 < 0.05), software A and software C (P = 0.017 < 0.05) and software B and software C (P = 0.000 < 0.05). The task 2 operation time for software A (M = 5.556, Sd = 3.491) was significantly shorter than that for software B (M = 56.788, Sd = 26.800) and software C (M = 24.176, Sd = 8.354).

Table 5. Post-hoc multiple comparison of task 2 operation time

	A	B	C
A		.000*	0.017*
B			.000*
C			

$\alpha = 0.05$, *P < 0.05

The third task was to find the function of contacting for maintenance. The results of post-hoc multiple comparison of task 3 operation time are shown in Table 6. There is a significant difference between software A and software B (P = 0.000 < 0.05) and software B and software C (P = 0.000 < 0.05). The task 3 operation time for software A (M = 6.93, Sd = 2.499) and software C (M = 8.96, Sd = 4.419) were both significantly shorter than that for software B (M = 36.682, Sd = 14.242). However, no significant difference was observed between software A and software C (P = 0.607 > 0.05).

Table 6. Post-hoc multiple comparison of task 3 operation time

	A	B	C
A		.000*	0.607
B			.000*
C			

$\alpha = 0.05$, *P < 0.05

4.3 Discussion

The results from the SUS questionnaire show that the interfaces of software C were best and very easy to use for the participants. The usability of the interfaces using fewer colors and a unified switch lock icon with sliding mode was considered significantly better than that of the interfaces using strong colors and the same button with different feedback designs for locking and unlocking.

The analysis of task operation time indicate that interface design can affect the usability of intelligent travel applications for electric bicycles. For the task of locking and unlocking an electric bicycle, the interfaces using strong and contrasting colors, two separate switch lock icons and many other scattered icons were the most inefficient. This might be because using two separate switch lock icons make the interface more complex and there is no feedback when the icons are clicked. Users may click the icon repeatedly to make sure that they have locked the electric bicycle successfully.

For the task of finding the functions of authorizing others to use the electric bicycle, the interfaces of software B using strong colors with fewer centralized icons were the most inefficient. Perhaps users need to click the bicycle icon on the interface of software B to enter the function selection area, but there is no visual cue about which one to click. The functional icon without good affordance can easily be ignored or misunderstood as a decoration.

For the task of finding the functions of contacting for maintenance, the interfaces of software B still were the most inefficient. A possible explanation for this phenomenon is that the after-sales function and cycling function are not on the same interface of software B, so it takes a longer time.

Through detailed analysis of the data collected from the experimental samples, it can be seen that interface design may lead to significant differences in the usability of intelligent travel applications.

5   Conclusion

This study explored how interface design affect the user experience of intelligent travel applications for electric bicycles. Three design recommendations contributed by this study are listed as follows: (1) Using a sliding button to lock and unlock an electric bicycle can improve users' subjective evaluations of usability and their efficiency. (2) The main functional icons need to be integrated into a clear interface and have good affordance to improve users' efficiency. (3) It is recommended to use fewer colors on the interfaces of intelligent travel applications.

Finally, the results obtained in this study may help the developers of intelligent travel applications manage their products more efficiently. Future studies may focus on the design of visual and auditory feedback for electric bicycles.

Acknowledgements. This work was funded by Philosophy and Social Science Planning Project of Guangdong Province [GD22XYS31], and STU Scientific Research Initiation Grant [STF22003].

References

1. Wang, L.: The market size of two-wheel electric vehicles will reach 100 billion, and the new national standard will intensify the industry reshuffle. Electr. Bicycle **2**, 3–4 (2020). (in Chinese)
2. Mu, D.: Where is the innovation and pride of domestic electric bicycles? China Internet Week **639**(09), 22–23 (2017). (in Chinese)
3. Reddy, V.M., Vinay, N., Pokharna, T., Jha, S.S.K.: Internet of things enabled smart switch. In: Proceedings of the Thirteenth International Conference on Wireless and Optical Communications Networks (WOCN), pp. 1–4. Hyderabad, India (2016)
4. Tian, C.Y.: Design and implementation of electronic lock security system based on smart phone controlled. University of Electronic Science and Technology of China (2020). (in Chinese)
5. Zhang, Z.F.: NB-IoT low-rate narrowband IoT communication technology status and development research. Wirel. Internet Technol. **15**(12), 12–13 (2018). (in Chinese)
6. Norman, D.A.: The Invisible Computer. MIT Press, Cambridge (1999)
7. Sharma, V., Tiwari, A.K.: A study on user interface and user experience designs and its tools. World J. Res. Rev. **12**(6), 41–44 (2021)
8. Cristina, M.Y., Pere, P., Javier, V., Francisco, J.P.: User experience to improve the usability of a vision-based interface. Interact. Comput. **22**(6), 594–605 (2010)
9. Brooke, J.: SUS: a quick and dirty usability scale. In: Jordan, P.W., Thomas, B., Weerdmeester, B.A., McClelland, A.L. (eds.) Usability Evaluation in Industry, pp. 189–194. Taylor and Francis, London (1996)

Tinkering in Sunway City: Sustainable Transportation and Mobility for Older Dwellers

Ka Po Wong[1,2(✉)], Pei-Lee Teh[3], and Jing Qin[1]

[1] Centre for Smart Health, School of Nursing, The Hong Kong Polytechnic University, Kowloon, Hong Kong
portia.wong@polyu.edu.hk
[2] Department of Applied Social Sciences, The Hong Kong Polytechnic University, Kowloon, Hong Kong
[3] School of Business, Gerontechnology Laboratory, Monash University Malaysia Selangor Darul Ehsan, 47500 Bandar Sunway, Malaysia

Abstract. Age-friendly transportation design is an important factor in fostering mobility for older adults. Mobility is associated with older adults' lifestyle, well-being and quality of life. The government of Malaysia is dedicated to developing an age-friendly city to address the rapid expansion of the ageing population. Sunway City is a township in Malaysia, seamlessly linking public transport such as Bus Rapid Transit (BRT), free shuttle buses and elevated canopy walk. Therefore, it is necessary to examine the design of transportation in Sunway City to achieve the aspiration of an age-friendly city. Focus groups and individual interviews were conducted to examine the attitudes and experiences towards different transportation modes in Sunway City, in which 32 older adults were interviewed. It was found that the transportation design did not fully meet the criteria of age-friendly transportation suggested by the World Health Organization (WHO) because the physical design did not adequately address the needs of older people with physical and cognitive impairments. Education on respecting older adults should be enhanced among young adults for the purpose of creating an age-friendly community. The findings provide insights for Malaysian authorities to optimise the transportation systems and services in future.

Keywords: Sustainable Mobility · Transportation System · Age-Friendly City · Ageing Population · Active Ageing

1 Introduction

Ageing is one of the major impacts of ongoing global demographic change. According to the estimation of the World Health Organization (WHO) [1], there will be approximately 2 billion people aged 60 and over, representing 22% of the global population. In Malaysia, the Department of Statistics has reported that the percentage of people aged 65 or above is about 7.0% and it is estimated that the ageing population will reach 15% by 2030 [2]. This change in the demographics of the ageing population may affect the allocation of healthcare resources [3]. Growing costs in healthcare services may be induced by the ageing population due to the increasing use of treatment and health care.

© The Author(s), under exclusive license to Springer Nature Switzerland AG 2023
P.-L. P. Rau (Ed.): HCII 2023, LNCS 14022, pp. 417–428, 2023.
https://doi.org/10.1007/978-3-031-35936-1_31

Society value mobility in ageing as walking and driving are core to healthy ageing [4]. Maintaining mobility for older adults is not only good for their physical body, but also for their mental health. Staying active is beneficial to the bone, muscles and heart, emotions and wellbeing [5]. WHO advocated the necessity of an age-friendly environment for older adults that supportive and inclusive environments assist in coping with ill health, disability, dependence or loneliness among the ageing population [6]. The transportation system is the key factor contributing to active and healthy ageing. Barriers to transportation may result in less frequency of moving around in the communities among the ageing population. Visual and mobility impairments are the main physical challenges for older adults to use personal vehicles or public transportation services. Lacking an age-friendly design on transportation services may impact the health and wellbeing of older adults due to being unable to access healthcare appointments. With the ageing population in developing communities, the challenges were compounded [7].

A review regarding age-friendly communities conducted by Torku et al. [8] indicated only one age-friendly city and community research publication from Malaysia among the 98 extracted publications, possibly implying that the investigation of age-friendly creation and the importance of the age-friendly concept might be neglected in Malaysia. Although several empirical studies have examined the age-friendly environment of Malaysia (e.g. [9–11]), these studies did not attach great attention to sustainable mobility for older adults. Considering the lack of previous studies examining the mobility of Malaysia for older adults, it is crucial to conduct a study to gain insight into Malaysia's transport system and services and further improve them in response to an ageing population. The study aimed to explore the perceptions of older people about transportation and mobility at Sunway City in Kuala Lumpur. The findings informed local and central government policies to support the ongoing development of communities to achieve age-friendly goals.

2   Literature Review

A considerable volume of research has explored sustainable transportation systems for active ageing and evaluated the effects of ageing-friendly transportation systems design. The study of Yuan et al. [12] accessed the ten dimensions affecting the use of bus services among older passengers in Harbin, China, including, reliability, time schedule, route characteristics, ticketing, driver service, convenience, safety and security, cleanliness, comfort, and information services. It was found that the older adults emphasized the dimensions of safety, convenience and driver service, while time schedule and reliability were less important to the participants. Han et al. [13] pointed out that public transportation accessibility was an important factor influencing ageing mobility. The criteria of public transportation accessibility included travel connectivity to destinations, public transport frequency and reliability, and proximity to bus stops on foot. Reinhard et al. [14] argued that free bus passes were related to the increased use of public transportation among the ageing population, which could promote their cognitive health. Sustainable transportation provides various benefits for active ageing, whereas the inappropriate design of transportation systems may lead to different levels of difficulties and harm to older adults.

The growth of the ageing population implied the number of older pedestrians, drivers and cyclists increases. Extensive literature demonstrated the decline of pedestrian and driving skills in older adults [15, 16]. An inconsiderate design of transportation systems and services might hamper the mobility of older adults and adversely affect their health at different levels. Adorno et al. [17] indicated that unsuitable transportation designs limited older adults to access health care, products and services, resulting in cutting off from familiar habits and social networks as well as marginalising the ageing population. Age-friendly transportation systems affect not only the mobility of the ageing population but also their physical lifestyles and wellbeing. Casado-Sanz et al. [18] stated that the ageing population was associated with different levels of road accidents, leading to severe injuries and fatal outcomes.

Given the importance of sustainable transportation for the ageing population, improving the transportation systems and services for older adults in Sunway City is of utmost importance. We examined the transportation in accordance with the age-friendly strategy for transportation suggested by WHO includes 1) affordability and reliability to all older adults, 2) adequate connecting routes in all areas, 3) safety and accessibility shelters, stops and stations, 4) provision of priority seating on all transportation options and 5) safe and comfortable transportation options [1]. These strategies have been applied in many studies regarding sustainable transportation for ageing.

3 Materials and Methods

3.1 Sampling

A purposive sampling method was adopted in this study. Participants who were living in Sunway City and aged 50 years old or above were eligible. Participants were recruited via advertisements in social media and community centers. The potential participants were contacted, and the aims and entire nature of the study were clearly explained to the participants. The informed and written consent was obtained. Ethical approval was received from The Monash University Human Research Ethics Committee study (Review Reference: 2020–19083-41584).

3.2 Studied Field

The field of this study is Sunway City, which is a transect of the population typical of those who live in Malaysia. The site includes a variety of built environments and infrastructure which poses challenges and opportunities in older adults' mobility. All participants took the bus rapid transit (BRT) Sunway line and Sunway free shuttle bus and experienced the Canopy Walk in Sunway (see Fig. 1). BRT is interconnected with the Kelana Jaya Line and the KTM Line. The free shuttle bus is a circular line with 13 stops departing from Persiaran Lagoon or Sunway Pyramid. Canopy Walk connects Sunway Pyramid, Menara Sunway, The Pinnacle Sunway, Sunway Geo Residence, Sunway Lagoon Club, Palm Ville Condominium, Sunway Medical Centre, Sunway University, Monash University, Sunway Lagoon BRT Station.

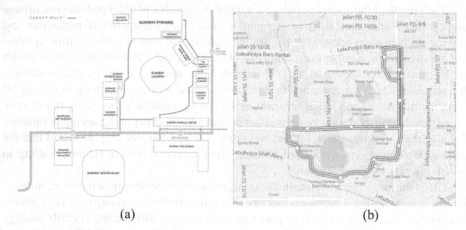

(a)   (b)

Fig. 1. (a) The grey line shows the route of the BRT and the green line shows the route of Canopy Walk. (Source: https://www.sunway.city/kualalumpur/getting-around/); (b) The orange line indicates the route map of the free shuttle bus and the white spots indicate the locations of 13 stops. (Source: https://moovitapp.com/index/en/public_transit-line-SCTY-Kuala_Lumpur-1082-901524-66255888-0)

3.3 Data Collection

Two research team members undertook the focus groups and individual interviews. An interview guideline was provided for the interviewers to ensure the key subject areas were addressed in the interview. Examples of questions in the interview guideline included "What did you dislike about travelling by public transportation system (i.e. using a smartphone app, walking to BRT station, waiting at the shuttle bus station etc.) within Sunway City?", "What do you think about the specialized transportation services for people with disabilities in Sunway City?" and "Do you feel that Sunway Free Shuttle Bus can help to improve mobility within Sunway City?". The participants were allowed to share any relevant opinions at the end of the interview or discussion.

All focus groups and individual interviews were digitally recorded and transcribed verbatim. All participants were assigned pseudonyms and identifying information was removed to ensure anonymity. All focus groups and individual interviews were conducted in the Gerontechnology Laboratory of Monash University Malaysia and were approximately 30–60 min in duration.

3.4 Data Analysis

The collected data were input into NVivo 12 Pro software for qualitative data analysis. The analysis usually involved a three-step coding process, namely, open coding, axial coding and selective coding [19, 20]. In the first step, the verbatim data are progressively scrutinized. We segmented, detected and categorised the data to identify various conditions. The direct responses and reactions of the participants towards the conditions were clearly identified as codes. In the second step, we combined the categories and subcategories and constructed unique categories from each related code for explaining

Table 1. Demographic characteristics

Variables	Example	Frequency ($n = 32$)	Percentage (%)
Gender	Male	21	65.6%
	Female	11	34.4%
Marital status	Married	22	68.8%
	Divorced	2	6.3%
	Never married	4	12.5%
	Widowed	4	12.5%
Educational level	Postgraduate	5	15.6%
	Degree/ Professional	9	28.1%
	Diploma/ Pre-U	8	25%
	Secondary	9	28.1%
	Primary or below	1	3.1%
Employment status	Retired	19	59.4%
	Full time	6	18.8%
	Part time	4	12.5%
	Others	3	9.4%
Ethnicity	Chinese	24	75%
	Indian	4	12.5%
	Malay	2	6.3%
	Others	2	6.3%

the phenomena. We repeatedly collected, interpreted and inducted the data until no new data or the existence of saturated categories and subcategories. In the third step, we construct a core category to link all categories.

4   Results

A total of 32 participants were interviewed, with nine focus groups and 10 individual face-to-face interviews. All interviews were conducted from October 2019 to January 2020. 65.6% of the participants were females. The age range of all participants was 50-year-old to 84-year-old and the median age is 64. About 68.8% of the participants were married and 68.7% of them had at least a degree in tertiary education. 10 participants were still working. The demographic characteristics of the participants are shown in Table 1.

The analysis of the data mainly demonstrated the four aspects of the transportation systems and services in Sunway City, including (1) BRT, (2) free shuttle bus, (3) canopy walkway and (4) the overall condition of Sunway City. For BRT and free shuttle bus, internal design, linking facilities and other relevant issues were categorised.

4.1 Bus Rapid Transit

The positive impression of BRT was mainly convenient, accessible, well-maintained, clean, air-conditioned, timely, frequent, comfortable and user-friendly.

The dissatisfaction with the internal design of BRT included not enough seats, inappropriate arrangement of seats (upper level with more seats, lower level with seats), no priority seats for disabled people and older adults, unobvious signs, not enough language on the signs, unobvious announcements and small bus size.

"Seats are not so many a... the bus I'm in this, should have more seats" PID_010, S10_G10

"You see the bus there are two tiers, the upper, consider the upper level more seats, the lower-level lesser seats, right? So, that part of it also needs to improve. But what if they are more, say more older people it's not so convenient for them to climb upstairs." PID_027, S10_G10

"Even in back to BRT and shuttle bus also I don't see priority seats for handicapped and the elderly." PID_085, S15_G15

The facilities linking BRT that the participants were rather unhappy with were no shelter and seating in the station, a large platform gap, a lack of waiting area in the stations, small station size, no ramp for disabilities with wheelchairs, unclear signages in the station, more stops to go to other places, provision of more shuttle buses, lifts and elevators in under maintenance state and no location guide of lifts and elevators.

"There was no shelter [at the waiting area of BRT]." PID_023, S17_G17.

"The gap between the platform and the bus looks a bit threatening, but it can't be helped." PID_013, S6_G06

"I tell you they should have ramps for the disabled and that keeps knocking off my mind just now." PID_016, S7_G07

"Probably the signage is actually before that is not so big... Not visible." PID_018, S11_G11

Other issues related to BRT were costly bus fares, low bus frequency, inconsiderate drivers, lack of courtesy among young adults, insufficient promotion of the service, and inadequacy and no police patrol for traffic management.

"Maybe a little bit lower fare... Maybe RM0.70" PID_069, S18_G18.

"I believe the driver. He may slow down a bit, I don't think there is a need to hurry. He may slow down a bit in the... around while driving down and the curve has basically, the curve was when a bit em... bad. Into the curve." PID_016, S7_G07

"But it is never mentioned can you please give up your seats for the elderly people? And this never happens, when you are on the bus, it is either the young people sitting down there, pretending to be sleeping or they are playing with their phone. They just don't care, a damn about the elderly people." PID_030, S9_G09.

4.2 Free Shuttle Bus

Most older participants were satisfied with the driver's comfort, air-conditioned environment, accessibility, cleanliness, safety, patience and courtesy.

The internal design of the free shuttle bus that the participants were disappointed with included insufficient seats, no priority seats for disabled people and older adults, no designated areas for wheelchair users, small bus size, and unclear and small signage.

"I don't see any priority seats. Ah, not as like in the LRT they put the priority seats ...[it] need to improve on this." PID_063, S12_G12

"For senior citizens, for that mobility challenged, I am not talking about wheelchairs for people who are on walking sticks and all those there is no place for them." PID_032, S9_G09

"[Free shuttle bus]'s too small. People get on it and before you know it its full and the seats are taken up." PID_004, S2_G02

The other comments about facilities linking free shuttle bus were no ramp for wheelchair users, no seats and shelter areas at the station, no waiting areas for disabled people and older adults, small signage at the bus station and inadequate stations to connect more places.

"I think they might want to consider wheel-chair users...you might have a rump...you know? And that could be a gadget which should help them either, no they could roll onto it and the thing could be mechanically raised and they could roll into the bus." PID_004, S2_G02

"The waiting area is not proper. I mean there is no proper waiting or sitting la to wait for the bus." PID_069, S18_G18

Other feedback related to the free shuttle bus included low bus frequency, irregular bus timings, considerate drivers (car jerking), lack of courtesy among youngsters, insufficient promotion of the free shuttle bus, inconsiderate drivers, and no specific area catering for bicycles. Some participants complained that the application (app) was not reliable, they did not know how to download and use it, and the app did not contain enough description.

"We didn't have the chance. The waiting time is too long. One hour till the bus is not here." PID_027 & PID_010, S10_G10

"We don't know how to use or never install [app] then he cannot use this service." PID_064, S12_G12.

4.3 Canopy Walkway

Positive feedback for canopy walkways among older residents includes convenience, cleanliness, safety, adequate space for wheelchair users, top cover, and adequate connections to different places.

Regarding the design of the canopy walkway the participants were relatively discontented with the materials of the road, insufficient branches in the walkway to connect different places, unclear and small signage, no signage at the junctions, no cover or shelter on the side of the walkway, long distance, steep ramps, no air-conditioners, the inadequacy of elevator and lift, lifts and elevators in under maintenance state and inconvenience for wheelchair users. Some participants also pointed out that there was an insufficient promotion for the elevated canopy walk and thus they might not be aware of it.

"Dislike maybe during the raining season because it will be slippery." PID_001, S1_G01

"But I have experience before there is a puddle of water you know. I took the how a… I park somewhere near the medical centre there. The shops there then I walk using that pedestrian… using that canopy walk. I walk to the medical centre Sunway. I think it was maybe after the rain. So there was a lot of water." PID_069, S18_G18

"Whether the side cover-up…is there any cover-up. Because sometime when it rains, the water will flood." PID_060, S19_G19

"That sign a, earlier when coming to the junction there is no sign." PID_033, S11_G11

"But the lift [the BRT station lift to push up to the Canopy Walk] also not working." PID_063, S12_G12.

4.4 Sunway City

Most seniors are satisfied with greenery, landscaping, well-maintained facilities, safety, cleanliness, and comfort.

The most concerning issues among all participants in Sunway city were the lack of parking areas and severely congested traffic. The transportation systems and services that needed to be improved also included interlocking pavers that make buses a bit bumpy, poor condition of roads (e.g., popped-up tiles or pavers), imprecise signages, signages being blocked by different objects, some potholes, negative behaviour patterns of taxi drivers, steep staircase, inadequate travel information and insufficient specialized transportation services for older people and people with disabilities.

"Then sometimes the drain cover is not properly I mean sometimes is missing or sometimes there is a hole there very dangerous. Especially even main road sometimes porthole also they don't repair quick enough which is very dangerous." PID_069, S18_G18

"I find Malaysian signages quite confusing. Even at the BRT station. The signages are quite confusing also. Probably you might get used to it, then you might understand what it's trying to do." PID_002, S3_G03

"Taxi [drivers] are very selective, they choose the hour, and they choose the place you go. They reject you." PID_060, S19_G19

"The staircase [I] go up and down [are] very steep. That's the steepest staircase I've ever seen." PID_013, S6_G06.

5 Discussion

This qualitative study demonstrated that the transportation systems and services in Sunway City might not fully meet the expectations of older adults. There is clearly an opportunity for improvement in the mobility of Sunway City's ageing population because the older adults have numerous recommendations on current transportation systems and services, for instance, lowering the fare, increasing the connecting routes in some areas, installation of more shelters, stops and stations and provision of more priority seating on all transportation options and improving the overall accessibility of transport.

The government of Malaysia is dedicated to transforming the capital city and its surrounding municipalities into a vibrant and livable metropolitan area [21]. Malaysia Smart City Framework (MSCF) has been formulated by the government to guide different stakeholders to plan, develop and implement smart city initiatives in Malaysia [22]. The findings of this study indicated that the ongoing development of smart city plans in Malaysia may have neglected the initiatives in addressing the dynamically increasing ageing population, especially from the perspective of transportation systems and services. The participants pointed out several problems hindering their use of the transport systems in Sunway City. The results further support the argument of Yuan et al. [12] that older adults cared about the safety and convenience of transportation and the attitudes of drivers. The findings corroborate the ideas of Reinhard et al. [14] that affordability was an important factor affecting mobility among the ageing population. The lower the fare, the more use of public transport. It was found that accessibility of the transportation systems tremendously affected the mobility of older adults, which is consistent with previous research [13].

The results of this study highlighted the need for developing age-friendly transportation systems and services for older dwellers in Sunway City. Physical and cognitive impairment in older adults probably reduces the use of transportation and age-friendly transportation systems may improve their mobility. The design of the transportation system in Sunway City seems to neglect the needs of older adults. For instance, vision impairments or physical disabilities are common among older people, whereas the word font in the signage was small, insufficient priority seats were provided, the pavements were uneven with potholes and the lifts and elevators were always not functioning. Furthermore, it is important to promote community, education, training and awareness (CETA) among the young adults in Sunway City as some participants commented that some young people, who used mobile phones and pretended to sleep, did not voluntarily give them a seat on the buses. In addition, all participants indicated that inadequate public parking is problematic in Sunway City. The parking issues may affect the accessibility to healthcare services among older people [17], which might negatively affect their health in the long run.

The findings of this study suggest that the design of the transportation systems and services in Sunway City is not fully age-friendly and sustainable enough. The government and municipal authorities may need to consider the changes in the physical and cognitive functions of older adults in the process of designing transportation systems and services. The practical strategies included the increase of font size on signages, provision of clear directions and more languages on signages, provisions of more priority seats for older people and disabilities, facilities for disabled with wheelchairs and shelter areas and increasing the connecting route between different places. Increasing the number of public parking is the key challenge for the government of Malaysia. Meanwhile, the concept of respecting and caring for senior citizens should be strengthened among civilians. Combining the tangible age-friendly built environment and intangible respect for older adults can enhance the harmony between different generations in the community.

This study was not without limitations. First, the small sample size may not completely reflect the insufficiency of the transportation systems and services. Thus, more older adults need to be interviewed in the future to solicit their lived experience which possibly provides more insights for the local authorities to optimise the systems and facilities. Second, this study utilised a qualitative method for data analysis. Therefore, empirical studies are recommended to conduct in future to identify the causation between the design of age-friendly transportation and mobility for ageing. The weightings and significance of the factors of sustainable transportation and mobility can be identified through empirical studies. Third, the completeness of the interviews might be affected by the unwillingness to spend much time on the interview among the participants. Some interviewees seem to answer in a rush, possibly leading to the omission of details related to their commuting experiences. In-depth interviews are suggested to undertake in future studies. The key steps of conducting in-depth interviews included making a list of topics that must be covered, scheduling an interview at a time and date chosen by the respondents, setting a maximum duration with less exhaustion, observing the body expressions and gestures, and maintaining ethics throughout the process.

6 Conclusion

The study set out to explore the perceptions of older dwellers about transportation and mobility at Sunway City in Kuala Lumpur. Findings are based on the focus groups and individual interviews with 32 older adults residing in Sunway City. It was found the affordability, reliability, connecting routes of different areas, safety accessibility of shelters, stops and stations, provision of priority seating and the comfortability of transportation had different levels of shortcomings. These limitations may affect the mobility of the ageing and their physical and mental wellbeing. The government may formulate more strategies to promote an age-friendly community and implement policies to enhance the built environment to be age-friendly.

Acknowledgement. This project was supported by Monash University Malaysia (Grant Code: SCG-2018–02-SCI) and a grant of Project of Strategic Importance of The Hong Kong Polytechnic University (project no 1-ZE2Q).

References

1. World Health Organization: Global age-friendly cities: A guide (2007). https://www.jcafc. hk/uploads/docs/Global-Age-friendly-Cities-A-Guide-1.pdf
2. Yang, S.L., Woon, Y.L., Teoh, C.C.O., Leong, C.T., Lim, R.B.L.: Adult palliative care 2004–2030 population study: estimates and projections in Malaysia. BMJ Support. Palliat. Care **12**, 1–8 (2020). https://doi.org/10.1136/bmjspcare-2020-002283

3. Mafauzy, M.: The problems and challenges of the aging population of Malaysia. Malays. J. Med. Sci. **7**(1), 1–3 (2000)
4. Satariano, W.A., Guralnik, J.M., Jackson, R.J., Marottoli, R.A., Phelan, E.A., Prohaska, T.R.: Mobility and aging: new directions for public health action. Am. J. Public Health **102**(8), 1508–1515 (2012). https://doi.org/10.2105/ajph.2011.300631
5. Liotta, G., et al.: Active ageing in Europe: adding healthy life to years. Front. Med. **5**, 123 (2018). https://doi.org/10.3389/fmed.2018.00123
6. World Health Organization: Creating age-friendly environments in Europe. A tool for local policy-makers and planners. (2016)
7. Steels, S.: Key characteristics of age-friendly cities and communities: a review. Cities **47**, 45–52 (2015). https://doi.org/10.1016/j.cities.2015.02.0
8. Torku, A., Chan, A.P.C., Yung, E.H.K.: Age-friendly cities and communities: a review and future directions. Ageing Soc. **41**(10), 2242–2279 (2020). https://doi.org/10.1017/S01446 86X20000239
9. Elsawahli, H., ShahAli, A., Ahmad, F., AlObaidi, K.M.: Evaluating potential environmental variables and active aging in older adults for age-friendly neighborhoods in Malaysia. J. Hous. Elderly **31**(1), 74–92 (2017). https://doi.org/10.1080/02763893.2016.1268
10. Hamid, M.B.B.: Domains influencing Malaysia in achieving age-friendly nation status. Asian Proc. Soc. Sci. **9**(1), 321–322 (2022). https://doi.org/10.31580/apss.v9i1.2387
11. Tiraphat, S., et al.: Age-friendly environments in ASEAN plus three: case studies from Japan, Malaysia, Myanmar, Vietnam, and Thailand. Int. J. Environ. Res. Public Health **17**(12), 4523 (2020). https://doi.org/10.3390/ijerph17124523
12. Yuan, Y., Yang, M., Wu, J., Rasouli, S., Lei, D.: Assessing bus transit service from the perspective of elderly passengers in Harbin. China. Int. J. Sustain. Transp. **13**(10), 761–776 (2019). https://doi.org/10.1080/15568318.2018.1512
13. Han, J., Chan, E.H.W., Qian, Q.K., Yung, E.H.K.: Achieving sustainable urban development with an ageing population: an "age-friendly city and community" approach. Sustainability **13**(15), 8614 (2021). https://doi.org/10.3390/su13158614
14. Reinhard, E., Carrino, L., Courtin, E., van Lenthe, F.J., Avendano, M.: Public transportation use and cognitive function in older age: a quasiexperimental evaluation of the free bus pass policy in the United Kingdom. Am. J. Epidemiol. **188**(10), 1774–1783 (2019). https://doi. org/10.1093/aje/kwz149
15. Castellucci, H.I., Bravo, G., Arezes, P.M., Lavallière, M.: Are interventions effective at improving driving in older drivers?: A systematic review. BMC Geriatr. **20**, 125 (2020). https://doi.org/10.1186/s12877-020-01512-z
16. Di Stefano, M., Macdonald, W.: Assessment of older drivers: relationships among on-road errors, medical conditions and test outcome. J. Safety Res. **34**(4), 415–429 (2003). https:// doi.org/10.1016/j.jsr.2003.09.010
17. Adorno, G., Fields, N., Cronley, C., Parekh, R., Magruder, K.: Ageing in a low-density urban city: transportation mobility as a social equity issue. Ageing Soc. **38**(2), 296–320 (2018). https://doi.org/10.1017/S0144686X16000994
18. Casado-Sanz, N., Guirao, B., Gálvez-Pérez, D.: Population ageing and rural road accidents: analysis of accident severity in traffic crashes with older pedestrians on Spanish crosstown roads. Res. Transp. Bus. Manage. **30**, 100377 (2019). https://doi.org/10.1016/j.rtbm.2019. 100377
19. Corbin, J., Strauss, A.: Basics of Qualitative Research: Techniques and Procedures for Developing Grounded Theory, 3rd edn. Sage, Thousand Oaks (2008)
20. Eaves, Y.D.: A synthesis technique for grounded theory data analysis. J. Adv. Nurs. **35**(5), 654–663 (2001). https://doi.org/10.1046/j.1365-2648.2001.01897.x

21. Yau, K.L.A., Lau, S.L., Lin, M.W.Q., Rahman, M.S.A.: Towards a smart city: the case of greater Kuala Lumpur in Malaysia. In: International Conference on Frontiers of Communications, Networks and Applications (ICFCNA 2014 –Malaysia), pp. 1–6 (2014). https://doi.org/10.1049/cp.2014.1393

22. Lim, S.B., Malek, J.A., Hussain, M.Y., Tahir, Z.: Malaysia smart city framework: a trusted framework for shaping smart Malaysian citizenship? In: Augusto, J.C. (ed.) Handbook of Smart Cities, pp. 1–24. Springer International Publishing, Cham (2020). https://doi.org/10.1007/978-3-030-15145-4_34-1

Study on Narrative Visualization Design of Rare and Endangered Plants in Deserts

Jinxuan Xie and Jun Wu(⊠)

School of Art and Design, Division of Arts, Shenzhen University, Guangdong,
Shenzhen 518061, People's Republic of China
junwu2006@hotmail.com

Abstract. Protection of rare and endangered plants remains to be the world hot topic all the time. As an important part of the ecological system, rare and endangered plants possess ecological value, economic value, medicinal value, etc., and play a very important role in ecological environmental protection. Narrative visualization combines narratology with information visualization to form a visualization mode for various territories, and creates a new dissemination mode for rare and endangered plants. This study puts forward a study architecture for exploring narrative visualization of rare and endangered plants in deserts, and designs the narrative visualization design path for rare and endangered plants in deserts based on analysis of the dissemination of existing rare and endangered plants to provide reference for following dissemination and popularization.

Keywords: Rare and endangered plants · narrative visualization · desert protection · environmental protection dissemination

1 Preface

Biodiversity provides the material basis for human survival. China attaches great importance to biodiversity conservation [1]. However, because of the lack of knowledge about rare and endangered plants, people's awareness of conservation is weak [2]. In recent years, due to human destruction and deteriorating natural environment, many rare and endangered plants have been severely damaged. In addition, the number of plentiful rare and endangered plants has declined dramatically, thus leading to extinction [3]. However, these rare and endangered plants are valuable in the development of ecology, economy, and medicine, etc. Also, they play a significant role in ecological environment protection [4]. Biodiversity provides the material basis for the development of human society [5]. With the increasing impact of human activities and climate change, biodiversity is facing an unprecedented crisis [6]. Research shows that there are nine rare and endangered plants under national key protection in the Kubuqi Desert area of Inner Mongolia. The nine plants are Ammopiptanthus nanus, Tetraena mongolica Maxim, sacsaoul, liquorice, Potaninia mongolica Maxim, Calligonum mongolicum Turcz, Amygdalus mongolica (Maxim.) Ricker, Ephedra intermedin Schrenk, and Populus euphratica. These plants, with obvious regional characteristics, are valuable in wind prevention, sand fixation,

P.-L. P. Rau (Ed.): HCII 2023, LNCS 14022, pp. 429–443, 2023.
https://doi.org/10.1007/978-3-031-35936-1_32

and soil improvement, playing a significant role in local ecological protection [7]. From 1991 to 2017, through the protection of rare and endangered plants and other methods, progress was achieved in desertification control in the Kubuqi Desert, and the sand areas were reduced from 45.76% to 28.66% [8], which provides a good reference for global desertification control. Because of human activities such as excessive grazing, reclamation, excavation, and truncation [2], every year, a large number of rare and endangered plants become extinct with the drastic declining in their numbers [3]. Nearly 200 of the 4000 ~ 5000 types of endangered plant species in China have become extinct [9]. In the process of combating desertification, apart from carrying out scientific work related to desertification control and sand fixation, it's also important to promote and popularize the knowledge related to desertification control and protection of endangered desert plants. It is worthwhile to study how to make more people aware of the importance of desert management and take active part in protecting endangered desert plants through communication methods. The existing programs are mainly based on science popularization, focusing on infographics, popular science videos, and other traditional forms of science popularization. However, these traditional science popularization methods are scattered in content distribution and insufficient in breadth and depth [10].

Narrative visualization is an emerging comprehensive study formed by the integration of narratology and visualization. It utilized certain narrative rhetoric to endow visualization results with a story-like effect, which can improve people's efficiency and memory in interpreting data and information [11], thus making it easier for users to obtain and understand scientific knowledge. Therefore, studying the ecological value of rare and endangered plants in the Kubuqi Desert is important for global biodiversity conservation. On one hand, it can help people understand the ecological value of these plants; on the other hand, it can establish the awareness of preserving biodiversity and protecting rare and endangered plants, and also provide a reference for biodiversity conservation.

This study, based on the research of three rare and endangered plants (namely, ammopiptanthus nanus, Tetraena mongolica Maxim, and sacsaoul) in the Kubuqi Desert of Inner Mongolia, aims to popularize and disseminate the ecological value of the rare and endangered plants of the desert through narrative visualization and touchscreen interaction. The goals of this study are as follows.

1) To investigate existing dissemination of rare and endangered plants in the Kubuqi Desert.
2) To present the ecological value of rare and endangered plants by narrative visualization so as to appeal to people for protecting rare and endangered plants.

2   Literature Review

2.1   Studies on Dissemination of Rare and Endangered Plants

Effective preserving and rational utilizing plant diversity are the basis of sustainable development of the human society [12]. However, rare and endangered plants occur only in some specific ecological environments due to natural factor and human factor [1]. They may become extinct if not being well protected. According to data, the extinction rate of plants is 100 to 1000 folds of the natural extinction rate [13]. The extinction of rare and endangered plants has an influence not only on biodiversity, but also on the survival environment of the human being. As an important part of biodiversity, rare and endangered plants have attracted much attention of the international community for rational studying and protecting them [14].

As for study on dissemination of rare and endangered plants, most of existing studies focus on basis from the perspectives of botany and environmentology [14, 15]. As for botany, most of exiting studies disseminate rare and endangered plants mainly by images and texts. As for environmentology, most of existing studies disseminate rare and endangered plants mainly by books and figures. Although these studies play a part in study on dissemination of rare and endangered plants, their designs are not original enough, their method consists mainly of the conventional media, their contents are boring, and thus they cannot attract enough attention of common citizens. The arcane contents and single dissemination means can hardly attract interest of people, and as a result people little about the related contents and the dissemination works poorly.

2.2 Study on Narrative Visualization

At present, most visualizations are interpreted by data, texts, etc. However, when people read the information by themselves, they always have cognitive problems of lacking interest in reading, difficulties in understanding, and forgetting [16]. Narrative visualization design is a visual expression means for enhancing people's cognitive ability by studying visual representation of abstract data [17]. It can simplify complex concepts, reveal trends and information hidden in data [11], and help users to acquire and remember presented information [18]. Narrative visualization can be used in various fields, can well convert information in various formats into story editions, and build the emotional connection with users more quickly to help users understand information better [19].

Narrative visualization is featured by story which helps us understand the past of things and deduce future. Johnson and MacIntyre think storytelling supasses communication and can arouse violent affective commitment and resonance of readers [16]. Normally, visualized works only present knwoledge of the topic logically and simply, but they are a little boring and are hard to be understood by users [20]. Narrative visualization design presents design activity connotations by narratology theory and method, and reveals the story behind data to users by arranging, organizing and expressing a series of data [21]. It meets both visual and spiritual requirements of users, enables users to participate in data, builds and leads communication, arouse users' insight, feelings, association and affective commitment to enhance users' thinking and understanding on dissiminated scientific knowledge [22]. However, only a few practices and studies are narrative visualization design for protecting rare and endangered plants, and these theoretical studies are not complete enough. Most narrative visualization studies are for computer, medical treatment, etc., and only a small amount are for dissemination of protection of rare and endangered plants.

Narrative visualization design is significant for dissemination of rare and endangered plants. Narrative visualization design is more narrative than information visualization, enhances relevance among complex information, builds the emotional connection with users [23]. Arouses emotional resonance of users, and can more easialy builds awarness of users for protecting vegetation diversity. Compared with the single and boring conventional scientific knowledge dissemination means, it can systematically analyze and design cumbersome data and text information, transmit extracted information to audiences simply and efficiently in the form of picture elements to convert logic texts into visual images, make dissemination of scientific knowledge more jaunty [24], help users to understand the knoweldge and enhance the efficiency of information acquisition by users.

Based on narrative visualization design, this study enriches the disseminated scientific knowledge of rare and endangered plants in the Kubuqi Desert and makes it more visual and interesting mainly by encoding of images and story edition in order to make users more willing to and more easily undestand ecological value of related rare and endangered plants, better protect them and biodiversity.

3   Methodology

Information visualization design encodes knowledge by graphic symbols [25]. It is for storying information and helping users to acquire knowledge during interaction, and possesses the application value of simplifying concepts, building emotional connection and helping users remember information [22].

The narrative visualization design for rare and endangered plants in deserts focuses on data information from the perspective of narrative visualization, see Fig. 1, in four steps, "knowledge layer-structural layer-visual layer-interaction layer" as below:

1) Searching literatures to collect, collate and analyze related information
2) Classifying information and constructing hierarchy
3) Information visualization design for easy understanding
4) Interactive design development for promoting transmission and acquisition

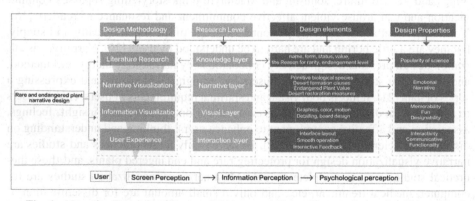

Fig. 1. Narrative Property of Rare and Endangered Plants (Source: drawn for this study)

In the phase of collecting information on rare and endangered plants in the Kubuqi Desert, the author investigated and researched related data of rare and endangered plants by literature review, sorted the information, classified the acquired data set into 4 parts, and constructed the hierarchy of the story: the original plant specifies in the Kubuqi Desert, ecological damage of the Kubuqi Desert by human factor and natural factor, ecological value of rare and endangered plants in the Kubuqi Desert, and measures for restoring ecological environment of the Kubuqi Desert by human being, which forms the structural layer. In the visualization phase, the author thought how to design visualization from the perspectives of colors, images, formats, etc. according to previously analyzed data conclusion, extracted and analyzed the contents of the four data sets and the emotions to be transmitted, converted abstract knowledge into symbolic design elements to construct the visual layer [26]; at last, the author studied users to construct the interaction layer, cut cognitive difficulties and improve users' experience, see Fig. 2.

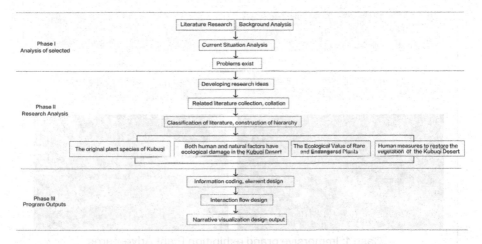

Fig. 2. Study Flow (Source: drawn for this study)

4 Case Analysis and Design

4.1 Analysis on Design Cases of Rare and Endangered Plants

The work *Immersive PLants Exhibition* (Fig. 3) presents immersive interactive spaces with mountains, rivers, plants, etc. as images in the spaces to make users trigger interactive devices in the spaces by exploration and understand the 58 rare and endangered plants in the spaces exploringly. Users can touch, listen, and see them in the exhibition following their own paths for exploratory learning and understanding rather than following a given path. Upon a plant card is fit to the proximity card, the rare and endangered plant image will be highlighted for people to understand the morphological characteristics. The design provides some functions and interactions for the interactive layer, but provides little knowlege mainly by the image display in the visual layer, so it needs to be improved for dissminating more scientific knowledge.

The work *Infographics of Endangerd Plants in Mulinzi State Reserve* (Fig. 4) presents static illustrations and texts on rare and endnagered plants in Mulinzi State Reserve

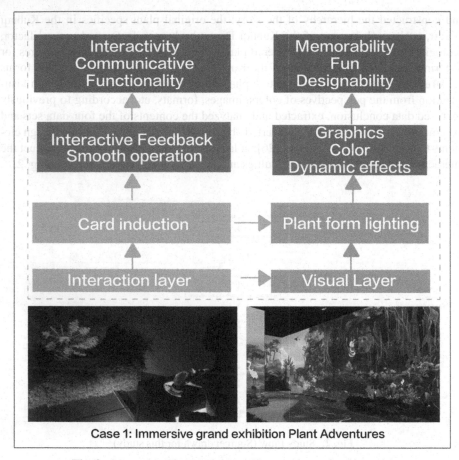

Case 1: Immersive grand exhibition Plant Adventures

Fig. 3. Immersive *Plants Exhibition* (Source: drawn for this study)

mainly in the form of information visualization in order to visually display looks, values, distribution, habits and characteristics, etc. of rare and endangered plants to users, make them recognize and understand these rare and endangered plants and build awarness of protecting the plants. This work can dissminate some scientfic knowledge of rare and endangered plants mainly by illustratins and texts. Although it presents fairly abundant knowledge and can popularize scientific knowledge to some extent, its contents are too boring and hard to understand, and thus cannot arouse much interest of users and cannot disseminate the knowledge widely. As for the visual layer, the work presents mainly static images, colors and formats which are lack of interestingness, and thus can hardly help users think and remember.

The work *Hey, Pagoda Mountain* (Fig. 5) presents rare and endangered plants mainly in the form of narrative electronic picture book. As for the visual layer, it presents mainly static illustrations. Users need to turn pages to learn about the story, and at the same time they need to click rare and endangered plants according to image prompts in order to learn about related information of rare and endangered plants, like names, looks,

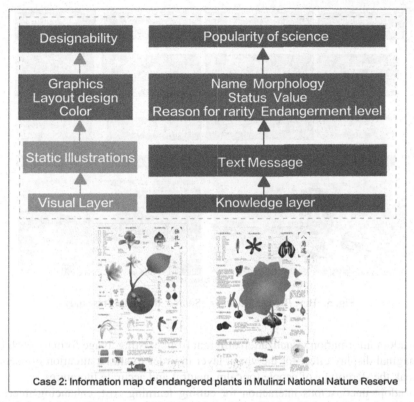

Case 2: Information map of endangered plants in Mulinzi National Nature Reserve

Fig. 4. *Infographics of Endangered Plants in Mulinzi State* Reserve (Source: drawn for this study)

habitats, etc. The visual layer of the electronic picture book consists mainly of pictures, colores and compositions of a piacture, and is single and boring. The knowledge layer does not present enough scientific knowledge, and can not well polularize the knowledge of rare and endangered plants. The interative layer consists mainly of sliding and click, is poor in interactive response to click, and thus poor in functionality and interactivity.

According to the foregoing analysis on design cases of rare and endangered plants, we can see that existing designs of rare and endangered plants are mainly in the form of poster, picture book, interactive exhibition, etc. The study method is fairly single, mainly by visual expression, presents little knowledge of rare and endangered plants, are lack of scientific knowledge polularization capabity, can hardly arouse interest of readers and thus can hardly build the awarness of users for protecting rare and endangered plants. In order to solve these problems, the design goals of this study are as below:

1. To increase knowledge elements to enhance scientific knowledge for the knowledge layer.
2. To add story background to enhance the work's narrativity and emotionality for the narrative layer.

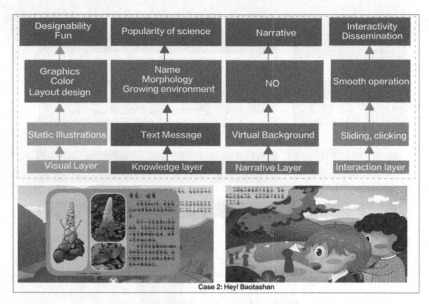

Fig. 5. Hey, *Pagoda Mountain* (Source: drawn for this study)

3. To adopt information visualization different from existing image form to reach fairly imaginal display effect for the visual layer in order to attract attention of users and break the stereotype of people for calm, neutral and accurate literatures.
4. To adopt unconscious interaction for cutting learning cost, enhancing interactive feedback and work's interactivity for the interactive layer.

In addition, because target users are common people, the author needs to adequately consider accuracy and instantaneity of information and at the same time cut technical terms and concepts as far as possible. If any technical term and concept are necessary, they need to be attached with explainations to avoid cognitive bias and consequent poor user experience.

4.2 Narrative Visualization Design of Rare and Endangered Plants in Deserts

Knowledge layer. This layer focuses on displaying information of rare and endangered plants in derserts to make audiences learn more about names, functions, backgrounds, etc. of plants and enhance scientific knowledge. It presents species and names of the original vegetations in the Kubuqi Desert [7, 27], analyzes causes for forming the Kubuqi Desert [28–30], the ecological values of the three rare and endangered plants in the Kubuqi Desert, ammopiptanthus nanus, Tetraena mongolica Maxim, and sacsaoul [31–36], and presents measures for restoring ecological enviroment of the Kubuqi Desert [37, 38].

Structural Layer. This study arranges and reorganizes the collected data, and constructes the hierarchy based on the three historical phases of the Kubuqi Desert, and divides the work into 4 chapters as follow (Fig. 6): the original plant species of the Kubuqi Desert, causes for forming the ecological environment of the Kubuqi Desert, ecological values of rare and endangered plants in the Kubuqi Desert, and human activities for restoring ecological environment of the Kubuqi Desert. The four chapters act in cooperation with each other and are progressive to narrate the story of the Kubuqi Desert changing from the original thick vegetation to desert and to the last rare and endangered plants, and how the plants coexist harmoniously with human being to reserve the Kubuqi.

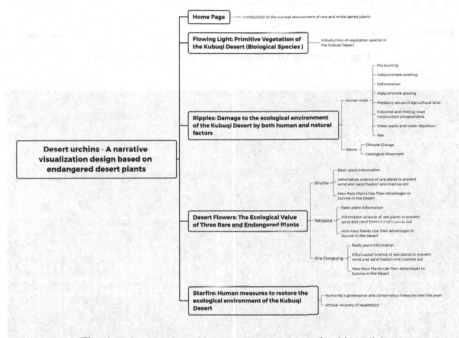

Fig. 6. Information Architecture (Source: drawn for this study)

Visual Layer. Visualization coding is the core of visualization design. This study consists of four chapters. The author analyzed data of each chapters, and designed imaginal elements according to the topic and emotion of each chapter to be transmitted to audiences (Fig. 7). As the information visualization design of rare and endangered plants, information presentation is the main part, the background of the visualization design is black and images are concise and lively white assisted with green and red in order to highlight main information.

The first chapter Oasis main displays the original vegetation species of the Kubuqi Desert. At that time, the Kubuqi Desert was covered by thick vegetation, and thus the main color is lively green, and the images are stream and rain drops to transmit vitality and luxuriance. In addition, the texts and dynamic effects at the beginning are designed according to rain drops. After user turns to the information page, they can see strems representing lively plants and simulating flowing sense of the grassland and feel the original lively scene of the Kubuqi Desert. Users can click different rain drops to learn about vegetation names of the Kubuqi Desert (Fig. 8).

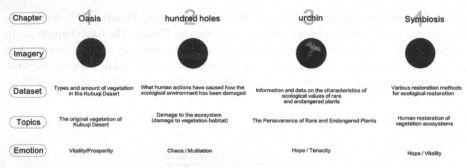

Chapter	Oasis	hundred holes	urchin	Symbiosis
Imagery				
Dataset	Types and amount of vegetation in the Kubuqi Desert	What human actions have caused how the ecological environment has been damaged	Information and data on the characteristics of ecological values of rare and endangered plants	Various restoration methods for ecological restoration
Topics	The original vegetation of Kubuqi Desert	Damage to the ecosystem (damage to vegetation habitat)	The Perseverance of Rare and Endangered Plants	Human restoration of vegetation ecosystems
Emotion	Vitality/Prosperity	Chaos / Mutilation	Hope / Tenacity	Hope / Vitality

Fig. 7. Element UI Design (Source: drawn for this study)

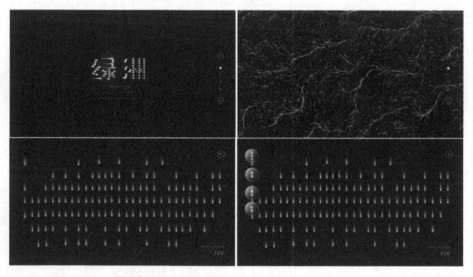

Fig. 8. Page Design (Source: drawn for this study)

The second chapter Damage main presents the human activites and natural factor damaging habitat of plants in the Kubuqi Desert. Ihe main color is crisis red, main image is ripples, and transmitted emotions are chaos and incompleteness. The ripples generated by flashing of rain drops represent the damange of the Kubuqi Desert by human activites and natural factor. This chapter presents a badly damaged ecological environment of the Kubuqi Desert to people. Users can click different red dots to learn about various damage factors (Fig. 9).

The third chapter Dogged Plants presents mainly wind break and sand fixation by rare and endangered pkants, characteristics and concrete data of improved soil. The main color is sacred white and main images are blooming flowers in the desert. The flowers represent the standing fast of rare and endangered plants and transmit tenacity and holiness of them. The three different flowers represent the three plants, ammopiptanthus nanus, Tetraena mongolica Maxim and sacsaoul. Users can click them to view the information about the three rare and endangered plants (Fig. 10).

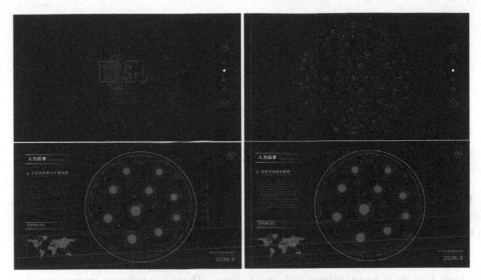

Fig. 9. Page Design (Source: drawn for this study)

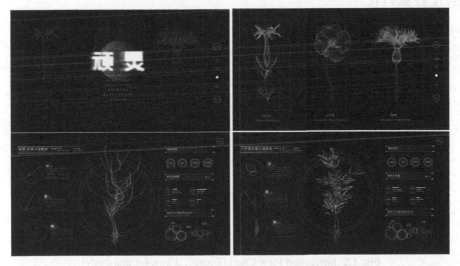

Fig. 10. Page Design (Source: drawn for this study)

The fourth chapter Coexistence presents mainly the data and concrete information about how the Kubuqi Desert's vitality is restored year by year with the joint efforts of human being and rare and endangered plants. The main color is lively green, and main images are sparks of fire. A single spark of fire can start a prairie fire. The restoration activities are just like sparks of fire, and they affect the whole prairie and restore the vitality of the prairie. Users can slide the time shaft to select year, particles gather to form proper density and text information presenting concrete restoration measures occur at the right lower corner in order to display ecological restoration visually to users (Fig. 11).

Fig. 11. Page Design (Source: drawn for this study)

Interactive Layer. In order to enhance transmissibility, functionality and interactivity, this study constructs an interactive device. The interactivity increased enhances involvement degree of users, enables users to participate in topic exploration, learn about the past and future of endangered plants, experience the complete story and remember the information well. Besides, users can learn about the information by click or Mouse Over and trigger various dynamic effects and sound effects. These can enhance interactive interestingness and experience sense, attract more people and thus enhance dissemination (Figs. 12 and 13).

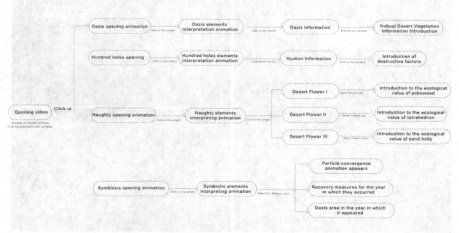

Fig. 12. Interaction Flow Chart (Source: drawn for this study)

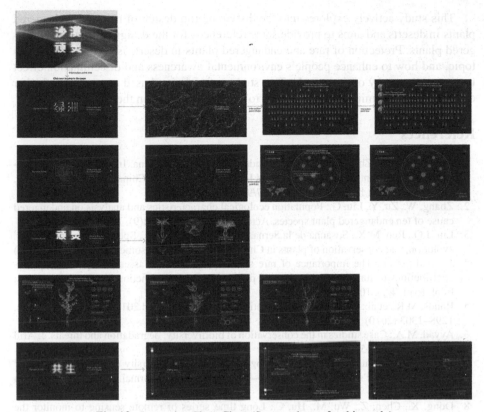

Fig. 13. Interacion Flow Chart (Source: drawn for this study)

5 Conclusions and Suggestions

According to investigation and research results of current dissemination of rare and endangered plants, the main dissemination means of rare and endangered plants is visualization, which can present only a little knowedge, cannot reach scientific knowledge polularization, is normally monotonous and boring, hard to understand and lack of information depth and breadth.

1) From the perspective of knowledge contents, the knowledge of rare and endangered plants is abundant and covers a very long time range, and is hard to be clearly presented by separate study. The narrative visualization elements of "the knowledge layer, structural layer, visual layer and interactive layer" can integrate separate studies.

2) From the perspective of design method, the information visualization, narrativity and interactive design of narrative visiualization design are integrated to enhance science popularization, interestingness, memorability, interactivity and transmissibility and solve the difficulties of the current rare and endangered plants dissmination, "hard to understand, accept and experience".

This study actively explores into the dissemination design of rare and endangered plants in deserts and aims to provide some references for the design of rare and endangered plants. Protection of rare and endangered plants in deserts is an important study topic, and how to enhance people's environmental awareness and dissemination effect by design is worthy of deep study. This study is for design based on analysis of other cases, and its dissemination effect needs to be further studied in the future.

References

1. Qin, H., Jin, X., Zhao, Lina: Rare and endangered plants in China. In: Ren, Hai (ed.) Conservation and Reintroduction of Rare and Endangered Plants in China, pp. 21–31. Springer, Singapore (2020). https://doi.org/10.1007/978-981-15-5301-1_2
2. Zhang, W., Zu, Y., Liu, G.: Population ecological characteristics and analysis on endangered cause of ten endangered plant species. Acta Ecologica Sinica. **22**(9), 1512–1520 (2002)
3. Liu, J.Q., Ren, M.X., Susanna de la Serna, A., & López-Pujol, J., Special issue on Ecology, evolution, and conservation of plants in China: Introduction and some considerations (2015)
4. Jain, M., et al.: The importance of rare species: a trait-based assessment of rare species contributions to functional diversity and possible ecosystem function in tall-grass prairies. Ecol. Evol. **4**(1), 104–112 (2014)
5. Rands, M.R., et al.: Biodiversity conservation: challenges beyond 2010. Science. **329**(5997), 1298–1303 (2010)
6. Ayyad, M.A.: Case studies in the conservation of biodiversity: degradation and threats. J. Arid Environ. **54**(1), 165–182 (2003)
7. Jiang, C.Y.: The attraction of Inner Mongolia desert plant diversity and its protection and research (Amaster's degree thesis, pp. 45–48. Inner Mongolia normal university) (2016). (in Chinese)
8. Dong, X., Chen, Z., Wu, M., Hu, C.: Long time series of remote sensing to monitor the transformation research of Kubuqi Desert in China. Earth Sci. Inf. **13**(3), 795–809 (2020). https://doi.org/10.1007/s12145-020-00467-4
9. Personal Libraries. http://www.360doc.com/content/20/0228/11/141793_895401831.shtml. Accessed 8 Feb 2023. (in Chinese)
10. Li, J.X., Hu, Y.: Research on the development dilemma and response strategies of science popularization short video under the perspective of digital publishing. Publ. Sci. **04**, 67–77 (2022). (in Chinese)
11. Segel, E., Heer, J.: Narrative visualization: telling stories with data. IEEE Trans. Visual. Comput. Graph. **16**(6), 1139–1148 (2010)
12. Caro, T.M., O'Doherty, G.: On the use of surrogate species in conservation biology. Conserv. Biol. **13**(4), 805–814 (1999). https://doi.org/10.1046/j.1523-1739.1999.98338.x
13. Wilson, E.O.: Biodiversity, National Forum on Biodiversity, Washington D.C. 1986 (1988)
14. Xu, J., Xiao, P., Li, T., Wang, Z.: Research progress on endangered plants: a bibliometric analysis. Biodivers. Conserv. **31**(4), 1125–1147 (2022)
15. Y, X. F.: Information System of Rare and Endangered Plants in the Three Gorges Reservoir Area, pp. 11–20. (Master's thesis, Southwest Normal University) (2001). (in Chinese)
16. Anupama Kumar, S., Vijayalakshmi, M.N., Koppad, S.H., Dharani, A.: Narrative and text visualization: a technique to enhance teaching learning process in higher education. In: Anouncia, S.M., Gohel, H.A., Vairamuthu, S. (eds.) Data Visualization, pp. 1–13. Springer, Singapore (2020). https://doi.org/10.1007/978-981-15-2282-6_1
17. Fuling, J., Yong, W.: Data analysis and expression methods in epidemic visualization design: taking data visualization analysis of covid-19 epidemic in Chongqing as an example. Ind. Eng. Des. **2**(02), 32–38 (2020)

18. Figueiras, A.: How to tell stories using visualization. In: 2014 18th International Conference on Information Visualisation, p. 18. IEEE, July 2014
19. Lee, B., Riche, N. H., Isenberg, P., Carpendale, S.: More than telling a story: transforming data into visually shared stories. IEEE Comput. Graph. Appl. **35**(5), 84–90 (2015)
20. Kim, N.W.: From exploration to explanation: designing for visual data storytelling (Doctoral dissertation, Harvard University) (2019)
21. Dove, G., Jones, S.: Narrative visualization: sharing insights into complex data (2012)
22. Figueiras, A:. Narrative visualization: a case study of how to incorporate narrative elements in existing visualizations. In: 2014 18th International Conference on Information Visualisation, pp. 46–52. IEEE, July 2014
23. Li, Z.: Research on the Narrative Design of Information Visualization in Epidemic Science (Master's thesis, Shandong University), pp. 14–15 (2021). (in Chinese)
24. Reng, Y.T., Wang, J.: Narrative research and application of information visualization design. Design **09**, 27–31 (2022). (in Chinese)
25. Liu, Y.: Information visualization-based study on interactive design of elderly health management application. In: Kurosu, M. (ed.) Human-Computer Interaction. Design and User Experience. LNCS, vol. 12181, pp. 614–624. Springer, Cham (2020). https://doi.org/10.1007/978-3-030-49059-1_45
26. Jiang, F.L, Wang, Y.: Research on data analysis and expression methods in epidemic visualization design: a case study of "Visualization Analysis of Novel Coronavirus pneumonia epidemic Data in Chongqing". Indus. Eng. Des. **02**, 24–39 (2020). (in Chinese)
27. Tie, L.: Preliminary Survey of Wild Plant Resources in Kubqi Desert (Master's Thesis, Inner Mongolia Normal University), pp. 17–65 (2015). (in Chinese)
28. Huang, Y.Z.: Nearly 2000 desertification process and the causes of ordos plateau research (Ph.D. Dissertation, Lanzhou University), pp. 90–108 (2009). (in Chinese)
29. Yao, X .R.: Vegetation change on Ordos Plateau and its relationship with climate and human activities (Master's thesis, Inner Mongolia University), pp. 52–56 (2012). (in Chinese)
30. Li, C.S., Ding, Y.H., Li, Z.C., Hou, Y.Y., Yang, X.H., Ci, L.J.: A preliminary study on the impact of climate change on the ecological environment of Kubuqi Desert and its adaptive measures. Desert Oasis Meteorol. **05**, 1–5 (2007). (in Chinese)
31. Rong, Z.R.: Research on the effectiveness of evergreen shrub sand holly in sandy areas for wind protection and sand fixation and soil modification. J. Gansu Agric. Univ. **01**, (1994). (in Chinese)
32. Xu, X.Y., et al.: Quantitative study on wind and sand resistance of Ilex mongolicum and several common species. Chin. Agric. Sci. Bull. **04**, 21–25 (2011). (in Chinese)
33. Yang, X.H., Zhao, Q.S., Duan, J.J.: A rare drought-resistant plant in North China: Tetrahedrin. Pratacult. Animal Husb. **01**, 28+33 (2012). (in Chinese)
34. Liu, J.L., et al.: Effects of desert relictplant Tetracycline on soil Archaea community. Acta Ecologica Sinica. **09**, 3548–3563 (2021). (in Chinese)
35. Zhao, X., Gao H.L., Long, J.M., Liu., Y.X., Li., X., He X.E.: Temporal and spatial distribution of dark septate endophytic fungi and their response to rhizosphere soil environment in the sandy region of Northwest China. J. Fungus. **10**, 2716–2734 (2021). (in Chinese)
36. Wei., Y.J., et al.: Soil improvement effect of different age of the artificial Ammodendron L. J. Northeast Forest. Univ. **02**, 46+42–63 (2019). (in Chinese)
37. He, G., Yang, C.F.: Spring returns to Kubuqi. Liaoning People's Publ. House. 18–105 (2019). (in Chinese)
38. Yang, W.B., Zhang, T.Y., Yan, D.R., et al.: Natural environment and comprehensive management of Kubuqi Desert, pp. 57–260. Mongolia University Press (2005). (in Chinese)

Cross-Cultural Perspectives on Consumer Behavior

The Study of Cultural Differences in Consumers' Visual Perception of Parametric Shape Arrangement Products Between East and West : Applying to Consumer Electronics as Example

Syu-Wei Chen and Tseng-Ping Chiu(✉)

Department of Industrial Design, National Cheng Kung University, Tainan, Taiwan
{p36104097,mattchiu}@gs.ncku.edu.tw

Abstract. In recent years, the globalization of product design has developed rapidly. When a product is sold and displayed in the market, people with different cultural backgrounds may have different views and feelings about the product. In this era of focusing on consumer feelings, cross-cultural cognitive differences must be considered in product design. However, the past literature shows two different self-construction models between East and West, and self-construction will affect a person's cognition, emotion, and motivation. Therefore, the common "shape" elements in product design have different cognitive differences between East and West consumers. Thus, through three experiments, this study compares cross-cultural visual perceptions of product designs with "shape" elements by consumers with different cultural self-construction. (1) The first experiment explores the differences in aesthetic preferences of cross-cultural self-construction for geometric arrangement samples. Through the sample design of round and angular arrangement, the differences in aesthetic preferences of self-construction of different cultures are investigated; (2) The second experiment is a study on the design dimension of consumers' arrangement of product surface shapes, which mainly explores consumers' definition of design dimensions for product surface shape arrangement, including the relationship between aesthetic, functional, and symbolic design characteristics; (3) The third stage is the discussion of consumers' physiological visual perception, using eye trackers to explore consumers' visual perception of shape-arranged products. These studies provide a prospective insight into cross-cultural product design and deliver a reference for designers to apply the "shape" element in products.

Keywords: Cross-cultural self-construction · Cross-cultural aesthetic differences · Visual perception · Parametric shape arrangement products · Eye tracking

1 Introduction

Eyes are basically the most direct way for human beings to understand the world. Among the visual stimuli we receive, besides the shape of the object, we are also stimulated by the material, and the color and surface treatment accompanying the material will bring

© The Author(s), under exclusive license to Springer Nature Switzerland AG 2023
P.-L. P. Rau (Ed.): HCII 2023, LNCS 14022, pp. 447–463, 2023.
https://doi.org/10.1007/978-3-031-35936-1_33

us different feelings and stimuli. In recent years, the globalization of product design has developed rapidly. Therefore, products designed by different cultures are everywhere in the world. When a product is sold and displayed in the market, people with different cultural backgrounds may have different views and feelings on the product. In this era of paying attention to consumers' feelings, it is bound to consider the differences in cross-cultural perception into product design.

The past literature shows that there are two different self-construction models between East and West. Easterners emphasize harmony and interdependence with others, so they are described as "interdependent self-construction" and "collectivism"; In contrast, Westerners are described as "independent self-construction" and "individualism", because they are related to conflict and confrontation, and emphasize personal will and independence from others [1]. In addition, self-construction can affect one's cognition, emotion, and motivation. For example, when researchers studied trademarks in the past, they found that the collectivist culture preferred the round outline, mainly because the round shape symbolized a sense of harmony and closeness. Therefore, it corresponds to the characteristics of aesthetic preference in the context of interdependent self-construction; On the other hand, individualistic culture prefers the edge of the angular shape, mainly because the angular shape represents a sense of conflict and strength, etc. Therefore, it corresponds to the characteristics of aesthetic preference in the context of independent self-construction [2].

However, in recent years, more and more "shape arrangement" elements have been applied to surface details in product design, such as consumer electronics, vehicles, and sportswear... etc. (Fig. 1). The emergence of parametric software allows designers to build on generative logic. Through the mastery of design concepts, they can clarify the correlation between relevant parameters, and more quickly and accurately control the shape, arrangement, density, composition, rules, and proportions of product surface details. In general, how to properly use the parametric design application of "shape arrangement" to make the visual perception of products more attractive to consumers of different cultures is the subject of this study.

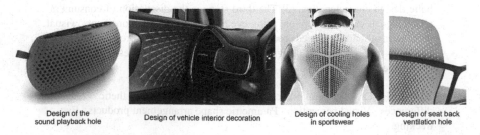

| Design of the sound playback hole | Design of vehicle interior decoration | Design of cooling holes in sportswear | Design of seat back ventilation hole |

Fig. 1. Application of parametric shape arrangement to surface details of product design.

Therefore, the purpose of this study is to: (1) Understand the differences in aesthetic preferences of consumers with self-construction in different cultures for patterns arranged in different shapes; (2) Discusses the design dimension of the product surface shape arrangement by consumers, and the design characteristics of aesthetic, functional and symbolic aspects; (3) To explore the physiological information through the eye movement instrument, and to study the visual perception of consumers on products arranged in shape with scientific methods; (4) Finally, the above experimental results will be applied to the design of hole shape arrangement of audio products, and different parameters will be controlled through the parametric software Grasshopper in the modeling software Rhinoceros (Rhino for short), hoping to more accurately design audio products that meet the visual aesthetic preferences of self-construction of different cultures.

2   Literature Review

2.1   The Self-construction of "Individualism" and "Collectivism"

"Self-construction" is defined as "the relationship between self and others" [3]. The past literature shows that there are two different self-construction models between East and West. Easterners emphasize harmony and collaboration with others, so they are described as "interdependent self-construction"; In contrast, Westerners are described as "independent self-construction", because they are related to conflict and confrontation, and emphasize personal will and independence from others [1]. As shown in "Fig. 2", people with independent are less closely connected with those around them and belong to "individualistic self-construction"; while interdependent people are closely connected with those around them, which is more of a "collectivist self-construction".

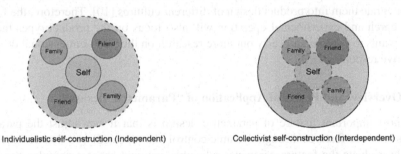

Individualistic self-construction (Independent)   Collectivist self-construction (Interdependent)

Fig. 2. "Individualistic self-construction" and "Collectivist self-construction".

2.2   Aesthetic Preference of "Shape"

Different shapes produce different perceptions and associations. For example, "angular shapes" tend to evoke symbols of energy, toughness, and strength; while "rounded shapes" evoke harmony, friendship, and friendliness. In addition, self-construction affects a person's cognition, emotion, and motivation. For example, when researchers studied trademarks in the past, they found that collectivist culture preferred the "round outline", while individualistic culture preferred "angular edges" [2]. In addition, Tzeng, Trung, and Rieber (1990) found that students in Mexico, Colombia and Japan have different opinions on the same icons and graphics. For example, Japanese students think that circular graphics are powerful and beautiful, while Colombian students think they are ugly and weak [4]. In addition, Simonson and Schmitt (2009) discussed the building of the "Bank of China Tower in Hong Kong" in the book "Marketing Aesthetics", which is composed of typical angular and triangular elements. They believe that in a culture that values harmony, although this structure symbolizes the display of authority and power, it also symbolizes conflict, conflict and bad luck for them [5].

Therefore, the above theories and cases show that in individualistic culture, in terms of shape alone, "angular shapes" are generally considered to be more attractive; In contrast, the "round shapes" is more popular and attractive in the collectivist culture.

2.3 Three Dimensions of Product Design

Product design can be mainly divided into three dimensions, namely Aesthetics, Functionality and Symbolism [6]. "Aesthetic dimension" refers to the appearance and aesthetics of a product [7]; "Functional dimension" refers to the user's perception of the degree to which a product can fulfill its purpose [8]; "Symbolic dimension" refers to the perceived information that a product conveys to users and others about the user's self-image [8]. According to the previous scholar Batra and Ahtola (1991), a product has the characteristics of all three design dimensions, that is, a product is not aesthetic, functional or symbolic, but displays these dimensions at the same time in different degrees [9].

These dimensions are crucial to design, especially for "cross-cultural design", because successful products can capture the characteristics of these three categories and integrate them into product design of different cultures [10]. Therefore, the follow-up research and experimental operation will also focus on the product types that this study wants to explore and carry out more research on the three-dimensional design of cognitive response.

2.4 Overview and Practical Application of "Parametric Design"

The most important feature of parametric design is that it can adjust the parameter values between features through dynamic control and repeatedly, so that designers can quickly evaluate the feature parameter rules they set, and process complex parameter operations by computer, which greatly reduces the time of manual processing. Coupled with the advancement of today's digital manufacturing technology, it not only provides a new design method, but also accelerates the overall design process [11]. In addition, parametric design enables the presentation of complex structures that were previously impossible to achieve. By changing some elements of the design into variables of a function, and by changing the variables of a function, or by changing the algorithm to generate new design elements, in addition to enabling the product to display a varied and rich aesthetic feeling, it also promotes the visual presentation effect of the product to be more diversified and can meet the personalized needs of consumers. The most important thing is to make the design very rational [12].

As shown in "Fig. 3" we use the parametric software "Grasshopper" to conduct a demonstration. By adjusting different parameters, we can accurately control the appearance, hole shape and density of the air cleaner, so that the same product can produce hundreds of thousands of possibilities at the same time.

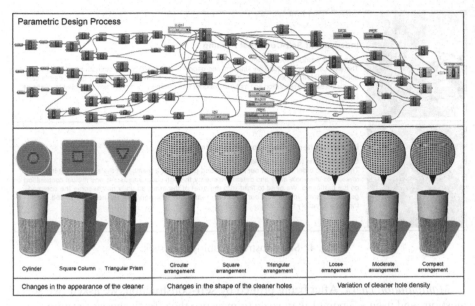

Fig. 3. Parametric software applied to air cleaner design.

3   Method

3.1   Experiment 1 – A Study of the Differences in Aesthetic Preferences of Cross-Cultural Self-construction for Geometric Arrangement Samples

This study was a between-subjects, 2 (self-construal priming: independent vs. interdependent) by 2 (shape: angular vs. round) by 2 (shape arrangement: angular arrangement and round arrangement) experiment. Therefore, it is mainly through the design of round and angular arrangement samples to investigate the different effects of different cultural self-construction on aesthetic preferences for shape arrangement. To confirm whether the round and angular shapes are the same as the aesthetic preference theory of shapes in the literature after being arranged.

1. Participants
In the experiment, a total of 120 people participated in the experiment (62 women and 58 men). We randomly divided these 120 participants into four groups (30 participants in each group), and named the groups "Group 1, 2, 3, 4".

2. Procedure
Self-construal priming. In the first part of the questionnaire, we used the priming method to help establish the causal effect of self-construal. Ybarra and Trafimow (1998) supported the materials for priming self-construal were adapted [13]. Participants were asked to read the text of a character story and watch a picture (Fig.4). Among them, two groups (groups 1 and 2) were selected to priming the independent self-construction, and the other two groups (groups 3 and 4) were selected to priming the interdependent self-construction.

Independent Self-Construal Priming

As a brave warrior, I exist to defend my kingdom.
Therefore, in order to defend my kingdom and people, I must enhance my strength and confrontation ability and defeat the enemy through my strength on the battlefield. I hope my heroic deeds can greatly increase my reputation and make my kingdom and people proud of me and respected by everyone.

Interdependence Self-Construal Priming

Our army exists to protect our kingdom.
Therefore, in order to protect our kingdom and people, as a member of the army, I must integrate myself into the whole army and defeat the enemy through countermeasures and mutual cooperation on the battlefield. We need to fight with the goal of the army, so unity has become the common goal of our army. In this way, our army can bear the responsibility for failure together and share the glory of victory together.

Fig. 4. Self-construal priming materials.

Manipulation check. After being primed by self-construction, we asked two sets of questions and used a 7-point Likert scale to measure the effectiveness of priming.

Participants subject to "independent priming" :(1) Do you think you belong to your independent self? (2) Do you think you are quite different and unique? ; Participants subject to "interdependent priming" :(1) Do you think you are part of this army? (2) Do you think the interests of the military are more important than yourself?

Shape arrangement pattern sample stimuli. After the self-construal primed, the participants were asked to watch the shape arrangement pattern sample in the second part of the questionnaire (Fig.5). Among them, we asked the participants (group 1) who were primed by the independent self-construction materials and the participants (group 3) who were primed by the interdependent self-construction materials to watch the "pattern of angular frame with round arrangement", and "pattern of angular frame with angular arrangement"; on the contrary, we asked the participants (group 2) who were primed by the independent self-construction material and the participants (group 4) who were primed by the interdependent self-construction material to watch the "pattern of round frame with round arrangement", and "pattern of round frame with angular arrangement". After the participants watched the sample of the shape arrangement pattern, we used the 7-point Likert scale to measure the degree of preference and adaptability.

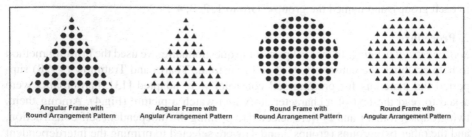

Angular Frame with Round Arrangement Pattern | Angular Frame with Angular Arrangement Pattern | Round Frame with Round Arrangement Pattern | Round Frame with Angular Arrangement Pattern

Fig. 5. Shape arrangement pattern sample stimuli materials.

Self-Construction Scale. In the third part of the questionnaire, we used a self-construction scale with 30 items [14] to measure the participants' cultural self-construction scores for reference in the subsequent analysis of data.

3.2   Experiment 2 – Definition of Design Dimensions for Product Surface Shape Arrangement

This experiment is mainly to understand consumers' definition of design dimensions for product surface shape arrangement, and explores the relationship between aesthetics, functionality, and symbolic design characteristics.

1. Participants
In the experiment, a total of 3 graduate students in the field of industrial design participated in the experiment (1 women and 2 men).

2. Procedure
Collect samples. In the first part of this experiment, we asked the three graduate students to collect many product image samples with "shape arrangement" elements.

Image classification. In the second part of the experiment, we asked these three graduate students to classify the collected image samples by the KJ method.

Design dimension definition. In the third part of the experiment, we discussed and defined the aesthetic, functional and symbolic design characteristics of the classified products through the focus group method.

3.3   Experiment 3 – A Study of Consumers' Visual Perception of Shape-Arranged Products

This experiment is a study on consumers' physiological visual perception, using eye-tracking equipment (Tobii pro nano) to explore physiological information, and scientifically researching consumers' visual perception of shape-arranged products. The purpose of this experiment is to confirm the importance of the "shape arrangement" element in product design.

1. Participants
In the eye tracker experiment, a total of 10 people participated in the experiment (5 females and 5 males).

2. Procedure
Select experimental samples. In the first part of this experiment, we selected 12 product types from the product image samples classified in Experiment 2, among which 6 product surface shape arrangement elements were classified as more "aesthetic" dimensions; and the other 6 product surface shape-arranged elements of are classified as more "functional" dimension.

Classify experimental samples. In the second part of the experiment, we post-processed the samples of these 12 products, respectively processed the pictures in grayscale and removed the product trademarks, and removed and retained the "shape arrangement" elements on the surface of the products at the same time. The purpose is to generate an experimental group and a control group. Therefore, there are 24 product image samples in this experiment (Fig. 6).

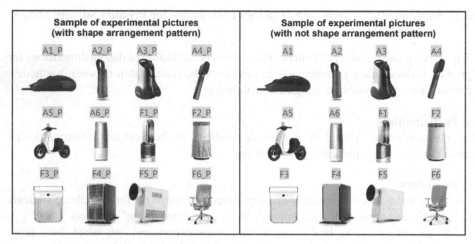

Fig. 6. Sample images from eye tracker experiment.

Experimental space configuration. The space for carrying out the eye movement instrument experiment is a research room of about ten square meters. There are two tables in the configuration of this space, and one screen is placed on each table, and the other is the screen operated by the experimenter; the other is the screen for the eye movement measurement of the participants (Fig. 7).

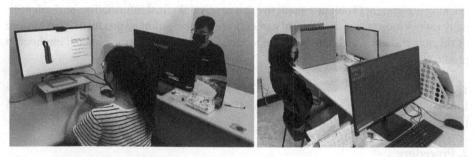

Fig. 7. Experimental space configuration.

Eye tracker instrument. The eye tracker is Tobii pro nano, which can be attached to the bottom of the computer screen and is mainly used for the observation of eye movement on the computer screen (Fig. 8).

Eye tracker experiment. In the third part of the experiment, we divided 10 participants into two groups to carry out the eye tracker experiment. The purpose of the experiment

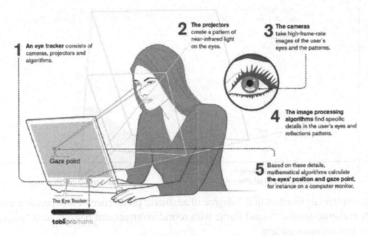

Fig. 8. Schematic diagram of eye tracker technology.

was to ensure that the image samples of the same product with and without shape arrangement elements would not be seen by the same participant. In addition to recording the physiological information of the participants, the experiment also conducted interviews with five questions to facilitate further discussion.

4   Result

4.1   The Result of "Experiment 1" (a Study of the Differences in Aesthetic Preferences of Cross-Cultural Self-construction for Geometric Arrangement Samples).

The result of self-construal priming. The priming of self-construction was effective, even though the 120 participants were all Taiwanese (with more interdependent self-construction), the participants of group 1 and group 2 who were independently primed (M = 5.08, SD = 1.544) thought they were more independent thinking mode during the experiment; while the participants in groups 3 and 4 who were primed by interdependence (M = 5.43, SD = 1.267) strengthened their own interdependent thinking mode.

   The result of the aesthetic preference of cross-cultural self-construction to the samples of shape arrangement. In this experiment, the priming of self-construction was effective. An examination of "Fig. 9" suggests that compared with the participants in group 3 who were primed by interdependence (M = 3.50, SD = 1.137), the participants in group 1 who were primed independently (M = 4.53, SD = 1.167) thought that the pattern of angular frame with angular arrangement had a higher preference, F (1, 59) = 4.589, p < .05; Conversely, compared with the participants in group 2 who were primed by independence (M = 3.80, SD = 1.540), the participants in group 4 who were primed interdependently (M = 5.23, SD = 1.357) thought that the pattern of round frame with round arrangement had a higher preference, F (1, 59) = 7.951, p < .05.

   In addition, the examination of "Fig. 10" suggests that compared with the participants in group 1 who were primed by independence (M = 3.90, SD = 1.094), the participants

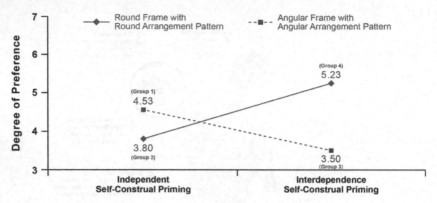

Fig. 9. The result analysis chart of the degree of aesthetic preference of independent and interdependent self-construction for "round frame with round arrangement pattern" and "angular frame with angular arrangement pattern".

in group 3 who were primed interdependently (M = 3.97, SD = 1.217) thought that the pattern of angular frame with round arrangement had a higher preference, although the difference was not significant at p =. 05; Conversely, compared with the participants in group 4 who were primed by interdependence (M = 3.73, SD = 1.202), the participants in group 2 who were primed independently (M = 3.87, SD = 1.525) thought that the pattern of round frame with angular arrangement had a higher preference, although the difference was not significant at p =. 05.

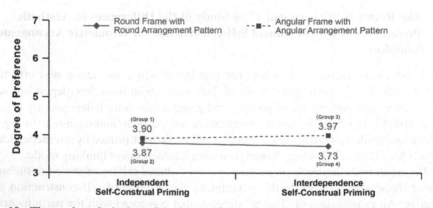

Fig. 10. The result analysis chart of the degree of aesthetic preference of independent and interdependent self-construction for "round frame with angular arrangement pattern" and "angular frame with round arrangement pattern".

4.2 The Result of "EXPeriment 2" (Definition of Design Dimensions for Product Surface Shape Arrangement).

This experiment is mainly to understand consumers' definition of design dimensions for product surface shape arrangement. Therefore, we searched for 3 graduate students majoring in industrial design to explore the relationship between aesthetic, functional and symbolic design characteristics of the shape arrangement product pictures classified in the second part of the experiment (Fig. 11), and will conduct the following classification and integration of the discussed results:

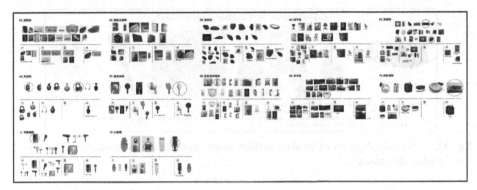

Fig. 11. KJ classification and integration of product images in shape arrangement.

1. Classification of "aesthetics dimension" (Fig. 12):

(1) The "holes" and "textures" in the shape of the product surface are not related to the operation of the product. Generally, it will be classified into aesthetic dimension.
(2) The product surface has the shape element details of "light arrangement", which is not related to the operation of the product. Generally, it will be classified into aesthetic dimension.

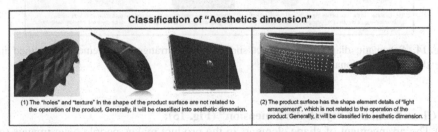

Fig. 12. Schematic diagram of product surface shape arrangement elements classified into "aesthetic dimension".

2. Classification of "functional dimension" (Fig. 13):

(1) The "holes" and "textures" arranged on the surface of the product are related to the operation of the product (ex: heat dissipation, ventilation, anti-slip, broadcasting…). Generally, it will be classified into functional dimension.
(2) The elements of "holes design" on the product surface are presented in a neat and orderly arrangement and are related to the operation of the product. Generally, it will be classified into functional dimension.

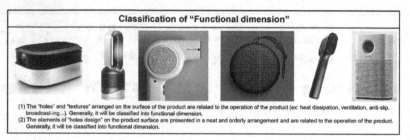

Fig. 13. Schematic diagram of product surface shape arrangement elements classified into " functionality dimension".

3. Classification of both "aesthetic and functional dimensions" (Fig. 14):

(1) The surface of the product has the element of "holes design", which is related to the operation of the product (ex: heat dissipation, water spray, broadcasting…), and has the "changes in pattern composition rules" (ex: gradual change, rhythm). Generally, it will be classified into both aesthetic and functional dimensions.

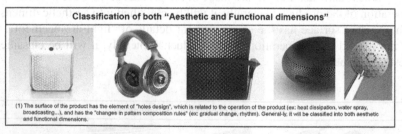

Fig. 14. Schematic diagram of product surface shape arrangement elements classified into "aesthetic and functional dimension".

4. Classification of "symbolic dimension" (Fig. 15):

(1) The arrangement of shape elements in the product makes people have images (ex: sense of momentum, sense of technology, sense of retro…), or makes people have connections or associations (ex: totem, memory of the past). Generally, it will be classified into symbolic dimensions.

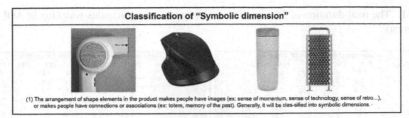

Classification of "Symbolic dimension"

(1) The arrangement of shape elements in the product makes people have images (ex: sense of momentum, sense of technology, sense of retro...), or makes people have connections or associations (ex: totem, memory of the past). Generally, it will be clas-sified into symbolic dimensions.

Fig. 15. Schematic diagram of product surface shape arrangement elements classified into " symbolic dimension".

4.3 The Result of "Experiment 3" (A Study of Consumers' Visual Perception of Shape-Arranged Products).

In this experiment, we first draw the AOI (Area of interest) for the product sample in "Fig. 6", which is mainly to frame the areas of "with shape arrangement" and "without shape arrangement" elements in the shape arrangement product through eye tracker software (Tobii Pro Lab) and calculate the data of participants in each AOI through the software, and then compare and analyze each other (Fig. 16).

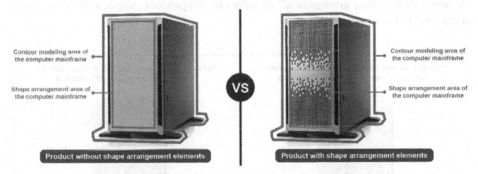

Fig. 16. Schematic diagram of product drawing area of interest (AOI).

"Table 1" is the total duration of fixation in AOI of the two groups of participants in this experiment. The "orange areas" of the two charts are the elements "with shape arrangement" in the product sample; the "blue areas" are the element "without shape" arrangement in the product sample. Therefore, by comparing the "blue" and "orange" areas in the rightmost column (total duration of fixation in AOI) of the two charts, it can be clearly seen that the area "with shape arrangement elements" in the product sample will attract the participants to have more staring attention time.

Table 1. The total duration of fixation of the "Group-01" of participants watching in AOI (area of interest).

Total duration of fixation in AOI_Group-01						
AOI / Participant	P01	P02	P03	P04	P05	Total
A-1	0.72	0.40	0.62	0.38	1.72	3.84
A-2	0.6	2.43	1.1	2.41	0.93	7.47
A-3	0.00	0.78	1.39	0.23	0.23	2.63
A-4_P	3.28	0.43	0.58	0.55	0.68	5.52
A-5_P	0.22	2.37	1.27	0.00	0.65	4.51
A-6_P	1.73	2.96	3.10	3.46	3.96	15.21
F-1_P	3.21	1.74	1.37	0.6	2.25	9.17
F-2_P	4.65	2.07	3.71	4.03	3.48	17.94
F-3_P	3.35	1.63	5.56	2.6	3.86	17
F-4	3.01	4	1.77	0.62	2.84	12.24
F-5	0.5	0.7	0.86	0.97	0.85	3.88
F-6	2.07	3.14	1.72	3.11	4.8	14.84

- The units of numbers in the table are "seconds".
- The numbers "A-1 to A-3" and "F-4 to F-6" of the experimental samples of the leftmost column of the eye tracker are products "without shape arrangement" elements (blue area).
- The numbers "A-4_P to A-6_P" and "F-1_P to F-3_P" of the experimental samples of the leftmost column of the eye tracker are products "with shape arrangement" elements (orange area).

Total duration of fixation in AOI_Group-02						
AOI / Participant	P01	P02	P03	P04	P05	Total
A-1_P	1.48	2.43	2.78	1.88	4.11	12.68
A-2_P	3.06	6.08	6.88	4.64	4.83	25.49
A-3_P	2.94	3.37	0.88	0.97	0.5	8.66
A-4	1.11	1.44	1.05	0.22	0.00	3.82
A-5	0.00	0.00	0.00	0.17	0.00	0.17
A-6	1.90	1.8	1.93	1.22	2.71	9.56
F-1	2.17	2.65	0.45	1.10	2.3	8.67
F-2	1.25	2.12	0.37	2.28	0.75	6.77
F-3	0.82	3.4	0.97	1.15	0.32	6.66
F-4_P	5.51	4.94	6.37	7.38	5.48	29.68
F-5_P	3.58	4.12	6.11	5.05	3.77	22.63
F-6_P	0.70	3.9	3.81	2.71	3.75	14.87

- The units of numbers in the table are "seconds".
- The numbers "A-4 to A-6" and "F-1 to F-3" of the experimental samples of the leftmost column of the eye tracker are products "without shape arrangement" elements (blue area).
- The numbers "A-1_P to A-3_P" and "F-4_P to F-6_P" of the experimental samples of the leftmost column of the eye tracker are products "with shape arrangement" elements (orange area).

In addition, more visual methods can also be used for observation. For example, "Fig. 17" is the "heap map (hot spot map)" generated by the participants when viewing the product sample in the experiment. The red area in the "Fig. 17" is regarded as the hot area of the spot of sight. Therefore, it can also be clearly seen from this figure that the areas "with shape arrangement" elements in the product sample will attract more attention from the participants.

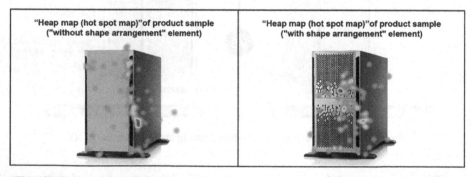

| "Heap map (hot spot map)"of product sample ("without shape arrangement" element) | "Heap map (hot spot map)"of product sample ("with shape arrangement" element) |

Fig. 17. Schematic diagram of comparison of visual "heap map (hot spot map)" of products.

5 Conclusion and Discussion

In the past, many literatures have investigated the aesthetic preference between culture and shape. In addition to re-examining the aesthetic preference of cultural self-construction for angular and round shapes, our research also examined the impact of angular and round arrangement on the aesthetic preference of different cultural self-construction. Our research found that compared with the participants who were primed by interdependence (M = 3.50, SD = 1.137), the participants who were independently primed (M = 4.53, SD = 1.167) thought that the pattern of angular frame with angular arrangement had a higher preference, F (1, 59) = 4.589, p < .05; Conversely, compared with the participants who were primed independently (M = 3.80, SD = 1.540), the participants who were primed by interdependence (M = 5.23, SD = 1.357) thought that the pattern of round frame with round arrangement had a higher preference, F (1, 59) = 7.951, p < .05. Therefore, the analysis results show that cross-cultural self-construction has a significant impact on the angular and round arrangement, which also makes us more actively explore the relationship between "shape arrangement", "product design", and" cultural self-construction".

In the past literature, it has been mentioned that a product has the characteristics of three design dimensions. A product is not aesthetic, functional, or symbolic, or displays these dimensions at the same time in different degrees. In addition, we also believe that when consumers evaluate products, they will affect perception and evaluation due to the characteristics of different design dimensions. Therefore, in the part of experiment 2, we discussed the definition of design dimensions of consumers for the elements of product surface shape arrangement. In the experiment, we defined and classified shape-arranged products through three graduate students from the department of industrial design (Figs. 12, 13 , 14 and 15), and clearly defined the characteristics and indicators of different design dimensions of shape-arranged products. In addition to giving other designers a clear understanding of the corresponding design dimensions when using the "shape arrangement" elements, it also helps us to logically divide the experimental samples into "aesthetic" and "functional" when operating experiment 3. However, the reason why Experiment 3 does not include "symbolic" experimental samples is that the definition of symbolic dimension involves the generation of images, links and associations, and these definitions will vary from person to person and vary greatly, so they are not included in the presentation of our experimental samples.

In the part of experiment 3, we further explore the physiological information through the eye tracker and use scientific methods to study consumers' visual perception of shape-arranged products. Our research found that the area with "shape arrangement" elements in the product sample will attract consumers to spend more time staring and paying attention. That is to say, the areas "with shape arrangement" elements in product design will attract more attention from consumers, and the interview after the experiment also found that compared with the product samples "without shape arrangement" elements, the product samples "with shape arrangement" elements will generally increase consumers' preference. Therefore, the above research gives product designers a new inspiration. In addition to the product appearance and function, the use of "shape arrangement" elements in products also needs to be considered more carefully, so as to improve consumers' preference for products.

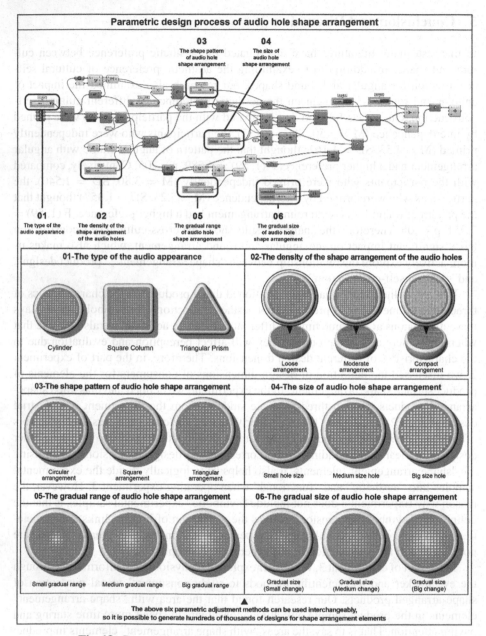

Fig. 18. Parametric design process of audio hole shape arrangement.

Finally, this study applies the experimental results to the design of the shape arrangement of the holes in the broadcast of audio products (Fig. 18). The reason why we choose the audio holes for the design application is that the design of the audio holes belongs to the category of "aesthetic" and "functional" through the design dimension defined in our experiment 2. Therefore, it is quite suitable to be used as an application example of the experimental design in this study. In this design application, we use the modeling software Rhinoceros (Rhino for short) to construct the audio appearance, and use the parametric software Grasshopper in Rhinoceros to generate the pattern of shape arrangement, and can generate hundreds of thousands of shape arrangement possibilities through parameter adjustment. However, in the unit type of shape arrangement, we choose the independent self-construction universal preference "angular shape" and the interdependent self-construction universal preference "round shape", as well as the quite common use of "square shape" in product design, which are the main unit types. In terms of the large appearance of the audio, we also choose the above three shapes as the main design.

Although the design application of "Fig. 18" seldom considers the actual design vocabulary or functions, but the core value of this study lies in the relationship between "shape arrangement", "product design" and "cultural self-construction". Therefore, it is expected that the design application of "Fig. 18" can give other designers a good example. In the future, this study will also expand more cross-cultural studies of shape arrangement, and hope that the results and data of the study can contribute to the design practice.

References

1. Markus, H.R., Kitayama, S.: Culture and the self: Implications for cognition, emotion, and motivation. Psychol. Rev. **98**(2), 224–253 (1991)
2. Henderson, P.W., et al.: Building strong brands in Asia: selecting the visual components of image to maximize brand strength. Int. J. Res. Mark. **20**(4), 297–313 (2003)
3. Zhang, Y., Feick, L., Price, L.J.: The impact of self-construal on aesthetic preference for angular versus rounded shapes. Pers. Soc. Psychol. Bull. **32**(6), 794–805 (2006)
4. Tzeng, O.C., Trung, N.T., Rieber, R.W.: Cross-cultural comparisons on psychosemantics of icons and graphics. Int. J. Psychol. **25**(1), 77–97 (1990)
5. Simonson, A., Schmitt, B.H.: Marketing Aesthetics. Free Press (2009)
6. Homburg, C., Schwemmle, M., Kuehnl, C.: New product design: concept, measurement, and consequences. J. Mark. **79**(3), 41–56 (2015)
7. Desmet, P., Hekkert, P.: Framework of product experience. Int. J. Des. **1**, 57–66 (2007)
8. Bloch, P.: Product design and marketing: reflections after fifteen years. J. Prod. Innov. Manag. **28**, 378–380 (2011)
9. Batra, R. and O. Ahtola, measuring the hedonic and utilitarian sources of consumer attitudes. Mark. Lett. 2 (1991)
10. Rubin, Z.L.: A Framework for Cross-cultural Product Design. Georgia Institute of Technology (2012)
11. Li, S.-Y., 參數式設計應用於產品創作與探討 (2013)
12. 陳秀杏, 參數化建模應用架構研究-以Grasshopper建構樓梯為例 (2019)
13. Ybarra, O., Trafimow, D.: How priming the private self or collective self affects the relative weights of attitudes and subjective norms. Personal. Soc. Psychol. Bull. **24**(4), 362–370 (1998). https://doi.org/10.1177/0146167298244003
14. Singelis, T.M.: The measurement of independent and interdependent self-construals. Pers. Soc. Psychol. Bull. **20**(5), 580–591 (1994)

Does the Visual Background Matter for East Asians?
The Study of Cross-Cultural Differences in Consumer's Visual Perception and Recognition of Merchandise with Contextual Display between Americans and Taiwanese

Tseng-Ping Chiu(✉) (iD)

Industrial Design Department, National Cheng Kung University, Tainan 701, Taiwan, R.O.C.
mattchiu@gs.ncku.edu.tw

Abstract. Past research has shown visual perception differs based on cultural variation. However, there is little research investigating merchandising displays on the E-commerce platform. In this research, we tend to investigate the cultural differences in consumers' visual perception and attention interest between Western (e.g., the United States) and Eastern countries (e.g., Taiwan) by applying Signal Detection Theory (SDT) to analyze their recognition memory of the focal product displayed on the online platform of cross-border e-commerce. This research uses qualitative and quantitative methods to analyze consumers' visual perception and cognitive responses cross-culturally. We expect to organize and establish precise online merchandise visual presentation and marketing strategy design cross-culturally.

Keywords: Cross-Border E-Commerce · Cross-Cultural Differences · Cultural Cognition · Visual Perception · Eye-Tracking · Online Merchandise Visual Presentation · Consumer Behavior

1 Introduction

Digital information has dominated and changed how people live. Mainly, shopping online is the most influential activity in the Post-Pandemic Area. Consequently, the rapid development of e-commerce increases sharply year by year [1]. Since there is a high demand for digital information on the e-commerce platform worldwide, it causes great differences in visual perception between Eastern and Western consumers. For example, when a product's visual information is displayed on the online platform, people of different cultural backgrounds might pay attention to the product differently. As a result, it may cause diverse intentions to the visual presentation of the product in the marketplace. Due to cross-cultural cognition studies, past research showed there is a significant difference in visual perception between Easters and Westers. However, little is known about how cultural differences in people's visual perception and attention to online merchandise visual design. This research is to investigate consumers' visual perception and attention to the merchandising display of e-commerce platforms.

P.-L. P. Rau (Ed.): HCII 2023, LNCS 14022, pp. 464–478, 2023.
https://doi.org/10.1007/978-3-031-35936-1_34

In the social psychology domain, many studies showed that people originating from different countries prefer to perceive visual information differently between East and West [2–4]. This difference in visual perception originated from cultural cognition and thinking style. Past research has shown Westerners tend to be more analytic in their thinking, while East Asians tend to be holistic by attending to the entire field. Consequently, Westerners are described as "Context-independent" because they focus on a focal object rather than its context. In contrast, East Asians are "Context-dependent" by attending to the relationship between the focal object and its context [5, 6]. In addition, the research has shown East Asians were more easily affected by contextual information than Westerners in perception tasks, which indicates visual background is an indispensable element for East Asians when they perceive visual images and information.

Although there is a significant cross-cultural difference in visual perception related to the social psychology domain, few studies apply cognitive psychology to explore those cultural differences in visual merchandising displays on the e-commerce platform. In this research, we tend to investigate the cultural differences in consumers' visual perception and attention interest between Western (e.g., the United States) and Eastern countries (e.g., Taiwan) by applying Signal Detection Theory (SDT) to analyze their recognition memory of the focal product displayed on the online platform of cross-border e-commerce. To simulate the actual merchandise visual scene on the website, we examine various combinations of merchandising visual display, including focal products in context-independent or context-dependent visual presentation. According to past cross-cultural research, we hypothesize East Asians would prefer the focal product presented in a context-dependent scenario and cause greater attention to the focal product and contextual information simultaneously compared to Westerners.

There are two main studies of this research. Study 1 is to investigate consumers' aesthetic preference for the product's visual presentation within contextual information. We separate the product visual information into two parts: (1) focal product itself and (2) background information, respectively. We would examine the differences between Eastern and Western consumer visual preference on the product visual presentation on the e-commerce platform. In addition, Study 2 is to investigate cross-cultural differences in consumers' visual perception of merchandising displays by measuring their recognition memory of the focal product within various contextual backgrounds. We apply Signal Detection Theory (SDT) to measure consumers' sensitivity to the focal object and background information between East Asians (e.g., Taiwanese) and Westerners (e.g., Americans). The goal of this research is to understand how consumers in different cultures respond to visual scenes using by quantitative approach. This research applies both qualitative and quantitative methods to analyze consumers' visual perception and cognitive response cross-culturally. We expect to organize and establish precise online merchandise visual presentation and marketing strategy design in the future.

2   Literature Review

2.1   Cultural Difference in Visual Perception

Prior work in cultural psychology has shown that cultures vary in the extent of attention paid to contextual information [5–8]. Visual perception has been shown to differ based on cultural background of who people originated from (Nisbett, 2003). Westerners tend to be more analytic in their thinking, while East Asians tend to be holistic, attending to the entire field [5, 6]. In perceptual tasks, Westerners are described as "context-independent" because they focus on a salient object rather than its context, whereas East Asians attend to the relationship between an object and its context [9, 10]. Americans prefer context-exclusive images more than Japanese, consistent with analytic vs. holistic patterns of attention [5, 8, 9]. As compared to people engaged in European American cultures (European Americans in short), those engaged in East Asian cultures (East Asians in short) are described as more holistic in cognitive style and thus context-dependent. This finding of cultural cognition has been extended in various ways in subsequent studies, such as the aesthetic appeal of portraits with variations in the size of the model and background [11], the amount of information on the website homepage [12], and artistic expressions of visual artwork [13, 14]. Based on the evidence of cultural variation in attentional patterns, we may expect that the context effect on the online visual merchandising display would be more pronounced for East Asians than for European Americans. To test these possibilities, we recruited two cultural groups—North Americans and Taiwanese—to investigate the cultural variation in the attentional pattern of visual scenes, including the focal object and background visual information.

2.2   Recognition Memory: Signal Detection Theory

To investigate the difference in visual perception between East and West, we apply Signal Detection Theory to examine consumers' recognition memory of the focal object and its background information. Signal Detection Theory (SDT) is widely accepted and applied to different domains. It moved to psychology [15] initially as part of sensation and perception. Further, it was an attempt to understand some of the features of human behavior when detecting very faint stimuli (signals) among other stimuli (noise) that were not being explained by traditional theories of thresholds [16]. Moreover, Signal Detection Theory targeted marketing and consumer research [17].

SDT can be applied whenever two possible stimulus types must be discriminated. In our study, we used one of the most popular tasks: the yes/no task, to test recognition memory. A yes/no task involves signal trails, which present old (target), and noise trails, which present new (distractor). A typical SDT usually encompasses a detection task. With the detection task, a mix of stimuli contains signals and noise. Signals are stimuli to be detected, while noise is the background, which is not to be detected. For example, in a recognition task, signals are exposed items in the study phase, whereas noise consists of new items never exposed before. The detection task is to find the signals in a max of signals and noise. When subjects respond to a signal (old or target) as "yes" it is called a "Hit"; otherwise, it is a "Miss." When subjects respond to a noise (new or distractor) as "yes" it is called a "False Alarm"; otherwise, it is a "Correct Rejection" (see Fig. 1).

	Signal trails (Target)	Noise trails (Distractor)
	Stimulus Present	**Stimulus Absent**
Response "Yes"	Hit	False Alarm
Response "No"	Miss	Correct Rejection

Fig. 1. Signal Detection Theory of Yes/No task to test recognition memory

According to SDT, the subjects in a yes/no task base their response on the value that a decision variable achieves during each trial. If the decision variable is sufficiently high during a given trial, the subject responds yes; otherwise, the subject responds no. The value that defines sufficiently high is called the criterion. The hit rate (the probability of responding yes on signal trails) equals the proportion of the signal distribution that exceeds the criterion, whereas the false-alarm rate (the probability of responding yes on noise trails) equals the proportion of the noise distribution that exceeds the criterion. Therefore, the hit and false-alarm rate fully describe performance on a yes/no task. Also, the SDT is measured by two components, which are sensitivity and response bias. Sensitivity is specified by the signal-to-noise ratio. More specifically, the sensitivity of strength is the standardized mean difference of the strength between the signal and noise distributions, which means the discriminability of signal and noise trails. If the sensitivity is high, the subject is effective in detecting the presence of signals. On the other hand, the response bias is distinct from its sensitivity. It specifies how certain one must be before one is willing to say "yes, a signal is present." The response bias is based on the decision variable (criterion). If the criterion is set lower, it will produce mostly yes responses in signal trails and a high hit rate but also produce a high proportion of yes responses on noise trails and a high false-alarm rate. The lower criterion of response bias is called liberal bias, which means the subject is willing to say yes on both signal and noise trail and cause a high hit rate and false-alarm rate. Conversely, if the criterion is set higher, it will produce mostly no response in signal trails and a low hit rate but also produce a high proportion of no response in noise trails and a low false-alarm rate. The higher criterion of response bias is called conservative bias, which means the subject is willing to say no on both signal and noise trials and causes a low hit rate and false-alarm rate. According to the sensitivity and response bias of SDT, we could verify and test the subject's recognition memory and performance (see Fig. 2).

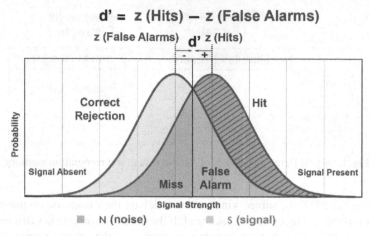

d' = z (Hits) − z (False Alarms)

Fig. 2. Signal Detection Theory of sensitivity of signal distribution

3 Study 1

In Study 1, we would like to investigate cross-cultural differences in consumers' visual preference for merchandising displays on e-commerce. We manipulated the visual scenes, including focal product and contextual information, and investigated consumers' visual aesthetic preference between East Asians (e.g., Taiwanese) and Westerners (e.g., Americans). The goal of Study 1 is to understand how consumers in different cultures respond to visual scenes using by quantitative approach.

We collect the best-selling merchandise as our product visual information between Eastern and Western e-commerce platforms, including Amazon in the United States, Argos in the United Kingdom, Rakuten in Japan, and Momo in Taiwan. In addition, we decompose the product visual information into two parts—focal product and background information, respectively. According to past research on cultural differences in visual perception tasks, we hypothesize that the performance of recognition memory for East Asians would be influenced by the visual scene within contextual information (e.g., a product with many visual background scenes) rather than Westerners do.

3.1 Method

Material

Visual Stimuli Selection

A collection of home products, including furniture (e.g., chairs), kitchen products (e.g., kettles, air flyers), lighting (e.g., floor lamps, desk lamps), home appliances (e.g., air-purifier, vacuums), and consumer electronic product (e.g., mouses, keyboards,) was used in the study. The first product selection criterion is the product could fit into the revenant contextual information (e.g., the kettle could be placed on the dining table). The second product selection criterion is that all the products were best-seller or have high customer reviews on each E-commerce platform (e.g., the best-seller air flyer on Amazon and Rakuten). We avoided the strong brand image and identity for the product selection to make the product as neutral as possible. Each product was shown in perspective containing its outline, shape, color, material, and detail. There were six product categories, including 20 focal product stimuli in total. Each product category includes 40 product stimuli: dining chair, floor lamp, kettle, air flyer, dinner plate set, and air purifier, respectively.

In addition, each product's visual stimuli are designed as two visual presentations: (1) Context-independent Scenario (2) Context-interdependent condition. For the Context-independent condition, there is only the focal product itself without any contextual information (e.g., an air flyer display on a white background). On the other hand, Context-interdependent Scenario is the product displayed within a suitable scenario (e.g., an air flyer display on the table of the kitchen). In total, there were 40 stimuli, including 20 stimuli without background (Context-independent condition) and 20 stimuli within visual background scenario (Context-interdependent condition) (see Fig. 3).

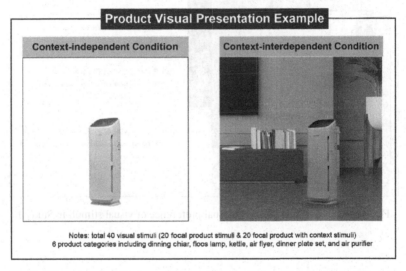

Fig. 3. The example of two conditions of Product Visual Presentation of Study 1

Participants

We recruited 206 European Americans via Qualtrics.com online survey service (M_{age} = 34.9, 45.6% male, 54.4% female), and 98 Taiwanese participated in the laboratory at the large southern university in Taiwan (M_{age} = 22.5, 35.8% male, 64.2% female). Whereas European Americans and Taiwanese both received $USD 10 when they finished the study.

Procedure

In the beginning, participants were informed that they would be shown a series of objects one at a time and asked to focus on the focal product only. The object was marked by a red arrow (see Fig. 4). Participants were first asked two questions about object attractiveness: *"Do you think the product is beautiful?"* and *"Do you like the product itself?"* The third question was a measure used to check the effectiveness of the context manipulation, *"How well do you think the product fits into this context?"* They were then given two additional questions on the attractiveness of the entire scene: *"Do you like the product in this context?"* and *"Overall, do you like the whole picture?"* Participants responded using a 7-point scale). At the end of the study, participants completed a demographic questionnaire, reporting age, education, occupation, race, parents' race, citizenship, duration of living in the U.S., location of birth, and English language ability.

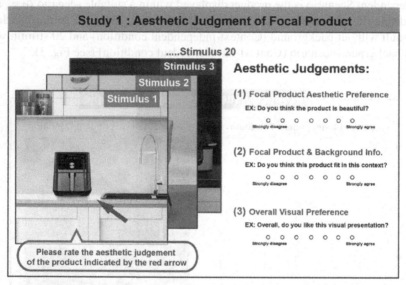

Fig. 4. Aesthetic judgments and visual preference of visual stimuli in Study 1

3.2 Results

The result showed the overall viewing time of American consumers (M = 9.72, SD = 6.36) is significantly greater than Taiwanese consumers (M = 3.17, SD = 1.90). In addition, Taiwanese consumers spend more time on Context-interdependent condition (M = 3.87, SD = 2.81) rather than Context-independent condition (M = 2.46, SD = 0.99). It showed contextual information of visual presentation draws more attention for East Asians, which corresponded to cultural variation in visual perception. Interestingly, American spent considerable viewing time on the Context-independent condition (14.43, SD = 6.70) as opposed to Context-interdependent condition (M = 5.03, SD = 6.02), which indicated that European American prefer to apply an analytical thinking style to focus on the product itself (see Fig. 5).

For the aesthetic judgment, the result demonstrated that Taiwanese consumers were higher evaluated on the Context-interdependent condition than on Context-independent condition, including focal product, the fitness of focal product and context, and purchase

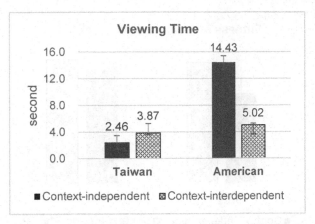

Fig. 5. Viewing time of visual stimuli between East and West in Study 1

intention (see Table 1). It indicated that East Asian consumer prefer the product visual presentation within the contextual information such as a suitable scenario or diverse background. In particular, in the rating of fitness of focal product and context—"*Do you think the product fit in this context?*", there is a significant difference between Context-interdependent condition (M = 4.70, SD = 0.66) and Context-independent condition (M = 3.76, SD = 0.80) for East Asians (see Fig. 6).

Table 1. Study 1 aesthetic judgments of visual stimuli for two experimental conditions

	Context-independent condition				Context-interdependent condition			
	Taiwan		American		Taiwan		American	
	M	SD	M	SD	M	SD	M	SD
Focal product aesthetic judgment	4.17	0.77	4.67	1.27	4.39	0.66	4.65	1.58
Fitness of focal product & context	3.76	0.80	4.58	1.35	4.70	0.66	4.79	1.37
Visual preference	3.65	0.86	4.64	1.36	4.42	0.73	4.77	1.41
Purchase intention	3.84	0.90	4.63	1.33	4.35	0.79	4.58	1.52
Viewing Time	2.46	0.99	14.43	6.70	3.87	2.81	5.02	6.03
Sample size (N)	49		105		49		101	

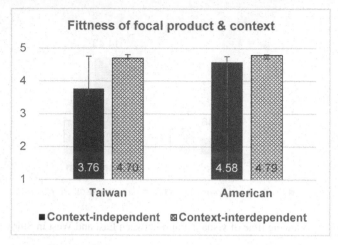

Fig. 6. Fitness rating of the visual scene in Study 1

4 Study 2

Study 2 is to investigate cross-cultural differences in consumers' visual perception of merchandising displays by measuring their recognition memory of the focal product within the two experimental conditions (Context-independent vs. Context-interdependent background). We apply Signal Detection Theory (SDT) to measure consumers' sensitivity to the focal object and background information between East Asians (e.g., Taiwanese) and Westerners (e.g., Americans). We added new sets of focal products as the distractor to manipulate the signal and noise trials. On the other hand, all the contextual information for signal and noise stimuli stays the same. Due to the cross-cultural variation in visual perception research, East Asians prefer to apply holistic thinking to attend to the entire visual scene, including object and context simultaneously. Hence, we hypothesize the recognition memory performance for East Asians in Context-interdependent condition would be poorer than Context-independent condition.

4.1 Methods

Material

Signal and Distractor Visual Stimuli Selection
For Study 2, all the signal stimuli of focal products were the same as in Study 1. We added another similar set of focal products as the distractor for the recognition memory test. In addition, all the contextual information is the same as in the previous study because we only ask participants to recognize the focal product. The standardized contextual information could help us to manipulate the visual element trial by trails. For example, a dining chair in the living room background (Context-independent condition) was in Study 1 as the signal. Another new dining chair in the same living room background showed in Study 2 as the distractor (see Fig. 7). Each product was shown in perspective containing its outline, shape, color, material, and detail. There were 40 visual stimuli in

Study 2, including 20 signal focal products and 20 distractor focal product visual stimuli in total. There are six product categories in total: dining chair, floor lamp, kettle, air flyer, dinner plate set, and air purifier, respectively.

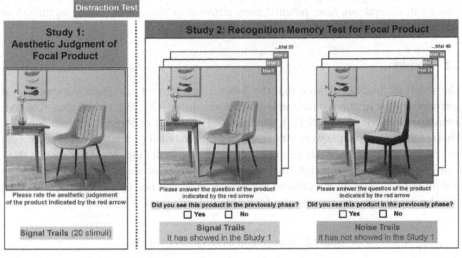

Fig. 7. Recognition memory test procedure in Study 2

Participants
Participants were the same as in Study 1. There were 206 European Americans (M_{age} = 34.9, 45.6% male, 54.4% female) and 98 Taiwanese (M_{age} = 22.5, 35.8% male, 64.2% female) respectively.

Procedure
After the participants finished Study 1 (Aesthetic judgments of visual stimuli), we asked participants to engage in a 10-min-long distraction test, which is unrelated to preference and recognition tasks. The purpose of conducting a distraction test before the recognition phase is to clean the participant's working memory of the previous preference phase. It will help to standardize their memory performance for the following recognition phase.

Next, participants were given a series of distractive focal products, which were similar to the signal focal product presented in previous Study 1. To clarify the task, we informed participants to recognize the focal product only, and they were shown a sample picture informing them which focal product in the picture is the signal stimulus indicated by a red arrow and the rest of the visual scene is the background before they started to official trials. The only difference in pictorial stimuli between Study 1 and Study 2 is the replacement of focal products. We substitute a similar set of distractors in the recognition phase for the focal product in Study 1. The rest of the background information remained the same (see Fig. 7 above). Participants were asked to identify as fast as possible the focal product that had actually appeared in the previous phase.

They responded with the *"Yes, I have seen it before"* or *"No, I have not seen it before"* keys to indicate whether they had previously seen the focal product. In sum, there are 40 stimuli in the recognition memory phase in Study 2, including 20 original signal focal products and 20 distractive focal products with the same background information. At the end of the study, participants completed a demographic questionnaire, reporting age, education, occupation, race, parents' race, citizenship, duration of living in the US or Taiwan, location of birth, and English language ability.

4.2 Results

The result of Study 2 showed that the general accuracy of recognition memory was performed well in the Context-independent condition (77.2%) rather than Context-interdependent condition (69.1%), whether for Easterners or Westerners (see Table 2). This result showed people were influenced by the contextual cue on the visual perception task. It provided evidence that people could recognize better the signal trials when there is no other contextual visual information. It led us to focus on the context-interdependent condition to investigate the cultural differences in visual perception when the product visual presentation accompanies by contextual information.

Table 2. Recognition memory test of Study 2

	Context-independent condition		Context-interdependent condition	
	Taiwan	American	Taiwan	American
Hit rate	0.91	0.69	0.76	0.62
False Alarm rate	0.13	0.38	0.20	0.41
Sensitivity (d')	2.57	0.94	1.70	0.59
Response Bias (β)	−0.10	−0.12	0.07	−0.04
Accuracy	89.0%	65.4%	78.2%	60.0%
Sample size(N)	49	105	49	101

In addition, the result of Taiwanese consumers showed the sensitivity of recognition memory in the Context-interdependent condition ($d' = 1.70$) was significantly low than Context-independent condition ($d' = 2.57$). It indicated that Taiwanese consumers were easily affected by contextual visual cues when they recognized the focal visual stimuli. When a signal visual stimulus is placed in the same contextual visual scene, Taiwanese consumers both pay attention to the focal object and context simultaneously. Hence, when a noise visual stimulus of focal product is displayed in the same context, Taiwanese consumers are vulnerable to recognizing the signal focal product because contextual information interferes with their visual perception. The result of recognition memory of sensitivity for East Asians provides evidence of cultural visual patterns between East and West. While East Asians matter the contextual visual cue when they apply holistic thinking style, it causes a higher weight of visual preference on the contextual information. In contrast, for Americans, there were no significant differences of the sensitivity of recognition memory between Context-independent condition ($d' = 0.94$) and Context-interdependent condition ($d' = 0.59$). It indicated the discriminability of focal product was not affected by the contextual visual scene for Americans (see Fig. 8).

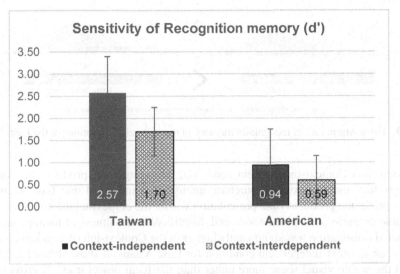

Fig. 8. Sensitivity of recognition memory of Study 2

Moreover, we found there is a dramatic cultural difference in the False Alarm (FA) rate of the recognition memory test. When subjects respond to a noise (new or distractor) as "yes" it is called a "False Alarm." Hence, the meaning of False Alarm rate represents the magnitude of attraction by the distractor in the visual perception. The higher False Alarm rate shows a higher possibility of making errors in discriminating the target object. The result of False Alarm for Taiwanese consumers in Context-interdependent condition (FA = 0.20) is significantly higher than Context-independent condition (FA = 0.13) (see Fig. 9). Conversely, there are no differences between Context-interdepend condition (FA = 0.41) and Context-independent condition (FA = 0.38) for Americans. This indicated that East Asians were likely to recognize the focal object with the assistance of contextual visual cues, whether it was a signal or noise visual stimuli. Consequently, contextual information lures the accuracy of recognizing the correct focal product.

5   Conclusion and Discussion

Two studies demonstrated the cultural difference in visual merchandising display on the E-commerce website. Study 1 investigated East Asian (Taiwanese) and European American (North American) consumers' aesthetic preferences regarding the product visual presentation within contextual information. We separate the product visual information into two parts: (1) focal product itself and (2) background information, respectively. We found that Taiwanese consumers were higher evaluated on the Context-interdependent

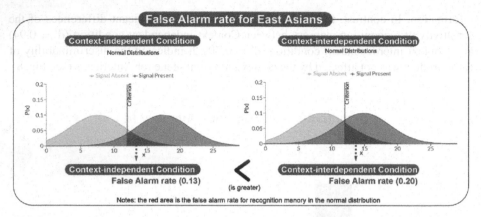

Fig. 9. False Alarm rate of recognition memory in the normal distribution for the East Asians

condition than Context-independent condition, including focal product, the fitness of focal product and context, and purchase intention. It indicated that East Asian consumers prefer the product visual presentation within the contextual information such as a suitable scenario or diverse background. Specifically, the fitness of focal product and contextual information was significantly higher in the Context-interdependent condition rather than Context-independent condition for East Asians. It showed that East Asians valued the whole visual scene more rather than the focal object itself. It provides evidence that East Asians do matter the contextual visual cue. Thus, East Asians apply the holistic thinking style to perceive visual stimuli and prefer to adopt these visual stimuli within contextual information.

Study 2 is to investigate cross-cultural differences in consumers' visual perception of merchandising displays by measuring their recognition memory of the focal product within various contextual backgrounds. We apply Signal Detection Theory (SDT) to measure consumers' sensitivity to the focal object and background information between East Asians (e.g., Taiwanese) and Westerners (e.g., Americans). Signal Detection Theory is to measure human recognition memory by manipulate the detection of signal or noise visual stimuli. It can be applied whenever two possible stimulus types must be discriminated. In Study 2, we used one of the most popular tasks: yes/no task, to test recognition memory. A yes/no task involves signal trails, which present old (target), and noise trails, which present new (distractor). A typical SDT usually encompasses a detection task. With the detection task, a mix of stimuli contains signals and noise.

Hence, we added new sets of focal products as the distractor to manipulate the signal and noise trials. On the other hand, all the contextual information for signal and noise stimuli stays the same. Due to the cross-cultural variation in visual perception research, we assumed East Asians prefer to apply holistic thinking to attend to the entire visual scene, including object and context simultaneously. Consequently, we hypothesize the recognition memory performance for East Asians in Context-interdependent condition would be poorer than Context-independent condition.

The result of recognition memory showed the sensitivity for discriminating the focal object was influenced by the contextual visual cue for East Asians. In addition, the False

Alarm rate supported that East Asians tended to make an error when they responded to the signal or noise visual stimuli depending on the contextual cue. When East Asians try to discriminate the focal product in the recognition memory test, they take the contextual information as one of the considerations. As a result, the False Alarm rate goes higher in the Context-interdependent condition. On the other hand, there are no significant differences in the False Alarm rate between Context-independent and Context-interdependent conditions for Americans.

Study 1 and Study 2 clearly indicated that when East Asians perceive the visual scene, they adopt holistic thinking to view the focal product and context at the same time. It means "Contextual Visual Scene Do Matter for East Asians," whether in the visual preference and cognitive process of sensing the target object in the context.

5.1　Contributions

In general, this present study identified that visual merchandising display and product visual representation on e-commerce could be influenced by the suitability of contextual information cross-culturally. The context moderates the cultural variations in the aesthetic judgment of the focal product. When a merchandise is displayed on the e-commerce platform worldwide, the variety of visual scenes attracts consumers' attention differently. Past research has shown the distinct visual pattern between East and West, which indicates that people from different cultural backgrounds might perceive the same visual presentation on the e-commerce platform differently. This research shed light on product visual presentation variations on the e-commerce platform cross-culturally. For example, Amazon's U.S. sites displays products visual information individually with minimal context, while the Japanese Amazon site shows products with relevant scenarios or contexts. This evidence of visual presentation on e-commerce is fascinating, but little research has explored the phenomenon before. This present study appears to be the first to establish the visual preference of cultural differences in product representation with contextual information. Moreover, we apply psychological experiment to investigate consumer's visual perception on the combination of focal product and context. Our results demonstrated that the aesthetic judgment of products and appreciation of the whole visual scenes are affected by cultural influences. We assert that current findings are generalizable and identify several important implications for the research field of cultural visual perception and marketing application. It contributes to cross-cultural design in the domain of cultural psychology and marketing to understand the underlying psychological mechanisms of visual perception.

5.2　Limitations and Future Research

We wish to acknowledge a few limitations of the current work. First, the current finding of the visual presentation was based on focal product and contextual visual scene only. Specifically, the contextual visual scenes for our experimental setting only show the visual information without any text or functional description. Future work should elaborate on the contextual information in detail to examine what contextual visual elements influence East Asians the most. Secondly, we will expand more Eastern and Western E-commerce platforms in the future to investigate the cross-cultural variations in visual merchandising display globally. Lastly, we will apply eye-tracking equipment to collect the physiological response of visual scenes to understand consumer's visual fixation and area of interest on the e-commerce platform. In sum, we expect to organize and establish precise online merchandise visual presentation design cross-culturally in the future.

References

1. UNCTAD: UNCTAD estimates of global e-commerce 2019 (2020). United Nations Conference on Trade and Development. https://unctad.org/news/global-e-commerce-hits-256-tri llion-latest-unctad-estimates
2. Kitayama, S., et al.: Perceiving an object and its context in different cultures: a cultural look at new look. Psychol. Sci. 14(3), 201–206 (2003)
3. Masuda, T., et al.: Cognition and perception. In Cohen, D., Kitayama, S. (eds.) Handbook of Cultural Psychology, 2nd edn., pp. 431–475. The Guilford Press, New York (2019)
4. Masuda, T., Batdorj, B., Senzaki, S.: Culture and attention: future directions to expand research beyond the geographical regions of WEIRD cultures. Front. Psychol. 11(1394) (2020)
5. Masuda, T., Nisbett, R.: Attending holistically versus analytically: comparing the context sensitivity of Japanese and Americans. J. Pers. Soc. Psychol. 81(5), 922–934 (2001)
6. Nisbett, R., et al.: Culture and systems of thought: holistic versus analytic cognition. Psychol. Rev. 108(2), 291–310 (2001)
7. Markus, H.R., Kitayama, S.: Culture and self: implications for cognition, emotions, and motivation. Psychol. Rev. 98(2), 224–253 (1991)
8. Nisbett, R.: The Geography of Thought: How Asians and Westerns think differently...and why. Living Together vs. Going It Alone 2003. Simon and Schuster, New York (2003)
9. Nisbett, R., Miyamoto, Y.: The influence of culture: holistic versus analytic perception. TRENDS Cogn. Sci. 9(10), 467–473 (2005)
10. Chua, H.F., Boland, J.E., Nisbett, R.: Cultural variation in eye movements during scene perception. Proc. Natl. Acad. Sci. U. S. A. 102(35), 12629–12633 (2005)
11. Masuda, T., et al.: Culture and aesthetic preference: comparing the attention to context of East Asians and Americans. Pers. Soc. Psychol. Bull. 34(9), 1260–1275 (2008)
12. Wang, H., et al.: How Much Information? East Asian and North American Cultural Products and Information Search Performance. Pers. Soc. Psychol. Bull. 38(12), 1539–1551 (2012)
13. Masuda, T., et al.: Culture and cognition: implications for art, design, and advertisement. In: Okazaki, S. (ed.) Handbook of Research on International Advertising. Edward Elgar, Cheltenham, UK, Northampton, MA, USA, pp. 109–132 (2012)
14. Senzaki, S., Masuda, T., Nand, K.: Holistic versus analytic expressions in artworks: cross-cultural differences and similarities in drawings and collages by Canadian and Japanese school-age children. J. Cross Cult. Psychol. 45(8), 1297–1316 (2014)
15. Green, D.M., Swets, J.A.: Signal Detection Theory and Psychophysics, New York (1966)
16. Snodgrass, J.G., Berger, G.L., Haydon, M.: Human Experimental Psychology. Oxford University Press, Oxford (1985)
17. Tashchian, A., White, J.D., Pak, S.: Signal detection analysis and advertising recognition: an introduction to measurement and interpretation issues. J. Mark. Res. 25(4), 397–404 (1988)

A Discussion on Consumer Kansei Over the Relative Position and Price of Commodities

Yen-Chieh Huang(✉) 🆔 and Yen Hsu 🆔

The Graduate Institute of Design Science, Tatung University, New Taipei, Taiwan
d11117011@o365.ttu.edu.tw, yhsu@gm.ttu.edu.tw

Abstract. This study mainly explored whether the relative position of the visual elements of price and product in the design of an online shopping page affects consumer preferences. The objective of this study is to determine whether the position of the two design elements of price and product to each other affects consumers' preference for the product.

The results of the analysis of the questionnaires collected by the statistical software are as follows: (1) Combining the two categories of products, it was found that the order of consumers' preference for the placement of price and product is: "product picture on the right and price on the left", "product picture on the left and price on the right", "product picture on top and price at the bottom", and "product picture at the bottom and price on top". (2) The orders of preference for price and product of the three representative products of daily appliances are the same, i.e. (3) According to the analysis of consumers' preference for the relative position of price and product by age, those aged 15 to 25 and 26 to 35 preferred the "product picture on the left and price on the right", while those aged 36 to 45 and 46 to 55 preferred the "product picture on the right and price on the left". The results of this study reveal what patterns consumers prefer when viewing product advertisements in the current rise of e-commerce shopping platforms, which in turn leads to a positive impression of consumers on the product.

Keywords: Kansei engineering · consumer preferences · price-product left-right up-down placement

1 Introduction

1.1 Research Background and Motives

In recent years, consumers have shifted from shopping offline to online due to the COVID-19 pandemic, which has facilitated many shops that were originally based on physical sales to slowly transform and expand their online sales models. According to the SHOPLINE Online Store White Paper, online orders grow by up to 85% in 2020 from 2019, suggesting a significant change in the way consumers buy products. However, when potential consumers visit a shopping website, the advertisements on the page affect them to have different opinions and ideas about the brand and the products, and improving their preference for the product can increase the chance of the product being

P.-L. P. Rau (Ed.): HCII 2023, LNCS 14022, pp. 479–493, 2023.
https://doi.org/10.1007/978-3-031-35936-1_35

selected. Therefore, in the marketing of products on online shopping platforms, the layout design of advertisements can be an important way for merchants to promote their products. In advertising design, apart from the product pictures, the price will also be included. The increased adoption of this design technique has highlighted the importance of the layout between product and price. Nonetheless, Cai et al. (2012) expressed the difference between left and right through a mental number line, noting that in life, numbers are always from left to right, which indirectly affects consumers' preference for the advertising page. Therefore, the position of products and prices is an issue worth exploring.

This study mainly explored whether the relative position of the visual elements of price and product in the layout design of an online shopping page affects consumer preferences. The following purposes of this study provide a clearer understanding: (1) Consumer preference is influenced by the position of the design elements of price and product to each other in the design layout. (2) Whether consumer preferences for the position of price and product are influenced by the different product categories. (3) Whether consumer preferences for the placement of price and product on an advertising page vary according to age and gender.

2 Literature Review

2.1 Evaluation Relationship of Relative Position of Product and Price

Potential consumers are often influenced by advertisements and have different opinions and attitudes towards a product or image, which further influences their purchases. Therefore, it is crucial for marketing managers and researchers to understand what design techniques they should use to draw customers' attention to the products they intend to sell, as perceptions of products, positions, promotions, and related objects are central to the interaction between the market and consumers (Krishna 2012). Advertising designers should gain a clear picture of the product attributes to effectively improve consumer preference for the product when they view the advertising page, and help consumers to understand and purchase the product (Nelson and Simmons 2009). As the product packaging design is validated to affect consumer preferences, the attributes and the position relevance of a product cannot be neglected (Nelson and Simmons 2009; Holbrook and Moore 1981). Clearly, the position of the product picture in an advertisement is absolutely relevant to consumer preference for the advertisement. Scholars (Valenzuela et al. 2012) suggest that the more expensive the product, the more it should be placed to the right, and the older the consumer group to whom it is sold, the more it should be placed to the right. According to Deng and Kahn (2009), if a product is placed on the left of the page, the product looks heavy and gives consumers a sense of security to buy it.

The position of a product affects the degree to which consumers prefer the advertisement, and Christman and Pinger (1997) used eye-tracking instruments to understand the order in which consumers read advertisements. Consumers will spend the most time on the product picture regardless of the number of advertising elements. Through a comparison of the time by the position of the product picture, consumers spend significantly longer time on the product picture on the right than the left. The reading habits of consumers have a lot to do with the beginning and end of the advertisement, so many advertisers create dynamic advertisements with products placed from left to right, so that consumers can focus more on the product itself (Fuhrman and Boroditsky 2010). Thus, the readability of advertisements makes consumers more willing to view the content and remember the content of smooth advertisements better (Ferraro et al. 2009).

Among the various consumption ad space, basic elements, such as product pictures, prices, and the logo of the business or the slogan of the product, are the most often used and will leave a deep impression on consumers. In the case of a horizontal printed product advertisement, the product, price, and logo should be presented in a level position which is more preferred by consumers. Chae and Hoegg (2013) argued that the position of a product on the advertising page affects consumer preferences for the product and that different consumer groups have different preferences. Some scholars have also explored the differences in consumer preferences between vertical and horizontal advertising. Simons and Rensink (2005) held that in the layout of a vertical advertisement, a long slogan being divided into too many lines will make consumers lose interest in the product because it is not easy to read. Therefore, when designing a vertical advertisement, the copy must be concise. Shapiro and Nielsen (2013) studied and compared the position of products in vertical and horizontal advertisements and found that horizontal advertisements were more suitable for describing and explaining the product, whereas vertical ones were more suitable for explaining the context in which the product was used. However, in today's advertising layouts, it is rare to see only one product on the page, with no copy, logo, or price for the product. If other elements are added to the advertising page, are consumer preferences for the layout still the same as described in the literature above? Therefore, this study took two design elements of price and product to explore consumer preferences.

2.2 Evaluation Relationship of the Impact of Product Category on Product Position and the Relative Position of Price

The fast-moving society of today is full of a wide range of products, some of which are ever-changing and some of which have been existing for a long time. Whether or not consumer preferences vary for advertisements of products in different categories. Meier and Robinson (2006) suggested that for consumers, if a product has been placed at a fixed point for a long time, or if the product is older and its appearance is less likely to change over time, they will prefer the product as it gives them a great sense of trust and certainty when it is placed on the left. When placed on the left side, consumers will feel a sense of trust and certainty about the product and thus prefer it. New and high-tech products placed on the left can be greatly favored by consumers by virtue of their novelty (Ouellet et al. 2010), while light or technology-based products (e.g., snacks and computer equipment) can be perceived as unstable by consumers due to their attributes, so it is recommended that these categories of products are placed on the left. We can see that the category of the product does have a significant impact on consumer preference for the layout (Deng and Kahn 2009).

2.3 Relationship of Preference and Age-Based Perception

According to previous studies, the younger the consumers, the more they prefer ornate packaging designs, while adults prefer plain packaging designs. Therefore, the packaging design should be appropriate for the target consumers (Raheem et al. 2014). In addition, the printed information aims to attract consumers and stimulate them to buy the product (Silayoi and Speece 2004; Butkeviciene et al. 2008). Teenagers prefer a direct and simple introduction to the product, which can induce curiosity from this group about the product and lead to purchase. On the contrary, the middle-aged group prefers an imaginative presentation of products with an aesthetic concept when making a selection (Deng and Kahn 2009).

Guo (2013) studied the popularity of online shopping and the preference of consumers in Taiwan and found that the personal utilization rate of online community services reached 67.62% and that of online shopping services was 59.62%. The majority of these online community users are under the age of 44, while users aged 20–24 accounted for the highest proportion (89.5%). Furthermore, they use online community services due to the influence of their peers. In terms of the age distribution of online shoppers, the highest proportion of shoppers is aged 22–44, who use online shopping because it is convenient to shop from home and preferential prices are provided online. It can be seen that digital media has become the most important procurement partner for consumers in Taiwan, with the vast majority of them reading large amounts of information online and frequently shopping on various websites. With the popularity of the internet in Taiwan, online shopping or marketing through media to prompt consumers to buy products is bound to increase. Therefore, four age groups were defined as the main respondents for this study: 15 to 25, 26 to 35, 36 to 45, and 46 to 55 years old.

3 Experimental Design

The main objective of this study is to figure out whether the relative position of the visual design elements of price and product affects consumer preferences, and whether different product categories and age groups have the same preference level.

3.1 Selection of Representative Samples from the Questionnaire

To study this issue, it is important to confirm that consumers of all age groups have the same knowledge and understanding of each product category. Hence, the questionnaire stimuli were selected from two product categories, namely, daily appliances and 3C home appliances, to explore consumers' perceptions of different product categories. Products selected from the category of daily appliances included tumblers, lamps, and chairs, while those selected from the category of 3C home appliances included over-ear headphones, mouses, and Bluetooth speakers. Representative and suitable samples of questionnaires were acquired from various online shopping platforms, for which the screening criteria are to avoid samples with ambiguous appearances or difficult for the test subjects to recognize their initial functions, and the collected pictures were subject to post-production image processing. The six product samples are shown in Fig. 1.

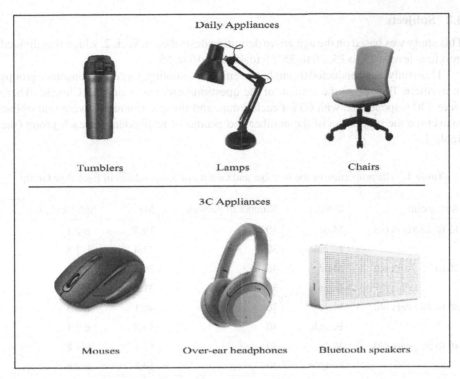

Fig. 1. Appearance of Tested Samples

The post-production image process includes resizing the image, coloring the image in greyscale to avoid color effects on the screening, removing the brand logo to avoid any personal preference of the test subject due to brand association and any accompanying objects to avoid visual interference, and lowering the corresponding price of the products below current market price in Taiwan to avoid price interference. The appearance of the products screened is shown in Fig. 2.

Fig. 2. Picture Production of Tested Samples

3.2 Subjects

This study was based on the age group definition described in Sect. 2, which was divided into four levels: 15 to 25, 26 to 35, 36 to 45, and 46 to 55.

This study was conducted through convenience sampling, targeting consumer groups in northern Taiwan, so the content of the questionnaire was mainly in Chinese. There were 240 respondents, with 60 for each group, and the questionnaires were sent online to average the proportion of the number and gender of respondents in each group (see Table 1).

Table 1. The proportion of the Number and Gender of Respondents in Each Age Group

Age group	Gender	Number of persons	Mean	Std. Deviation
15 to 25 years old	Male	30	19.5	± 2.1
	Female	30	21.4	± 1.8
26 to 35 years old	Male	30	29.8	± 1.6
	Female	30	31.5	± 2.0
36 to 45 years old	Male	30	40.1	± 2.5
	Female	30	39.8	± 2.1
46 to 55 years old	Male	30	51.4	± 1.8
	Female	30	53.5	± 2.8

3.3 Questionnaire Design

The survey was conducted with an online questionnaire, and the two layout design elements of price and product were arranged for each respondent. The preferences were measured using a Likert scale and divided into seven levels, with 7 representing "strongly like" and 1 representing "strongly dislike". Each level has a corresponding adjective so that the respondent can answer clearly. The preference questionnaire is shown in Fig. 3.

Fig. 3. Preference Questionnaire Response

The questionnaire was divided into two parts, namely the basic information of the respondents and the content of the questionnaire. Before filling in the questionnaire, the respondents were informed of the purpose of this study and invited to respond to these representative samples, regardless of factors such as brand, material, color, and price.

4 Research Results Analysis

Before proceeding with the findings, the corresponding representative symbols for the narrative sample sentences, which are repeated several times in this chapter, are shown in Table 2 for ease of reading.

Table 2. Corresponding Representative Symbols for the Narrative Sample Sentences Repeated Several Times in This Chapter

Narrative sample sentence	Representative symbol
Product picture on the right and price on the left	A
Product picture on the left and price on the right	B
Product picture at the bottom and price on top	C
Product picture on top and price at the bottom	D

4.1 Preference of All Respondents for the Position of the Two Layout Design Elements of "Price" and "Product"

The purpose of this stage is to figure out whether the preference for the two layout design elements, price and product, in an advertisement is the same for all the respondents and analyze the data obtained from all the respondents. The mean and standard deviation statistics of the preferences of the tested samples are shown in Table 3.

Table 3. Preference of All Respondents for the Position of Layout Design Elements

	Mean	Std. Deviation
A	5.94	0.64
B	5.40	0.74
C	3.34	0.75
D	3.16	0.73

All products were sorted by price position in descending order of mean as follows: product picture on the right and price on the left (M = 5.94, SD = 0.64), product picture on the left and price on the right (M = 5.40, SD = 0.74), product picture at the bottom and price on top (M = 3.34, SD = 0.75), and the product picture on top and price at the bottom (M = 3.16, SD = 0.73).

4.2 Preference of All Respondents for the Position of the Layout Design Elements of 3C Home Appliances and Daily Appliances

Six products were selected for this study, including tumblers, lamps, and chairs from the category of daily appliances and over-ear headphones, mouses, and Bluetooth speakers from the category of 3C home appliances. The two major product categories were used to analyze the preferences of all respondents.

The mean and standard deviation statistics of preferences of all respondents for the samples in the category of 3C home appliances are shown in Table 4.

Table 4. Preference of All Respondents for the Position of the Layout Design Elements of 3C Home Appliances and Daily Appliances

	3C home appliances		Daily appliances	
	Mean	Std. Deviation	Mean	Std. Deviation
A	5.59	1.05	6.28	0.67
B	5.72	0.88	5.08	0.99
C	4.23	1.02	3.71	1.03
D	2.61	1.12	2.45	1.07

The preference for 3C home appliances is ranked in descending order of average as follows: Price on the right of the product picture (M = 5.72, SD = 0.88), product picture on the right and price on the left (M = 5.59, SD = 1.05), product picture at the bottom and price on top (M = 4.23, SD = 1.02), and the product picture on top and price at the bottom (M = 2.61, SD = 1.12).

The preference for daily appliances is ranked in descending order of average as follows: product picture on the right and price on the left (M = 6.28, SD = 0.67), product picture on the left and price on the right (M = 5.08, SD = 0.99), product picture at the bottom and price on top (M = 3.71, SD = 1.03), and the product picture on top and price at the bottom (M = 2.45, SD = 1.07).

4.3 Preference of Respondents in Different Age Groups for the Position of Layout Design Elements

In this study, the respondents were divided into four groups: 15–25 years old, 26-35 years old, 36–45 years old, and 46–55 years old, and their preferences for products and prices were analyzed by the groups. The data are shown in Table 5.

The preference of respondents aged 15–25 for the relative position of the two layout design elements of price and product is: product picture on the right and price on the left (M = 6.34, SD = 0.41), product picture on the left and price on the right (M = 5.26, SD = 0.95), product picture at the bottom and price on top (M = 3.33, SD = 0.76), and the product picture on top and price at the bottom (M = 3.03, SD = 0.76).

The preference of respondents aged 26–35 for the relative position of the two layout design elements of price and product is: product picture on the right and price on the left

(M = 6.28, SD = 0.43), product picture on the left and price on the right (M = 5.15, SD = 0.74), product picture at the bottom and price on top (M = 3.26, SD = 0.68), and the product picture on top and price at the bottom (M = 2.95, SD = 0.67).

Table 5. Preference of Respondents in Different Age Groups for the Position of Layout Design Elements

	Age	N	Mean	Std. Deviation	Minimum	Maximum
A	15–25	60	6.34	0.41	5.17	7.00
	26–35	60	6.28	0.43	5.17	7.00
	36–45	60	5.57	0.61	4.00	6.67
	46–55	60	5.57	0.61	4.00	6.83
	Total	240	5.94	0.64	4.00	7.00
B	15–25	60	5.26	0.95	2.50	6.67
	26–35	60	5.15	0.74	3.17	6.50
	36–45	60	5.59	0.55	4.33	6.67
	46–55	60	5.60	0.53	4.33	6.67
	Total	240	5.40	0.74	2.50	6.67
C	15–25	60	3.33	0.76	1.83	6.00
	26–35	60	3.26	0.68	2.17	5.50
	36–45	60	3.38	0.77	1.17	4.83
	46–55	60	3.39	0.77	1.17	4.83
	Total	240	3.34	0.75	1.17	6.00
D	15–25	60	3.03	0.76	1.67	5.17
	26–35	60	2.95	0.67	1.67	4.67
	36–45	60	3.33	0.72	2.00	5.17
	46–55	60	3.34	0.72	2.00	5.17
	Total	240	3.16	0.73	1.67	5.17

The preference of respondents aged 36–45 for the relative position of the two layout design elements of price and product is: product picture on the left and price on the right (M = 5.59, SD = 0.55), product picture on the right and price on the left (M = 5.57, SD = 0.61), product picture at the bottom and price on top (M = 3.38, SD = 0.77), and the product picture on top and price at the bottom (M = 3.33, SD = 0.72).

The preference of respondents aged 46–55 for the relative position of the two layout design elements of price and product is: product picture on the left and price on the right (M = 5.60, SD = 0.53), product picture on the right and price on the left (M = 5.57, SD = 0.61), product picture at the bottom and price on top (M = 3.39, SD = 0.77), and the product picture on top and price at the bottom (M = 3.34, SD = 0.72).

4.4 Significance Comparison of Preference of Respondents in Different Age Groups for the Position of the Layout Design Elements of 3C Home Appliances and Daily Appliances

In this chapter, the six product samples were categorized into two categories of 3C home appliances and daily appliances, and the relationship between the position of price and product in the two categories and the four age groups is shown in Table 5 and Table 6.

Table 6. Preference of Respondents in Different Age Groups for the Position of the Layout Design Elements of 3C Home Appliances

	Age	N	Mean	Std. Deviation	Minimum	Maximum	F	Post inspection
A	15–25	60	6.35	1.038	1	7	30.05^{***}	15–25 > 36–45
	26–35	60	6.28	1.120	1	7		15–25 > 46–55
	36–45	60	6.35	1.106	1	7		26–35 > 36–45
	46–55	60	6.14	1.509	1	7		26–35 > 46–55
	Total	240	6.28	1.208	1	7		
B	15–25	60	5.28	1.652	1	7	7.65^{***}	36–45 > 15–25
	26–35	60	4.98	1.658	1	7		36–45 > 26–35
	36–45	60	4.99	1.499	1	7		46–55 > 15–25
	46–55	60	5.06	1.518	1	7		46–55 > 26–35
	Total	240	5.08	1.585	1	7		
C	15–25	60	2.52	1.786	1	7	5.95^{**}	36–45 > 26–35
	26–35	60	2.44	1.804	1	7		46–55 > 26–35
	36–45	60	2.42	1.778	1	7		
	46–55	60	2.42	1.778	1	7		
	Total	240	2.45	1.783	1	7		
D	15–25	60	3.67	1.778	1	7	5.81^{**}	36–45 > 26–35
	26–35	60	3.49	1.722	1	7		46–55 > 26–35
	36–45	60	3.84	1.581	1	7		
	46–55	60	3.84	1.581	1	7		
	Total	240	3.71	1.671	1	7		

The preference of respondents in different age groups for 3C home appliances being placed on the right is: Respondents aged 15–25 preferred 3C home appliances being placed on the right more significantly than those aged 36–45 and 46–55. Respondents aged 26–35 preferred 3C home appliances being placed on the right more significantly than those aged 36–45 and 46–55.

The preference of respondents in different age groups for 3C home appliances being placed on the left is: Respondents aged 36–45 preferred 3C home appliances being placed on the left more significantly than those aged 15–25 and 26–35. Respondents aged 46–55 preferred 3C home appliances being placed on the left more significantly than those aged 15–25 and 26–35.

The preference of respondents in different age groups for 3C home appliances being placed at the bottom is: Respondents aged 36–45 preferred 3C home appliances being placed at the bottom more significantly than those aged 26–35. Respondents aged 46–55 preferred 3C home appliances being placed at the bottom more significantly than those aged 26–35.

The preference of respondents in different age groups for 3C home appliances being placed on top is: Respondents aged 36–45 preferred 3C home appliances being placed on top more significantly than those aged 26–35. Respondents aged 46–55 preferred 3C home appliances being placed on top more significantly than those aged 26–35 (Table 7).

Table 7. Preference of Respondents in Different Age Groups for the Position of the Layout Design Elements of Daily Appliances

	Age	N	Mean	Std. Deviation	Minimum	Maximum	F	Post inspection
A	15–25	60	6.33	.783	4	7	46.92***	15–25 > 36–45
	26–35	60	6.27	.845	3	7		15–25 > 46–55
	36–45	60	4.78	2.205	1	7		26–35 > 36–45
	46–55	60	4.99	2.029	1	7		26–35 > 46–55
	Total	240	5.59	1.752	1	7		
B	15–25	60	5.23	1.575	1	7	28.69***	36–45 > 15–25
	26–35	60	5.32	1.523	1	7		36–45 > 26–35
	36–45	60	6.20	.960	3	7		46–55 > 15–25
	46–55	60	6.13	.988	3	7		46–55 > 26–35
	Total	240	5.72	1.367	1	7		
C	15–25	60	4.15	1.451	1	7	4.75**	36–45 > 15–25
	26–35	60	4.09	1.540	1	7		36–45 > 26–35
	36–45	60	4.33	1.422	1	7		46–55 > 15–25
	46–55	60	4.36	1.401	1	7		46–55 > 26–35
	Total	240	4.23	1.456	1	7		
D	15–25	60	2.38	1.435	1	7	5.11**	36–45 > 15–25
	26–35	60	2.41	1.401	1	7		36–45 > 26–35
	36–45	60	2.82	1.554	1	7		46–55 > 15–25
	46–55	60	2.83	1.509	1	7		46–55 > 26–35
	Total	240	2.61	1.489	1	7		

The preference of respondents in different age groups for daily appliances being placed on the right is: Respondents aged 15–25 preferred daily appliances being placed on the right more significantly than those aged 36–45 and 46–55. Respondents aged 26–35 preferred daily appliances being placed on the right more significantly than those aged 36–45 and 46–55.

The preference of respondents in different age groups for daily appliances being placed on the left is: Respondents aged 36–45 preferred daily appliances being placed on the left more significantly than those aged 15–25 and 26–35.Respondents aged 46–55 preferred daily appliances being placed on the left more significantly than those aged 15–25 and 26–35.

The preference of respondents in different age groups for daily appliances being placed at the bottom is: Respondents aged 36–45 preferred daily appliances being placed at the bottom more significantly than those aged 15–25 and 26–35. Respondents aged 46–55 preferred daily appliances being placed at the bottom more significantly than those aged 15–25 and 26–35.

The preference of respondents in different age groups for daily appliances being placed on the top is: Respondents aged 36–45 preferred daily appliances being placed on the top more significantly than those aged 15–25 and 26–35. Respondents aged 46–55 preferred daily appliances being placed on the top more significantly than those aged 15–25 and 26–35.

4.5 Preference of Consumers in Different Age Groups for the Position of

This chapter mainly explores whether there is a significant relationship between the preferences and the four age groups of consumers by changing the position of the two layout design elements of price and product of eight different product samples. The relationship is shown in Table 8.

The preference of respondents in different age groups for all products being placed on the right is: Respondents aged 15–25 preferred all products being placed on the right more significantly than those aged 36–45 and 46–55. Respondents aged 26–35 preferred all products being placed on the right more significantly than those aged 36–45 and 46–55.

The preference of respondents in different age groups for all products being placed on the left is: Respondents aged 36–45 preferred all products being placed on the left more significantly than those aged 15–25 and 26–35. Respondents aged 46–55 preferred all products being placed on the left more significantly than those aged 15–25 and 26–35.

The preference of respondents in different age groups for all products being placed at the bottom is: Respondents aged 36–45 preferred all products being placed at the bottom more significantly than those aged 26–35. Respondents aged 46–55 preferred all products being placed at the bottom more significantly than those aged 26–35.

The preference of respondents in different age groups for all products being placed on the top is: Respondents aged 36–45 preferred all products being placed on the top more significantly than those aged 26–35.Respondents aged 46–55 preferred all products being placed on the top more significantly than those aged 26–35.

Table 8. Preference of Respondents in Different Age Groups for the Position of Layout Design Elements of All Products.

	Age	N	Mean	Std. Deviation	Minimum	Maximum	F	Post inspection
A	15–25	60	6.34	.918	1	7	29.46***	15–25 > 36–45
	26–35	60	6.28	.991	1	7		15–25 > 46–55
	36–45	60	5.57	1.911	1	7		26–35 > 36–45
	46–55	60	5.57	1.875	1	7		26–35 > 46–55
	Total	240	5.94	1.543	1	7		
B	15–25	60	5.26	1.612	1	7	8.54***	36–45 > 15–25
	26–35	60	5.15	1.598	1	7		36–45 > 26–35
	36–45	60	5.59	1.395	1	7		46–55 > 15–25
	46–55	60	5.60	1.387	1	7		46–55 > 26–35
	Total	240	5.40	1.514	1	7		
C	15–25	60	3.33	1.819	1	7	6.51**	36–45 > 26–35
	26–35	60	3.26	1.867	1	7		46–55 > 26–35
	36–45	60	3.38	1.871	1	7		
	46–55	60	3.39	1.869	1	7		
	Total	240	3.34	1.855	1	7		
D	15–25	60	3.03	1.737	1	7	5.32**	36–45 > 26–35
	26–35	60	2.95	1.660	1	7		46–55 > 26–35
	36–45	60	3.33	1.647	1	7		
	46–55	60	3.34	1.625	1	7		
	Total	240	3.16	1.675	1	7		

5 Conclusion and Suggestions

5.1 Research Findings

The results of this study are positive in terms of whether the relative position of the visual elements of price and product in the online shopping pages affects consumer preferences. In particular, products with the price on the right or left of the product picture were highly preferred by all respondents. It was suspected that as mentioned in Sect. 2, this finding had much to do with consumers' reading habits and the beginning and end of the advertisement (Fuhrman and Boroditsky 2010).

According to the results of this study on consumer preferences for the relative position of the two layout design elements of price and product, regardless of the product category, background, and attribute (e.g., technology-based), consumers preferred horizontal layouts in No. 1 and No. 2. In particular, in terms of the layout design of 3C home appliances, the participants' preference for the layout in No. 1, i.e., the product picture on the left and price on the right, is the same as that mentioned in the literature in Sect. 2, that is, technology-based products placed on the left are greatly favored by consumers (Ouellet et al. 2010).

In terms of the significance of each age group, respondents aged 15 to 25 and 25 to 35 significantly preferred horizontal layouts with the product picture on the left and price on the right than those aged 36 to 45 and 46 to 55; respondents aged 36 to 45 and 46 to 55 significantly preferred horizontal layouts with the product picture on the right and price on the left picture than those aged 15 to 25 and 25 to 35. This is a significant trend for future designers to consider when designing. This provides a reference for designers in the future.

5.2 Recommendations for Future Research

This study used quantitative research methods to obtain responses from respondents through an online questionnaire. In the future, it is suggested that a more qualitative method, such as fieldworks, can be used for cross-comparison, which will provide more direct insights into consumers' perceptions of product layouts.

In this study, although the distance between the product and price has been adjusted to eliminate its effect on the judgment of the main experimental purpose, the distance between the two elements may cause different perceptions and preferences of consumers in the configuration of the advertising space. Therefore, future studies can incorporate price, product, and distance into the discussion.

References

Krishna, A.: An integrative review of sensory marketing: engaging the senses to affect perception, judgment and behavior. J. Consum. Psychol. **22**(3), pp. 332–351 (2012)

Butkeviciene, V., Stravinskiene, J., Rütelione, A.: Impact of consumer package communication on consumer decision making process. Econ. Eng. Decis. **1**(56), 57–65 (2008)

Cai, F., Shen, H., Hui, M.K.: The effect of location on price estimation: understanding number-location and number-order associations. J. Mark. Res. **49**(5), 718–724 (2012)

Chae, B., Hoegg, J.: The future looks "right": effects of horizontal location of advertising images on product attitude. J. Consum. Res. **40**(2), 223–238 (2013)

Christman, S., Pinger, K.: Lateral biases in aesthetic preferences: pictorial dimensions and neural mechanisms. Laterality **2**(2), 155–175 (1997)

Deng, X., Kahn, B.E.: Is your product on the right side? The 'location effect' on perceived product heaviness and package evaluation. J. Mark. Res. **46**, 725–738 (2009)

Ferraro, R., Bettman, J.R., Chartrand, T.L.: The power of strangers: the effect of incidental consumer brand encounters on brand choice. J. Consum. Res. **35**, 729–741 (2009)

Fuhrman, O., Boroditsky, L.: Cross-cultural differences in mental representations of time: evidence from an implicit nonlinguistic task. Cogn. Sci. **34**, 1430–1451 (2010)

Holbrook, M.B., Moore, W.L.: Feature inter actions in consumer judgments of verbal versus pictured presentations. J. Consum. Res. **8**, 103–113 (1981)

Nelson, L.D., Simmons, J.P.: On southbound ease and northbound fees: literal consequences of the metaphoric link between vertical position and cardinal direction. J. Mark. Res. **46**, 715–724 (2009)

Meier, B.P., Robinson, M.D.: Does 'feeling down' mean seeing down? Depressive symptoms and vertical selective attention. J. Res. Pers. **40**, 451–461 (2006)

Ouellet, M., Santiago, J., Funes, M.J., Lupianez, J.: Thinking about the future moves attention to the right. J. Exp. Psychol. Hum. Percept. Perform. **36**, 17–24 (2010)

Peracchio, L.A., Meyers-Levy, J.: Evaluating persuasion-enhancing techniques from a resource-matching perspective. J. Consum. Res. **24**, 178–191 (1997)

Raheem, R., Ahmad, N., Vishnu, P., Imamuddin, K.: Role of packaging and labeling on Pakistani consumers purchase decision. Eur. J. Sci. Res. **10**(16), 464–473 (2014)

Shapiro, S.A., Nielsen, J.H.: What the blind eye sees: incidental change detection as a source of perceptual fluency. J. Consum. Res. **39**(6), 1202–1218 (2013)

Silayoi, P., Speece, M.: Packaging and purchase decisions: an exploratory study on the impact of involvement level and time pressure. Br. Food J. **106**(8), 607–628 (2004)

Simons, D.J., Rensink, R.A.: Change blindness: past, present, and future. Trends Cogn. Sci. **9**, 16–20 (2005)

Valenzuela, A., Raghubir, P., Mitakakis, C.: Shelf space schemas: myth or reality? J. Bus. Res. (2012). https://doi.org/10.1016/j.jbusres.2011.12.006

A Comparative Study on the Cultural Difference of Users' Preference of Library Website Interface Design Between Korea and the United States

Mi-seul Jo[1], Lin Wang[1(✉)], and Zhe Chen[2]

[1] Incheon National University, Incheon 22012, Republic of Korea
linwang0@gmail.com
[2] Beihang University, Beijing 100191, China

Abstract. The interface of the library website should be designed in a way that provides a good user experience to users. However, the same user interface may have different user experiences in different cultures. This study investigated the cultural differences in users' preference for library website interface design factors including background colors, amounts of information presented, and image-based vs. text-based interfaces in Korea and the US. A survey was used as the research method. It was found both Koreans and Americans preferred a concise interface, meaning that too much information should not be presented on the homepage of library websites. There was a significant difference between the Korean subjects' and American subjects' preference for image vs. text-based interface. Koreans preferred text-based interfaces. On the opposite, Americans significantly preferred image-based interfaces. Due to the small sample size of this study, although there was no significant difference found, Korean subjects preferred no-color background more, and American subjects preferred colorful background more on the opposite. It is hoped that the results of this study can help libraries provide better services to users.

Keywords: Cultural Difference · Library Websites · Interface Design · Korean · American

1 Introduction

The spread of the Internet and web technology has created an environment where people all over the world can share information. Cultural difference is a variable that cannot be ignored in the field of human-computer interaction [1–4]. Due to the heterogeneity of traditional culture and lifestyle, users from different cultural backgrounds may have different user experiences with the same design elements [5]. Therefore, when designing a website, it is important to understand and respect the differences between different cultures [6]. Accordingly, designers need to understand the differences between different cultures and design a website suitable for the cultural background.

P.-L. P. Rau (Ed.): HCII 2023, LNCS 14022, pp. 494–502, 2023.
https://doi.org/10.1007/978-3-031-35936-1_36

Accordingly, this study examines the interface design factors of library websites and compares the preferences of Korean users in an eastern culture and American users in a western culture. The specific research process is as follows. First, the interface characteristics of the current Korean and American library web pages were analyzed. Five major libraries in Korea and the United States were chosen respectively. Second, based on the analyzed information, the interface design factors were defined. After that, a survey was conducted to compare users' preferences of the factors to find if there was a cultural difference.

2   Literature Review

2.1   Theories of Cultural Differences

Comparative study between cultures is an essential method for understanding other cultures. Through this, it is possible to reveal cultural universality and specificity. Regarding theories of cultural comparison, Hofstede's model [7] and Hall's model [8] are widely used as cross-cultural analysis models. Hofstede's cross-country cultural comparative analysis model is based on a 1983 study of IBM's 100,000 employees in more than 40 countries, which divides culture into five dimensions: Individualism-collectivism dimension, uncertainty avoidance dimension, power distance dimension, masculinity dimension, and long-term orientation dimension. The model has empirical numerical comparisons and comparative items that can be universally applied across countries.

As the objective of this study is to compare the cultural differences in preferences of interface design factors of library websites in Korea and the US, numerical differences in the Hofstede cultural dimensions are compared between the two countries, as shown in Fig. 1. By Hofstede's cultural dimensions, Korea has a relatively higher power distance, low individualism, relatively lower masculinity, high uncertainty avoidance, and high long-term orientation. On the opposite, the US has a relatively lower power distance, high individualism, relatively higher masculinity, lower uncertainty avoidance, and low long-term orientation.

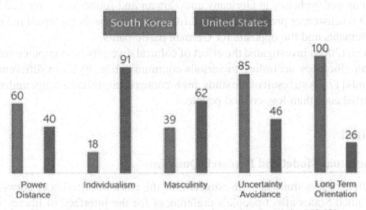

Fig. 1. Hofstede's cultural dimensions of Korea and the US [9]

In cultures with high individualism, the consciousness of 'I' is strongly affected. Competition rather than cooperation is encouraged, individual goals take precedence over group goals, and people tend not to depend on organizations. These cultures emphasize individual initiative and achievement and value individual decision-making [10]. On the other hand, collectivist cultures, in contrast to individualistic cultures, prioritize group or organizational goals. Korean consciousness is influenced by Confucianism. It is the expression of consciousness that distinguishes the group to which one belongs (in-group) and the group to which one does not belong (out-group). Koreans value harmony and harmony in interpersonal relationships [11].

2.2 Factors of Web Interface Design

Regarding the factors of webpage interface design, Hong et al. (2009) found that web interface design elements including color, image, and layout significantly influenced the users' emotional experience of the websites in their study [12].

Lee (2004) found that if the color was properly used, it could be used to improve the efficiency of information expression in a wide range. But if used inappropriately, it could significantly reduce the function of the display system [13].

In Callahan's research (2005), it was found that the homepage image was the most interesting element among the elements that appeared on the homepage screen. It was an element that attracted the attention of users and arouses curiosity because it had direct, implicit, and symbolic characteristics compared to text [14].

2.3 Cultural Differences in Interface Design

Cheng and Kim (2022) studied the cultural differences between action movie posters in Korea, China, and Japan based on differences in masculinity and femininity dimensions in Hofstede's cultural dimensions [15]. As a result, compared to Korean and Chinese, Japanese action movie posters used relatively high-chroma and high-contrast colors. Also, when comparing the layout of the posters, close-up of the main character's facial expressions and logos were exaggerated in Japanese posters, resulting in a visual interface design difference in a high-masculinity country. A study by Cheng, Wu, and Reiner (2019) compared websites in Germany and Taiwan and found that color had a significant effect on customer preference [16]. Taiwanese participants preferred red to blue in website elements and the opposite for German participants.

Xie et al. (2008) investigated the effect of cultural diversity on computer-based communication efficiency according to various communication styles in different cultural backgrounds [17]. As a result of the study, high-context people had a better understanding of non-verbal cues than low-context people.

3   Method

3.1   Conceptual Model and Research Questions

The objective of this study is to investigate how the cultural differences between Korea and the United States affect people's preferences for the interface of library websites. Further, whether there is a significant difference exists between Korean and US users' preferences of library websites' background color, the amount of information, and image-based vs. text-based interface. The conceptual model is shown in Fig. 2.

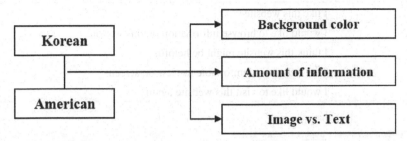

Fig. 2. Conceptual model

Research question 1: Are there differences in background color preferences for library website interfaces between Koreans and Americans?

Research question 2: Are there differences in preferences for the amount of information for library website interfaces between Koreans and Americans?

Research question 3: Are there differences in image-based interface vs. text-based interface preferences for library websites between Koreans and Americans?

3.2 Questionnaire Construction and Survey Procedure

A survey was conducted. Based on the selected library homepages, as shown in Table 1, library website prototype interfaces were generated for comparison in the survey, as shown in Fig. 3. The interfaces were shown to the subjects by mobile phones. The subjects rated each item to indicate the degree of agreement with the statement listed in Table 2. 5-point Likert scales were used (from completely disagree to strongly agree).

Table 1. Selected library homepage for reference of prototype interface.

Selected Korean Libraries	Selected US libraries
National Library of Korea https://www.nl.go.kr/	Library of Congress https://www.loc.gov/
Seoul Metropolitan Library https://lib.seoul.go.kr/	the New York Public Library https://www.nypl.org/
Incheon Metropolitan City Office of Education Integrated Public Library https://lib.ice.go.kr/ice/index.do	Seattle Public Library https://www.spl.org/
Gwangju Central Library https://lib.gen.go.kr/jungang/	Columbia Public Library https://www.dbrl.org/
Gyeonggi-do Cyber Library https://www.library.kr/cyber/index.do	Las Vegas-Clark County Library https://thelibrarydistrict.org/

Table 2. The statements used in the questionnaire

No.	Statement
1	I like this website
2	I would like to browse information on this website
3	I think this website might be helpful
4	This website is comfortable to view on screen
5	I would like to visit this website again

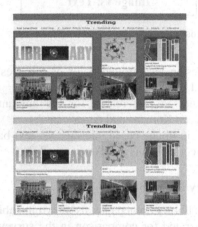

a. colorful background

b. no-color background

c. small amount of information

d. large amount of information

e. image-based interface

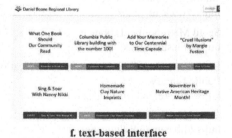

f. text-based interface

Fig. 3. Library website interface prototypes used in the survey

3.3 Subject

There were total ten Koreans and five Americans participated in this study. All Korean subjects were female and there were four females and one male US subject. The age range for Korean subjects was as: 6 subjects in their 30's, 2 subjects in their 40's, and 2 subjects in their 50's. The age range for American subjects was as: 1 participant in her 10's, 3 subjects in their 20's, and 1 participant in her 50's. For the educational background, all Korean subjects had college or higher education. All American subjects had college or higher education except for one high school student.

4 Result

4.1 Website Background Color Preference

For Korean subjects, the average preference for colorful backgrounds was 2.76, and the average for no-color backgrounds was 3.32, indicating Korean subjects had a higher preference for no-color backgrounds. On the opposite, for American subjects, the average preference for the colorful background was 3.28, and the average for no-color backgrounds was 2.60, indicating American subjects had a higher preference for colorful backgrounds, which was different from Korean subjects, as shown in Table 3. Although there was no significant difference in the statistical test for the comparison, a large part was due to the small sample size of this study.

Table 3. Library website background color preference of Korean and American subjects

Culture	Color	Mean	SD	F	p
Korean	colorful	2.76	1.22	1.307	0.268
	no-color	3.32	0.95		
American	colorful	3.28	1.03	0.991	0.349
	no-color	2.60	0.80		

4.2 Preference for the Amount of Information

Both Korean and American subjects preferred a small amount of information. Korean subjects' significantly ($F = 10.065$, $p = 0.005$) preferred a small amount of information (mean $= 3.48$, SD $= 0.71$) on the library websites over a large amount of information (mean $= 2.32$, SD $= 0.91$). Similarly, American subjects significantly ($F = 101.531$, $p < 0.001$) preferred a small amount of information (mean $= 3.64$, SD $= 0.30$) on the library websites than a large amount of information (mean $= 1.36$, SD $= 0.41$) (Table 4).

Table 4. Information amount preference of Korean and American subjects

Culture	Amount of information	Mean	SD	F	p
Korean	small	3.48	0.71	10.065	**0.005***
	large	2.32	0.91		
American	small	3.64	0.30	101.531	**<0.001***
	large	1.36	0.41		

Note: * means p < 0.05

4.3 Preference of Image vs. Text

Korean subjects preferred text-based interface (mean = 3.20, SD = 0.88) rather than image-based interface (mean = 2.56, SD = 1.22). On the opposite, American subjects significantly (F = 47.361, p < 0.001) preferred the image-based interface (mean = 4.16, SD = 0.50) rather than the text-based interface (mean = 1.80, SD = 0.58) which is different from Korean subjects (Table 5).

Table 5. Image vs. text preference of Korean and American subjects

Culture	image vs. text	Mean	SD	F	p
Korean	image	2.56	1.22	1.808	0.195
	text	3.20	0.88		
American	image	4.16	0.50	47.361	**<0.001***
	text	1.80	0.58		

Note: * means p < 0.05

5 Conclusion

The library website interface should be designed in a way that provides a good user experience to users. The user experience might be affected by various factors such as background color, amount of information, and whether the interface is image-based or text-based. In this study, users' preferences for library websites' background color, amount of information, and image-based vs. text-based interface were investigated in the cultures of Korea and the United States.

A survey was conducted. The result showed that there were significant differences between Korean subjects' and American subjects' preferences on the above interface design factors. First, for the website background colors, due to the small sample size, although there was no statistically significant difference found, it could still be seen that Korean subjects preferred a background without color, while Americans preferred a colored background. Second, for the amount of information, both Korean subjects and

American subjects preferred an interface with a small amount of information. But at present, most Korean libraries are presenting quite a lot of information on their home pages. According to the result of this study, users may wish to reduce the amount of information on the homepages of library websites. Last, there was a significant difference in Korean subjects' and American subjects' preference for image-based vs. text-based interfaces. Korean subjects preferred text-based interfaces. On the opposite, American subjects significantly preferred image-based interfaces.

The biggest limitation of this study should be that the sample was too small. In addition, only three interface design factors were studied. In future studies, it is necessary to investigate the influence of other design factors on the website interface. Also, to increase the reliability and credibility of the study, more participants should be involved.

References

1. Chen, J., Wang, L., Wang, H., Kang, H., Hwang, M.-H., Lee, D.G.: Influences of PM2.5 pollution on the public's negative emotions, risk perceptions, and coping behaviors: a cross-national study in China and Korea. J. Risk Res. https://doi.org/10.1080/13669877.2022.216 2106
2. Liu, P., Wang, L., Vincent, C.: Self-driving vehicles against human drivers: equal safety is far from enough. J. Exp. Psychol. Appl. **26**(4), 692 (2020)
3. Liu, P., Du, Y., Wang, L., Da Young, J.: Ready to bully automated vehicles on public roads? Accid. Anal. Prev. **137**, 105457 (2020)
4. Wang, L., Ali, M., Kim, H.J., Lee, S., Hernandez Perlines, F.: Individual entrepreneurial orientation, value congruence, and individual outcomes: does the institutional entrepreneurial environment matter? Bus. Strategy Environ. **30**(5), 2293–2312 (2021)
5. Li, T., Wang, L., Liu, J., Yuan, J., Liu, P.: Sharing the roads: robot drivers (vs. human drivers) might provoke greater driving anger when they perform identical annoying driving behaviors. Int. J. Hum. Comput. Interact. **38**(4), 309–323 (2022)
6. Marcus, A., Gould, E.W.: Crosscurrents: cultural dimensions and global Web user-interface design. Interactions **7**(4), 32–46 (2000)
7. Hofstede, G.: Geert Hofstede cultural dimensions (2009)
8. Hall, J. M.: Hellenicity: Between Ethnicity and Culture. University of Chicago Press, Chicago (2002)
9. Hofstede Insights. https://www.hofstede-insights.com/fi/product/compare-countries/. Accessed 21 Dec 2022
10. Dierdorff, E.C., Bell, S.T., Belohlav, J.A.: The power of "we": effects of psychological collectivism on team performance over time. J. Appl. Psychol. **96**(2), 247(2011)
11. Kim, M.S.: Cross-cultural comparisons of the perceived importance of conversational constraints. Hum. Commun. Res. **21**(1), 128–151 (1994)
12. Hong, S.-Y., Lee, H.-J., Jin, K.-N.: The analysis of design characteristic in web interface according to the classification of emotion. Arch. Des. Res. **22**(4), 197–209 (2009)
13. Lee, W.-H.: A study on evaluation of sensitivity in website interface design: focus on development of an evaluation methodology for website design. A thesis on a master's degree in Korea. Major in multimedia advertising. Graduate School of Advertising and Public Relations Hong-Ik University (2004)
14. Callahan, E.: Cultural similarities and differences in the design of university web sites. J. Comput. Mediat. Commun. **11**(1), 239–273 (2005)

15. Cheng, C., Kim, E.H.: A study on the relationship between the differences of Korean-Chinese-Japanese action movie posters and the Hofstede MAS. J. Korean Soc. Des. Cult. **28**(2), 323–337 (2022)
16. Cheng, F., Wu, C., Leiner, B.: The influence of user interface design on consumer perceptions: a cross-cultural comparison. Comput. Hum. Behav. **101**, 394–401 (2019)
17. Xie, A., Rau, P.-L.P., Tseng, Y., Su, H., Zhao, C.: Cross-cultural influence on communication effectiveness and user interface design. Int. J. Intercult. Relat. **33**(1), 11–20 (2009)

Leveraging Living Trust Networks for Socially-Aware Recommendations

Shin'ichi Konomi[1]([✉]), Xiangyuan Hu[2], Yu Chen[2], Tianyuan Yang[2], Baofeng Ren[2], and Chengzuo Yao[2]

[1] Faculty of Arts and Science, Kyushu University,
744, Motooka, Nishi-ku, Fukuoka 819-0395, Japan
konomi@artsci.kyushu-u.ac.jp
[2] Graduate School of Information Science and Electrical Engineering, Kyushu University, 744, Motooka, Nishi-ku, Fukuoka 819-0395, Japan

Abstract. Social contexts play critical roles when people provide and receive recommendations in the real world. However, existing recommender mechanisms, such as collaborative filtering, model social connections based on the similarity of users' interests, without fully considering their social ties at different strengths. Such mechanisms may fail to provide recommendations that fit human needs, ignoring important social relations such as trust and giving rise to so-called "filter bubbles" problems. In this paper, we propose a network-based model to represent multi-faceted relations of actors in local communities, which we call Living Trust Networks (LTNs), and discuss methods to create and manage LTNs based on different types of sensor data including location and proximity information. We also discuss a social recommendation model that can treat LTNs and "user-item interactions" in an integrated manner based on graph neural networks (GNNs). Finally, we present a study of the use of proximity-based LTNs to support people to obtain useful information in a university campus, and discuss the implications of our approach on the design of effective socially-aware recommendation environments based on LTNs.

Keywords: Recommender Systems · Social Networks · Sensing · Graph Neural Networks

1 Introduction

As smart devices pervade our everyday lives, people increasingly use them to share and recommend news and event information in local communities. Community members can also help others by sharing tips, advice, and recommendations about local issues by using pervasive devices such as smartphones [1]. The rapid increase in the amount, variety and speed of shared information in local communities can increase people's awareness about and activities in local communities, thereby potentially contributing to the revitalization of the communities and

© The Author(s), under exclusive license to Springer Nature Switzerland AG 2023
P.-L. P. Rau (Ed.): HCII 2023, LNCS 14022, pp. 503–518, 2023.
https://doi.org/10.1007/978-3-031-35936-1_37

the improvement of their members' Quality of Life (QOL). It can however cause many problems as well due to the excessive amount and the uncertain quality of the information shared by anyone, anywhere at anytime.

In this context, we aim to develop a novel social recommendation system that facilitates access to relevant and trustable information by the local community members. Social contexts play critical roles when people provide and receive recommendations in the real world. Conventional recommender mechanisms, such as collaborative filtering, however, model social connections based on the similarity of users' interests, without fully considering their social ties. They could thus fail to provide appropriate information to users by narrowly focusing on personal interests and potentially causing "filter bubbles."

In this paper, we propose a network-based model to represent multi-faceted relations of actors in local communities, which we call *Living Trust Networks (LTNs)*, and discuss methods to create and manage LTNs based on different types of sensor data including location and proximity information. We also discuss a social recommendation model that can treat LTN-based networks and "user-item interactions" in an integrated manner based on graph neural networks (GNNs). Finally, we present a study of a prototype that recommends answerers for a question asked in a university campus, and discuss the implications of our approach on the design of effective socially-aware recommendation environments based on LTNs.

The proposed socally-aware recommendation model can contribute to the development of a digital substrate of *smart local communities of the future*, which amplifies the potential of the communities and their members by supporting local community members to access relevant, trustable and valuable information based on LTNs.

2   Related Works

2.1   Location-Based and Social Q&A Systems

The idea to use location information and social networks in community-based information sharing is not new. For example, Burrell, et al. discuss a location-based mobile information sharing system in a university campus [2]. Park, et al. discuss the use of location-based social Q&A systems based on a study of Naver Kin "Here", focusing on spatial locality of Q&A interactions as well as unique motivators such as ownership of local knowledge and sense of local community [3]. Aardvark is a community Q&A system that considers the importance of expert knowledge and social networks in community-based information sharing [4] without fully exploiting location information and spatial contexts. Our preliminary work on a location-aware Q&A environment discusses a model that incorporates the interest, expertise, proximity, and locations to recommend relevant 'answerers' [5]. This paper builds on this work and proposes a networks-centric recommendation mechanism that is aware of richer social and physical contexts by incorporating social signals from small sensing devices.

2.2   Sensor-Based Social Networks and Their Applications

Researchers have explored the uses of pervasive sensors to capture relational data that can be used to construct social network graphs. The Sociometer uses wearable devices that are equipped with IR sensors, microphones, Bluetooth, and accelerometers, etc. to detect proximity [6]. Reality mining exploits Bluetooth devices to detect proximity relations between people and use them to infer their contexts [7]. Saquib, et al. use a proximity sensor network in a classroom setting [8]. Gashi, et al. use sensing devices that detect electrodermal activity (EDA), blood-volume pulse (BVP), skin temperature (ST) and acceleration (ACC) to analyze physiological synchrony [9]. This suggests the possibility to construct various types of social graphs using sensors, although noisy sensor data necessitates techniques to derive social graphs reliably [10]. Existing research projects use sensor-based social data to enable different types of applications including analysis of social behaviors [7–9], enhancement of social experiences [11], and improvement of information routing [12]. We propose to integrate sensor-based social networks to realize novel socially-aware recommendation mechanisms.

2.3   Social Recommender Systems

Existing social recommender systems leverage social networks to remedy the data sparsity issue in collaborative filtering mechanisms and provide useful recommendations. Earlier systems discussed such an approach in relation to trust relations among users [13]. Other researchers propose a social regularization method to incorporate social networks in matrix factorization-based recommendation systems [14]. Recent advances in graph neural networks, including graph attention networks [15], have enabled significant further developments in graph-based modeling techniques for social recommender systems. For example, Fan, et al. propose a graph neural network framework for social recommendations [16]. Wu, et al. propose a neural recommendation model that considers the diffusion of influence in social networks to improve the performance of social recommendation [17]. This paper builds on our recent work that discusses an extension of GNN-based social recommendation by incorporating location information [18,19]. Unlike existing GNN-based social recommender systems, our approach considers sensor-based social networks as well as online social networks to capture different facets of social influence.

3   Living Trust Networks (LTNs)

We next propose a model that can be used to represent sensor-based social graphs and discuss how they can be used to construct recommendation mechanisms.

3.1   Modeling LTNs

Social interactions take place not only in online environments but also in the physical world. We can use various types of sensors to track social interactions in the physical space. For example, location, proximity, and physiological data has been used to study different types of social interactions and relationships. Mobile, wearable, and pervasive sensors including GNSS devices, cameras, WiFi, Bluetooth, radio-frequency, infrared, and ultrasonic sensors in different form factors allow us to detect locations of people in indoor and outdoor spaces. These devices can also be used to detect proximity relations between people. Moreover, motion and physiological sensors allow us to detect time-based relations such as synchronicity.

The process to derive social graphs by using these sensors consists of two steps: the sensing step and the data processing step. The sensing step collects streams of raw data from different types of sensors, and performs some pre-processing to increase the reliability and deal with the heterogeneity of different types of sensor data. The data processing step uses different algorithms and rules to derive graph structures from the sensed data.

Some of the generated social graphs can be used as proxies of social trust networks. The social graphs can be updated in realtime, periodically, or lazily on demand, as sensors keep generating new data. We call the social graphs that are generated in this manner *Living Trust Networks (LTNs)*, and its derivation process can be modeled as the following representational transformations involving sensed data (D), actor relations (R_a), substrate graphs (G_s), and social graphs (G_{ltn}). That is:

$$D \rightarrow R_a \rightarrow G_s \rightarrow G_{ltn} \tag{1}$$

Sensed data D are associated with actors (e.g., users) by using some identification method. Processing sensed data and converting them into a tabular form generates actor relations R_a involving actors' IDs and relevant attributes. Substrate graphs G_s are graphs generated from actor relations based on *dyadic connection rules*. We can derive proximity relations of two actors by using a connection rule based on contextual co-location such as co-presence in space and time. Finally, nodes, edges and subgraphs of substrate graph G_s can be filtered, aggregated and/or converted to produce social graphs G_{ltn} that can be used as proxies for social contexts including trust networks. In this derivation process, each transformation can generate multiple representations. For example, multiple actor relations can be generated from the same sensed data, multiple substrate graphs can be generated from the same actor relations, and multiple social graphs can be generated from the same substrate graph.

3.2 Recommendation Mechanisms Based on LTNs

We next discuss a method to enhance a recommendation mechanism by exploiting G_{ltn}. The proposed method represents the social and physical contexts simultaneously to provide effective, socially-aware recommendations. We begin the discussion based on a scenario to recommend people in a local community who may be able to answer a question. In this scenario, users use an app on a location-aware smartphones and can attach tags to a question and rate answerers. Although this particular scenario considers the latent factor model (LFM) based recommendation, the proposed method can be generalized for other types of recommendation algorithms including the ones based on Graph Neural Networks (GNNs).

The system provides recommendations based on multiple metrics such as *interaction-based*, *location-based* and *social proximity-based* metrics.

Interaction-Based Metrics. Users' past interactions with items can be quantified in different manners. The user-item interaction matrices are often used in collaborative filtering-based recommendation systems. In case tags are attached to items, we can use the tags as well to improve recommendation. In the context of our current scenario, tags can be used to compute the expertise score E_s, which quantifies users' expertise in different topic areas.

We obtain the user latent matrix p_u, and the tag latent matrix q_t by using the following equation.

$$min \sum_{u,t \in S} (y_{ut} - p_u q_t)^2 + \lambda |p_u|_2 + \lambda |q_t|_2 \qquad (2)$$

In this equation, y_{ut} and λ represent the real score of a tag and the regularization coefficient, respectively. We multiply p_u and q_t to get the predicted score of the user expertise and normalize it to obtain E_s.

We can also quantify a specific aspect of individual users as well. For example, in the context of our current scenario, we may quantify the answer speed for each answerer based on past interaction records.

Location-Based Metrics. Location is a physical context that often influences users' needs and interests. Location information can be represented in different forms, including location labels, points in a 2D/3D space, and string-based representations such as Geohash.

Current and past location information can be considered in computing recommendations. Firstly, users' current location not only provides various clues regarding their needs and interests but also allows calculation of distances between the users and the recommended items (or answerers.) Secondly, users' historical location information can be used to quantify users' familiarity with relevant places, people, and objects.

Social Proximity-Based Metrics. We can calculate social proximity based on online-based and physically-based relationships. The distance between two people can be determined based on a 'friends' list in some online service. The distance between two people can also be determined based on the space/time distance in the physical space. Both types of distance can be represented as tuples that look like (`actor1`, `actor2`, `distance`, ...) in actor relation R_a. We can integrate online and physically-based distances by calculating each distance and simply obtaining a weighted sum.

$$d = w \times d_{online} + (1 - w) \times d_{physical}, \quad 0 \leq w \leq 1 \qquad (3)$$

In this calculation, d_{online} and $d_{physical}$ can be calculated in different ways. As for d_{online}, we can for example calculate the distance on the shortest path between the actors in the online social network. As for $d_{physical}$, we can for example calculate the distance based on the time duration t of co-presence within a certain spatial boundary (e.g., within a 60-meter range), i.e., $d_{physical} = t^{-1}$.

We can generate a social proximity graph G_{ltn} based on a dyadic connection rule with a threshold distance of θ, such that $d < \theta$.

Providing Recommendations. We can use *interaction-based, location-based,* and *social proximity-based* metrics to provide recommendations to users. Besides calculating an overall rating by aggregating them, we can store them separately to allow users to perform fine-grained control over the recommendation mechanism. In the context of our current scenario, the asker may specify their preferred values for the expertise score, social proximity, and answer speed using a graphical user interface. In that case, the system can select answerers that match detailed individual preferences.

4   Integrating LTNs in a GNN-Based Recommender Model

We next discuss how living trust networks can be integrated in a graph neural network-based social recommender model [18]. We expect that the integrated GNN model can provide effective recommendations for local community members who interact with each other in the physical space as well as in online environments. We describe the model as *socially-aware* since it is attentive to the socially-relevant information in digital and physical spaces.

4.1   An Extended Model for GNN-Based Social Recommendation

In our model, we handle the two main components in parallel, one of which is *user modeling* including item aggregation and social aggregation, while the other, *item modeling*, includes user aggregation and relation aggregation. Existing techniques such as GraphRec [16] use GNNs and masked-attention mechanisms to model the user embedding and item embedding. However, they do not fully consider information aggregation of items. Our model can consider relationships between items to model item representations (see Fig. 1). This allows us to make the model location-aware by incorporating location-based item relationships. Again, the model has two main components: *user modeling* and *item modeling*. The former exploits item aggregation and social-relation aggregation to model user embedding. The latter leverages user aggregation information and item-item relations to model item embedding.

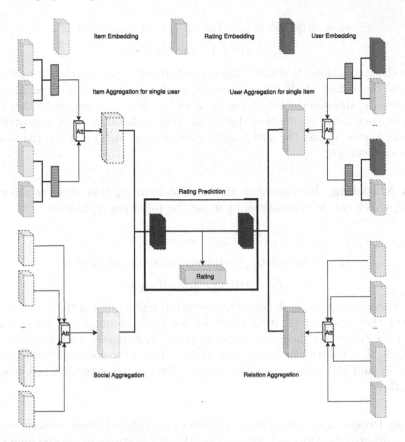

Fig. 1. An extended GNN-based social recommender model

User Modeling. The mean operator, which is often used as a means of aggregation, considers the contribution of each node equally. However, since the importance of each node can be quite different, we employ the masked attention mechanism [15] in our *user modeling* component.

We first concatenate the converted item embedding with their associated embedding. We then use an attention network to take this concatenation as the input to obtain the latent user embedding as the output.

We next feed the generated user embedding into another attention network that aggregates the social relations of the corresponding users to obtain the latent social embedding. In this process, we can use social proximity graph G_{ltn} as a representation of the social relations.

Finally, we concatenate the latent user embedding with the latent social embedding to obtain the user vector as the output.

The whole process can be presented as the following math equations:

$$Emb\ B_{i,j} = b_i \oplus r_{b_i,u_j} \tag{4}$$

$$s_j = Att(Emb\ B_{i,j}) \quad for\ all\ embeddings\ of\ user_j \tag{5}$$

$$S_j = Att(s_k) \quad for\ all\ users \tag{6}$$

In these equations, b_i denotes the converted embedding of the ith item, r_{b_i,u_j} denotes the rating of ith item given by $user_j$, $\oplus$ denotes the concatenation operation, s_j denotes the latent vector of $user_j$ after aggregating his/her rating towards each item, S_j denotes the latent user embedding after concatenating the user vector s_j and the social aggregated vector, $Att()$ denotes the masked-attention network.

Item Modeling. We aggregate the item-to-item relation with its associated rating, which can be represented by using the following equations:

$$Emb\ U_{i,j} = u_j \oplus r_{b_i,u_j} \tag{7}$$

$$t_r = Att(Emb\ U_{i,j}) \quad for\ all\ embeddings\ of\ item_i \tag{8}$$

$$T_r = Att(t_q) \quad for\ all\ items \tag{9}$$

In these equations, u_i denotes the converted embedding of the jth user, r_{b_i,u_j} denotes the rating of ith item given by $user_j$, $\oplus$ denotes the concatenation operation, t_r denotes the latent vector of $item_j$ after aggregating its rating from all users, T_r denotes the latent user embedding after concatenating the user vector s_j and the item aggregated vector. $Att()$ denotes the masked-attention network.

Rating Prediction. After getting the above aggregated latent vectors, we use a fully-connected feed-forward neural network with Softmax to get the final rating prediction:

$$\alpha_i = \frac{\exp(\alpha_i)}{\sum \exp(\alpha_i)} \tag{10}$$

4.2 Preliminary Performance Evaluation

We have conducted a preliminary performance evaluation of our proposed model using an existing dataset.

Dataset and Evaluation Metrics. We use the Yelp dataset for our evaluation study. Yelp is a well-known location-based restaurant recommendation website, and it allows users to add 'friends' and comment on restaurants. The rating scale is from 1 to 5 and restaurants have the location attribute. We selected Yelp-CA, a subset of the Yelp dataset including all items in California. The statistics of the Yelp-CA dataset are shown in Table 1.

In order to evaluate the performance of our model, we use two widely used metrics, Mean Absolute Error (MAE) and Root Mean Square Error (RMSE). Smaller values of MAE and RMSE indicate better performance.

Table 1. Statistic of the dataset

Dataset	Yelp-CA
Users	5945
Items	2491
Ratings	13980
Social Relation	37510
Rating Density	0.0943
Social Relation Density	0.1061

Effect of Attention Mechanisms. We use different attention mechanisms during user-item aggregation, item-user aggregation, user-user aggregation, and item-item aggregation, which are key components of our proposed model. We thus show the result of an ablation experiment on attention mechanisms in Table 2. We also performed experiments with and without the attention mechanism, and the result is shown in Table 2.

Table 2. Result of the ablation experiment

Model	RMSE	MAE
DREANRec	0.5550	0.2961
DREANRec **w/o** *B2B Graph*	0.5702	0.3210
DREANRec **w/o** Attention	0.5732	0.4116

We can see that RMSE and MAE for our method are fairly low. The model achieved a better performance compared with the model without the location information, which suggests the effectiveness of incorporating items' location information. In addition, the attention mechanism has shown a strong positive influence on the whole model.

5 Socially-Aware Recommendation: A User Study

In order to understand the implications of using LTNs for the provision of socially-aware recommendation, we have developed a prototype of a local information-sharing app that provides an LTN-based recommendation feature, and conducted a user study in a university campus.

5.1 Prototype Development

In this section, we will show the details of the design and implementation of our application. The general framework of QFami is shown in Fig. 2. We develop the application by using the Google Cloud service, node.js and Python. First, the asker input the question and tags to the cloud. Then, the server gets the question and calculates interaction-based, location-based and social proximity-based scores. Next, it returns the candidate answerers to the asker.

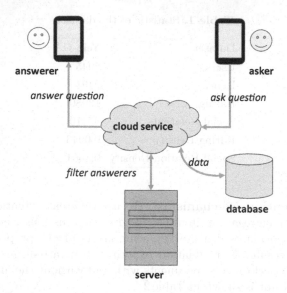

Fig. 2. Overview of the QFami system

Registration. Registering information is a crucial part of a system, which can effectively alleviate the user's cold start problem. Figure 3(a) shows the registration page of QFami. New users need to input their age, sex, province, department, laboratory, self-introduction, and interested areas. The system will initialize users' basic information by filling out this form. The information of province, department, laboratory, and interested areas will become personal tags and be attached to the user. The system will then initialize the score of each tag to 0.5. Also, they can modify their profiles anytime on the profile page.

Asking Question. Figure 3(b) shows the page where the user can ask questions. Here, the asker needs to input the title and detail of their questions. The title can make the problem clear at a glance. If users need to write an explanation of the question, they can add some more details in the input box below. Then, users need to add related tags by clicking #Add Tag button, and the interface will show all the tags ranked by popularity. They can choose one of them or input some keywords to search for related existing tags, and also, they can create new tags by inputting the words and clicking the Add button. After inputting the question, click next to the next page to decide the parameters. Figure 3(c) shows the page where the user can specify the values for the parameters. For the parameter of expertise, familiarity, and answer speed, if the asker drags them to the left, the system prioritize the answerers with a higher score. "0% top" corresponds to the maximum score, and "100% top" corresponds to the minimum score. For the distance parameter, the asker can search the answerers within 5 km. Finally, the asker needs to choose the number of recommended answerers. We set the minimum number as one, and the maximum number is ten.

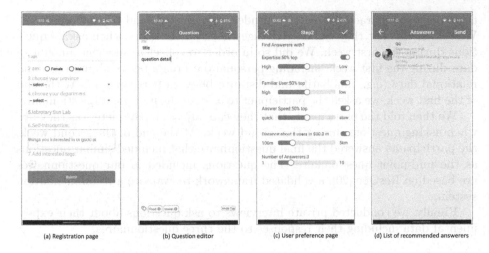

(a) Registration page   (b) Question editor   (c) User preference page   (d) List of recommended answerers

Fig. 3. Android-based prototype of QFami

Explanation. After sending the question, the system will return a page (see Fig. 3(d)), which shows the matched answerers. The grey text shows the reason for recommendation in dfferent aspects, including the expertise level, distance, social proximity, and answer speed. There are three types of expertise levels: very high, high, and low. If the asker chooses the distance parameter, the system will also show the accurate distance. The social proximity part will show whether they are friends or often stay in one building. Also, the asker can check the answerers' profile by clicking the profile image of the candidates, which shows the self-introduction. Finally, users can freely choose which candidates to send information to through this information. When the answerer answers the question, the asker can evaluate the answerer by clicking the hand button in the private room. Then, the system will add a point on these question tags of the answerer. Besides these functions, users can ask or answer questions anonymously, and they can reject or share questions.

5.2 User Experiment

We have conducted a user experiment to understand the use of QFami, in particular, how people control and prioritize personal and relational parameters to maximize the usefulness of a socially-aware recommendation mechanism.

Method. After acquiring the IRB approval, we recruited 17 students in our university, including seven females and ten males. We asked the participants to use the prototype of QFami for two weeks from the 7th of January, 2022 till the 21st of January, 2022. We paid 5,000 Japanese yen to those who completed the experimental tasks.

Participants answered a questionnaire at the start of the experiment, when they registered themselves in the system, and provided the information about their personal characteristics (e.g., gender, department, and self-introduction). We told them that they can only change the expertise score when asking questions during the first week. We did so in order to collect a sufficient amount of data during the first week, including personal data (e.g., personal interests) and relational data (e.g., familiarity and distance between participants). At the end of the first week, we asked the participant to answer the mid-point questionnaire.

We then told the participants that they can adjust all parameters as they like when asking questions during the second week. At the end of the second week, the participants answered the final questionnaire that included similar questions as the mid-point questionnaire. The questions included in our questionnaires are based on ResQue [20], a validated framework to evaluate a recommendation system.

Finally, we conducted private interviews to ask questions about their experimental data including their responses to the three questionnaires.

Key Results. Firstly, We analyzed the popular topics based on the tags attached to the questions that were asked during the experiment. The most popular tag is `lifestyle`, which was much more frequently used than any other tags. Other tags such as `study`, `cooking` and various hobby-related tags were also popular.

Secondly, we analyzed how people controlled and prioritized personal and relational parameters to obtain useful recommendations from QFami. Figure 4 shows the number of participants who thought each parameter was useful. In addition to the above questionnaire result, we used the system log data to analyze the parameter settings for all of the 179 questions that were asked during the second week of the experiment. As shown in Fig. 3(c), the *expertise, familiar user*, and *answer speed* parameters are controllable between 0 and 100. The *distance* parameter is controllable between 100m and 5km. We found that 97% of the questions used the *expertise* parameter, and its mean value is 57. Also, 54% questions used the *familiar user* parameter with the mean value of 52. Moreover, 25% questions used the *speed* parameter with the average value of 57. Finally, 21% questions used the *distance* parameter with the average value of 1700 m. Overall, most participants felt that *expertise* is a useful parameter and used it to control the recommendation. More than half participants felt that *familiar user* is a useful parameter and used it to control the recommendation. There are also participants who felt that the *answer speed* and *distance* were useful parameters and/or used them to control the recommendation.

Our in-depth interviews with each participant revealed some perceptions and behaviors that could be considered in designing socially-aware recommender systems. Firstly, users who used the *familiar user* parameter said that they used it hoping that friends can answer their questions rather than strangers. Their comments suggested that they felt that the answers from friends are of better quality and have higher credibility. Secondly, some participants created new friends by asking questions using QFami. This leads our attention to the fact that socially-aware recommender systems not only use but also generate social connections.

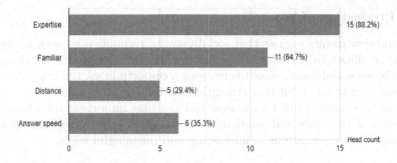

Fig. 4. Number of participants who thought each parameter was useful

Thirdly, some participants appreciated that the system allowed them to share information and chat, which enabled access to a broader range of sources of information than what had been already available. Fourthly, some participants felt that the system could have provided more explanations about the recommendations it gives. Users of the current QFami prototype can examine the "personal page" of the recommended answerers but the system does not provide any other means of explanations. Finally, several participants wished to avoid the situation in which they are provided with an empty list of recommendations when they change different parameter values, possibly selecting the values that may be "too high".

6 Discussion

What our study has revealed about the effectiveness of Living Trust Networks can inform the design of effective socially-aware recommender systems. This section discusses the results of our study from two perspectives: roles of social proximity in recommender systems and production of weak ties.

6.1 Roles of Social Proximity in Recommender Systems

Our questionnaire results as well as the system log data show that *expertise* and *familiar user* can be the most important factors in providing useful recommendations to users. This suggests that social proximity (cf. *familiar user*) as well as relevance of items (cf. *expertise*) can play significant roles in recommendation.

Existing studies often discuss the usefulness of social networks in remedying cold-start problems. However, our study highlights the impact of social proximity on the emotional and trust-related qualities of recommendations. Moreover, our sensor-based social networks can reflect non-verbal social effects in physical spaces [21]. Blending relevance and social proximity in recommender systems is not merely about alleviating cold-start problems and their balance would have to be explored with the understanding of their impact on trust and affective user experiences.

6.2 Production of Weak Ties

Our interview results suggest that socially-aware recommender systems can create opportunities to generate new social ties. As Living Trust Networks exploit sensor-based social connections to create such opportunities, the generated social ties would likely be of different strengths and include weak ties.

Weak ties connect different groups and can play important roles in information diffusion processes and community organization [22], suggesting a potential to change recommendations in interesting and meaningful ways.

6.3 Limitations

Our current study has some limitations including the small number of participants and the focus on a specific scenario. We thus acknowledge that our discussions cannot be generalized for diverse users and scenarios easily.

In addition, as the study is based on the latent factor model, we are yet to study the impact of our GNN-based social recommendation "in the wild" Finally, there is a need of future work to study the privacy and security issues of the proposed approach.

7   Conclusion

We have proposed a model that can be used to represent sensor-based social graphs and discussed how they can be used to construct recommendation mechanisms. The proposed model allows for recommendations on the basis of the interaction-based, location-based, and social proxy-based metrics, and can be integrated with a graph neural network-based recommender model.

We have also presented the user study of a socially-aware recommendation in a university campus based on our approach. The study is revealing about the effectiveness of Living Trust Networks in terms of the roles of social proximity in recommender systems and production of weak ties. We hope our work can inform the design of effective socially-aware recommender systems that can potentially alleviate some difficult problems such as "filter bubbles" and contribute to the development of a next-generation digital substrate for local communities.

Acknowledgements. We thank the participants of our user experiment. This work was supported by JSPS KAKENHI Grant Numbers JP17KT0154 and JP20H00622.

References

1. Sasao, T., Konomi, S., Kostakos, V., Kuribayashi, K., Goncalves, J.: Community reminder: participatory contextual reminder environments for local communities. Int. J. Hum.-Comput. Stud. **102**, 41–53 (2017). https://doi.org/10.1016/j.ijhcs. 2016.09.001

2. Burrell, J., Gay, G.K., Kubo, K., Farina, N.: Context-aware computing: a test case. In: Borriello, G., Holmquist, L.E. (eds.) UbiComp 2002. LNCS, vol. 2498, pp. 1–15. Springer, Heidelberg (2002). https://doi.org/10.1007/3-540-45809-3_1

3. Park, S., Kim, Y., Lee, U., Ackerman, M.: Understanding localness of knowledge sharing: a study of Naver KiN'here'. In: Proceedings of the 16th International Conference on Human-Computer Interaction with Mobile Devices & Services (Mobile-HCI 2014), pp. 13–22. (2014). https://doi.org/10.1145/2628363.2628407

4. Horowitz, D., Kamvar, S.D.: The anatomy of a large-scale social search engine. In: Proceedings of the 19th International Conference on World Wide Web (WWW 2010), pp 431–440. Association for Computing Machinery, New York, NY, USA (2010)

5. Hu, X., Konomi, S.: QFami: an integrated environment for recommending answers on campus. In: Stephanidis, C., Antona, M., Ntoa, S. (eds.) HCII 2021. CCIS, vol. 1498, pp. 119–125. Springer, Cham (2021). https://doi.org/10.1007/978-3-030-90176-9_17

6. Choudhury, T., Pentland, A.: Sensing and modeling human networks using the sociometer. In: Proceedings of the 7th IEEE International Symposium on Wearable Computers, White Plains, NY, USA, vol. 2003, pp. 216–222. IEEE (2003). https://doi.org/10.1109/ISWC.2003.1241414

7. Eagle, N., Pentland, A.: Reality mining: sensing complex social systems. Pers. Ubiquitous Comput. **10**, 255–268 (2006)

8. Saquib, N., Bose, A., George, D., Kamvar, S.: Sensei: sensing educational interaction. Proc. ACM Interac. Mob. Wearable Ubiquitous Technol. **1**(4), 1–27 (2018)

9. Gashi, S., Di Lascio, E., Santini, S.: Using unobtrusive wearable sensors to measure the physiological synchrony between presenters and audience members. In: Proceedings of the ACM on Interactive, Mobile, Wearable and Ubiquitous Technologies, vol. 3, no. 1, pp. 1–19. Association for Computing Machinery, New York, NY, USA (2019)

10. Martella, C., Dobson, M., Van Halteren, A., Van Steen, M.: From proximity sensing to spatio-temporal social graphs. In: Proceedings of the 2014 IEEE International Conference on Pervasive Computing and Communications (PerCom 2014), pp. 78–87. IEEE, Piscataway, NJ, USA (2014)

11. Paulos, E., Goodman, E.: The familiar stranger: anxiety, comfort, and play in public places. In: Proceedings of the SIGCHI Conference on Human Factors in Computing Systems (CHI 2004), pp. 223–230. Association for Computing Machinery, New York, NY, USA (2004)

12. Daly, E.M., Haahr, M.: Social network analysis for routing in disconnected delay-tolerant manets. In: Proceedings of the 8th ACM International Symposium on Mobile ad Hoc Networking and Computing, pp. 32–40. ACM, New York, NY, USA (2007)

13. Massa, P., Avesani, P.: Trust-aware recommender systems. In: Proceedings of the 2007 ACM conference on Recommender systems, pp. 17–24. Association for Computing Machinery, New York, NY, USA (2007)

14. Ma, H., Zhou, D., Liu, C., Lyu, M. R., King, I.: Recommender systems with social regularization. In: Proceedings of the Fourth ACM International Conference on Web Search and Data Mining, pp. 287–296. Association for Computing Machinery, New York, NY, USA (2011)

15. Veličković, P., Casanova, A., Lió, P., Cucurull, G., Romero, A., Bengio, Y.: Graph attention networks. In: Proceedings of the 6th International Conference on Learning Representations (ICLR 2018). OpenReview.net (2018). https://doi.org/10.17863/CAM.48429

16. Fan, W., et al.: Graph neural networks for social recommendation. In: Proceedings of the World Wide Web Conference (WWW 2019), pp. 417–426. Association for Computing Machinery, New York, NY, USA (2019). https://doi.org/10.1145/3308558.3313488

17. Wu, L., Sun, P., Fu, Y., Hong, R., Wang, X., Wang, M.: A neural influence diffusion model for social recommendation. In: Proceedings of the 42nd International ACM SIGIR Conference on Research and Development in Information Retrieval, pp. 235–244. ACM Press, New York, NY, USA (2019). https://doi.org/10.1145/3331184.3331214

18. Chen, Y., Yang, T., Ren, B., Yao, C., Xu, F., Konomi, S.: DREANRec: deep relation enhanced attention networks for social recommendation. In: Proceedings of the 85th National Convention of Information Processing Society of Japan (IPSJ). Information Processing Society of Japan, Tokyo (2023). (in press)

19. Yang, T., Chen, Y., Ren, B., Yao, C., Xu, F., Konomi, S.: Cost-efficiency analysis in deep relation-enhanced graph attention networks for social recommender systems. In: Proceedings of the 85th National Convention of Information Processing Society of Japan (IPSJ). Information Processing Society of Japan, Tokyo (2023). (in press)

20. Pu, P., Chen, L., Hu, R.: user-centric evaluation framework for recommender systems. In: Proceedings of the 5th ACM Conference on Recommender Systems (RecSys 2011), pp. 157–164. ACM Press, New York, NY, USA (2011)

21. van Kleef, G.A., Côté, S.: The social effects of emotions. Ann. Rev. Psychol. **73**, 629–658 (2022)

22. Granovetter, M.S.: The strength of weak ties. Am. J. Soc. **78**(6), 1360–1380 (1973)

Exploring the Influence of Social Interaction Characteristics on Advertising Attitudes Toward Online Video Platform Users

I-Chen Lo, Xiaojun Lai, and Pei-Luen Patrick Rau[✉]

Department of Industrial Engineering, Tsinghua University, Beijing 100084, China
rpl@mail.tsinghua.edu.cn

Abstract. The comprehensive evaluation of advertisements can be affected by the interactive relationships among the online video platforms and their user bases. These spontaneous interactions manifest sociability features and represent a unique cultural phenomenon on diverse video platforms. The purpose of the study is to understand the impact of social interaction characteristics on the attitudes of users toward online video advertising. A survey was conducted with responses from 297 participants. Results suggested that the perceived value of advertising can significantly predict the tendency of users' attitudes toward online video advertising. Social interaction characteristics are essential in positively shaping users' advertising attitudes. With a higher intensity of video platform engagement and social ties, users have a more positive perception of the advertisement.

Keywords: Online video advertising · Interactive characteristic · Advertising attitudes

1 Introduction

Online video platforms serve as a primary source of entertainment, information, and education for people worldwide, which have witnessed a significant increase in their usage. These platforms can be broadly categorized into two types based on their video content. The first type comprises platforms that primarily feature original content and employ a subscription-based model, such as Netflix, Disney+, and IQIYI. However, the second type focuses on user-generated content which has incorporated social interaction features, among the most representative ones are YouTube, Vimeo, and Bilibili.

Both types of video platforms provide a space for users to share and interact with others through video content and lead to the development of virtual social communities. By engaging in similar video content, users tend to feel more connected with others and form communities based on shared experiences. It can be asserted that social interaction characteristics play a significant role in promoting user engagement and offer prospects of contributing to sustainable growth for businesses.

For example, YouTube as the world's most widely used online video platform, constantly encourages user participation and creativity, leading to the expansion of interest

P.-L. P. Rau (Ed.): HCII 2023, LNCS 14022, pp. 519–529, 2023.
https://doi.org/10.1007/978-3-031-35936-1_38

groups among YouTubers and their fans. On the other hand, although Netflix offers licensed content to its users which does not provide the same level of community-driven creation that other platforms do, it has attempted to enhance interactive experiences through video-based interactive choices, reflecting the trend toward socialization.

Bilibili and IQIYI also achieved unprecedented commercial success in the market. IQIYI strengthens its position in the market through its comprehensive range of content and vast users. Specifically, Bilibili targets ACG (Animation, Comic, Game) content and attracts the young generation with close social associations. Through the sharing atmosphere in the platform, Bilibili has distinctive culture integrating active user participation to build a lot of cultural circles driven by interest.

With the continuous growth of user size, online video advertising has become an indispensable tool to generate profit. Given the significant role that user attitudes play in determining the success of online video advertising, it is crucial to evaluate advertising while also taking advertising attitudes into account. However, users' attitudes toward advertising may be influenced by several factors, including the unique interaction characteristics of the platforms, which have been rarely investigated in previous studies.

Understanding the relationships between social interaction characteristics on online video platforms and users' attitudes about advertising enables a more comprehensive evaluation of the success of advertising beyond existing indicators.

2   Literature Review

2.1   Perceived Advertising Value and Advertising Attitudes

A great deal of previous research into advertising attitudes has focused on the path of perceived advertising value. The concept of perceived advertising value specifically refers to comprehensive feelings of benefits or costs after exposure to advertising stimuli (Deraz, 2018). Advertising attitudes indicate the audience's subjective perception of advertisements, and the propensity to evaluate the overall performance of advertisements negatively or positively.

Firat (2019) found that the perceived benefits of YouTube ads positively influence advertising attitudes, and indirectly enhance product awareness and purchase intention. Pashkevich et al. (2012) reported benefits gained from advertisements can effectively reduce generally negative impressions in audiences' cognition, and users' engagement in advertisements can also improve advertising attitudes and effectiveness. Other studies came to similar results, namely that audience views regarding advertising can be either positive or negative depending on whether they receive specific benefits from the advertisement or not. In other words, how useful or worthy the audience perceived results in their assessment of the advertisement.

According to the model suggested by Ducoffe (1995), the three antecedents of accessing advertising value include informativeness, irritation, and entertainment. Brackett and Carr (2001) discovered that the credibility factor is an important dimension in the advertising value model following Ducoffe's study. As a result, this study focuses on perceived entertainment value, informativeness value, and credibility value based on

Brackett's model. Advertising attitudes are measured by the widely used indexes defined by Friedman and Friedman (1979). Proposed hypothesis 1.

H1: Users' advertising perceived value positively influences their advertising attitudes.

2.2 Impact of Social Interaction Factors on Advertising Attitudes

Haridakis and Hanson (2009) confirmed that interpersonal activities and social interaction are unique social resources in online media platforms, which can influence users' attitudes toward the platform content.

Granovetter (1973) found that the weak connections between people who are not well acquainted with each other in social networks could increase information transit efficiency; while strong connection makes an impact on individuals' attitudes and behaviors and enhances positive emotions. Since the bullet screen or live comments are widely used in online video platforms, users can express their emotions and find resonance through these functions. Gradually cluster into a group with shared interests with strong relationship characteristics.

Bansal and Voyer (2000) reported that strong social ties between people can strengthen their attention on the advertisement during the progress of advertising acceptance and influence their attitudes propensity. Zhen et al. (2020) proved that the relationship between users' advertising perceived value and advertising attitudes can be positively promoted by social connection. Considering the high interpersonal interaction in online video platforms, users can build intimate relationships and gain interpersonal utility in the platforms, hypothesis 2 is proposed.

H2: Social strength tie can positively affect the relationship between users' advertising perceived value and advertising attitudes.

Other studies suggested that exploring how video platforms affect users is valuable in assessing their attitudes toward online video advertising. Meanwhile, the relationship between users and video platforms is confirmed as a novel type of consumer network, indicating that the higher level of media platforms engagement results in a positive assessment of the advertisement. Voorveld et al. (2018) confirmed that engagement with a social media platform is positively associated with advertising evaluations in some cases. Consequently, it is important to consider how users and video platforms interact. Proposed hypothesis 3.

H3: Online video platform engagement can positively affect the relationship between users' advertising perceived value and advertising attitudes.

In summary, a model of the comprehensive relationship between advertising perceived value and advertising attitude is constructed, as shown in Fig. 1.

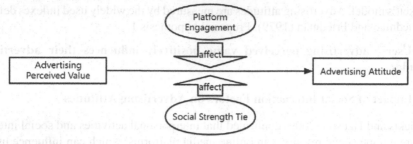

Fig. 1. Research model

3 Methodology

3.1 Scale Design

Take perceived advertising value, platform engagement, and social strength tie as the independent variables, and advertising attitudes as the dependent variable. The scale of four constructs refers to the previous literature, then modifies some measurements for the purpose of research. The source of the measurement scale is shown in Table 1, with 21 items on the scale using 5-point Likert scale questions to measure.

3.2 Data Source

An online questionnaire is adopted for this research. The data collection was carried out for a week on the platform "Wenjuanxing".

There are 340 participants who responded to the online questionnaire during a week. All of them come from China and the most frequently used platforms reported are IQIYI and Bilibili, therefore, the subsequent data analysis will be based on the two platforms.

To avoid data being biased, the responses from repetitive IP or finish less than a minute were removed, leading to a final sample of 297 valid users, with an efficiency rate of 87.4%. Among the data, the group aged 18–25 accounted for the largest proportion (81.1%), with the majority of the undergraduate degree (82.2%). The income is mostly in the section of CNY1,000 to CNY5,000 per month (61.6%). The sample distribution is consistent with the core persona of Bilibili and IQIYI reported by Kong et al. (2021) and data from QuestMobile company, well representing the actual situation to a certain extent.

Table 1. Indicators of the survey

Construct	Item	Description	References
Perceived Advertising Value	AV1	Informativeness	Brackett and Carr (2001) and Yang et al. (2017)
	AV2	Entertainment	
	AV3	Credibility	
Platform Engagement	SE1	Information	Voorveld (2018)
	SE2	Entertainment	
	SE3	Irritation	
	SE4	Stimulation	
	SE5	Identification	
	SE6	Social factor	
	SE7	Practical use	
	SE8	Social interaction	
	SE9	Innovation	
	SE10	Topicality	
Social Strength Tie	SI1	Relationship with others	Granovetter (1973) and Bansal and Voyer (2000)
	SI2	Pleasing communication	
	SI3	Interaction frequency	
	SI4	Likelihood of sharing	
	SI5	community atmosphere	
Advertising Attitudes	ATT1	Attractive	Friedman and Friedman (1979)
	ATT2	Ignored	
	ATT3	Positive	

4   Results and Discussion

Data were analyzed in SPSS 26 and AMOS 22 to perform a structural model and validate the relationships between all constructs.

4.1   Model Testing

The obtained Cronbach's α and KMO values are acceptable, indicating that the collected data is appropriate for subsequent factor analysis. The data demonstrates great convergent and discriminant validity, with factor loadings exceeding 0.5 for all measured items, a composite reliability value exceeding 0.75, and an average variance extracted value ranging between 0.3 to 0.5, indicating the effective measurement of the latent constructs and significant differentiation among them.

Model relationships are tested by fit indices to confirm the sample data can well fit the model. Some common indexes including CMIM/Df, AGFI, TLI, RMR, GFI, CFI, and

RMESA, are taken into consideration in the research (Hooper et al., 2008; Hu & Bentler, 1999; Kaiser & Rice, 1974; Kline, 2016; MacCallum & Hong, 1997). The testing results, presented in Table 1, indicate that all fit indices meet the general criteria and support the impact of social interaction characteristics on online video advertising attitudes.

Table 2. The proposed model fit indices for the structural model

X2/df	RMESA	GFI	AGFI	CFI	TLI	RMR
2.485	0.071	0.871	0.837	0.912	0.9	0.055

4.2   The Universal Effect of Perceived Advertising Value on Advertising Attitudes

Conducting the path analysis to explore the universal relationship between perceived advertising value and advertising attitudes proven in prior studies. According to the categorical variables divided into Bilibili users and IQIYI users, the direct path test results show in Table 3.

Table 3. Estimation of the direct path

	Direct path	Estimate	S.E	C.R	P
Bilibili	Perceived Advertising Value –> Advertising Attitudes	0.947	0.11	8.64	***
IQIYI	Perceived Advertising Value –> Advertising Attitudes	0.703	0.104	6.776	***

***.p < 0.001, **.p < 0.01, *.p < 0.05.

Users' advertising perceived value can significantly influence their advertising attitudes on both Bilibili and IQIYI platforms, indicating that the perceived informativeness, entertainment, and credibility of advertising can adjust the propensity of users advertising attitudes to be positive or negative. Hypothesis 1 is supported.

In contrast to conventional advertising mediums, such as television, newspapers, and public transportation, online video advertisements present a multitude of dynamic scenes and expressions, thereby providing a more engaging and captivating format. Additionally, the lack of expression limitations in online video advertisements allows users to be more receptive to product information without feeling coerced. This can mitigate the potential for advertisements to cause more disruption than utility as users to weigh the costs and benefits of consuming advertising content.

Online video advertisements enhance the expression of advertising content by leveraging various multimedia scenarios, including user-generated content advertisements commonly found on Bilibili. Content creators on Bilibili integrate product information from advertisers into their video content by blending advertising content with the plot of their videos, thus not only conveying information but also promoting the development of the original stories. With regard to minimizing the potential for user interference and maximizing the value of advertising to some extent, online video advertisements on both platforms yield favorable outcomes.

4.3   The Special Social Interaction Characteristics Shape Positive Advertising Attitudes

To determine whether social interaction characteristics influence users' advertising attitudes, testing the mediation and moderation effect of both platform engagement and social strength tie on the path of advertising perceived value to advertising attitudes with SPSS PROCESS macro (Preacher & Hayes, 2004).

By performing bootstrap analysis with 5000 resamplings, if the 95% confidence interval of the indirect effect does not contain zero, indicating the model exists mediation or moderation effect. The results of the bootstrap present that there is a moderating effect of platform engagement and social strength tie in Bilibili, while there is a mediating effect in IQIYI. Tables 4 and 5 show the moderation and mediation model results separately.

Table 4. Moderating effect of platform engagement and social strength tie in Bilibili

Advertising Attitudes in Bilibili					
Regression model	β	SE	t	95% Confidence Interval	
				LLCI	ULCI
Constant	2.5998	0.038	68.482***	2.5251	2.6745
Perceived Advertising Value	0.6919	0.0554	12.4960***	0.5829	0.8008
Platform Engagement	0.1837	0.0705	2.6025***	0.0449	0.3225
Interaction	0.2136	0.071	3.0073***	0.0738	0.3534
Constant	2.6038	0.0384	67.8661***	2.5283	2.6793
Perceived Advertising Value	0.6501	0.0577	11.2573***	0.5364	0.7637
Social Strength Tie	0.1876	0.0545	3.4395***	0.0803	0.295
Interaction	0.136	0.0556	2.4474***	0.0266	0.2454

***.p < 0.001, **.p < 0.01, *.p < 0.05.

In Bilibili's term, considering the direct path of perceived advertising value on advertising attitudes when platform engagement and social strength tie are at high and low levels respectively. Figures 2 and 3 show that the direct path is stronger at a higher level of platform engagement or social strength tie than at a lower level, suggesting that these two variables strengthen the path relationship between advertising perceived value and advertising attitudes, which is supporting hypotheses 2 and 3.

Table 5. Fitting coefficients of mediating effect in IQIYI

Regression Model		Fitting Index			Significance	
Dependent Variable	Independent Variable	R	R^2	F	β	t
Platform Engagement	Perceived Advertising Value	0.628	0.394	102.193	0.507	10.109***
Social Strength Tie	Platform Engagement	0.76	0.586	110.406	0.817	9.447***
	Perceived Advertising Value				0.209	2.995***
Advertising Attitudes	Social Strength Tie	0.787	0.620	84.247	0.211	2.894***
	Platform Engagement				0.226	2.285**
	Perceived Advertising Value				0.487	7.435***

***.p < 0.001, **.p < 0.01, *.p < 0.05.

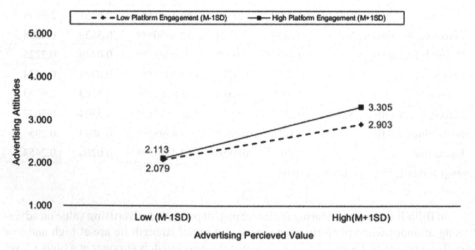

Fig. 2. Moderating effect of platform engagement in Bilibili

These results confirm the users' platform engagement and social strength tie play a part in bolstering the direct path on the advertising attitudes. As the majority of online video advertisements on Bilibili are primarily implanted advertisements by video creators, the content of the video is interpreted by the creator themselves and also expresses

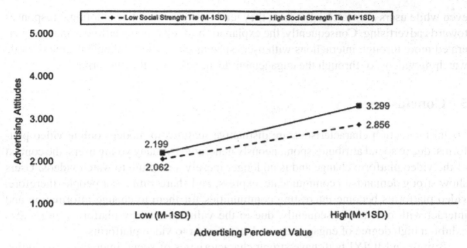

Fig. 3. Moderating effect of social strength tie in Bilibili

their approval of the product, making the advertisements more credible to users. Meanwhile, users can interact with others while watching the videos through various interactive features, such as bullet screens, and share their experience of using the products to gain more useful information through this interesting way.

In IQIYI's term, testing the effect of the direct and indirect path with mediating effect model. Table 6 indicates that the degree of platform engagement and social strength tie involved in the influence path of the advertising perceived value on the advertising attitude on IQIYI. Proving hypotheses 2 and 3.

Table 6. The mediating effect size of platform engagement and social strength tie in IQIYI

Path	Effect	SE	LLCI	ULCI	Effect Size
Total effect	0.7334	0.0544	0.6259	0.8408	100%
Direct effect	0 .4870	0.0655	0.3567	0.6164	66.40%
Indirect effect path 1	0.1146	0.0521	0.0123	0.2179	15.63%
Indirect effect path 2	0.0442	0.0248	0.0064	0.102	6.02%
Indirect effect path 3	0.0876	0.0368	0.0229	0.1671	11.94%

Indirect Path 1: Perceived Advertising Value -> Platform Engagement -> Advertising Attitude.
Indirect Path 2: Perceived Advertising Value -> Social Strength Tie -> Advertising Attitude.
Indirect Path 3: Perceived Advertising Value -> Platform Engagement -> Social Strength Tie ->
Advertising Attitude.

The results demonstrate that the intensity of platform engagement and social strength tie serve as mediating factors, partly substituting for the direct effect of perceived advertising value on users' advertising attitudes. Since pre-video advertisements are the primary advertising format employed by IQIYI, which may appear during natural pauses or even while users are watching videos, they tend to trigger negative emotional responses towards advertising. Consequently, the explanation of advertising attitudes may be generated more through interactions with users such as comments and bullet screens while watching videos, or through the engagement feedback from the platforms.

5 Conclusion

Social interaction characteristics are distinctive features in modern online video platforms, due to social attributes spontaneously generated by many young users, the context of the video platform change and is no longer merely a medium to watch videos. Users show strong demands to communicate, express, and share with other people, therefore, video platforms become interesting communities for them to change information and interact with others. Consequently, due to the value offered by platforms, users also exhibit a high degree of engagement and attachment to video platforms.

Bilibili and IQIYI both have strong characteristics of social interaction, including the close social tie between users and active participation in the platforms. Although two interaction characteristics affect the user's attitudes toward advertising in different models, there is no doubt that social features in the platforms positively influence advertising attitudes, benefit companies and advertising agencies further.

Especially in Bilibili, which focuses on user-generated advertisements compared to IQIYI pre-video advertisements, the intensity of platform engagement and social tie directly strengthen the relationship between perceived advertising value and advertising attitudes. In other words, the fundamental formation of advertising attitudes is driven by the advertising value, however, the social interaction characteristics present as the key factors in positively shaping the users' advertising attitudes.

References

Bansal, H.S., Voyer, P.A.: Word-of-mouth processes within a services purchase decision context. J. Serv. Res. **3**(2), 166–177 (2000). https://doi.org/10.1177/109467050032005

Brackett, L.K., Carr, B.N.: Cyberspace advertising vs. other media: consumer vs. mature student attitudes. J. Advert. Res. **41**(5), 23–32 (2001). https://doi.org/10.2501/JAR-41-5-23-32

Deraz, H.: Social networking sites-consumers' assessment of the value of advertisements (extended model) (2018). https://doi.org/10.13140/RG.2.2.11612.64645

Ducoffe, R.H.: How consumers assess the value of advertising. J. Curr. Issues Res. Advert. **17**(1), 1–18 (1995). https://doi.org/10.1080/10641734.1995.10505022

Ducoffe, R.H., Curlo, E.: Advertising value and advertising processing. J. Mark. Commun. **6**(4), 247–262 (2000). https://doi.org/10.1080/135272600750036364

Firat, D.: YouTube advertising value and its effects on purchase intention. J. Glob. Bus. Insights **4**(2), 141–155 (2019). https://doi.org/10.5038/2640-6489.4.2.1097

Friedman, H.H., Friedman, L.: Endorser effectiveness by product type. J. Advert. Res. **19**, 63–71 (1979)

Granovetter, M.S.: The strength of weak ties. Am. J. Sociol. **78**(6), 1360–1380 (1973). https://doi.org/10.1086/225469

Haridakis, P., Hanson, G.: Social interaction and co-viewing with YouTube: blending mass communication reception and social connection. J. Broadcast. Electron. Media **53**(2), 317–335 (2009). https://doi.org/10.1080/08838150902908270

Hooper, D., Coughlan, J., Mullen, M.: Structural equation modelling: guidelines for determining model fit. Electro. J. Bus. Res. Methods **6**(1), 53–60 (2008)

Hu, L., Bentler, P.M.: Cutoff criteria for fit indexes in covariance structure analysis: conventional criteria versus new alternatives. Struct. Equ. Model. **6**(1), 1–55 (1999). https://doi.org/10.1080/10705519909540118

Kaiser, H.F., Rice, J.: Little Jiffy, Mark Iv. Educ. Psychol. Measur. **34**(1), 111–117 (1974). https://doi.org/10.1177/001316447403400115

Kline, R.B.: Principles and Practice of Structural Equation Modeling, 4th edn. The Guilford Press (2016)

Kong, R., Wu, L., Jiang, M.H., Yang, Y.C.: Three Questions on Bilibili (BILI.US/9626.HK): The Midfield Battle of 'Little Broken Stations'. TF Securities Co., Ltd. (2021)

MacCallum, R.C., Hong, S.: Power analysis in covariance structure modeling using GFI and AGFI. Multivar. Behav. Res. **32**(2), 193–210 (1997). https://doi.org/10.1207/s15327906mbr3202_5

Pashkevich, M., Dorai-Raj, S., Kellar, M., Zigmond, D.: Empowering online advertisements by empowering viewers with the right to choose: the relative effectiveness of skippable video advertisements on YouTube. J. Advert. Res. **52**(4), 451–457 (2012). https://doi.org/10.2501/JAR-52-4-451-457

Preacher, K.J., Hayes, A.F.: SPSS and SAS procedures for estimating indirect effects in simple mediation models. Behav. Res. Methods Instrum. Comput. **36**(4), 717–731 (2004). https://doi.org/10.3758/BF03206553

Voorveld, H.A.M., van Noort, G., Muntinga, D.G., Bronner, F.: Engagement with social media and social media advertising: the differentiating role of platform type. J. Advert. **47**(1), 38–54 (2018). https://doi.org/10.1080/00913367.2017.1405754

Yang, K.-C., Huang, C.-H., Yang, C., Yang, S.Y.: Consumer attitudes toward online video advertisement: YouTube as a platform. Kybernetes **46**(5), 840–853 (2017). https://doi.org/10.1108/K-03-2016-0038

Zhen, H., Zhang, Y., Lu, Y.: The curvilinear relationship between perceived value and advertising attitude: an empirical study based on moderating effect of social attributes. J. China Univ. Pet. (Ed. Soc. Sci.) **04**, 41–47 (2020)

Text Mining of the Attractiveness Dimensions of Internet Celebrity Products: Taking Li Ziqi's Snail Noodles for Example

Xiaolin Tan[1,2], Yixuan Chang[1], and Runting Zhong[1(✉)] 🆔

[1] School of Business, Jiangnan University, 1800 Lihu Avenue, Wuxi 214122, Jiangsu, People's Republic of China
zhongrt@jiangnan.edu.cn
[2] School of Economics and Management, Southeast University, 2 Southeast Avenue, Nanjing 211189, Jiangsu, People's Republic of China

Abstract. In this study, we explored the attractiveness dimensions of Internet celebrity products through text mining. Via descriptive statistical analysis and Canopy+K-means clustering, the most frequently mentioned word was "taste". The attractiveness dimensions of consumers' attention to Internet celebrity products were clustered into five categories in terms of mention frequency, namely, functional value, Internet celebrity marketing, service value, cost value, and design value. The five categories of attractiveness dimensions contained text ratings of 43.53%, 4.54%, 5.74%, 26.48%, and 19.71% of the overall number of reviews, respectively. Among them, the functional value was the most critical influence dimension. This study offers a method to analyze the attractiveness dimensions of Internet celebrity products. Product providers were recommended to focus on ingredient selection, improve product quality, and enhance product taste according to consumer tastes.

Keywords: Attractiveness · Internet Celebrity Products · Multi-source Data

1 Introduction

The Top 10 Food Internet Celebrities of 2020 showed that food video blogger Li Ziqi topped the list of Chinese Internet celebrities [1]. As of July 1, 2022, Li Ziqi's YouTube subscribers numbered up to 17 million, the Chinese channel with the largest number of subscribers on the platform and the highest number of individual video plays, exceeding 80 million [2]. Compared with Li Jiaqi and other marketing Internet celebrities, Li Ziqi, a food video Internet celebrity, has come out with a unique *"video + self-owned store"* development route. Her videos are positioned as *"ancient style + food + traditional culture"*. By creating a personal brand and setting up a professional company to operate it, she has turned the network flow and heat into money in a short period [3].

In the snail noodle market, *"Li Ziqi snail noodle"* (as shown in Fig. 1) is also a hot Internet celebrity product. Li Ziqi made a unique taste of snail noodles through her strict

P.-L. P. Rau (Ed.): HCII 2023, LNCS 14022, pp. 530–540, 2023.
https://doi.org/10.1007/978-3-031-35936-1_39

selection in her video in 2019. Subsequently, the hot sale of the Li Ziqi brand snail noodles has also made snail noodles more widely known to consumers [4]. According to the data from Li Ziqi's flagship store, the top-selling Li Ziqi snail noodles sold nearly 1.5 million copies per month [5]. As one of the most popular products, Li Ziqi snail noodles sold 6.7 million bags on the *"Double 11"* in 2020, a year-on-year increase of more than four times [6]. In contrast, the exact product produced in the same factory as Li Ziqi snail noodles, with the same packaging and lower retail price, sold only a fraction of her sales [7]. Compared to ordinary products, how can such Internet celebrity products have such a strong appeal to consumers?

This study aims at exploring the attractiveness dimensions of Internet celebrity products through text mining. The results form a better understanding of consumer attitudes towards Internet celebrity products.

Fig. 1. Li Ziqi snail noodles

2 Literature Review

2.1 Attractiveness Dimensions of Internet Celebrity Products

To evaluate the attractiveness dimensions of Internet celebrity products, many models such as stimulus-organism-response (SOR), source credibility theory and the Technology Acceptance Model (TAM) were constructed [8–14]. Tan et al. developed an instrument to measure the attractiveness of Internet celebrity products. Via exploratory factor analysis and regression analysis, a model of the attractiveness source of Internet celebrity products was constructed based on the survey and interview. The results showed that the attractiveness of Internet celebrity products was mainly affected by the products' practical value, hedonic value, and Internet celebrity product purchase experience, with regression coefficients of 0.710, 0.164, and 0.193, respectively [8]. Wang took the SOR model as the theoretical framework. Internet celebrity's information source was regarded as stimulus variables. Consumer cognitive and emotional attitudes were regarded as body variables. The result showed that the information source credibility of Internet celebrities could be divided into four factors: trustworthiness, perceived expertise, attractiveness, and consistency between influencers and products [9]. Gao established a research model based on the SOR model to study the influence of the word-of-mouth information characteristics of Internet celebrities and their own attribute characteristics on consumers' purchase intention in online platforms. The results finally validated the model that the emotional response was used as a mediator to explore its mediating role and quasi-social interaction was introduced as a regulating variable [10]. Liu et al. used a combination of qualitative and quantitative research to construct a theoretical framework for the influence of Internet celebrities' lives on consumer decision-making. Through in-depth interviews, the characteristics of the information sources that consumers follow Internet celebrities were summarized and classified into four dimensions: credibility, professionalism, interactivity, and attractiveness. The Internet celebrity live stream pop-ups were crawled through big data Python crawler technology. The Internet celebrity information source characteristics were evaluated and weighted statistically with the help of the fuzzy hierarchical evaluation method, which further supported the research conclusions [11]. Nyambayar constructed a model based on the source credibility theory and the TAM [12]. Three dimensions of credibility proposed by Ohanian [13] and two dimensions of perceived ease of use and perceived usefulness proposed by Davis [14] were used to test Instagram's social media influencers' impact on the purchase intention of Mongolian young female consumers. The study found that the trustworthiness, expertise, attractiveness, usefulness, and ease of use of Instagram influencers influenced the attitude and purchase intention of female young Mongolian consumers. The positive correlation hypothesis between consumer attitude and consumer intention was also valid [12].

2.2 Text Mining Methods for Online Reviews

Online reviews refer to the content published on online platforms based on consumers' experience of using them and their opinions and attitudes [15], a form of Internet Word-of-Mouth (IWOM) [16]. Online reviews impact consumers' purchasing decisions [17] and product performance [18]. Online consumers can obtain product-related information from online reviews to inform their purchasing decisions [19]. Online reviews also promote value co-creation between companies and customers [20]. Companies must be able to perceive quickly and respond to customer needs in the product development process [21]. Thus, absorbing customer information is crucial for product development [22]. Online reviews contain much information about customer needs and are considered a more reliable source of information [23, 24]. Many companies try to improve customer agility by mining online review information to gain product competitiveness [25].

Text mining usually uses Python software to crawl review data, and through text pre-processing, descriptive statistics, and relevant machine learning algorithms [26], consumers' emotional tendencies towards products are informed. Python has the advantages of simplicity, ease of use, power, cross-platform, high development efficiency, open source, portability, and support for a large number of third-party repositories [27, 28]. Python has been widely used in scientific statistics, artificial intelligence development, and web crawling. Python provides many libraries to implement crawler technology [29]. It is fast to use Python to build web crawlers with high development efficiency [30]. Text pre-processing is a necessary step before deep text analysis, facilitating the standardization of complex data information. The main process includes text separation, text cleaning, deactivation of words, etc. Word frequency statistics is an important element of descriptive statistics on word frequency. It refers to counting the number and frequency of occurrences of individual words in a text, which has developed into a scientific quantitative research method [31]. Word cloud mapping enables visualization of text mining results [32]. Machine learning algorithms include the bag-of-words model, frequency-of-words-inverse document frequency (TF-IDF) algorithm, clustering, etc. [33]. Text clustering is the process of dividing text data into multiple classes based on similarity. Macqueen proposed that K-means clustering is a commonly used unsupervised clustering algorithm [34].

3 Method

3.1 Data Acquisition and Text Processing

We applied Python crawler to Li Ziqi snail noodles, an Internet celebrity product on Jingdong's owned platform [35]. The latest 100 pages of online review text before February 19, 2021, were crawled in chronological order of release. The crawled text data was de-duplicated to filter out comments that had no real meaning or contained text that was too short for analysis [36]. Meaningless reviews refer to reviews that have no connection to goods, services, and logistics. Comments with content such as "*random Chinese, garbled codes and other product advertisements*" are mainly included. After the primary data cleaning, 1167 valid samples were collected, with approximately 400,000 words of original data retained.

In order to evaluate what attracts consumers to choose the Internet celebrity product (Li Ziqi snail noodles), the study used the Jieba word splitting tool system in Python to split the collected reviews into words [37]. In this study, Baidu's deactivation word list [38] was used as the basis for selection. Relevant deactivation words, such as "*think, buyback, at first*", etc., were added manually after browsing and judging the product reviews to filter the textual vocabulary better. Without many contextual descriptions for machine analysis, ordinary common lexicons had some bias in identifying words. For example, the word "*snail noodles*" was broken down into two separate words, "*snail*" and "*noodles*", because the lexicon did not include a specific expression for this food. Therefore, we used a custom dictionary to supplement the original lexicon. The core text processing code is presented in Fig. 2.

```
# Divide sentences into words
def seg_sentence(sentence):
    sentence_seged=jieba.cut(sentence.strip())
    stopwords=stopwordlist('D:\idea\pythontest\Jupyter\stopwords.txt')
    outstr=''
    segment=["Li Ziqi","Snail noodles","Eat till you drop","Adequate ingredients","Ingredient packs","Li Ziqi's"]
    for ii in segment:
        jieba.suggest_freq(ii, tune=True)
    for word in sentence_seged:
        if word not in stopwords:
            if word !='\t':
                outstr+=word
                outstr+=" "
    return outstr
```

Fig. 2. Text processing code

3.2 Statistical Analysis

Descriptive Statistics. The comment word count box plot, word frequency statistics, and word cloud are used for descriptive statistics analysis. A box plot is a statistical chart used to show the dispersion of a set of data. It shows the maximum, minimum, median, upper and lower quartiles of a set of data [39]. Word frequency analysis is used to extract product attributes that are highly relevant to Internet celebrity product reviews [37]. High word frequency means that consumers pay more attention to this aspect of Internet celebrity products, and the attractiveness of this attribute of Internet celebrity products is more prominent. Word clouds, which are visual representations of text data, are used to display large amounts of text data. The importance of each word is displayed in font size or color, making it easy to quickly perceive the most prominent text. The top 100 words in terms of word frequency were selected for word cloud display. Words with higher word frequency had larger fonts in the word cloud [37].

Clustering Model. In this study, we mainly used a hybrid clustering algorithm to analyze the attraction dimensions of Internet celebrity products. The study assumed that each consumer review could be classified into a specific evaluation dimension category, such as focusing on the product's functional value, design value, or service function. Canopy+K-means clustering was used to analyze the type of review that should be attributed to each review [40].

4   Results

4.1 Descriptive Statistics Analysis of Online Reviews

Based on the actual word count of each review, a box plot of the word count of the overall sample was generated. As shown in Fig. 3, the mean word count of reviews was 70 words, with a standard deviation of 41.5. 75% of the reviews were under 100 words. Nevertheless, six customers made detailed experience reviews of over 200 words, with the longest review reaching 286 words.

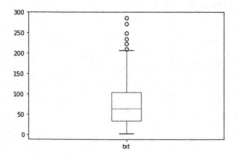

Fig. 3. Comment word count box plot

Based on the above processing, word frequencies can be calculated for online review texts. In this study, the top 20 feature words in word frequency were selected, as shown in Table 1, and the subsequent data analysis was carried out.

Table 1. Word frequency statistics (N = 3807)

Feature word	Word frequency	Part of speech	Feature word	Word frequency	Part of speech
Taste	736	n	Repurchase	121	v
Delicious	421	adj	Flavor	108	n
Like	329	v	Brand	101	n
Li Ziqi	322	n	Recommend	93	v
Packaging	244	n	Quickly	90	adv
JD.COM	242	n	Express Delivery	84	n
Quite Tasty	196	adj	Brand	83	n
Ingredient	154	n	Authentic	75	adj
Logistics	137	n	Activity	74	n
Buy	124	v	Price	73	n

Note: v.-verb n.-noun adj.-adjective adv.-adverb.

The results showed that the most frequently mentioned word was "*taste*", followed by "*delicious*", which meant that consumers paid more attention to the taste (quality) of the product, which corresponded to the food properties of the product itself. The words "*like*" and "*recommend*" expressed consumers' subjective emotional evaluation. The frequency of the word "*Li Ziqi*" exceeded that of objective evaluation indicators, such as "*packaging*", "*logistics*", and "*price*". It meant that the celebrity effect had an important influence on the attractiveness of this online product.

The top 100 words from the word frequency statistics above were selected for word cloud presentation, thus visualizing the data. The word cloud of the evaluation of Li Ziqi snail noodles coded through Python is plotted in Fig. 4.

From the word cloud chart, we can see that words about product quality (taste), the Internet celebrity herself, product design, additional services, and cost assessment, such as taste, Li Ziqi, packaging, JD.COM, delivery, price, and like, appeared more frequently. In this regard, it can be tentatively determined that the Jingdong review dimension of Li Ziqi snail noodles was five categories. Later on, a clustering algorithm will be used to determine the attractiveness dimensions of online products that consumers follow.

Fig. 4. Word cloud display

4.2 Cluster Analysis of Online Reviews

This study used Canopy+K-means clustering to classify each feature word into a dimension. Clustering algorithms can be divided into coarse and fine clustering. Using the Canopy algorithm, we performed coarse clustering on the comment data and got 5 clusters. Therefore, the K value was initially determined of 5. Then the K-means algorithm was used to perform fine clustering, draw the clustering graph, and extract the keywords of the five categories of text evaluation. The clustering diagram is shown in Fig. 5.

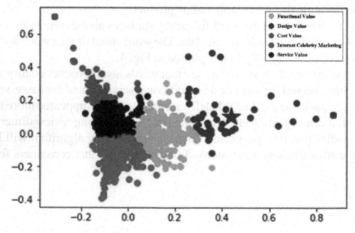

Fig. 5. K-means clustering effect diagram

By referring to the previous literature study [40], the maximum number of iterations was chosen to be 50 in the clustering model of this study. After clustering, the text of each dimension was aggregated. Five types of high frequency matrices can be directly machine classified according to Python code. The top three occurrences in each category of text were extracted as high-frequency feature words.

From the number mentioned in each dimension of product reviews, the clustering algorithm can classify the attractiveness dimensions of online products that consumers follow into five categories, as shown in Table 2.

Table 2. K-means clustering text number distribution

Dimension	Text number	Percentage	High-frequency feature words
Functional Value	508	43.53%	Delicious, Taste, Ingredient
Design Value	53	4.54%	Packaging, A Big Bag, Brand
Cost Value	67	5.74%	Price, Repurchase, Activity
Internet Celebrity Marketing	309	26.48%	Internet Celebrity, Li Ziqi, Authentic
Service Value	230	19.71%	Logistics, Express Delivery, Place an Order
Effective	1167	100%	/

The first attractiveness dimension contains 508 text evaluations, accounting for 43.53% of the reviews, which is the highest proportion of the overall evaluation. The core words of this category were "*delicious*" and "*ingredients*", focusing on the functional quality of the Internet celebrity product itself, which was named as the functional value in this study.

The second attractiveness dimension contains 53 text evaluations, accounting for 4.54% of the reviews, which is a slightly smaller percentage. It was named as design value in this study, which was influenced by the "*packaging*" and "*brand*" factors, responding to the design aesthetics and emotional symbols conveyed by Internet celebrity products.

The third attractiveness dimension contains 67 text evaluations, accounting for only 5.74% of the number of reviews, which is a small proportion of the overall evaluations. This type of consumer was more concerned about "*repurchase*" and "*price*", showing a tendency to repeat purchases under controlled cost; so this study named this dimension as cost value.

The fourth attractiveness dimension contains 309 text evaluations, accounting for 26.48% of the number of reviews, which is the larger category of the overall evaluations. The factors that attracted consumers in this category are mainly related to "*Internet celebrity*" and "*Li Ziqi*". The influence of product marketing and Internet celebrity was similar to the text evaluation (with "*Li Ziqi*" as the main focus). They were combined into a new category of attractiveness dimensions: Internet celebrity marketing.

The fifth attractiveness dimension contains 230 text evaluations, accounting for 19.71% of the comments, which is in the middle of the overall percentage. This category of consumers paid more attention to "*logistics*" and "*order*", i.e., the quality and speed of services attached to Internet celebrity products. This study named this dimension as service value.

5 Conclusion

In this study, we explored the attractiveness dimensions of Internet celebrity products through text mining. Via descriptive statistical analysis and Canopy+K-means clustering, the most frequently mentioned word was found to be "taste". The attractiveness dimensions of consumers' attention to Internet celebrity products were clustered into five categories in terms of mention frequency, namely, functional value, Internet celebrity marketing, service value, cost value, and design value. Among them, functional value was the most critical influence dimension. This study offers a method to analyze the attractiveness dimensions of Internet celebrity products. Product providers are recommended to focus on ingredient selection, improve product quality, and enhance product taste according to consumer tastes.

Acknowledgements. This study was supported by a National Natural Science Foundation of China (grant number 72101100).

References

1. Top 10 food internet celebrities of 2020. https://www.yezicc.com/renwu/2021032322211. html. Accessed 23 Mar 2021. (in Chinese)
2. Feng, W., Ren, H., Wu, D.: How to tell Chinese stories to the world in the short video era: a study of Li Ziqi's cross-cultural communication strategy on the YouTube platform. Media **16**, 65–68 (2022)
3. How to go further as a country Internet celebrity. Advis. Peasant Families (4), 135–138 (2022)
4. Gong, M.: Analysis of the way of Liuzhou snail noodles "out of the circle" and development strategy in the new media era. J. News Res. **13**(12), 181–183 (2022)
5. Zhou, J., Shu, X., Peng, X.: Exploring the short video marketing model of agricultural products based on the phenomenon of Li Ziqi becoming popular. Contemp. Econ. **3**, 65–67 (2021)
6. Jiang, Y., Shu, X., Du, S., et al.: Research on short video of agricultural products in China-taking Li Ziqi's model as an example. China Bus. Trade **4**, 51–53 (2022)
7. Ji, Z.: Research on Li Ziqi's short food video in the context of consumer culture. West China Broadcast. TV **41**(16), 4–6 (2020)
8. Tan, X., Han, S., Zhong, R.: Evaluating the attractiveness factors of internet celebrity products using survey data. In: Rau, PL.P. (eds.) HCII 2022. LNCS, vol. 13313, pp. 68–81. Springer, Cham (2022). https://doi.org/10.1007/978-3-031-06050-2_6
9. Wang, S.: Research on the Impact of Internet Celebrity's Information Source Credibility on Consumers' Purchase Intention on Short Video Platform. Beijing Jiaotong University, Beijing (2021)
10. Gao, H.: Research on the Influence of Internet Celebrity's Word-of-Mouth on Consumers' Purchase Intention. Shandong University, Shandong (2020)
11. Liu, F., Meng, L., Chen, S., Duan, K.: The impact of network celebrities' information source characteristics on purchase intention. Chinese J. Manag. **17**(01), 94–104 (2020)
12. Nyambayar, J.: The Research on Instagram Social Media Influencer's Impact on Mongolian Young Female Consumers' Purchase Intention. Chang'an University, Shaanxi (2020)
13. Ohanian, R.: Construction and validation of a scale to measure celebrity endorsers' perceived expertise, trustworthiness, and attractiveness. J. Advert. **V19**(3), 39–52 (1990)
14. Davis, F., Bagozzi, R., Warshaw., P.: User acceptance of computer technology: a comparison of two theoretical models. Manag. Sci. **V35**, 982–1003 (1989)

15. Chen, Y., Xie, J.: Online consumer review: word-of-mouth as a news element of marketing communication mix. Manag. Sci. J. Inst. Manag. Sci. **54**(3), 477–491 (2008)
16. Chen, J.: Analysis of factors influencing online reviews on consumers' purchase intention in the context of "Internet+." Mod. Mark. (Bus. Ed.) **6**, 96–97 (2019)
17. Sun, M.: How does the variance of product ratings matter? Manag. Sci. J. Inst. Manag. Sci. **58**(4), 696–707 (2012)
18. Yang, B., Liu, Y., Liang, Y., et al.: Exploiting user experience from online customer reviews for product design. Int. J. Inf. Manag. **46**, 173–186 (2019)
19. Jin, W.: An empirical analysis of the impact of online reviews on hotel consumers' booking decisions. Econ. Res. Guid. **3**, 47–49 (2021)
20. Yao, S.: Driving impact of intellectual capital on customer participation: from the perspective of transformative learning. J. Manag. Sci. **29**(2), 77–92 (2016)
21. Sun, J., Zheng, Y., Chen, J.: The influence of credibility of online reviews on consumers' trust: the moderating role of uncertainty. Manag. Rev. **32**(4), 146–159 (2020)
22. Jayachandran, S., Hewett, K., Kaufman, P.: Customer response capability in a sense-and-respond era: the role of customer knowledge process. J. Acad. Mark. Sci. **32**(3), 219–233 (2004)
23. He, L., Zhang, N., Yin, L.: The evaluation for perceived quality of products based on text mining and fuzzy comprehensive evaluation. Electron. Commer. Res. **18**(2), 277–289 (2018). https://doi.org/10.1007/s10660-018-9292-0
24. Franke, N., Piller, F.: Key research issues in user interaction with user toolkits in a mass customization system. Int. J. Technol. Manag. J. Technol. Manag. Technol. Eng. Manag. Technol. Policy Strategy **26**(5/6), 578–599 (2003)
25. Yi, C., Jiang, Z., Li, X., et al.: Leveraging user-generated content for product promotion: the effects of firm-highlighted reviews. Inf. Syst. Res. **30**(3), 711–725 (2019)
26. Wu, J., Jia, L.: Public opinion analysis and sentiment analysis based on text mining - an example of Sina official microblog comments of Le'shan normal college. Inf. Rec. Mater. **23**(2), 163–166 (2022)
27. Li, G.: Python Madness Handout. Electronic Industry Press, Beijing (2018)
28. Jiang, C, Meng, L.: A Python-based automated test application example. Ind. Control Comput. **34**(10), 109–110, 113 (2021)
29. Python Basic Web Crawler Tutorial, pp. 5–6. People's Post and Telecom Press, Beijing (2022)
30. Luo, K.: The design and implementation of cloud singing system based on python crawler. Mod. Comput. **28**(9), 78–81 (2022). https://doi.org/10.3969/j.issn.1007-1423.2022.09.015
31. Zhai, Q., Cheng, J.: The educational values of the president's speech at the opening ceremony: based on the word frequency analysis of 36 world–class university presidents. Jiangsu High. Educ. **6**, 42–50 (2021). https://doi.org/10.13236/j.cnki.jshe.2021.06.006
32. Chen, N., Li, J., Man, Y., et al.: Analysis of approach landing risk factors based on civil aviation safety information text mining. J. Saf. Sci. Technol. **18**(3), 5 (2022). https://doi.org/10.11731/j.issn.1673-193x.2022.03.001
33. Wang, X.: Sentiment analysis of tourism reviews based on semantic lexicon and machine learning. Comput. Digit. Eng. **44**(4), 578–582,766 (2016). https://doi.org/10.3969/j.issn.1672-9722.2016.04.004
34. Macqueen: 190. attitudes of health visitors to possible developments. Nurs. Res. **16**(2), 206 (1967)
35. Li Ziqi snail noodles on Jingdong's owned platform. https://item.jd.com/100004251875.html. Accessed 23 Mar 2021
36. Zhou, M., Xin, Y.: Research on sentiment analysis of film and TV pop-ups based on text mining. Technol. Innov. Appl. **11**(24), 51–53 (2021)

37. He, Y., Wen, Y.: Text mining and topic extraction of factors influencing customer online shopping satisfaction. Softw. Guide **21**(6), 147–151 (2022). https://doi.org/10.11907/rjdk. 211848

38. Baidu's deactivation word list. https://github.com/goto456/stopwords. Accessed 23 Mar 2021

39. Wang, H., Li, X., Zhao, L.: Cable segmentation method based on box-plot and turning point threshold boundary. Comput. Appl. Softw. **38**(9), 244–249 (2021). https://doi.org/10.3969/j. issn.1000-386x.2021.09.038

40. Zhang, L., Mu, X.: Chinese text clustering algorithm based on Canopy+K-means. Libr. Trib. **38**(6), 113–119 (2018). https://doi.org/10.3969/j.issn.1002-1167.2018.06.021

The Bottomline Usability Measurement and Evaluation System for Enterprise Products

Yun Xu[✉], Yuxuan Wang, and Jianing Feng

Fourth Paradigm (Beijing) Technology Co., Ltd., Beijing, China
xuyun@4paradigm.com

Abstract. In the business service industry, product experience is a key factor for winning customer trust and securing business opportunities. However, because enterprise products are usually deployed at the customer side as a private asset and require a long iteration cycle, fixing the issue of usability in a timely manner is challenging. Therefore, controlling the quality of product experience before the release of products into the market is an urgent requirement to the business service industry. In this paper, a set of bottom-line usability measurement and an evaluation system are proposed with regard to the characteristics of enterprise products. With an aim to fulfill the customer's task, a system of primary indicators has been set up. Based on the characteristics of enterprise products, classic design principle, and high frequency experience problems, an evaluation system of secondary indicators is set up. To ensure market adaptability, multilevel evaluation is set up based on the product versions and the size of market demands. By adopting such usability measurement tools, the development cost can be minimized and the enterprises can be provided more benefits. This evaluation system allows the enterprise products to secure their core competitiveness, as well as enable the customers in various industries to accomplish their business goals.

Keywords: Enterprise products · Bottom-line measurement · Usability

1 Research Background

1.1 Customer Experience is the Key to the Success of Enterprise Product Providers

Enterprise products usually refer to the services provided to enterprises, covering all aspects aiming at reproduction in the process of enterprise development. The buyers are usually formal organizations, which also determines the basic characteristics of enterprise products that are generally different from ToC (To customer) products.

Generally, enterprise products have the following four characteristics [7]:

Highly Professional. Compared with the customers from ToC products, enterprise-level customers are often from professional fields; therefore, various high-technology and complex business processes are involved.

Long Purchase Decision Chain. Generally, the decision-making process for enterprise products is more cautious and complex because of the high average transaction value and

P.-L. P. Rau (Ed.): HCII 2023, LNCS 14022, pp. 541–554, 2023.
https://doi.org/10.1007/978-3-031-35936-1_40

wide-ranging influence. Many participants are involved in various links from initiation, decision-making, and approval, and many factors affect decision-making. Therefore, buyers have to be especially cautious. Providers of enterprise products need to promote their brand to win customer trust.

More Customization Needs. Because of factors, such as the enterprise scale and location of customers, different customers can have different perspectives and different levels of understanding about the product, even for the same business in the same field. This means that the "customization" of enterprise products can widely exist at a certain stage. This type of standard and customization puts forward certain requirements of agility for the efficiency of product providers.

Less Number of Customers, Longer Service Cycle. Compared with ToC products that have a wider range of customer groups, less contact, and short-term services, providers of enterprise products often win benchmark customers in subdivided fields with their professional abilities with a relatively less number of customers. During the process, they communicate with customers many times, and the maintenance services often last for months or even years. Therefore, to gain higher customer satisfaction, providers of enterprise products should produce value in many aspects, such as product performance, product experience, service quality, and after-sales, and increase competitiveness and brand reputation.

The popularization and rise of big data, artificial intelligence (AI), and other technologies have greatly promoted the transformation of all walks of life. Because enterprise products have quietly entered the stage of digital intelligence, enterprises need more powerful enterprise products to achieve their business goals. Customer experience is the key to the success of enterprise products. Good customer experience, in addition to giving full play to the key technologies and truly helping customers effectively achieve their business goals, is the foundation for the survival of providers of enterprise products. Therefore, attaching importance to customer experience is one of the inevitable trends of enterprise products in the era of digital intelligence.

1.2 Product Usability is an Important Measure of Customer Experience

Customer experience is a complex concept. There are four significant dimensions of customer experience, which can be summarized as follows:

Interactive Experience. It refers to the experience during the communication and interaction between the customer and the enterprise.

Product/Service Experience. It refers to the customer's experience with the product, including product practicability, ease of use, and consistency with customer demands.

Brand Awareness. It refers to the views on company values and industry status.

Price. It refers to the value judgment of the product.

According to the 2019 Gartner Report [6], product/service experience has the greatest impact on customer loyalty, which accounts for more than 36%. Therefore, customer experience can be enhanced by continuously improving product/service experience, followed by interactive experience, brand awareness, and price.

1.3 Necessity and Feasibility Analysis of Adopting Bottom-Line Usability Measurement Mechanism

Necessity. Enterprise products are mainly used in specific business scenarios, and the customers usually pay for the product that can achieve the key task. The usability of enterprise products is reflected in the following aspects: improving the transmission efficiency of product information, improving the efficiency of task operation, decreasing repeated operations and failures, and improving experience consistency. Therefore, usability is a crucial measurement tool of enterprise products.

Contrastingly, the business is usually highly professional for enterprise products. The more complex the product, the more difficult it is to ensure a good user experience. While using the product, every new feature, function, and step increases the risk of failure in user experience. The interface serves as a bridge between users and products, and the "language" of the interface should ensure smooth and effective "communication" between the business users and technical products, which suggests extremely high requirements for the ease of use and learnability of enterprise products.

Finally, owing to the long iteration cycle and high deployment cost of these products, establishing an experience feedback mechanism through data event tracking is difficult for the manufacturers of enterprise products, and exposing usability problems promptly is also challenging. However, for enterprise products, a certain ripple effect exists among different product versions or different products of the same series [8]. The usability of each product can affect the company's reputation as a high-quality product supplier. Poor usability can have a drastic impact on the sales of an entire product series. Therefore, before the product enters the market, it is crucial to vigilantly determine product usability when it is released as basic quality assurance.

Reasons for Replacing Regular Usability Testing with "Bottom-Line Usability Measurement".

Different fundamental purposes. Choosing bottom-line usability measurement instead of conventional usability testing is crucial because their purposes are different. Of note, the purpose of usability testing before release is to find as many usability problems as possible or to verify solutions, which is fundamentally different from the purpose of bottom-line usability measurement. We aim to set an experience baseline before release of products and to ensure customer success at the lowest cost. To achieve this goal, the bottom-line usability measurement is more targeted, and the implementation cost is lower.

Conventional usability testing is divided into the following stages: developing objectives, recruiting testers, designating tasks, and testing measurements [1]. However, difficulties often appear in the first link of "inviting customers"—testers (development/testing/business/designers) contacting customers in advance is difficult and risky. For instance, sales representatives may worry that testers can affect the business relationship when contacting customers, or the customer does not want to provide their internal employees to be the test object [9]. Owing to the time/risk cost brought by its dependence on external users, there can be certain obstacles to implementing usability testing.

Regular testing lacks standard for judging the suitability of the collected user feedback for version release. There is no reasonable standard for the user feedback obtained from regular usability testing to define the problems that are not suitable for product release when they are not resolved and those that can be solved in subsequent versions. Therefore, in the case of tight product release time and limited R&D resources, providers of enterprise products usually prioritize testing and optimization of functions, performance, stability, compatibility, and security. In the subsequent iteration plan, it can even directly skip the problems of usability testing, burying hidden dangers for customer experience. Furthermore, the customization features of enterprise products also require manufacturers to agilely and promptly respond to market needs. Therefore, setting a bottom line for a low-cost experience at a critical stage of release is necessary.

When implementing the bottom-line usability measurement, we optimized it based on the following four aspects:

- **Decrease the number of users invited externally.** Enterprise product users play a distinct role in an organization. Regardless of differences in gender, age, or region, they play the same role with relatively consistent professional attributes. Therefore, the main basis for the functional design of the product is the enterprise's business positioning and assessment objectives of the role. Therefore, on the theoretical basis that five people can find 85% of the usability problems proposed by Nielsen [1], we further decreased the number of external users. Meanwhile, we included experts in the design field and business fields during the implementation to improve testing efficiency and neutralize the situation of the small number of external users to a certain extent.

- **Measurement based on tasks and cancel subjective satisfaction evaluation.** The degree of satisfaction is a crucial feature that distinguishes bottom-line usability measurement from user experience measurement. User satisfaction is undeniably an important factor in product development iterations; however, we did not consider it during the release stage. It is the inverting result of measuring the purpose.

  Our purpose is to ensure that the product reaches the usability bottom line at the minimum cost, the products entering the market may not have a negative impact on the brand reputation, and the products have a certain guarantee for the experience.

  Therefore, we believe that the core of the investigation should be whether our products can effectively help enterprises complete their tasks or goals. Furthermore, based on the complexity of enterprise products, we included an important factor that affects customer satisfaction—whether the product is the ease of learning as a more specific measurement. To conclude, because our ultimate goal is to improve brand reputation, the standardization of brand vision is also included in the measurement.

- **User testing + expert heuristic evaluation.** It is well-known that expert heuristic evaluation is highly efficient and low-cost usability testing [2]. In the measurement stage, the real-user testing is integrated, and the advantages of combining the experience of the walk-throughs of experts and business experts are as follows: first, it includes a small number of external testers. Furthermore, experts are more sensitive when experiencing problems. Furthermore, the expert walk-through setup during the implementation process is not completely independent of user testing but is also a part of the observation during the user testing process. It can provide a professional perspective for problems ignored by users and for situations that are difficult to define.

- **Establish a multi-layer measurement system based on the release situation to avoid the disadvantages brought by the one-size-fits-all model.** Because it is the "bottom line," its tightness decides whether the product can be released successfully. If all products are treated equally with the same evaluation method, it can be difficult to achieve flexibility for different markets, and there can be some resistance from the business side, which can make the implementation of the mechanism difficult or fail the plan. Therefore, through different product sales plans and different market influences, we have set up many levels. The indicators of each level are the same, but the measurements of whether the test passes are different.

To conclude, relatively low implementation costs, reasonable goals, applicable indicators for enterprise products, and multilevel measurements for different markets are sufficient criteria for bottom-line usability measurement to obtain consensus among different parties within the manufacturers of enterprise products, which include high-level executives, product business parties, and designers.

2   Research Process

To ensure the bottom-line product experience before release of products, we constructed a model of bottom-line usability measurement for enterprise products. The specific building process is divided into the following steps:

2.1   Establishing the Indicators of Bottom-Line Usability Measurement

With the development of society, usability measurements are also updated iteratively, from the early CSAT measurements [10] to the product experience measurements models introduced by leading companies in the Internet era. Different development stages have given rise to different product forms and corresponding experience measurement tools. Any rule or model has its target and scope of application. For bottom-line usability measurement, our scope of application is largely for enterprise products, and we must fully consider the characteristics of such products. Further, because the implementation stage is in the release stage, we also selected the indicators most directly related to the goal to ensure low cost and high efficiency.

We extensively analyzed the existing measurement models. We prioritized its usability measurements, and secondly due to the modern measurement models are often based on classical theories. Thus, we refer to the system usability scale (SUS), 10 Nielsen heuristics, and relatively common usability measurement principles. Finally, combined with the characteristics of enterprise products, such as users often having no choice, enterprise-level privatization deployment, and data security, we comprehensively considered the selection of the indicators.

Selection of First-Level Evaluation Dimensions. Combined with the goals of bottom-line usability measurement, we established 6 primary dimensions and 20 secondary indicators. There were two measurements for the primary dimensions, one was based on the task, emphasized the achievement of user goals and the learnability of the system, whereas the other was closely related to the goal, as reflected in the inclusion of brand normality in the scope of examination. They were as follows:

- **Practicality.** We focused on whether user goals could be achieved through the product.
- **Learnability.** In terms of presenting the content through the interface, we established indicators around factors, including the product's information structure, visual elements, and functional concepts, and focused on the ease of understanding of the product.
- **Efficiency.** From the perspective of functional operation, we established indicators based on whether operational steps to complete the task were convenient and concise and whether multi-role collaborative support was provided; we focused on user efficiency when completing the task.
- **Memorability.** We included the time dimension in the usability measurement to ensure that the product provided a certain memory during its long-term use.
- **Error.** We evaluated the fault tolerance function during product use.
- **Visual brand.** We mainly focused on the standardization of the use of brand vision, copyright issues, and customization compliance.

Establishing Secondary Measurement Indicators. After setting the primary indicators, we sorted out and summarized the experience problem pool of existing products and established subdivided secondary inspection indicators based on high-frequency experience problems that were encountered. There are 20 items as follows:

- **Practicality**

  1. Overall, using the product/feature enabled the users to achieve the aforementioned goals.

- **Learnability**

  1. When using the product/feature, the users could always clarify the tasks of the current interface.
  2. When using the product/feature, problems could be solved through the explanation provided in the product or the manual.
  3. When using the product/feature, the existing concepts that the users were exposed to matched their cognition.
  4. When using the product/feature, the users could find a clear explanation of the unique concept of the product.
  5. When using the product/feature, the users felt that the navigation division of the product was reasonable.
  6. When using the product/feature, the operation required by the users could be found by them.
  7. When using the product/feature, the users believed that the colors, icons, and illustrations used in the product were identifiable and matched their cognition.

- **Efficiency**

  1. When using the product/feature, the users did not have to perform any extensive and repetitive operations to complete the task.

2. When using the product/feature, the users did not have to perform any difficult precise control to complete the task.
3. When using the product/feature, tasks involving multiple roles and different permissions conformed to the users' collaboration mode.

- **Memorability**

  1. When using the product/feature, the users did not have to memorize any information that did not belong to the current operational interface.
  2. When using the product/feature, the users needed to be aware of the state of the object they were operating at any time.

- **Error**

  1. When using the product/feature, unless a warning was provided to the users before any operation, all key operations allowed the users to undo.
  2. When using the product/feature, the users could return to the previous page/source page at any time.
  3. When using the product/feature, the users received a second confirmation every time before executing a risky command; hence, they could understand the operational risks.
  4. When using the product/feature, if an error occurred, the users could obtain an easy-to-understand description of the cause of the error and a solution to the error.

- **Brand vision**

  1. The brand and logo used in this product/feature complied with company regulations.
  2. Design elements, including fonts, icons, and pictures used in this product/feature, had no copyright infringement.
  3. There was no error in information related to customization, including the brand, logo, and copy of this product/feature.

Clarifying the Measurements for the Prioritization of the Indicators. When establishing the indicator system, we closely focused on user tasks. Therefore, the division of the priorities of the 20 secondary indicators was mainly based on their impact on the completion of the tasks. There were five types of division:

- **Block (P0).** The core tasks that the users wanted to perform were completely unavailable. If such issues are not fixed, users will feel that they cannot accomplish their goals through the product.
- **Critical (P1).** Some core features were unavailable. If such issues are not fixed, users will think that the product makes them feel irritated or painful.
- **Major (P2).** Products could be used normally, but user efficiency was greatly affected. If such issues are not fixed, users will perceive the product experience as unfriendly.
- **Minor (P3).** Professional users from the non-experience industry could perceive the issues of interface styles and interactive dynamic effects. If such issues are not fixed, users will think the product design is of low quality.

- **Trivial (P4).** Only professional users from the non-experience industry could perceive these minor interface issues. If such issues are not fixed, they will not affect overall user satisfaction with the product (Table 1).

Table 1. Indicator system for bottom-line usability measurement

Type of assessment	Level of important	Specific inspection items
Practicality	Block (P0)	1. Overall, using the product enables the user to achieve the goals defined above
Learnability	Block (P0) Critical (P1) Major (P2) Major (P2) Major (P2) Critical (P1) Major (P2)	2. The user can always clarify the tasks of the current interface 3. Problems can be solved through the explanation provided in the product or the manual 4. The existing concepts that users are exposed to match their cognition 5. The user can find a clear explanation of the unique concept of the product 6. The user thinks that the navigation division of the product is reasonable 7. The operation required by the user can be found by the user 8. The user believes that the colors, icons, and illustrations used in the product are identifiable and match their cognition
Efficiency	Major (P2) Major (P2) Major (P2)	9. The user does not have to perform any extensive and repetitive operations to complete the task 10. The user does not have to perform any difficult precise control to complete the task 11. Tasks involving multiple roles and different permissions conform to the user's collaboration mode
Memorability	Major (P2) Major (P2)	12. The user does not have to memorize any information that does not belong to the current operational interface 13. The user should be aware of the state of the object he is operating at any time
Error	Major (P2) Critical (P1) Major (P2) Critical (P1)	14. Unless a warning is provided to the user before the operation, all key operations should allow the user to undo 15. Users can return to the previous page/source page at any time 16. Users will receive a second confirmation every time before executing a risky command, so that they can understand the operational risks 17. If an error occurs, the user can obtain an easy-to-understand description of the cause of the error and a solution to the error

(continued)

Table 1. (*continued*)

Type of assessment	Level of important	Specific inspection items
Brand vision	Critical (P1) Major (P2) Critical (P1)	18. The brand and logo used in this product/feature comply with company regulations 19. The fonts, icons, pictures and other design elements used in this product/feature have no copyright infringement 20. There is no error in the brand, logo, copy and other information related to customization in this product

2.2 Establishing Graded Evaluation Standards

After the indicators were determined, evaluation standards were formulated in the next step. To apply to the release of different product versions, we formulated evaluation standards and scopes for different versions based on the number of customers the product could be sold to. In other words, connecting and binding the evaluation standards of bottom-line usability measurement with the management of different versions. The basis for the classification of the levels of product version usability was as follows (Table 2):

Table 2. Classification of the usability levels of product versions

Type of version	The maximum number of customers that can be supported	Version standards
Concept	1	1. No block-level experience problems
Pre-release	10	1. No block-level experience problems 2. No critical experience problems 3. The rest of the interactive experience
Customization	XX customer exclusive	1. Boundary: The boundary determined and recognized by the customer 2. Red line: The red line meets the standard, and the part that does not meet the standard provides a plan
Release	30	1. No block-level experience problems 2. No critical experience problems 3. Major-level experience problems
Experience	5	1. No block-level experience problems 2. The rest of the experience
GA	More than 30	1. No block-level experience problems 2. No critical experience problems 3. No major experience problems

2.3 Combining User Evaluation and Expert Heuristic Evaluation as an Implementation Method

During implementation, we set up a team of design and business experts to perform heuristic evaluations in addition to external target users.

Heuristic evaluation refers to having a group of evaluators for examining pages in conjunction with usability principles. The advantage of this evaluation method is that the evaluation based on expert experience is faster and more convenient, and the research cost is lower. The disadvantage is that the problems found are relatively subjective [2]. Therefore, in addition to heuristic evaluation, an expert review was also arranged to observe how the real users performed tasks, with the actual user test results as the main reference and the results of the heuristic evaluation as a supplement. The final evaluation was combined with double considerations.

During the implementation, these experts participated as a review team. They played the roles of both experienced experts and process supervisors. The expert review process was as follows:

Step 1. The experts confirmed the usability requirements corresponding to version classification according to the project approval materials of the product.

Step 2. The experts confirmed the demand range and level according to the project approval materials of the product to review whether the task process given by the business side was reasonable.

Step 3. The experts confirmed the task process and understood version features before testing, simulated the users to complete a specific task independently, and reviewed the achievement of the indicators based on the task.

Step 4. The experts observed the usage during the test, combined the task completion and walked through the results to review the results of each indicator, integrated the version usability requirements, and communicated with several experts to give the final consistent review results.

2.4 Establishing the Rules for Bottom-Line Usability Measurement

Selecting appropriate users and testing tasks is the prerequisite to ensure the validity of the measurement results. In addition, because the release involves the interests of multiple parties, multiple roles, such as business sides, designers, and project managers, need to reach an agreement in participation. The relevant rules used in this study were as follows:

The Rules for User Selection (Persona, Quantity). The main principle for selecting the testers was those who could represent the expected users of a product. The skills and knowledge reserves needed to be consistent with the end user persona. Before the test, the users' positioning, permissions, usage scenarios, and behavioral characteristics/rules were not 50% different from the persona of target users. In addition, from the perspective of reducing costs, no fewer than two real users were allowed to participate.

The Rules for Measurement Task Selection. The selection principle of the measurement task was mainly that the task should best represent the usage after the system was released and should cover important parts of the system interface. The selection of "core tasks" covered the full functionality of the current version of the core process defined in the product management mechanism.

The Rule of Multiparty Participation. To ensure that the test results were true and effective, the consensus and efforts of multiple personnel related to the product needed to be inseparable. In addition to a panel of experts and designers as hosts, the measurement process also involved product and project managers. Among them, the product managers were responsible for inviting real users, confirming a stable and operational test environment, preparing tasks, and preparing manuals and other materials. The product managers needed to be present to observe the real-user testing. The project managers were responsible for supervising the on-time implementation of the test, as well as notifying the scheduling plan by email and subsequent scheduling if it failed.

3 Application

The implementation is described in detail below in conjunction with the bottom-line usability test of the company's intelligent supply chain product version 1.0 (hereinafter referred to as the "experience red line" test).

3.1 Preparation Stage

The Business Side Determined the Testers. Before testing, the business side needed to clarify the persona of the target users of the product to the review group and invite the real users as test objects.

The Business Side Determined the Evaluation Boundary. The business side needed to clarify the tasks of the test, and the scope of tasks was consistent with the main tasks in the published materials. Moreover, the business side needed to clarify the preset scenarios provided to the users during the test (Figs 1 and 2).

Designers Completed Specific Test Scripts Based on Main Tasks and Scenarios.

Product Name: Intelligent Supply Chain Predictive Replenishment Platform V1.0.0 Grading and Evaluation boundarys: Concept version; no block-level experience problems		User Position : supply chain managers	
Process		**Problem statistics**	
1. The business side provides the evaluation scope, including information on users, objectives, tasks, scenarios, etc., in order to clarify the evaluation boundary		Block (P0) Problem	0
2. Based on the information provided by the business side, the product manager and the contact designer provide usability test scripts, environment and other information to conduct tests before the release		Critical (P1) Problem	1
3. Based on the test, record the problems encountered by users. If more than half of the users in the test encounter the same problem, the problem will be recorded in the check items of the red line below		Major (P2) Problem	19
4. count the number of problems in each red line check item		Total	
5. get the number of problems under each level according to the level of each check item, and alert according to the overall quality standard			20
Scope			
User	How many kinds of target users can a product be divided into? What are the abilities and limitations of these roles?	Have planning authority and high level of business proficiency	
Target	What goals does the product/feature aim to meet?	To assist planners with promotion and clearance decisions with sales data, inventory data and machine learning forecasting technology	
Task	What tasks do users need to complete in order to achieve these goals?	Complete the basic setup of the system; complete the operation of the promotion program to achieve the purpose of promotion; complete the operation of clearing the stagnant inventory	
Scenarios	What are the typical scenarios for users to use the product? Are there limitations such as environment/platform/device?	Inventory management of goods in the clear stagnation and commodity promotion price decision Constraints: The product is responsible for the auxiliary decision making part, and will provide price suggestions to users for promotion decisions. The specific implementation needs to rely on the corresponding hard promotion system to make specific price reduction operations	

Fig. 1. The evaluation scope of the experience redline report

User information						
Name	**	Position		Supply Chain Director	Match deviation	Low
Time	2021/6/28			Test site	Office	
Sequence Number	Task List					
	1	Log in				
	2	Please complete the sales forecast setting				
	3	Please complete the complementary settings				
	4	Browse the home page				
	5	Check the overall sales forecast				
	6	Search Products Sales Forecast				
	7	Complete inventory plan inquiry and export				
	8	Complete replenishment plan inquiry and confirmation				
	9	Create unscheduled replenishment orders				
	10	Complete the inquiry and confirmation of the transfer plan				
	11	Complete refund plan inquiry and closure				

Detail Task List				
Task 1. Log in				
Step	Additional Information	Standard	Feedback	Notes
1. Find the login page	URL: http://172.24.15.157:30001/home	Whether the page is displayed properly		
2.Enter the user name and password	Username: test password: test123456			
3.Go to home page		Home page correctly displayed		
Task 2: Please complete the sales forecast setting				
Step	Additional Information	Standard	Feedback	Notes
1. Go to the sales forecast setting page		The entry can be found and the interface is displayed normally		
2. Completion of forecast target setting		Complete the required field settings and submit correctly		

Fig. 2. Part of the task form

3.2   Execution Stage

Key points in execution stage:

- To avoid the real users from being nervous or disturbed during the test, the members of the review team were not in the same space as the users, and the review team viewed real-user operations through shared screens.

- During the test, the users were allowed to receive a certain degree of help according to the release plan. For example, if the product itself promised to provide customers with assistance, such as user manuals and telephone consultations, during the test, the users were allowed to provide support within this scope.
- During the usability test, the review team recorded the problems in the indicators encountered by the participants.
- The expert team studied the tasks and performed expert heuristic evaluations a day before testing.

3.3 Statistical Review Stage

In the statistical review stage, the review group counted the number of problems in each indicator. According to the level of importance of each inspection item, the number of problems at each level was obtained and reviewed according to the overall quality standard.

If the test failed, the business side needed to synchronize the problem with the relevant personnel and explain the reason for the failure, and the project managers needed to re-book a new round of testing after modifications.

4 Conclusions

The bottom-line usability measurement mechanism was implemented within the company in April 2021, and more than 30 measurements have been organized so far, which involve more than 10 products in various industries such as finance, retail, and manufacturing. It has successfully intercepted five unreleased products with usability problems and recorded more than 100 experience problems.

The bottom-line usability measurement mechanism is a new usability measurement mechanism that aims to minimize costs and control quality of the product delivery experience. Unlike the traditional usability test, this mechanism innovates the indicator system, implementation method, evaluation standards, and personnel composition in combination with the characteristics of Enterprise products. On this basis, we established a multi-party consensus on relevant roles where the test objective met the common interest of multiple parties. The cost of testing could be controlled within the scope of limited resources. Combined with the company's existing product version management mechanism, the fairness of its measurement basis was ensured. Product usability was ensured to reach the bottom line of helping customers succeed in tasks under limited development resources, which could help companies control the product experience quality from the source of release and build long-term brand trust.

References

1. Nielsen, J., Mack, R.L.: Usability Inspection Methods. Wiley, New York (1994)
2. Nielsen, J.: Usability Engineering. Academic Press, New York (1993)
3. Dong, J., Fu, L., Rao, P.: Human-Computer Interaction: User-Centered Design and Evaluation. Tsinghua University Press, Beijing (2013)

4. Brooke, J.: SUS: a retrospective. J. Usability Stud. **8**(2), 29–40 (2013)
5. Iresearch: 2020 China enterprise service research report. https://www.iresearch.com.cn/Det ail/report?id=3571&isfree=0 (2020)
6. Gartner: inc-creating a high impact customer experience strategy. https://www.gartner.com/ en/marketing/research/creating-a-high-impact-customer-experience-strategy (2019)
7. Liu, Y.: Win at End B: B2B Brand Marketing Growth Handbook. China Textile & Apparel Press, China (2021)
8. Grudin, J.: Why CSCW applications fail: problems in the design and evaluation of organizational interfaces. In: Proceedings of ACM CSCW'88 Conference Computer-Supported Cooperative Work, pp. 85–93(1988)
9. Grudin, J.: The case against user interface consistency. Commun. ACM **3210**, 1164–1173 (1989)
10. Cardozo, R.N.: An experimental study of customer effort, expectation, and satisfaction. J. Mark. Res. **2**(3), 244–249 (1965)

Cross-Cultural Research on the Construction of Digital Media Takes Virtual Idol Landscape as an Example

Rui Xu[1,2](✉), Yen Hsu[1], and Hanlin MI[2]

[1] The Graduate Institute of Design Science, Tatung University, Taipei 104, Taiwan
635524937@qq.com, yhsu@gm.ttu.edu.tw
[2] School of Art and Design, Fuzhou University of International Studies and Trade,
Fuzhou 350202, China

Abstract. Research background: In the context of digital media globalization, virtual idols, as a new type of media with its own relationship, is an extension of human strong relationship. Virtual idols add relationship attributes to content, making it easier for some audiences to be noticed and recognized, and they are more influential. With the influence of virtual idols or virtual assistants, content and products can touch the target audience group (fans or students) more quickly. It is not only an important medium for students to define and present themselves, but also an important way for students to project self-image, obtain identity marks and create self-value. In the era of digital virtual idol technology, virtual idols carry a new algorithm based on relationship logic, which can help the communicator find the target audience more quickly (Atkinson, R. K. 2002). At the same time, the target audience is also more willing to accept the content related to the favorite virtual idols because of the relationship between them and their idols. In addition, in online education activities all over the world, teaching agents can be designed as human or non-human roles. Human roles can be visualized as videos of human tutors, as well as roles which are calculated and generated, and can effectively avoid the problem of students' distraction in learning. The latter can be visualized as static or animated images, so that virtual idols have full opportunities to enter the field of digital education. With the help of virtual imaging, virtual idols break the boundary between anime and three-dimensional (Clark & Mayer, 2002), and interact with fans, students and other groups with more realistic individual images.

Keywords: virtual idols · digital media · media literacy · online education platform

1 Introduction

Thanks to the application of multiple new technologies such as dynamic capture, real-time rendering, face recognition and character modeling, compared with a single virtual idol, the new generation of virtual idols can make multi-path interaction with the student community possible with a more distinctive "personality charm": which not

P.-L. P. Rau (Ed.): HCII 2023, LNCS 14022, pp. 555–563, 2023.
https://doi.org/10.1007/978-3-031-35936-1_41

only can accurately control facial expression changes, make appropriate facial and voice responses, but also can achieve real-time singing, dancing, talk show, voice prompt (Bendel, 2003), teaching, etc. More importantly, there are more platforms that can carry virtual idols. Virtual idols are active in various digital media, such as short video platforms, live broadcast platforms, and online education portals. They can easily be downloaded by mobile phones and computers to achieve real-time interaction and multiple exchanges. The purpose of the study to explore the differences and future teaching models of virtual idols as teaching assistants of intelligent courses under different driving forces, and discuss the changes of virtual idols and teachers' roles in the process of continuous development and upgrading of digital, information, intelligent platforms and tools. At the same time, this article also aims at taking college students as the target audience, discussing whether the target users are more willing to accept the education and teaching content related to their favorite virtual idols in the online platform or digital media field because of the relationship addition. In addition, by organizing students to participate in the questionnaire survey, we can discuss that in the digital education environment, the emergence of virtual idol assistants can effectively improve the learning effect of students. The research results: the use of virtual idol assistants has an important effect on improving the media literacy of students in the online education environment, and also helps students improve their learning effect to a certain extent. Therefore, in the process of digital education in the future, we can promote the development of digital education through the intermediary of virtual idols, which requires multiple efforts. Educators should pay attention to the new field of digital education opened up by effective use of virtual idols, improve the ability of personal media literacy and digital literacy of using virtual idols, create an industry ecosystem that guarantees the healthy texture of virtual idols, and build an external barrier to promote the orderly development of virtual idols.

2 Introduction

In the long history, from the primitive society's totem worship of nature to the later worship of mythological characters and ancestors, and then to the real worship of heroes, celebrities, stars and other real people, it has gone through a process of gradually fading the mysterious veil. It is obvious that people in different historical periods place different expectations and dreams on their idols. Idol itself is an extended carrier of "relational media", which is "a new type of media with its own relational attributes". "relational" indicates that the existence of idols depends on the recognition, pursuit or worship of others, while "media" indicates that it has the symbol function of conveying meaning, and there is a process of meaning construction and interpretation that is encoded and decoded. As a digital medium with fictional and technical color, the encoding and decoding of virtual idol is more constructive. The virtual idol is an abstract cultural product that interacts with intelligent information technology, anime culture and fan culture. It uses digital symbols as the medium to build a virtual world, and presents landscape representations such as virtual presence, virtual social interaction and virtual personality setting. It forms an online/offline, virtual/real interaction and call with young audiences, so as to create a free space for self-expression and cultural attitude of young students. It is not a new thing or concept to preserve and establish the field of its own meaning reserve. The birth of virtual idols can be traced back to the 1970s and 1980s. However, due to the continuous progress of AI, AR, VR, 3D motion capture, holographic image and other related digital technologies in recent years, under the background of the industry where the real idols often prove to be notorious and cause negative discussion in the whole society, the virtual idols industry, as one of the main tracks of the universe, began to rise, leading the new consumption trend of youth student group in culture, education and entertainment. According to the Research Report on the Development of China's Virtual Idol Industry and Internet Users in 2021, 82% of Internet users in Chinese Mainland have ever had "idols", and 64% of them have "virtual idols". The proportion of young people among virtual idol lovers is 92%. The special technical practice and participatory cultural practice of virtual idols not only dredge young people's desire for the real world, but also dispel young people's subjectivity, critical consciousness and transcendence dimension, and deepen the virtualization of social culture. Through the analysis of the landscape characteristics of virtual idols and the value orientation, cultural mentality and identity of young subcultural groups in the digital era reflected by them, the digital education platform can be used to investigate the construction and value of the current digital subculture, thus subtly affecting the learning status, efficiency and final results of young students. In addition to the large audience of young students, it provides new thinking for digital education and teaching. The study of virtual idols has also received academic attention (Sweller, J., 2003). From the perspective of research literature in recent years, there are two types of research paths: the first is industrial path analysis, focusing on the planning and operation of virtual idols. Generally, according to the driving force behind the development of virtual idols, virtual idols are divided into three categories: content-driven, technology-driven and industry-driven, and according to their types and the degree of idol operation, it discusses the differences in the operation strategies and realization methods of virtual idols under different driving forces. In the era of Internet virtual idol technology, virtual idol carries a new algorithm based on relationship logic. The second is media communication analysis and some studies suggest that media literacy education based on young student users and virtual idols should highlight how to correctly understand and make new media an auxiliary tool for their study and life, and avoid excessive addiction. It is necessary to improve the media literacy of college students, including research on media cognition and responsibility literacy, media use and technology literacy, information production and consumption literacy, social communication and participation literacy, etc. The third is the cultural analysis path, emphasizing the cultural characteristics and functions of virtual idols and the cultural interpretation of virtual idol fans. It also uses the theory of emotional design to analyze the virtual idol and its interaction with fans. In addition to these theoretical analyses, some young scholars have carried out empirical research on the fans of virtual idols, including qualitative and quantitative research. The relevant content includes the study of the interaction between fans and virtual idols, and the existence of a quasi-social relationship between fans and virtual idols, which is "shouting through the air". It also analyzes the cultural practice of "building identity through specific code transmission, creating regenerative text and relational imagination within the fan community". It can be said that as a specific medium, virtual idols are not only an important medium for young people to define and present themselves, but also an important way for young people to project self-image

(Clark, R. E., 2005)., obtain identity identification and create self-value. The virtual idol landscape reflects the unique cultural mentality and "meaning world" of the youth in the modern time, and is a complex of youth group psychology, spiritual needs, lifestyle, behavior patterns and values. Virtual idols, represented by intelligent terminals, digital symbols and holographic imaging, create the unique existence, expression and cultural attitude of the youth in the modern time. This unique network cultural landscape builds a new "field" for youth's ideological cognition and behavior activities, and becomes an important carrier for the youth in the modern time to express themselves, participate in the production, creation and consumption of network culture, and reflect the aesthetic taste, the discourse style, value orientation and cultural mentality of the youth in the modern time. It is necessary to conduct in-depth perspective and overall study. In the critical period of youth socialization, the personality traits, behavior patterns and value tendencies embodied in life models and positive energy idols will imperceptibly affect the cognitive style (Dirkin, K. H., Mishra, P., 2005), thinking concepts and cultural mentality of young people, become the spiritual power of youth growth, and play an important role in the process of youth growth.

Therefore, based on the above contents, this study attempts to analyze the multidimensional patterns of virtual idols and cultural mentality of youth reflected by them, and integrate them into youth values education as an effective educational resource, which has important value implications for giving play to the educational function of digital culture and building a new climate and new ecology of Internet culture in the intelligent information era. This paper expects to use virtual idols as teachers' intelligent teaching assistants to carry out relevant research from this perspective and explore the following core issues:

- Theoretical evaluation and discussion of virtual idols based on various types of models.
- Based on a literature review, this study attempts to explain the importance of virtual idols as a digital medium for teaching.
- Taking virtual idols as an example, this study anticipates the important role of virtual idols as digital teaching assistants in various disciplines.

3   Virtual Idols and Education

At present, the traditional classroom teaching mode has been criticized for many existing problems. The reform of the new curriculum standards and the change of the evaluation method also have new demands on the teaching mode. With the continuous development of virtual idol technology, digital information technology and virtual idol technology (Clarebout, G., 2006), the application in the field of education has brought a new direction to the optimization of the classroom (Holmes, J., 2007)., and also provided a new support for the realization of intelligent and collaborative classroom teaching. It makes intelligent technology reach or even exceed the "level" of human teachers in specific fields, such as the maturity of intelligent speech synthesis and intelligent speech evaluation technology in the field of English teaching. In the field of music teaching, virtual idols can recognize the piano sound "more intelligently" through digital technology, and the key technical indicators that effectively improve the accompaniment effect through intelligent learning assistants. The current digital technology has been able to accurately "independently understand" the content that children are playing, such as which section they are playing, and they are playing with the left hand or the right hand... Which is far beyond the original way of "only passively recognize the specified music score" of the same type of technology. In the process of Chinese learning, the information intelligence system, represented by Tsinghua Natural Language and Social Humanities Computing Laboratory, focuses on the frontiers of natural language processing with Chinese as the core, and the Poetry Creation System of Nine Odes is developed by the laboratory (Baylor, A. L., 2003). The "Nine Odes" can be trained and learned based on 800000 previous poems. Compared with other poetry generation systems on the market, the system of Nine Odes can achieve multi-genre, multi-style and human-computer interactive creation. By inputting keywords, sentences, etc. into the system, and selecting the style to be created (quatrains, metrical poems, collection poems, and word boards), we can obtain a work that meets the requirements of ancient poetry creation. The operation is simple and fast, and the created poems basically meet the rules in terms of rhyme, tone, antithesis, adhesion, and so on, which solves the pain points of rhythm in poetry creation. In the field of art teaching, virtual idol technology learning digital portrait is similar to painting. It is to use a dynamic learning data to depict it stereoscopically and visually after analyzing the psychological and behavioral characteristics of learners. This needs to rely on key technologies such as intelligent data mining and machine learning algorithms. By portraying three-dimensional and visible digital portraits for learners, it can provide more targeted and personalized education services. Due to the limitation of current market environment factors and the impact of evaluation methods, products that can focus on classroom teaching have problems such as low intelligence and low synergy, and the process of classroom intelligence is slightly stagnant. Obviously, from the perspective of the integration of virtual idol technology and traditional classroom, it is necessary and feasible to design and develop an intelligent teaching assistant that can be applied to classroom teaching and give full play to "teacher wisdom" and "virtual idol wisdom". Under the above background, this study is guided by the design concept of "human-computer cooperation", and aims at improving the teaching effect and quality (Baylor, A. L, 2005). It uses the research methods of literature research, content analysis, and investigation to explore virtual idol technology and the research and application of virtual idol technology in teaching. The representative intelligent teaching products on the market are selected for in-depth research and analysis to understand the advantages and disadvantages of existing products and provide ideas and guidance for the design and development of intelligent teaching assistants.

4 Discussion

4.1 Cooperation and Coexistence: Realize Efficient Teaching of Human-Computer Cooperation

Virtual idol technology has special significance for teachers. It can free teachers from tedious, mechanical and repetitive mental work and become valuable tools and partners for teachers. On the one hand, virtual idol technology can replace a single skill of teachers to complete tedious and mechanical work in daily work such as checking and correcting homework, and liberate teachers from repetitive and mechanical affairs; On the other hand, virtual idol technology will become an integral part of teachers' work in the future, and intelligent work will be completed by human-computer cooperation. The education service system for the individual development of students is difficult to support by teachers alone. Especially in Chinese Mainland, a teacher often has to face dozens of students. Thus, without technical support, it is difficult to accurately understand the characteristics of students and without the support of virtual idol technology, it is also impossible to implement personalized teaching that varies from person to person. In the era of virtual idol technology, on the basis of comprehensive collection and analysis of students' learning process data, human-computer interaction can not only realize the large-scale support of group classes, but also realize personalized teaching that adapts to the development of each individual. The education in the industrial era is a uniform and large-scale processing. Education in the future is to focus on the development of individual personality, just like building an ecosystem, where there are towering trees, small grass, and a variety of animals and plants, each taking its place and supporting each other. The assembly-line examination-oriented education ultimately turns students into homogeneous people, that is, people with strong examination-oriented ability. We should abandon this single education because students are diverse in all aspects. Future education should change from cultivating artificial forests to cultivating ecosystems. To build an ecosystem, teachers are required to pay attention to the competitive and interdependent relationship between each individual, the needs of each individual in the ecosystem, the personality of students, the cultivation of students' personality, and the promotion of students' personality development. To achieve these goals, it is difficult to achieve them by teachers alone without the external intellectual support of virtual idol technology representatives. Therefore, the future teachers are human teachers and virtual idol technology teachers who jointly undertake teaching tasks. Both of them play their respective advantages and assume their roles in teaching. The earliest chat machine, Eliza, originating at MIT, plays the role of a psychologist, with the purpose of making text conversation more vivid. Today, with the development of virtual idol technology, the application of intelligent dialogue technology in the field of education is widely concerned. In the non-educational field, virtual idol technology provides people with the functions of consultation, transaction processing, chat, psychological consultation, virtual chat, etc., involving office, business and personal leisure and entertainment, and has the characteristics of convenience, entertainment, emotion, intelligence, etc. In the field of education, the scope of application involves the auxiliary and supporting functions of teachers, students, courses, schools and other aspects, including the functions of effective and harmonious communication between students and teachers, question consultation, question answering, tutoring language learning, simulating teachers and auxiliary teaching work, as shown in the table. Previous studies have shown that intelligent classroom assistants support personalized tutoring, question-and-answer interaction, emotional communication and other functions, create autonomous learning and interactive learning environment, provide learning resources, exercise simulation, emotional regulation, course knowledge guidance and other services. There are many obstacles and deficiencies in classroom teaching based on question teaching method, such as teachers' active questioning and students' passive answering mechanical questioning.

Modern information technology urges colleges and universities to use a large number of question-answering systems to support the application of question teaching methods in classroom teaching. For example, MIT uses Smart to answer questions about geography, history, culture, science and technology, entertainment and other aspects; Power - Aqua system is an intelligent question and answer system based on knowledge base, which contains information knowledge base in various fields; The intelligent real-time English chat system and the intelligent question and answer system provide a simulated context for English conversation practice. According to the survey of the application of modern technology in question teaching, there are few question answering systems that integrate emotional analysis and natural language processing technology. The application of technology integrating natural language and emotional analysis can make up for the shortcomings of traditional classroom problem teaching, create a virtual communication environment for students, and interact with intelligent classroom assistants as teachers and learning partners.

The future education needs to change the way students acquire knowledge. The teaching function of teachers teaching knowledge will be replaced by virtual idol technology. The main job of teachers is to cultivate students' ability. Teachers need to carefully design questions, learning resources, learning tools, learning activities, and learning evaluation. Accompanied by teachers, students can learn, acquire knowledge, learn to learn independently, think independently, collaborate, transfer and apply knowledge through problem-solving, so as to develop comprehensive quality and ability. Teachers' company, organization, supervision and inspection are very important for students' independent learning. The future form of learning must be the integration of three kinds of studying including online learning for students, problem-solving oriented project learning in the field of practice, and offline supervision, management, and accompanying of teachers, rather than a single form dominated by classroom teaching. However, virtual idol technology still cannot replace human beings. There are many differences between people and machines: people find problems, and machines solve problems. Therefore, education should focus on cultivating students' ability to find problems in addition to cultivating students' ability to solve problems. Machines do not have social attributes. Most of the time, computers communicate with people through virtual answers prepared in advance, without active social interaction ability. Thirdly, Machines do not have psychological properties. It will not feel happy or depressed. Therefore, compared with machines, teachers should pay more attention to their unique value as human beings, improve students' social value, psychological value and ability to use global resources, and assume the social responsibility of cultivating students to create the future rather than following the future (Johnson, W. L., 2000).

5   Conclusion

Higher requirements are put forward for teachers. In the future, the teacher team will be divided into two directions: on the one hand, it includes all-round teachers supported by virtual idol technology, that is, teachers should not only provide personalized support for each individual, but also provide support for groups with ecological nature, which requires them to master not only subject knowledge, but also teaching method knowledge, technical knowledge, and knowledge related to cognition, brain science development, and physical and mental health of young students. They should also understand various social attributes and have leadership and social cooperation ability, which is difficult for ordinary teachers to be competent. However, with the support of virtual idol technology, it is possible to have all-round teachers and professional teachers who are responsible for the physical and mental health and overall development of young students. In the future, teachers will have a fine and personalized division of labor. It is not possible for every teacher to become an all-around master, but some teachers can do their best in some aspects. In the future, there will be teachers who are specialized in practice guidance, project design, students' psychological problems, teachers for teaching, teachers for teaching design, etc. The division of teachers' roles is becoming more and more detailed, just like in making movies, there are screenwriters, actors, directors, cameramen and post-production workers. Therefore, teachers need to be good at carrying out education services based on large-scale social cooperation. With the change of teachers' roles and functions in the future, the future curriculum will also change. It is impractical to expect teachers to complete comprehensive courses across multiple fields alone, which must be supported by the structure of collaborative environment between teachers, and teachers and virtual idol technology. In the future, a course may be in the charge of more than one teacher, including subject experts, instructional designers, knowledge transmitters, activity designers, virtual idol technology assistants or other roles (Bartneck, C., 2009). It can be predicted that the design and teaching of future courses will be jointly completed by virtual idol teacher assistants and teachers of other disciplines, and even high-quality resources related to virtual idol technology such as universities and enterprises may be included in the classroom. The boundaries of disciplines, classes and schools will be gradually broken. The interconnection of all things on the Internet has changed social organizations and large-scale social systems. In the future, the curriculum will complete education services based on the social collaborative division of labor across the boundaries of schools. The transformation education of the institutional system and thinking system of human-machine integration of virtual idol technology, first of all, embodies various intelligent educational equipment and intelligent educational environment. Secondly, it is the educational business process and system embedded in virtual idol technology services, and finally it is the transformation of human-machine integration thinking mode. Virtual idol technology can develop rapidly and iteratively, but the transformation of education system, teachers' knowledge structure, teachers' teaching habits and teachers' concepts is a long and painful process (Kruger et al., 2004). The construction of the new education system must go through a difficult process. To give full play to the role of virtual idol technology, it is necessary to break through the original system, embed virtual idol technology services into business processes, create new paradigms, new processes, new structures, and new business forms to serve our education and generate new education form. In the era of virtual idol technology, we should also be good at using the thinking mode of human-computer combination. At present, data, information and knowledge are expanding rapidly, and the gap between them and everyone's learning time and cognitive ability is becoming greater. The survival of a complex society in the era of big data calls for the educational intelligence of human-computer integration (Atkinson, R. K., 2005). The era of our survival with the help of intelligent devices has come. Only by using the thinking mode of human-machine integration can education not only achieve large-scale coverage, but also achieve personalized development matching with individual capabilities. We should use external tools or smart devices to develop our own intelligence, and cognitive outsourcing will become the normal condition. Human-machine integrated thinking system is an important transformation direction of our future thinking mode. Human intelligence is limited. With mobile phones, computers and virtual idol technology, we can handle the total amount of information and data, and our ability to deal with emergencies will be greatly improved. The combination of human and computer can break through the limits of human individual cognition, enable us to control complex situations that exceed the limits of individual cognition, handle massive amounts of information that exceed individual cognitive ability, and cope with rapid changes that exceed the limits of individual cognitive ability.

Fund Name. The 2020 Fuzhou City Teachers' school-level scientific research project "Virtual Idol: College Community Culture and Fan Empowerment", No.: Research Results of FXW20015.

References

Atkinson, R.K.: Optimizing learning from examples using animated pedagogical agents. J. Educ. Psychol. **94**, 416–427 (2002)

Atkinson, R.K., Mayer, R.E., Merril, M.M.: Fostering social agency in multimedia learning: Examining the impact of an agent's voice. Contemp. Educ. Psychol. **30**, 117–139 (2005)

Bartneck, C., Croft, E., Kulic, D., Zoghbi, S.: Measurement instruments for the anthropomorphism, animacy, likeability, perceived intelligence, and perceived safety of robots. Int. J. Soc. Robot. **1**, 71–81 (2009)

Baylor, A.L., Kim, Y.: Simulating instructional roles through pedagogical agents. Int. J. Artif. Intell. Educ. **15**(1), 95–115 (2005)

Baylor, A.L., Ryu, J.: The effects of image and animation in enhancing pedagogical agent persona. J. Educ. Comput. Res. **28**, 373–395 (2003)

Clarebout, G., Elen, J.: Open learning environments and the impact of pedagogical agents. J. Educ. Comput. Res. **35**, 211–226 (2006)

Clark, R.E., Choi, S.: Five design principles for experiments on the effects of animated pedagogical agents. J. Educ. Comput. Res. **32**, 209–225 (2005)

Dirkin, K.H., Mishra, P., Altermatt, E.: All or nothing: levels of sociability of a pedagogical software agent and its impact on student perceptions and learning. J. Educ. Multimedia Hypermedia **14**, 113–127 (2005)

Holmes, J.: Designing agents to support learning by explaining. Comput. Educ. **48**, 523–547 (2007)

Johnson, W.L., Rickel, J.W., Lester, J.C.: Animated (2000)

Kalyuga, S., Ayres, P., Chandler, P., Sweller, J.: Theexpertise reversal effect. Educ. Psychol. **38**(1), 32 (2003)

Kruger, J., Wirtz, D., Van Boven, L., Altermatt, T.W.: The effort heuristic. J. Exp. Soc. Psychol. **40**(1), 91–98 (2004)

The Application and Expression of Product Modeling Design from Cross-Cultural Perspective

Songsen Zeng[1], Rui Xu[2]([✉]), and Shazhou Huang[1]

[1] School of Art and Design, Fuzhou University of International Studies and Trade, Fuzhou 350200, Fujian, China
[2] Institute of Design Science, Tatung University, Taipei 11604, Taiwan
635524937@qq.com

Abstract. With the development of society and the change of the times, the trend of economic globalization has further strengthened and accelerated the arrival of cultural globalization. The modernization of society, the internationalization of design, and the intermingling of cultural diversity are becoming evident. The international exchange and collision of diverse cultures gradually form a cross-cultural environment. The relationship between culture and design has become increasingly close, and cross-cultural product design has slowly become an important initiative to promote cultural development and increase the added value of products.

Cross-cultural product design means that designers must understand the differences between various cultures around the world, break the barriers of regional and national cultures, break the bonds of their own culture, and cross the cultural divide formed by history so that the designed products are "culturally" humanized and designed to be "global." We create "global" products. The cross-cultural design needs to understand the culture of the target region to make a targeted design. This paper attempts to overcome the current product design in different cultural backgrounds in other groups can not be better expressed in the core of its products, proposes a product design in the cross-cultural environment to quantify the research method, and through the introduction of Hofstede cultural dimension theory into the design process to assist in completing the product design, enhance the expression of the product's modeling semantics to reduce user learning costs. We propose an effective method to make the final product shape accurate in its representation. From the perspective of cross-cultural communication, it is of far-reaching significance to explore the expression of product styling and promote the development of products towards internationalization. The paper also describes the development trend of cross-cultural product design, the current situation, and the cross-cultural nature and cultural attributes accordingly.

Through preliminary investigation and related experiments, the results show that multiple factors influence cross-cultural product design, and people growing up in different cultures form differences in values. Users' habits and behavior patterns vary in other cultures, so in cross-cultural design, the designed products can be accepted by user groups in different cultural circles by exploring cross-cultural product styling design methods. By examining the ways of cross-cultural product design, the theoretical model of product design is obtained with the help

P.-L. P. Rau (Ed.): HCII 2023, LNCS 14022, pp. 564–579, 2023.
https://doi.org/10.1007/978-3-031-35936-1_42

of theoretical approaches. It is brought into the cross-cultural integration product design to verify the feasibility and validity of the cross-cultural product design model. The long-term significance of cross-cultural product design also lies in the coordination of the "human-product-environment-society. The long-term significance of cross-cultural product design is also to harmonize the relationship between "people-product-environment-society" and to have a positive impact on the formation of a sustainable human living environment and a way of life that integrates global and regional cultures, scientific and humanistic cultures.

Keywords: product design · cross-cultural · product semantics · styling

1 Background and Status of the Selected Topic

With the development of science and technology and productivity, the globalization of the economy has been strengthened, and the process of globalization has been further strengthened after the information revolution has gradually become a consensus. Communication between regions has become more convenient and efficient. The first and foremost is cultural exchange, with more frequent contact between different cultures and more tension between differences and conflicts between them. The development of cross-border trade and the high-speed circulation of markets has made the geographical boundaries of products themselves more blurred, and products have shifted from a single-oriented to a more diversified market, which has become a key point worth exploring for cross-cultural product design and an essential requirement for modern design product designers.

The formation of culture is influenced by the corresponding living environment, ideals and beliefs, institutional models, and other factors, which will also lead to differences in the way of thinking, different norms of behavior, different forms of organization, and their impact, forming the difference in culture between regions.

Fixed paradigm similarities in language, human environment, ecology, and production methods shape a region's culture. There are two main research directions in cross-regional cultural studies: one is to compare the mutually similar or similar parts of different cultures, and the other is to compare the interaction and communication between different cultures, and cross-regional cultural studies are to go from comparing the mutual parts of each region in the traditional culture to focusing on the communication, interaction, and influence across cultural boundaries. Culture, as a critical element of product design, must be fully understood in terms of cultural practices and differences in the target region to avoid conflicts and consider the possibility of cultural crossover in the design process.

Cross-cultural connections refer to the complex connections between participants' ability to rely not only on their codes, practices, perceptions, and ways of behaving but also to experience and understand the codes, practices, perceptions, and ways of behaving of others in the process of interaction. There still needs to be more research on cross-cultural knowledge and product design, where people's understanding of products, intercultural communication, and intercultural bonding place greater demands on product design. The influence of interculturalism is expanding with the development of internationalization and is generally attracting the attention of all sectors of society. As an essential aid to human behavior and an auxiliary product for life, product design activities are also inevitably closely related to human behavior, thought, life patterns, and other human elements. With the rapid development of computer technology after the Industrial Revolution, the concept of cross-cultural product design has come to the forefront, and the "human-centeredness" of design means that any design activity takes human needs as its essential starting point and achieves the highest goal of human survival, continuity and development from all angles and at all levels [1]. It is a conscious activity to achieve a specific goal and foreseeable task. It is also an activity to carefully explore and select the ideal alternative to achieve a particular requirement.

In the late 1980s, the scope of research on intercultural communication began to expand gradually in China. Its leading research objects include the language community and the fields of intercultural communication, intercultural communication methods, and interdisciplinary advertising communication [2]. The research on intercultural communication is gradually expanding in China. Cross-cultural" will also become another focus of modern product design and will be studied by design science, and there are still many gaps in the scope of cross-cultural design. Cross-cultural studies have become a trend in product design in industrial countries. Japan's domestic market is limited, but its exports can have a substantial global impact. Japanese products not only retain their traditional stylistic characteristics but also take into account the cultural customs and lifestyles of the destination country, which is a critical factor in the success of Japanese products. Products should be designed from a cultural perspective, and design priorities should be considered. In Italy, aesthetic appearance is crucial, while the British are more concerned with comfort, and the Germans focus on product quality. An essential task of product design is to deeply understand, study, and master this difference, so that the product can meet the new international requirements.

Cross-cultural product design means that the designer should have an in-depth understanding of the differences between various cultures around the world, break the boundaries of regional and national cultures, break the limitations of his own culture, and cross the cultural divide formed by history so that the designed products have human characteristics in the "cultural," thus designing "globalized" products. They have globalized" products. The globalized market requires cross-cultural carrier research to be oriented to the cross-cultural cognitive differences of different cultural backgrounds, and cross-cultural design can integrate the results of cognitive differences research into the shaping of cross-cultural carriers to meet the needs of cross-cultural objects, effectively promoting cultural exchange and improve the cultural added value of products.

2   Purpose and Significance of the Study

Cross-cultural research in the design field covers a single area, and the combination of methodology and design practice has some deviations. However, the study of product theory is more in-depth, and the dissolution of cross-cultural differences expressed in some product designs at this stage is far-fetched. The purpose of this paper is to clarify the primary attributes of cross-cultural product design and to reduce the learning cost of users by introducing Hofstede's theoretical approach to the design to help complete the product design and shape the semantic expression of the product itself. A relatively complete set of theories for cross-cultural product design has been developed to enable accurate representation in the final product design.

With the development trend of China's international economy, cross-cultural design has become an inevitable trend, a further extension of the existing design theory and an essential part of modern product design. It is an extension of existing design theories and a vital part of modern product design. The cross-cultural design will also become a trend in the global market and will become a key focus in evaluating future product design. However, intercultural design should be more comprehensive than traditional perspectives, cultures, and levels but should go beyond traditional understanding bases. The design of the corresponding regional culture can significantly improve the user's recognition of the product, as well as reduce its learning costs to avoid unnecessary disputes and improve the influence of the product.

3 Current Status of Domestic and International Research

The disciplinary distribution of intercultural studies is mainly in language, education, psychology, society, and media. The difference between Chinese intercultural research and international, intercultural research disciplines is that media studies account for a high proportion. In contrast, international, intercultural research has a high proportion of educational studies and linguistics. Many scholars have summarized different theories of cross-cultural studies according to different research needs and backgrounds, combining social sciences, natural sciences, and other research methods and theories, mainly in education, psychology, and linguistics. Cultural studies refer to the new wave of cultural studies that emerged in the international community in the late twentieth century, aiming at a comprehensive and reasonable understanding of cultural phenomena, traditions, and customs that are different or contradictory to our civilization and accepting and adapting to them in a more tolerant way [3]. There are also many studies on interculturalism in China. Zeng Yanbing et al. [4] Zeng Yanbing and others have studied the relationship between literature and culture, foreign and Chinese literature, literary translation, and translated literature; He et al. [5] The new areas of cross-cultural studies are reviewed: the study of the "other," the cross-cultural study of religion, the study of the cross-cultural diffusion of scientific and technological knowledge, and the study of the impact of cross-regional exchange of goods, species, people, and ideas; Yingying Wang [6] Based on Hofstede's theory of cultural dimensions, she explores how to improve intercultural communication skills by taking Chinese and American cultural perceptions as an example. International theories on students' essential competencies: Byram [7] explored the five elements of basic intercultural competence (attitude, learning, understanding, discovery, criticality); Hofstede [8] examined dimensional models of essential competencies: individuality and collectivism, uncertainty avoidance, power distance, masculinity and femininity, long-term and short-term perspectives, freedom of Indulgence and restraint, and summarized various basic competency dimensional variables in different countries and regions of the world, and Beyond culture [9] In turn, theories of cultural paradox, cultural identity, differently. By applying Hofstede's cultural hierarchy theory to guide cross-cultural design, Linghao Zhang and Guangmei Yang [10] give an opinion for innovative development based on Hofstede's socio-cultural hierarchy theory and hierarchy of needs theory for the cases of innovative development in Wuxi and Milan communities in China;ssing Zhou Jian [11] used the view to give five value levels to study the product styling image and summarized the method of cross-socio-cultural commodity styling design. The research object has been extended from traditional industrial services to digital interactive product service methods, but how to carry out specific applications needs further in-depth research.

4 Research Content and Methods

4.1 Research Content

This paper generally follows the research idea of viewpoint formulation - theoretical derivation - case study - methodological summary. The section on "Point of View" analyzes the concept of cross-cultural design and proposes the expression of cross-cultural product design; the section on "Theoretical Reasoning" is the definition of cross-cultural design research and the difference between cross-cultural design and localization, and the combing of the current situation of cross-cultural product design and the construction of Hofstede's theoretical model. The "Case Study" section focuses on the characteristics of cross-cultural research, the acquisition and analysis of cross-cultural objects, and the selection of corresponding models to avoid bias in the process of cross-cultural difference research; "Methodology Summary "The generalization of Hofstede's cultural dimension theory and the case analysis with the data of six dimensions are based on cross-cultural design research, combined with Hofstede's model and classic cases to propose on cross-cultural product design methods.

4.2 Research Methodology

(1) **Quantitative research method**

Quantitative research, also known as quantitative research, is scientific research that determines the quantitative prescriptiveness of an aspect of something [12]. It is the research method and process of quantifying problems and phenomena and then analyzing, testing, and explaining them to obtain meaning.

(2) **Literature analysis method**

The study will use literary analysis to collect and organize the research results related to product design theory and Hofstede theory, to analyze and summarize the work and research results of previous studies, to understand the current status of the development of the theory and the similarities and differences of the development, and to understand the characteristics and complementarities between the selected theories.

(3) **Case study method**

The analysis of representative cross-cultural products leads to a practical research framework through analysis.

5 Research on Cross-Cultural Product Design Methods

5.1 Definition

In cross-cultural design, the design intent is expressed in the product carrier so that its meaning is reflected and the needs of the cross-cultural object in a specific context are met. By analyzing the products of different regions in depth in terms of market, social and human needs and understanding the direction and overview of the development of the modern product modeling design, we can derive some attributes of cross-cultural product modeling design. In the context of economic globalization, the diversity and complexity of the world's cultures, and the high-speed circulation of the market economy, cross-cultural product design take the diverse cultures of different regions as the main object. It reflects the intercultural blend in the final designed products. In addition to the product's essential characteristics, the product of intercultural product design should also consider cultural communication, which is one of the essential characteristics of intercultural products. The relationship between design and society cleverly links interculturalism as a background to product styling.

5.2 Differences Between Localization

Cross-cultural design is another extension of modern design and is inextricably linked to and very different from localized design, which often needs clarification. Localized design is the traditional cultural design, mainly from the relationship between peoples.[13] Traditional Design Traditional design combines inherent traditional elements and products that can be rigidly applied to form a symbolic product with vital national attributes so that the product design has personality and market competitiveness. The localized design has excellent market potential and has been recognized by major companies as a strategic focus for brands, and localized design has also gained rapid development. Currently, localized design is mainly a simple design based on cultural modeling. It is a strong attachment of local symbols to the product shape. Localized product design takes Chinese localized product design (or Chinese traditional cultural product design) as an example; localized product design mainly focuses on extracting the symbolic features of the traditional shape relative to the ground. The localized product design, for example, localized Chinese product design (or Chinese traditional cultural product design), focuses on extracting the relative local symbolic features of traditional shapes, converting the patterns and images of traditional Chinese culture into product features, and directly combining them with the product design concept, and emphasizing these localized products with Chinese characteristics as truly "Chinese" designs, which are directly associated with the word "China" when you see the product. The word "China" is directly associated with the product.

The core concept of localized design is the hope that design guides the recovery of the original local traditional cultural characteristics and cultural phenomena or gets cultural identity. Cross-regional artistic design, on the other hand, refers to the differences and conflicts that arise between different regional cultures. Product design is designed under the conditions of different socio-cultural backgrounds. The designer analyzes the differences and commonalities within them and uses cultural factors to guide the conduct and realization of product design, leading the design of the product through the analysis of the relationship between social cultures. Cross-regional cultural product design, on the other hand, focuses on the cultural aspects of cultural organization. The need for "cultural identity" is the same for both. The results of cross-cultural design research can be more creatively applied in the design process.

5.3 Research on Cross-Cultural Product Design Theory

By distinguishing design characteristics through understanding cultural hierarchy, the relationship between design and culture can be visually sorted out clearly. Design characteristics can be distinguished into explicit and implicit characteristics. As the most direct level of artifacts, it represents the tools and products of the culture. The design features that the senses can directly perceive through the observation of the product and that can be expressed and interpreted through external forms are called explicit features of design, such as shapes, textures, materials, techniques. The implicit features of the cross-cultural design are the organizational and value layers of the cultural hierarchy, which are the inner thoughts of the culture. The senses cannot directly accept it, so it is called the implicit characteristics of design instead of the explicit characteristics. Such as structure, properties, functions, semantics. In cross-cultural design, some structural and functional parts of the organizational level can be differentiated by observing and analyzing human behavior. However, the value level is elusive, so it is necessary to use some theoretical research results of cross-cultural studies to analyze them and summarize the design characteristics of the core value level for designers to analyze the design. Among the many schools of cross-cultural theory, Horstad's cultural scale model to analyze the corresponding product design is relevant to the implicit elements generated in the conceptual layer.

Hofstede's theory of socialist cultural perspectives: using an extensive analysis to study the variables or factors of the relationship between various civilizations, taking as the main scope of the study the regions that differ from people's behavior and exploring the human attributes specific to their regions, the socialist cultural perspective theory has a higher starting point of foundation, a more ambitious and comprehensive scope, and can provide guidance for cross-cultural product design research, Gilt Hofstede Tate gives six socialist cultural perspectives: Power Distance, Uncertainty Avoidance, Individualism, Masculinity and Femininity, and Medium- and Short-term Orientation. Long-term and Short-term) and Indulgence.[15].

Power distance is "the degree of acceptance and expectation of inequality in the distribution of power among the disadvantaged groups in social relations," Power distance is the degree to which socially recognized rights are equitably distributed among social institutions. The meaning of the immense power distance is the ranking in the order of status, as everyone is in a high or low social status, and the role in the image of the commodity is relatively luxurious. Therefore, people demand luxury and atmosphere for commodity image, reflecting their role in status and position, and when people, after being limited by their current cultural level, can find another way to convert a more simple form of life, wearing or imitating big brand clothing, in order to show the impression of luxury given by the commodity to people, to realize their own needs.

Individualism distinction: the basic meaning of "individual" and "collective," individualism refers to the loose social structure of a group, as opposed to collectivist values, which are characterized by the strictest social structure, the strictest family system in the group; there is the distinction between internal and external groups. This dimension is expressed in the image of the product, which is more individual. Human behavior is always closely linked to the whole family or social group, so people are more repressed in their expression of individuality. On the one hand, they want to be different and reflect their personality; on the other, they want to be accepted and have a sense of belonging. The expression in the shape or color of the goods is more restrained. However, there must be specific characteristics, that is, to be able to express their requirements, that is, to make these characteristics in the collective can be accepted and recognized by them, and not overly fancy.

The value dimension of masculinity and femininity is an index of the right to socialize gender roles, which means that this perspective of values indicates the level of "male" and "female" values in modern society. They also believe that gender roles are clearly defined in the real world, and the definition of survival value is significant to them. Based on these beliefs, product design can focus on showing the comfortable and harmonious relationship between products and modern life, thus inspiring positive emotional feelings and spiritual experiences. In designing products for the female consumer market, the product image should also show the importance and care of society for women.

The uncertainty avoidance dimension is the degree to which community members feel uneasy about uncertainty and ambiguity. Uncertainty avoidance is evaluated as high if competitors are not afraid of risk and lower if they are not. In the aesthetics of the shape, the beauty of the focus is not more on the object, the object. However, the association and rhythm focus more on the performance of the inner life context rather than the honesty of imitation and reproduction of credibility. For the product form, the focus is more on the beauty of the context rather than the fear of life's fatalism or pessimism of the sublime. In product design, the focus is on the humanistic quality of the product design and the function of the goods in the overall space in which they are located, on the harmony between the goods and the entire natural environment, on the shaping of imagery, and the embodiment of a subtle aesthetic. For example, the design of cell phones, by and large, shows a non-decorative trend. In addition to the direct influence of Western product design functionalism, it is also related to cultural characteristics.

Long-term value dimension: the individual's basic concept of time and orientation is based on whether the group is willing to adhere to the values and beliefs in the long term. The design should emphasize nature, greenery, and environmental protection. The details and materials of the real, and the durable, durable sense of shape to meet people's long-term aesthetic orientation. Such as the iPhone's tight curve, body shape, and silky smooth material in people's minds to produce a positive image of good quality sound quality to achieve a better role.

The indulgence dimension is the degree to which people control their original desires and nature.

The product is an artificial combination of cultural characteristics of natural objects, and the various manifestations of the product reflect the different aspectsristics it contains. [16] The products represent the diverse cultural backgrounds of consumers. The product represents a group of consumers from different cultural backgrounds, other event cultural requirements, and feelings towards development. How to make products for consumers from different cultural backgrounds, Hofstede gives better ideas on six levels in the cultural dimension study: to describe the strength of the cultural dimension in the form of a scale of 0 ~ 100, to show through the comparison of data, to analyze cultural differences based on specific data, to summarize the semantic characteristics of products at different cultural levels, and to provide a reference basis for the judgment of product types, the socialist cult aspectistics can reflect the product design element and this element respectively and shows The judgment of cross-cultural product design element divided and to the intuitive cultural dimensions and In contrast, the implicit design elements corresponding at the level of core values are analyzed using Hofstede's cultural scale model, which is of practical significance for the analysis of culture to design and then from design to culture.

6 Cross-Cultural Product Design Classic Case Study

Intercultural design is a design process that accurately recognizes and redefines the characteristics of cultural construction, can integrate the cultures of other countries in the world, and can better meet the needs of the target users in their own countries in terms of culture and art forms, and is designed with an accurate understanding of the historical and cultural backgrounds of the target countries as well as the users. Hofstede's cultural dimensional theory has been used to analyze the differences between each regional culture in six dimensions; quantitative analysis has been made, as these scale indicators can guide cross-cultural product design.

The first typical case is the "Oriental Legend" kitchenware; see Fig. 1, a cross-cultural product jointly launched by the National Palace Museum in Taiwan and the Italian brand Alessi. The product is a cross-cultural product launched by the National Palace Museum in Taiwan and the Italian brand Alessi. [17] The brand's "Oriental Legend" spirit is to "see the Oriental story from a Western perspective." The product design is more fashionable and modern, and the design concept is more in-depth. The design not only maintains the traditional Chinese style elements but also integrates the Chinese, Western, and modern design ideas, thus linking the exchange between the East and West civilizations. The target users of "Oriental Legend" are mainly the European and American groups represented by Italians; therefore, the designers take the historical Culture of Chinese cultural relics collected by the Palace Museum as the inspiration for the image design and interpret the traditional Chinese elements, such as various animals, floral forms, and auspicious objects such as monkeys and koi, as oriental style. The abstract expression is simplified into simple geometry that is easy to understand, and the minimalist design style breaks with the traditional simple and complicated decoration. This is also in line with the Italian "uncertainty avoider" design characteristics: the rejection of ambiguity in the actual situation and a preference for products that can be expressed in a straightforward manner in product design. In terms of color, the designers chose four primary colors representing ancient Chinese socialist civilization: red, yellow, green, and blue, as the primary colors of the product, in conjunction with black: through a high degree of abstraction in shape, with some of the higher purity colors clashing with each other, not only buffering the overall sense of solemnity, while maintaining the cultural elements but also in line with the "power Low distance," "distinct individualism" and "restrained socialism" are traditional values. The shape of the bottles and jars of the previous household utensils is wholly broken and replaced with a more modern and sensual experience and a humorous hip-hop flavor. The Banana Boy pepper shaker set of the same spray shakers reflects the product design's systematic nature by modifying some of the shapes while keeping the functionality intact. This is the same as Italian "masculinity," which emphasizes practical value and functionality. The use of plastic as the raw material for the product is light, stable, and artistic, and the use of complex processes for the product material shows a high artistic and practical value, which is in line with the requirements of "long-term goals."

The second typical example is the modern "Chinese chair" created by Hans Wegner, which is influenced by the traditional Chinese chair, see Fig. 2. [18] See Fig. 2. The first chair of the China series, based on the Chinese Ming-style circle chair, see Fig. 3 "changed," is close in appearance to the design of the shape of the circle chair. However, Wegner understood the essence of the design of the Ming-style circle chair, not precisely following the design of the shape of the Ming furniture, but through modern technology to reproduce the complete classical furniture. Another improvement is that the semi-circular back of the chair is connected to the sleek armrests, which is different from the traditional wedge nail method and the conventional wedge and tenon method, using the finger joint inlay method. However, the joint is still in a three-stage structure. The refinement of the back of the Ming-style chair and the repositioning of the backrest panel to fit the curve of the body give the overall design style a Chinese solid flavor and a more straightforward emotional expression: it fits the low "power distance" and low "uncertainty avoidance" dimensions of Danish Culture. The cushion on the replaced "China Chair" is made of natural paper rope weave, which gives full play to the characteristics of the material and shows the details of the texture of the material by hand-tied, expressing his Chinese feelings, but also showing the fit between product design ideas and Chinese national culture, without the mechanical indifference of the modern international style, and the natural material of the chair surface made of natural materials provides a challenging and comfortable feeling effect: in line with the "feminist" and "individualist" dimensions of Danish Culture. The science of wood construction provides perfect lines and touch, and a four-legged support system fully supports the seat. This solid construction eliminates the need for additional support in the seat frame. In addition, the simplified Ming-style chair seat frame under the drum leg Pentooth, but also without the elaborate shape, replaced by a simple wood panel, more prominent in the design culture of Scandinavian minimalist style, maintains a uniquely Nordic style, emphasizing the abstract beauty of the imagery and functional human-machine combination design: both "short-term goals" and The dimension of "indulgence." Through the above two typical examples, we find that Hofstede's dimensional model clarifies the different values of each country's culture at different levels, which provides a reasonable basis for studying consumer habits and behavior patterns and can help designers to study the value orientation of the target consumer groups, as well as the behavior and product orientation under the influence of value orientation.

Table 1. Case studies of classic cross-cultural products using Hofstede's cultural dimension theory

Case 1 Italian Alessi "Oriental Legend" kitchenware series		
Target geography	Dimensional Cultural Characteristics	Hofstede cultural dimension values
Take Italian culture as an example	The product is positioned for everyday use, but the symbolic element of power is still sought after	Right distance 60
	The selection of open, individual design elements	Individualism:80
	Rational, focus on product features	Masculinity and Femininity:65
	Straightforward modeling language	Uncertainty avoidance: 81
	Pragmatism, attention to quality and performance	Long-term value: 56
	Value-based	Indulgence: 25
Case 2 Hans Wegner "China Chair", Denmark		
Target geography	Dimensional Cultural Characteristics	Hofstede cultural dimension values
Take Danish culture as an example	Reduce the sense of distance and design more humane	Right distance:20
	Selection of personalized design elements	Individualism:68
	Emotionalization	Masculinity and Femininity:12
	Simple shape	Uncertainty avoidance: 18
	Young sense, fashion sense	Long-term value: 40
	Enjoy life and focus on comfort	Indulgence: 82

Fig. 1. Alessi "Legend of the East"

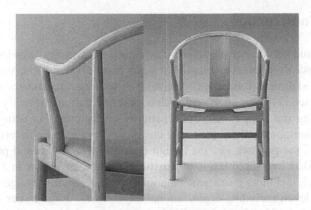

Fig. 2. Hans Wegner The China Chair

Fig. 3. Chinese Ming yellow pear circle chair

7 Model Construction

From the case study, it is easy to find that both value orientation and behavioral orientation strongly influence the product orientation of target product consumers. Value orientation is the aspect most directly influenced by values, i.e., the target consumers' needs in terms of values reflected in the product; while behavioral orientation is directly influenced by values, reflecting the unique behavioral patterns of customers in using the product; and product orientation reflects the target customers' preferences in terms of external shape design of the product, i.e., the design concept of cross-cultural products. Fee's content is divided into three levels of artistic elements, as shown in Fig. 4: (1) the conceptual level, including characters, emotions, and particular messages in art; (2) the organizational level, including organizational capabilities, usage issues, usability, and safety; and (3) the artifact level, including colors, patterns, shapes, accessories, surface design, line expression, and details [19]. The ten characteristic elements of cultural product design can be summarized by eliminating the characteristic elements that are not clearly expressed or complicated. The comprehensive cross-cultural image analysis model and the design research model of the cultural environment given in the paper have an inherent unity in terms of practical orientation, behavioral orientation, and product orientation. Therefore, after synthesizing the above two basic models, a model of cross-cultural product design based on Hofstede's cultural dimension theory can be derived, as shown in Fig. 5.

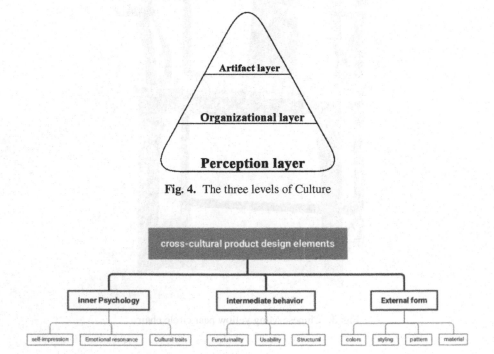

Fig. 4. The three levels of Culture

Fig. 5. Model of product design elements of cultural dimension theory

7.1 Process of Using the Model

By studying the cultural differences of the target consumers, this model solves the fundamental problem of accurately understanding the cultural background of consumers when designing and provides a basis for design expression in product development. [21] This model provides a basis for design expression in product development. Taking the cross-cultural product design using regional elements as an example, the application process is as follows. First, a cultural scene is established to clarify the core user, the primary culture of the region, and the contrasting culture. With the target user as the core of product design, the subject Culture is the regional cultural background in which the target user is located, while the comparative social culture refers to the national culture or the cultural background of the country that the designer knows better, so there are generally differences or contradictions between the subject culture and the comparative social culture; second, firstly, carry out the research on the differences of the target user: the six dimensions in Hofstede's dimensions unfold the subject Second, firstly, we conduct a study of the differences between the target users: the six dimensions of Hofstede's dimensions develop a study of the differences between the subject culture and the comparative regional culture, explain the value orientation of the product, and thus explain the socio-cultural background of the target users; then, we explore the behavior of the target consumers under the role of regional cultural ideology by studying the behavior orientation of the product, and propose a theoretical basis for the functional design of the product; then, we study the product design orientation through the product value orientation and action orientation, and derive the target consumers' Third, determine the cultural elements of product design: select appropriate cultural elements and pay attention to the degree of avoidance of traditional culture; fourth, based on the identified cultural elements, carry out research on the elements of product design: based on the values derived from the cultural difference research layer and extract the factors of product design, and finally refine the design elements. Fourth, based on the identified cultural elements, we will conduct a study on the elements of product design: based on the values derived from the cultural difference research layer and extracting the product design factors, finally refining the design elements and combining them with the cultural difference analysis to obtain a suitable product design expression.

8 Summary and Outlook

8.1 Summary

This paper provides a new mode of expression of commodity styling design from a cross-cultural perspective through a model that integrates Hofstede's cultural dimension theory and product design elements, bringing a product design mindset that translates from the local culture for designers. The use of socialist cultural dimension data to transform the design characteristics of product styling helps to design products that are recognized and favored by the user community, according to the six levels of Hofstede's Humanistic Value Hierarchy Theory classification from personality (uncertainty avoidance index), association with nature (uncertainty index), ability orientation (masculinity index), relationship (free time index, individualism index), and association with the times (long-term index). It is not mechanical but works through the influence on consumer culture and thus has strong possibilities. At present, local Chinese products do not have their semantic system and are more often "fetishistic" and unconcerned, lacking socialist cultural content and taste that integrate local Chinese characteristics. The introduction of Hofstede's concept of cultural dimension value level undoubtedly raises the product's primary cultural value and the product's shaping to a higher level. After studying those mentioned local culture-oriented product design, we can get the following conclusions: that is, the cultural image of national products must fit the characteristics of regional culture and drive people to change from the understanding of culture to the understanding of products, and through such deeper communication and resonance of humanistic values, people can form a continuous favorable feeling towards the market and products; secondly, cultural strategy. Secondly, cultural or national brand strategy has become the best way of cross-cultural marketing. With the development of the market economy and world integration process, the success stories of multinational brands entering the target regional markets have also caused national introspection: they first did not seize the target market to grasp the benefits and talk about turnover but made a lot of market research, consumer mentality analysis, the study of consumer culture categorization, humanistic value orientation, and finally confirmed the cultural model, using humanistic communication to obtain a more sustainable social and economic benefits. Third: an in-depth exploration of the essence of the local culture, extracted on behalf of the traditional cultural heritage of the modeling symbols and used in product design modeling. Of course, this is a deep-seated cultural reconstruction and not simply rigid;our think the most critical is the requirement that the product design as a whole can express a certain mood, and this imagery gives people the natural feeling that the product design is there This imagery gives people a natural feeling that the product design is "tasty," not "style." In order for the fourth product to go to the global market, it is necessary to have a fuller understanding of the culture of the region to which the product belongs so that the shape of the product can be accurately decoded in terms of the underlying semantics of Chinese Culture, and then genuinely realize the correct cognition of the cultural connotation of both sides, to achieve the effective transmission of the brand across cultures.

8.2 Outlook

As today's world is constantly changing, the degree of multicultural convergence and the complexity of traditional cultures is also changing, so cross-cultural product styling is also analyzing new product designs centered on traditional cultures from a multifaceted perspective. The cross-cultural, intercultural product design and creation process is an innovative addition to the design development process. The cross-regional artistic design approach will be applied in more areas with the globalization of culture. Therefore, the formation of a systematically comprehensive and designer-led update of a comparative table of cultural design avoidance elements is of great importance for future design. This study uses Hofstede's theory to focus on cross-cultural product styling and design methods. In contrast, the study of Hofstede's theory in product design and other applications can gradually deepen. It is hoped that theoretical research and practice can be increased in future research. This study is only a brick in the wall for cross-cultural product design methods, and we hope that later researchers can pool their ideas to find better design methods.

Acknowledgements. The 2021 Fuzhou Students School-level Scientific Research Project: "Research on Product Modeling Innovation of Lacquer Ware Based on Semiotics Theory", NO: FWXXS21120.

References

1. Renke, H.: History of Industrial Design. Beijing Institute of Technology Press, Beijing (2000). (in Chinese)
2. Xie, S.: Cross-cultural product design research. The Nanjing University of Aeronautics and Astronautics, Nanjing (2012). (in Chinese)
3. Lexi, Z., Yongcheng, Z., Fubin, D.: A review of cross-cultural product design and internationalization. Mechatron. Eng. **25**(6), 108–110 (2008)
4. Yanbing, Z.: Research on teaching foreign literature in cross-cultural context. Foreign Lit. Res. Res. **2**, 161–167 (2006)
5. He, P.: Theories and methods of cross-cultural research. Stud. Hist. Theory (4), 68–78+160–161 (2014). (in Chinese)
6. Wang, Y.: A study on the differences in cultural perceptions between China and the United States from a cross-cultural perspective. Xi'an Engineering University (2015)
7. Byram, M.: Teaching and Assessing Intercultural Communicative Competence. Shanghai Foreign Language Education Press, Shanghai (2014)
8. Hofstede, G., Hofstede, G.J., Minkov, M.: Cultures and organizations, software of the mind. intercultural cooperation and its importance for survival. Southern Med. J. **13**(3), S219-S222 (2010)
9. Hall, E.T.: Beyond culture, Chicago (1976)
10. Linghao, Z., Guangmei, Y.: Cross-cultural reflections on the sustainability of social innovation service design - a case study of Milan and Wuxi. Creativity Des. **03**, 66–70 (2015)
11. Jian, Z., Binbin, L.: Cross-cultural theory analysis and product design. Art Des.: Theory Ed. **9**, 248–250 (2009). (in Chinese)
12. Zheng, L.: Research and application of cultural composition design methodology. Zhejiang University, Hangzhou (2016)
13. Zhang, L., et al.: Cross-cultural design. J. Nanjing Art Inst., 7–15 (2012)
14. Hu, J.: Cultural interpretation of modern home design. Qingdao University of Technology (2010)
15. Wang, L.-W.: Cross-culture theory for the study of TCL mobile phone brand culture expansion. Jiangnan University, Wuxi (2006)
16. Xu, H.: Design aesthetics. Tsinghua University Press, Beijing (2006)
17. Xue, Y.: On giovannis emotion-based product design style. Nanjing Arts Institute, Nanjing (2011)
18. Zhang, R.: A study of Hans Wegener's furniture design. Nanjing University, Nanjing (2014)
19. Wu, T.Y., Cheng, H., Lin, R.: The study of culture interface in Taiwan aboriginal twin-cup. In: HCI International, no. 4, pp. 22-27 (2005)
20. Li, W.-J.: Hofstede's culture dimensions and inter-cultural studies. J. Soc. Sci. (12) (2009).(in Chinese)
21. Chunfu, L., Xiaoling, Q., Jiao Dongfang, W., Jianfeng.: A study on cross-cultural product design based on Hofstede's cultural dimension theory. Packag. Eng. **41**(12), 117–124 (2020). https://doi.org/10.19554/j.cnki.1001-3563.2020.12.017. (in Chinese)

Study on the Weightings of Evaluation Indicators for Factors Influencing Eastern and Western Consumers' Purchase Intentions in Live Streaming E-Commerce Based on the Triangular Fuzzy Number

Ruoqiao Zhao[✉] and Tseng Ping Chiu

National Cheng Kung University, Industrial Design Department, Strategic Design Group, Tainan City, Taiwan
zhaoruoqiao163@gmail.com, mattchiu@gs.ncku.edu.tw

Abstract. This study aims to explore the preferences of factors influencing Eastern and Western consumers' purchase intentions in E-commerce live streaming under different cultural backgrounds. On the theoretical basis of Individualism/Collectivism, Uncertainty Avoidance, Long Term Orientation & Short Term Orientation in the Hofstede (2011) model and High Context & Low Context proposed by Hall (1976), a questionnaire for evaluation indicators was designed for Eastern and Western consumers. Three groups, i.e., Chinese local consumers (n = 44), Chinese consumers having lived in the West for over half a year (n = 43), and Western consumers having lived in China for over half a year (n = 30), were invited to take part in this study. According to the fundamentals of Triangular Fuzzy Number, through data collection, this article statistically analyzed the evaluation indicators influencing the willingness of Eastern and Western consumers to watch live-streaming shopping, quantified the importance of evaluation indicators with weights, and then analyzed the willingness, needs and preferences of Eastern and Western consumers watching live-streaming shopping. The findings showed that both Eastern and Western consumers considered visual display and anchors' professionalism as the most important indicators. Eastern consumers represented by Chinese consumers placed more weight on being able to buy more affordable goods with guaranteed quality in live-streaming shopping while Western consumers represented by European and American consumers were more concerned about the personality of anchors. This study will have some reference value for the cross-cultural study on live-streaming shopping and related industry network operations.

Keywords: Live-streaming shopping · consumer behaviors · eastern and Western Consumers · purchase intention

© The Author(s), under exclusive license to Springer Nature Switzerland AG 2023
P.-L. P. Rau (Ed.): HCII 2023, LNCS 14022, pp. 580–598, 2023.
https://doi.org/10.1007/978-3-031-35936-1_43

1 Introduction

Live-streaming shopping is a new way of shopping started since 2016 that integrates E-commerce, live-streaming, and social networking. In 2019, it became one of the popular ways of shopping (Xuan & Sun, 2020). Since 2020, due to COVID-19, people have had more time to watch live-streaming shopping at home, and many retailers have shifted from physical stores to live-streaming shopping. The new way of shopping is characterized by high interactivity, entertainment, authenticity, and visibility (Feng, 2021). Being more interactive than traditional online shopping, it has an important influence on consumers' purchase intentions (Shi et.al, 2021).

Qing & Jin (2022) suggested that factors such as the service quality (SEQ), information quality (IQ) and system quality (SQ) of E-commerce live streaming will influence consumers' purchase intentions; perceived usefulness (PU), perceived ease of use (PEU), perceived trust (PT) and perceived value (PV) will also influence consumers' purchase intentions. Xu & Lyu (2022) found that anchors' professionalism, the reciprocal expectation of live streaming, and consumers' social connections can effectively increase consumers' purchase intentions, and negative public events will reduce consumers' purchase intentions. Yan et.al, (2022) noted that the credibility, charm, perceived enjoyment, perceived trust, and perceived usefulness of online celebrities will influence consumers' impulse buys through consumers' attitudes toward anchors. The persuasiveness in anchors' style of language will cause consumers to change their purchase intentions, thereby affecting the sales of products sold (Luo et.al, 2021). Chen et.al, (2017) argued that live streaming has a great influence on consumers' online purchasing behaviors, especially in the context of cross-border E-commerce. It can influence consumers' purchasing behaviors by improving information transparency, so that merchants can gain a competitive edge in cross-border markets (Xu et.al, 2021).

Most of the previous live-streaming shopping studies focus on Chinese consumers, with few on Western consumers. There are even fewer studies on live-streaming shopping in different cultures. In this sense, investigating the preferences of cross-cultural consumers for live-streaming shopping is of great significance. Learning the preferences of Eastern and Western consumers for, and differences in, the factors influencing live-streaming shopping from a cross-cultural perspective can provide a new perspective for studies in related fields. The findings can provide a better reference for live-streaming sales to E-commerce and cross-border platforms in different cultures.

This study mainly aims to explore the preferences of Eastern and Western consumers for the factors influencing live-streaming shopping in different cultures. However, human thinking is complex and uncertain, and cannot be clearly defined in determining evaluation indicators. The Analytic Hierarchy Process (AHP) proposed by Saaty (1977) is currently the most commonly used method for determining the indicators evaluating information resources. It integrates the evaluation values of the groups evaluated with the concept of average, lacks the distribution information determined by the evaluators, and therefore cannot reflect complete information. To fully reflect the results of all evaluators, the concept of the fuzzy number has to be added to integrate the comments of groups. In order to truly express the differences in subjective judgments in actual circumstances and to include more complete information in evaluation, this study will process the survey data with triangular fuzzy semantics to determine the fuzzy weight of pointers.

2 Cultural Difference Theories

Consumer behaviors are largely influenced by cultures. Hofstede (2011) summarized a six-dimension model for national cultures: power distance, uncertainty avoidance, individualism/collectivism, masculinity/femininity, long-term/short-term orientation, and indulgence/restraint, as shown in Fig. 1.

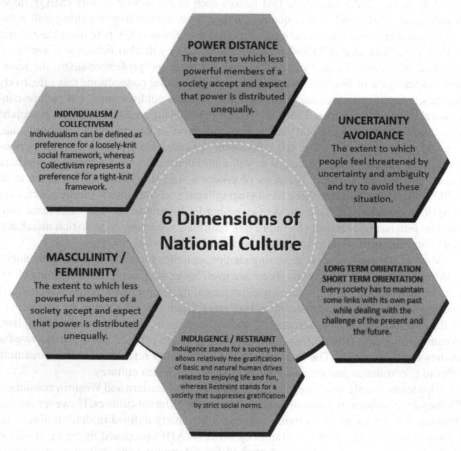

POWER DISTANCE
The extent to which less powerful members of a society accept and expect that power is distributed unequally.

INDIVIDUALISM / COLLECTIVISM
Individualism can be defined as preference for a loosely-knit social framework, whereas Collectivism represents a preference for a tight-knit framework.

UNCERTAINTY AVOIDANCE
The extent to which people feel threatened by uncertainty and ambiguity and try to avoid these situation.

6 Dimensions of National Culture

MASCULINITY / FEMININITY
The extent to which less powerful members of a society accept and expect that power is distributed unequally.

LONG TERM ORIENTATION SHORT TERM ORIENTATION
Every society has to maintain some links with its own past while dealing with the challenge of the present and the future.

INDULGENCE / RESTRAINT
Indulgence stands for a society that allows relatively free gratification of basic and natural human drives related to enjoying life and fun, whereas Restraint stands for a society that suppresses gratification by strict social norms.

Fig. 1. Hofstede Model: six dimensions of national culture (Hofstede, 2011)

This study will mainly start from the theoretical basis of Individualism/Collectivism, Uncertainty Avoidance, Long Term Orientation & Short Term Orientation in the Hofstede (2011) model and High Context & Low Context proposed by Hall (1976).

Individualism/Collectivism refers to the integration of individuals into groups. Individualism represents a loosely-knit social framework, whereas Collectivism describes a tight-knit framework (Hofstede, 2011). The Individualist culture emphasizes individual rights and freedoms, very loosely organized into the social framework. The collectivist culture advocates harmony among members, by which individuals must serve the collective interests. Chua et al., (2005) monitored eye movements and found that North Americans in an individualistic culture attend longer to focal objects, whereas Asian participants in a collectivist culture attend more to contextual information. The findings suggested that East Asians may view photographs overall and look more at how the background is related to the objects while Westerners may fix more on focal objects. Therefore, in E-commerce live streaming, factors such as interfacing and furnishings in the room may influence consumers of different cultures in watching live-streaming shopping.

Uncertainty Avoidance refers to the extent to which people feel threatened by uncertainty and ambiguity. People are used to establishing more formal rules and relying on knowledge and expert evaluation to avoid unexpected circumstances (Hofstede, 2011). Online shopping is different from offline shopping in that consumers are unable to personally try and experience products. Therefore, anchors' professional knowledge, understanding of products, and product display and interpretation become particularly important in live streaming.

Long Term Orientation & Short Term Orientation refer to the extent to which members of a culture can accept delayed gratification of their material, social, and emotional needs (Hofstede, 2011), or whether these people have the ability to judge their behaviors with future orientation. In previous studies, China was considered a long-term-oriented country, which is more concerned about product pricing and practicality and less concerned about brands. Western consumers place greater importance on the quality, grade and service represented by brands (De & Hofstede, 2011).

High Context & Low Context was proposed by Hall (1976) to describe the diversity of world cultures based on the differences between high and low contexts. High Context is used to describe communication in a collectivist culture, where people are dependent more on the current domain than words, so there are many indirect, non-verbal codes (hints, facial expressions). Low Context is used to describe communication in an individualistic culture, where people will carry their messages directly in words that should be accurate, so that listeners do not need to guess if there are other meanings. The latter is characterized by less non-verbal, direct, explicit, detailed, and individualist communication.

3   Study Design

3.1   Methodology

This study first took a look at how Eastern consumers represented by Chinese consumers and Western consumers represented by US consumers know about live-streaming shopping, and then designed a questionnaire for evaluation indicators for Eastern and Western consumers by reference to the Online Questionnaire for China Live-streaming Shopping Consumer Satisfaction in 2020 and based on Individualism/Collectivism, Uncertainty Avoidance, Long Term Orientation & Short Term Orientation in the Hofstede (2011) model and High Context & Low Context proposed by Hall (1976). According to the questionnaire for live-streaming shopping consumer satisfaction, we established an evaluation scale, and explored how Eastern and Western consumers evaluated live-streaming shopping with the help of triangular fuzzy semantics, in the hope to provide a reference for related fields.

Definition and Rules of the Triangular Fuzzy Number Method. Triangular Fuzzy Number is defined as follows:

Definition 1: Let R be a set of real numbers, then a fuzzy set $M \in FR$ on R is called a fuzzy number:

(1) There is such $x_0 \in R$ that $\mu_M(x_0) = 1$;
(2) For any $\in 0,1, A_\lambda = [x : u_{A_\lambda}(x) \geq \lambda]$ is a closed interval.

Definition 2: The fuzzy number M on R is called a triangular fuzzy number. The membership function of M $\mu_M : R \to [0, 1]$ is the membership function of the triangular fuzzy number for the fuzzy semantic variable M, where l and u represent the lower and upper limits of M respectively, m is the median of M, and the triangular fuzzy number M is expressed as (l, m, u).

$$u_M(x) = \begin{cases} \frac{x-1}{m-1} & x \in [l, m] \\ \frac{x-u}{m-u} & x \in [m, u] \\ 0 & \text{other} \end{cases}$$

A general triangular fuzzy number can be expressed as $R = (l, m, u)$. In the number, l, u are used to determine fuzziness. A smaller value of $(u - l)$ represents lower fuzziness, and vice versa.

Let $R_1 = (l_1, m_1, u_1)$ and $R_2 = (l_2, m_2, u_2)$ be two triangular fuzzy numbers, then the following algorithms will be met:

$$R_1 \oplus R_2 = (l_1 + l_2, m_1 + m_2, u_1 + u_2)$$

$$R_1 \otimes R_2 = (l_1 l_2, m_1 m_2, u_1 u_2)$$

$$\lambda R_1 = (\lambda l_1, \lambda m_1, \lambda u_1)$$

$$1/R_1 = (1/u_1, 1/m_1, 1/l_1)$$

Representation of the Triangular Fuzzy Number of Influencing Factors. Convert-ing the original quantitative importance into an analyzable quantitative value in a rea-sonable way by applying the Triangular Fuzzy Number Method can help eliminate the unreasonableness resulting from subjective factors, thus making questionnaire weights more objective and accurate. In this study, semantic variables were included in a 5-point scale in the form of their fuzzy numbers, as shown in Table 1. The fuzzy language can be expressed as (a_1, a_2, a_3), where $a_1 \geq 1, 1 \leq a_2 \leq a_3 \leq 5$, a_1 is the most likely value, a_1 and a_3 represent the upper and lower limits of the fuzzy language respec-tively. Their semantic variables correspond to the triangular fuzzy numbers, as shown Fig. 2.

Table 1. Representation of the triangular symmetric fuzzy numbers of weights on evaluation indicators

Fuzzy number	Strongly disagree	Disagree	No opinion	Agree	Strongly agree
Representation of triangular fuzzy number	(1,1,2)	(1,2,3)	(2,3,4)	(3,4,5)	(4,5,5)

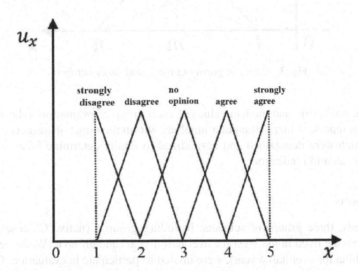

Fig. 2. Correspondence between semantic variables and triangular fuzzy numbers

Determination of Fuzzy Weights. The weights of E-commerce live streaming evaluation indicators reflect the influence of each indicator on the whole. In order to further overcome the subjective uncertainty, fuzzy numbers are used to obtain clear weights, which more truly reflect the judgment tendency of evaluators. In this study, center of gravity defuzzification was used to determine the weights. Let there be a fuzzy set M, its membership function $\mu_M(x), x \in X, DF_i(M)$ as the explicit value converted through center of gravity defuzzification, then:

$$DF_i(M) = \frac{\int_x x\mu_M(x)dx}{\int_x \mu_M(x)dx}$$

where the denominator is the area of $\mu_M(x)$, then $DF_i(M)$ represents the projected position of such area on axis x, as shown in Fig. 3:

DF_i was obtained after defuzzification with fuzzy triangle weights. Namely, weight ω was calculated in the following formula:

$$\omega = DF_i = [(u - l) + (m - l)]/3 + 1$$

where l and u represent the lower and upper limits of the triangular fuzzy number $M(l, m, u)$ respectively and m is the most likely value. The values composed of the

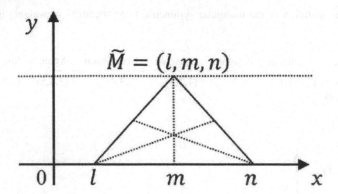

Fig. 3. Center of gravity of triangular fuzzy numbers

maximum, minimum, and median values of each group of evaluation indicators in the survey data represent fuzzy triangular numbers within the range of weights on all indicators, which were defuzzified and normalized to finally determine fuzzy weights on two-level evaluation indicators.

3.2 Subjects

In this study, three groups of subjects, including group a (native Chinese), group b (Chinese having lived in the West for over half a year) and group c (Westerners having lived in China for over half a year), were invited to participate in evaluation. Given that live-streaming shopping is mature in China, to ensure that most of the subjects were somewhat aware of live-streaming shopping, Westerners having lived in China for over half a year were selected to participate in the questionnaire.

A total of 243 responses were received. 44 of 101 responses from local subjects were valid. 43 of 104 responses from Chinese subjects having lived in the West were valid. With many female respondents in the two groups of Chinese subjects, some responses from female subjects who had answered in short time were excluded, so as to ensure a balance of male and female respondents. 30 of 38 responses from Western consumers were valid. The three groups of participants were aged 18–30, with an average age of 27. Their basic information is given in Table 2. Table 3 lists the consumers' knowledge of E-commerce live streaming, and subjects had not heard of live-streaming shopping were excluded and not to complete subsequent evaluation indicators.

3.3 Design of Evaluation Indicator Items

In this study, 10 primary indicators were designed, including visibility, interactivity, authenticity, entertainment, purchase intentions, anchors' popularity, anchors' professionalism, anchors' attractiveness, persuasion effectiveness, and language stimulation. 27 secondary indicators were provided out of the said primary indicators, so as to be more intuitive to the evaluators. E-commerce live streaming evaluation indicators are given in Table 4:

Table 2. Basic information on subjects

Basic information		a	b	c	Significance
Age	Average	27	27	27	0.16
	Standard deviation	3.48	3.85	3.98	
Gender	Male	23 (51%)	21 (48%)	18 (58%)	0.68
	Female	22 (49%)	23 (52%)	13 (42%)	
Total	Total number of subjects	45	44	31	

Table 3. Subjects' knowledge of live-streaming shopping

Question	Options	a	b	c
Have you heard of e-commerce live streaming (for marketing and shopping)?	Yes, I am aware of what e-commerce live streaming is	43(96%)	38(86%)	19(61%)
	I have heard of it, but I do not know what e-commerce live streaming is	1(2%)	5(11%)	11(35%)
	I have never heard of it	1(2%)	1(2%)	1(3%)
Number of persons filled in		45	44	31

Table 4. Evaluation indicators for factors influencing E-commerce live streaming consumers' shopping intentions

Indicator	Code	Description
Visibility (A)	A1	Interface (page) design
	A2	Overall visual design
	A3	Scene setting design
Interactivity (B)	B1	Interaction with anchors
	B2	Interaction with other consumers
	B3	Interactive behaviors
Authenticity (C)	C1	Quality and efficacy
	C2	Multi-angle display
	C3	Product description
Entertainment (D)	D1	Feel interesting

(continued)

Table 4. (*continued*)

Indicator	Code	Description
	D2	Feel relaxed
	D3	Bring fun
Purchase intentions (E)	E1	Purchase behavior
	E2	Purchase decision
	E3	Desire to purchase
Anchors' popularity (F)	F1	Word of mouth
	F2	Star
Anchors' professionalism (G)	G1	Professional knowledge
	G2	Professional display
Anchors' Attractiveness (H)	H1	Anchors' appearance
	H2	Anchors' personalities
	H3	Anchors' voices
	H4	Anchors' body language
Persuasion effectiveness (I)	I1	Description
	I2	Display effect
Language stimulation (J)	J1	Situational associative copywriting 1
	J2	Situational associative copywriting 2

4 Findings

4.1 Weights on E-Commerce Live Streaming Evaluation Indicators

Triangular fuzzy weights, explicit values and standard deviations for responses from subjects in group a, group b and group c were calculated respectively through the collation and analysis of all data in these responses. A standard deviation was used to describe the discrete trend of evaluators' assessment of the importance of an evaluation indicator. A smaller standard deviation reflects more concentration of the importance values of such evaluation indicator. Triangular fuzzy weights constituted the expression range of weights on evaluation indicators with the maximum, median and minimum values of importance, as shown in Table 5, Table 6, and Table 7.

Table 5. Importance of E-commerce live streaming evaluation indicators for subjects in group a

Group a: native Chinese		Triangular fuzzy weight	Explicit value	Standard deviation
Primary indicator	A	(0.527, 0.777, 0.941)	0.748	0.062
	B	(0.401, 0.64, 0.832)	0.624	0.019
	C	(0.46, 0.706, 0.904)	0.69	0.043
	D	(0.273, 0.515, 0.742)	0.51	0.014
	E	(0.273, 0.51, 0.741)	0.508	0.008
	F	(0.299, 0.523, 0.75)	0.524	0.026
	G	(0.512, 0.762, 0.938)	0.737	0.051
	H	(0.321, 0.57, 0.806)	0.566	0.064
	I	(0.412, 0.622, 0.878)	0.651	0.054
	J	(0.398, 0.642, 0.861)	0.634	0.033
Secondary indicator	A1	(0.529, 0.780, 0.942)	0.75	0.064
	A2	(0.528, 0.778, 0.942)	0.749	0.064
	A3	(0.523, 0.773, 0938)	0.774	0.059
	B1	(0.420, 0.659, 0.847)	0.642	0.022
	B2	(0.420, 0.659, 0.847)	0.642	0.012
	B3	(0.364, 0.602, 0.801)	0.589	0.023
	C1	(0.330, 0.574, 0.807)	0.57	0.033
	C2	(0.3557, 0.801, 0.955)	0.771	0.061
	C3	(0.494, 0.744, 0.909)	0.716	0.034
	D1	(0.290, 0.534, 0.761)	0.528	0.014
	D2	(0.25, 0.494, 0.727)	0.491	0.027
	D3	(0.278, 0.517, 0.739)	0.511	0.002
	E1	(0.25, 0.489, 0.722)	0.487	0.018
	E2	(0.284, 0.517, 0.744)	0.515	0.002
	E3	(0.284, 0.523, 0.756)	0.521	0.005
	F1	(0.364, 0.591, 0.801)	0.585	0.047
	F2	(0.233, 0.455, 0.699)	0.462	0.004
	G1	(0.517, 0.767, 0.938)	0.741	0.048
	G2	(0.506, 0.756, 0.938)	0.733	0.054
	H1	(0.278, 0.523, 0.767)	0.523	0.059
	H2	(0.375, 0.625, 0.841)	0.614	0.04

(*continued*)

Table 5. (*continued*)

Group a: native Chinese

	H3	(0.313, 0.563, 0.801)	0.559	0.08
	H4	(0.318, 0.568, 0.813)	0.566	0.078
	I1	(0.443, 0.693, 0.892)	0.676	0.045
	I2	(0.381, 0.631, 0.864)	0.625	0.062
	J1	(0.375, 0.619, 0.841)	0.612	0.021
	J2	(0.42, 0.665, 0.881)	0.655	0.044

Table 6. Importance of E-commerce live streaming evaluation indicators for subjects in group b

Group b: Chinese having lived in the West for over half a year

		Triangular fuzzy weight	Explicit value	Standard deviation
Primary indicator	A	(0.510, 0.754, 0.911)	0.755	0.007
	B	(0.306, 0.527, 0.743)	0.525	0.05
	C	(0.364, 0.606, 0.826)	0.599	0.023
	D	(0.2, 0.407, 0.643)	0.417	0.022
	E	(0.215, 0.43, 0.665)	0.437	0.125
	F	(0.256, 0.468, 0.704)	0.476	0.036
	G	(0.483, 0.733, 0.936)	0.717	0.073
	H	(0.314, 0.545, 0.785)	0.548	0.085
	I	(0.361, 0.602, 0.837)	0.6	0.03
	J	(0.341, 0.576, 0.788)	0.568	0.021
Secondary indicator	A1	(0.488, 0.733, 0901)	0.707	0.001
	A2	(0.5, 0.744, 0.913)	0.720	0.018
	A3	(0.541, 0.785, 0.919)	0.748	0.001
	B1	(0.279, 0.494, 0715)	0.496	0.057
	B2	(0.291, 0.517, 0733)	0.514	0.014
	B3	(0.349, 0.570, 0.780)	0.567	0.052
	C1	(0.256, 0.488, 0.721)	0.488	0.003
	C2	(0.407, 0.657, 0.866)	0.643	0.034
	C3	(0.43, 0.674, 0.89)	0.665	0.031
	D1	(0.221, 0.448, 0.68)	0.45	0.017
	D2	(0.169, 0.366, 0.610)	0.382	0.005

(*continued*)

Table 6. (*continued*)

Group b: Chinese having lived in the West for over half a year				
	D3	(0.209, 0.407, 0.640)	0.419	0.045
	E1	(0.203, 0.407, 0.640)	0.417	0.03
	E2	(0.238, 0.459, 0.698)	0.465	0.014
	E3	(0.203, 0.424, 0.657)	0.428	0.33
	F1	(0.285, 0.494, 0.727)	0.502	0.043
	F2	(0.227, 0.442, 0.680)	0.45	0.029
	G1	(0.477, 0.727, 0.930)	0.711	0.065
	G2	(0.488, 0.738, 0.942)	0.723	0.08
	H1	(0.25, 0.477, 0.721)	0.483	0.004
	H2	(0.355, 0.587, 0.826)	0.589	0.01
	H3	(0.32, 0.547, 0.774)	0.547	0.004
	H4	(0.331, 0.570, 0.820)	0.547	0.032
	I1	(0.372, 0.616, 0.843)	0.61	0.025
	I2	(0.349, 0.587, 0.831)	0.589	0.035
	J1	(0.297, 0.529, 0.738)	0.521	0.036
	J2	(0.384, 0.622, 0.837)	0.614	0.005

Table 7. Importance of E-commerce live streaming evaluation indicators for subjects in group c

Group c: Westerners having lived in China for over half a year				
		Triangular fuzzy weight	Explicit value	Standard deviation
Primary indicator	A	(0.433, 0.475, 0.866)	0.658	0.011
	B	(0.266, 0.471, 0.702)	0.48	0.063
	C	(0.301, 0.532, 0.776)	0.536	0.101
	D	(0.170, 0.362, 0.609)	0.38	0.059
	E	(0.244, 0.439, 0.673)	0.452	0.067
	F	(0.246, 0.452, 0.711)	0.453	0.086
	G	(0.385, 0.625, 0.827)	0.612	0.075
	H	(0.346, 0.575, 0.796)	0.572	0.023
	I	(0.313, 0.543, 0.770)	0.542	0.025
	J	(0.337, 0.558, 0.785)	0.56	0.02

(*continued*)

Table 7. (*continued*)

Group c: Westerners having lived in China for over half a year				
Secondary indicator	A1	(0.394, 0.642, 0.837)	0.624	0.028
	A2	(0.442, 0.683, 0.885)	0.67	0.004
	A3	(0.462, 0.699, 0.875)	0.678	0.001
	B1	(0.240, 0.442, 0.673)	0.452	0.062
	B2	(0.288, 0.481, 0.712)	0.494	0.062
	B3	(0.269, 0.490, 0.721)	0.493	0.066
	C1	(0.173, 0.394, 0.635)	0.401	0.095
	C2	(0.365, 0.596, 0.837)	0.599	0.16
	C3	(0.365, 0.606, 0.856)	0.609	0.04
	D1	(0.231, 0.433, 0.673)	0.446	0.036
	D2	(0.163, 0.365, 0.615)	0.381	0.006
	D3	(0.115, 0.288, 0.538)	0.314	0.135
	E1	(0.260, 0.452, 0.692)	0.468	0.115
	E2	(0.212, 0.404, 0.644)	0.42	0.019
	E3	(0.260, 0.462, 0.683)	0.468	0.066
	F1	(0.231, 0.442, 0.673)	0.449	0.065
	F2	(0.260, 0.462, 0.692)	0.471	0.107
	G1	(0.404, 0.644, 0.846)	0.631	0.141
	G2	(0.365, 0.606, 0.827)	0.6	0.008
	H1	(0.279, 0.5, 0.74)	0.506	0.009
	H2	(0.442, 0.683, 0.885)	0.67	0.014
	H3	(0.317, 0.538, 0.76)	0.539	0.042
	H4	(0.346, 0.577, 0.798)	0.574	0.025
	I1	(0.269, 0.490, 0.712)	0.49	0.04
	I2	(0.356, 0.596, 0.712)	0.593	0.009
	J1	(0.288, 0.5, 0.731)	0.506	0.027
	J2	(0.385, 0.615, 0.837)	0.612	0.012

4.2 Sorting of Important Values of Live-Streaming Shopping Evaluation Indicators

Fuzzy weights on evaluation indicators were obtained according to the calculation formula for center of gravity defuzzification, and then fuzzified and normalized to determine the weights on two-level evaluation indicators. Local weights and global weights were collected on the selection tendency of subjects, as shown in Table 8, Table 9 and Fig. 4.

Table 8. Local weights on the importance of E-commerce live streaming consumer evaluation indicators (Primary indicator)

Primary indicator	Group a	Group b	Group c
	Local weight		
A	0.12	0.13	0.12
B	0.1	0.09	0.09
C	0.11	0.11	0.1
D	0.08	0.07	0.07
E	0.08	0.08	0.09
F	0.09	0.08	0.09
G	0.12	0.13	0.12
H	0.09	0.1	0.11
I	0.11	0.11	0.1
J	0.1	0.1	0.11

As can be seen from Table 5, Table 6 and Table 7 together with Table 8 and Table 9, the importance of live-streaming shopping evaluation indicators for group a Chinese local subjects is sorted as follows: Visibility (A) > Anchors' professionalism (G) > Authenticity (C) > Persuasion effectiveness (I) > Language stimulation (J) > Interactivity (B) > Anchors' attractiveness (H) > Anchors' popularity (F) > Entertainment (D) > Purchase intentions (E).

The importance of live-streaming shopping evaluation indicators for group b Chinese subjects having lived in the West for over half a year is sorted as follows: Visibility (A) > Anchors' professionalism (G) > Persuasion effectiveness (I) > Authenticity (C) > Anchors' attractiveness (H) > Language stimulation (J) > Interactivity (B) > Anchors' popularity (F) > Purchase intentions (E) > Entertainment (D).

The importance of live-streaming shopping evaluation indicators for group c Western subjects having lived in China for over half a year is sorted as follows: Visibility (A) > Anchors' professionalism (G) > Anchors' attractiveness (H) > Language stimulation (J) > Persuasion effectiveness (I) > Authenticity (C) > Interactivity (B) > Anchors' popularity (F) > Purchase intentions (E) > Entertainment (D).

Table 9. Local weights and global weights on the importance of E-commerce live streaming consumer evaluation indicators (Secondary indicator)

Secondary indicator	Group a		Group b		Group c	
	Local weight	Global weight	Local weight	Global weight	Local weight	Global weight
A1	0.33	0.04	0.33	0.04	0.32	0.04
A2	0.33	0.04	0.33	0.04	0.34	0.04
A3	0.34	0.05	0.34	0.05	0.34	0.05
B1	0.34	0.03	0.32	0.03	0.31	0.03
B2	0.34	0.03	0.33	0.03	0.34	0.03
B3	0.31	0.03	0.36	0.04	0.34	0.03
C1	0.27	0.03	0.27	0.03	0.26	0.03
C2	0.37	0.04	0.36	0.04	0.37	0.04
C3	0.34	0.04	0.37	0.04	0.38	0.04
D1	0.34	0.03	0.36	0.03	0.39	0.03
D2	0.32	0.03	0.31	0.02	0.33	0.02
D3	0.33	0.03	0.33	0.02	0.28	0.02
E1	0.31	0.03	0.33	0.03	0.35	0.03
E2	0.33	0.03	0.35	0.04	0.32	0.03
E3	0.34	0.03	0.33	0.03	0.35	0.03
F1	0.55	0.05	0.53	0.04	0.49	0.04
F2	0.44	0.04	0.47	0.04	0.51	0.04
G1	0.5	0.06	0.5	0.06	0.53	0.06
G2	0.49	0.06	0.5	0.06	0.49	0.06
H1	0.23	0.02	0.22	0.02	0.22	0.02
H2	0.23	0.02	0.23	0.02	0.23	0.02
H3	0.24	0.02	0.25	0.02	0.25	0.03
H4	0.25	0.02	0.26	0.03	0.26	0.03
I1	0.51	0.05	0.51	0.05	0.45	0.04
I2	0.48	0.05	0.49	0.05	0.55	0.06
J1	0.48	0.05	0.48	0.05	0.45	0.05
J2	0.52	0.05	0.54	0.05	0.55	0.06

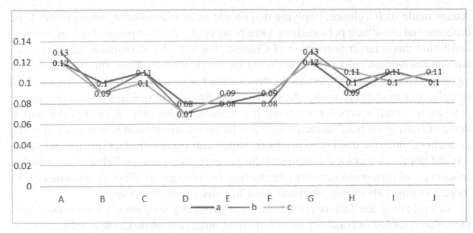

Fig. 4. Statistical chart of weights on E-commerce live streaming consumer evaluation indicators

5 Discussion and Analysis

According to the above findings, when Eastern and Western consumers are watching live-streaming shopping, overall visual design is the most important to consumers, and interface design, overall visual design and furnishings in the live-streaming room are the most important factors influencing consumers watching live-streaming shopping. Then comes anchors' professionalism, or whether anchors have professional knowledge of the product and the ability to display the product professionally.

Chinese local subjects (group a) and Chinese subjects having lived in the West (group b) considered authenticity and persuasion effectiveness to be important. Authenticity means whether the subjects believe that sellers present authentic product quality and efficacy, multiple-angle display, and product introduction during live-streaming shopping. In such shopping, there will be discounts on the same products. In China, a long-term-oriented country, consumers are more concerned about product cost performance (De & Hofstede, 2011). Persuasion effectiveness means the effect of anchors' description and display of products. As China is considered to be a country with a high culture of uncertainty avoidance, multi-angle display and interpretation can help consumers better understand products and avoid buying products beyond expectations. Therefore, the importance of these two evaluation indicators for Chinese subjects was greater than that for Western subjects.

Western subjects considered anchors' attractiveness to be more important in live-streaming shopping. Anchors' attractiveness evaluation indicators include anchors' appearance, personalities, voices and body language. Secondly, language stimulation was also very important to Western subjects. Language stimulation means that anchors use language copywriting to stimulate consumers' desire to purchase when recommending a product. For example, an anchor recommends eye shadow, saying that "When you use this eye shadow, it is as beautiful as the stars falling on your eyes"; or "When you wear this watch, you will be the center of attention". Kim & Markus (1999) found that 74% of European Americans selected a pen with an uncommon color, whereas only 24% of East

Asians made such a choice, implying that people in an individualist culture prefer to be different and show their personalities. Otterbring et al., (2022) replicated this experiment and found that a larger proportion of Chinese, but not US, participants selected a pen with an uncommon color now than during the original study. Thus, the study indicates a potential transmission of certain Western values to cultures traditionally characterized by collectivism and conformity. As shown in the findings of this study, local consumers gave high overall scores for watching live-streaming shopping. Although the importance of scoring anchors' attractiveness and language stimulation was not as important as anchors' intuitive display of products, which can ensure product quality and value, this did not mean that local consumers did not care about anchors' charm and whether products could bring uniqueness to themselves. In comparison, Western consumers were more concerned about this when watching live-streaming shopping.

In evaluating the factors influencing live-streaming shopping, Chinese local subjects also regarded interactivity as an important indicator, while Chinese subjects living in the West and Western subjects did not see interactivity as that important as other indicators. Ou & Davison (2009) concluded that why eBay lost to Taobao in China was because Taobao allowed instant communication between buyers and sellers through Aliwangwang, an instant communication tool embedded in Taobao. Similarly, China is a high-context country, while the West consists of low-context countries. Chinese consumers can interact more directly with other consumers and anchors by watching live streaming, so as to obtain more product information more quickly, listen to more consumers' suggestions and evaluations, and improve their trust in sellers.

Seen from the evaluation weights, the three groups of subjects thought that anchors' popularity, entertainment of live streaming, and whether watching live streaming can influence consumers' purchase intentions were not that important. Nowadays, live-streaming shopping has adopted many ways, such as inviting stars and writing script stories, to attract consumers' attention, in a way to increase the number of people watching live streaming to some extent. Simply in terms of the importance of factors influencing live-streaming shopping to consumers, entertainment, celebrities attracting traffic, and whether consumers purchase products through live streaming channels are not the main purpose of consumers actually watching live-streaming shopping.

6   Conclusion and Suggestions

In this study, triangular fuzzy weights were calculated with the main purpose to learn about the preferences for, and differences in, the willingness to watch live-streaming shopping between Eastern and Western consumers due to cultural differences. It was found that the most important factor for Eastern consumers represented by Chinese consumers in watching live-streaming shopping is the desire to buy affordable, high-quality products, while Western consumers represented by US consumers watch live-streaming shopping mostly due to the personal charm of anchors themselves or language stimulation and in the hope that they can purchase products showing personalities as described by anchors.

So far, there have been many studies on live-streaming shopping, with few studies on the influence of cultural differences on live-streaming shopping. This study was conducted to try in this field. According to the evaluation weighting scores, the average weighted evaluation score for watching live-streaming shopping was high for Chinese local consumers, lower for Chinese local consumers having lived in the West than that for Chinese local consumers, and lowest for Western consumers. This may be because many Western subjects participating in this study just had limited knowledge of live-streaming shopping and had not actually experienced live-streaming shopping. In this sense, live-streaming shopping is not so appealing to Western consumers. Future studies may further work on the differences in, and reasons for, Eastern and Western consumers watching live-streaming shopping, and then learn about why live-streaming shopping is very popular in Eastern countries, but not very popular in Western countries.

Live streaming shopping is closely related to consumers' vision and attention. If future related studies are conducted to test consumers' eye movement responses and EEG responses in watching live streaming through experimental design by using eye trackers and ERP equipment, collecting the physiological data of Eastern and Western consumers can help better learn about the realities of Eastern and Western consumers watching live-streaming shopping.

References

Chen, A., Lu, Y., Wang, B.: Customers' purchase decision-making process in social commerce: a social learning perspective. Int. J. Inf. Manage. **37**(6), 627–638 (2017)

Chua, H.F., Boland, J.E., Nisbett, R.E.: Cultural variation in eye movements during scene perception. Proc. Natl. Acad. Sci. **102**(35), 12629–12633 (2005)

De Mooij, M., Hofstede, G.: Cross-cultural consumer behavior: a review of research findings. J. Int. Consum. Mark. **23**(3–4), 181–192 (2011)

Feng, Y.: Research on consumers' purchase intention of webcast shopping platform time honored brand marketing (02), 75–76 (2021)

Hall, E.T.: Beyond Culture. Garden city, Anchor, NY (1976)

Hofstede, G.: Dimensionalizing cultures: the Hofstede model in context. Online Read. Psychol Cult. **2**(1), 2307 (2011)

Kim, H., Markus, H.R.: Deviance or uniqueness, harmony or conformity? A cultural analysis. J. Pers. Soc. Psychol. **77**(4), 785–800 (1999)

Luo, H., Cheng, S., Zhou, W., Yu, S., Lin, X.: A study on the impact of linguistic persuasive styles on the sales volume of live streaming products in social e-commerce environment. Mathematics **9**(13), 1576 (2021)

Otterbring, T., Bhatnagar, R., Folwarczny, M.: Selecting the special or choosing the common? A high-powered conceptual replication of Kim and Markus' (1999) pen study. J. Soc. Psychol., 1–7 (2022)

Ou, C.X., Davison, R.M.: Technical opinion Why eBay lost to TaoBao in China: the Glocal advantage. Commun. ACM **52**(1), 145–148 (2009)

Qing, C., Jin, S.: What drives consumer purchasing intention in live streaming e-commerce?. Front. Psychol., 3655 (2022)

Saaty, T.L.: Modeling unstructured decision problems—the theory of analytical hierarchies. Math. Comput. Simul. **20**(3), 147–158 (1978)

Shi, Y., Ma, C., Bao, X.: Journal of Shandong Institute of Business and Technology (2021)

Xuan, Y., Sun, J., From rationality to impulse: the influencing factors model of user behavior in live shopping and its development and changes during the fight against COVID-19. J. Commun. Univ. Chin. (Nat. Sci. Edn) (06), 25–35 (2020). https://doi.org/10.16196/j.cnki.issn.1673-479 3,2020.06.004

Xu, P., Cui, B.J., Lyu, B.: Influence of streamer's social capital on purchase intention in live streaming E-commerce. Front. Psychol. **12**, 6194 (2022)

Xu, Y., Jiang, W., Li, Y., Guo, J.: The influences of live streaming affordance in cross-border e-commerce platforms: an information transparency perspective. J. Glob. Inf. Manage. (JGIM) **30**(2), 1–24 (2021)

Yan, M., Kwok, A.P.K., Chan, A.H.S., Zhuang, Y.S., Wen, K., Zhang, K.C.: An empirical investigation of the impact of influencer live-streaming ads in e-commerce platforms on consumers' buying impulse. Internet Res. (ahead-of-print) (2022)

Author Index

P.-L. P. Rau (Ed.): HCII 2023, LNCS 14022, pp. 599–602, 2023.
https://doi.org/10.1007/978-3-031-35936-1

Printed in the United States
by Baker & Taylor Publisher Services